WORD
BIBLICAL
COMMENTARY

WORD
BIBLICAL
COMMENTARY

VOLUME 47ʙ

Hebrews 9-13

WILLIAM L. LANE

THOMAS NELSON PUBLISHERS

Nashville

Word Biblical Commentary
HEBREWS 9–13
Copyright © 1991 by Word, Incorporated

Library of Congress Cataloging in Publication Data
Main entry under title:

Word biblical commentary.

>Includes bibliographies.
>1. Bible—Commentaries—Collected works.
BS491.2W67   220.7'7   81–71768
ISBN 0–8499–0935–X (vol. 47B) AACR2

Printed in Colombia

Unless otherwise indicated, Scripture quotations in the body of the commentary are from the New International Version of the Bible, copyright © 1973 by New York Bible Society International, or are the author's own. The author's own translation of the text appears in italic type under the heading "Translation."

03 04 05 06 07 08 09 QWB 15 14 13 12 11 10

EDITOR'S NOTE

For the convenience of the reader, page numbers for both volumes of this commentary on Hebrews (47A and 47B) are included in the Contents. Page numbers for the volume in hand are printed in boldface type, while those for the other volume are in lightface.

In addition, all of the front matter from Vol. 47A but the *Introduction* has been repeated in Vol. 47B so that the reader may have abbreviations, bibliography, and other pertinent information readily at hand.

Contents

Editorial Preface

The launching of the *Word Biblical Commentary* brings to fulfillment an enterprise of several years' planning. The publishers and the members of the editorial board met in 1977 to explore the possibility of a new commentary on the books of the Bible that would incorporate several distinctive features. Prospective readers of these volumes are entitled to know what such features were intended to be; whether the aims of the commentary have been fully achieved time alone will tell.

First, we have tried to cast a wide net to include as contributors a number of scholars from around the world who not only share our aims, but are in the main engaged in the ministry of teaching in university, college, and seminary. They represent a rich diversity of denominational allegiance. The broad stance of our contributors can rightly be called evangelical, and this term is to be understood in its positive, historic sense of a commitment to Scripture as divine revelation, and to the truth and power of the Christian gospel.

Then, the commentaries in our series are all commissioned and written for the purpose of inclusion in the *Word Biblical Commentary.* Unlike several of our distinguished counterparts in the field of commentary writing, there are no translated works, originally written in a non-English language. Also, our commentators were asked to prepare their own rendering of the original biblical text and to use those languages as the basis of their own comments and exegesis. What may be claimed as distinctive with this series is that it is based on the biblical languages, yet it seeks to make the technical and scholarly approach to a theological understanding of Scripture understandable by—and useful to—the fledgling student, the working minister, and colleagues in the guild of professional scholars and teachers as well.

Finally, a word must be said about the format of the series. The layout, in clearly defined sections, has been consciously devised to assist readers at different levels. Those wishing to learn about the textual witnesses on which the translation is offered are invited to consult the section headed *Notes.* If the readers' concern is with the state of modern scholarship on any given portion of Scripture, they should turn to the sections of *Bibliography* and *Form/Structure/Setting.* For a clear exposition of the passage's meaning and its relevance to the ongoing biblical revelation, the *Comment* and concluding *Explanation* are designed expressly to meet that need. There is therefore something for everyone who may pick up and use these volumes.

If these aims come anywhere near realization, the intention of the editors will have been met, and the labor of our team of contributors rewarded.

General Editors: *David A. Hubbard*
Glenn W. Barker †
Old Testament: *John D. W. Watts*
New Testament: *Ralph P. Martin*

Author's Preface

When the invitation arrived to contribute the volume on Hebrews in the Word Biblical Commentary, I was advancing some preliminary studies toward a monograph on the christology of Hebrews. That research had made me alert to the distinctiveness and richness of the writer's understanding of Jesus and redemption, and to the depth of his pastoral concern for a community in crisis. I welcomed the opportunity to immerse myself in the text and the discussion it had prompted. I was convinced that I would be able to advance both projects in tandem. I had forgotten that an invitation to prepare a comprehensive commentary, especially on a document as complex and richly textured as Hebrews, is an invitation to humiliation. You never know enough. Confidence outstrips competence. And then confidence can falter.

When I took my place at the table among those who were vigorously engaged in the discussion of the text, I quickly realized that it was presupposed that all the participants were linguistically competent. They were speaking at least eleven Western European languages. And to make matters worse, there was no consensus among them. They all claimed to have listened to the text, but they had a tendency not to listen to each other or to learn from one another. The writing of a commentary is often an exercise in discrimination of the relative merits among competing arguments and opinions. Responsible interpretation is never a private affair. The writing of a commentary is a collaborative event. There is no autonomy of insight.

I have frequently had to disengage myself from the discussion of the text within the academy and simply to sit before the text itself, learning again how to listen to the text both in its detail and its totality. The past twelve years have been devoted to a sustained dialogue with the text in order to sharpen my ability to listen responsibly. I have just as frequently returned to the discussion prompted by the text because listening is not accomplished in isolation. Some of my colleagues have grown impatient while waiting for this commentary. When they ask me what I have been doing, I respond that I have been dismantling the mufflers erected between me and the text.

The task of a commentator is not only to organize and summarize the discussion of the text but to contribute to that discussion in a substantial way. For one who makes a theological commitment to the authority of the text in its canonical form, that is a demanding task. One cannot make facile decisions and then move on. At stake is the determination of the meaning of a text of ultimate significance and the expression of that meaning in a clear modern idiom that is faithful to the original and that communicates its intention forcefully to a contemporary reader. I have sought to contribute to the discussion of the text by introducing lesser-known participants in the discussion as well as by my own synthetic response to the text. Undergirding the commentary presented here is the conviction that commitment to the claims of the text is the essential condition for creative exegetical insight.

I have been encouraged and instructed by those who have prepared commentaries, especially O. Michel and C. Spicq, monographs, dissertations, and articles.

They have stimulated me to look at the text from different angles of vision. It has been a high privilege to interact with so many gifted scholars who have sought to interpret the witness of Hebrews. The divergence in their conclusions was an incentive to a fresh investigation of the text. I am especially indebted to those who called my attention to unpublished dissertations on Hebrews and who frequently assisted me by securing them for me. I was in the Netherlands when H. W. Attridge's commentary on Hebrews in the Hermeneia series became available, and regrettably I enjoyed access to it only when this commentary was in its final stage.

A major problem in the preparation of a commentary is that concentration on issues of a textual, grammatical, syntactical, rhetorical, or theological nature within a unit of text can foster a fragmented perception of the unit as a whole, just as concentration upon an individual section can interfere with the discernment of the document as a whole. A serious problem in making use of a commentary is that the concerns of the commentator in an individual section can direct the attention to the details of the text but divert it from the flow of the statement within the section and the document as a whole. In this commentary readers will be advised to read the *Introduction* to each of the five major divisions discerned in Hebrews before consulting the commentary on a particular section. This will allow the pastoral thrust of the document, as opposed to the section, to be grasped. When turning to individual sections, it will be helpful to read first the *Explanation* for an overview of the section before consulting the commentary on individual units of the text.

This commentary has been prepared for professional colleagues and seminary students, but also for pastors and teachers in the churches. I have sought to expose myself to the significant work that has been done on Hebrews in any Western European language in order to make that research accessible to those who work primarily in English. This has been a labor of love for the Church. This commentary will provide a resource for determining the state of scholarship on Hebrews. It will also seek to advance the claims of the text for unwavering commitment to God, who continues to speak decisively in his Son to a culture not unlike that to which Hebrews was addressed, one that appears to lack order, structure, and meaning.

Hebrews has acquired a reputation for being formidable and remote from the world in which we live. Consequently, it has been neglected in the liturgy and preaching of the churches, in the curriculum of seminaries, and in the devotional reading of the laity. There has been no dearth of commentaries, monographs, dissertations, and articles on Hebrews. In the course of my own research, I have come to appreciate that significant descriptive phrase from the computer age, "informational overload." But Hebrews tends to remain unappreciated and unused in the classroom, the pulpit, and the pew.

Ironically, Hebrews is a call for ultimate certainty and ultimate commitment. James Olthuis has described Hebrews as a "certitudinal Book": it concerns itself with the issue of certainty by confronting ultimate questions about life and death with ultimate realities. Its presentation of the way in which God responds to the human family as one who speaks, creates, covenants, pledges, calls, and commits himself is intended to breathe new life into men and women who suffer a failure of nerve because they live in an insecure, anxiety-provoking society. Hebrews participates in the character of Scripture as gift. It is a gift the Church sorely needs.

My debts to others are large, but not easy to define. I am especially indebted to the two mentors who did so much to train me for scholarship, to whose memory this volume is dedicated. A number of graduate students have assisted me in my research: Robert Herron, Kern Trembath, Joseph Causey, Paul Schmidgall, Bedford Smith, Jack Thomas, Bill Bailey, Alan Carter, David Wornam, Michael Card, Brian Yorton, Chris Steward, Pat Cely, Greg Salyer, Roy Swisher, and Alan Lewis. To each of them I express my appreciation. I owe a special debt of gratitude to my colleagues Joe Trafton and Jim Davis, with whom I discussed decisions to which I felt driven by the text, but for which I could find no other support. The writing of a commentary is happily a collegial experience. I am grateful to Robert Hanna of Seminario Evángelico in Maracay, Aragua, Venezuela, who responded to my grammatical questions and kindly presented me with a prepublication copy of his helpful *Grammatical Aid.*

Access to the splendid collection and the ideal setting for scholarship at Tyndale House in Cambridge, England, first in 1981, and then again in 1988 and 1989, was indispensable to the beginning of my research and to its completion. A year spent at the Institute for Ecumenical and Cultural Research in Collegeville, MN, in 1981-82, and the warm support of the director, Dr. Robert Bilheimer, made it possible for me to draft the commentary on the first eight chapters of Hebrews. A year spent in community in Amsterdam in 1988-89, with the men and women of Youth With A Mission, made it possible to return to the task of completing the commentary in a supportive environment and to sharpen my perspective through engagement in mission. I am appreciative of the careful editing of the manuscript by Dr. R. P. Martin and Dr. L. A. Losie, and for those on the editorial staff at Word Books who have seen the manuscript through the press.

My deepest debt is to my wife, Brenda, who believed in me when I felt inadequate to the task and who has been a source of constant encouragement. We talked at length about the problems presented by the text with which I was wrestling. Her ability to ask instinctively the right questions consistently pointed me in the direction of a solution. She has rejoiced in the completion of every section of the commentary and typed the bulk of the manuscript. I especially appreciate the counsel she gave me one day on a slip of paper tucked in with my work sheets: "The commentary is the Lord's. Do it in his strength!" I also appreciate the commitment to the project of my daughter, Debra Gensheimer, who completed the typing of the manuscript and the preparation of the copy for the publisher. I would be remiss if I did not mention the gracious hospitality of Dr. and Mrs. Ben Burgoyne, who made available to me a portion of their home in an exquisite setting where I was able to prepare the pages for the Introduction without distraction.

The writing of this commentary has been an act of love and devotion to God and to the Church. May it serve the Church and the guild well by directing attention to the remarkable gift we possess in the discourse that we call Hebrews.

July 12, 1991   WILLIAM L. LANE
School of Religion
Seattle Pacific University
Seattle, Washington

Abbreviations

A. General Abbreviations

A	Codex Alexandrinus
ad	comment on
Akkad.	Akkadian
ℵ	Codex Sinaiticus
act	active
adj	adjective
adv	adverb
aor	aorist
Ap. Lit.	Apocalyptic Literature
Apoc.	Apocrypha
Aq.	Aquila's Greek Translation of the OT
Arab.	Arabic
Aram.	Aramaic
B	Codex Vaticanus
C	Codex Ephraemi Syri
c.	*circa*, about
cent.	century
cf.	*confer*, compare
chap(s).	chapter(s)
cod., codd.	codex, codices
conj	conjunction
consec	consecutive
contra	in contrast to
D	Codex Bezae
dittogr	dittography
DSS	Dead Sea Scrolls
ed.	edited by, editor(s)
e.g.	*exempli gratia*, for example
et al.	*et alii*, and others
ET	English translation
EV	English Versions of the Bible
f., ff.	following (verse or verses, pages, etc.)
fem	feminine
frag.	fragments
FS	*Festschrift*, volume written in honor of
ft.	foot, feet
fut	future
gen	genitive
Gk.	Greek
hap. leg.	*hapax legomenon*, sole occurrence
haplogr	haplography

Heb.	Hebrew
Hitt.	Hittite
ibid.	*ibidem*, in the same place
id.	*idem*, the same
i.e.	*id est*, that is
impf	imperfect
ind	indicative
inf	infinitive
infra	below
in loc.	*in loco*, in the place cited
lat	Latin
lit.	literally
loc. cit.	the place cited
LXX	Septuagint
masc	masculine
mg.	margin
MS(S)	manuscript(s)
MT	Masoretic text (of the Old Testament)
n.	note
n.d.	no date
Nestle[26]	E. & E. Nestle (ed.), *Novum Testamentum Graece*[26], rev. by K. Aland et al.
NHC	Nag Hammadi Codex
no.	number
nom	nominative
n.s.	new series
NT	New Testament
obj	objective, object
obs.	obsolete
OG	Old Greek
OL	Old Latin
o.s.	old series
OT	Old Testament
p., pp.	page, pages
pace	with due respect to, but differing from
//	parallel(s)
par.	paragraph, parallel(s)
pass	passive
passim	elsewhere
pf	perfect
pl	plural
poss	possessive
prep	preposition

Pseudep.	Pseudepigrapha	Theod.	Theodotion
ptcp	participle	TR	Textus Receptus
Q	Quelle ("Sayings" source for the Gospels)	tr.	translator, translated by
		UBSGNT	The United Bible Societies Greek NT
q.v.	*quod vide*, which see		
rev.	revised, reviser, revision	Ugar.	Ugaritic
Rom.	Roman	UP	University Press
Sam.	Samaritan recension	u.s.	*ut supra*, as above
sc.	*scilicet*, that is to say	v, vv	verse, verses
Sem.	Semitic	viz.	*videlicet*, namely
sg	singular	Vg	Vulgate
subj	subjective, subject	*v.l.*	*varia lectio*, alternative reading
Sumer.	Sumerian		
s.v.	*sub verbo*, under the word	vol.	volume
sy	Syriac	x	times (2x = two times, etc.)
Symm.	Symmachus		
Tg.	Targum		

Note: The textual notes and numbers used to indicate individual manuscripts are those found in the apparatus criticus of *Novum Testamentum Graece*, ed. E. & E. Nestle, rev. K. Aland et al., 26th ed. (Stuttgart: Deutsche Bibelgesellschaft, 1979). This edition of the Greek NT is the basis for the *Translation* sections.

B. Abbreviations for Translations and Paraphrases

AmT	Smith & Goodspeed, *The Complete Bible, An American Translation*	Moffatt	J. Moffatt, *A New Translation of the Bible* (NT 1913)
		NAB	*The New American Bible*
ASV	American Standard Version of Revised Version (1901)	NASB	*The New American Standard Bible*
AV	Authorized Version = KJV	NCV	New Century Version
Basic	*The New Testament in Basic English*	NEB	*The New English Bible*
		NIV	The New International Version (1978)
Beck	W. F. Beck, *The New Testament in the Language of Today*	NJB	*New Jerusalem Bible* (1985)
		Phillips	J. B. Phillips, *The New Testament in Modern English*
GNB	*Good News Bible* = Today's English Version		
JB	*Jerusalem Bible*	RSV	Revised Standard Version (NT 1946, OT 1952, Apoc. 1957)
JPS	Jewish Publication Society, *The Holy Scriptures*		
KJV	King James Version (1611) = AV	RV	Revised Version, 1881–85
		TEV	Today's English Version
Knox	R. A. Knox, *The Holy Bible*		

C. Abbreviations of Commonly Used Periodicals, Reference Works, and Serials

AB	Anchor Bible	*Aeg*	*Aegyptus*
ACR	*Australasian Catholic Record*	*AEPHE*	*Annuaire de l'École practique des Hautes Études*
ACW	Ancient Christian Writers		

AER	American Ecclesiastical Review	BAG	W. Bauer, W. F. Arndt, and F. W. Gingrich, Greek-English Lexicon of the NT (1957)
AIPHO	Annuaire de l'Institute de Philologie et d'Histoire Orientales		
AJBA	Australian Journal of Biblical Archaeology	BAGD	W. Bauer, W. F. Arndt, F. W. Gingrich, and F. W. Danker, Greek-English Lexicon of the NT (1979)
AJBI	Annual of the Japanese Biblical Institute		
AJPh	American Journal of Philosophy	BASOR	Bulletin of the American Schools of Oriental Research
AJT	American Journal of Theology		
ALBO	Analecta lovaniensia biblica et orientalia	BBB	Bonner biblische Beiträge
		BDF	F. Blass, A. Debrunner, and R. W. Funk, A Greek Grammar of the NT
ALGHJ	Arbeiten zur Literatur und Geschichte des hellenistischen Judentums		
		BenM	Benediktinische Monatsschrift zur Pflege religiösen und geistigen Lebens
ALUOS	Annual of Leeds University Oriental Society	BeO	Bibbia e oriente
AnBib	Analecta biblica	BETL	Bibliotheca ephemeridum theologicarum lovaniensium
Ang	Angelicum		
Angelos	Angelos: Archiv für neutestamentliche Zeitgeschichte und Kulturkunde	BETS	Bulletin of the Evangelical Theological Society
		BFCL	Bulletin des Facultés Catholiques de Lyon
ANRW	Aufstieg und Niedergang der römischen Welt	BFCT	Beiträge zur Förderung christlicher Theologie
Anton	Antonianum		
Anvil	Anvil	BGBE	Beiträge zur Geschichte der biblischen Exegese
APOT	R. H. Charles (ed.), Apocrypha and Pseudepigrapha of the Old Testament	BHK	R. Kittel, Biblia hebraica⁷
		Bib	Biblica
		BibLeb	Bibel und Leben
ARG	Archiv für Reformationsgeschichte	BibOr	Biblica et orientalia
		BibRev	Biblical Review
ASem	Asbury Seminarian	BibTh	Biblical Theology
AsiaJT	Asia Journal of Theology	BIOSCS	Bulletin of the International Organization for Septuagint and Cognate Studies
ASNS	Annuaire de la societé Nathan Söderblom		
AsSeign	Assemblées du Seigneur		
ASTI	Annual of the Swedish Theological Institute	BIRBS	Bulletin of the Institute for Reformation Biblical Studies
ATh	L'Année Théologique Augustinienne	BJRL	Bulletin of the John Rylands University Library of Manchester
ATR	Anglican Theological Review		
AusBR	Australian Biblical Review		
AUSS	Andrews University Seminary Studies	BLit	Bibel und Liturgie
		BR	Biblical Research
BA	Biblical Archaeologist	BSac	Bibliotheca Sacra

BT	*The Bible Translator*	EAJT	*East Asia Journal of Theology*
BTB	*Biblical Theology Bulletin*	EBib	Études bibliques
BU	Biblische Untersuchungen	EE	*Estudios Eclesiásticos*
Burg	*Burgense*	EEv	*Études Evangéliques*
BV	*Biblical Viewpoint*	EKKNT	Evangelisch-Katholischer
BVC	*Bible et vie chrétienne*		Kommentar zum Neuen
BW	*The Biblical World*		Testament
BZ	*Biblische Zeitschrift*	Enc	*Encounter*
BZNW	Beihefte zur *ZNW*	ErJb	*Eranos Jahrbuch*
CB	*Cultura bíblica*	ERT	*Evangelical Review of*
CBQ	*Catholic Biblical Quarterly*		*Theology*
CBQMS	Catholic Biblical Quar-	EstBib	*Estudios bíblicos*
	terly—Monograph	EstFran	*Estudios Franciscanos*
	Series	ETL	*Ephemerides theologicae*
CCER	*Cahiers du Cercle Ernest-*		*lovanienses*
	Renan	ETR	*Études théologiques et*
CentBibQ	*Central Bible Quarterly*		*religieuses*
CGTC	Cambridge Greek Testa-	EuA	*Erbe und Auftrage:*
	ment Commentaries		*Benediktinische*
Chr	*Christus*		*Monatsschrift*
CJT	*Canadian Journal of Theology*	EV	*Esprit et Vie*
ClBib	Clarendon Bible	EvJ	*Evangelical Journal*
CleM	Clergy Monthly	EvMz	*Evangelische*
ClRev	*The Classical Review*		*Missionszeitschrift*
CMech	*Collectanea Mechliniensia*	EvQ	*Evangelical Quarterly*
CNT	Commentaire du Nouveau	EvT	*Evangelische Theologie*
	Testament	Exp	*Expositor*
Coll	*Colloquium*	ExpTim	*Expository Times*
CollTh	*Collectanea Theologica*	FGNK	Forschungen zur
ConNT	*Coniectanea neotestamentica*		Geschichte des
CQR	*Church Quarterly Review*		neutestamentlichen
CrozQ	*Crozer Quarterly*		Kanons und der
CSion	Cahiers Sioniens		altkirchlichen Literatur
CSEL	Corpus scriptorum	FM	*Faith and Mission*
	ecclesiasticorum	FRLANT	Forschungen zur Religion
	latinorum		und Literatur des Alten
CTJ	*Calvin Theological Journal*		und Neuen Testaments
CTM	Concordia Theological	FV	*Foi et Vie*
	Monthly	GBTh	Gegenwartsfragen
CTom	*Ciencia Tomista*		biblischer Theologie
CurrThMiss	*Currents in Theology and*	GCS	Griechischen christlichen
	Mission		Schriftsteller
CV	*Communio Viatorum*	GJ	*Grace Journal*
DACL	*Dictionnaire d'archéologie*	GOTR	*Greek Orthodox Theological*
	chrétienne et de liturgie		*Review*
DBSup	*Dictionnaire de la Bible,*	Greg	*Gregorianum*
	Supplément	GThT	*Gereformeered Theologisch*
Div	*Divinitas*		*Tijdschrift*
DivThom	*Divus Thomas*	GTJ	*Grace Theological Journal*

G.	*Geist und Leben*	JSNT	*Journal for the Study of the New Testament*
HBK	Herders Bibel Kommentar		
HDR	Harvard Dissertations in Religion	JSNTSup	JSNT Supplement Series
		JSOT	*Journal for the Study of the Old Testament*
Her	*Hermathena*		
Hermes	*Hermes: Zeitschrift für klassische Philologie*	JSS	*Journal of Semitic Studies*
		JTSB	*Jahrbuch der theologischen Schule Bethel*
HeyJ	*Heythrop Journal*		
HibJ	*Hibbert Journal*	JTS	*Journal of Theological Studies*
Hist	*Historia*		
HKNT	Handkommentar zum Neuen Testament	Jud	*Judaism*
		KD	*Kerygma und Dogma*
HNT	Handbuch zum Neuen Testament	KNT	Kommentar zum Neuen Testament
HNTC	Harper's NT Commentaries	LCC	Library of Christian Classics
HTR	*Harvard Theological Review*	LCL	Loeb Classical Library
HUCA	*Hebrew Union College Annual*	LD	Lectio divina
IB	*Interpreter's Bible*	LexTQ	*Lexington Theological Quarterly*
IBS	*Irish Biblical Studies*		
ICC	International Critical Commentary	LPGL	G. W. H. Lampe, *Patristic Greek Lexicon*
IDB	G. A. Buttrick (ed.), *Interpreter's Dictionary of the Bible*	LQHR	*London Quarterly and Holborn Review*
		LSJ	Liddell-Scott-Jones, *Greek-English Lexicon*
IEJ	*Israel Exploration Journal*		
IlRev	*Iliff Review*	LV	*Lumière et Vie*
Int	*Interpretation*	LQ	*Lutheran Quarterly*
It	*Itala*	MCM	*Modern Churchman*
ITQ	*Irish Theological Quarterly*	Mel Theol	*Melita Theologica*
JAC	*Jahrbuch für Antike und Christentum*	MeyerK	H. A. W. Meyer, *Kritisch-exegetischer Kommentar über das Neue Testament*
JBL	*Journal of Biblical Literature*		
JBR	*Journal of Bible and Religion*		
JDT	*Jahrbuch für deutsche Theologie*	MGWJ	*Monatsschrift für Geschichte und Wissenschaft des Judentums*
JETS	*Journal of the Evangelical Theological Society*		
JHS	*Journal of Hellenic Studies*	MM	J. H. Moulton and G. Milligan, *Vocabulary of the Greek Testament*
JJS	*Journal of Jewish Studies*		
JNES	*Journal of Near Eastern Studies*	MNTC	Moffatt NT Commentary
JPTh	*Jahrbücher für protestantische Theologie*	MPTh	*Monatsschrift für Pastoral Theologie*
JQR	*Jewish Quarterly Review*	MQR	*Methodist Quarterly Review*
JRS	*Journal of Roman Studies*	MTS	Münchener theologische Studien
JSJ	*Journal for the Study of Judaism in the Persian, Hellenistic and Roman Period*	MTZ	*Münchener theologische Zeitschrift*
		Mus	*Muséon*

NAWG	Nachrichten der Akademie der Wissenschaften in Göttingen	PG	J. Migne, *Patrologia graeca*
		PRS	*Perspectives in Religious Studies*
NBl	*New Blackfriars*	PSB	*Princeton Seminary Bulletin*
NC	*Nineteenth Century*	PTR	*Princeton Theological Review*
NedTTs	*Nederlands theologisch Tijdschrift*	QuartRev	*Quarterly Review*
		RAC	*Reallexikon für Antike und Christentum*
Neot	*Neotestamentica*		
NewDocs	*New Documents Illustrating Early Christianity*, ed. G. H. R. Horsley	RB	*Revue biblique*
		RBén	*Revue bénédictine*
		RCB	*Revista de cultura bíblica*
NGWG	*Nachrichten der Gesellschaft der Wissenschaften zu Göttingen*	RDT	*Revue Diocésaine de Tournai*
		RefRev	*The Reformed Review*
		REJ	*Revue des études juives*
NIBC	New International Biblical Commentary	ResQ	*Restoration Quarterly*
		RevExp	*Review and Expositor*
NICNT	New International Commentary on the New Testament	RevistB	*Revista bíblica*
		RevistCal	*Revista Calasancia*
		RevistCatT	*Revista Catalana de Teologia*
NIDNTT	*New International Dictionary of New Testament Theology*	RevQ	*Revue de Qumran*
		RevRéf	*Revue Réformee*
NJDT	*Neue Jahrbücher für Deutsche Theologie*	RevScRel	*Revue des sciences religieuses*
		RGG	*Religion in Geschichte und Gegenwart*
NKZ	*Neue kirchliche Zeitschrift*		
NorTT	*Norsk Teologisk Tidsskrift*	RHPR	*Revue d'histoire et de philosophie religieuses*
NovT	*Novum Testamentum*		
NovTSup	Novum Testamentum, Supplements	RHR	*Revue de l'histoire des religions*
		RivB	*Revista biblica*
NPNF	Nicene and Post-Nicene Fathers	RNT	Regensburger Neues Testament
NRT	*La nouvelle revue théologique*	RPLHA	*Revue de Philologie de Littérature et d'Histoire Anciennes*
NTD	Das Neue Testament Deutsch		
NThS	*Nieuwe Theologische Studiën*	RSPT	*Revue des sciences philosophiques et théologiques*
NTS	*New Testament Studies*		
NTStud	*The New Testament Student*		
NTTS	New Testament Tools and Studies	RSR	*Recherches de science religieuse*
		RTP	*Revue de théologie et de philosophie*
OCD	*Oxford Classical Dictionary*		
OGI	*Orientis Graeci Inscriptiones Selectae*, ed. W. Dittenberger	RTR	*Reformed Theological Review*
		SacDoc	*Sacra Doctrina*
		Sal	*Salesianum: Pontificio ateneo salesiano*
OLZ	*Orientalische Literaturzeitung*		
OPTT	*Occasional Papers in Translation and Textlinguistics*	SB	Sources bibliques
		SBFLA	*Studii Biblici Franciscani Liber Annuus*
OTS	*Oudtestamentische Studiën*	SBLASP	Society of Biblical Literature Abstracts and Seminar Papers
PCSBR	*Papers of Chicago's Society of Biblical Research*		

SBLDS	SBL Dissertation Series	*TCh*	*The Churchman*
SBLMS	SBL Monograph Series	*TD*	*Theology Digest*
SBLSCS	SBL Septuagint and Cognate Studies	*TDNT*	G. Kittel and G. Friedrich (ed.), *Theological Dictionary of the New Testament*
SBT	Studies in Biblical Theology		
SC	Sources chrétiennes		
ScC	*Scuola cattolica: Revista di scienze religiose*	*TF*	*Theologische Forschung*
		TGl	*Theologie und Glaube*
ScEccl	*Sciences ecclésiastiques*	*ThBullMDC*	*Theological Bulletin: McMaster Divinity College*
Schol	Scholastik		
ScEs	*Science et Esprit*	*ThEduc*	*Theological Educator*
Scr	*Scripture*	*Th*	*Theology*
ScrHier	*Scripta hierasolymitana*	*Theol(A)*	*Theologia*
SE	Studia Evangelica	THKNT	Theologischer Handkommentar zum Neuen Testament
SEÅ	Svensk exegetisk årsbok		
Sem	Semitica		
Serv	*Servitium*	*ThEv*	*Theologica Evangelica*
SJT	*Scottish Journal of Theology*	*ThRev*	*Theological Review*
SNT	Studien zum Neuen Testament	*ThViat*	*Theologia Viatorum*
		TLZ	Theologische Literaturzeitung
SNTSMS	Society for New Testament Studies Monograph Series	TNTC	Tyndale New Testament Commentaries
		TPQ	*Theologisch-Praktische Quartalschrift*
SNTU	Studien zum Neuen Testament und seiner Umwelt, Series A	*TRev*	*Theologische Revue*
		TRu	*Theologische Rundschau*
SP	*Studia Patristica*	*TS*	*Theological Studies*
SPAW	Sitzungsberichte der preussischen Akademie der Wissenschaften	TSK	*Theologische Studien und Kritiken*
		TToday	*Theology Today*
SPB	Studia postbiblica	*TTZ*	*Trierer theologische Zeitschrift*
SpTod	*Spirituality Today*	TU	Texte und Untersuchungen
SR	*Studies in Religion/Sciences religieuses*		
		TY	*Tantur Yearbook*
ST	*Studia theologica*	*TynBul*	*Tyndale Bulletin*
STK	*Svensk teologisk kvartalskrift*	*TZ*	*Theologische Zeitschrift*
Str-B	[H. Strack and] P. Billerbeck, *Kommentar zum Neuen Testament*	UCB	Die Urchristliche Botschaft
		USQR	*Union Seminary Quarterly Review*
StudBibTh	*Studia Biblica et Theologica*	*VC*	*Vigiliae christianae*
StudNeot	Studia neotestamentica, Studia	*VD*	*Verbum domini*
		VL	Vetus Latina
SUNT	Studien zur Umwelt des Neuen Testaments	*VoxEv*	*Vox Evangelica*
		VS	Verbum salutis
SWJT	*Southwestern Journal of Theology*	*VSpir*	*Vie spirituelle*
		VT	*Vetus Testamentum*
TBei	*Theologische Beiträge*	VTSup	Vetus Testamentum, Supplements
TBl	*Theologische Blätter*		
TBT	*The Bible Today*	*WesThJ*	*Wesleyan Theological Journal*

WMANT	Wissenschaftliche Monographien zum Alten und Neuen Testament	ZKT	Zeitschrift für Katholische Theologie
Wor	Worship	ZNW	Zeitschrift für die neutestamentliche Wissenschaft
WTJ	Westminster Theological Journal	ZRGG	Zeitschrift für Religions- und Geistesgeschichte
WUNT	Wissenschaftliche Untersuchungen zum Neuen Testament	ZST	Zeitschrift für systematische Theologie
WW	Word and World	ZTK	Zeitschrift für Theologie und Kirche
ZAW	Zeitschrift für die alttestamentliche Wissenschaft	ZWT	Zeitschrift für wissenschaftliche Theologie
		ZZ	Zeichen der Zeit

D. Abbreviations for Books of the Bible, the Apocrypha, and the Pseudepigrapha

OLD TESTAMENT

Gen	1 Sam	Esth	Lam	Mic
Exod	2 Sam	Job	Ezek	Nah
Lev	1 Kgs	Ps(Pss)	Dan	Hab
Num	2 Kgs	Prov	Hos	Zeph
Deut	1 Chr	Eccl	Joel	Hag
Josh	2 Chr	Cant	Amos	Zech
Judg	Ezra	Isa	Obad	Mal
Ruth	Neh	Jer	Jonah	

NEW TESTAMENT

Matt	1 Cor	1 Thess	Philem	1 John
Mark	2 Cor	2 Thess	Heb	2 John
Luke	Gal	1 Tim	Jas	3 John
John	Eph	2 Tim	1 Pet	Jude
Acts	Phil	Titus	2 Pet	Rev
Rom	Col			

APOCRYPHA

1 Kgdms	1 Kingdoms	Wis	Wisdom of Solomon	Sus	Susanna
2 Kgdms	2 Kingdoms			Bel	Bel and the Dragon
3 Kgdms	3 Kingdoms	Sir	Ecclesiasticus (Wisdom of Jesus the son of Sirach)		
4 Kgdms	4 Kingdoms			Pr Man	Prayer of Manasseh
1 Esd	1 Esdras			1 Macc	1 Maccabees
2 Esd	2 Esdras			2 Macc	2 Maccabees
Tob	Tobit	Bar	Baruch	3 Macc	3 Maccabees
Jdt	Judith	Ep Jer	Epistle of Jeremy	4 Macc	4 Maccabees
Add Esth	Additions to Esther	S Th Ch	Song of the Three Children (or Young Men)		
4 Ezra	4 Ezra				

E. Abbreviations of the Names of Jewish, Pseudepigraphical, and Early Patristic Books

Adam and Eve	*Life of Adam and Eve*	*Gos. Pet.*	*Gospel of Peter*
Apoc. Abr.	*Apocalypse of Abraham* (1st to 2nd cent. A.D.)	*Gos. Thom.*	*Gospel of Thomas*
		Prot. Jas.	*Protevangelium of James*
2–3 Apoc. Bar.	Syriac, Greek *Apocalypse of Baruch*	*Barn.*	*Barnabas*
		1–2 Clem.	*1–2 Clement*
Asc. Isa.	*Ascension of Isaiah*	*Did.*	*Didache*
Apoc. Mos.	*Apocalypse of Moses*	*Diogn.*	*Diognetus*
As. Mos.	(See *T. Mos.*)	*Herm. Man.*	Hermas, *Mandates*
Apoc. Elijah	*Apocalypse of Elijah*	*Sim.*	*Similitudes*
1–2–3 Enoch	Ethiopic, Slavonic, Hebrew *Enoch*	*Vis.*	*Visions*
		Ign. Eph.	Ignatius, *Letter to the Ephesians*
Ep. Arist.	*Epistle of Aristeas*		
Jub.	*Jubilees*	*Magn.*	*Letter to the Magnesians*
Mart. Isa.	*Martyrdom of Isaiah*	*Phld.*	*Letter to the Philadelphians*
Odes Sol.	*Odes of Solomon*	*Pol.*	*Letter to Polycarp*
Pss. Sol.	*Psalms of Solomon*	*Rom.*	*Letter to the Romans*
Sib. Or.	*Sibylline Oracles*	*Smyrn.*	*Letter to the Smyrnaeans*
T. 12 Patr.	*Testaments of the Twelve Patriarchs*	*Trall.*	*Letter to the Trallians*
		Jos., Ag. Ap.	Josephus, *Against Apion*
T. Abr.	*Testament of Abraham*	*Ant.*	*The Jewish Antiquities*
T. Judah	*Testament of Judah*	*J. W.*	*The Jewish War*
T. Levi	*Testament of Levi*, etc.	*Life*	*The Life*
		Mart. Pol.	*Martyrdom of Polycarp*
Apoc. Pet.	*Apocalypse of Peter*	*Pol. Phil.*	Polycarp, *Letter to the Philippians*
Apost. Const.	*Apostolic Constitutions*		
Gos. Eb.	*Gospel of the Ebionites*	*Iren. Adv.*	Irenaeus, *Against*
Gos. Eg.	*Gospel of the Egyptians*	*Haer.*	*All Heresies*
Gos. Heb.	*Gospel of the Hebrews*	*Tert. De*	Tertullian, *On the*
Gos. Naass.	*Gospel of the Naassenes*	*Praesc. Haer.*	*Proscribing of Heretics*

F. Abbreviations of Names of Dead Sea Scrolls and Related Texts

CD	Cairo (Genizah text of the) Damascus (Document)	1QapGen	*Genesis Apocryphon* of Qumran Cave 1
Hev	Nahal Hever texts	1QH	*Hôdāyôt* (*Thanksgiving Hymns*) from Qumran Cave 1
Mas	Masada texts		
Mird	Khirbet Mird texts	1QIsa^a,b	First or second copy of Isaiah from Qumran Cave 1
Mur	Wadi Murabbaᶜat texts		
P	Pesher (commentary)	1QpHab	*Pesher on Habakkuk* from Qumran
Q	Qumran		
1Q, 2Q,		1QM	*Milḥāmāh* (*War Scroll*)
3Q, etc.	Numbered caves of Qumran, yielding written material; followed by abbreviation of biblical or apocryphal book	1QS	*Serek hayyaḥad* (*Rule of the Community, Manual of Discipline*)
QL	Qumran literature	1QSa	Appendix A (*Rule of the Congregation*) to 1QS

1QSb	Appendix B (*Blessings*) to 1QS	4QTestim	*Testimonia* text from Qumran Cave 4
3Q15	Copper Scroll from Qumran Cave 3	4QTLevi	*Testament of Levi* from Qumran Cave 4
4QFlor	*Florilegium* (or *Eschatological Midrashim*) from Qumran Cave 4	4QPhyl	Phylacteries from Qumran Cave 4
4QMess ar	Aramaic "Messianic" text from Qumran Cave 4	11QMelch	*Melchizedek* text from Qumran Cave 11
4QPrNab	Prayer of Nabonidus from Qumran Cave 4	11QtgJob	*Targum of Job* from Qumran Cave 11

G. Abbreviations of Targumic Material

Tg. Onq.	*Targum Onqelos*	*Tg. Ps.-J.*	*Targum Pseudo-Jonathan*
Tg. Neb.	*Targum of the Prophets*	*Tg. Yer. I*	*Targum Yerušalmi I**
Tg. Ket.	*Targum of the Writings*	*Tg. Yer. II*	*Targum Yerušalmi II**
Frg. Tg.	*Fragmentary Targum*	*Yem. Tg.*	*Yemenite Targum*
Sam. Tg.	*Samaritan Targum*	*Tg. Esth. I, II*	*First or Second Targum of Esther*
Tg. Isa.	*Targum of Isaiah*		
Pal. Tgs.	*Palestinian Targums*		
Tg. Neof.	*Targum Neofiti I*	*optional title	

H. Abbreviations of Other Rabbinic Works

ʾAbot R. Nat.	*ʾAbot de Rabbi Nathan*	*Pesiq. R.*	*Pesiqta Rabbati*
ʾAg. Ber.	*ʾAggadat Berešit*	*Pesiq. Rab Kah.*	*Pesiqta de Rab Kahana*
Bab.	*Babylonian*	*Pirqe R. El.*	*Pirqe Rabbi Eliezer*
Bar.	*Baraita*	*Rab.*	*Rabbah* (following abbreviation for biblical book: *Gen. Rab.* = *Genesis Rabbah*)
Der. Er. Rab.	*Derek Ereṣ Rabba*		
Der. Er. Zuṭ.	*Derek Ereṣ Zuṭa*		
Gem.	*Gemara*	*Sem.*	*Semaḥot*
Kalla	*Kalla*	*Sipra*	*Sipra*
Mek.	*Mekilta*	*Sipre*	*Sipre*
Midr.	*Midraš*; cited with usual abbreviation for biblical book; but *Midr. Qoh.* = *Midraš Qohelet*	*Sop.*	*Soperim*
		S. ʿOlam Rab.	*Seder ʿOlam Rabbah*
		Talm.	*Talmud*
		Yal.	*Yalqut*
Pal.	*Palestinian*		

I. Abbreviations of Orders and Tractates in Mishnaic and Related Literature

Sources of tractates are indicated as follows: *m.* (Mishnah), *t.* (Tosepta), *b.* (Babylonian Talmud), and *y.* (Jerusalem Talmud).

ʾAbot	*ʾAbot*	*Beṣa*	*Beṣa* (= *Yom Tob*)
ʿArak.	*ʿArakin*	*Bik.*	*Bikkurim*
ʿAbod. Zar.	*ʿAboda Zara*	*B. Meṣ.*	*Baba Meṣiʿa*
B. Bat.	*Baba Batra*	*B. Qam.*	*Baba Qamma*
Bek.	*Bekorot*	*Dem.*	*Demai*
Ber	*Berakot*	*ʿEd.*	*ʿEduyyot*

ʿErub.	ʿErubin	Ohol.	Oholot
Giṭ.	Giṭṭin	ʿOr.	ʿOrla
Ḥag.	Ḥagiga	Para	Para
Ḥal.	Ḥalla	Peʾa	Peʾa
Hor.	Horayot	Pesaḥ.	Pesahim
Ḥul.	Ḥullin	Qinnim	Qinnim
Kelim	Kelim	Qidd.	Qiddušin
Ker.	Keritot	Qod.	Qodašin
Ketub.	Ketubot	Roš. Haš.	Roš Haššana
Kil.	KilʾPayim	Sanh.	Sanhedrin
Maʿaśʾ.	Maaʿśʾerot	Šabb.	Šabbat
Mak.	Makkot	Šeb.	Šebiʿit
Makš.	Makširin (= Mašqin)	Šebu.	Šebuʿot
Meg.	Megilla	Šeqal.	Šeqalim
Meʿil.	Meʿila	Sota	Sota
Menaḥ.	Menahot	Sukk.	Sukka
Mid.	Middot	Taʿan.	Taʿanit
Miqw.	Miqwaʾot	Tamid	Tamid
Moʿed	Moʿed	Tem.	Temura
Moʿed Qaṭ.	Moʿed Qaṭan	Ter.	Terumot
Maʿaś. Š.	Maʿaśer Šeni	Ṭohar.	Toharot
Našim	Našim	T. Yom	Tebul Yom
Nazir	Nazir	ʿUq.	ʿUqṣin
Ned.	Nedarim	Yad.	Yadayim
Neg.	Negaʿim	Yebam.	Yebamot
Nez.	Neziqin	Yoma	Yoma (= Kippurim)
Nid.	Niddah	Zabim	Zabim
		Zebaḥ	Zebaḥim
		Zer.	Zeraʿim

J. Abbreviations of Nag Hammadi Tractates

Acts Pet. 12 Apost.	Acts of Peter and the Twelve Apostles	Exeg. Soul	Exegesis on the Soul
		Gos. Eg.	Gospel of the Egyptians
		Gos. Phil.	Gospel of Philip
Allogenes	Allogenes	Gos. Thom.	Gospel of Thomas
Ap. Jas.	Apocryphon of James	Gos. Truth	Gospel of Truth
Ap. John	Apocryphon of John	Great Pow.	Concept of our Great Power
Apoc. Adam	Apocalypse of Adam	Hyp. Arch.	Hypostasis of the Archons
1 Apoc. Jas.	First Apocalypse of James	Hypsiph.	Hypsiphrone
2 Apoc. Jas.	Second Apocalypse of James	Interp. Know.	Interpretation of Knowledge
Apoc. Paul	Apocalypse of Paul	Marsanes	Marsanes
Apoc. Pet.	Apocalypse of Peter	Melch.	Melchizedek
Asclepius	Asclepius 21–29	Norea	Thought of Norea
Auth. Teach.	Authoritative Teaching	On Bap. A	On Baptism A
Dial. Sav.	Dialogue of the Savior	On Bap. B	On Baptism B
Disc. 8–9	Discourse on the Eighth and Ninth	On Bap. C	On Baptism C
		On Euch. A	On the Eucharist A
Ep. Pet. Phil.	Letter of Peter to Philip	On Euch. B	On the Eucharist B
Eugnostos	Eugnostos the Blessed	Orig. World	On the Origin of the World

Paraph. Shem	*Paraphrase of Shem*	*Thom. Cont.*	*Book of Thomas the Contender*
Pr. Paul	*Prayer of the Apostle Paul*	*Thund.*	*Thunder, Perfect Mind*
Pr. Thanks	*Prayer of Thanksgiving*	*Treat. Res.*	*Treatise on Resurrection*
Prot. Jas.	*Protevangelium of James*	*Treat. Seth*	*Second Treatise of the Great*
Sent. Sextus	*Sentences of Sextus*		*Seth*
Soph. Jes. Chr.	*Sophia of Jesus Christ*	*Tri. Trac.*	*Triparite Tractate*
Steles Seth	*Three Steles of Seth*	*Trim. Prot.*	*Trimorphic Protennoia*
Teach. Silv.	*Teachings of Silvanus*	*Val. Exp.*	*A Valentinian Exposition*
Testim. Truth	*Testimony of Truth*	*Zost.*	*Zostrianos*

Commentary Bibliography

Andriessen, P., and **Lenglet, A.** *De Brief aan de Hebreeën.* Roermond: Roman and Zonen, 1971. **Aquinas, T.** "Ad Hebraeos." In *Super Epistolas S. Pauli Lectura.* Ed. R. Cai. Turin/Rome: Marietti, 1953. **Attridge, H. W.** *A Commentary on the Epistle to the Hebrews.* Hermeneia. Philadelphia: Fortress, 1989. **Barclay, W.** *The Epistle to the Hebrews.* Daily Study Bible. Philadelphia: Westminster, 1957. **Bénétreau, S.** *L'Épître aux Hébreux.* Vol. 1. Commentaire Evangélique de la Bible 10. Vaux-sur-Seine: ÉDIFAC, 1989. **Bleek, F.** *Der Brief an die Hebräer, erläutert durch Einleitung, Uebersetzung und fortlaufenden Kommentar.* 2 vols. in 3. Berlin: Dümmler, 1828–40. **Bonsirven, J.** *Saint Paul, Épître aux Hébreux.* 2nd ed. VS 12. Paris: Beauchesne, 1953. **Bose, W. P. du.** *High Priesthood and Sacrifice: An Exposition of the Epistle to the Hebrews.* New York: Longmans, Green, 1908. **Bourke, M. M.** *The Epistle to the Hebrews.* Englewood Cliffs, NJ: Prentice Hall, 1990. **Bowman, G. M.** *Don't Let Go! An Exposition of Hebrews.* Phillipsburg: Presbyterian & Reformed, 1982. **Bowman, J. W.** *Hebrews.* Richmond: Knox, 1962. **Braun, H.** *An die Hebräer.* HNT 14. Tübingen: Mohr, 1984. **Bristol, L. O.** *Hebrews: A Commentary.* Valley Forge, PA: Judson, 1967. **Brown, R.** *Christ above All: The Message of Hebrews.* Downers Grove, IL: Inter-Varsity Press, 1982. **Bruce, A. B.** *The Epistle to the Hebrews, The First Apology for Christianity: An Exegetical Study.* 2nd ed. Edinburgh: Clark, 1899. **Bruce, F. F.** *The Epistle to the Hebrews.* NICNT. Grand Rapids: Eerdmans, 1964. **Buchanan, G. W.** *To the Hebrews.* AB 36. Garden City, NY: Doubleday, 1972. **Calvin, J.** *The Epistle of Paul the Apostle to the Hebrews.* Tr. W. B. Johnston. Grand Rapids: Eerdmans, 1963. **Casey, J.** *Hebrews.* Dublin: Veritas Publications, 1980. **Caudill, R. P.** *Hebrews: A Translation with Notes.* Nashville: Broadman, 1985. **Chadwick, G. A.** *The Epistle to the Hebrews.* London: Hodder & Stoughton, n.d. **Chilstrom, H. W.** *Hebrews: A New and Better Way.* Philadelphia: Fortress, 1984. **Chrysostom, J.** "Homiliae xxxiv in Epistolam ad Hebraeos." *PG* 63 (1862) 9–256. ———. *Homilies on the Gospel of John and the Epistle to the Hebrews.* Tr. P. Schaff and F. Gardiner. NPNF 14. New York: Scribner's, 1889. **Corbishley, T.** *Good News in Hebrews: The Letter to the Hebrews in Today's English Version.* Cleveland: Collins & World, 1976. **Davidson, A. B.** *The Epistle to the Hebrews.* Edinburgh: Clark, 1882. **Davies, J. H.** *A Letter to Hebrews.* Cambridge Bible Commentary. Cambridge: UP, 1967. **Delitzch, F. J.** *Commentary on the Epistle to the Hebrews.* 2 vols. Tr. T. L. Kingsbury. Edinburgh: Clark, 1871–72. **Edwards, T. C.** *The Epistle to the Hebrews.* New York: A. C. Armstrong and Son, 1903. **Ellingworth, P.** and **Nida, E.** *A Translator's Handbook on the Letter to the Hebrews.* New York: United Bible Societies, 1983. **Evans, L. H.** *Hebrews.* The Communicator's Commentary 10. Waco, TX: Word, 1985. **Farrar, F. W.** *The Epistle of Paul the Apostle to the Hebrews.* CGTC. Cambridge: UP, 1894. **Feld, H.** *Der Hebräerbrief.* Beiträge der Forschung. Darmstadt: Wissenschaftliche Buchgesellschaft, 1985. **Gooding, D.** *An Unshakeable Kingdom: The Letter to the Hebrews for Today.* Grand Rapids: Eerdmans, 1989. **Graf, J.** *Der Hebräerbrief.* Freiburg i/B: Wagner, 1918. **Grässer, E.** *An die Hebräer: 1. Hebr 1–6.* EKKNT 17/1. Zürich: Benziger, 1990. **Gromacki, R. G.** *Stand Bold in Grace: An Exposition of Hebrews.* Grand Rapids: Baker Book House, 1984. **Grosheide, F. W.** *De Brief aan de Hebreeën en de Brief van Jakobus.* 2nd ed. Kampen: Kok, 1955. **Guthrie, D.** *The Letter to the Hebrews.* TNTC. Grand Rapids: Eerdmans, 1983. **Haering, T.** *Der Brief an die Hebräer.* Stuttgart: Calwer, 1925. **Hagner, D. A.** *Hebrews.* Good News Commentaries. San Francisco: Harper & Row, 1983. ———. *Hebrews.* NIBC 14. Peabody, MA: Hendrickson, 1990. **Hegermann, H.** *Der Brief an die Hebräer.*

THKNT 16. Berlin: Evangelische Verlangsanstalt, 1988. **Héring, J.** *L'Épître aux Hébreux.* CNT 12. Neuchâtel: Delachaux & Niestlé, 1954. [ET *The Epistle to the Hebrews.* Tr. A. W. Heathcote and P. J. Allcock. London: Epworth, 1970.] **Hewitt, T.** *The Epistle to the Hebrews.* TNTC. London: Tyndale Press, 1960. **Hillmann, W.** *Der Brief an die Hebräer.* Düsseldorf: Patmos, 1965. **Hollmann, G.** *Der Hebräerbrief.* Die Schriften des Neuen Testaments 3. Ed. W. Bousset and W. Heitmüller. 3rd ed. Göttingen: Vandenhoeck & Ruprecht, 1917. **Hudson, J. T.** *The Epistle to the Hebrews.* Edinburgh: Clark, 1937. **Hugedé, N.** *Le sacerdoce du Fils: Commentaire de l'Épître aux Hébreux.* Paris: Editions Fischbacher, 1983. **Hughes, P. E.** *A Commentary on the Epistle to the Hebrews.* Grand Rapids: Eerdmans, 1977. **Javet, J. J.** *Dieu nous parla: Commentaire sur l'Épître aux Hébreux.* Collection "L'Actualité Protestante." Neuchâtel/Paris: Delachaux & Niestlé, 1945. **Jewett, R.** *Letter to Pilgrims: A Commentary on the Epistle to the Hebrews.* New York: The Pilgrim Press, 1981. **Johnsson. W. G.** *Hebrews.* Knox Preaching Guides. Atlanta: John Knox, 1980. **Keil, K. F.** *Kommentar über den Brief an die Hebräer.* Leipzig: Deichert, 1885. **Kendrick, A. L.** *Commentary on the Epistle to the Hebrews.* Philadelphia: American Baptist, 1889. **Kent, H. A.** *The Epistle to the Hebrews, A Commentary.* Grand Rapids: Baker, 1972. **Ketter, P.** *Hebräerbrief, Jakobusbrief, Petrusbrief, Judasbrief: Übersetzt und erklärt.* HBK 16/1. Freiburg: Herder, 1950. **Kistemaker, S. J.** *Exposition of the Epistle to the Hebrews.* New Testament Commentary. Grand Rapids: Baker Book House, 1984. **Klijn, A. F. J.** *De Brief aan de Hebreeën.* Nijkerk: Callenbach, 1975. **Kuss, O.** *Der Brief an die Hebräer.* RNT 8/1. Regensburg: Pustet, 1966. **Lane, W. L.** *Call to Commitment: Responding to the Message of Hebrews.* Nashville: Nelson, 1985. **Lang, G. H.** *The Epistle to the Hebrews.* London: Paternoster, 1951. **Laubach, F.** *Der Brief an die Hebräer.* Wuppertal: Brockhaus, 1967. **Lenski, R. C. H.** *The Interpretation of the Epistle to the Hebrews and the Epistle of James.* Columbus, OH: Wartburg, 1946. **Lightfoot, N. R.** *Jesus Christ Today: A Commentary on the Book of Hebrews.* Grand Rapids: Baker, 1976. **Lünemann, G.** *Kritisch-exegetischer Handbuch über den Hebräerbrief.* MeyerK 13. Göttingen: Vandenhoeck & Ruprecht, 1878. **März, C.-P.** *Hebräerbrief.* Die neue echter Bibel, Neues Testament 16. Würzburg: Echter, 1989. **MacDonald, W.** *The Epistle to the Hebrews: From Ritual to Reality.* Neptune, NJ: Loizeaux, 1971. **McCaul, J. B.** *The Epistle to the Hebrews: A Paraphrastic Commentary with Illustrations from Philo, the Targums, the Mishna and Gemara, etc.* London: Longmans, Green, 1871. **Médebielle, A.** *Épître aux Hébreux: Traduite et commentée.* 3rd ed. SB 12. Paris: Letouzey et Ané, 1951. **Michel, O.** *Der Brief an die Hebräer.* 12th ed. MeyerK 13. Göttingen: Vandenhoeck & Ruprecht, 1966. **Moffatt, J.** *A Critical and Exegetical Commentary on the Epistle to the Hebrews.* ICC. Edinburgh: Clark, 1924. **Montefiore, H.** *A Commentary on the Epistle to the Hebrews.* HNTC. New York: Harper, 1964. **Morris, L.** *Hebrews.* Bible Study Commentary. Grand Rapids: Zondervan, 1983. **Nairne, A.** *The Epistle to the Hebrews.* CGTC. Cambridge: UP, 1917. ———. *The Epistle to the Hebrews.* Cambridge Bible for Schools and Colleges. Cambridge: UP, 1921. **Narborough, F. D. V.** *Epistle to the Hebrews.* Clarendon Bible. Oxford: Clarendon, 1930. **Neighbour, R. E.** *If They Shall Fall Away: The Epistle to the Hebrews Unveiled.* Miami Springs: Conlay & Schaettle, 1940. **Neil, W.** *The Epistle to the Hebrews.* 2nd ed. TBC. London: Black, 1959. **Newell, W. R.** *Hebrews: Verse by Verse.* Chicago: Moody Press, 1947. **Obiols, S.** *Epístoles de Sant Pau: Als Hebreus.* Montserrat: Monestir de Montserrat, 1930. **Owen, J.** *An Exposition of the Epistle to the Hebrews.* 7 vols. Edinburgh: Ritchie, 1812. **Pfitzner, V. C.** *Chi Rho Commentary on Hebrews.* Adelaide, S. Australia: Lutheran Publishing House, 1979. **Purdy, A. C.,** and **Cotton, J. H.** "The Epistle to the Hebrews." *IB* 11 (1955) 575–763. **Reisner, E.** *Der Brief an die Hebräer.* Munich: Beck, 1938. **Rendall, F.** *The Epistle to the Hebrews.* London: Macmillan, 1888. **Riggenbach, E.** *Der Brief an die Hebräer.* 3rd ed. KNT 14. Leipzig: Deichert, 1922. **Robinson, T. H.** *The Epistle to the Hebrews.* 8th ed. MNTC. London: Hodder & Stoughton, 1964. **Schierse, F. J.** *The Epistle to the Hebrews.* Tr. B. Fahy. London: Burns & Oates, 1969. **Schlatter, A.** *Der Brief an die Hebräer ausgelegt für Bibelleser.*

Stuttgart: Calwer, 1950. **Schneider, J.** *The Letter to the Hebrews.* Tr. W. A. Mueller. Grand Rapids: Eerdmans, 1957. **Schulz, D.** *Der Brief an die Hebräer.* Breslau: Holaufer, 1818. **Seeberg, A.** *Der Brief an die Hebräer.* KNT. Leipzig: Quelle & Meyer, 1912. **Smit, E.** *Die Brief aan die Hebrëers.* Pretoria: N. G. Kerkboekhandel Transval, 1982. **Smith, R. H.** *Hebrews.* Augsburg Commentary on the New Testament. Minneapolis: Augsburg, 1984. **Snell, A. A.** *New and Living Way: An Explanation of the Epistle to the Hebrews.* London: Faith, 1959. **Soden, H. von.** *Der Hebräerbrief.* 3rd ed. HKNT 3/2. Freiburg/Leipzig/Tübingen: Mohr, 1899. **Spicq, C.** *L'Épître aux Hébreux.* 2 vols. EBib. Paris: Gabalda, 1952–53. ———. *L'Épître aux Hébreux: Traduction, notes critiques, commentaire.* SB. Paris: Gabalda, 1977. **Stibbs, A. M.** *So Great Salvation: The Meaning and Message of the Letter to the Hebrews.* Exeter: Paternoster Press, 1970. **Strathmann, H.** *Der Brief an die Hebräer, übersetzt und erklärt.* 7th ed. NTD 9. Göttingen: Vandenhoeck & Ruprecht, 1963. **Strobel, A.** *Der Brief an die Hebräer.* NTD 9/2. Göttingen: Vandenhoeck & Ruprecht, 1975. **Stuart, M.** *A Commentary on the Epistle to the Hebrews.* 4th ed. Andover: W. F. Draper, 1876. **Teodorico, P.** *L'epistola agli Ebrei.* Torino/Rome: Marietti, 1952. **Theodoret.** *Interpretatio Epistulae ad Hebraeos.* PG 82. **Thompson, J. W.** *The Letter to the Hebrews.* Austin: Sweet, 1971. **Vaughan, C. J.** *The Epistle to the Hebrews.* London: Macmillan, 1890. **Weiss, B.** *Der Brief an die Hebräer.* 6th ed. MeyerK 13. Göttingen: Vandenhoeck & Ruprecht, 1897. **Westcott, B. F.** *The Epistle to the Hebrews: The Greek Text with Notes and Essays.* 3rd ed. London/New York: Macmillan, 1903. **Wettstein, J. J.** *Η ΚΑΙΝΗ ΔΙΑΘΗΚΗ: Novum Testamentum Graecum editionis receptae cum lectionibus variantibus Codicum MSS, editionum aliarum, versionum et patrum nec non commentario pleniore ex scriptoribus veteribus hebrais, graecis et latinis historiam et vim verborum illustrante.* Vol. 2. Amsterdam: Dommer, 1752. **Wickham, E. C.** *The Epistle to the Hebrews.* London: Methuen, 1910. **Williamson, R.** *The Epistle to the Hebrews.* London: Epworth, 1965. **Wilson, R. McL.** *Hebrews.* New Century Bible Commentary. Grand Rapids: Eerdmans, 1987. **Windisch, H.** *Der Hebräerbrief.* 2nd ed. HNT 14. Tübingen: Mohr, 1931.

Main Bibliography

Ahern, A. A. "The Perfection Concept in the Epistle to the Hebrews." *JBR* 14 (1946) 164–67. **Alexander, J. P.** *A Priest for Ever: A Study of the Epistle Entitled "To the Hebrews."* London: Clarke, 1937. **Alfaro, J.** "Cristo glorioso, revelador del Padre." *Greg* 39 (1958) 220–70. **Anderson, C. P.** "The Epistle to the Hebrews and the Pauline Letter Collection." *HTR* 59 (1966) 429–38. ———. "Hebrews among the Letters of Paul." *SR* 5 (1975–76) 258–66. ———. "The Setting of the Epistle to the Hebrews." Dissertation, Columbia University, 1969. ———. "Who Wrote 'The Epistle from Laodicea'?" *JBL* 85 (1966) 436–40. **Anderson, R.** *The Hebrews Epistle in the Light of the Types.* London: Nisbet, 1911. **Andriessen, P.** *En lisant l'Épître aux Hébreux: Lettre au R. P. A. Vanhoye, Professeur à l'Institute Biblique Pontifical sur l'interprétation controversée de certain passages.* Vaals: Abby St. Benedictusberg, 1977. ———. "L'Eucharistie dans l'Épître aux Hébreux." *NRT* 94 (1972) 269–77. **Appel, H.** *Der Hebräerbrief: Ein Schreiben des Apollos an Judenchristen der korinthischen Gemeinde.* Leipzig: Deichert, 1918. **Archer, G. L.,** and **Chirichigne, G.** *Old Testament Quotations in the New Testament.* Chicago: Moody, 1983. **Asting, R.** *Die Heiligkeit im Urchristentum.* FRLANT 29. Göttingen: Vandenhoeck & Ruprecht, 1930. **Atkinson, B. F. C.** *The Theology of Prepositions.* London: Tyndale, 1944. **Attridge, H. W.** "Paraenesis in a Homily (λόγος παρακλήσεως): The Possible Location of, and Socialization in, the 'Epistle to the Hebrews.'" *Semeia* 50 (1990) 211–26. **Aune, D.** *The New Testament in Its Literary Environment.* Philadelphia: Westminster, 1987. **Ayles, H. H. B.** *Destination, Date, and Authorship of the Epistle to the Hebrews.* London: Clay, 1899. ———. "The References to Persecution in the Epistle to the Hebrews." *Exp* 8th ser. 12 (1916) 69–74. **Badcock, F. J.** *The Pauline Epistles and the Epistle to the Hebrews in Their Historical Setting.* London: SPCK, 1937. **Bacon, B. W.** "The Doctrine of Faith in Hebrews, James and Clement of Rome." *JBL* 19 (1900) 12–21. **Baigent, J. W.** "Jesus as Priest: An Examination of the Claim that the Concept of Jesus as Priest May Be Found outside of the Epistle to the Hebrews." *VoxEv* 12 (1981) 33–44. **Ballarini, T.** "Il peccato nell 'epistola agli Ebrei.'" *ScC* 106 (1978) 358–71. **Barbel, J.** *Christos Angelos: Die Anschauung von Christus als Bote und Engel in der gelehrten und volkstümlichen Literatur des christlichen Altertums.* Bottrop: Postberg, 1941. **Barnes, A. S.** "St. Barnabas and the Epistle to the Hebrews." *HibJ* 30 (1931–32) 103–17. **Barrett, C. K.** "The Eschatology of the Epistle to the Hebrews." In *The Background of the New Testament and Its Eschatology.* Ed. W. D. Davies and D. Daube. Cambridge: Cambridge UP, 1954. **Barth, M.** "The Old Testament in Hebrews: An Essay in Biblical Hermeneutics." In *Current Issues in New Testament Interpretation.* Ed. W. Klassen and G. F. Snyder. New York: Harper & Row, 1962. **Bartlet, J. V.** "The Epistle to the Hebrews Once More." *ExpTim* 34 (1922–23) 58–61. **Bartlet, V.** "Barnabas and His Genuine Epistle." *Exp* 6th ser. 6 (1902) 28–30. ———. "The Epistle to the Hebrews as the Work of Barnabas." *Exp* 6th ser. 8 (1903) 381–96. **Barton, G. A.** "The Date of the Epistle to the Hebrews." *JBL* 57 (1938) 195–207. **Batdorf, I. W.** "Hebrews and Qumran: Old Methods and New Directions." *FS F. Wilbur Gingrich.* Ed. E. H. Barth and R. E. Cocroft. Leiden: Brill, 1972. **Bates, W. H.** "Authorship of the Epistle to the Hebrews Again." *BSac* 79 (1922) 93–96. **Batiffol, P.** "L'attribution de l'Épître aux Hébreux à S. Barnabé." *RB* 8 (1899) 278–83. **Beare, F. W.** "The Text of the Epistle to the Hebrews in P⁴⁶." *JBL* 63 (1944) 379–96. **Behm, J.** *Der Begriff Διαθήκη im Neuen Testament.* Berlin: Runge, 1912. **Berger, K.** *Exegese des Neuen Testaments: Neue Wege vom Text zur Auslegung.* 2nd ed. Heidelberg: Quelle & Meyer, 1984. **Bickerman, E. J.** "En marge de l'Écriture." *RB* 88 (1981) 19–41. **Bieder, W.** "Pneumatologische Aspekte im Hebräerbrief." In *Neues Testament und Geschichte.* FS O. Cullmann. Ed. H. Baltensweiler and B. Reicke. Tübingen: Mohr, 1972. **Biesenthal, J. H. R.** *Das Trostschreiben des Apostels Paulus an die Hebräer.* Leipzig: Fernau,

1878. **Bietenhard, H.** *Die himmlische Welt im Urchristentum und Spätjudentum.* WUNT 2. Tübingen: Mohr, 1951. **Black, D. A.** "The Problem of the Literary Structure of Hebrews." *GTJ* 7 (1986) 163–77. ————. *Linguistics for Students of New Testament Greek: A Survey of Basic Concepts and Applications.* Grand Rapids: Baker, 1988. **Black, M.** "The Christological Use of the Old Testament in the New Testament." *NTS* 18 (1971–72) 1–14. **Blass, F.** "Die rhythmische Komposition des Hebräers." *TSK* 75 (1902) 420–60. **Bligh, J.** *Chiastic Analysis of the Epistle to the Hebrews.* Heythrop: Athenaeum, 1966. ————. "The Structure of Hebrews." *HeyJ* 5 (1964) 170–77. **Bodelschwingh, F. V.** "Jesus der Mittler des Neuen Testaments nach dem Zeugnis des Hebräerbriefs." In *Lebendig und Frei:* Bethel bei Bielefeld: Anstalt Bethel, 1949. **Bolewski, H.** "*Christos Archiereus:* Über die Entstehung der hohepriesterlichen Wurdenamens Christi." Dissertation, Halle, 1939. **Bonnard, P.** "Actualité de l'Épître aux Hébreux." *FV* 62 (1963) 283–88. **Bonsirven, J.** "La sacerdoce et le sacrifice de Jésus-Christ après l'Épître aux Hébreux." *NRT* 71 (1939) 641–60, 769–86. **Bornhäuser, K.** *Empfänger und Verfasser des Briefes an die Hebräer.* BFCT 35/3. Gütersloh: Bertelsmann, 1932. **Borchet, L.** "A Superior Book: Hebrews." *RevExp* 82 (1985) 319–32. **Bornkamm, G.** "Das Bekenntnis im Hebräerbrief." *TBl* 21 (1942) 56–66. **Bover, J. M.** "La esperanza en la Epístola a los Hebreos." *Greg* 19 (1938) 110–20. ————. "Inspiración divina del redactor de la Epístola a los Hebreos." *EE* 14 (1935) 433–66. **Braun, H.** "Die Gewinnung der Gewissenheit in dem Hebräerbrief." *TLZ* 96 (1971) 321–30. ————. "Das himmlische Vaterland bei Philo und im Hebräerbrief." In *Verborum Veritas.* FS G. Stählin. Ed. O. Böcher and K. Haacker. Wuppertal: Brockhaus, 1970. **Bristol, L. O.** "Primitive Christian Preaching and the Epistle to the Hebrews." *JBL* 68 (1949) 89–97. **Brooks, W. E.** "The Perpetuity of Christ's Sacrifice in the Epistle to the Hebrews." *JBL* 89 (1970) 205–14. **Brown, J. V.** "The Authorship and Circumstances of 'Hebrews'—Again!" *BSac* 80 (1923) 505–38. **Brown, R.** "Pilgrimage in Faith: The Christian Life in Hebrews." *SWJT* 28 (1985) 28–35. **Bruce, F. F.** "Christianity under Claudius." *BJRL* 44 (1961–62) 309–26. ————. "Kerygma of Hebrews." *Int* 23 (1969) 3–19. ————. "Recent Contributions to the Understanding of Hebrews." *ExpTim* 80 (1969) 260–64. ————. "The Structure and Argument of Hebrews." *SWJT* 28 (1985) 6–12. ————. "'To the Hebrews' or 'To the Essenes'?" *NTS* 9 (1963) 217–32. **Brüll, A.,** ed. *Das samaritanische Targum zum Pentateuch.* 5 vols. Frankfurt: Kaufmann, 1874–79. **Buchanan, G. W.** "The Present State of Scholarship on Hebrews." In *Judaism, Christianity and Other Greco-Roman Cults.* FS Morton Smith. Ed. J. Neusner. Vol. 1. Leiden: Brill, 1975. **Büchel, C.** "Der Hebräerbrief und das Alte Testament." *TSK* 79 (1906) 508–91. **Büchsel, F.** *Die Christologie des Hebräerbriefs.* BFCT 27/2. Gütersloh: Bertelsmann, 1922. **Bullock, M. R.** "The Recipients and Destination of Hebrews." Dissertation, Dallas Theological Seminary, 1977. **Burch, V.** *The Epistle to the Hebrews: Its Sources and Its Message.* London: Williams & Norgate, 1936. ————. "Factors in the Christology of the Letter to the Hebrews." *Exp* 47 (1921) 68–79. **Burggaller, E.** "Das literarische Problem des Hebräerbriefes." *ZNW* 9 (1908) 110–131. ————. "Neue Untersuchungen zum Hebräerbrief." *TRu* 13 (1910) 369–81, 409–17. **Burns, D. K.** "The Epistle to the Hebrews." *ExpTim* 47 (1935–36) 184–89. **Burtness, J. H.** "Plato, Philo, and the Author of Hebrews." *LQ* 10 (1958) 54–64. **Burton, E. D.** *Syntax of the Moods and Tenses in New Testament Greek.* 3rd ed. Edinburgh: Clark, 1898. **Cabantous, J.** *Philon et l'Épître aux Hébreux ou essai sur les rapports del la christologie de l'Épître aux Hébreux avec la philosophie Judéo-Alexandrine.* Montauban: Granié, 1895. **Caird, G. B.** "The Exegetical Method of the Epistle to the Hebrews." *CJT* 5 (1959) 44–51. ————. *The Language and Imagery of the Bible.* London: Duckworth, 1980. **Cambier, J.** "Eschatologie ou héllenisme dans l'Épître aux Hébreux: Une étude sur μένειν et l'exhortation finale de l'épître." *Sal* 11 (1949) 62–96. [Reissued as ALBO 2/12. Bruges/Paris: Descles de Brouwer, 1949.] **Campbell, A. G.** "The Problem of Apostasy in the Greek New Testament." Dissertation, Dallas Theological Seminary, 1957. **Campbell, J. C.** "In a Son: The Doctrine of the Incarnation in the Epistle to the Hebrews." *Int* 10 (1956) 24–38. **Campbell, J. Y.** *Three New Testament Studies.* Leiden: Brill, 1965. **Campos, J.** "A Carta aos Hebreus como Apolo ã superasão de 'Certa

Religiosidade Popular.'" *RCB* 8 (1984) 122–24. **Carlston, C.** "Eschatology and Repentance in the Epistle to the Hebrews." *JBL* 78 (1959) 296–302. ———. "The Vocabulary of Perfection in Philo and Hebrews." In *Unity and Diversity in New Testament Theology.* FS G. E. Ladd. Ed. R. A. Guelich. Grand Rapids: Eerdmans, 1978. **Casey, R. P.** "The Earliest Christologies." *JTS* 10 (1959) 253–77. **Cason, D. V.** "*ΙΕΡΕΥΣ* and *ΑΡΧΙΕΡΕΥΣ* (and Related Contexts) in Hebrews: An Exegetical Study in the Greek New Testament." Dissertation, Southern Baptist Theological Seminary, 1931. **Castelvecchi, I.** *La homologia en la carta a los Hebreos: Estudio exegetico-teológico.* Montevideo: Pellegrini Impresares, 1964. **Cazelles, H.** et al. *Moïse, l'homme de l'alliance.* CSion 8:2–3–4. Paris/Tournai: Desclée, 1954. **Chapman, J.** "Aristion, Author of the Epistle to the Hebrews." *RBén* 22 (1905) 50–64. **Clarkson, M. E.** "The Antecedents of the High Priest Theme in Hebrews." *ATR* 29 (1947) 89–95. **Cleary, M.** "Jesus, Pioneer and Source of Salvation: The Christology of Hebrews 1–6." *TBT* 67 (1973) 1242–48. **Clements, R. E.** "The Use of the Old Testament in Hebrews." *SWJT* 28 (1985) 36–45. **Cody, A.** *Heavenly Sanctuary and Liturgy in the Epistle to the Hebrews: The Achievement of Salvation in the Epistle's Perspectives.* St. Meinrad, IN: Grail, 1960. **Collins, R. F.** *Letters That Paul Did Not Write: The Epistle to the Hebrews and the Pauline Pseudepigrapha.* Wilmington, DE: Glazier, 1988. **Combrink, H. J. B.** "Some Thoughts on the Old Testament Citations in the Epistle to the Hebrews." *Neot* 5 (1971) 22–36. **Conner, W. T.** "Three Theories of the Atonement." *RevExp* 43 (1946) 275–90. ———. "Three Types of Teaching in the New Testament on the Meaning of the Death of Christ." *RevExp* 43 (1946) 150–66. **Constable, T. L.** "The Substitutionary Death of Christ in Hebrews." Dissertation, Dallas Theological Seminary, 1966. **Coppens, J.** "Les affinités Qumrâniennes de l'Épître aux Hébreux." *NRT* 84 (1962) 128–41, 257–82. [Reissued as ALBO 4/1 (1962).] ———. "La portée messianique du Ps CX." *ETL* 32 (1956) 1–23. **Cothenet, E., LeFort, P., Prigent, P.,** and **Dussaut, L.** *Les écrits de Saint Jean et l'Épître aux Hébreux.* Paris: Desclée, 1984. **Cotterell, P.,** and **Turner, M.** *Linguistics and Biblical Interpretation.* Downers Grove, IL: Inter-Varsity, 1989. **Cox, W. L. P.** *The Heavenly Priesthood of Our Lord.* Oxford: Blackwell, 1929. **Craddock, F. B.** *The Pre-Existence of Christ in the New Testament.* Nashville: Abingdon Press, 1968. **Cullmann, O.** *The Christology of the New Testament.* Rev. ed. Philadelphia: Westminster, 1963. **Culpepper, R. H.** "The High Priesthood and Sacrifice of Christ in the Epistle to the Hebrews." *ThEduc* 32 (1985) 46–62. **Custer, S.** "Annotated Bibliography on Hebrews." *BV* 2 (1968) 45–68. **Dahms, J. V.** "The First Readers of Hebrews." *JETS* 20 (1977) 365–75. **Dalbert, P.** *Die Theologie der hellenistisch-jüdischen Missionsliteratur unter Ausschluss von Philo und Josephus.* TF 4. Hamburg: Evangelischer, 1954. **Daly, R. J.** "The New Testament Concept of Christian Sacrificial Activity." *BTB* 8 (1978) 99–107. **D'Angelo, M. R.** *Moses in the Letter to the Hebrews.* SBLDS 42. Missoula, MT: Scholars, 1979. **Daniélou, J.** "La session à la droite du Père." *SE* 1 (1959) 689–98. **Daube, D.** "Rabbinic Methods of Interpretation and Hellenistic Rhetoric." *HUCA* 22 (1949) 239–64. **Dautzenberg, G.** "Der Glaube in Hebräerbrief." *BZ* 17 (1963) 161–77. **Davies, J. H.** "The Heavenly Work of Christ in Hebrews." *SE* 4 (1968) 384–89. **Déaut, R. le.** "Apropos a Definition of Midrash." *Int* 25 (1971) 259–82. ———. *La nuit pascale.* Rome: Institute Biblique Pontificale, 1963. **Deichgräber, R.** *Gotteshymnus und Christushymnus in der frühen Christenheit: Untersuchungen zu Form, Sprache und Stil der frühchristlichen Hymnen.* SUNT 5. Göttingen: Vandenhoeck & Ruprecht, 1967. **Descamps, A.** "La Sacerdoce du Christ d'après l'Épître aux Hébreux." *RDT* 9 (1954) 529–34. ———. "La structure de l'Épître aux Hébreux." *RDT* 9 (1954) 333–38. **Dey, L. K. K.** *The Intermediary World and Patterns of Perfection in Philo and Hebrews.* SBLDS 25. Missoula, MT: Scholars, 1975. **De Young, J. C.** *Jerusalem in the New Testament.* Kampen: Kok, 1960. **Dibelius, F.** *Der Verfasser des Hebräerbrief: Eine Untersuchung zur Geschichte des Urchristentums.* Strassburg: Heitz & Mundel, 1910. **Dibelius, M.** "Der himmlische Kultus nach dem Hebräerbrief." In *Botschaft und Geschichte: Gesammelte Aufsätze II: Zum Urchristentum und zur hellenistischen Religionsgeschichte.* Tübingen: Mohr, 1956. [Reprinted from *TBl* 21 (1942) 1–11.] **Dickie, J.** "The Literary Riddle of the 'Epistle to the Hebrews.'" *Exp* 8th ser. 5 (1913) 371–78. **Díez Macho, A.** *Neophyte 1: Targum*

Palestinense MS de la Biblioteca Vaticana. 6 vols. Madrid/Barcelona: Consejo Superior de Investigaciones Científicas, 1968–79. **Dimock, N.** *The Sacerdotium of Christ.* London: Longmans, Green, 1910. **Dinkler, E.** "Hebrews, Letter to the." *IDB* 2 (1962) 571–75. **Dobschütz, E. von.** "Rationales und irrationales Denken über Gott in Urchristentum: Eine Studie besonders zum Hebräerbrief." *TSK* 95 (1923–24) 235–55. **Dubarle, A. M.** "Rédacteur et destinataires de l'Épître aux Hébreux." *RB* 48 (1939) 506–29. **Dukes, J. G.** "Eschatology in the Epistle to the Hebrews." Dissertation, Southern Baptist Theological Seminary, 1956. **Dunbar, D. G.** "The Relation of Christ's Sonship and Priesthood in the Epistle to the Hebrews." Dissertation, Westminster Theological Seminary, Philadelphia, 1974. **Dupont, J.** "'Assis à la droite de Dieu': L'interpretation du Ps 110,1 dans le Nouveau Testament." In *Resurrexit: Actes du Symposium International sur la Résurrection de Jésus, Rome, 1970.* Ed. E. Dhanis. Rome: Vaticana, 1974. **Dussaut, L.** *Synopse structurelle de l'Épître aux Hébreux: Approche d'analyse structurelle.* Paris: Desclée, 1981. **Dyck, T. L.** "Jesus Our Pioneer: *ΑΡΧΗΓΟΣ* in Heb. 2:5–18; 12:1–3, and Its Relation in the Epistle to Such Designations as *ΠΡΩΤΟΤΟΚΟΣ ΑΙΤΟΣ, ΠΡΟΔΡΟΜΟΣ, ΑΡΧΙΕΡΕΥΣ, ΕΓΓΥΟΣ, ΜΕΣΙΤΗΣ, ΠΟΙΜΗΝ* and to the Recurring Theme of Pilgrimage in Faith along the Path of Suffering Which Leads to Glory." Dissertation: Northwest Baptist Theological Seminary, 1980. **Eagar, A. R.** "The Authorship of the Epistle to the Hebrews." *Exp* 6th ser. 10 (1904) 74–80, 110–23. ———. "The Hellenistic Elements in the Epistle to the Hebrews." *Her* 11 (1901) 263–87. **Eccles, R. S.** "Hellenistic Mysticism in the Epistle to the Hebrews." Dissertation, Yale University, 1952. ———. "The Purpose of the Hellenistic Patterns in the Epistle to the Hebrews." In *Religions in Antiquity.* FS E. R. Goodenough. Ed. J. Neusner. Leiden: Brill, 1968. **Edgar, S. L.** "Respect for Context in Quotations from the Old Testament." *NTS* 9 (1962–63) 55–62. **Elbogen, I.** *Der jüdische Gottesdienst in seiner geschichtlichen Entwicklung.* 3rd ed. Frankfurt: Kaufmann, 1931. **Ellingworth, P.** "The Old Testament in Hebrews: Exegesis, Method and Hermeneutics." Dissertation, University of Aberdeen, 1977. **Ellis, E. E.** "Midrash, Targum and New Testament Quotations." In *Neotestamentica et Semitica.* FS Matthew Black. Ed. E. E. Ellis and M. Wilcox. Edinburgh: Clark, 1969. **English, E. S.** *Studies in the Epistle to the Hebrews.* Traveler's Rest, SC: Southern Bible House, 1955. **Etheridge, J. W.,** ed. *The Targums of Onkelos and Jonathan ben Uzziel on the Pentateuch.* London: Longmans, Green, 1962–65. **Fairhurst, A. M.** "Hellenistic Influence in the Epistle to the Hebrews." *TynBul* 7–8 (1961) 17–27. **Feld, H.** "Der Hebräerbrief: Literarische Form, religionsgeschichtlicher Hintergrund, theologische Fragen." *ANRW* 2.25.4 (1987) 3522–3601. ———. *Martin Luthers und Wendelin Steinbachs Vorlesungen über den Hebräerbrief: Eine Studie zur Geschichte der neutestamentlichen Exegese und Theologie.* Wiesbaden: Steiner, 1971. ———. "Die theologischen Hauptthemen der Hebräerbrief-Vorlesung Wendelin Steinbachs." *Augustiniana* 37 (1987) 187–252. **Fensham, F. C.** "Hebrews and Qumran." *Neot* 5 (1971) 9–21. **Fenton, J. C.** "The Argument in Hebrews." *SE* 7 (1982) 175–81. **Fernández, J.** "La teleíosis o perfección cristiana en la epistola a los Hebreos." *CB* 13 (1956) 251–59. **Feuillet, A.** "L'attente de la Parousie et du Jugement dans l'Épître aux Hébreux." *BVC* 42 (1961) 23–31. ———. "Les points de vue nouveaux dans l'eschatologie de l'Épître aux Hébreux." *SE* 2 (1964) 369–87. ———. *The Priesthood of Christ and His Ministers.* Garden City: Doubleday, 1975. **Field, F.** *Notes on the Translation of the New Testament.* Cambridge: Cambridge UP, 1899. **Field, J. E.** *The Apostolic Liturgy and the Epistle to the Hebrews.* London: Rivertons, 1882. **Filson, F. V.** "The Epistle to the Hebrews." *JBR* 22 (1954) 20–26. ———. *"Yesterday": A Study of Hebrews in the Light of Chapter 13.* SBT 2nd ser. 4. Naperville: Allenson, 1967. **Fiorenza, E. Schüssler** "Der Anführer und Vollender unseres Glaubens: Zum theologischen Verständnis des Hebräerbriefes." In *Gestalt und Anspruch des Neuen Testaments.* Ed. J. Schreiner. Würzburg: Echter, 1969. **Fitzer, G.** "Auch der Hebräerbrief legitimiert nicht eine Opfertodchristologie zur Frage der Intention des Hebräerbriefes und seiner Bedeutung für die Theologie." *KD* 15 (1969) 294–319. **Fitzmyer, J. A.** "The Use of Explicit Old Testament Quotations in Qumran Literature and in the New Testament." *NTS* 7 (1960–61) 297–333. **Floor, L.** "The General

Priesthood of Believers in the Epistle to the Hebrews." *Neot* 5 (1971) 72–82. **Fonseca, L. G. da.** "Διαθήκη—Foedus an testamentum?" *Bib* 8 (1927) 31–50, 161–81, 290–319, 418–41; 9 (1928) 26–40, 143–60. **Ford, J. M.** "The First Epistle to the Corinthians or the First Epistle to the Hebrews." *CBQ* 28 (1966) 402–16. ———. "The Mother of Jesus and the Authorship of the Epistle to the Hebrews." *TBT* 82 (1976) 683–94. **Forkman, G.** *The Limits of the Religious Community.* Lund: Gleerup, 1972. **Fransen, I.** "Jésus Pontife parfait du parfait sanctuaire (Épître aux Hébreux)." *BVC* 20 (1957) 262–81. ———. "Jesus, wahrer Hoherpriester des wahren Bundeszeltes." *BLit* 25 (1957–58) 172–82, 218–25, 261–69. **Friedrich, G.** "Beobachtungen zur messianischen Hohepriestererwartung." *ZTK* 53 (1956) 265–311. **Galinsky, G. K.** *The Herakles Theme.* Leiden: Brill, 1972. **Galot, J.** "Le sacrifice rédempteur du Christ selon l'Épître aux Hébreux." *EV* 89 (1979) 369–77. **Gamble, J.** "Symbol and Reality in the Epistle to the Hebrews." *JBL* 45 (1926) 162–70. **Gammie, J. G.** "A New Setting for Psalm 110." *ATR* 51 (1969) 4–17. ———. "Paraenetic Literature: Toward the Morphology of a Secondary Genre." *Semeia* 50 (1990) 41–77. **Gardiner, F.** "The Language of the Epistle to the Hebrews as Bearing upon Its Authorship." *JBL* 7 (1887) 1–25. **Garrard, L. A.** "The Diversity of New Testament Christology." *HibJ* 55 (1956–57) 213–22. **Gayford, S. C.** *Sacrifice and Priesthood.* 2nd ed. London: Methuen, 1953. **Gelin, A.** "Le sacerdoce du Christ d'après l'Épître aux Hébreux." In *Études sur le Sacrement de l'Ordre.* Lyon: LePuy, 1957. **Gemés, I.** "Alianca no Documento de Damasco e na Epístola aos Hebreus: Una contribuicão a questão: Qumran e as origens do Christianismo." *RCB* 6 (1969) 28–68. **Gifford, E. H.,** ed. *Eusebii Pamphilli Evangelicae Praeparationis.* 4 vols. Oxford: Oxford University, 1903. **Gilbert, G. H.** "The Greek Element in the Epistle to the Hebrews." *AJT* 14 (1910) 521–32. **Giversen, S.** "Evangelium Veritatis and the Epistle to the Hebrews." *ST* 13 (1959) 87–96. **Glaze, R. E.** "Introduction to Hebrews." *ThEduc* 32 (1985) 20–37. ———. *No Easy Salvation: A Careful Examination of Apostasy in Hebrews.* Nashville: Broadman, 1966. **Gnilka, J.** "Der Erwartung des messianisches Hohepriesters in den Schriften von Qumran und im Neuen Testament." *RevQ* 2 (1960) 395–426. **Goguel, M.** "La seconde géneration chrétienne." *RHR* 136 (1949) 31–57, 180–208. **Gooding, D.** *An Unshakeable Kingdom: Studies on the Epistle to the Hebrews.* Toronto: Everyday Publications, 1976. **Goodspeed, E. J.** "First Clement Called Forth by Hebrews." *JBL* 30 (1911) 157–60. ———. "The Problem of Hebrews." *JBR* 22 (1954) 122. **Goppelt, L.** *Typos: Die typologische Deutung des Alten Testaments im Neuen.* BFCT 2/43. Gütersloh: Bertelsmann, 1939. **Gordon, V. R.** "Studies in the Covenantal Theology of the Epistle to the Hebrews in Light of Its Setting." Dissertation, Fuller Theological Seminary, 1979. **Gornatowski, A.** *Rechts und Links im antiker Aberglauben.* Breslau: Nischkowsky, 1936. **Gotaas, D. S.** "The Old Testament in the Epistle to the Hebrews, the Epistle of James, and the Epistle of Peter." Dissertation, Northern Baptist Theological Seminary, 1958. **Gourgues, M.** *A la droite de Dieu: Résurrection de Jésus et actualisation du Psaume 110:1 dans le Nouveau Testament.* EBib. Paris: Gabalda, 1978. ———. "Lecture christologique du Psaume CX et fête de la Pentecôte." *RB* 83 (1976) 5–24. ———. "Remarques sur la 'structure centrale' de l'Épître aux Hébreux." *RB* 84 (1977) 26–37. **Graham, A. A. K.** "Mark and Hebrews." *SE* 4 (1968) 411–16. **Grass, K. K.** *Ist der Brief an die Hebräer an Heidenchristen gerichtet?* St. Petersburg: Köhne, 1892. **Grässer, E.** "Zur Christologie des Hebräerbriefes: Eine Auseinandersetzung mit Herbert Braun." In *Neues Testament und christliche Existenz.* FS H. Braun. Tübingen: Mohr, 1973. ———. "Die Gemeindevorsteher im Hebräerbrief." In *Vom Amt des Laien in Kirche und Theologie.* FS G. Krause. Ed. H. Schröer and P. G. Müller. Berlin: de Gruyter, 1982. 67–84. ———. *Der Glaube im Hebräerbrief.* Marburg: Elwert, 1965. ———. "Der Hebräerbrief 1938–1963." *TRu* 30 (1964) 138–236. ———. "Der historische Jesus im Hebräerbrief." *ZNW* 56 (1965) 63–91. ———. "Rechtfertigung im Hebräerbrief." In *Rechtfertigung.* FS E. Käsemann. Ed. J. Friedrich, W. Pöhlmann, and P. Stuhlmacher. Tübingen: Mohr, 1976. ———. "Das wandernde Gottesvolk zum Basismotiv des Hebräerbriefes." *ZNW* 77 (1986) 160–79. ———. *Texte und Situation.* Gütersloh: Mohn, 1973. **Greer, R. A.** "The Antiochene Exegesis of Hebrews."

Dissertation, Yale University, 1965. ———. *The Captain of Our Salvation: A Study in the Patristic Exegesis of Hebrews.* BGBE 15. Tübingen: Mohr, 1973. **Griffin, H.** "The Origin of the High Priestly Christology of the Epistle to the Hebrews." Dissertation, University of Aberdeen, 1978. **Grogan, G. W.** "The New Testament Interpretation of the Old Testament." *TB* 18 (1967) 54–76. **Grothe, J. F.** "Was Jesus the Priestly Messiah? A Study of the New Testament's Teaching of Jesus' Priestly Office against the Background of Jewish Hopes for a Priestly Messiah." Dissertation, Concordia Seminary, 1981. **Guthrie, D.** "The Epistle to the Hebrews." In *New Testament Introduction.* Vol. 3. Chicago: Inter-Varsity, 1962. **Guthrie, G. H.** "The Structure of Hebrews: A Textlinguistic Analysis." Dissertation, Southwestern Baptist Theological Seminary, 1991. **Gyllenberg, R.** "Die Christologie des Hebräerbriefes." *ZST* 11 (1934) 662–90. ———. "Die Komposition des Hebräerbriefs." *SEÅ* 22–23 (1957–58) 137–47. **Haering, T.** "Gedankengang und Grundgedanken des Hebräerbriefs." *ZNW* 18 (1917–18) 145–64. **Hagen, K.** *Hebrews Commenting from Erasmus to Beza 1516–1598.* BGBE 23. Tübingen: Mohr, 1981. ———. *A Theology of Testament in the Young Luther: The Lectures on Hebrews.* Leiden: Brill, 1974. **Hagner, D. A.** "Interpreting the Epistle to the Hebrews." In *The Literature and Meaning of Scripture.* Ed. M. A. Inch and C. H. Bullock. Grand Rapids: Baker, 1981. 217–42. ———. *The Use of the Old and New Testaments in Clement of Rome.* Leiden: Brill, 1973. **Hamerton-Kelly, R. G.** *Pre-Existence, Wisdom, and the Son of Man: A Study of the Idea of Pre-Existence in the New Testament.* SNTSMS 21. Cambridge: Cambridge UP, 1973. **Hammer, P.** "The Understanding of Inheritance (κληρονομία) in the New Testament." Dissertation, Heidelberg University, 1958. **Hamp, V.** "Ps 110, 4b und die Septuaginta." In *Neues Testament und Kirche.* FS R. Schnackenberg. Ed. J. Gnilka. Freiburg: Herder, 1974. **Hanna, R.** *A Grammatical Aid to the Greek New Testament.* Vol. 2: *Romans to Revelation.* Hidalgo, Mexico: Saenz, 1979. **Hanson, A. T.** "Christ in the Old Testament according to Hebrews." *SE* 2 (1964) 393–407. ———. "The Gospel in the Old Testament according to Hebrews." *Theol* 52 (1949) 248–52. **Harder, G.** "Die Septuagintazitate des Hebräerbriefs: Ein Beitrag zum Problem der Auslegung des Alten Testaments." In *Theologia Viatorum.* Ed. M. Albertz. Munich: Kaiser, 1939. **Harnack, A.** "Probabilia über die Adresse und den Verfasser des Hebräerbriefs." *ZNW* 1 (1900) 16–41. **Harris, J. R.** "Menander and the Epistle to the Hebrews." *ExpTim* 44 (1932–33) 191. ———. "An Orphic Reaction in the Epistle to the Hebrews." *ExpTim* 40 (1928–29) 449–51. ———. "Side-Lights on the Authorship of the Epistle to the Hebrews." In *Side-Lights on New Testament Research.* London: Kingsgate, 1908. **Harrison, E. F.** "The Theology of the Epistle to the Hebrews." *BSac* 121 (1964) 333–40. **Harrison, M. P.** "Psalm 110 in the Epistle to the Hebrews." Dissertation, Southern Baptist Theological Seminary, 1950. **Harrop, C. K.** "The Influence of the Thought of Stephen upon the Epistle to the Hebrews." Dissertation, Southern Baptist Theological Seminary, 1955. **Harvill, J.** "Focus on Jesus: The Letter to the Hebrews." *SpTod* 37 (1985) 336–47. ———. "Focus on Jesus (Studies in the Epistle to the Hebrews)." *ResQ* 22 (1979) 129–40. **Hatch, E.,** and **Redpath, H. A.** *A Concordance to the Septuagint and the Other Greek Versions of the Old Testament.* 2 vols. Oxford: Clarendon, 1897. **Hatch, W. H. P.** "The Position of Hebrews in the Canon of the New Testament." *HTR* 29 (1936) 133–51. **Hay, D. M.** *Glory at the Right Hand: Psalm 110 in Early Christianity.* SBLMS 18. Nashville: Abingdon, 1973. **Heigl, B.** *Verfasser und Adresse des Briefes an die Hebräer: Eine Studie zur neutestamentlichen Einleitung.* Freiburg i/B: Wagner, 1905. **Henderson, M. W.** "The Priestly Ministry of Jesus in the Gospel of John and the Epistle to the Hebrews." Dissertation, Southern Baptist Theological Seminary, 1965. **Héring, J.** "Eschatologie biblique et idéalisme platonicien." In *The Background of the New Testament and Its Eschatology.* Ed. W. D. Davies and D. Daube. Cambridge: Cambridge UP, 1954. **Heris, C. V.** *The Mystery of Christ, Our Head, Priest and King.* Cork/Liverpool: Mercier, 1950. **Herrmann, L.** "L'épître aux (Laodicéens et l'apologie aux) Hébreux." *CCER* 15 (1968) 1–16. **Hession, R.** *From Shadow to Substance: A Rediscovery of the Inner Message of the Epistle to the Hebrews Centered around the Words "Let Us Go On."* Grand Rapids: Zondervan, 1977. **Higgins, A. J. B.** "The Priestly Messiah." *NTS* 13 (1967) 211–39. **Hill, D.** *Greek Words* *and Hebrew Meanings.* SNTSMS 5. Cambridge: Cambridge UP, 1967. **Hill, H. E.** "Messianic Expectation in the Targum of the Psalms." Dissertation, Yale University, 1955. **Hillmann, W.** "Glaube und Verheissung: Einführung in die Grundgedanken des Hebräerbriefes (10,32–13,25)." *BibLeb* 1 (1960) 237–52. ———. "Der Höhenpriester der künftigen Güter: Einführung in die Grundgedanken des Hebräerbriefes (4,14–10,31)." *BibLeb* 1 (1960) 157–78. ———. "Lebend und wirksam ist Gottes Wort: Einführung in die Grundgedanken des Hebräerbriefes (1,5–4,13)." *BibLeb* 1 (1960) 87–99. ———. "Das Wort der Mahnung: Einführung in die Grundgedanken des Hebräerbriefes." *BibLeb* 1 (1960) 17–27. **Hillmer, M. R.** "Priesthood and Pilgrimage: Hebrews in Recent Research." *ThBullMDC* 5 (1969) 66–89. **Hoekema, A. A.** "The Perfection of Christ in Hebrews." *CTJ* 9 (1974) 31–37. **Hoennicke, G.** "Der Hebräerbrief und die neuer Kritik." *NKZ* 29 (1918) 347–68. ———. "Die sittlichen Anschauungen des Hebräerbriefes." *ZWT* 45 (1902) 24–40. **Hofius, O.** *Katapausis: Die Vorstellung vom endzeitlichen Ruheort im Hebräerbrief.* WUNT 11. Tübingen: Mohr, 1970. ———. *Der Vorhang vor dem Thron Gottes: Eine exegetisch-religions-geschichtliche Untersuchung zu Hebräer 6,19f. und 10,19f.* WUNT 14. Tübingen: Mohr, 1972. **Holbrook, F. B.,** ed. *Issues in the Book of Hebrews.* Silver Spring, MD: Biblical Research Institute, 1989. **Holtz, T.** "Einführung in die Probleme des Hebräerbriefes." *ZZ* 23 (1969) 321–27. **Holtzmann, O.** "Der Hebräerbrief und das Abendmahl." *ZNW* 10 (1909) 251–60. **Hoppin, R.** *Priscilla, Author of the Epistle to the Hebrews and Other Essays.* New York: Exposition, 1969. **Horton, C. D.** "The Relationship of the Use of Tenses to the Message in the Epistle to the Hebrews." Dissertation, Southern Baptist Theological Seminary, 1953. **Hoskier, H. C.** *A Commentary on the Various Readings in the Text of the Epistle to the Hebrews in the Chester Beatty Papyrus P*[46]. London: Quaritch, 1938. **Houlden, J. L.** "Priesthood in the New Testament and the Church Today." *SE* 5 (1968) 81–87. **Howard, G.** "Hebrews and the Old Testament Quotations." *NovT* 10 (1968) 208–16. **Howard, W. F.** "Studia Biblica, XIII: The Epistle to the Hebrews." *Int* 5 (1951) 80–91. **Hughes, G.** *Hebrews and Hermeneutics: The Epistle to the Hebrews as a New Testament Example of Biblical Interpretation.* SNTSMS 36. Cambridge: Cambridge UP, 1979. **Hughes, P. E.** "The Blood of Jesus and His Heavenly Priesthood in Hebrews." *BSac* 130 (1973) 99–109, 195–212, 305–14; 131 (1974) 26–33. ———. "The Christology of Hebrews." *SWJT* 28 (1985) 19–27. **Humphrey, J. F.** "The Christology of the Epistle to the Hebrews." *LQHR* 14 (1945) 425–32. **Hunt, B. P. W. S.** "The 'Epistle to the Hebrews': An Anti-Judaic Treatise?" *SE* 2 (1964) 408–10. **Hunter, A. M.** "Apollos the Alexandrian." In *Biblical Studies.* FS William Barclay. Ed. J. R. McKay and J. F. Miller. Philadelphia: Westminster, 1976. 147–56. **Hurst, L. D.** "Apollos, Hebrews, and Corinth: Bishop Montefiore's Theory Examined." *SJT* 38 (1985) 505–13. ———. "The Background and Interpretation of the Epistle to the Hebrews." Dissertation, Oxford University, 1981. [Published as *The Epistle to the Hebrews: Its Background of Thought.* SNTSMS 65. Cambridge: Cambridge UP, 1990.] ———. "Eschatology and 'Platonism' in the Epistle to the Hebrews." SBLASP (1984) 41–74. **Hutaff, M. D.** "The Epistle to the Hebrews: An Early Christian Sermon." *TBT* 99 (1978) 1816–24. **Huxhold, H. N.** "Faith in the Epistle to the Hebrews." *CTM* 38 (1967) 657–61. **Immer, K.** "Jesus Christus und die Versuchten: Ein Beitrag zur Christologie des Hebräerbriefes." Dissertation, Halle, 1943. **Jansen, A.** "Schwäche und Vollkommenheit des Hohepriesters Christus: Ein Beitrag zur Christologie des Hebräerbriefes." Dissertation, Gregorian Pontifical University, 1957. **Jeffrey, P. J.** "Priesthood of Christ in the Epistle to the Hebrews." Dissertation, University of Melbourne, 1974. **Johnson, S. L.** "Some Important Mistranslations in Hebrews." *BSac* 110 (1953) 25–31. **Johnsson, W. G.** "The Cultus of Hebrews in Twentieth-Century Scholarship." *ExpTim* 89 (1977–78) 104–8. ———. "Defilement and Purgation in the Book of Hebrews." Dissertation, Vanderbilt University, 1973. ———. "Issues in the Interpretation of Hebrews." *AUSS* 15 (1976–77) 169–87. ———. "The Pilgrimage Motif in the Book of Hebrews." *JBL* 97 (1978) 239–51. **Jones, C. P. M.** "The Epistle to the Hebrews and the Lucan Writings." In *Studies in the Gospels.* FS R. H. Lightfoot. Ed. D. E. Nineham. Oxford: Oxford University, 1957. **Jones, E. D.** "The Authorship of Hebrews xiii." *ExpTim*

46 (1934–35) 562–67. **Jones, P. R.** "The Figure of Moses as a Heuristic Device for Understanding the Pastoral Intent of Hebrews." *RevExp* 76 (1979) 95–107. **Kallenbach, W. D.** *The Message and Authorship of the Epistle "To the Hebrews."* St. Paul: Northland, 1938. **Käsemann, E.** *Das wandernde Gottesvolk: Eine Untersuchung zum Hebräerbrief.* 4th ed. FRLANT 55. Göttingen: Vandenhoeck & Ruprecht, 1961. [ET: *The Wandering People of God.* Tr. R. A. Harrisville and I. L. Sandberg. Minneapolis: Augsburg, 1984.] **Katz, P.** "The Quotations from Deuteronomy in Hebrews." *ZNW* 49 (1958) 213–23. **Keck, L. E.** "The Presence of God through Scripture." *LexTQ* 10 (1975) 10–18. **Kennedy, G. A.** *New Testament Interpretation through Rhetorical Criticism.* Chapel Hill, NC: University of North Carolina Press, 1984. **Kennedy, H. A. A.** "The Significance and Range of the Covenant-Conception in the New Testament." *Exp* 8th ser. 10 (1915) 385–410. **Kidner, D.** "Sacrifice—Metaphors and Meaning." *TynBul* 33 (1982) 119–36. **Kirkpatrick, E.** "Hebrews: Its Evangelistic Purpose and Literary Form." Dissertation, Southern Baptist Theological Seminary, 1941. **Kistemaker, S.** *The Psalm Citations in the Epistle to the Hebrews.* Amsterdam: Van Soest, 1961. **Kitchens, J. A.** "The Death of Jesus in the Epistle to the Hebrews." Dissertation, New Orleans Baptist Theological Seminary, 1964. **Klappert, B.** *Die Eschatologie des Hebräerbriefs.* Munich: Kaiser, 1969. **Knox, E. A.** "The Samaritans and the Epistle to the Hebrews." *TCh* 22 (1927) 184–93. **Knox, W. L.** "The Divine Hero Christology of the New Testament." *HTR* 41 (1948) 229–49. **Koester, H.** *Introduction to the New Testament.* Vol. 2: *History and Literature of Early Christianity.* Philadelphia: Fortress, 1982. **Koester, W.** "Platonische Ideenwelt und Gnosis im Hebräerbrief." *Schol* 4 (1956) 545–55. **Kögel, J.** "Der Begriff τελειοῦν im Hebräerbrief." In *Theologische Studien Martin Kähler dargebracht.* Leipzig: Deichert, 1905. **Kosmala, H.** *Hebräer, Essener, Christen: Studien zur Vorgeschichte der frühchristlichen Verkündigung.* SPB 1. Leiden: Brill, 1959. **Kuss, O.** "Über einige neuere Beiträge zur Exegese des Hebräerbriefes." *TGl* 42 (1952) 186–204. ———. "Der theologische Grundgedanke des Hebräerbriefes: Zur Deutung des Todes Jesu im Neuen Testament." *MTZ* 7 (1956) 233–71. ———. "Der Tod Jesu im Hebräerbrief." *MTZ* 7 (1956) 1–22. ———. "Zur Deutung des Hebräerbriefes." *TRev* 53 (1957) 247–54. ———. "Der Verfasser des Hebräerbriefes als Seelsorger." *TTZ* 67 (1958) 1–12, 65–80. **Lach, S.** "Les Ordonnances du culte Israélite dans la Lettre aux Hébreux." In *Sacra Pagina: Miscellanea Biblica Congressus Internationalis Catholici de Re Biblica.* Ed. J. Coppens, A. Descamps, and E. Massaux. Paris: Gabalda, 1959. **Laflamme, R.,** and **Gervais, M.,** eds. *Le Christ hier, aujourd'hui et demain: Colloque de Christologie tenu à l'Université Laval (21 et 22 mars 1975).* Québec: l'Université Laval, 1976. **Lampe, G. W. H.** "Hermeneutics and Typology." *LQHR* 190 (1965) 17–25. ———. "Typological Exegesis." *Theol* 56 (1953) 201–8. **Lane, W. L.** "Hebrews: A Sermon in Search of a Setting." *SWJT* 28 (1985) 13–18. **Larcher, C.** *L'actualité chrétienne de l'Ancien Testament d'après le Nouveau Testament.* Rome: Institute Biblique Pontifical, 1962. **Larrañaga, V.** *L'Ascension de Notre-Seigneur dans le Nouveau Testament.* Rome: Institute Biblique Pontifical, 1938. **Larsson, E.** "Om Hebréerbrevets syfte." *SEÅ* 37–38 (1972–73) 296–309. **LaSor, W. S.** "The Epistle to the Hebrews and the Qumran Writings." In *The Dead Sea Scrolls and the New Testament.* Grand Rapids: Eerdmans, 1972. 179–90. **Laub, F.** *Bekenntnis und Auslegung: Die paränetische Funktion der Christologie im Hebräerbrief.* BU 15. Regensburg: Pustet, 1980. **Legg, J. D.** "Our Brother Timothy: A Suggested Solution to the Problem of Authorship of the Epistle to the Hebrews." *EvQ* 40 (1968) 220–23. **Lehne, S.** *The New Covenant in Hebrews.* JSNTSup 44. Sheffield: JSOT, 1990. **Leivestad, R.** *Christ the Conqueror: Ideas of Conflict and Victory in the New Testament.* New York: Macmillan, 1954. ———. "Jesus som forbillede ifølge Hebréerbrevet." *NorTT* 74 (1973) 195–206. **Leon, H. J.** "The Jews of Rome in the First Centuries of Christianity." In *The Teacher's Yoke.* FS H. Trantham. Ed. E. J. Vardaman and J. L. Garrett. Waco, TX: Baylor UP, 1964. **Leonard, W.** *The Authorship of the Epistle to the Hebrews.* London/Vatican: Polyglott, 1939. **Leschert, D.** "Hermeneutical Foundations of the Epistle to the Hebrews: A Study in the Validity of Its Interpretation of Some Core Citations from the Psalms." Dissertation, Fuller Theological Seminary, 1991. **Lewis, T. W.** "The Theological Logic in Hebrews 10:19–12:29

and the Appropriation of the Old Testament." Dissertation, Drew University, 1965. **Lewis, W. M.** "St. Paul's Defense before King Agrippa, in Relation to the Epistle to the Hebrews." *BW* 13 (1899) 244–48. **Lidgett, J. S.** *Sonship and Salvation: A Study of the Epistle to the Hebrews.* London: Epworth, 1921. **Lindars, B.** *New Testament Apologetic: The Doctrinal Significance of the Old Testament Quotations.* London: SCM, 1961. ———. "The Rhetorical Structure of Hebrews." *NTS* 35 (1989) 382–406. **Linss, W. C.** "Logical Terminology in the Epistle to the Hebrews." *CTM* 37 (1966) 365–69. **Linton, O.** "Hebréerbrevet och 'den historiske Jesus.'" *STK* 26 (1950) 335–45. **Loader, W. R. G.** "Christ at the Right Hand: Ps. cx. 1 in the New Testament." *NTS* 24 (1977–78) 199–217. ———. *Sohn und Hoherpriester: Eine traditionsgeschichtliche Untersuchung zur Christologie des Hebräerbriefes.* WMANT 53. Neukirchen/Vluyn: Neukirchener Verlag, 1981. **Loane, M. L.** "The Unity of the Old and New Testaments as Illustrated in the Epistle to the Hebrews." In *God Who is Rich in Mercy.* FS D. B. Knox. Ed. P. T. O'Brien and D. G. Peterson. Homebush West, NSW: Lancer, 1986. 255–64. **LoBue, F.** "The Historical Background to the Epistle to the Hebrews." *JBL* 75 (1956) 52–57. **Loew, W.** *Der Glaubensweg des Neuen Bundes: Eine Einführung in den Brief an die Hebräer.* UCB. Berlin: Akademie, 1941. **Loewerich, W. von.** "Zum Vertändnis des Opfergedankens im Hebräerbrief." *TBl* 12 (1933) 167–72. **Lohmann, T.** "Zur Heilsgeschichte des Hebräerbriefes." *OLZ* 79 (1984) 117–25. **Longacre, R. E.** *An Anatomy of Speech Notions.* Lisse, Belgium: de Ridder, 1976. ———. "Some Fundamental Insights of Tagmemics." *Language* 41 (1965) 66–76. ———. *Tagmemics.* Waco, TX: Word, 1985. **Longenecker, R. N.** *Biblical Exegesis in the Apostolic Period.* Grand Rapids: Eerdmans, 1975. **Louw, J. P.** *The Semantics of New Testament Greek.* Philadelphia: Fortress, 1982. **Luck, U.** "Himmlisches und irdisches Geschehen im Hebräerbrief: Ein Beitrag zum Problem des 'historischen Jesus' im Urchristentum." *NovT* 6 (1963) 192–215. **Lueken, W.** *Michael: Eine Darstellung und Vergleichung der jüdischen und der morgenländisch-christlichen Tradition vom Erzengel Michael.* Göttingen: Vandenhoeck & Ruprecht, 1898. **Lussier, E.** *Christ's Priesthood according to the Epistle to the Hebrews.* Collegeville, MN: Liturgical, 1975. **Luther, J. H.** "The Use of the Old Testament by the Author of Hebrews." Dissertation, Bob Jones University, 1977. **Luther, M.** *Vorlesungen über den Hebräerbrief.* Ed. E. Hirsch and H. Rückert. Berlin: de Gruyter, 1929. **Lyonnet, S.** "Bulletin d'exégèse paulinienne (V): Épître aux Hébreux." *Bib* 33 (1952) 240–57. ——— and **Sabourin, L.** *Sin, Redemption and Sacrifice.* AnBib 48. Rome: Pontifical Biblical Institute, 1970. **Maar, O.** "Philo und der Hebräerbrief." Dissertation, Vienna, 1964. **Mack, B. L.** *Logos und Sophia: Untersuchungen zur Weisheitstheologie im hellenistischen Judentum.* SUNT 10. Göttingen: Vandenhoeck & Ruprecht, 1973. ———. *Rhetoric and the New Testament.* Minneapolis, MN: Fortress, 1990. **MacKay, C.** "The Argument of Hebrews." *CQR* 168 (1967) 325–38. **MacNeil, H. L.** *The Christology of the Epistle to the Hebrews.* Chicago: Chicago University, 1914. **MacRae, G. W.** "Heavenly Temple and Eschatology in the Letter to the Hebrews." *Semeia* 12 (1978) 179–99. **Madsen, N. P.** *Ask and You Will Receive: Prayer and the Letter to the Hebrews.* St. Louis: CBP Press, 1989. **Maeso, D. G.** "Lengua original, autor y estilo de la epístola a los Hebreos." *CB* 13 (1956) 202–15. **Manson, T. W.** *Ministry and Priesthood: Christ's and Ours.* Richmond: John Knox Press, 1958. ———. "The Problem of the Epistle to the Hebrews." *BJRL* 32 (1949–50) 1–17. **Manson, W.** *The Epistle to the Hebrews: An Historical and Theological Reconsideration.* London: Hodder & Stoughton, 1951. **Marchant, G. J. C.** "Sacrifice in the Epistle to the Hebrews." *EvQ* 20 (1948) 196–210. **Marcos, J. R.** *Jesús de Nazaret y su glorificación: Estudio de la exegésis patrística de la formula "Sentado a la diestra de Dios" hasta el Concilio de Niceo.* Salamanca/Madrid: Instituto Superior de Pastoral, 1974. **Marshall, I. H.** *Kept by the Power of God: A Study of Perseverance and Falling Away.* London: Epworth, 1969. **Mauro, P.** *God's Apostle and High Priest.* New York: Revell, 1912. ———. *God's Pilgrims: Their Danger, Their Resources, Their Rewards.* Rev. ed. Boston: Hamilton Brothers, 1918. **Maxwell, K. L.** "Doctrine and Parenesis in the Epistle to the Hebrews, with Special Reference to Pre-Christian Gnosticism." Dissertation, Yale University, 1952. **Mayser, E.** *Grammatik der griechischen Papyri aus der Ptolemäerzeit, mit Einschluss der gleichzeitigen Ostraka und der in*

Äegypten verfassten Inschriften. 2 vols. Berlin/Leipzig: Teubner, 1906–34. **McCown, W. G.** "Holiness in Hebrews." *WesThJ* 16 (1981) 58–78. ———. "*Ο ΛΟΓΟΣ ΤΗΣ ΠΑΡΑΚΛΗΣΕΩΣ:* The Nature and Function of the Hortatory Sections in the Epistle to the Hebrews." Dissertation, Union Theological Seminary, Richmond, 1970. **McCullough, J. C.** "Hebrews and the Old Testament." Dissertation, Queen's University, Belfast, 1971. ———. "The Old Testament Quotations in Hebrews." *NTS* 26 (1979–80) 363–79. ———. "Some Recent Developments in Research on the Epistle to the Hebrews." *IBS* 2 (1980) 141–65. **McDonald, J. I. H.** *Kerygma and Didache: The Articulation and Structure of the Earliest Christian Message.* SNTSMS 37. Cambridge: Cambridge UP, 1980. **McGaughey, D. H.** "The Hermeneutic Method of the Epistle to the Hebrews." Dissertation, Boston University, 1963. **McNamara, M.** *The New Testament and the Palestinian Targum to the Pentateuch.* AnBib 27. Rome: Pontifical Biblical Institute, 1966. ———. *Targum and Testament: Aramaic Paraphrases of the Hebrew Bible, A Light on the New Testament.* Shannon: Irish UP, 1972. **McNicol, A. J.** "The Relationship of the Image of the Highest Angel to the High Priest Concept in Hebrews." Dissertation, Vanderbilt University, 1974. **McNicol, J.** "The Spiritual Value of the Epistle to the Hebrews." *BibRev* 15 (1930) 509–22. **McRay, J.** "Atonement and Apocalyptic in the Book of Hebrews." *ResQ* 23 (1980) 1–9. **Mealand, D. L.** "The Christology of the Epistle to the Hebrews." *MCM* 22 (1979) 180–87. **Méchineau, L.** *L'Epistola agli Ebrei secondo le risposte della Commissione Biblica.* Rome: Pontifical Biblical Commission, 1917. **Médebielle, A.** *L'Expiation dans l'Ancien Testament et Nouveau Testament.* 2 vols. Rome: Institut Biblique Pontifical, 1923. **Medico, M. dal.** *L'auteur de l'Épître aux Hébreux.* Rome: Pontifical Biblical Institute, 1914. **Meeter, H. H.** *The Heavenly High Priesthood of Christ.* Grand Rapids: Eerdmans-Sevensma, 1916. **Ménégoz, E.** *La théologie de l'Épître aux Hébreux.* Paris: Fischbacher, 1894. **Mercier, R.** "La Perfección de Cristo y de los Cristiános en la carta a los Hebreos." *RevistB* 35 (1973) 229–35. **Merle, G.** *La christologie de l'Épître aux Hébreux.* Montauban: Granié, 1877. **Metzger, B. M.** "The Formulas Introducing Quotations of Scripture in the NT and the Mishnah." *JBL* 70 (1951) 297–307. ———. *A Textual Commentary on the Greek New Testament: A Companion Volume to the United Bible Societies' Greek New Testament (third edition).* London/New York: United Bible Societies, 1971. **Michaelis, W.** *Zur Engelchristologie im Urchristentum.* GBTh 1. Basel: Maier, 1942. **Michel, O.** "Die Lehre von der christlichen Vollkommenheit nach der Anschauung des Hebräerbriefes." *TSK* 106 (1934–35) 333–55. **Mickelsen, A. B.** "Methods of Interpretation in the Epistle to the Hebrews." Dissertation, University of Chicago, 1950. **Miller, P. D.** *The Divine Warrior in Early Israel.* Cambridge, MA: Harvard UP, 1973. **Milligan, G.** "The Roman Destination of the Epistle to the Hebrews." *Exp* 4 (1901) 437–48. ———. *The Theology of the Epistle to the Hebrews with a Critical Introduction.* Edinburgh: Clark, 1899. **Milligan, W.** *The Ascension and Heavenly Priesthood of Our Lord.* London: Macmillan, 1891. **Minear, P. S.** "An Early Christian Theopoetic?" *Semeia* 12 (1978) 201–14. ———. *New Testament Apocalyptic.* Nashville: Abingdon, 1981. **Moe, O.** "Der Gedanke der allgemeinen Priestertums im Hebräerbrief." *TZ* 5 (1949) 161–69. ———. "Das Priestertum Christi im NT ausserhalb des Hebräerbriefs." *TLZ* 72 (1947) 335–38. **Moffatt, J.** "The Christology of the Epistle to the Hebrews." *ExpTim* 28 (1916–17) 505–8, 563–66; 29 (1917–18) 26–30. ———. *Jesus Christ the Same.* The Shaffer Lectures for 1940 in Yale University Divinity School. New York: Abingdon-Cokesbury, 1940. **Molero, X. R.** "El sacerdocio celeste de Cristo." *EstBib* 22 (1963) 69–77. **Monod, V.** *De titulo epistolae vulgo ad Hebraeos inscriptae.* Montalbani: Granié, 1910. **Mora, G.** *La Carta a los Hebreos como Escrito Pastoral.* Barcelona: Herder, 1974. ———. "Ley y sacrificio en la carta a los Hebreos." *RCB* 1 (1976) 1–50. **Morgenthaler, R.** *Statistik des neutestamentlichen Wortschatzes.* Zürich: Gotthelf, 1958. **Morin, J.** "L'Église dans l'Épître aux Hébreux." In *L'Église dans la Bible.* Paris/Bruges: Desclée de Brouwer, 1962. **Morris, L.** *The Apostolic Preaching of the Cross.* Grand Rapids: Eerdmans, 1955. **Moule, C. F. D.** "Commentaries on the Epistle to the Hebrews." *Theol* 61 (1958) 228–32. ———. *An Idiom-Book of New Testament Greek.* 2nd ed. Cambridge: UP, 1960. ———. "The Influence of Circumstances on the Use of Christological Terms." *JTS* n.s. 10 (1959)

247–63. ———. "The Influence of Circumstances on the Use of Eschatological Terms." *JTS* n.s. 15 (1964) 1–15. ———. *The Sacrifice of Christ.* Greenwich: Seabury Press, 1957. **Moulton, J. H.** *A Grammar of New Testament Greek: I. Prolegomena.* 3rd ed. Edinburgh: Clark, 1908. ——— and **Howard, W. F.** *A Grammar of New Testament Greek: II. Accidence and Word-Formation.* Edinburgh: Clark, 1920. **Moulton, W. F.**, and **Geden, A. S.** *A Concordance to the Greek Testament according to the Texts of Westcott and Hort, Tischendorf and the English Revizers.* 4th ed. Rev. H. K. Moulton. Edinburgh: Clark, 1963. **Moxnes, H.** *Theology in Conflict.* NovTSup 53. Leiden: Brill, 1980. **Müller, P. G.** *ΧΡΙΣΤΟΣ ΑΡΧΗΓΟΣ: Der religionsgeschichtliche und theologische Hintergrund einer neutestamentlichen Christusprädikation.* Frankfurt a/M.: Lang, 1973. ———. "Die Funktion der Psalmzitate im Hebräerbrief." In *Freude an der Weisung des Herrn.* Ed. E. Haag and F. L. Hossfeld. Stuttgart: Katholisches Bibelwerk, 1986. 223–42. **Murray, J.** "The Heavenly, Priestly Activity of Christ." In *Collected Writings of John Murray.* Ed. I. Murray. Vol. 1. Edinburgh: Banner of Truth Trust, 1976. 44–58. ———. "Jesus the Son of God." In *Collected Writings of John Murray.* Vol. 4. Edinburgh: Banner of Truth Trust, 1982. 58–81. **Murray, R.** "Jews, Hebrews and Christians: Some Needed Distinctions." *NovT* 24 (1982) 194–208. **Nairne, A.** *The Epistle of Priesthood: Studies in the Epistle to the Hebrews.* Edinburgh: Clark, 1913. **Nakagawa, H.** "Christology in the Epistle to the Hebrews." Dissertation, Yale University, 1955. **Nash, R. H.** "The Notion of Mediator in Alexandrian Judaism and the Epistle to the Hebrews." *WTJ* 40 (1977) 89–115. **Nauck, W.** "Zum Aufbau des Hebräerbriefes." In *Judentum, Urchristentum, Kirche.* FS J. Jeremias. Ed. W. Eltester. BZNW 26. Giessen: Töpelmann, 1960. **Neeley, L. L.** "A Discourse Analysis of Hebrews." *OPTT* 3–4 (1987) 1–146. **Nellessen, E.** "Lateinische Summarien zum Hebräerbrief." *BZ* 14 (1970) 240–51. **Nestle, E.** "On the Address of the Epistle to the Hebrews." *ExpTim* 10 (1898–99) 422. **Neufeld, V. H.** *The Earliest Christian Confessions.* NTTS 5. Grand Rapids: Eerdmans, 1963. **Nicolau, M.** "El 'Reíno des Dios' en la carta a los Hebreos." *Burg* 20 (1979) 393–405. **Nicole, R.** "C. H. Dodd and the Doctrine of Propitiation." *WTJ* 17 (1955) 117–57. **Nida, E. A., Louw, J. P.**, et al. *Style and Discourse: With Special Reference to the Text of the Greek New Testament.* Cape Town: Bible Society, 1983. **Nikiprowetsky, V.** "La Spiritualisation des sacrifices et le cult sacrificial au Temple de Jérusalem chez Philon d'Alexandrie." *Sem* 17 (1967) 98–114. **Nissilä, K.** *Das Hohepriestmotiv in Hebräerbrief: Eine exegetische Untersuchung.* Helsinki: Oy Liitun Kirjapaino, 1979. **Nomoto, S.** "Herkunft und Struktur der Hohepriestervorstellung im Hebräerbrief." *NovT* 10 (1968) 10–25. ———. "Die Hohenpriester-Typologie im Hebräerbrief: Ihre traditionsgeschichtliche Herkunft und ihr religionsgeschichtlicher Hintergrund." Dissertation, Hamburg, 1965. **Norden, E.** *Agnostos Theos: Untersuchungen zur Formengeschichte religiöser Rede.* Leipzig: Teubner, 1913. **Oepke, A.** *Das neue Gottesvolk in Schrifttum, Schauspiel, bildender Kunst und Weltgestaltung.* Gütersloh: C. Bertelsmann, 1950. **Olson, S. N.** "Wandering but Not Lost." *WW* 5 (1985) 426–33. **Osborne, G.** "Soteriology in the Epistle to the Hebrews." In *Grace Unlimited.* Ed. C. Pinnock. Minneapolis: Bethany Fellowship, 1975. **Otto, C. W.** *Der Apostel und Hohepriester unseres Bekenntnis.* Leipzig: Deichert, 1861. **Oudersluys, R. C.** "Exodus in the Letter to the Hebrews." In *Grace upon Grace.* FS L. J. Kuyper. Ed. J. I. Cook. Grand Rapids: Eerdmans, 1975. 143–52. **Padolski, M. V.** *L'idée du sacrifice de la Croix dans l'Épître aux Hébreux.* Paris: Gabalda, 1935. **Padva, P.** *Les citations de l'Ancien Testament dans l'Épître aux Hébreux.* Paris: Danzig, 1904. **Parker, H. M., Jr.** "Domitian and the Epistle to the Hebrews." *IlRev* 36 (1979) 31–43. **Perdelwitz, R.** "Das literarische Problem des Hebräerbriefs: 1. Der literarische Charakter des Schreibens. 2. Der Verfasser. 3. Die Addressaten." *ZNW* 11 (1910) 59–78, 105–23. **Perdue, L. B.** "The Social Character of Paraenesis and Paraenetic Literature." *Semeia* 50 (1990) 5–39. **Perkins, D. W.** "A Call to Pilgrimage: The Challenge of Hebrews." *ThEduc* 32 (1985) 69–81. **Perowne, T. T.** *Our High Priest in Heaven.* 2nd ed. London: E. Stock, 1894. **Pevella, C. M.** "De justificatione secundum Epistolam ad Hebraeos." *Bib* 14 (1933) 1–21, 150–69. **Pérez, G.** "Autenticidad y canonicidad de la Carta a los Hebreos." *CB* 13 (1956) 216–26. **Perry, M.** "Method and Model in the Epistle to the Hebrews." *Theol* 77 (1974) 66–74. **Peterson, D. G.**

"An Examination of the Concept of 'Perfection' in the 'Epistle to the Hebrews.'" Dissertation, University of Manchester, 1978. [Published as *Hebrews and Perfection: An Examination of the Concept of Perfection in the "Epistle to the Hebrews."* Cambridge: Cambridge UP, 1982.] ————. "The Ministry of Encouragement." In *God Who Is Rich in Mercy.* FS D. B. Knox. Ed. P. T. O'Brien and D. G. Peterson. Homebush West, NSW: Lancer, 1986. 235–53. ————. "Towards a New Testament Theology of Worship." *RTR* 43 (1984) 65–73. **Pinto, L. di.** *Volontà di Dio e legge antica nell' Epistola agli Ebrei: Contributo ai fondementi biblici della teologia morale.* Naples: Gregorian, 1976. **Pittard, C. R.** "The Person and Work of Christ in the Epistle to the Hebrews." Dissertation, Southern Baptist Theological Seminary, 1926. **Plessis, P. J. du.** *ΤΕΛΕΙΟΣ: The Idea of Perfection in the New Testament.* Kampen: Kok, 1959. **Ploeg, J. van der.** "L'exégèse de l'Ancien Testament dans l'Épître aux Hébreux." *RB* 54 (1947) 187–228. **Plooij, D.** *Studies in the Testimony Book.* Amsterdam: Noord-Hollandsche, 1932. **Plumptre, E. H.** "The Writings of Apollos." *Exp* n.s. 1 (1885) 329–48, 409–35. **Pollard, E. B.** "Notes on the Old Testament Citations in the Epistle to the Hebrews." *CrozQ* 1 (1924) 447–52. **Powell, C. H.** *The Biblical Concept of Power.* London: Epworth, 1963. **Powell, D. L.** "Christ as High Priest in the Epistle to the Hebrews." *SE* 7 (1982) 387–99. **Pretorius, E. A. C.** "Christusbeeld en Kerkmodel in die Hebräerbrief." *ThEv* 15 (1982) 3–18. ————. "*Diathēkē* in the Epistle to the Hebrews." *Neot* 5 (1971) 37–50. **Prince, A.** "An Investigation into the Importance of Perseverance in the Christian Life as Presented in Five Warning Passages in Hebrews." Dissertation, Southwestern Baptist Theological Seminary, 1980. **Prümm, K.** "Das neutestamentliche Sprach- und Begriffsproblem der Vollkommenheit." *Bib* 44 (1963) 76–92. **Purdy, A. C.** "The Purpose of the Epistle to the Hebrews." *Exp* 8th ser. 19 (1920) 123–39. ————. "The Purpose of the Epistle to the Hebrews in the Light of Recent Studies in Judaism." In *Amicitiae Corolla.* Ed. H. G. Wood. London: University of London, 1933. **Quentel, J.** "Les destinataires de l'Épître aux Hébreux." *RB* 9 (1912) 50–68. **Rábanos, R.** "Sacerdocio de Melquisedec, sacerdocio de Aarón, sacerdocio de Cristo." *CB* 13 (1956) 264–75. **Rahlfs, A.,** ed. *Septuaginta: Id est Vetus Testamentum graece iuxta LXX interpretes.* 4th ed. 2 vols. Stuttgart: Württembergische Bibelanstalt, 1950. **Ramsay, W. M.** "The Date and Authorship of the Epistle to the Hebrews." In *Luke the Physician.* London: Hodder & Stoughton, 1908. **Rawlingson, A. E. J.** "Priesthood and Sacrifice in Judaism and Christianity." *ExpTim* 60 (1949) 116–21. **Reid, R.** "The Use of the Old Testament in the Epistle to the Hebrews." Dissertation, Union Theological Seminary, New York, 1964. **Rendall, F.** *Theology of the Hebrew Christians.* London: Macmillan, 1886. **Rendall, R.** "The Method of the Writer to the Hebrews in Using Old Testament Quotations." *EvQ* 27 (1955) 214–20. **Renner, F.** *An die Hebräer: Ein pseudepigraphischen Brief.* Münsterschwarz: Vier-Türme, 1970. **Rice, G. E.** "Apostasy as a Motif and Its Effect on the Structure of Hebrews." *AUSS* 23 (1985) 29–35. **Riddle, D. W.** "Hebrews, First Clement, and the Persecution of Domitian." *JBL* 43 (1924) 329–48. **Riehm, E.** *Der Lehrbegriff des Hebräerbriefes.*[2] Basel: Balmer & Riehm, 1867. **Rienecker, F.** *A Linguistic Key to the Greek New Testament.* Grand Rapids: Zondervan, 1976. **Riggenbach, E.** "Der Begriff der ΔΙΑΘΗΚΗ im Hebräerbrief." In *Theologische Studien.* FS T. Zahn. Leipzig: Deichert, 1908. ————. "Der Begriff der ΤΕΛΕΙΩΣΙΣ im Hebräerbrief: Ein Beitrag zur Frage nach der Einwirkung der Mysterienreligion auf Sprache und Gedankenwelt des Neuen Testaments." *NKZ* 34 (1923) 184–95. ————. *Historische Studien zum Hebräerbrief.* Vol. 1: *Die ältesten lateinischen Kommentare zum Hebräerbrief.* FGNK 8/1. Leipzig: Deichert, 1907. **Rissi, M.** *Die Theologie des Hebräerbriefs.* WUNT 44. Tübingen: Mohr, 1987. **Ritschl, A.** "Über die Leser des Hebräerbriefs." *TSK* 39 (1866) 89–102. **Robertson, A. T.** *A Grammar of the Greek New Testament in the Light of Historical Research.* Nashville: Broadman, 1934. **Robertson, O. P.** "The People of the Wilderness: The Concept of the Church in Hebrews." Dissertation, Union Theological Seminary, Richmond, 1966. **Robinson, J. A. T.** *Redating the New Testament.* London: SCM, 1976. **Robinson, W.** *The Eschatology of the Epistle to the Hebrews.* Birmingham, AL: Overdale College, 1950. ————. "The Eschatology of the Epistle to the Hebrews: A Study in the Christian Doctrine of

Hope." *Enc* 22 (1961) 37–51. **Rogers, E. W.** *Him That Endured.* London: Pickering & Inglis, 1965. **Roloff, J.** "Der mitleidende Hohepriester: Zur Frage nach der Bedeutung des irdischen Jesus für die Christologie des Hebräerbriefes." In *Jesus Christus in Historie und Theologie.* FS H. Conzelmann. Ed. G. Strecker. Tübingen: Mohr, 1975. **Ross, A.** "The Message of the Epistle to the Hebrews for Today." *ExpTim* 51 (1942–43) 161–68. **Rowell, J. B.** "Our Great High Priest." *BSac* 118 (1961) 148–53. **Rusche, H.** "Glauben und Leben nach dem Hebräerbrief." *BibLeb* 12 (1971) 94–104. **Rylaarsdam, J. C.** "Jewish-Christian Relationships: The Two Covenants and the Dilemmas of Christology." In *Grace upon Grace.* FS L. J. Kuyper. Ed. J. I. Cook. Grand Rapids: Eerdmans, 1975. **Sabourin, L.** "Auctor Epistulae ad Hebraeos ut interpres Scripturae." *VD* 46 (1968) 275–85. ———. "Il sacrìficio di Gèsu e le Realtà cultuali." *BeO* 10 (1968) 25–37. ———. *Priesthood: A Comparative Study.* Leiden: Brill, 1973. ———. "Sacrificium et liturgia in Epistula ad Hebreos." *VD* 46 (1968) 235–58. **Saito, T.** *Die Mosevorstellungen im Neuen Testament.* Bern/Frankfurt: Lang, 1977. **Salmon, G.** "The Keynote of the Epistle to the Hebrews." *Exp* 2nd ser. 3 (1882) 81–93. **Salom, A. P.** "*Ta Hagia* in the Epistle to the Hebrews." *AUSS* 5 (1967) 59–70. **Sandegren, C.** "The Addressees of the Epistle to the Hebrews." *EvQ* 27 (1955) 221–24. **Sanders, J. T.** *The New Testament Christological Hymns.* SNTSMS 15. Cambridge: Cambridge UP, 1971. **Sanford, C. J.** "The Addressees of Hebrews." Dissertation, Dallas Theological Seminary, 1962. **Saydon, P. P.** "The Master Idea of the Epistle to the Hebrews." *MelTheol* 13 (1961) 19–26. **Schaefer, J. R.** "The Relationship between Priestly and Servant Messianism in the Epistle to the Hebrews." *CBQ* 30 (1968) 359–85. **Schäfer, K. T.** *Untersuchungen zur Geschichte der lateinischen Übersetzungen des Hebräerbriefes.* Freiburg: Herder, 1929. **Scheller, E. J.** *Das Priestertum Christi im Anschluss an den hl. Thomas von Aquin.* Paderborn: Schöniagh, 1934. **Schenke, H. M.** "Erwägungen zum Rätsel des Hebräerbriefes." In *Neues Testament und christliche Existenz.* FS H. Braun. Tübingen: Mohr, 1973. **Schick, E.** *Im Glauben Kraft empfangen Betrachtungen zum Brief an die Hebräer.* Stuttgart: Katholisches Bibelwerk, 1978. **Schiele, F. M.** "Harnack's 'Probabilia' Concerning the Address and the Author of the Epistle to the Hebrews." *AJT* 9 (1905) 290–308. **Schierse, F. J.** *Verheissung und Heilsvollendung: Zur theologischen Grundfrage des Hebräerbriefes.* MTS 1/9. Munich: Zink, 1955. **Schildenberger, J.** "Psalm 109 (110): Christus, König und Priester." *BenM* 20 (1938) 361–74. **Schille, G.** "Die Basis des Hebräerbriefes." *ZNW* 48 (1957) 270–80. ———. "Erwägungen zur Hohenpriesterlehre des Hebräerbriefes." *ZNW* 46 (1955) 81–109. ———. *Frühchristliche Hymnen.* Berlin: Akademie, 1962. **Schillebeeckx, E.** "Die Welt der Zukunft und die grosse Gnade Gottes: Der Hebräerbrief." In *Christus und die Christen.* Freiburg: Herder, 1977. **Schlatter, A.** *Der Glaube im Neuen Testament.* 5th ed. Stuttgart: Calwer, 1963. **Schmidgall, P.** "The Influence of Jewish Apocalyptic Literature on the Book of Hebrews." Dissertation, Western Kentucky University, 1980. **Schmitz, O.** *Die Opferanschauung des späteren Judentums und die Opferaussagungen des Neuen Testaments: Eine Untersuchung ihres geschichtlichen Verhältnisses.* Tübingen: Mohr, 1910. **Schoonhoven, C. R.** "The 'Analogy of Faith' and the Intent of Hebrews." In *Scripture, Tradition, and Interpretation.* FS E. F. Harrison. Ed. W. W. Gasque and W. S. LaSor. Grand Rapids: Eerdmans, 1978. 92–110. **Schröger, F.** "Der Gottesdienst der Hebräerbriefgemeinde." *MTZ* 19 (1968) 161–81. ———. "Der Hebräerbrief—paulinisch?" In *Kontinuität und Einheit.* FS F. Mussner. Ed. P. G. Müller and W. Stenger. Freiburg/Basel/Vienna: Herder, 1981. 211–22. ———. "Das hermeneutische Instrumentarium des Hebräerbriefverfassers." *TGl* 60 (1970) 344–59. ———. *Der Verfasser des Hebräerbriefes als Schriftausleger.* Regensburg: Pustet, 1968. **Schubert, P.** "Der Verbindung von Königtum und Priestertum in der Vorgeschichte der Christusoffenbarung: Eine Voruntersuchung der Christologie des Hebräerbriefs." Dissertation, Leipzig, 1955. **Scott, E. F.** "The Epistle to the Hebrews and Roman Christianity." *HTR* 13 (1930) 205–19. ———. *The Epistle to the Hebrews: Its Doctrine and Significance.* Edinburgh: Clark, 1923. **Scott, W. M. F.** "Priesthood in the New Testament." *SJT* 10 (1957) 399–415. **Selph, B. K.** "The Christology of the Book of Hebrews." Dissertation, Southwestern Baptist Seminary, 1948. **Sen, F.** "La Carta a los Hebreos en el Canon y en el corpus paulino." *CB* 25 (1968) 35–40.

Shuster, I. "I destinatari dell' epistola agli Ebrei." *ScC* 66 (1938) 641–65. **Siegman, E. F.** "The Blood of the Covenant." *AER* 136 (1957) 167–74. **Silva, M.** *Biblical Words and Their Meanings: An Introduction to Lexical Semantics.* Grand Rapids: Zondervan, 1983. ———. "Perfection and Eschatology in Hebrews." *WTJ* 39 (1976) 60–71. **Simon, M.** *Hercule et le Christianisme.* Paris: Publications de la faculté de Strasbourg, 1955. **Simpson, E. K.** "The Vocabulary of the Epistle to the Hebrews." *EvQ* 18 (1946) 35–38, 187–90. **Slot, W.** *De Letterkundige Vorm van de Brief aan de Hebreeën.* Gröningen: Wolters, 1912. **Smalley, S. S.** "The Atonement in the Epistle to the Hebrews." *EvQ* 33 (1961) 36–43. **Smith, J.** *A Priest for Ever: A Study of Typology and Eschatology in Hebrews.* London/Sydney: Sheed and Ward, 1969. **Smith, L.** "Metaphor and Truth in Hebrews." *NBl* 57 (1976) 227–33. **Smith, R. B.** "Apostasy in the Book of Hebrews." Dissertation, Southern Baptist Theological Seminary, 1959. **Smith, R. W.** *The Art of Rhetoric in Alexandria: Its Theory and Practice in the Ancient World.* The Hague: Nijhoff, 1974. **Smits, C.** *Oud-testamentische Citaten in het Nieuw Testament.* Malmberg: Hertogenbosch, 1963. **Soden, H. von.** "Der Hebräerbrief." *JPTh* 10 (1884) 435–93, 627–56. **Solari, J. K.** "The Problem of *Metanoia* in the Epistle to the Hebrews." Dissertation, Catholic University of America, 1970. **Sowers, S. G.** *The Hermeneutics of Philo and Hebrews: A Comparison of the Interpretation of the Old Testament in Philo Judaeus and the Epistle to the Hebrews.* Richmond: Knox, 1965. **Spicq, C.** "Alexandrinismes dans l'Épître aux Hébreux." *RB* 58 (1951) 481–502. ———. "Contemplation, théologie et vie morale d'après l'Épître aux Hébreux." *RSR* 39 (1951) 289–300. ———. "L'Épître aux Hébreux, Apollos, Jean-Baptiste, les Hellénistes et Qumran." *RevQ* 1 (1958–59) 365–90. ———. "Hébreux (Épître aux)." DBSup 7: 226–79. ———. "L'Origine johannique de la conception du Christ-prêtre dans l'Épître aux Hébreux." In *Aux sources de la tradition chrétienne.* FS M. Goguel. Neuchâtel/Paris: Delachaux & Niestlé, 1956. ———. "La perfection chrétienne d'après l'Épître aux Hébreux." In *Bibliothèque de la faculté Catholique de Théologie de Lyon* 5. FS J. Chaine. Ed. G. Villepelet. Lyon: Facultés Catholiques, 1950. ———. "Le Philonisme de l'Épître aux Hébreux." *RB* 56 (1949) 542–72; 57 (1950) 212–42. ———. "La théologie des deux alliances dans l'Épître aux Hébreux." *RSPT* 33 (1949) 15–30. ———. *Vie chrétienne et pérégrination selon le Nouveau Testament.* LD 71. Paris: Cerf, 1972. **Stadelmann, A.** "Zur Christologie des Hebräerbriefes in der neueren Diskussion." In *Theologische Berichte.* Vol. 2. Ed. J. Pfammatter and F. Furger. Zürich: Zwingli, 1973. **Stagl, H.** "Pauline Authorship of the Epistle to the Hebrews according to Mt. Sinai Arabic Manuscript 151." *RefRev* 21 (1961) 14, 51–53. **Staples, A. F.** "The Book of Hebrews in Its Relationship to the Writings of Philo Judaeus." Dissertation, Southern Baptist Theological Seminary, 1951. **Stine, D. M.** "The Finality of the Christian Faith: A Study of the Unfolding Argument of the Epistle to the Hebrews, Chapters 1–7." Dissertation, Princeton Theological Seminary, 1964. **Stöger, A.** "Der Hohepriester Jesus Christus." *TPQ* 100 (1952) 309–19. **Stott, W.** "The Conception of 'Offering' in the Epistle to the Hebrews." *NTS* 11 (1962–63) 62–67. **Stuart, S. S.** "The Exodus Tradition in Late Jewish and Early Christian Literature: A General Survey of the Literature and a Particular Analysis of the Wisdom of Solomon, II Esdras and the Epistle to the Hebrews." Dissertation, Vanderbilt University, 1973. **Suárez, P. L.** "Cesárea, lugar de composición de la Epístola a los Hebreos?" *CB* 13 (1956) 226–31. ———. "Casárea y la Epístola 'ad Hebraeos.'" In *Studiorum Paulinorum Congressus Internationalis Catholici 1961.* AnBib 17–18. Rome: Pontifical Biblical Institute, 1963. **Swetnam, J.** "Form and Content in Hebrews 1–6." *Bib* 53 (1972) 368–85. ———. "Form and Content in Hebrews 7–13." *Bib* 55 (1974) 333–48. ———. *Jesus and Isaac: A Study of the Epistle to the Hebrews in the Light of the Aqedah.* AnBib 94. Rome: Biblical Institute Press, 1981. ———. "On the Literary Genre of the 'Epistle' to the Hebrews." *NovT* 13 (1969) 261–69. **Synge, F. C.** *Hebrews and the Scriptures.* London: SPCK, 1959. **Tabachovitz, D.** *Die Septuaginta und das Neue Testament.* Lund: Gleerup, 1956. **Tasker, R. V. G.** *The Gospel in the Epistle to the Hebrews.* London: Tyndale, 1956. ———. "The Text of the 'Corpus Paulinum.'" *NTS* 1 (1954–55) 180–91. **Taylor, C. D.** "A Comparative Study of the Concepts of Worship in Colossians and Hebrews." Dissertation, Southern Baptist Theological Seminary, 1957.

Tenney, M. C. "A New Approach to the Book of Hebrews." *BSac* 123 (1966) 230–36. **Teodorico, P.** "Alcuni aspetti dell' ecclesiologia della Lettera agli Ebrei." *Bib* 24 (1943) 125– 61, 323–69. ———. *La Chiesa della Lettora agli Ebrie.* Torin/Rome: Marietti, 1945. ———. "Il sacerdozio celeste di cristo della lettera agli Ebrei." *Greg* 39 (1958) 319–34. **Terra, J. E. M.** "A Libertação Escatológica na Epístola aos Hebreus: O Povo de Deus a Caminho do Santúario." *RCB* 2 (1978) 325–43. **Thayer, J. H.** "Authorship and Canonicity of the Epistle to the Hebrews." *BSac* 24 (1867) 681–722. **Theissen, G.** *Untersuchungen zum Hebräerbrief.* SNT 2. Gütersloh: Mohn, 1969. **Thien, F.** "Analyse de l'Épître aux Hébreux." *RB* 11 (1902) 74–86. **Thiselton, A.** "Semantics and New Testament Interpretation." In *New Testament Interpretation: Essays on Principles and Methods.* Ed. I. H. Marshall. Grand Rapids: Eerdmans, 1977. 75–104. **Thomas, J.** "The Use of Voice, Moods and Tenses in the Epistle to the Hebrews." Dissertation, Western Kentucky University, 1980. **Thomas, K. J.** "The Old Testament Citations in Hebrews." *NTS* 11 (1964–65) 303–25. ———. "The Use of the Septuagint in the Epistle to the Hebrews." Dissertation, University of Manchester, 1959. **Thompson, J. W.** *The Beginnings of Christian Philosophy: The Epistle to the Hebrews.* CBQMS 13. Washington, DC: The Catholic Biblical Association of America, 1981. ———. *Strategy for Survival: A Plan for Church Renewal from Hebrews.* Austin, TX: Sweet, 1980. ———. "'That Which Abides': Some Metaphysical Assumptions in the Epistle to the Hebrews." Dissertation, Vanderbilt University, 1974. ———. "The Underlying Unity of Hebrews." *ResQ* 18 (1975) 129–36. **Thrall, M. E.** *Greek Particles in the New Testament.* Linguistic and Exegetical Studies. Grand Rapids: Eerdmans, 1962. **Thurston, R. W.** "Philo and the Epistle to the Hebrews." *EvQ* 58 (1986) 133–43. **Thüsing, W.** "Erhöhungsvorstellung und Parusieerwartung in der ältesten nach-österlichen Christologie." *BZ* 11 (1967) 95–108, 205–22; 12 (1968) 54–80. ———. "Das Opfer der Christen nach dem Neuen Testament." *BibLeb* 6 (1965) 37–50. **Thyen, H.** *Der Stil der jüdisch-hellenistischen Homilie.* FRLANT 47. Göttingen: Vandenhoeck & Ruprecht, 1955. **Tiede, D. L.** *The Charismatic Figure as Miracle Worker.* SBLDS 1. Missoula, MT: Scholars, 1972. **Torm, F.** "Om τελειοῦν: Hebraeerbrevet." *SEÅ* 5 (1940) 116–25. **Torrance, J. B.** "The Priesthood of Jesus." In *Essays in Christology for Karl Barth.* Ed. T. H. L. Parker. London: Lotterworth Press, 1956. 153–73. **Torrey, C. C.** "The Authorship and Character of the So-Called 'Epistle to the Hebrews.'" *JBL* 30 (1911) 137–56. **Toy, C. H.** *Quotations in the New Testament.* New York: Scribner's, 1884. **Trinidad, J.** "De sacrificio Christi in Epistola ad Hebraeos." *VD* 19 (1939) 180–86, 207–12. **Trites, A. A.** *The New Testament Concept of Witness.* SNTSMS 31. Cambridge: Cambridge UP, 1977. **Tucker, M. A. R.** "The Gospel according to Prisca." *NC* 73 (1913) 81–98. **Turner, G. A.** *The New and Living Way: A Fresh Exposition of the Epistle to the Hebrews.* Minneapolis: Bethany Fellowship, 1975. **Turner, N.** *A Grammar of New Testament Greek: III. Syntax.* Edinburgh: Clark, 1963. ———. *A Grammar of New Testament Greek: IV. Style.* Edinburgh: Clark, 1976. **Ubbrink, J. T.** "De Hoogepriester en zijn Offer in de Brief aan de Hebreeën." *NThS* 22 (1939) 172–84. **Ungeheuer, J.** *Der grosse Priester über dem Hause Gottes: Die Christologie des Hebräerbriefes.* Würzburg: Stürtz, 1939. **Vaccari, A.** "Las citas del Antiquo Testamento en la Epístola a los Hebreos." *CB* 13 (1956) 239–43. **Vaganay, L.** "Le Plan de l'Épître aux Hébreux." In *Mémorial Lagrange.* Paris: Gabalda, 1940. **Vandenbroucke, F.** *Les Psaumes et le Christ.* Louvain: Abbé Mont-César, 1955. **Vanhoye, A.** "Cristo Sumo Sacerdote." *RCB* 2 (1978) 313–23. ———. "De 'aspectu' oblationis Christi secundum Epistolam ad Hebraeos." *VD* 37 (1959) 32–38. ———. "Discussion sur la structure de l'Épître aux Hébreux." *Bib* 55 (1974) 349–80. ———. "De Sacerdotio Christi in Hebr." *VD* 47 (1969) 22–30. ———. "De sessione celesti in epistola ad Hebraeos." *VD* 44 (1966) 131–34. ———. *Epistolae ad Hebraeos: Textus de Sacerdotio Christo.* Rome: Pontifical Biblical Institute, 1968–69. ———. *Homilie für haltbedürftige Christen: Struktur und Botschaft des Hebräerbriefes.* Regensburg: Pustet, 1981. ———. "L'Épître aux Éphésiens et l'Épître aux Hébreux." *Bib* 59 (1978) 198–230. ———. "Le Dieu de la nouvelle alliance dans l'Épître aux Hébreux." In *Le notion biblique de Dieu.* BETL 41. Louvain: Louvain UP, 1976. 315–30. ———. "Les indices de la structure littéraire de l'Épître aux Hébreux." *SE* 2 (1964) 493–509. ———. "Literarische Struktur und theologische Botschaft des Hebräerbriefs." *SNTU* 4 (1979) 119–47; 5 (1980) 18–49. ———. *Le message de l'Épître aux Hébreux.* Paris: Cerf, 1977. ———. *Our Priest in God: The Doctrine of the Epistle to the Hebrews.* Rome: Biblical Institute Press, 1977. ———. *Prêtres anciens, prêtre nouveau selon le Nouveau Testament.* Paris: Cerf, 1980. ———. "Sacerdoce du Christ et culte chrétien selon l'Épître aux Hébreux." *Chr* 28 (1981) 216–30. ———. *Situation du Christ, Hébreux 1–2.* LD 58. Paris: Cerf, 1969. ———. *Structure and Message of the Epistle to the Hebrews.* Rome: Pontificio Instituto Biblico, 1989. ———. *A Structured Translation of the Epistle to the Hebrews.* Tr. J. Swetnam. Rome: Pontifical Biblical Institute, 1964. ———. "La structure centrale de l'Épître aux Hébreux (Héb 8/1–9/28)." *RSR* 47 (1959) 44–60. ———. *La structure littéraire de l'Épître aux Hébreux.* 2nd ed. StudNeot 1. Paris/Bruges: Desclée de Brouwer, 1976. **Vansant, A. C.** "The Humanity of Jesus in the Epistle to the Hebrews." Dissertation, Southern Baptist Theological Seminary, 1951. **Venard, L.** "L'utilisation des Psaumes dans l'Épître aux Hébreux." In *FS E. Podechard.* Lyons: Faculté Catholique, 1945. **Viard, A.** "Le salut par la foi dans l'Épître aux Hébreux." *Ang* 58 (1981) 115–36. **Vis, A.** *The Messianic Psalm Quotations in the New Testament.* Amsterdam: Hertberger, 1936. **Vitti, A. M.** "Le bellezze stilistiche nella Lettera agli Ebrei." *Bib* 7 (1936) 137–66. ———. "La lettera agli Ebrei." *RivB* 3 (1955) 289–310. ———. "Il sacerdozio di Gesù Cristo." In *Conferenze Bibliche.* Rome: Pontifical Biblical Institute, 1934. ———. "Ultimi studi sulla Lettera agli Ebrei." *Bib* 22 (1941) 412–32. **Vos, G.** "Hebrews—the Epistle of the *Diathēkē*." *PTR* 13 (1915) 587–632; 14 (1916) 1–61. ———. "The Priesthood of Christ in the Epistle to the Hebrews." *PTR* 4 (1907) 423–47, 579–604. ———. *The Teaching of the Epistle to the Hebrews.* Ed. and rev. J. Vos. Grand Rapids: Eerdmans, 1956. **Voulgaris, C. H.** *Η ΠΡΟΣ ΕΒΡΑΙΟΥΣ ΕΠΙΣΤΟΛΗ: ΠΕΡΙΣΤΑΤΙΚΑ, ΠΑΡΑΛΗΠΤΑΙ, ΣΥΓΓΡΑΦΕΥΣ, ΤΟΠΟΣ ΚΑΙ ΧΡΟΝΟΣ ΣΥΓΓΡΑΦΗΣ.* Athens: University of Athens, 1986. **Vuyst, J. de.** *"Oud en nieuw Verbond" in de Brief aan de Hebreeën.* Kampen: Kok, 1964. **Waal, C. van der.** "The 'People of God' in the Epistle to the Hebrews." *Neot* 5 (1971) 83–92. **Waddell, H. C.** "The Readers of the Epistle to the Hebrews." *Exp* 8th ser. 26 (1923) 88–105. **Walden, H. E.** "The Christology of the Epistle to the Hebrews." Dissertation, Southern Baptist Theological Seminary, 1944. **Warfield, B. B.** "Christ Our Sacrifice." In *The Person and Work of Christ.* Ed. S. G. Craig. Philadelphia: Presbyterian and Reformed, 1950. 391–426. **Watson, J. K.** "L'Épître aux Hébreux." *CCER* 15 (1968) 10–16. ———. "L'Épître aux Hébreux et l'historicité." *CCER* 20 (1972) 1–13. **Webster, J. H.** "The Epistle to the Hebrews." *BSac* 85 (1928) 347–60. **Wengst, K.** *Christologische Formeln und Lieder des Urchristentums.* SNT 7. Gütersloh: Bertelsmann, 1972. **Wenschkewitz, H.** "Die Spiritualisierung der Kultusbegriffe Tempel, Priester und Opfer im Neuen Testament." *Angelos* 4 (1932) 70–230. **Werner, E.** *The Sacred Bridge.* London: Dobson, 1959. **Wette, W. M. L. de.** "Über die symbolisch-typische Lehrart des Briefes an die Hebräer." *TZ* 3 (1822) 1–51. **Whitley, W. T.** "The Epistle to the Hebrews." *RevExp* 3 (1906) 214–29. **Wiefel, W.** "The Jewish Community in Ancient Rome and the Origins of Roman Christianity." In *The Romans Debate.* Ed. K. P. Dornfried. Minneapolis: Augsburg, 1977. **Wikgren, A.** "Patterns of Perfection in the Epistle to the Hebrews." *NTS* 6 (1959–60) 159–67. ———. "Some Greek Idioms in the Epistle to the Hebrews." In *The Teacher's Yoke.* FS H. Trantham. Ed. E. J. Vardaman and J. L. Garrett. Waco, TX: Baylor UP, 1964. **Williams, A. H.** "An Early Christology: A Systematic and Exegetical Investigation of the Traditions Contained in Hebrews." Dissertation, Mainz, 1971. **Williams, S. K.** *Jesus' Death as Saving Event: The Background and Origin of a Concept.* HDR 2. Missoula, MT: Scholars, 1975. **Williamson, R.** "The Background to the Epistle to the Hebrews." *ExpTim* 87 (1975–76) 232–37. ———. "The Eucharist and the Epistle to the Hebrews." *NTS* 21 (1974–75) 300–12. ———. "Hebrews and Doctrine." *ExpTim* 81 (1969–70) 371–76. ———. *Philo and the Epistle to the Hebrews.* ALGHJ 4. Leiden: Brill, 1970. ———. "Philo and New Testament Christology." In *Studia Biblica 1978* III. JSNTSup 3. Sheffield: JSOT Press, 1980. 439–45. ———. "Platonism and Hebrews." *SJT* 16 (1963) 415–24. **Willis, C. G.** "St. Augustine's Text of the Epistle to the Hebrews." *SP* 6 (1962) 543–47. **Wilson, R. McL.** "Coptisms in the Epistle to the Hebrews?" *NovT* 1 (1956) 322–24. **Winter, A.** "ἅπαξ, ἐφάπαξ im Hebräerbrief." Dissertation, Rome, 1960. **Worden, T.** "Before Reading the Epistle to the Hebrews." *Scr* 14 (1962) 48–57. **Worley, D. R.** "God's Faithfulness to Promise: The Hortatory Use of Commissive Language in Hebrews." Dissertation, Yale University, 1981. **Wrede, W.** *Das literarische Rätsel des Hebräerbriefs.* FRLANT 8. Göttingen: Vandenhoeck & Ruprecht, 1906. **Yadin, Y.** *The Art of Warfare in Biblical Lands in the Light of Archaeological Study.* 2 vols. Tr. M. Pearlman. New York: McGraw-Hill, 1963. ———. "The Dead Sea Scrolls and the Epistle to the Hebrews." *ScrHier* 4 (1958) 36–55. **Young, F. M.** "Christological Ideas in the Greek Commentaries on the Epistle to the Hebrews." *JTS* 20 (1969) 150–63. ———. *Sacrifice and the Death of Christ.* London: SPCK, 1975. ———. "The Use of Sacrificial Ideas in Greek Christian Writers from the New Testament to John Chrysostom." Dissertation, Cambridge University, 1967. **Young, J. A.** "The Significance of Sacrifice in the Epistle to the Hebrews." Dissertation, Southwestern Baptist Theological Seminary, 1963. **Zedda, S.** *Lettera agli Ebrei: Versione, introduzione, note.* Rome: Edizioni Paoline, 1967. **Zerwick, M.** *Biblical Greek, Illustrated by Examples.* Tr. J. Smith. Rome: Pontifical Biblical Institute, 1963. ——— and **Grosvenor, M.** *A Grammatical Analysis of the Greek New Testament.* Vol. 2: *Epistles-Apocalypse.* Rome: Pontifical Biblical Institute, 1979. **Zimmer, F.** *Exegetische Probleme des Hebräer- und Galaterbriefes.* Hildburghausen: Gradow, 1882. **Zimmermann, H.** *Das Bekenntnis der Hoffnung: Tradition und Redaktion im Hebräerbrief.* BBB 47. Cologne/Bonn: Hanstein, 1977. ———. *Die Hohepriester-Christologie des Hebräerbriefes.* Paderborn: F. Schöningh, 1964. ———. *Neutestamentliche Methodenlehre: Darstellung der historische-kritischen Methode.* 7th ed. Stuttgart: Katholisches Bibelwerk, 1982. **Zorn, R.** "Die Fürbitte und Interzession im Spätjudentum und im Neuen Testament." Dissertation, Göttingen, 1957. **Zuntz, G.** *The Text of the Epistles: A Disquisition upon the 'Corpus Paulinum.'* Schweich Lectures, 1946. London: The British Academy, 1953. **Zupez, J.** "Salvation in the Epistle to the Hebrews." *TBT* 37 (1968) 2590–95.

F. The Necessity for New Cultic Action (9:1–10)

Bibliography

Andriessen, P. "L'Eucharistie dans l'Épître aux Hébreux." *NRT* 94 (1972) 269–77. **Attridge, H. W.** "The Uses of Antithesis in Hebrews 8–10." *HTR* 79 (1986) 1–9. **Beavis, M. A.** "The New Covenant and Judaism." *TBT* 22 (1984) 24–30. **Brown, J. R.** *Temple and Sacrifice in Rabbinic Judaism.* Evanston, IL: Seabury Western Theological Seminary, 1963. **Camacho, H. S.** "The Altar of Incense in Hebrews 9:3–4." *AUSS* 24 (1986) 5–12. **Casalini, N.** *Dal simbolo alla realtà: L'espiazione dall'Antica alla Nuova Alleanza secondo Ebr 9,1–14: Una proposta esegetica.* Studium Biblicum Franciscanum 26. Jerusalem: Franciscan Press, 1989. ————. "I sacrifici dell'antica alleanza nel piano salvifico di Dio secondo la Lettera agli Ebrei." *RivB* 35 (1987) 443–64. **Cody, A.** *Heavenly Sanctuary and Liturgy.* 133, 145–50. **D'Angelo, M. R.** *Moses in the Letter to the Hebrews.* 225–43. **Delporte, L.** "Les principes de la typologie biblique et les éléments figuratifs du sacrifice de l'expiation." *ETL* 3 (1926) 307–27. **Dibelius, M.** "Der himmlische Kultus nach dem Hebräerbrief." *TBl* 21 (1942) 1–11. **Dulière, W. L.** "Les chérubins du troisième temple à Antioch." *ZRGG* 13 (1961) 201–19. **Dunkel, F.** "Expiation et Jour des expiations dans l'Épître aux Hébreux." *RevRéf* 33 (1982) 63–71. **Ellingworth, P.** "Jesus and the Universe." *EvQ* 58 (1986) 337–50. **Fabris, R.** "La lettera agli Ebrei e l'Antico Testamento." *RivB* 32 (1984) 237–52. **Fischer, J.** "Covenant, Fulfilment and Judaism in Hebrews." *ERT* 13 (1989) 175–87. **Harnack, A.** "Zu Hebräerbrief ix.3–4." *TSK* 49 (1876) 572–74. **Hofius, 0.** "Das 'erste' und das 'zweite' Zelt: Ein Beitrag zur Auslegung von Hbr 9:1–10." *ZNW* 61 (1970) 271–77. ————. *Der Vorhang vor dem Thron Gottes.* 60–65. **Johnsson, W. G.** "The Cultus of Hebrews in Twentieth-Century Scholarship." *ExpTim* 89 (1977–78) 104–8. ————. "Defilement and Purgation in the Book of Hebrews." Dissertation, Vanderbilt University, 1973. 27–290. **Koester, C. R.** *The Dwelling of God: The Tabernacle in the Old Testament, Intertestamental Jewish Literature, and the New Testament.* CBQMS 22. Washington, DC: Catholic Biblical Association, 1989. **Lach, S.** "Les ordonnances du culte israélite dans la lettre aux Hébreux." In *Sacra Pagina: Miscellanea Biblica Congressus Internationalis Catholici de Re Biblica.* Ed. J. Coppens, A. Descamps, and E. Massaux. Paris: Gabalda, 1952. 2:390–403. **Langhe, R. de.** "L'autel d'or du temple de Jérusalem." *Bib* 40 (1959) 476–94. **Laub, F.** *Bekenntnis und Auslegung,* 191–96. **Lindeskog, G.** "The Veil of the Temple." *ConNT* 11 (1947) 132–37. **Loader, W. G. R.** *Sohn und Hoherpriester.* 161–66, 171–80, 187–89. **Loewenich, W. von.** "Zum Verständnis des Opfergedankens im Hebräerbrief." *TBl* 12 (1933) 167–72. **Luck, U.** "Himmlisches und irdisches Geschehen im Hebräerbrief." *NovT* 6 (1963) 192–215. **McNicol, A. J.** "The Relationship of the Image of the Highest Angel to the High Priest Concept in Hebrews." Dissertation, Vanderbilt University, 1974. 148–71. **Moe, O.** "Das irdische und das himmlische Heiligtum: Zur Auslegung von Hebr. 9, 4f." *TZ* 9 (1953) 23–29. **Mora, G.** "Ley y sacrificio en la carta a los Hebreos." *RevistCatT* 1 (1976) 1–50. **Nikiprowetsky, V.** "La spiritualization des sacrifices et le cult sacrificial au temple de Jérusalem chez Philon d'Alexandrie." *Sem* 17 (1967) 98–114. **Omanson, R. L.** "A Superior Covenant: Hebrews 8:1–10:18." *RevExp* 82 (1985) 361–73. **Peterson, D. G.** "An Examination of the Concept of 'Perfection' in the 'Epistle to the Hebrews.'" Dissertation, University of Manchester, 1978. 227–35. **Pierce, C. A.** *Conscience in the New Testament.* Chicago: Allenson, 1955. **Purton, J. S.** "The Golden Censer: A Note on Hebrews 9:4." *Exp* 3rd ser. 6 (1881) 469–71. **Raurell, F.** "Certain Affinities between Ez-LXX and the Epistle to the Hebrews with Regard to the 'Doxa' and the Cherubins." *EstFran* 86 (1985) 209–32. **Salom, A. P.** "*Ta Hagia* in the Epistle to the Hebrews." *AUSS* 5 (1967) 59–70. **Schröger, F.** *Der Verfasser des Hebräerbriefes.* 206, 229–35. **Selby,**

G. S. "The Meaning and Function of συνείδησις in Hebrews 9 and 10." *RestQ* 28 (1985–86) 145–54. **Spicq, C.** "La conscience dans le Nouveau Testament." *RB* 47 (1938) 50–80. **Stelzenberger, J.** *Syneidēsis im Neuen Testament.* Paderborn: Schöningh, 1961. 56–65. **Swetnam, J.** "Hebrews 9,2 and the Uses of Consistency." *CBQ* 32 (1970) 205–21. ———. "On the Imagery and Significance of Hebrews 9,9–10." *CBQ* 28 (1966) 155–73. **Thompson, J.** "Hebrews 9 and Hellenistic Concepts of Sacrifice." *JBL* 98 (1979) 567–78. **Turner, J. M.** "After Liberation—What? (Heb. 9:4)." *ExpTim* 96 (1984) 22–23. **Vernet, J. M.** "Cristo, él que abre el camino." *Sal* 47 (1985) 419–31. **Wenschkewitz, H.** "Die Spiritualisierung der Kultusbegriffe: Tempel, Priester, Opfer im Neuen Testament." *Angelos* 4 (1932) 131–49, 162–66. **Williamson, R.** "The Eucharist and the Epistle to the Hebrews." *NTS* 21 (1974–75) 300–312. **York, A. D.** "The Arrangement of the Tabernacle Furniture (Hebrews 9)." *BV* 2 (1968) 28–32. **Young, N. H.** "The Gospel according to Hebrews 9." *NTS* 27 (1980–81) 198–210. **Zimmermann, H.** *Das Bekenntnis der Hoffnung.* 181–88.

Translation

[1]*Now*[a] *the first covenant*[b] *had regulations for cultic worship and a sanctuary which was earthly.*[c] [2]*For a tabernacle was set up: it consisted of the front compartment*[d] *in which were the lampstand and the table together with*[e] *the consecrated bread.*[f] *This was called the "Holy Place."*[g] [3]*Behind*[h] *the second curtain was a compartment called "the Most Holy Place,"* [4]*containing the golden altar of incense*[i] *and the gold-covered*[j] *ark of the covenant in which*[k] *were the gold jar containing the manna, Aaron's rod that had blossomed, and the stone tablets of the covenant.* [5]*Above the ark were the cherubim of the Glory,*[l] *overshadowing the place of atonement.*[m] *We cannot speak in detail*[n] *now about these things.*

[6]*When*[o] *these things had been arranged like this, the priests entered*[p] *continually into the front compartment as they performed their ritual functions,* [7]*but only the high priest entered the rear compartment,*[q] *and that only once a year, and never without blood, which he offered for himself and also for the sins the people had committed in ignorance.* [8]*The Holy Spirit was showing by this that the way into the real sanctuary*[r] *had not yet been disclosed while the first compartment*[s] *had cultic status.*[t] [9]*This is an illustration pointing to the present time, according to which the gifts and sacrifices being offered are unable to bring decisive purgation*[u] *to the worshiper so far as his conscience is concerned,* [10]*[but] only on the basis of*[v] *food and drink and various ceremonial washings, regulations pertaining to the human order*[w] *which were imposed until the time of correction.*[x]

Notes

[a] The expression μὲν οὖν appears to be transitional, simply denoting continuation (cf. 7:11; 8:4). So Hanna, *Grammatical Aid,* 155; cf. Moule, *Idiom-Book,* 163. The UBSGNT adds in brackets the particle καί, but it should be omitted with P[46] B 1739 *al* sa bo co sy[p] Origen. The inclusion of καί conveys the impression that the old order is being described as parallel to the new, when, in fact, it is the writer's intention to contrast the old and new orders. On this question see Zuntz, *Text of the Epistles,* 209–10.

[b] The term ἡ πρώτη, "the first," is to be understood as modifying the unexpressed word "covenant," as in 8:13.

[c] An adj in predicate use is sometimes equivalent to a relative clause of the type that in English is preceded by a comma. This is the case in the expression τό τε ἅγιον κοσμικόν, where Zerwick translates "'(its) sanctuary, which (however) was a terrestrial one' [in opposition to the sanctuary of the new covenant (8:5; 9:11)]" (*Biblical Greek* §187). The term κοσμικός does not mean "cosmic" (cf. Sowers, *Hermeneutics,* 108–9, who translates "the tabernacle with its cosmic symbolism"), but rather ἐπίγειος, "earthly," and so the opposite of terms used by the writer to qualify the heavenly sanctuary: ἀληθινός, "true" (8:2; 9:24), ἐπουράνιος, "heavenly" (8:5), οὐ χειροποίητος, "not made with hands" (9:11),

and οὐ ταύτης τῆς κτίσεως, "not of this creation" (9:11). There is a complete absence of cosmic speculation in Hebrews. See Hofius, *Vorhang*, 61; J. Thompson, 569–70; Theissen, *Untersuchungen*, 102.

d The term ἡ πρώτη is used elliptically for ἡ πρώτη σκηνή and expresses a rare spatial sense ("the front"), found only here in the NT (Michaelis, *TDNT* 6:866; 7:376). Cf. JB: "There was a tent which comprised two compartments: the first . . ."; NIV: "A tabernacle was set up: in its first room . . . ." The recognition of the spatial sense of πρώτη in vv 2, 6, and 8, and of τὴν δευτέραν in v 7 is a significant corrective to those interpreters who hold that the writer spoke of two separated tents, a "first tent" and a "second tent" (NEB) or an "outer" and "inner tent" (RSV, TEV; Michel, 298, 301; Kuss, 113; Schröger, *Verfasser*, 230; Schierse, *Verheissung*, 26–29; et al.).

e The expression ἡ τράπεζα καὶ ἡ πρόθεσις τῶν ἄρτων is a hendiadys meaning "the table together with the loaves displayed upon it," table and loaves being regarded as a single unit. The writer's formulation is similar to 2 Chr 13:11 LXX, where πρόθεσις ἄρτων means "the display of the loaves" (Zerwick and Grosvenor, *Grammatical Analysis*, 672).

f After the reference to the consecrated bread several witnesses (B sa^mss) add καὶ τὸ χρυσοῦν θυμιαστήριον, "and the golden altar of incense," bringing the text into conformity with the OT description of the Holy Place (Exod 30:1–6). These same witnesses delete the reference to the golden altar of incense in v 4. The transposition was clearly a scribal attempt to remove the difficulty concerning the writer's statement regarding the location of the golden altar of incense in the tabernacle (see Metzger, *Textual Commentary*, 666).

g This is the only occurrence in Hebrews of the anarthrous use of ἄγια (neuter pl) to denote "the Holy Place." Elsewhere the writer uses the neuter pl with the article to designate "the Most Holy Place" in the Tabernacle or its heavenly prototype (e.g., 9:25; 13:11; but see 9:24 where the anarthrous ἄγια denotes the inner sanctuary). The proposal that the phrase ἥτις λέγεται Ἅγια is a marginal gloss that later entered the text at the wrong place (i.e., "which is called the Most Holy Place": so H. Koester, "'Outside the Camp': Hebrews 13:9–14," *HTR* 55 [1962] 309, n. 34) is unsupported by the MS tradition. Synge (*Hebrews and the Scriptures*, 26) and Vanhoye (*La structure*, 144, n. 2) argue that the term should be construed not as a neuter pl (ἄγια) but as a fem sg (ἀγία), in which case it is used adjectivally and describes the compartment as "holy." The only other use of anathrous ἄγια in Hebrews, however, is certainly to be read as a neuter pl (9:24), and at 9:2 Codex B actually reads τὰ ἄγια. On the grounds of the supposed inconsistency in the writer's practice, if ἄγια here means "the Holy Place," Swetnam proposed that the entire phrase qualifies not the front compartment but the consecrated bread that is designated as "holy," in keeping with LXX practice (e.g., Lev 24:9; cf. "Hebrews 9,2 and the Uses of Consistency," 207–14; but see in response Schröger, "Der Gottesdienst der Hebräerbriefgemeinde," *MTZ* 19 [1968] 165). It is appropriate to regard ἄγια as a neuter pl and to recognize that the use of this form to describe the front compartment in 9:2 is exceptional (so Spicq, 2:249; Michel, 298–99; N. H. Young, *NTS* 21 [1980–81] 198).

h In the NT the prep μετά followed by the accusative means "after" in a temporal sense, except in this one instance where it denotes a spatial sense, "behind" or "beyond" (Moule, *Idiom-Book*, 60; cf. BDF §236).

i The translation of the noun θυμιατήριον (from the verb θυμιᾶν, "to burn incense") has been debated. The New Confraternity Version, following the Vg of Jerome (*turibulum*), renders "having a golden censer." The reference is to the incense-shovel or vessel used for carrying live coals from the altar of burnt offering in the courtyard into the Most Holy Place on the Day of Atonement, where the high priest mingled incense with the coals in order to generate an aromatic cloud that would envelop the ark. The Gk. term is used with this nuance in classical Greek (Herodotus 4.162; Thucydides 6.46) and in the LXX (2 Chr 26:19; Ezek 8:11; 4 Macc 7:11; cf. Exod 8:11; 27:3; 38:3; Num 4:14), and this meaning has been adopted by Riggenbach, 241–43, n. 73; Lach, "Les ordannances," 402–3; and is preferred by Zerwick and Grosvenor, *Grammatical Analysis*, 672.

There are, however, strong objections to this interpretation. The censer was cast in brass, not gold, and there is no mention in the OT of a *golden* censer. Moreover, there is no Jewish tradition according to which the censer was left in the Most Holy Place (Str-B 3:376). Most significantly, the term θυμιατήριον is used in writings contemporary or near contemporary with Hebrews to designate the golden altar of incense (Philo, *Who is the Heir?* 226; *Moses* 2.94, 101, 105; Jos., *J. W.* 5.214, 218; *Ant.* 3.147, 198; 4.35, 54, 55; Exod 30:1 Theod. and Symm.). Cf. Michaelis, *TDNT* 4:264; P. E. Hughes, 309–14.

j The term πάντοθεν means "on all sides, entirely" (BAG 613), and has reference to the fact that both the inside and outside of the ark were covered with gold.

ᵏ Lach ("Les ordonnances," 395) has argued that the prep expression ἐν ᾗ does not signify "in which" but "next to which" or "close to." He points out that the Gk. prep ἐν, united to an impersonal obj in the dative, indicates not only the circumstance of place but also a situation accompanying the main verb, as for example in 9:25, ἐν αἵματι ἀλλοτρίῳ, "with blood of another." The writer in 9:4*b* wishes to accentuate the fact that there was preserved in the Most Holy Place, besides the ark, three other objects, according to Lach. This solution to an old exegetical problem would be attractive were it not that the same prep expression, ἐν ᾗ, occurs in v 2, and there it must mean "in which." It seems necessary to translate the two expressions in the same way.

ˡ The term δόξης in the expression χερουβὶν δόξης, "cherubim of the Glory," signifies the divine presence. The expression is calculated to emphasize that the Most Holy Place was the place that was to be associated with the presence of God in glory (cf. Cody, *Heavenly Sanctuary*, 147).

ᵐ Nouns ending in -τήριον form a class, generally indicating a local area. Here ἱλαστήριον denotes the seat of propitiation or "mercy seat" (A. T. Robertson, *Grammar*, 154).

ⁿ The expression κατὰ μέρος exhibits the distributive use of the prep with the accusative, signifying here "in detail" (Moule, *Idiom-Book*, 60).

ᵒ 9:6–10 is a periodic sentence, which has been broken up in translation out of consideration for English style.

ᵖ The literary form εἰσίασιν occurs for εἰσέρχονται, "they enter in" (cf. BDF §99[1]).

�q The numerical expression τὴν δευτέραν is used with a spatial nuance and denotes the rear compartment as opposed to the front compartment mentioned in v 6. The πρώτη and δευτέρα are respectively the Holy Place and the Most Holy Place, as in vv 2–3. Vv 6–7 are tightly linked together by the μέν . . . δέ construction: "on the one hand into the front compartment . . . but on the other hand into the rear compartment" (cf. N. H. Young, *NTS* 21 [1980–81] 199).

ʳ The gen τῶν ἁγίων stands, as in 10:19, for εἰς τὰ ἅγια, "into the sanctuary," with reference to the heavenly sanctuary, the presence of God (BDF §163; so already Lünemann, 283, followed by Riggenbach, 249; Michel, 306, n. 2; Hofius, *Vorhang*, 62; N. H. Young, *NTS* 21 [1980–81] 199–201, 209).

ˢ The meaning of τῆς πρώτης σκηνῆς is disputed. It has been argued that the reference in πρώτη is temporal and that the expression refers to the whole Mosaic tabernacle. In that case the phrase will be translated "former" or "earlier tabernacle" (so NEB; NIV; Spicq, 2:253–54; F. F. Bruce, 194–95). The syntactical structure of the periodic sentence, which extends from 9:6–10, however, lends little support to this understanding. The spatial reference in τὴν πρώτην σκηνήν in v 6 is incontestable. An unannounced shift to a temporal idea within such a short compass would be unnecessarily harsh and abrupt. It is better to recognize that ἡ πρώτη σκηνή consistently means "the front compartment" in vv 2, 6, and 8 (so RSV; Michel, 307; N. H. Young, *NTS* 21 [1980–81] 200–201). The temporal significance of the front compartment is expressed by the particle ἔτι, "still, yet, while."

ᵗ The expression ἔτι . . . ἐχούσης στάσιν conveys more than the literal sense of "while being in existence" or "still standing" (RSV; NEB; JB; NIV; TEV). Used with the previous ptcp, the phrase means "retaining its status," in reference to the God-ordained cultic status and currency of the front compartment. The meaning is analogous to the use of ἱστάναι in 10:9 ("to establish as valid/to have status"; so Riggenbach, 249; Hofius, *Vorhang*, 62–63; Peterson, "Examination," 228–29).

ᵘ It is difficult to express the nuance of τελειῶσαι in this context. Clearly there is an inner connection between τελειοῦν (9:9; 10:1) and καθαρίζειν, "to cleanse, purify" (9:14; 10:2), but the simple equation of the two terms (as in Michel, 333, n. 4) is inappropriate. Peterson argues that τελειοῦν is not synonymous with καθαρίζειν but involves the latter as a most significant element. The primary notion, however, is that of relationship to God. He translates the phrase "to perfect the worshiper with respect to conscience" ("Examination," 234–35). The translation adopted for the commentary follows Johnsson who seeks to take into account the fact that τελειοῦν in Hebrews connotes finality and that the immediate context concerns the decisive purging of the consciousness of sin ("Defilement," 282, 450). Cf. Maurer, *TDNT* 7:918.

ᵛ The prep ἐπί with the dative here means "on the basis of" or "in accordance with," as in 8:6 (BDF §235[2]). Rienecker has made the alternative proposal to translate the prep "in the matter of" (*Linguistic Key*, 349).

ʷ The expression δικαιώματα σαρκός is almost invariably understood as a pejorative term for statutes relating to the "flesh" or "body" (e.g., RSV; NEB; NASB; cf. Michel, 308–9). In Heb 2:14; 5:7; 12:9, however, σάρξ is a neutral term and simply refers to the human sphere. The expression in v 10 echoes the related phrase in v 1, where δικαιώματα denotes "regulations" for public worship in an earthly tabernacle. There is no dichotomy intended between "conscience" (v 9) and σάρξ in v 10 (so Johnsson,

"Defilement," 288–89, who translates the expression "human regulations"; cf. Schweizer, *TDNT* 7:142, who proposes the rendering "statutes of the earthly sphere").

ˣ The term διόρθωσις in the phrase μέχρι καιροῦ διορθώσεως denotes "the making straight of what has shifted from its true position" (Preisker, *TDNT* 5:450). The use of the word in the papyri and in hellenistic Greek indicates that it expresses the notions of correction, reconstruction, improvement, or amendment (Williamson, *Philo*, 117–18). Preisker proposes the translation "until the time of the true order" (cf. BAG 198: "the time of the new order").

Form/Structure/Setting

In 9:1–10 the writer concentrates narrowly upon the disposition of the tabernacle and its provisions for cultic worship. The comparison of Jesus as priestly ministrant and mediator of the new covenant with the Levitical arrangement under the terms of the Sinaitic covenant in 8:1–13 established a context for the statement that τὴν πρώτην, "the first covenant," had been regarded by God as obsolete (8:13). In 9:1 the writer repeats the catchword ἡ πρώτη (denoting "the first covenant") as the point of transition for explicating one aspect of the Sinaitic covenant, namely, its cultic regulations. By repeating the catchword at the beginning of the new unit, the writer skillfully enhances a sense of continuity between the sections of the homily as he shifts from one aspect of his subject to another. In this instance the shift from the discussion of covenant (8:6–13) to the consideration of the tabernacle services (9:1–10) is indicated by the transitional particle οὖν ("now," "indeed") in 9:1.

The thematic introductory sentence in 9:1 announces the exposition of two subjects, namely, regulations for cultic worship (δικαιώματα λατρείας) and the earthly tabernacle (τὸ ἅγιον κοσμικόν). In characteristic fashion, the writer develops them in inverse order. He considers first the arrangement of the tabernacle (9:2–5) and then the regulations for cultic worship (9:6–10). The point of transition between the two paragraphs is clearly marked by the summarizing comment in v 5b ("We cannot speak in detail now about these things"), which prepares the reader for the new development in vv 6–10. In the initial paragraph (9:2–5), the writer seeks to stress as strongly as possible the distinction and independent significance of the front and rear compartments of the desert sanctuary (Riggenbach, 238). This emphasis prepares for the argument in 9:6–10 concerning the meaning of the cultic actions that reflect these arrangements.

The cultic regulations are of primary importance to the writer, and he has underscored this fact by using the term δικαιώματα, which occurs only here in Hebrews, to indicate the structural limits of the section. Corresponding to the expression δικαιώματα λατρείας, "regulations for cultic worship," in v 1 is the complementary expression δικαιώματα σαρκός, "regulations pertaining to the human order," in v 10. The writer is most concerned to stress that the disposition of the tabernacle and its cultic regulations expressed symbolically the imperfect and provisional character of the old Sinaitic covenant. His description emphasizes limited access and the inadequacy of the offerings. The facts demonstrated that the way into the presence of God was not yet disclosed (hence, the arrangement was provisional, 9:8) and that the gifts and sacrifices offered could not provide decisive purgation (hence, the arrangement was imperfect, 9:9–10) (cf. Vanhoye, "La structure centrale," *RSR* 47 [1959] 49; *La structure*, 144–45; Hofius, *ZNW* 61 [1970] 271, n. 1).

As a unit, 9:1–10 sets the stage for the account of the priestly ministry of Christ in the heavenly sanctuary in 9:11–10:18. In contrast to the limited access to God provided under the Levitical arrangement and the inadequacy of its offerings, the writer will stress the unhindered access provided by the eschatological high priest and the finality of his offering in the heavenly sanctuary. Accordingly, 9:1–10 is to be interpreted as a unit describing the old cultus in preparation for the ensuing exposition. The argument is developed in distinctly cultic terms. The significant element in 9:1–10 is the introduction of the cultic terminology and its leading motif: access to God is possible only through the medium of blood (9:7; cf. Johnsson, "Defilement," 222).

Comment

In his comments on the place of worship and its divisions, the writer draws upon the tabernacle of the Israelites in the wilderness rather than upon the temple in any of its forms. The reason for this is almost certainly to be traced to the prior use of Exod 25:40, instructing Moses to erect a sanctuary according to the pattern God showed to him on Mount Sinai (8:5). The matter of the sanctuary is to be considered in relation to the old and new covenants, and the contrast between the two. It is only natural, therefore, that the tabernacle be used rather than the temple because of the association of the desert sanctuary with the establishment of the old covenant at Sinai. The fact that the argument is developed in terms of the tabernacle indicates that the present tenses in the account should be taken as "timeless," rather than as reflections of a continuing temple liturgy in Jerusalem.

The division of the tabernacle into two parts, the front and rear compartments, a division that is essentially spatial, becomes temporal in the writer's typological exposition. His concern is with the elaboration of a theology of salvation that recognizes the eschatological newness of the period introduced with Christ. The appeal to the cultic appointments and actions in the tabernacle demonstrates the ultimate inadequacy of the Levitical institution and the necessity for the new cultic action of Christ, which brings a definitive and better order of salvation with unlimited access to the presence of God (cf. Cody, *Heavenly Sanctuary,* 146–60).

The manner in which the writer develops his argument forces the interpreter to give serious consideration to the use of cultic terminology in 9:1–10:18. It is imperative that this terminology be recognized as religious language. It calls for a study of the text in religious perspective, with an openness to the internal logic of the argument from the cultus. It is within a religious perspective that an earnest concern with access to the presence of God and with the decisive purgation of the defilement of sin is thrown into sharp relief (see especially Johnsson, "Defilement," 89–205).

1   The thematic first sentence of this unit makes the point that the preceding covenant (ἡ πρώτη) had its own cultic regulations for worship and that these were related to what transpired within the precincts of the tabernacle. The significance of the expression δικαιώματα λατρείας, "regulations for cultic worship," is clarified in vv 6–10, where the writer repeats the term λατρείας (in reference to the cultic ministry of the priests) in v 6 and the term δικαιώματα in v 10.

Initially the emphasis falls on the phrase τό τε ἅγιον κοσμικόν, "and a tabernacle which was earthly." In Hebrews the neuter singular form τὸ ἅγιον clearly refers to the whole sanctuary (cf. N. H. Young, *NTS* 21 [1980–81] 198). The predicate adjective κοσμικόν qualifies the tabernacle as belonging to the earth, as distinct from the heavenly sanctuary in which the eschatological high priest now ministers. The description recalls the contrast developed between the sanctuary "which the Lord pitched, not man" (8:2) and the sanctuary constructed by Moses in accordance with the divine instructions (8:5). The expression anticipates the pejorative term χειροποίητα, "made by human hands," which qualifies the sanctuary in 9:24. The term κοσμικόν does not reflect the contemporary view that the tabernacle was a symbolic reflection of the world (e.g., Philo, *On the Special Laws* 1.66; *Moses* 2.77–80; Jos., *J. W.* 4.324). The writer views the OT sanctuary as taking its pattern from the heavenly prototype, not from the creation (8:5; cf. Michel, 298; Hofius, *Vorhang*, 61). As an earthly sanctuary, the tabernacle is not only transitory but participates in the imperfection of the present world. The description is accordingly pejorative (Thompson, 569–70; Theissen, *Untersuchungen*, 102).

2 The detail of the construction of the tabernacle that the writer emphasizes is the division of the sanctuary into two compartments. This distinction appears to be fundamental for the interpretation of 9:1–10. In vv 2–3 the writer uses the standard designations Ἅγια, "the Holy Place," and Ἅγια Ἁγίων, "the Most Holy Place," but throughout the section he distinguishes between the two compartments by the numerical terms πρώτη, "first" (vv 2, 6, 8), and δευτέρα, "second" (v 7). These terms do not designate two separate tents but rather one tent that was divided into a "front" sanctuary and a "rear" sanctuary, assigning to πρώτη and δευτέρα the rare spatial nuance in these terms (Michaelis, *TDNT* 6:866; 7:376; Riggenbach, 238, 240). The writer's distinctive formulation is not attested elsewhere (but cf. Jos., *Ant.* 3.122–23, where the tabernacle is divided into τρία μέρη, "three parts," and the designation τρίτον μέρος, "the third part," denotes the Most Holy Place). Michel suggested that the distinction into πρώτη σκηνή and δευτέρα σκηνή (understood as a first tent and a second tent) reflected a false understanding of the LXX text of Exod 25–26 (298, n. 3). A linguistic parallel to the rare spatial use of πρῶτος and δεύτερος, however, occurs in Josephus, who describes the whole temple area as ἱερόν (*J. W.* 5.184, 186) but designates the outer court, which was accessible to the Gentiles, as τὸ πρῶτον ἱερόν, "the front courtyard," and the inner court, accessible to the Jews, as τὸ δεύτερον ἱερόν, "the rear courtyard" (*J. W.* 5.193–95). Twice Josephus speaks of the antechamber of the temple as ὁ πρῶτος οἶκος, "the front house" (*J. W.* 5.208–9; see Hofius, *ZNW* 61 [1970] 274–75). The descriptive terminology in v 2 indicates the writer envisages the sanctuary in use: entering the tabernacle from the courtyard, the appointed priest enters first the Holy Place and then passes through the separating second curtain into the Most Holy Place (D'Angelo, *Moses*, 226–27).

Of the furnishings of the front chamber the writer mentions two items. The menorah (λυχνία, "lampstand") was placed at the south side of the Holy Place (Exod 26:35). It was constructed of beaten gold, with three branches springing from either side of a main stem. The main stem and all six branches each supported a flower-shaped lamp holder that was kept lit day and night (Exod 25:31–39; 27:20–21 LXX; cf. Michaelis, *TDNT* 4:324–27). The table together with the consecrated bread stood at the north side of the front compartment (Exod 25:23–30; 26:35; Lev 24:6; cf. Goppelt, *TDNT* 8:209–11). The twelve "loaves" of bread were arranged in two rows of six loaves each. The consecrated bread was unleavened, a fact that is not mentioned in the OT but is reported unanimously by witnesses contemporary with the writer of Hebrews (Philo, *On the Special Laws* 2.161; *On the Preliminary Studies* 168; *Moses* 81; Jos., *Ant.* 3.142, 255; cf. *Sipra* on Lev 2:11 [7c, 15], *m. Menah* 5:1; *b. Menah* 77b). There is at this point no mention of the golden altar of incense, which was placed just before the second curtain at the rear of the front chamber (Exod 30:1–10; see *Comment* below, v 4).

3–5a In describing the front compartment the writer began with (*a*) an enumeration of the furnishings and concluded with (*b*) the qualification that it was designated the Holy Place. In vv 3–5a he immediately supplies (*b'*) the qualification that the rear compartment was designated the Most Holy Place and then proceeds to mention (*a'*) the items it contained, giving to the presentation a chiastic disposition (Michel, 298).

The rear compartment was "behind the second curtain." The expression τὸ δεύτερον καταπέτασμα denotes the inner curtain that screened the rear sanctuary from the antechamber where the priests carried on their daily ministry (Exod 26:31–33; Lev 16:2, 12; 21:23; 24:3; Philo, *Moses* 2.86, 101; Jos., *Ant.* 8.75). This screen was made of fine twisted linen woven with blue, purple, and scarlet yarn and was embroidered with figures of cherubim (Exod 26:31). Behind this curtain was the inner sanctuary designated Ἅγια Ἁγίων. The force of this expression is that of an emphatic superlative ("the Most Holy Place"). The common designation "the Holy of Holies" translates an alternative expression τὸ ἅγιον τῶν ἁγίων (Exod 26:33 LXX). The plural form employed by the writer in v 3 is also found in the LXX (1 Kgs 8:6; 2 Chr 4:22; 5:7).

The location of the χρυσοῦν . . . θυμιατήριον, "golden altar of incense," within the Most Holy Place is problematical because it was well known that it stood in the Holy Place just before the inner curtain (Exod 30:6; 40:26; for the history of this altar see de Langhe, *Bib* 40 [1959] 476–94). The scribal tradition represented by Codex B and certain of its allies recognized this problem and sought to resolve it by textual alteration (see above, *Note* g). In the course of Israel's subsequent history the golden altar was placed within the inner sanctuary (1 Kgs 6:20, 22), and one source nearly contemporary with Hebrews reflects that liturgical tradition (*2 Apoc. Bar.* 6:7; cf. Rev 8:3; 9:13). The ceremonial prescriptions for the Day of Atonement, however, plainly indicate that this altar was located in the Holy Place (Lev 16:18; for the ministry at this altar see *m. Tamid* 1:4; 3:1, 6, 9; 6:1), and this is confirmed by sources contemporary with Hebrews (Philo, *Moses* 2.94–95, 101–4; *Who is the Heir?* 226; Jos., *J. W.* 5.216–18; *Ant.* 3.139–47, 198; Luke 1:8–11).

The description in v 4 corresponds to the Samaritan Pentateuch recension of Exodus, in which Exod 30:1–10 is inserted between Exod 26:35 and 36. This was one of the factors that led Scobie to deduce that the writer of Hebrews was representative of Samaritan Christianity ("The Origin and Development of Samaritan Christianity," *NTS* 19 [1972–73] 412–13). The correspondence should be seen rather as evidence of the variety of text–types extant before the standardization of the MT. Although no Greek text reflecting the proto-Samaritan text of Exod 26 has as yet been recovered, it is probable that the writer of Hebrews was following this textual tradition (Grothe, "Was Jesus the Priestly Messiah?" 132, n. 31).

The ark of the covenant was the most important object located within the Most Holy Place. It was a chest made of acacia wood and was covered on all sides with gold, with rings of gold in each corner through which the staves for lifting and transporting the ark from one place to another were to be permanently inserted (Exod 25:10–15; 37:1–5). The lid of the chest was the focal point for atonement (see *Comment* on v 5). Moreover, God promised to manifest his presence in the inner sanctuary above the ark and to meet with Israel there (Exod 25:22).

The statement that the ark contained, in addition to the stone tablets of the covenant, the golden jar of manna and Aaron's rod that blossomed, is not attested elsewhere. These objects were deposited in the Most Holy Place in accordance with the command of God, but the biblical accounts state only that they were placed "before the witness," i.e., in front of the ark (Exod 16:32–34; Num 17:10–11). According to all of the texts and versions known of the OT, only the tablets of the covenant were actually placed within the ark (Exod 25:16, 21; Deut 10:1–2; cf. 1 Kgs 8:9; 2 Chr 5:10). J. van der Ploeg (*RB* 54 [1947] 219) suggested that the writer adopted a tradition according to which subsequently other objects were placed within the ark, a tradition presupposed in certain strands of the rabbinic evidence (cf. *b. B. Bat.* 14a; *t. Yoma* 3.7; ʾ*Abot R. Nat.* 41 [67a]). In describing the jar containing the omer of manna, the MT, followed by *Tg. Neof.* Exod 16:33, is neutral; *Tg. Ps.-J.* Exod 16:33 actually specifies "an earthenware jar." The writer's statement in v 4 follows the LXX, which specifies χρυσοῦν, "a gold jar," and this tradition is supported by Philo (*On the Preliminary Studies* 100).

The description of the ark is extended with the mention of the cherubim, the two-winged figures made of gold that stood facing each other on top of the ark, their wings outstretched over the lid of the chest (Exod 25:18–20, 22; 37:7–9). Together with the cover they were seen as the throne bearing the divine glory (Exod 25:22; Num 7:89; cf. A. Jacoby, P. Dhorme, and L. H. Vincent, "Les chérubins," *RB* 35 [1926] 328–58, 481–95; W. F. Albright, "What were the Cherubim?" *BA* 1 [1938] 1–3). The writer follows the LXX in designating the lid on the ark of the covenant ἱλαστήριον, "an atonement cover" (Exod 25:17, 21; cf. Philo, *On the Cherubim* 25; *On Flight and Finding* 100; *Moses* 2.95). The lid was sprinkled with the blood of the sin-offering on the Day of Atonement (Lev 16:14–15).

5b The discussion of the two compartments and their respective furnishings ends abruptly with the declaration, "We cannot speak in detail now about these things." That statement makes it clear that the writer has no interest in any hidden significance of the two compartments or the sanctuary furnishings (cf. Hofius, *Vorhang*, 61; N. H. Young, *NTS* 21 [1980/81] 200). He does not intend to give a typological exposition of the cultic objects he has briefly enumerated. Biblical typology is not allegory. The writer exploits only those aspects of the biblical account of the tabernacle and its cultic ministry that are to be applied to his own exposition, omitting entirely those elements that are not to the point (cf. Delporte, *ETL* 3 [1926] 307–27). In vv 2–5 his attention is attracted by the division of the Mosaic tabernacle into two compartments, which is simply accentuated by the enumeration of the furnishings. The division of the desert sanctuary into two parts is also emphasized in the application which the writer makes of the disposition of the old sanctuary. He distinguishes between the priests, who continually entered the front compartment in the course of their cultic tasks (v 6), and the

high priest, who alone was permitted to enter the rear compartment on the Day
of Atonement (v 7).

6–7 In these two verses, which are closely linked by a μέν . . . δέ construction
("on the one hand . . . but on the other"), the writer advances his argument by
taking up the cultic provisions of the preceding covenant, mentioned in v 1
(δικαιώματα λατρείας, "regulations for cultic worship"). In the term δικαίωμα
the nuance of authorization is prominent. It connotes the cultic actions of the
priests of the old covenant, which were authorized by the divine commands
(Hofius, *Vorhang,* 62). In the LXX the term λατρείας denotes cultic service or
worship (Strathmann, *TDNT* 4:60), and this meaning is reflected in the use of
the word in v 6.

The introductory phrase τούτων δὲ οὕτως κατεσκευασμένων, "when these things
had been arranged like this," sums up the preparatory paragraph, vv 2–5, and
introduces a series of contrasts between the cultic functions of the priests (v 6)
and of the high priest (v 7). The priests enter εἰς μὲν τὴν πρώτην σκηνήν, "into
the front compartment"; the high priest enters εἰς δὲ τὴν δευτέραν, "into the rear
compartment." They enter διὰ παντός, "continually"; he enters ἅπαξ τοῦ ἐνιαυτοῦ,
"once a year." Their entry is unqualified, apart from the fact that it was related to
the discharge of cultic duties; his entry is qualified as being οὐ χωρὶς αἵματος, "not
without blood." These contrasts serve to underscore the distinction between the
front and rear compartments. The principal cultic functions of the priests in
the Holy Place (v 6) concerned the trimming of the lamps of the menorah (Exod
27:20–21) and the burning of incense on the golden altar (Exod 30:7–8) in the
morning and evening of each day. Once each week the appointed priests were
responsible for replacing fresh "loaves" of the unleavened consecrated bread on
the table (Lev 24:8–9). These cultic functions could be discharged by any priest
appointed to this ministry.

In the statement concerning the high priest (v 7), the reference to the Day of
Atonement is unmistakable. The high priest alone was permitted to enter the
inner sanctuary (Lev 16:32–33). He was not to do so arbitrarily, but only once a
year (Lev 16:2, 34), and then only under strictly prescribed conditions (Lev 16:3–
17). The one condition the writer specifies is οὐ χωρὶς αἵματος, "never without
blood," which the high priest offered for his own sins and for the sins committed
in ignorance by the people (see *Comment* on 5:1–3; 7:27). It was prescribed that
the blood of a slaughtered bull had to be sprinkled on the cover of the ark of the
covenant and in front of it for the high priest's own sins, and that this action had
to be repeated with the blood of a slaughtered goat as the sin-offering of the
people (Lev 16:14–17). In this way atonement was made "for the Most Holy Place
because of the uncleanness and rebellion of the Israelites" (Lev 16:16). The formulation of Lev 16:16 is significant, because it describes sin as defilement and
specifies that blood may act as the purging medium (cf. A. B. Davidson, 204–6).
In fact, blood was used to cleanse both compartments of the sanctuary and all its
furnishings (Lev 16:16; see *Comment* on 9:21).

Johnsson has rightly insisted that this understanding of defilement and purgation is crucial to the argument in Heb 9–10 ("Defilement," 223–27 and passim).
The reference to blood (αἷμα), which occurs for the first time in a cultic sense in
v 7, prepares for the repeated introduction of this term in a cultic context in the
ensuing sections (9:12, 13, 14, 18, 20, 21, 22; 10:4, 19, 29; cf. 11:28; 12:24; 13:11,

12, 20). Moreover, the writer drives home his point by repeating, with only slight variation, the significant phrase χωρὶς αἵματος, "without blood," in 9:18 and 9:22. His point is that blood is the medium of approach to God, and this fact underscores the importance of the reference to Christ's blood in the ensuing argument.

The writer's departure from the language of the LXX to describe the action of the high priest is striking. The singular use of the verb προσφέρειν, "to offer," in reference to the application of blood in the Most Holy Place is without parallel in the biblical cultic material. The translators of the LXX used the verbs ῥαίνειν, "to sprinkle," and ἐπιτιθέναι, "to apply," to denote the act of aspersion. The subsequent use of προσφέρειν in reference to Christ's death (9:14, 25, 28; 10:12) suggests that the writer has described the annual sprinkling of blood in the inner sanctuary in this way in order to prepare his readers to recognize the typological parallel between the high point of the atonement ritual under the old covenant and the self-offering of Christ on the cross. This inference finds support when the writer applies the Day of Atonement ritual to Christ in 9:25–28. The annual entrance of the high priest for blood aspersion in the Most Holy Place finds its eschatological fulfillment in Christ's death (προσφορά, "offering"; 10:10, 14). The creative use of unusual terminology to describe the atonement ritual in v 7 is indicative that the writer's interpretation of the Levitical rite is controlled by the Christ-event (N. H. Young, *NTS* 21 [1980–81] 207–10).

8–10 The deeper significance of the disposition of the tabernacle into two parts and of the cultic ordinances reviewed in vv 6–7 has been disclosed by the Holy Spirit. The phrase τοῦτο δηλοῦντος τοῦ πνεύματος τοῦ ἁγίου, "the Holy Spirit showing by this," connotes more than an acknowledgment of the Spirit's role in the inspiration of the text of Scripture (cf. P. E. Hughes, 321). It constitutes a claim to special insight which was not previously available to readers of the OT but which has clarified the meaning and purpose of the cultic provisions for Israel in the light of the fulfillment in Christ (Michel, 306; Peterson, "Examination," 228–30). The Holy Spirit disclosed to the writer that, so long as the front compartment of the tabernacle enjoyed cultic status, access to the presence of God was not yet available to the congregation (so Riggenbach, "Begriff," 249; Michel, 306; Hofius, *Vorhang*, 62–63, 65).

As in vv 2 and 6, the reference to ἡ πρώτη σκηνή in v 8 is spatial and clearly refers to the front compartment (see above, *Note* d). A temporal significance is drawn from the spatial metaphor of the front compartment and is expressed by the temporal particle ἔτι, "while." The formulation is strongly oriented toward redemptive history. So long as the cultic ordinances of the Sinaitic covenant were a valid expression of God's redemptive purpose and the front compartment ἐχούσης στάσιν, "had cultic status" (see above, *Note* t), entrance into the Most Holy Place was not yet (μήπω) accessible. There can be access only after the front compartment has been set aside. The "front compartment" represents the sanctuary as the sphere of cultic activity, which constituted a barrier to the presence of God (cf. Synge, *Hebrews and the Scriptures*, 27; Johnsson, "Defilement," 281; N. H. Young, *NTS* 21 [1980–81] 200–201).

Several interpreters relate the clauses introduced by the relative pronouns in v 9, ἥτις . . . καθ' ἥν ("this . . . according to which"), to the whole preceding context (vv 6–8), explaining the feminine gender (ἥτις for ὅτι) as due to attraction to the feminine noun παραβολή, "illustration" (e.g., Windisch, 77; Michel, 307;

F. F. Bruce, 195–97; cf. NEB: "all of this is symbolic"). Elsewhere in Hebrews, however, the writer consistently uses ἥτις to refer to a specific antecedent, and the gender and number are modified accordingly (2:3; 8:6; 9:2 [where the antecedent is ἡ πρώτη σκηνή, "the front compartment"]; 10:9, 11, 35; 12:5). It is preferable, therefore, to refer both ἥτις and καθ᾿ ἥν, and thus vv 9–10, back to the immediate antecedent in v 8, τῆς πρώτης σκηνῆς, "the front compartment" (so Lünemann, 285; Moffatt, 118; N. H. Young, NTS 21 [1980–81] 201). The writer's distinctive use of πρώτη, "first," and δευτέρα, "second," to describe spatially the two compartments of the tabernacle recalls his use of these numerical terms to designate the old and new covenants (8:7, 13). The "front compartment" (ἡ πρώτη σκηνή) becomes a spatial metaphor for the time when the "first covenant" (ἡ πρώτη διαθήκη) was in force. As an illustration for the old age, which is now in process of dissolution (8:13), it symbolizes the total first covenant order with its daily and annual cultic ritual (9:6, 7). Once the first has been invalidated, the second becomes operative (see 10:9). In the figurative language of the writer, the front compartment of the tabernacle was symbolic of the present age (τὸν καιρὸν τὸν ἐνεστηκότα), which through the intrusion of the καιρὸς διορθώσεως, "the time of correction" (v 10), has been superseded (Klappert, Eschatologie, 25; cf. Synge, Hebrews and the Scriptures, 26; Hofius, ZNW 61 [1970] 276; N. H. Young, NTS 21 [1980–81] 201–2, 205).

The redemptive historical significance of this fact is traced in vv 9–10, which focus upon a particular weakness in the cultic provisions of the first covenant. The gifts and sacrifices that were offered in the earthly tabernacle were unable to achieve "decisive purgation of the worshiper with respect to his conscience" (v 9). This deficiency extended to all the participants in the OT cultus. The term τὸν λατρεύοντα is not to be restricted to "the priest in the act of sacrifice" (so Michel, 308; Strathmann, TDNT 4:63–64; Delling, TDNT 8:83, n. 22). Considerations of context indicate that the expression is to be interpreted in accordance with LXX usage where λατρεύειν denotes cultic worship generally (e.g., Exod 3:12; 4:23; 7:26). The expression describes the individual in his role as worshiper, who would "draw near to God" (10:1). The quest for a cleansed conscience through the observance of the cultic prescriptions was the concern of priests and lay persons alike (so Meeter, Heavenly High Priesthood, 164–65; Peterson, "Examination," 230–31, who points to the parallel between 9:9 and 10:1–2).

The use of the verb τελειοῦν, "to perfect," in this context is significant. In his treatment of Heb 7:11–19, Peterson showed that the perfecting of believers in terms of a relationship to God is the primary thought ("Examination," 174–222; see above, Note u). The writer now specifies that this relationship cannot be perfected until the conscience is cleansed decisively from the defilement of sin. Defilement extends to the conscience as well as to the body and is inimical to the approach to the living God. "Perfection" in this context involves purgation. The fact that the most solemn ceremonies of the preceding covenant, those of the Day of Atonement, had to be repeated annually (9:7, 25; 10:1–3) underscores the inability of the old cultus to effect a permanent purgation (Johnsson, "Defilement," 253, 273, 282, who finds confirmation for this interpretation in the qualification of κεκαθαρισμένους by ἅπαξ in 10:2: "cleansed once for all"). The parallel to the writer's statement in v 9 is provided in 9:14: the conscience must be cleansed in order that one may serve God effectively. The concept of "perfection" refers to the whole process by which the community is consecrated to the service of God (Peterson, "Examination," 234–35). As used by the writer, τελειοῦν envisions a relationship to God such as is "not grasped and established by the law but by the sacrifice of Christ and his covenant" (Michel, 308).

The particular focus of concern in v 9 is the perfecting of the worshiper κατὰ συνείδησιν, "with respect to conscience." The term συνείδησις appears to have come into common currency only in the first century B.C. (cf. Pierce, *Conscience*, 13–59; Maurer, *TDNT* 7:900–918). Its use in the LXX was restricted to the wisdom literature (Job 27:6; Wis 17:11). In Hebrews the term has deeply religious overtones; the "conscience" is directed toward God and embraces the whole person in his relation to God (9:9, 14; 10:2, 22; 13:18). Apart from 13:18, the term has negative connotations: it is the "uneasy conscience" with its internal witness that defilement extends to the heart and mind. It is not engaged in moral decision making, but in remembering. Although the ritual of the Day of Atonement might effect temporary relief, the renewal was short lived. The annual repetition of the solemn ceremonies indicated that sin had again come into remembrance (10:3–4). The collective awareness of the congregation necessitates an annual observance of the Day of Atonement. Moreover, in the statements concerning συνείδησις in Hebrews, it is the community, not the individual, which is primarily in view (cf. Pierce, *Conscience*, 99–102; Johnsson, "Defilement," 282–88; on the relationship between συνείδησις and the cultus, Stelzenberger, *Syneidesis*, 56–61). The defiled conscience is an obstacle to the worship of God and calls for decisive purgation (see *Comment* on 9:14).

The inadequacy of the old cultic provisions justifies putting them on the same level as the peripheral statutes governing the life of ancient Israel. No special emphasis is intended in the reference to "food and drink and various ceremonial washings" (v 10; cf. Behm, *TDNT* 1:643; Goppelt, *TDNT* 6:145). These terms are representative of the δικαιώματα σαρκός, "regulations for the human order" (see above, *Note* w), which were imposed at Sinai but which have lost their validity under the new covenant. The perfection of the relationship to God came only with the new age, the καιρὸς διορθώσεως, which introduced "the ripe time of a correction of perspectives and of the whole order of salvation" (Cody, *Heavenly Sanctuary*, 133). The provisions of decisive purgation extending to the conscience (9:11–14) and of free access to the heavenly sanctuary (10:19–20) through Christ throw into bold relief what the cultic provisions of the old covenant could *not* achieve. The entire cultic ministry of the tabernacle was only a temporary provision in the outworking of God's redemptive purpose for his people, having validity "until the time of correction." With the inception of the new age, the cultic regulations of the old covenant are no longer in force, and the earthly tabernacle with its cultic provisions has lost its significance and status (Hofius, *Vorhang*, 64–65).

Explanation

The writer's concern in 9:1–10 is to assess the deficiency of the preceding covenant by referring to its cultic provisions for worship. The tabernacle and its ritual provide him with a vocabulary and grammar with which he is able to express the insights that have been disclosed to him by the Holy Spirit (9:8).

A distinction between the sphere of cultic ministry (9:2–5) and the discharge of cultic actions (9:6–7) is clearly established. The listing of the furnishings of the Holy Place and of the Most Holy Place serve to define the two compartments of the desert sanctuary. The division of the tabernacle into a front and rear compartment was significant, for it indicated that approach to God was not an easy matter. The old sanctuary consisted of a system of barriers between the worshiper and God. The reason for detailing the arrangement of the tabernacle and its furnishings in 9:2–5 is manifestly to show the lack of access to God under the old cultus. This, in turn, provides a framework for the development of certain deficiencies in the cultic regulations that had been imposed under the terms of the Sinaitic covenant in 9:6–10.

The brief review of the respective cultic ministries of the priests and the high priest in 9:6–7 reinforces the impression that access to God was barred. The cultic provisions allowed the people to approach God only through their representatives, the priests and the high priest. The stress falls on the annual entry of the high priest into the Most Holy Place, which was symbolic of the actual presence of God, on the Day of Atonement. The writer finds a double significance in this solemn occasion. First, the high priest alone is allowed to enter the rear compartment, and then only once a year under strictly prescribed conditions. He must never enter without the sacrificial blood, which is the medium of access. This first observation indicates that the way into the real, heavenly sanctuary, where there is free access to the presence of God, had not yet been disclosed (9:8). Secondly, it was mandatory that the high priest enter the rear compartment once a year. This indicates that the cultic regulations of the old covenant were unable to provide definitive purgation of the worshiper with respect to conscience (9:9). It was necessary to repeat sacrifices that were never adequate to effect the removal of sin and to achieve an unbroken relationship with God. The review of the cultic provisions of the old covenant and its defects demonstrates the necessity for new cultic action by God. Heb 9:1–10 thus sets the stage for the account of the ministry of Christ, the true and final high priest, in the heavenly sanctuary (9:11–28).

G. Decisive Purgation through the Blood of Christ (9:11–28)

Bibliography

Andriessen, P. "Das grössere und vollkommenere Zelt (Hebr 9, 11)." *BZ* 15 (1971) 76–92. Attridge, H. W. "The Uses of Antithesis in Hebrews 8–10." *HTR* 79 (1986) 1–9. Beavis, M. A. "The New Covenant and Judaism." *TBT* 22 (1984) 24–30. Berényi, G. "La portée de διὰ τοῦτο en Hé 9,15." *Bib* 69 (1988) 108–12. Bieder, W. "Pneumatologische Aspekte im Hebräerbrief." In *Verborum Veritas*. FS G. Stählin. Wuppertal: Brockhaus, 1970. 251–59.

Bourgin, C. "Heb. 9,11–15: Le sang du Christ et le culte spirituel." *AsSeign* 34 (1963) 26–53. **Bover, J. M.** "Las variantes μελλόντων y γενομένων en Hebr. 9,11." *Bib* 32 (1951) 232–36. **Brooks, W. E.** "The Perpetuity of Christ's Sacrifice in the Epistle to the Hebrews." *JBL* 89 (1970) 205–14. **Campbell, K. M.** "Covenant or Testament? Heb. 9:16, 17 Reconsidered." *EvQ* 44 (1972) 107–11. **Carr, A.** "Covenant or Testament? A Note on Hebrews 9:16–17." *Exp* 7th ser. 7 (1909) 347–52. **Casalini, N.** "Ebr 9,11: la tenda più grande e più perfetta: Una proposta per la soluzione del problema." *SBFLA* 36 (1986) 111–70. ———. "I Sacrifici dell'antica alleanza nel piano salvifico di Dio secondo la Lettera agli Ebrei." *RivB* 35 (1987) 443–64. **Cody, A.** *Heavenly Sanctuary and Heavenly Liturgy.* 47–73, 138–41, 146–51, 156–202. **Courthial, P.** "La portée de diathēcē en Hébreux 9:16–17." *EEv* 36 (1976) 36–43. **Culpepper, R. H.** "The High Priesthood and Sacrifice of Christ in the Epistle to the Hebrews." *ThEduc* 32 (1985) 46–62. **DaFonseca, L. G.** "Διαθήκη: Foedus an Testamentum?" *Bib* 8 (1927) 31–50, 161–81, 290–319, 418–41; 9 (1928) 26–40, 143–60. **Dunkel, F.** "Expiation, et Jour des expiations dans l'Épître aux Hébreux." *RevRéf* 33 (1982) 63–71. **Dussaut, L.** *Synopse structurelle de l'Épître aux Hébreux.* 73–83. **Estes, D.** "An Interpretation of Hebrews 9:16–17." *RevExp* 1 (1904) 177–86. ———. "Some Thoughts as to the Effect of the Death of Christ." *RevExp* 6 (1909) 600–620. **Fabris, R.** "La lettera agli Ebrei e l'Antico Testamento." *RivB* 32 (1984) 237–52. **Feldman, E.** *Biblical and Post-Biblical Defilement and Mourning: Law as Theology.* New York: Ktav, 1977. 41–45. **Feuillet, A.** "L'attente de la Parousie et du Jugement dans l'Épître aux Hébreux." *BVC* 42 (1961) 23–31. **Fitzer, G.** "Auch der Hebräerbrief legitimiert nicht eine Opfertodchristologie: Zur Frage der Intention des Hebräerbriefes und seiner Bedeutung für die Theologie." *KD* 15 (1969) 294–319. **Fritsch, C. T.** "*TO 'ANTITYΠON.*" In *Studia Biblica et Semitica.* FS T. C. Vriezen. Ed. W. C. van Unnik and A. S. van der Woude. Wageningen: Veenman, 1966. 100–107. **Gardiner, F.** "On διαθήκη in Hebrews 9:16, 17." *JBL* 5 (1885) 8–19. **Graystone, K.** "Salvation Proclaimed: III. Hebrews 9:11–14." *ExpTim* 93 (1982) 164–68. **Guest, T. H.** "The Word 'Testament' in Hebrews 9." *ExpTim* 25 (1913–14) 379. **Hofius, O.** *Der Vorhang vor dem Thron Gottes.* 50–59, 65–73. **Hughes, J. J.** "Hebrews ix 15ff. and Galatians iii 15ff.: A Study in Covenant Practice and Procedure." *NovT* 21 (1979) 27–96. **Hughes, P. E.** "The Blood of Jesus and His Heavenly Priesthood: Part III: The Meaning of 'The True Tent' and 'The Greater and More Perfect Tent.'" *BSac* 130 (1973) 305–14. **Hurst, L. D.** "The Background and Interpretation of the Epistle to the Hebrews." Dissertation, Oxford University, 1981. 24–29, 30–34, 41–59, 67–68. ———. "How 'Platonic' are Heb. viii. 5 and ix. 23f.?" *JTS* 34 (1983) 156–68. **Johnsson, W. G.** "The Cultus of Hebrews in Twentieth-Century Scholarship." *ExpTim* 89 (1977–78) 104–8. ———. "Defilement and Purgation in the Book of Hebrews." Dissertation, Vanderbilt University, 1973. 206–75, 290–338. **Kilpatrick, G. D.** "Διαθήκη in Hebrews." *ZNW* 68 (1977) 263–65. **Köster, W.** "Platonische Ideenwelt und Gnosis im Hebräerbrief." *Schol* 4 (1956) 545–55. **Lach, S.** "Les ordonnances du culte Israélite dans la Lettre aux Hébreux." In *Sacra Pagina: Miscellanea Biblica Congressus Internationalis Catholici de Re Biblica.* Ed. J. Coppens, A. Descamps, and E. Massaux. Paris: Gabalda, 1952. 2:390–403. **Laub, F.** *Bekenntnis und Auslegung.* 168–79, 185–203, 207–21. **Lehne, S.** *The New Covenant in Hebrews.* JSNTSup 44. Sheffield: JSOT, 1990. **Letter, P. de.** "The Judgment after Death 'post mortem iudicium' Hebr. 9,27." *CleM* 27 (1963) 365–74. **Loader, W. R. G.** *Sohn und Hoherpriester.* 54–55, 60–61, 166–80, 182–86, 189–202. **Luck, U.** "Himmlisches und irdisches Geschehen im Hebräerbrief." *NovT* 6 (1963) 192–215. **MacRae, G. W.** "Heavenly Temple and Eschatology in the Letter to the Hebrews." *Semeia* 12 (1978) 179–99. **McCarthy, D. J.** "Further Notes on the Symbolism of Blood and Sacrifice." *JBL* 92 (1973) 205–20. **McGrath, J. J.** *"Through the Eternal Spirit": An Historical Study of the Exegesis of Hebrews 9:13–14.* Rome: Pontificia Universitas Gregoriana, 1961. **McNeile, A. H.** "A Note on Heb. ix.12." *JTS* 24 (1923) 402. **Moffatt, J.** "Dead Works." *Exp* 8th ser. 15 (1918) 1–18. **Morris, L.** "The Biblical Use of the Term 'Blood.'" *JTS* n.s. 3 (1952) 216–27. ———. "The Day of Atonement and the Work of Christ." *RTR* 14 (1955) 9–19. **Nairne, A.** "Two Questions of Text and Translation." *JTS* 11 (1910) 560–62. **Nomoto, S.** "Herkunft und Struktur der Hohenpriestervorstellung im Hebräerbrief." *NovT* 10 (1968) 10–25. **Olson, S. N.** "Wandering but Not Lost." *WW* 5 (1985) 426–33. **Omanson, R. L.** "A Superior Covenant: Hebrews 8:1–10:18." *RevExp* 82 (1985) 361–73. **Peterson, D. G.** "An Examination of the Concept of 'Perfection' in the 'Epistle to the Hebrews.'" Dissertation, University of Manchester, 1978. 235–49. **Ramaroson, L.** "Contre les 'temples faits de main d'homme.'" *RPLHA* 43 (1969) 217–38. **Riggenbach, E.** "Der Begriff der *ΔIAΘHKH* im Hebräerbrief." In *Theologische Studien T. Zahn zum 10 Oktober, 1908 dargebracht.* Leipzig: Deichert, 1908, 289–316. **Rose, C.** "Verheissung und Erfüllung: Zum Verständnis von *ἐπαγγελία* im Hebräerbrief." *BZ* 33 (1989) 60–80. **Sabourin, L.** "Sacrificium et liturgia in Epistula ad Hebraeos." *VD* 46 (1968) 235–58. **Schaefer, J. R.** "The Relationship between Priestly and Servant Messianism in the Epistle to the Hebrews." *CBQ* 30 (1968) 359–85. **Schierse, F. J.** *Verheissung und Heilsvollendung.* 26–59. **Schlosser, J.** "La médiation du Christ d'après l'Épître aux Hébreux." *RevScRel* 63 (1989) 169–81. **Schröger, F.** "Der Gottesdienst der Hebräerbriefgemeinde." *MTZ* 19 (1968) 161–81. ———. *Der Verfasser des Hebräerbriefes.* 168–72, 203, 206, 235–39. **Selby, G. S.** "The Meaning and Function of *συνείδησις* in Hebrews 9 and 10." *RestQ* 28 (1985–86) 145–54. **Sisti, A.** "Il sacrificio della nuova alleanza (Ebr. 9, 11–15)." *BibOr* 9 (1967) 25–37. **Spicq, C.** "La théologie des deux alliances dans l'Épître aux Hébreux." *RSPT* 33 (1949) 15–30. **Stott, W.** "The Conception of 'Offering' in the Epistle to the Hebrews." *NTS* 9 (1962) 62–67. **Swetnam, J.** "Christology and the Eucharist in the Epistle to the Hebrews." *Bib* 70 (1989) 74–95. ———. "Sacrifice and Revelation in the Epistle to the Hebrews: Observations and Surmises on Hebrews 9,26." *CBQ* 30 (1968) 227–34. ———. "A Suggested Interpretation of Hebrews 9,15–18." *CBQ* 27 (1965) 373–90. ———. "'The Greater and More Perfect Tent': A Contribution to the Discussion of Hebrews 9, 11." *Bib* 47 (1966) 91–106. **Tetley, J.** "The Priesthood of Christ in Hebrews." *Anvil* 5 (1988) 195–206. **Thompson, J. W.** "Hebrews 9 and Hellenistic Concepts of Sacrifice." *JBL* 98 (1979) 567–78. **Thornton, T. C. G.** "The Meaning of *αἱματεκχυσία* in Heb. IX. 22." *JTS* n.s. 15 (1964) 63–65. **Vanhoye, A.** "De instauratione novae dispositionis (Heb 9,15–23)." *VD* 44 (1966) 113–30. ———. "Esprit éternel et feu du sacrifice en He 9,14." *Bib* 64 (1983) 263–74. ———. "L'intervention decisive du Christ, He 9,24–28." *AsSeign* 63 (1971) 47–52. ———. "Mundatio per sanguinem (Heb 9,22 s.v.)." *VD* 44 (1966) 177–91. ———. "'Par la tente plus grande et plus parfaite . . .' (Hebr 9,11)." *Bib* 46 (1965) 1–28. **Villapadierna, C. de.** "La alianza en la Epístola a los Hebreos: Ensayo de nueva interpretación a Hebreos 9,15–20." *EstBib* 21 (1962) 273–96. **Williamson, R.** "Platonism and Hebrews." *SJT* 16 (1963) 415–24. ———. "The Eucharist and the Epistle to the Hebrews." *NTS* 21 (1974–75) 300–312. **Young, F. M.** *The Use of Sacrificial Ideas in Greek-Christian Writers.* 145–58. **Young, N. H.** "The Gospel according to Hebrews 9." *NTS* 27 (1980–81) 198–210. **Zimmermann, H.** *Das Bekenntnis der Hoffnung.* 188–202. **Zupez, J.** "Salvation in the Epistle to the Hebrews." *TBT* 37 (1968) 2590–95.

Translation

[11] *But*[a] *when Christ appeared as high priest of the good things that have now come,*[b] *passing through*[c] *the greater and more perfect compartment*[d] *not made with hands, that is to say, not of ordinary building,*[e] [12] *he entered once for all into the real sanctuary, thus obtaining*[f] *eternal*[g] *redemption. He did not enter by means of the blood of goats and calves, but by means of his own blood.* [13] *For if*[h] *the blood of goats and bulls, and the sprinkled ashes of a heifer, sanctify those who have been ceremonially defiled to the extent of the purging of the flesh,* [14] *how much more will the blood of Christ purge our*[i] *conscience from acts that lead to death, so that we may worship the living God, seeing that he*[j] *offered himself through the eternal Spirit*[k] *as an unblemished sacrifice to God!*

[15]*And for this reason he is the mediator of a new covenant,*[l] *in order that, a death having occurred for redemption from transgressions committed on the basis of*[m] *the former covenant,*[n] *those who are called might receive the promised eternal inheritance.*[o] [16]*(For where there is a covenant,*[p] *it is necessary for the death of the one who ratifies it*[q] *to be brought forward,*[r] [17]*for a covenant is made legally secure*[s] *on the basis of the sacrificial victims,*[t] *since it is never valid*[u] *while the ratifier lives.* [18]*This is why not even the former covenant*[v] *was confirmed*[w] *without blood.* [19]*When each commandment of the law had been proclaimed by Moses to all the people, taking the blood of calves,*[x] *together with water, crimson wool and sprigs of hyssop, he sprinkled both the book itself and all the people,* [20]*saying, "This is the blood of the covenant which God has enjoined upon you."* [21]*He also sprinkled the tabernacle and all the cultic vessels*[y] *likewise with blood.* [22]*In fact everything, it might almost be said, is purged with blood*[z] *according to the law, but*[aa] *without the application of blood*[bb] *there is no definitive purgation.*[cc]*)*

[23]*It was necessary, then, for the suggestions*[dd] *of things in heaven to be purged by these means, but the heavenly things themselves*[ee] *with better sacrifices than these.* [24]*For Christ did not enter a sanctuary made with hands that was only a representation*[ff] *of the true one; he entered heaven itself, now to appear in the presence of God on our behalf.* [25]*Nor did he enter heaven*[gg] *in order to offer himself*[hh] *many times, like the high priest enters the Most Holy Place year by year*[ii] *bringing blood with him*[jj] *that is not his own;* [26]*otherwise,*[kk] *it would have been necessary for him to suffer death*[ll] *many times since the foundation of the world. But as a matter of fact,*[mm] *he has appeared once for all at the climax of the ages*[nn] *for the annulling of sin by his sacrifice.* [27]*And just as*[oo] *it is reserved for men to die once, and after this to experience judgment,* [28]*so also Christ, after having been offered once to bear the sin of many, will appear a second time to those who are eagerly waiting for him, without reference to sin*[pp] *but for salvation.*[qq]

Notes

[a] The adversative particle δέ is the complement of the μὲν οὖν clause of 9:1 ("Now on the one hand. . . . But on the other hand"), announcing a major shift in the argument. It establishes a counterpoint between what has been said in 9:1–10 and what is to be said now (so also Michel, 304–5; Thompson, *JBL* 98 [1979] 568–69; N. H. Young, *NTS* 21 [1980–81] 202).

[b] Although the variant reading μελλόντων, "which are to come," is supported by the majority of witnesses (‫א‬ A D^c I^vid K L P 0142 many minuscules it vg sy^h mg co arm aeth Eus Cyr Chr), the quality of the attestation for the reading γενομένων, "which have already come," is superior both in age and in diversity of textual type (r^46 B D* 1611 1739 2005 d e sy^p.h.pal Or Cyr J). This reading is also favored by considerations intrinsic to style and context. Copyists appear to have assimilated the reading in the majority of the witnesses to the expression τῶν μελλόντων ἀγαθῶν in 10:1 (see Metzger, *Textual Commentary*, 668; Zuntz, *Text of the Epistles*, 119; and especially Bover, *Bib* 32 [1951] 232–36).

It is necessary to regard the aor tense as inceptive: with the high priestly ministry of Christ the good things associated with the promised messianic redemption have begun to be experienced (so Bover, *Bib* 32 [1951] 235).

[c] The context (παραγενόμενος . . . εἰσῆλθεν, "when Christ appeared . . . he entered") indicates that διά relates to a space and must be understood in a local sense ("through the compartment") rather than in an instrumental sense (cf. Moffatt, 121; Hofius, *Vorhang*, 67; Andriessen, *BZ* 15 [1971] 921; Johnsson, "Defilement," 293–97). In the continuous statement set forth in vv 11–12 διά is used three times with reference to the work of Christ. Since the last two are clearly instrumental in function it has been held that considerations of syntax demand that the first instance of διά must also be instrumental (e.g., Westcott, 256; H. Montefiore, 151–52). Hofius, however, has demonstrated that elsewhere in the NT the same prep may function in a different sense even though in immediate succession (see *Vorhang*, 81–82). The use of the prep διά in two different senses (local διά with the gen in v 11*b*, instrumental διά with the gen twice in v 12*a*) is motivated rhetorically (see below on 10:20 for another case of this practice). In the translation of the long periodic sentence, the order of the clauses in v 12

has been rearranged to exhibit the distinction between the local use of διά in v 11 and the two uses of διά in an instrumental sense. See further Andriessen, *En lisant*, 32–38.

ᵈ The translation of σκηνή as "compartment" takes into account the consistent use of the term in a local sense in Hebrews (8:2, 5; 9:2, 3, 6, 8) and the comparison ("greater and more perfect") with the nearest antecedent use of σκηνή (in 9:8), where the writer refers to the "front compartment" of the earthly tabernacle.

ᵉ For this translation of the phrase οὐ ταύτης τῆς κτίσεως, see Zerwick and Grosvenor, *Grammatical Analysis*, 673. Field had already called attention to the particular nuance in ταύτης at this point (*Notes*, 229). The phrase means that it was not of the same order as the earthly tabernacle specified in 9:1.

ᶠ The temporal nuance of the ptcp εὑράμενος is unclear. When the ptcp stands second to the main verb (here εἰσῆλθεν, "he entered"), only exegesis can determine whether antecedent or coincident or subsequent action is intended. Although some grammarians reject the fact that the aor ptcp expresses subsequent action in Koine Greek (A. T. Robertson, *Grammar*, 861–63; Moulton, *Grammar*, 1:132–34), a good case has been made for the fact that it does (see C. D. Chambers, "On the Use of the Aorist Participle in Some Hellenistic Writers," *JTS* 24 [1922–23] 183–87, supported by W. F. Howard, "The Futuristic Use of the Aorist Participle in Hellenistic," *JTS* 24 [1922–23] 403–6). A. T. Robertson (*Grammar*, 809), McNeile (*JTS* 24 [1923] 402), and Moule (*Idiom-Book*, 100, n. 1) favor antecedent action ("having obtained . . . he entered"; cf. NIV, TEV), but Burton (*Moods and Tenses*, §145) and Cody (*Heavenly Sanctuary*, 178–80) argue strongly for subsequent or coincident action (cf. RSV, NEB). This latter position is supported in the translation, since in this context it is difficult to understand the meaning of εὑράμενος apart from entrance into the heavenly sanctuary (see 8:3–4).

ᵍ For the proposal to translate αἰωνίαν as "eschatological" rather than "eternal," see J. J. Hughes, *NovT* 21 (1979) 33, n. 20. Hughes observes that the writer seems never to have employed αἰώνιος in a purely temporal sense (cf. 5:9; 6:2; 9:12, 14, 15; 13:20); in each case the predominant emphasis seems to be upon an eschatological state or event. He argues that in Hebrews the temporal nuance is derivative from and subsidiary to this qualitative nuance.

ʰ The use of a first-class conditional clause (εἰ with the ind of reality, indicating that the condition is considered "a real case"; cf. BDF §§371, 372) is appropriate to the argument from the lesser to the greater in vv 13–14. It could be translated "since . . . the sprinkled ashes of a heifer sanctify."

ⁱ The external evidence for the two readings ἡμῶν ("our": A D* K P 1739* *al*) and ὑμῶν ("your": ℵ Dᶜ 33 81 1739ᶜ *al*) is rather evenly balanced. Elsewhere the writer has used the direct address only in the hortatory sections of his sermon. This factor tips the balance toward ἡμῶν (Metzger, *Textual Commentary*, 668).

ʲ The use of the relative pronoun ὅς in a causal sense to mean "because he" or "seeing that he" reflects a classical idiom (see A. W. Argyle, "The Causal Use of the Relative Pronoun in the Greek New Testament," *BT* 6 (1955) 165–69, who argues that the *a fortiori* character of the argument in vv 13–14 seems to require a causal force in the relative pronoun).

ᵏ The interpretation of the expression διὰ πνεύματος αἰωνίου is extremely difficult. The translation reflects the conviction that the expression is a periphrasis for the Holy Spirit (so also Michel, 314; Büchsel, *TDNT* 4:339; F. F. Bruce, 205; Peterson, "Examination," 238–39; RSV, JB, NIV). This understanding accounts for the clearly secondary reading διὰ πνεύματος ἁγίου ("through the Holy Spirit") found in ℵ² D* P *al* it vg bo. The anarthrous formulation πνεύματος ἁγίου is found in 2:4 and 6:4. An alternative proposal to translate the expression "through [his] eternal spirit" (so Phillips) is supported by Vos, *PTR* 5 (1907), 590–92; Moffatt, 124; Riggenbach, 264–66; P. E. Hughes, 358–59; Schweizer, *TDNT* 6:446, among others.

ˡ There is a virtual consensus that, apart from 9:16–17, διαθήκη in Hebrews means "covenant," and that this usage is rooted in the LXX where διαθήκη is the translation of the Heb. term בְּרִית, *bĕrît*, 270 times (plus 5 times in Sirach). Among modern commentators only Riggenbach was prepared to argue that every occurrence of διαθήκη in Hebrews denotes "testament," interpreting the term in the light of its hellenistic usage outside the LXX ("Begriff," 300–310, and reiterated in his commentary, 268–79; cf. now Swetnam, *CBQ* 27 [1965] 373–90; Swetnam interprets διαθήκη throughout vv 15–18 as "testament," arguing that the writer regarded even the Sinai διαθήκη as a type of testament). The reference to Christ as μεσίτης, "mediator," would seem to exclude the meaning of "testament" for διαθήκη in v 15, since the office of μεσίτης is unknown in conjunction with wills and testaments (J. J. Hughes, *NovT* 21 [1979] 64–65).

ᵐ The prep ἐπί with the dative ordinarily carries the nuance "on the basis of," "in accordance with," "under" (cf. 8:6; 9:10; so BDF §235[2]). Alternatively, it may be understood in a temporal sense, "in the days of," "at the time of" (so Zerwick and Grosvenor, *Grammatical Analysis*, 673–74).

n The syntactical construction of v 15 is very tight. The ὅπως clause (ὅπως . . . τὴν ἐπαγγελίαν λάβωσιν οἱ κεκλημένοι τῆς αἰωνίου κληρονομίας) is a final clause expressing the purpose for which Christ is the mediator of a new covenant. The participial phrase θανάτου γενομένου εἰς ἀπολύτρωσιν τῶν ἐπὶ τῇ πρώτῃ διαθήκῃ παραβάσεων, which occurs within the ὅπως clause, specifies the attendant circumstances. It is employed in a retrospectively cumulative circumstantial manner, which reflects back upon vv 11–14 and summarizes them (J. J. Hughes, *NovT* 21 [1979] 33).

o In the phrase τὴν ἐπαγγελίαν . . . τῆς αἰωνίου κληρονομίας, the genitival construction is epexegetical of ἐπαγγελίαν and specifies the content of the promise. What is received is not the promise of eschatological inheritance but that eschatological inheritance itself (cf. Zerwick and Grosvenor, *Grammatical Analysis*, 674).

p The major translations (RSV, NEB, JB, TEV, NIV) and most commentators are in agreement that in vv 16–17 διαθήκη refers to a will or testament. (Only the NASB translates διαθήκη everywhere in Hebrews as "covenant.") It is assumed that the writer resorted to a play on words, using διαθήκη in its secular sense (i.e., "will"/"testament") to undergird his point concerning the διαθήκη as it is employed in the LXX (i.e., "covenant"; vv 15 and 18). According to the prevailing point of view, the writer has in mind an analogy between the necessity of a death in establishing the validity of a will and the necessity of death in inaugurating the new covenant (cf. Moffatt, 125–31; Spicq, 2:260–65, 285–99; Michel, 315–22; F. F. Bruce, 209–14; Buchanan, 150–53, among others).

A recent review of this argument has demonstrated that it is impossible to translate διαθήκη in vv 16–17 as "will" or "testament" and to harmonize the writer's statements with any known form of hellenistic, Egyptian, or Roman legal practice. There is no evidence in classical or papyriological sources to substantiate that a will or testament was legally valid only when the testator died. A will became operative as soon as it was properly drafted, witnessed, and notarized. Moreover, inheritance did not occur only after the death of the testator, since it was common legal practice for an inheritance, as parental distribution *inter vivos* ("among the survivors"), to take place before death. This practice was especially widespread in Egypt and provided for the transfer of unrestricted ownership during the lifetime of the parents (J. J. Hughes, *NovT* 21 [1979] 59–65).

Syntactically, the tightly knit use of particles in 9:15–18 militates against the assignment of a different meaning to διαθήκη in vv 16–17 from the one it has in vv 15 and 18. The meaning of διαθήκη in vv 16–17 is qualified by its meaning in v 15, since vv 16–17 parenthetically explain the necessity of Christ's death. Moreover, the ὅπου γάρ . . . γάρ . . . ὅθεν ("for where . . . for . . . this is why") construction in vv 16–18 requires that v 18 be read as the logical conclusion of the argument in vv 16–17. Since διαθήκη clearly means "covenant" in v 18, it must have the same meaning in vv 16–17 (so Westcott, 263–70, 298–302; cf. J. J. Hughes, *NovT* 21 [1979] 32–35; K. M. Campbell, *EvQ* 44 [1972] 108). Lexical and semantic considerations indicate that the writer has employed διαθήκη in a consistent way in 9:15–18 to mean "covenant" (cf. J. J. Hughes, *NovT* 21 [1979] 35–59; Johnsson, "Defilement," 308–18).

q The translation of τοῦ διαθεμένου (v 16) and of ὁ διαθέμενος (v 17) as "the one who ratifies" or "the ratifier" takes account of the fact that in the LXX διατίθεσθαι διαθήκην is the standard legal expression referring to the inauguration or ratification of a covenant, corresponding to the Heb. idiom כָּרַת בְּרִית, *kārat běrît* ("to cut [i.e., make] a covenant"; cf. Heb 8:10; 10:16). The one who ratified the διαθήκη would be considered ὁ διαθέμενος, as in Ps 49(50):5 LXX (cited by J. J. Hughes, *NovT* 21 [1979] 40). This nuance was already recognized by T. H. Guest, who rendered the expression in vv 16 and 17 "the Covenant-ratifier" (*ExpTim* 25 [1913–14] 379). It should be noted that διατίθεσθαι is not used elsewhere in the NT for the making of a will.

r The verb φέρειν, according to a very common usage of the word, means "to bring forward" (i.e., to represent). The "representative" nuance of φέρεσθαι in v 16 is a function of the ability of φέρειν to mean "to bring into the picture," "to introduce" (e.g., John 18:29; 2 Pet 2:11; *1 Clem* 55:1). J. J. Hughes points out that φέρειν is not a hellenistic legal term and is never found in extrabiblical sources in conjunction with διαθήκη or διατίθεσθαι (in the context of making a will). However, in the LXX it functions as a cultic term, denoting either the bringing of sacrifices to be offered or the act of offering itself. The offerer is represented in and by his sacrifice. Hughes understands φέρεσθαι in v 16 in a cultic LXX sense of bringing sacrifices to be offered so that the (symbolic) death of the one who ratifies a covenant is represented as a sacrificial death (*NovT* 21 [1979] 40–43, 65–66).

s The technical term βεβαία denotes "legally guaranteed security" and has reference to the ratifying or confirming of something (see 2:2, 3; 3:6; 6:16; cf. MM 107; Schlier, *TDNT* 1:602–3). It could be translated as "secured" or "confirmed" (so J. J. Hughes, *NovT* 21 [1979] 45: "for a covenant is confirmed").

ᵗ In the expression ἐπὶ νεκροῖς (lit., "on the basis of the dead bodies") it is important to recognize the (neuter?) pl νεκροῖς in conjunction with the sg διαθήκη. There does not appear to be any evidence that the phrase can be translated idiomatically "at death" (RSV; cf. NEB, JB, TEV, NIV), which would require the sg ἐπὶ νεκρῷ or ἐπὶ νεκρώσει. The use of the pl νεκροῖς is more appropriate in terms of covenantal, and not testamentary, practice. The expression in v 17 finds an exact parallel in the reference to covenant sacrificial victims in Ps 49(50):5 LXX ἐπὶ θυσίαις, "on the basis of sacrifices." In its context νεκροῖς conveys the notion of covenant ratification by means of a self-maledictory rite involving the cutting up of the dead bodies of the sacrificial victims (cf. J. J. Hughes, *NovT* 21 [1979] 43–44; Kilpatrick, *ZNW* 68 [1977] 263–65; Johnsson, "Defilement," 311).

ᵘ On the basis of the negative particle μήποτε with the present ind of the verb, it has been stated that the subordinate clause in v 17 is clearly interrogative (BDF §428[5]; cf. F. F. Bruce, 207, n. 104: the negative particle μή is appropriate in a question expecting the answer "no"). But in later Gk. μή is found in causal clauses where οὐ would be expected; μήποτε with the ind is simply a strong negative particle meaning "never." In classical Gk. the usage is found in general relative clauses and with participles and subordinate clauses where a condition is present. In v 17 there is both a generalization, as the μήποτε may indicate, and a latent condition. It is therefore quite possible to take the clause as a negative statement of fact (so A. Wikgren, "Some Greek Idioms," 151–52 [with examples from hellenistic Greek]; N. Turner, *Grammar,* 3:284).

ᵛ The expression ἡ πρώτη ("the first," "the former") is used elliptically for ἡ πρώτη διαθήκη, as in 8:7, 13; 9:1.

ʷ The word ἐγκεκαίνισται must be understood as a cultic term meaning "to consecrate and inaugurate," and thus to render valid and ratify (cf. Num 7:11; 8:8; 3 Kgdms 8:63; 2 Chr 7:5; 1 Macc 4:36, 54; 5:1; 2 Macc 2:9). The perfect tense underscores the permanent character of the confirmation of the covenant (cf. Behm, *TDNT* 3:454).

ˣ A strongly attested reading (א* A C D P many minuscules it vg co arm) refers to "calves and goats," with some variation in the position of [τῶν] τράγων, but it is probable that the text was expanded by copyists under the influence of the formulation in v 12. The offering of goats had no place in the sacrifice to which the passage refers (cf. Exod 24:5). The text without kai; tw'n travgwn, "and goats," is supported by an impressive combination of witnesses (P⁴⁶ א² K L Ψ 181 1241 1739 syᵖ·ʰ·ᵖᵃˡ Or Chr) and is intrinsically superior (so Beare, *JBL* 63 [1944] 394; Zuntz, *Text of the Epistles,* 54–55; Hunzinger, *TDNT* 6:982, n. 29).

ʸ The cultic nuance in the expression τὰ σκεύη τῆς λειτουργίας reflects the influence of the LXX, which used λειτουργεῖν and its cognates for divine service only (cf. BAGD 471, 754).

ᶻ The prep ἐν in the expression ἐν αἵματι may retain its original locative sense (cf. A. T. Robertson, *Grammar,* 584–91): everything is purged *in* blood. Blood is the medium of purgation rather than the agent (cf. Westcott, 268; Oepke, *TDNT* 2:538).

ᵃᵃ The placement of the phrase κατὰ τὸν νόμον, "according to the law," limits the writer's point concerning legal qualification to v 22a and suggests that the second καί is adversative: according to the law almost everything is purged in blood, *but* for decisive purgation blood is essential. For the καί . . . καί construction as a means of introducing contrasts, see BDF §230.

ᵇᵇ The word αἱματεκχυσία is unknown prior to this reference and occurs nowhere else in the NT. In later writings it serves exclusively Christian purposes (cf. BAGD 23). The term may have been coined by the writer for the purpose of his argument. It is a compound of αἷμα, "blood," with ἐκχύννειν, which has a general sense of "to pour out." The use of the compound in a sacrificial context is consistent with the LXX which uses the verb ἐκχεῖν and αἷμα to denote the pouring out of blood as a sin offering upon the base of the altar (Exod 29:12; Lev 4:7, 18, 25, 30, 34; 8:15; 9:9). Rabbinic sources (e.g., *b. Zebaḥ* 6a, 8a, 26b, 36a, 36b, 51a, 51b, 89b) confirm that the reference is not to the shedding of the blood of the sacrificial victim but to *the application* of sacrificial blood to the altar in order to effect atonement. Cf. *b. Zebaḥ* 26b: "once the blood has reached the altar, the owners are cleansed" (cf. Johnsson, "Defilement," 320–25; Thornton, *JTS* n.s. 15 [1964] 63–65).

ᶜᶜ The rendering of ἄφεσις as "the forgiveness of sins" (RSV) is unwarranted; there is no reference to ἁμαρτία, "sin," or its equivalent in the immediate context. The translation "forgiveness" (NEB, TEV, NIV) or "remission" (JB) tends to convey the same unwarranted notion. It seems necessary to interpret the nuance in ἄφεσις in the light of the argument of the passage and, in view of the reference to the old cultus, of the unique use of ἄφεσις in the LXX translation of Leviticus (where twenty-one of the forty-nine occurrences of ἄφεσις in the LXX are found). The sole instance where ἄφεσις occurs in a cultic setting in the LXX is Lev 16:26, where τὸν διεσταλμένον εἰς ἄφεσιν, "commanded for letting go," has reference to the goat released "to Azazel" on the Day of Atonement. On the basis of a thorough review of the evidence, Johnsson proposed that the term in v 22 be translated "definitive putting away [of defilement]" or "decisive purgation," as consistent with its usage in a cultic setting ("Defilement," 325–29; cf. Moffatt, 130, who recognized that ideas of purgation cannot be excluded from ἄφεσις here). This is clearly the sense in which ἄφεσις is used in its only other occurrence in Hebrews (see below, 10:18).

dd For this nuance in the expression τὰ ὑποδείγματα see *Note* i on 8:1–13 and the discussion of E. K. Lee, "Words Denoting 'Pattern' in the New Testament," *NTS* 8 (1961–62) 167–69.

ee For the proposal that τὰ ἐπουράνια is the equivalent of τὰ ἐν τοῖς οὐρανοῖς and should be translated "the heavenly sanctuary," see Zerwick and Grosvenor, *Grammatical Analysis,* 674.

ff For the note of correspondence and representation in the term ἀντίτυπα, see Cody, *Heavenly Sanctuary,* 152, n. 9; Fritsch, "*TO 'ANTITYΠON,*" 100–101; Goppelt, *TDNT* 8:258 (who translates the word as "counterpart").

gg A long periodic sentence, extending from 9:24–26, has been broken up in the translation out of consideration for English style, but the main clause has been repeated from v 24 in order to indicate the direction of the thought.

hh The subjunctive mood of προσφέρῃ is appropriate to the use of the verb in a negative purpose clause. The present tense emphasizes continuous action and may be viewed here as iterative ("to offer himself over and over again").

ii In the expression κατ' ἐνιαυτόν the prep is used distributively, "year by year," "annually" (cf. MM 323; BAG 266).

jj The use of the prep in the phrase ἐν αἵματι is an example of the associative dative (BDF §198[2]). The translation follows Zerwick, who suggests that under Sem. influence ἐν is practically reduced to the expression of a general notion of association or accompaniment (*Biblical Greek* §117).

kk In accordance with a classical idiom, ἐπεί introduces a second-class conditional clause (contrary to fact), with the condition omitted in an elliptical construction. The condition is implied in the construction ἐπεί . . . παθεῖν ("since [if that were true], it would have been necessary for him to suffer death many times"). See N. Turner, *Grammar,* 3:90, 318; Burton, *Moods and Tenses* §249.

ll Whenever the writer refers to the death of Jesus he uses the verb πάσχειν ("to suffer") and its derivatives. Accordingly, παθεῖν carries the nuance "to suffer death" (see above on 2:9; cf. Michaelis, *TDNT* 5:917, 934–35). Cf. 13:12.

mm The translation assumes that νυνὶ δέ, following a sentence expressing an unreal condition (v 26a), is used in a nontemporal way to introduce the real situation (so Thrall, *Greek Particles,* 31). It has been argued, however, that the contrast is not between the hypothetical repetition of Christ's suffering of death many times and the factuality of his once-for-all death, but between two ages, the one the age of repeated sacrificial offerings and the other the new age of the definitive sacrifice. In that case νυνὶ δέ should be translated temporally, "But now he has appeared" (so Grothe, "Was Jesus the Priestly Messiah?" 165–66, n. 146).

nn In the phrase ἐπὶ συντελείᾳ τῶν αἰώνων the prep is used in a transferred sense in an expression of time to denote what English expresses by "at" (cf. Moule, *Idiom-Book,* 50). The pl τῶν αἰώνων occurs only here in the NT in this phrase, and may reflect an apocalyptic view of world history as a succession of ages (e.g., Dan 9:27 LXX, συντέλειαν καιρῶν, "the consummation of the times").

oo In accordance with classical idiom, vv 27 and 28 are joined together by the relative phrase καθ' ὅσον, "just as," and the correlative οὕτως καί, "so also," in v 28 (cf. A. T. Robertson, *Grammar,* 963, 966–67).

pp The phrase χωρὶς ἁμαρτίας carries the nuances of "without any relation to sin," i.e., not with the purpose of atoning for sin (so BAGD 891; cf. RSV; JB: "not to deal with sin").

qq In the phrase εἰς σωτηρίαν, the prep expresses purpose or result, as in v 15 (εἰς ἀπολύτρωσιν, "for redemption") and v 26 (εἰς ἀθέτησιν, "for annulling").

Form/Structure/Setting

In 9:1–10 two serious limitations in the cultic provisions of the Sinaitic covenant were exposed: the severe restriction of access to God indicated that the arrangement was provisional (vv 7–8); the inadequacy of the sacrifices offered to provide decisive purgation indicated that the arrangement was imperfect (vv 9–10). This situation remained in force "until the time of correction" (v 10). The adversative δέ in 9:11, which must be given its full force, announces a shift in argument and the introduction of a new section. In direct contrast to the arrangements under the old cultus, the writer points to the high priestly liturgy of Christ, focusing upon the issues of sacrifice and sanctuary. Christ did not approach God with the sacrificial blood of bulls and goats (cf. 9:7, 12, 25) but with his own blood (9:12, 14, 26, 28). Consequently, he has been able to achieve decisive purgation (9:14, 22, 28). He did not carry out his priestly office in an earthly tabernacle (cf. 9:1, 7) but in the heavenly sanctuary (9:11–12, 24). Consequently, he has been able to provide unrestricted access to God (9:14; cf. 10:19–20).

The efficacy of Christ's high priestly offering and ministry in the heavenly sanctuary was first introduced thematically in 8:1–4a, 6a. This theme is now developed in the light of the review of the atonement provisions of the old covenant in 9:1–10. The argument continues to be cast in the form of exposition, but there is a noticeable change in perspective. In 9:8–10 the deficiencies in the old cultic arrangements were emphasized. In the section introduced in 9:11, the cultic provisions of the Sinaitic covenant are presented positively as a point of departure for elaborating the results of Christ's offering of himself to God (9:13–14, 16–23). The writer uses both antithetic and complementary parallelism as he contrasts and compares the effective action of Christ with the cultic provisions for cleansing and atonement under the old covenant (cf. Vanhoye, *La structure*, 147–48, 150–51; Peterson, "Examination," 235).

Formal literary indications of structure are less evident in this section of the homily than elsewhere in Hebrews (correctly observed by Gourgues, *RB* 84 [1977] 28–31, 35–37, who insists on the importance of the content of the passage for the determination of structure and calls attention to the correspondences between chaps. 9 and 10). In delineating 9:11–28 as a recognizable unit, Vanhoye appealed to a "partial *inclusio*" based on the mention of "Christ" in 9:11 and 28. He also argued that the unit is framed by two paragraphs (9:11–14 and 9:24–28), which may be identified by an *inclusio* on the name "Christ" in 9:11 and 14 and in 9:24 and 28. Consequently, 9:15–23 must form a central subdivision (*La structure*, 43, 147–61). But the writer's use of an official title is a tenuous basis for speaking of an *inclusio*. Elsewhere in Hebrews this literary procedure entails the introduction of the same expression or phrase at the opening and close of a paragraph of integrated thought (see *Form/Structure/Setting* on 9:1–10). In the absence of formal literary indications it is preferable to establish the limits of the new section and its internal structure by tracing the course of the argument.

In 9:11–14 the writer develops the basis for the conclusion formulated in v 15: because Christ entered the heavenly sanctuary and obtained eschatological redemption, he is the mediator of a new covenant. His office as mediator is predicated upon the efficacy of his redemptive death and subsequent exaltation. He introduces vv 16–17 parenthetically to explain the necessity of Christ's death. These verses develop a principle basic to covenant practice, which in vv 18–22 is shown to have been operative in the former covenant. The internal logic of the argument indicates that vv 16–22 should be regarded as a parenthetical explanation of v 15, which in turn is the climax of vv 11–14. The discussion in vv 23–28 then resumes the theme of Christ's heavenly priestly ministry, which was introduced in vv 11–14 (so J. J. Hughes, *NovT* 21 [1979] 32–34). The course of the argument exhibits the tight coherence of a self-contained unit. When in 10:1 the writer turns abruptly to a consideration of the law and of the inadequacies of the cultic provisions of the old covenant, he signals the introduction of a different development (cf. Gourgues, *RB* 84 [1977] 32). An analysis based on content and the course of the argument indicates that the present section extends from 9:11 to 9:28 and consists of three interrelated paragraphs, 9:11–14, 9:15–22, and 9:23–28.

The initial paragraph specifies the character of "the new cultus" and summarizes its blessings in terms of the securing of eschatological redemption (9:11–12) and the provision of a purged conscience (9:13–14). The final two paragraphs (9:15–28) provide an explication of the basis for Christ's high priestly achievement. Accordingly, 9:11–14 may be considered the core of the writer's argument, at once contrasting the priestly action of Christ with the old cultus and outlining the subsequent discussion (Johnsson, "Defilement," 217–18).

Comment

The conception of Christ's death as a liturgical high priestly action is developed as a major argument in 9:11–28. Prior to this point in the homily, the high priesthood tended to be linked with Christ's present activity as heavenly intercessor (cf. 2:18; 4:15–16; 7:25; 8:1–2). The fact of his intercession provides assurance that the people of God will be able to endure stringent testing and will obtain the promised salvation. At specified points, however, the writer has anticipated the argument in the present passage. The general statement that every high priest is appointed to offer gifts and sacrifices for sins (5:1) arouses an expectation that reference will be made to the offering that Christ brought. It occurs for the first time in 7:27 when the writer contrasts the many sacrifices of the Levitical high priests with the definitive sacrifice of Christ, who "offered himself" for the sins of the people. When the generalization that every high priest is appointed to offer gifts and sacrifices is repeated in 8:3, the inference is drawn that it was necessary for the heavenly high priest to have "something to offer." That suggestive note is left undeveloped until 9:11–28, where the writer directs attention to Christ who "offered himself" to God (9:14, 25, 28).

The manner in which the argument is set forth presupposes the cultic orientation of 9:1–10 and its leading motif, that access to God is possible only through the medium of blood (9:7). The basis for the exposition in 9:11–28 is not primarily theological. It is the religious conviction that blood is the medium of purgation from defilement (9:12, 13, 14, 18, 19, 20, 21, 22, 25). The writer appeals not only to a typological parallel between the annual Day of Atonement ritual and the self-offering of Christ, but to other cultic occasions involving sacrifice and purgation. The essence of the two covenants is found in their cultic aspects; the total argument is developed in terms of cultus. Moreover, the categories of defilement and purgation are shown to be common to the old and new orders (9:13–14, 21, 23). As in the case of 9:1–10, it is necessary to recognize that the writer used cultic terminology as religious language. The interpreter must remain open to the internal logic of the argument from the cultus.

11–12 The review of the Levitical liturgy in 9:1–10 is summed up in the statement that the old cultus consisted of regulations that were obligatory "*until the time of correction*" (v 10). That pregnant formulation prepares for the subsequent argument in 9:11–14, where the writer balances the presentation of the precedents of redemption with the description of redemption itself. The transition is announced in v 11, the δέ having an adversative sense ("but when Christ appeared as high priest"). The installation of Christ as high priest indicates that "the time of correction" has begun. This understanding of v 11a is confirmed by the parallel statement in v 26 that Christ "appeared at the climax of the ages," where the reference is clearly eschatological in character and corresponds to "the time of correction" in v 10. With the transition from 9:1–10 to 9:11–14, the writer draws a temporal contrast between two successive periods of redemptive history and their respective provisions for salvation (cf. Bover, *Bib* 32 [1951] 235; N. H. Young, *NTS* 27 [1980–81] 204).

The concern with contrast in the immediate context is decisive for settling the issue of text in v 11: Christ appeared as high priest τῶν γενομένων ἀγαθῶν, "of the good things *that have now come*" (see above, *Note* b). The variant reading μελλόντων (of the good things "which are to come") would vitiate the contrast. That which was prefigured by the Levitical cultus had already begun to be experienced by the community for which the homily was prepared. The comprehensive expression τῶν ... ἀγαθῶν, "the good things," has reference precisely to those aspects of redemption that the old order could not provide, namely, decisive purgation and full access to God (see *Comment* on vv 8–9, 14). These blessings reflect the eschatological character of the redemption secured by Christ (cf. Hofius, *Vorhang*, 65; Johnsson, "Defilement," 290–93; Grundmann, *TDNT* 1:15).

Reference to Christ's entrance into the heavenly sanctuary has already been made earlier in the central division of the homily (see 6:19–20; 8:1–2). When that theme is introduced again in vv 11–12, Christ's high priestly action is depicted as closely analogous to the ritual of expiation on the annual Day of Atonement. The main clause of the periodic sentence in vv 11–12 asserts χριστὸς δὲ παραγενόμενος ἀρχιερεὺς ... εἰσῆλθεν ... εἰς τὰ ἅγια, "But when Christ appeared as high priest ... he entered ... into the [real] sanctuary." The subordinate clauses that qualify the assertion clarify the relative degree of continuity and discontinuity between the action of Christ and that of the Levitical high priest.

The continuity exists in that Christ, like the high priest, passed through the front compartment and entered the Most Holy Place by means of blood in order to secure atonement. But the accent falls on the degree of discontinuity in the action of Christ. The sphere of his priestly ministry was not an earthly tabernacle (9:1). He passed "through the greater and more perfect compartment" to enter "the [heavenly] sanctuary." The medium of his approach was not the blood of animals (9:7). He entered the presence of God not "by means of the blood of goats and calves, but by means of his own blood." The result of his cultic action was not the limited, recurrent redemption of the annual atonement ritual (9:9). He obtained "eternal redemption." Eschatological finality characterizes his ministration (cf. Thompson, *JBL* 98 [1979] 569; Peterson, "Examination," 235–36, 242–49).

This line of interpretation presupposes a local reference in the clause διὰ τῆς μείζονος καὶ τελειοτέρας σκηνῆς, "through the greater and more perfect compartment" (see above, *Note* c). If διά is understood in an instrumental sense (i.e., Christ obtained access to God "by means of the greater and more perfect σκηνῆς"), it becomes necessary to give to σκηνῆς a symbolic value, so that it signifies Christ's body in some way (so Westcott, 256–60; Vanhoye, *Bib* 46 [1965] 1–28; Swetnam,

Bib 47 [1966] 91–106; Cody, *Heavenly Sanctuary*, 155–65; among others; cf. Sabourin, *VD* 46 [1968] 238–48). Although precedents for such an interpretation can be traced back to the Greek and Latin patristic tradition (see Westcott, 257), it is not customary for the writer to use language so cryptically. When he refers to Christ's body, his characteristic term is σάρξ, "flesh," "body" (2:14; 5:7; 10:20). An instrumental interpretation of διά in v 11*b* runs counter to the immediate argument, to the context in which the argument is developed, and to parallel statements made elsewhere in Hebrews.

The immediate argument is developed in contrast to 9:1–10. The purpose of the subordinate clauses in vv 11*b*–12*a* is to establish why Christ's high priestly ministry was fully effective as opposed to the ministration of the high priest on the Day of Atonement. The superiority of Christ's cultic action derives from the uniqueness of the sanctuary that he entered and from the uniqueness of the sacrifice that he presented. These two factors have been formulated in antithesis to the explanation provided in 9:1–10, so that positive (A) and negative (B) statements are set forth in a chiastic arrangement:

A   διὰ τῆς μείζονος καὶ τελειοτέρας σκηνῆς
     "διά the greater and more perfect σκηνή"
  B οὐ χειροποιήτου, τοῦτ' ἔστιν οὐ ταύτης τῆς κτίσεως ... (v 11*b*)
     "not made with hands, that is to say, not of ordinary building ... "
  B' οὐδὲ δι' αἵματος τράγων καὶ μόσχων,
     "not by means of the blood of goats and calves,"
A'   διὰ δὲ τοῦ ἰδίου αἵματος (v 12*b*)
     "but by means of his own blood."

The two positive clauses (A/A') clarify the distinctive character of Christ's approach to the Most Holy Place. The two negative clauses (B/B') show that the entrance of Christ was not limited by the defects of the Levitical cultus. The second pair of negative and positive clauses does not simply repeat the thrust of the first pair; it introduces another factor in the development of the comparison. The first pair contrasts the cultic spaces, the second the medium of approach, under the old and new covenants. The order in which the clauses have been arranged corresponds to the structure of 9:1–10, where the concern was first with place (vv 1–7*a*) and then with instrumentality (v 7*b*). Once the antithesis of these statements to 9:1–10 is observed, it is clear that διά must be understood in a local sense: Christ passed *through* the σκηνή, "compartment," in order to enter "once for all into the [real] sanctuary" (so Hofius, *Vorhang*, 65–67; Andriessen, *BZ* 15 [1971] 84–89; Johnsson, "Defilement," 293–96; cf. Peterson, "Examination," 242–49).

This understanding draws support from the context in which the argument is developed. From 8:1–2 to this point in the homily, σκηνή has been used consistently in a local sense to designate the heavenly sanctuary (8:2) or the desert sanctuary (8:5), or to denote the front or rear compartments of the tabernacle (9:2, 3, 6, 8). The thrust of the argument is that the tabernacle with its division into two chambers was constructed according to the pattern or model shown to Moses on Mount Sinai (see on 8:5). The writer appears to have held a realistic understanding of Exod 25:40 and related texts, according to which a spatially conceived sanctuary consisting of two compartments existed in heaven and had provided the pattern for the desert sanctuary (cf. Hofius, *Vorhang*, 55–58). The formulation of v 11*b* would encourage a reader to compare the σκηνή through which Jesus passed to the closest antecedent reference. It is found in v 8, where σκηνή has reference to the front compartment of the earthly tabernacle (see *Comment* on 9:8). The compartment through which Christ passed is μείζονος καὶ τελειοτέρας, "greater and more perfect," because it more perfectly fulfilled its function: it actually led Christ, and ultimately his people (cf. 10:19–20), into the presence of God (9:24; cf. Michel, 309; Peterson, "Examination," 249; Brooks, *JBL* 89 [1970] 210–11).

The spatial imagery of v 11*b* is consistent with the writer's affirmation in 4:14 that Christians have a great high priest who "passed through the heavens" (διεληλυθότα τοὺς οὐρανούς, where the reference clearly has local significance) and with other parallel passages that speak of an entrance "behind the curtain" or into the presence of God (6:19–20; 9:24, 25). The qualifying phrase οὐ χειροποιήτου τοῦτ᾽ ἔστιν οὐ ταύτης τῆς κτίσεως, "not made with hands, that is to say, not of ordinary building" (cf. 8:2), indicates that the reference is not to a passage through the visible heavens but to heaven as the dwelling-place of God and the angels (so Hofius, *Vorhang*, 50–53, 65–69; Andriessen, *BZ* 15 [1971] 84–85; for the OT background, see L. I. J. Stadelmann, *The Hebrew Concept of the World*, AnBib 39 [Rome: Pontifical Biblical Institute, 1970] 49–52). The syntax of vv 11–12 demands that a distinction be made between the σκηνή, "front compartment," through which Christ passed and τὰ ἅγια, "the sanctuary," into which he entered. The way into the presence of God was through the heavenly counterpart to the front compartment of the earthly tabernacle (9:2, 6; so Michel, 310–11; Michaelis, *TDNT* 7:376–77; Cody, *Heavenly Sanctuary*, 148–50; Peterson, "Examination," 242–44).

Complementing the contrast between the place of access to God under the old and the new covenants in v 11*b* is the contrast between the medium of access in v 12*a* ("not by means of the blood of goats and calves, but by means of his own blood"). The term αἷμα, "blood," is clearly being used in a sacrificial sense and is pivotal for the argument in this section (vv 12, 13, 14, 18, 19, 20, 21, 22, 25). An offering of the blood of goats and calves was prescribed for the annual atonement sacrifices under the old covenant (Lev 16:3, 5–11, 15–16; see *Comment* on 9:7). The goat was provided for the sacrificial offering of the people, and the calf for the sacrifice offered by the high priest for himself and his household. The writer has already stated that the prescribed sacrifices were unable to achieve decisive purgation (9:9; cf. 10:4). The statement that Christ approached God by means of his own blood has specific reference to his death on the cross, which is the sacrifice of the new covenant corresponding to the animal sacrifices prescribed under the old covenant. Cody has correctly observed that just as the immolation of the calf and goat was an integral aspect of the Day of Atonement ritual, so are the passion and death of Christ regarded by the writer as an integral part of the heavenly liturgy (*Heavenly Sanctuary*, 170–72). Christ's sacrifice was qualitatively superior to the blood of goats and calves because it consisted in the offering of his life to God (9:14, 25, 26). The antithetic formulation of v 12*a* suggests a stark contrast between the involuntary, passive sacrifice of animals and the active obedience of Christ who willingly made himself the sacrifice for sins (9:26; 10:5–10).

Finally, in contrast to the Levitical high priest who was obligated to enter the Most Holy Place "year by year" (9:7), the writer qualifies Christ's entrance into the heavenly sanctuary by the word ἐφάπαξ, "once for all," a term that excludes both the necessity and the possibility of repetition. Christ's entry was definitive, and it achieved final redemption (Stählin, *TDNT* 1:383–84). In context Christ's death, ascension, and entrance into the heavenly sanctuary are seen retrospectively as a unity. The stress, however, falls on the arrival in the heavenly sanctuary and the achievement of eternal redemption. The participial phrase αἰωνίαν λύτρωσιν εὑράμενος, "obtaining eternal redemption," has a liturgical ring and may be a hymnic phrase (Michel, 312). Here it expresses action subsequent or coincident with the main verb (see above, *Note* f). Christ penetrated "behind the curtain" (6:19–20) in order to consummate the work of salvation in the presence of God (9:24–26; cf. Cody, *Heavenly Sanctuary,* 170–80). Christ's sacrifice on the cross requires no repetition or renewal; his exaltation and entrance into the real sanctuary consecrates the eternal validity of his redemptive ministry (Spicq, 2:256–58). The αἰωνία λύτρωσις, "eschatological redemption," he has obtained may be associated with the sustained offer of decisive purgation that is extended through Christ to the human family (9:15; 10:18; cf. Michel, 312–13; Peterson, "Examination," 236–37; Cody, 135).

13–14 A particular proof of the efficacy of Christ's sacrifice is presented in the *a fortiori* argument of vv 13–14. The argument is formulated in antithesis to vv 9–10, where the offerings prescribed under the old covenant are stigmatized as insufficient to provide the worshiper with decisive purgation of the conscience and as provisional regulations imposed until the time of correction. The presupposition for the argument is that blood is the medium of purgation (see Johnsson, "Defilement," 278–304). The writer again alludes to the sacrifices of the Day of Atonement with the phrase τὸ αἷμα τράγων καὶ ταύρων, "the blood of goats and bulls," though a broader reference to sacrifices in general may also be intended (e.g., Num 7:15–16, 87).

With these offerings he associates the occasional sacrifice of a heifer, the ashes of which were to be mixed with water and sprinkled upon any Israelite who had been defiled by contact with a corpse (Num 19:1–22; Jos., *Ant.* 4.80; cf. Feldmann, *Biblical and Post-biblical Defilement,* 41–45; I. Scheftelowitz, "Das Opfer der Roten Kuhn [Num. 19]," *ZAW* 39 [1924] 113–23; J. Milgrom, "Sin-offering or Purification Offering?" *VT* 21 [1971] 149–56; id., "The Paradox of the Red Cow (Num. xix)," *VT* 30 [1981] 62–72, who argues that it is the blood in the ashes which endows them with purgative power [67]). Although this rite is designated a "sin offering" (Num 19:9), its essential purpose was the removal of ceremonial defilement (Num 19:11–21). This fact is recognized by the writer's reference to τοὺς κεκοινωμένους, "those who have been defiled." The ritual of the red heifer aptly illustrates the external nature of the cultic provisions of the old covenant. It also demonstrates that a state of defilement is a hindrance to worship (Num 19:13, 20). By grouping "the blood of goats and bulls" and "the sprinkled ashes of a heifer," the writer implies that all the sacrifices of the old covenant were able to provide merely an external and symbolic removal of defilement. They sanctify πρὸς τὴν τῆς σαρκὸς καθαρότητα, "to the extent of the purging of the flesh."

The concession that blood cleanses from defilement under the old covenant provides the basis for the πόσῳ μᾶλλον argument ("how much more!") in v 14.

The writer rhetorically contrasts the limited efficacy of "the blood of goats and bulls" with the surpassing efficacy of "the blood of Christ." The effectiveness of the blood of Christ derives from the qualitatively superior character of his sacrifice. His sacrifice achieved what the old cultus could not accomplish, namely, the decisive purgation of conscience and the effective removal of every impediment to the worship of God (see *Comment* on v 9). The reference in the expression τὸ αἷμα τοῦ Χριστοῦ, "the blood of Christ," is not to the material substance but to the action of Christ who offered himself to God as an unblemished sacrifice, as the relative clause of v 14 makes clear (Michel, 314). The formulation is entirely appropriate to the immediate context as a graphic synonym for the death of Christ in its sacrificial significance. This understanding is confirmed when vv 11–14 are summarized retrospectively in v 15*b* in the phrase "a death having occurred for redemption from transgressions committed under the former covenant" (so J. J. Hughes, *NovT* 21 [1979] 33; Peterson, "Examination," 237–38). The self-sacrifice of Christ on Calvary qualified him to enter the heavenly sanctuary and to consummate his redemptive task in the presence of God.

The relative clause ὃς διὰ πνεύματος αἰωνίου ἑαυτὸν προσήνεγκεν ἄμωμον τῷ θεῷ, which is used in a causal sense ("seeing that he offered himself through the eternal Spirit as an unblemished sacrifice to God"; see above, *Note* j), indicates what makes Christ's sacrifice absolute and final. The word ἄμωμον has the ring of sacrificial terminology. In the LXX and elsewhere in Jewish hellenistic sources this term denotes the absence of defects in a sacrificial animal (e.g., Num 6:14; 19:2 LXX; Philo, *On the Sacrifices of Cain and Abel* 51). It was chosen to emphasize the perfection of Christ's sacrifice. The sinless high priest (4:15; 7:26) was also the spotless victim (cf. Hauck, *TDNT* 4:830–31). The free offering of himself to God was the culmination of a life of perfect obedience (cf. 5:8–9; 10:5–10). The fact that his offering was made διὰ πνεύματος αἰωνίου, "through the eternal Spirit," implies that he had been divinely empowered and sustained in his office. The formulation does not occur elsewhere in the NT or early Christian literature, but it may be understood as a designation for the Holy Spirit. A reference to the Spirit is appropriate in a section under the influence of Isaiah, where the Servant of the Lord is qualified for his task by the Spirit of God (Isa 42:1; 61:1, so F. F. Bruce, 205–6, 233, nn. 169–72; see *Comment* on v 28).

The main clause of v 14 summarizes the benefits experienced by Christians as a result of Christ's high priestly offering. The interest in the effect of Christ's sacrifice complements the concern with effect in v 13. In contrast to the limited effectiveness of the old cultic provisions ("sanctifies [ἁγιάζει] to the extent of the purging of the flesh"), the blood of Christ will purge (καθαριεῖ) the conscience from acts that lead to death. The community had first learned of the importance of repentance ἀπὸ νεκρῶν ἔργων, "from works that lead to death," in the catechetical instruction they had received (see *Comment* on 6:1). That foundational truth is now reviewed in the light of the redemptive accomplishment of Christ. In this context, where the discussion focuses upon purgation, the phrase reflects a concept of sin as defilement that is inimical to the approach to the living God (Johnsson, "Defilement," 232, 253, 305).

"Conscience" (συνείδησις) is the human organ of the religious life embracing the whole person in relationship to God (see *Comment* on v 9). It is the point at which a person confronts God's holiness. The ability of the defiled conscience to disqualify someone from serving God has been superseded by the power of the blood of Christ to cleanse the conscience from defilement. The purpose of this purgation is that the community may be renewed in the worship of God. The purpose clause εἰς τὸ λατρεύειν θεῷ ζῶντι, "so that we may worship the living God," has been formulated in antithesis to v 9, where the writer stressed the inability of the old cultus to provide τὸν λατρεύοντα, "the worshiper," with the needed purgation of conscience. The point is clear. The sacrifice that inaugurated the new covenant achieved the cleansing of the conscience that all worshipers lacked under the former covenant and that all had sought through prescribed gifts and offerings (10:1–2; so Peterson, "Examination," 231, n. 55). The writer's concern with the different effects of the cultic provisions of the old and new covenants upon worship indicates the pastoral orientation of the exposition.

15 A context for the discussion in vv 15–21 has been established in 8:6–13, where Christ was represented as the mediator of a superior covenant. In 9:1–10 the covenant theme was sustained with the exposition of the cultic provisions of the former covenant and their significance. This motif is now resumed in v 15, where διαθήκη clearly means "covenant" (see *Note* l). The reference to the purgation of conscience in v 14, which is the epitome of the promised benefits of the new covenant as reviewed in 8:10–12, accounts for the renewed discussion of covenant (so Johnsson, "Defilement," 312–13). The blood of Christ achieves what had been promised through Jer 31:31–34 and demonstrates that Jesus is διαθήκης καινῆς μεσίτης, "mediator of a new covenant." The emphasis, however, shifts at this point from the benefits conferred by the blood of Christ to the death of Christ, which was required for the ratification of the new covenant.

The introductory clause καὶ διὰ τοῦτο, "And for this reason," establishes a strong causal relationship between vv 11–14 and the result stated in v 15. Because Jesus freely offered his life in obedience to God, he became the priestly mediator of a new covenant (cf. 8:6). His entrance into the heavenly sanctuary confirms God's acceptance of his sacrifice and the ratification of the covenant he mediated. The office of μεσίτης, "mediator," is predicated on the efficacy of his redemptive death (cf. Michel, 329). The "eschatological redemption" he obtained (v 12) is now described as the actualization of God's promise to establish a new covenant with his people (Jer 31:31–34; cf. Heb 8:8–12; 10:16–17). The theme of Christ's heavenly redemptive ministry in vv 11–14 thus reaches its climax in v 15 (J. J. Hughes, *NovT* 21 [1979] 33–34, 47–48; Johnsson, "Defilement," 306–7).

In a tightly constructed final clause the writer exposes the purpose for which Christ is the priestly mediator of a new covenant and clarifies what this required of him (see above, *Note* n). The purpose is that those whom God has called might receive the promised eschatological inheritance that comprises the blessings of the new covenant. The promise concerns the enjoyment of eternal salvation (1:14; 3:1; 5:9; 10:36; cf. Cody, *Heavenly Sanctuary*, 136). In order to become the mediator of a new covenant, it was necessary for Jesus to die. The participial phrase θανάτου γενομένου εἰς ἀπολύτρωσιν τῶν ἐπὶ τῇ πρώτῃ διαθήκῃ παραβάσεων, "a death having occurred for redemption from transgressions committed on the basis of the former covenant," reflects on vv 11–14 and summarizes them in terms of covenant practice.

The old covenant exacted death for transgressions committed while it was in force (cf. 10:28). Those who had ratified the covenant had pledged their obedience to the stipulations of the covenant in a self-maledictory manner. Their transgressions were evidence that they had failed to keep their oath and put them in jeopardy of being cut off from God (cf. Deut 30:15–20). In his death Jesus identified himself with the transgressors and took upon himself the curse sanctions of the covenant that were invoked whenever the stipulations of the covenant were ignored. In an act of supreme obedience, Jesus died a representative death as the cursed one so that those whom he represents may receive the blessings of the covenant promised to those who obey its mandates. Christ's priestly self-offering accomplished redemption finally and perfectly because he made the definitive offering for sins. The concept of redemption is thus fully assimilated to the writer's sacrificial categories. From the perspective of covenant practice, Christ's death was a covenant sacrifice, which consummated the old order and inaugurated the new order. As the priestly mediator of a new covenant, he is able to administer the eschatological blessings that specify the newness of the διαθήκης καινῆς, "new covenant" (cf. J. J. Hughes, NovT 21 [1979] 38, 47–49, 55).

16–17 The extended unit that follows (vv 16–22) has been introduced parenthetically to explain the necessity for the death of Christ, to which reference was made in v 15b. This block of exposition is tied to the preceding verse by the explanatory γάρ, "for," in v 16 and by the inferential particle ὅθεν, "this is why," in v 18. In the flow of the argument the writer enunciates first a general principle based on the procedure for the ratification of a covenant (vv 16–17), and then shows that this procedure was illustrated in the case of the Sinaitic covenant mediated by Moses (vv 18–22). The striking association of διαθήκη, "covenant," and θάνατος, "death," in v 15 is reiterated in vv 16–17, which strongly suggests that διαθήκη continues to be used uniformly to mean "covenant." The meaning of διαθήκη in vv 16–17 is qualified by its meaning in v 15, where the proper frame of reference for the interpretation of v 15b is the death of the covenant-victim whose blood sealed and ratified the covenant (see above, Note p).

The recognition that the topic of vv 15–17 is covenant ratification indicates that vv 16–17 have been introduced to explain why Christ had to die in order to become the priestly mediator of the new covenant. The ὅπου γάρ διαθήκη clause of v 16 ("For where there is a covenant") explicates the circumstantial clause of v 15b ("a death having occurred"), not the final clause of v 15b ("in order that . . . they may receive the promised eternal inheritance"). As J. J. Hughes has observed, "the focus is upon death as it leads to priestly mediatorship of the new covenant, not death as it leads to inheritance. The writer is primarily concerned with christology, not with the soteriological blessings of inheritance" (NovT 21 [1979] 38–39).

The problematic phrase in v 16b, θάνατον ἀνάγκη φέρεσθαι τοῦ διαθεμένου, "it is necessary for the death of the ratifier to be brought forward," is to be interpreted in the light of covenant practice in general. The necessity for a death is rooted in covenant procedure. In the OT, ratification of a covenant based on sacrifice frequently entailed a self-maledictory procedure. The ratifying party invoked a curse upon himself when he swore commitment to comply with the terms of the covenant. In the transaction the ratifying party was represented by animals designated for sacrifice. The bloody dismemberment of representative animals signified the violent death of the ratifying party if he proved faithless to his oath (e.g., Gen 15:9–21; Exod 24:3–8; Ps 50:5; Jer 34:17–20; cf. G. E.

Mendenhall, "Ancient and Biblical Law," *BA* 17 [1954] 29; id., "Covenant Forms in Israelite Tradition," *BA* 17 [1954] 52).

The writer's familiarity with covenant procedure is evident in v 16*b*, where τοῦ διαθεμένου denotes "the one who ratifies" a covenant (cf. Ps 49[50]:5 LXX, where τοὺς διατιθεμένους designates collectively those who have made a covenant with God on the basis of sacrifices). For the ratification of a covenant it was necessary for the death of the ratifier to be represented symbolically. The writer's choice of the term φέρεσθαι, "to be introduced," "to be brought forward" (see *Note* r) was probably influenced by the cultic use of φέρειν in the LXX, where it is associated with the representative act of offering a sacrifice. The offerer is represented in and by the sacrifice he brings (J. J. Hughes, *NovT* 21 [1979] 65–66). In terms of OT covenant procedure, the death of sacrificial animals was brought forward on behalf of the one ratifying the covenant (cf. J. J. Hughes, *NovT* 21 [1979] 39–46; Kilpatrick, *ZNW* 68 [1977] 263–65; Johnsson, "Defilement," 313–17).

The assertion in v 16 is clarified and amplified in v 17: it was necessary to bring forward the death of the covenant-ratifier because a covenant was not in force until this had been done. The argument continues to be based on general covenant practice. Until the oath of allegiance had been sworn and validated by the action of cutting the animal in two and walking between the pieces (cf. Gen 15:10, 17; Jer 34:18), the covenant remained merely tentative. It was legally confirmed (βεβαία) on the basis of the dismembered bodies of the sacrificial victims. In its context, the unusual formulation ἐπὶ νεκροῖς, "on the basis of dead bodies," refers to the bodies of representative animals used in the self-maledictory rite of covenant ratification (see above, *Note* t). It finds an exact parallel in Ps 49[50]:5 LXX, where ἐπὶ θυσίαις means "on the basis of sacrificial animals." The thought is amplified with the strong negative assertion that a covenant is never operative ὅτε ζῇ ὁ διαθέμενος, "while the ratifier lives." The formulation accurately reflects the legal situation that a covenant is never secured until the ratifier has bound himself to his oath by means of a representative death (Johnsson, "Defilement," 313).

These general considerations explain why Christ had to die in order to become the priestly mediator of a new covenant. The ratification of a covenant required the presentation of sacrificial blood (cf. v 18). Such blood is obtained only by means of death. Christ's death was the means of providing the blood of the new covenant. His sacrificial death ratified or "made legally valid" the new covenant promised in Jer 31:31–34. Because he died a representative death (see on v 15*b*), those whom he represents may receive the blessings mediated through the new covenant. These ideas are deeply embedded in OT covenant practice, where the prerequisite for blessing and the reception of a promised inheritance was obedience displayed in an unbroken relationship with the Lord (cf. J. J. Hughes, *NovT* 21 [1979] 62–63; Johnsson, "Defilement," 313–14).

18–21 The concern with covenant procedure is sustained in vv 18–21, when the writer refers to the ratification of the covenant concluded with Israel at Sinai. The expression ἡ πρώτη, "the first," is used elliptically in v 18 for ἡ πρώτη διαθήκη, "the former covenant" (cf. 8:13; 9:1). The strong inferential particle ὅθεν, "this is why," shows that the conclusion drawn in v 18 has been derived on the basis of the legal principle developed in vv 16–17; the principle of representative death was operative in the inauguration of the former covenant. The inference is authorized because the argument continues to be centered on the reason for Christ's death and turns on the procedure for covenant-ratification. The Sinaitic covenant provides a particular example of the more general use of διαθήκη, "covenant," in v 16–17.

The central thrust of the argument is that there is an intimate relationship between covenant and sacrificial blood. The motif of blood is introduced in v 18 with the conclusion that "not even the former covenant had been confirmed without blood." The verb ἐγκαινίζειν denotes "solemnly to bring something new into effect" and is appropriate for describing the ratification of the solemn legal relationship binding Yahweh and his people (Behm, *TDNT* 3:454). The important phrase χωρὶς αἵματος, "without blood," recalls the earlier use of this formulation in v 7, where sacrificial blood is the medium of approach to God. It also anticipates the legal maxim in v 22*b* that there is no decisive purgation under the old or new covenants χωρὶς αἱματεκχυσίας, "without the application of blood." The covenant inaugurated at Sinai was ratified by blood and was made legally secure by death.

This fact is substantiated by reference to Exod 24:3–8, where it is clear that Moses functioned as a priest in the ratification of the old covenant (cf. C. Hauret, "Moïse était-il prêtre?" *Bib* 40 [1959] 516). The solemn occasion was observed by both burnt offerings and the sacrifice of young bulls for peace, or fellowship, offerings (Exod 24:5). After the blood had been collected in bowls, Moses sprinkled half of the blood on the altar. When he had read from the Book of the Covenant and the people had sworn obedience to the Lord, Moses sprinkled them with the other half of the blood, interpreting his action by reference to the covenant which the Lord had made with Israel (Exod 24:6–8). The act of sprinkling the blood sealed the ratification of the covenant, while the peace offerings attested to the fellowship between the covenant partners.

The allusion to this event in vv 19–21 displays some variations from the old biblical text. In addition to τὸ αἷμα τῶν μόσχων, "the blood of bulls," the writer refers to other traditional purgatives, water, crimson, wool, and sprigs of hyssop, possibly under the influence of Lev 14:4–7, 51–52 or Num 19:6. He may have inferred that the procedure described in Exod 24 implied the use of a sprinkling implement consisting of a cedar stick to which sprigs of hyssop were tied with crimson wool, which was dipped in blood diluted with water (cf. Exod 12:22; Lev 4:4; Num 19:18). This method of sprinkling appears to have been common (P. E. Hughes, 375–76). The statement that Moses sprinkled the book from which he had read the words of the Lord, as well as sprinkling the whole people, is not attested elsewhere. (Cf. Courthial, *EEv* 36 [1976] 41–42, who argues that the account in Exod 24 presupposes that the book had been placed within the altar, prior to the sprinkling of the altar. The writer's formulation emphasized in a symbolic manner that the sacrificial blood linked the people, who pledged themselves to be faithful, to the Lord, who was represented by his written word placed within the altar.) The further statement that Moses also sprinkled the tabernacle and all the cultic vessels with blood (v 21) may draw upon an independent Jewish tradition to which Josephus also had access. According to Exod 40:9, 16; Lev 8:11, Moses had anointed the tabernacle and its implements with oil at its dedication, but Josephus speaks of the use of both oil and blood (*Ant.* 3.206; N. H. Young, *NTS* 27 [1980–81] 205, calls attention to *b. Yoma* 4a where the oil is said to be symbolic of blood; cf. Johnsson, "Defilement," 318, n. 177).

The importance of blood is stressed repeatedly in these verses. The writer's intention is to show that the former covenant was ratified by sacrificial blood just as the new covenant was (Johnsson, "Defilement," 306–7; cf. Hunzinger, *TDNT* 6:982). The comparison of the blood by which the old covenant of Sinai was ratified with that of Christ clearly presupposes that the blood sprinkled by Moses had expiatory value. This point of view reflects later Jewish teaching on sacrifice, according to which all sacrifice, including the blood of the peace offerings, was expiatory in character. This tradition is reflected in *Tg. Onq.* and *Ps.-J.* Exod 24:8 where it is stated explicitly that "Moses took blood . . . *and sprinkled it on the altar to make atonement for the people* and he said: 'Behold the blood of the covenant which the Lord had made with you with all these words'" (cf. R. le Déaut, "Targumic Literature and New Testament Interpretation," *BTB* 4 [1974] 252).

The citation of Exod 24:8 in v 20 deviates in form from both the MT and the LXX. It is widely held that the substitution of τοῦτο for the ἰδού of the LXX text ("This is the blood of the covenant" for "Behold, the blood of the covenant") shows that the quotation has been brought into conformity with the eucharistic words of Christ, perhaps under the influence of a local liturgical tradition. The citation thus conveys a veiled allusion to the institution of the Lord's Supper (cf. Matt 26:28; Mark 14:24; so Spicq, 2:264; Michel, 319–20; Theissen, *Untersuchung*, 72; K. J. Thomas, *NTS* 11 [1964–65] 313–14; McCullough, *NTS* 26 [1979–80] 375; among others). Although this is not impossible, it is probable that the alteration of the LXX text by the change of ἰδού to τοῦτο, of διέθετο to ἐνετείλατο ("he inaugurated" to "he commanded," attested also in MS 71 of the LXX and in Philo, *Questions and Answers on Exodus* 2.36, which is known only in the Armenian version), and of κύριος to ὁ θεός ("Lord" to "God") was made to support the writer's carefully structured argument.

The purpose of the argument in vv 18–20 is to show that the covenant at Sinai, as a particular example of the more general use of "covenant" in vv 16–17, was ratified ἐπὶ νεκροῖς, "on the basis of dead bodies [of slain animals]." The presence of τοῦτο in v 20 underscores the fact that the old covenant was ratified by means of sacrificial blood obtained from slain animals. The substitution of ἐνετείλατο for διέθετο serves to avoid ambiguity. The writer used διατίθεσθαι to refer to the one who *ratified* the covenant (8:10; 9:16; 10:10). The retention of the LXX reading (διέθετο) in v 20 would have implied that God ratified the former covenant. By substituting ἐνετείλατο, the writer makes it clear that the people ratified what God had initiated by his authoritative word. Similarly, the writer's common tendency to use κύριος, "Lord," for Jesus called for the substitution of ὁ θεός for the LXX reading κύριος, in order to avoid any possible misunderstanding that it was Jesus who had commanded the Sinaitic covenant (cf. Schröger, *MTZ* 19 [1968] 169–70; J. J. Hughes, *NovT* 21 [1979] 46–47). Accordingly, there is no reference to Jesus' word over the cup at the institution of the Lord's Supper in v 20. The citation focuses upon the use of sacrificial blood in the ratification of the covenant.

22 The axiom formulated in v 22 functions as a general statement. It summarizes the previous verses and provides a transition to v 23 and the ensuing discussion concerning the heavenly sanctuary. The point made in v 22*a* that almost everything is purged by blood is limited to the period of the old cultus by the legal qualification κατὰ τὸν νόμον, "according to the law." The writer is prepared to recognize that when the former covenant was in force some provision was made for purgation without blood (e.g., Lev 5:11–13 [an offering of flour by a person too poor to purchase two doves]; Num 31:22–23 [purification by fire and water]). But he is quick to add that for decisive purgation blood is essential. On this understanding, the introductory καί in v 22b is adversative in force ("but") and introduces a principle that governs both the old and new cultus (see *Note* aa; cf. Johnsson, "Defilement," 318–20; H. Montefiore, 158–59).

The principle that defilement is purged by blood is extremely important to the argument being developed in this context. It provides the ground for comparing the animal sacrifices under the old covenant and the sacrifice of Christ that inaugurated the new covenant. The writer's concern with the quality of purgation achieved by the once-for-all offering of Christ's blood accounts for the presence of significant vocabulary in his formulation of a legal maxim to which close parallels can be cited in rabbinic literature (e.g., *b. Yoma* 5a; *b. Zebaḥ* 6a; *b. Menaḥ.* 93b, with appeal to Lev 17:11). The word αἱματεκχυσία may have been coined by the writer as a comprehensive term for the application of blood. Jewish sources indicate that in a cultic context the reference is not to the slaying of the sacrificial victims (i.e., "the shedding of blood"; so RSV, NEB, NIV; cf. Swetnam, *Jesus and Isaac*, 186–87), but to the final disposal of the blood upon the altar in order to effect atonement (see above, *Note* bb; cf. Exod 29:12; Lev 4:7, 18, 25, 30, 34; 8:15; 9:9 LXX, where αἷμα, "blood," and ἐκχύννειν, "to pour out," are used in conjunction with the pouring out of blood upon the altar). The term calls attention to the surpassing potency of blood as a religious force for dealing with defilement. The contrast between the two halves of v 22 is not between purgation ἐν αἵματι, "with blood," and αἱματεκχυσία, "the application of blood," but rather between the restrictive σχεδόν, "almost," and the inclusive οὐ, "no"/"none" (so Johnsson, "Defilement," 152–61, 322–23; cf. Thornton, *JTS* n.s. 15 [1964] 63–65).

The declaration in v 22b is the third of three postulates that have been formulated in a similar way to stress the crucial importance of sacrificial blood: blood was the medium of access to God (v 7); blood was the basis for the inauguration of the former covenant (v 18); blood is the medium of ἄφεσις (v 22b).

v 7　　οὐ χωρὶς αἵματος
　　　　"not without blood"
v 18　οὐδὲ ... χωρὶς αἵματος
　　　　"not even [the former covenant was inaugurated] without blood"
v 22　χωρὶς αἱματεκχυσίας οὐ
　　　　"without the application of blood [there is] no"

On each occasion the writer used χωρίς in a prepositional sense ("without") and cast his statement negatively.

The climactic character of the statement in v 22b requires that attention be given to the particular nuance in the term ἄφεσις. Throughout this section the writer has stressed the religious potency of blood: blood provides access (v 7); blood purges the conscience (v 14); blood inaugurates (v 18); blood consecrates the people (v 19); blood cleanses cultic implements (v 21); blood purges almost everything under the old law (v 22a). In light of the emphasis in the context Johnsson suggests that a ἄφεσις is a comprehensive term covering both the "subjective" and "objective" benefits of Christ's blood. Thus v 23 proceeds to direct attention to the purgation of heavenly things. The juxtaposing of καθαρίζειν, "to

purge," with ἄφεσις in v 22 and the resumption of καθαρίζειν in v 23 shows that
the meanings of these two words are closely connected. In this context, ἄφεσις
signals a definitive putting away of defilement or a decisive purgation ("Defilement," 324–29).

23 In the concluding paragraph (vv 23–28), the writer elaborates upon the
triumphant announcement of vv 11–12. His concern is to specify some of
the objective benefits of Christ's blood by reference to the heavenly sanctuary
and cultus and to the consummation of redemptive history. The preceding argument in vv 15–22 is clearly presupposed, as the inferential particle οὖν, "then,"
"therefore," in v 23 indicates, while the axiomatic character of the statement in
v 22b explains the necessity (ἀνάγκη) postulated. The canon concerning the application of blood extends not only to the purgation of the tabernacle and its
vessels but to the heavenly reality of which the earthly cultus was only an imperfect
suggestion. The formulation of v 23a reflects particularly on v 21 and defines the
significance of sacrifice in terms of blood as the medium of purgation. The use
of καθαρίζεσθαι, "to be purged," shows that the emphasis is placed upon the removal of impurity. Blood provides access to God by the removal of defilement
(Johnsson, "Defilement," 329–31).

The additional statement that the heavenly prototypes of the earthly tabernacle and its cultus required cleansing "by better sacrifices than these" clearly
implies that the heavenly sanctuary had also become defiled by the sin of the
people. Although this implication has been dismissed as "nonsense" (Spicq, 2:266–
67; cf. Moffatt, 132; F. F. Bruce, 218; among others), it is consistent with the
conceptual framework presupposed by the writer in 9:1–28. His thinking has been
informed by the Levitical conception of the necessity for expiatory purification.
Sin as defilement is infectious. An individual assumes his part in the community
through social relationships and cultic acts. Consequently, the effects of his defilement contaminate society (e.g., Lev 21:15; cf. Heb 12:15–16), the sanctuary
where God met with his people (cf. Lev 16:16; 20:3; 21:23; Num 19:20), and even
the inanimate vessels used in the cultus (cf. v 21).

That the effects of sin also extend to the heavenly world is a corollary of the
solidarity that the writer perceives between ultimate reality in heaven and its reflection on earth. The cultus on earth is inseparably linked to the situation in
heaven (cf. 8:5; 9:7, 11–12, 23; 12:18–24). As defilement reaches beyond the individual to taint society and the earthly cultus, it also pollutes heavenly reality.
The writer conceived of defilement as an objective impediment to genuine access
to God. It made necessary a decisive purgation that was comprehensive in its scope,
reaching even to the heavenly things themselves (so also Windisch, 85;
Riggenbach, 283; Cody, *Heavenly Sanctuary*, 81–91; Johnsson, "Defilement," 256–
61).

The full, perfect, and sufficient sacrifice of Christ purified the heavenly sanctuary from the defilement resulting from the sins of the people. The phrase
κρείττοσιν θυσίαις παρὰ ταύτας, "by means of better sacrifices than these," has
reference to the death of Christ on the cross. The plural form θυσίαις, "sacrifices," is to be explained as attraction to the plural form τούτοις, "by these means,"
in v 23a, with which it contrasts (N. H. Young, *NTS* 27 [1980–81] 206). The sacrificial blood with which the former covenant had been ratified and with which
the tabernacle had been dedicated and its vessels purged was insufficient to

remove the defilement that clung to αὐτὰ τὰ ἐπουράνια, "the heavenly things themselves." The superior sacrifice demanded was provided by the self-oblation of Christ. Cultic thinking thus demonstrates the necessity for Christ's death. In his concern with heavenly reality, the writer has not lost sight of the historical dimension, for the two cleansings envisioned in v 23 are depicted as temporally related to each other as first to second (Williamson, *SJT* 16 [1963] 420).

24–26 The cleansing of "the heavenly things themselves" is further specified by reference to the ascension of Christ and his appearance in the presence of God in the transcendent realm of "heaven itself." In focusing upon the definitive stage of Christ's access to God, the writer clarifies the conceptual scheme of heavenly priesthood and sacrifice, which had been approached in a cursory way in 8:3–5. The recapitulation of the theme of the heavenly sanctuary draws upon the Day of Atonement ritual, when it was the task of the high priest to appear before God. The keystone in the structure of the writer's thinking about the heavenly sanctuary and liturgy is the concept of the Most Holy Place (Cody, *Heavenly Sanctuary*, 165, 181–85). The contrasts developed in vv 24–26 clarify the basis of the superior sacrifice by which the heavenly sanctuary was purged. The writer establishes two contrasts.

(1) The sanctuary which Christ entered was not the earthly one, which was only a representation of the pattern or model shown to Moses on Mount Sinai (see *Comment* on 8:5), but heaven itself (v 24). The sharpness of the contrast is heightened by the pejorative term χειροποίητα, "made by hands" (cf. v 11), and the qualifying phrase ἀντίτυπα τῶν ἀληθινῶν, "a representation of the true one," which define the rear compartment of the earthly tabernacle. The heavenly sanctuary alone is true and genuine. Such descriptive phrases show that the old covenant with its cultic provisions is being evaluated and is judged to have had its validity only in reference to the eschatological reality associated with Christ's definitive sacrifice and exaltation. The comparison reflects upon the typological relation between the old and new covenants (Nomoto, *NovT* 10 [1968] 17–19; cf. Cody, *Heavenly Sanctuary*, 152, n. 9).

Christ entered εἰς αὐτὸν τὸν οὐρανόν, "into heaven itself," which is to be defined as the place of God's dynamic presence, which was only foreshadowed by the rear compartment of the tabernacle. Elsewhere in Hebrews the writer uses the plural form οὐρανοί, "heavens"; only in v 24 does he make use of the singular to denote the highest heaven in which the true sanctuary as the dwelling place of God is located (cf. Hofius, *Vorhang*, 70–71, who calls attention to the apocalyptic tradition in *T. Levi* 2:6–5:1: "the heavens" are opened [*T. Levi* 2:6] in order to permit the patriarch to pass through different realms until he reaches "the gate of heaven" where he sees the heavenly sanctuary and the Most High enthroned in glory [*T. Levi* 5:1]). The appearance of Christ in the presence of God ὑπὲρ ἡμῶν, "on our behalf," provides assurance that his saving action possesses eternal validity and will secure for his people unhindered access to God as well (see *Comment* on 6:20; 10:19–20). To see the face of God is to be certain of his presence and grace (Lohse, *TDNT* 6:733).

(2) The offering Christ made was not repeated, unlike the action of the high priest who year by year entered the Most Holy Place with the sacrificial blood of animals (vv 25–26). The high point of the annual atoning ritual under the old order was the sprinkling of the blood on the cover of the ark of the covenant. To

denote that cultic action, the writer had made singular use of the verb προσφέρειν, "to offer" (see *Comment* on v 7). When he applies the annual Day of Atonement ritual to Christ, he again uses the verb προσφέρειν. In this context it refers not to a corresponding action in the heavenly sanctuary but to the death of Christ on the cross. That becomes clear when the writer develops his thought hypothetically by means of a contrary-to-fact condition: if Christ had offered himself many times (on the analogy of the action of the high priest, v 25), it would have been necessary for him to suffer death many times, beginning with the foundation of the world (v 26a). In fact, he appeared ἅπαξ, "once," at the climax of history to cancel the force of sin through his sacrifice (v 26b). The antithesis to the πολλάκις, "many times," which qualifies the action of the Levitical high priest, is the ἅπαξ, "once," which qualifies the action of Christ. Thus the typological fulfillment of the Levitical high priest's annual sprinkling of blood in the Most Holy Place was Christ's death on Calvary. The contrast between the Levitical high priest and the heavenly high priest is displayed in the sequence of the projected action as well as in its frequency. The repeated entrance followed by the repeated act of sprinkling the sacrificial blood throughout the old order was displaced by the single, sufficient sacrifice upon the cross followed by the definitive entrance into the heavenly sanctuary. Christ's priestly action inaugurated the new covenant and introduced the new age of fulfillment (cf. Moffatt, 132; N. H. Young, *NTS* 27 [1980–81] 207–10).

The purpose of Christ's public appearance and single offering at a point in time in the past is expressed by means of a bold legal metaphor: he appeared εἰς ἀθέτησιν τῆς ἁμαρτίας, "for the annulling of sin," by means of the sacrifice of himself (v 26b; cf. MM 12). The cancelling of sin must in this context have primary reference to the purging of the "heavenly things" mentioned in v 23. This interpretation is consistent with the writer's emphasis on the objective accomplishment of the sacrifice of Christ. The subjective benefits to the new people of God do not seem to be directly in view here. On this understanding, vv 23–26 are closely integrated. The contrasts developed in vv 24–26 show that both the old cultus and the new cultus stand under the principle articulated in v 22, but the superior sacrifice of Christ achieved with finality what was quite impossible under the old order (so Johnsson, "Defilement," 336).

27–28 The uniqueness of Christ's sacrifice as an unrepeatable action that occurred ἅπαξ, "once," at the climax of history suggests a further line of argument. The common human experience that death occurs ἅπαξ provides an analogy for understanding the saving significance of Christ's priestly action. He was offered ἅπαξ to bear the sin of many, with the consequence that he will return to his people with the gift of salvation. The repetition of the term ἅπαξ ties vv 27–28 to v 26b and underscores the perfection of the sacrifice of Christ. By his single offering he dealt decisively with sin and secured final salvation (cf. Stählin, *TDNT* 1:381–83).

The observation that death is an unrepeatable experience has been made from the time of Homer (*Odyssey* 12.22: ἅπαξ θνῄσκουσ' ἄνθρωποι, "men die once"). The fact that death will be followed by divine judgment was commonly stressed in the preaching of the old synagogue. A record of the popular form this teaching could assume is preserved in the Palestinian Pentateuch Targum where Cain, the prototype of the godless person, argues that "there is no judgment, and there is no judge, and there is no other world, and there is no giving of a good reward to the just, and there is no retribution exacted from the wicked," while Abel, the prototype of the godly person, takes the contrary point of view (*Tg. Neof.* Gen 4:8). The truth that the human family stands under a divine appointment to die and to experience eternal judgment was part of the foundational teaching to which the community had been exposed when they first accepted the gospel (see *Comment* on 6:2). In v 27 it is cited axiomatically for the sake of the correlative clause in v 28*a*, οὕτως καὶ ὁ Χριστός, "so also Christ." The comparison extends to both terms, the once dying and the judgment.

The language of the clause ἅπαξ προσενεχθεὶς εἰς τὸ πολλῶν ἀνενεγκεῖν ἁμαρτίας, "after having been offered once in order to bear the sins of many," has a formal character, which may reflect an older catechetical formulation. It is striking that only here in Hebrews is there an allusion to the vicarious ministry of the servant of the Lord as set forth in Isa 53:12 LXX: καὶ αὐτὸς ἁμαρτίας πολλῶν ἀνήνεγκεν, "and he bore the sins of many." J. R. Schaefer has argued cogently that the source of the writer's interpretation of Jesus' death as a vicarious redemptive act was the servant christology of the early Church (cf. the similar formulation in 1 Pet 2:24). The decision to reinterpret servant christology in priestly terms enabled him to portray Jesus as both victim and priest. The sole trace of the primitive servant christology in Hebrews is the purpose clause "to bear the sins of many." By prefacing these words with the clause, "so also Christ, having been offered once," the writer introduced his distinctly priestly perspective. The reinterpretation of servant christology entailed a shift in emphasis from the passive submission of the servant to redemptive suffering (e.g., Acts 8:32–35; 1 Pet 2:21–24) to the active embracing of death as a priestly offering (see *Comment* on 10:9–10, 12). The vicariously redemptive quality of Jesus' death was of paramount importance to the argument. It permitted Jesus to enter the heavenly sanctuary and to appear in the presence of God as high priestly mediator (*CBQ* 30 [1968] 376–85; cf. Jeremias, *TDNT* 5:708).

The writer's distinctly priestly perspective is evident in the formulation of v 28*b* as well. The reference to Christ's return to those who wait for him draws its force in this context from the analogy with the sequence of events on the Day of Atonement. The people waited anxiously outside the sanctuary until the high priest emerged from the Most Holy Place after he had fulfilled his office (cf. Lev 16:17). His reappearance provided assurance that the offering he had made had been accepted by God. The scribe Joshua ben Sira commented on an occasion when the Oniad high priest Simon the Just (c. 200 B.C.) presided over the Day of Atonement ritual:

> How glorious he was when the people gathered round him as he came out of the inner sanctuary! (Sir 50:5).

An impression of the excitement with which Simon was greeted is conveyed by an accumulation of metaphors with which Ben Sira seeks to describe his appearance (Sir 50:6–10). The sequence of entrance into the sanctuary and return to the people is reflected in the development in vv 24–28. Christ entered the heavenly sanctuary to appear in the presence of God on behalf of his people (v 24). He will appear ἐκ δευτέρου, "a second time," to those who wait expectantly for him.

The parousia is not an event that can add anything to the sacrificial office Christ has already fulfilled. The force of sin has been decisively broken by his death. He will return χωρὶς ἁμαρτίας, "without reference to sin" (see *Note* pp). But his appearance will confirm that his sacrifice has been accepted and that he has secured the blessings of salvation for those whom he represented. For those who are the heirs of salvation (1:14; cf. 2:3, 10; 5:9; 6:9), it will mean full enjoyment of their inheritance. The parousia is thus the key event in the realization of salvation.

The comparative statement that as death occurs once and is followed by judgment so Christ's single offering is followed by his return with salvation declares that the issue in Christ's life is settled. His high priestly ministry has been fully effective. It poses for the community the issue whether they will allow the sequence of entrance into the sanctuary and return to inform their lives in a vital way so that they may persevere in faith and hope.

Explanation

The exposition in 9:11–28 is informed by a theology of salvation. The argument is developed in direct contrast to the brief review of the cultic arrangements under the old order in 9:1–10. The securing of salvation can be described in terms of a forward movement into the presence of God. Under the old covenant such movement was severely restricted. A tangible expression of this fact was the curtain separating the rear compartment of the tabernacle from the Holy Place. On one day of the year alone only the high priest could pass through the curtain to appear before God (9:7). That he must do so year after year indicated that the atonement he secured was merely provisional in character. The sacrifices he offered were inadequate to accomplish a decisive purgation of the defilement of sin. Against this backdrop the writer contrasts the efficacy of the unrepeatable action of Christ, whose single offering secured eschatological salvation and provided access to the inaccessible presence of God. The key to the typological exposition of salvation in 9:11–28 is that entrance into the heavenly sanctuary pertains to an eschatological and eternal order of salvation.

The writer's primary concern in this section is with objective salvation. The exposition is focused upon the saving work of Christ in relation to God in behalf of the redeemed community rather than upon salvation realized subjectively in Christians. The writer found in the ritual of the Day of Atonement a point of comparison with which to describe the significance of the death of Christ and his subsequent exaltation. The saving event by which Christ secured salvation is described under the symbolism of a liturgical action: Christ offered himself as an unblemished sacrifice to God and entered the heavenly sanctuary to consummate his priestly action in the presence of God. In the discussion, the "blood of Christ" provides a graphic synonym for the death of Christ in its sacrificial significance. The reference in the expression is not to the material substance but to the action of Christ who offered himself to God. The heavenly liturgy of Christ consists in his death, ascension, and appearance in the presence of God, viewed retrospectively as a unity. The consequence of his liturgical action is that every obstacle to union with God has been effectively removed. Since the great barrier to the presence of God is the defilement of sin, the writer structures his argument in terms of the securing of decisive purgation.

The leading motif of 9:11-28 is blood as the medium of lifegiving power. The total argument centers on the potency of blood. In the course of the exposition the writer refers to the daily sacrifices, to the rites of purification involving the ashes of the red heifer, to the sacrifices by which the covenant of Sinai was ratified, and to the ceremonies associated with the annual Day of Atonement. The elements that all of these occasions share in common are the presence of blood and a profound religious conviction concerning the potency of blood to provide access to God, to consecrate, to cleanse, to inaugurate covenant, and to achieve purgation from defilement. In each case the "material" character of blood is not in view but blood as a symbolic medium of power.

The writer's own religious understanding of blood is expressed most clearly when the sacrificial blood of animals is juxtaposed to the blood of Christ. The basis of the comparison is the concept that the death of Christ on the cross is the sacrifice of the new covenant corresponding to the animal sacrifices prescribed under the old covenant. The sacrificial blood of animals achieves the purgation of the flesh. It avails to consecrate, but it cannot provide full access to God. Moreover, it must be applied over and over. On the other hand, Christ's blood is the supreme purging medium. By his redemptive sacrifice he achieved the decisive purgation of conscience, which is prerequisite for the true worship of God (9:13-14). Consequently, the old pattern of fluctuation between defilement and purgation has been set aside. The argument presupposes that all sacrificial blood is powerful, but Christ's blood is the more powerful medium because it achieved decisive purgation and the removal of every impediment to the enjoyment of God.

H. The Ultimate Character of Christ's Single, Personal Sacrifice for Sins (10:1–18)

Bibliography

Andriessen, P. "Le seul sacrifice qui plait à Dieu: Hé 10,5–10." *AsSeign* 8 (1972) 58–63. **Armstrong, T. A.** "The Use of Psalm 40 in Hebrews 10." Dissertation, Trinity Evangelical Divinity School, 1975. **Attridge, H. W.** "The Use of Antithesis in Hebrews 8–10." *HTR* 79 (1986) 1–9. **Benoit, P.** "Préexistence et Incarnation." *RB* 77 (1970) 5–29. **Blank, J.** "Die Auslegung des Willens Gottes im Neuen Testament." In *Zum Thema Wille Gottes*. Ed. G. Denzler et al. Stuttgart: Calwer, 1973. 83–114. **Brandt, W.** "Die Wortgruppe λειτουργεῖν im Hebräerbrief und bei Clemens Romanus." *JTSB* 1 (1930) 145–76. **Byington, S. T.** "Hebrews x.1." *ExpTim* 55 (1943–44) 54. **Caird, G. B.** "Son by Appointment." In *The New Testament Age*. FS B. Reicke. Ed. W. C. Weinrich. Macon, GA: Mercer UP, 1984. 1:73–81. **Campbell, J. C.** "In a Son: The Doctrine of the Incarnation in the Epistle to the Hebrews." *Int* 10 (1956) 24–38. **Cantalamessa, R.** "Il papiro Chester Beatty III (p46) e la tradizione indiretta di Hebr. 10,1." *Aeg* 45 (1965) 194–215. **Casalini, N.** "I sacrifici dell'antica alleanza nel piano salvifico di Dio secondo la Lettera agli Ebrei." *RivB* 35 (1987) 443–64. **Deichgräber, R.** "Gehorsam und Gehorchen in der Verkündigung Jesu." *ZNW* 52 (1961) 119–22. **Dukes, J.** "The

Humanity of Jesus in Hebrews." *ThEduc* 32 (1985) 38–45. **Dussaut, L.** *Synopse structurelle de l'Épître aux Hébreux.* 83–91. **Ellis, E. E.** "Midrash, Targum and New Testament Quotations." 61–69. **Fabris, R.** "La lettera agli Ebrei e l'Antico Testamento." *RivB* 32 (1984) 237–52. **Gayford, S. C.** "The Aorist Participles in Heb. 1:3; 7:27; 10:12." *Th* 7 (1923) 282. **Ginn, R. J.** *The Present and the Past: A Study of Anamnesis.* Allison Park, PA: Pickwick, 1989. **Gourgues, M.** *A la droite de Dieu.* 110–19. ———. "Lecture christologique du Psaume cx et fête de la Pentecôte." *RB* 83 (1976) 5–24. **Hamm, D.** "Faith in the Epistle to the Hebrews: The Jesus Factor." *CBQ* 52 (1990) 270–91. **Hughes, P. E.** "The Blood of Jesus and His Heavenly Priesthood in Hebrews: Part II: The High Priestly Sacrifice of Christ." *BSac* 130 (1973) 195–212. **Johnsson, W. G.** "The Cultus of Hebrews in Twentieth-Century Scholarship." *ExpTim* 89 (1977–78) 104–8. ———. "Defilement and Purgation in the Book of Hebrews." Dissertation, Vanderbilt University, 1973. 338–51. **Kaiser, W. C.** "The Abolition of the Old Order and the Establishment of the New: A Study of Psalm 40:6–8 and Hebrews 10:5–10." In *Tradition and Testament.* Ed. J. S. and P. D. Feinberg. Chicago: Moody Press, 1981. 19–37. **Lacan, M. F.** "La source de l'assurance Chrétienne (Hébreux 10,1–39)." *BVC* 8 (1954–55) 89–94. **Lehne, S.** *The New Covenant in Hebrews.* JSNTSup 44. Sheffield: JSOT, 1990. **Levoratti, A. J.** "'Tú no has querido sacrificio ni oblación': Salmo 40,7; Hebreos 10,5." *RevistB* 48 (1986) 1–30, 65–87, 141–52, 193–237. **Loader, W. R. G.** "Christ at the Right Hand—Ps cx. 1 in the New Testament." *NTS* 24 (1977–78) 199–217. ———. *Sohn und Hoherpriester.* 170–80. **Nomoto, S.** "Herkunft und Struktur der Hohenpriestervorstellung im Hebräerbrief." *NovT* 10 (1965) 10–25. **Omanson, R. L.** "A Superior Covenant: Hebrews 8:1–10:18." *RevExp* 82 (1985) 361–73. **Peterson, D. G.** "An Examination of the Concept of 'Perfection' in the 'Epistle to the Hebrews.'" Dissertation, University of Manchester, 1978. 249–65. ———. "The Prophecy of the New Covenant in the Argument of Hebrews." *RTR* 38 (1979) 74–81. **Pinto, L. di.** *Volontà di Dio e legge antica nell'Epistola agli Ebrei.* Contributo ai fondamenti biblici della teologia morale. Naples: Pontificia Universitate Gregoriana, 1976. **Pryor, J. W.** "Hebrews and Incarnational Christology." *RTR* 40 (1981) 44–50. **Roark, D. M.** "The New Covenant." *ThEduc* 32 (1985) 63–68. **Schäfer, K. T.** "*ΚΕΦΑΛΙΣ ΒΙΒΛΙΟΥ.*" In *Weg zur Buchwissenschaft.* Ed. O. Wenig. Bonn: Bouvier, 1966. 1–10. **Schröger, F.** *Der Verfasser des Hebräerbriefes.* 172–79, 203–4, 206. **Selby, G. S.** "The Meaning and Function of *Syneidēsis* in Hebrews 9 and 10." *RestQ* 28 (1985–86) 145–154. **Sen, F.** "Se recupera la verdadera lectura de un texto muy citado, cuyo sentido cambia substancialmente (Hb 10:1)." *CB* 23 (1967) 165–68. **Smalley, S.** "Atonement in the Epistle to the Hebrews." *EvQ* 23 (1961) 36–43. **Stylianopoulos, T. G.** "Shadow and Reality: Reflections on Hebrews 10:1–18." *GOTR* 17 (1972) 215–30. **Taylor, F. J.** "The Will of God in the Epistle to the Hebrews." *ExpTim* 12 (1960–61) 167–69. **Vanhoye, A.** "Efficacité de l'offrande du Christ: He 10,11–14, 18." *AsSeign* 64 (1969) 41–46. ———. *Lectiones in Hebr. 10:1–39: De efficacia oblationis Christi et de vita christiana.* Rome: Biblical Institute, 1971–72 (*ad usum auditorum*). **Venard, L.** "L'utilization des Psaumes dans l'Épître aux Hébreux." 253–64. **Williamson, R.** "Platonism and Hebrews." *SJT* 16 (1963) 415–24. **Zimmermann, H.** *Das Bekenntnis der Hoffnung.* 116–28.

Translation

¹*For since the law possesses only a foreshadowing* [a] *of the good things which are to come, and not the actual form* [b] *of those realities,* [c] *it can* [d] *never decisively purge* [e] *those who draw near by the same sacrifices which are offered* [f] *continuously* [g] *year after year.* ²*(Otherwise,* [h] *would not these sacrifices have ceased to be offered, since the worshipers, once cleansed,* [i] *would have no consciousness of sins* [j] *any longer?* ³*In these sacrifices there is really* [k] *a reminder of sins year after year.)* ⁴*For it is impossible for the blood of bulls and goats to take away sins.*

⁵*So it is that when Christ* [l] *comes into the world he says,*

> *"You did not want sacrifice and offering,*
>   *but you have prepared a body*[m] *for me.*
> 6   *You did not like whole burnt offerings*
>   *and sin offerings.*[n]
> 7   *Then, I said,*
>   *'See, I have come*
>   *(it is written about me in the scroll*[o])
>   *to do your will, O God.'"*

[8] *After he said in the former part of the quotation,*[p] *"You did not want nor did you like sacrifices and offerings and whole burnt offerings and sin offerings" (namely those which are offered as the law prescribes*[q]*),* [9] *then he said, "See, I have come to do your will." He does away with*[r] *the first arrangement*[s] *in order to confirm the validity of*[t] *the second.* [10] *By that will*[u] *we have been consecrated through the offering of the body of Jesus Christ once for all.*[v]

[11] *Furthermore, every priest*[w] *stands*[x] *day after day performing his priestly service and offering repeatedly the same sacrifices such as can never remove sin utterly.*[y] [12] *But when this priest offered for all time*[z] *one sacrifice for sins, he sat down at God's right hand,* [13] *then waiting until his enemies are made*[aa] *his footstool,* [14] *because by one offering he has decisively purged*[bb] *forever those who are being consecrated.*[cc]

[15] *And the Holy Spirit also testifies to us. For after saying,*
> 16   *"'This is the covenant I will make with them*
>   *after that time,' declares the Lord,*
>   *'I will put my laws in their hearts*
>   *and inscribe them on their mind'";*
> 17 *then he adds,*[dd]
>   *"I will certainly not*[ee] *remember their sins and their*
>   *transgressions any longer."*

[18] *Now where there is a decisive putting away*[ff] *of these, an offering for sin is no longer necessary.*

Notes

[a] σκιάν is emphatic in the structure of the sentence. Moreover, when the ptcp ἔχων, "possessing," precedes the noun which it modifies, as here (ὁ νόμος, "the law"), it tends to add emphasis as well (see N. Turner, *Grammar*, 3:225).

[b] P[46], the earliest known copy of Hebrews, contains the unique reading καὶ τὴν εἰκόνα instead of οὐκ αὐτὴν τὴν εἰκόνα, giving the sense "since the law has only a shadow of the good things which are to come and the mere copy of those realities." The variant treats σκιά, "shadow," and εἰκών, "image," "copy," as complementary terms. This reading is defended as original by Cantalamessa (*Aeg* 45 [1965] 194–215) and Sen (*CB* 23 [1967] 165–68), and is regarded as possibly correct by Beare, *JBL* 63 (1944) 387–90. The construction of the sentence, however, implies a contrast between εἰκών and σκιά, which is well expressed by the formulation οὐκ αὐτὴν τὴν εἰκόνα, "not the actual form," which enjoys the combined weight of the rest of the textual tradition. The reading of P[46] should be rejected as an emendation of the original text by a scribe who was influenced by the traditional Platonic contrast of σκιά and εἰκών with reality itself (so Zuntz, *Text of the Epistles*, 20–23; Tasker, *NTS* 1 [1954–55] 182–83; Metzger, *Textual Commentary*, 669).

[c] The usage of the term πρᾶγμα in Hebrews is somewhat distinctive. Here it denotes reality itself (cf. 6:18: διὰ δύο πραγμάτων, "through two realities"). In both 6:18 and 10:1 the term is associated with God's eschatological promise of salvation.

[d] Although the pl form δύνανται is strongly attested (‭ℵ‬ A C D[1] P 33 81 *al*), it is incompatible with the sg form of the nom at the beginning of the sentence (ὁ νόμος, "the law"). It appears to be a

primitive error introduced by copyists who were influenced by the impersonal pl form προσφέρουσιν, "they offer" (so Zuntz, *Text of the Epistles,* 131; Metzger, *Textual Commentary,* 669). The sg form δύναται is supported by P[46] D[*,2] H K L Ψ 1739 *al.*

[e] For the shade of meaning in the verb τελειῶσαι in this context see *Note* u on the translation of the synonymous phrase τελειῶσαι τὸν λατρεύοντα, "decisively to purge the worshiper," in 9:9. This nuance has been recognized in *The New Testament in Basic English:* "to make . . . completely clean." See *Note* bb.

[f] The third person pl of the verb when used impersonally, as here, frequently has the force of a pass (cf. Zerwick, *Biblical Greek* §1; Moulton, *Grammar,* 1:58, 225).

[g] It has been argued that the adverbial expressions κατ' ἐνιαυτόν, "year after year," and εἰς τὸ διηνεκές, "for all time," are placed irregularly at the head of the clause to which they belong in order to emphasize the conceptions of annual repetition and perpetuity of effect, which characterize respectively the old and new covenants (e.g., Westcott, 305; H. Montefiore, 164; Michel, 331). This reading of the syntax is reflected in the NEB: "it can never bring the worshippers to perfection for all time." The use of εἰς τὸ διηνεκές in Hebrews, however, shows that in all other occurrences the adverbial expression follows the verb it qualifies (7:3; 10:12, 14). It should accordingly be applied to the preceding verb προσφέρουσιν rather than to the verb τελειῶσαι, which follows it. In this case it takes on the meaning "continually" and with κατ' ἐνιαυτόν reinforces the futility that attends the annual ritual of the Day of Atonement (see Peterson, "Examination," 252, n. 128; Stylianopoulos, *GOTR* 17 [1972] 229, n. 20).

[h] Reflecting a classical idiom, ἐπεί is used in an elliptical construction of a contrary-to-fact conditional clause cast in the form of a rhetorical question. The conj ἐπεί presupposes an implied protasis: "otherwise [if the law could have decisively purged its adherents], would these sacrifices not have ceased to be offered?" The same construction occurs in 9:26. The particle οὐκ in the interrogative expects the answer "Yes." Cf. Zerwick, *Biblical Greek* §313; BDF §§238–39, 260(2); Moule, *Idiom-Book,* 151.

[i] The perfect tense of the ptcp κεκαθαρισμένους implies a cleansing that is permanent.

[j] Elsewhere in Hebrews συνείδησις should be translated "conscience." Here, in combination with the obj gen ἁμαρτιῶν, it should be taken in the cognitive sense of "consciousness of sins" (Michel, 332, n. 4; cf. Maurer, *TDNT* 7:918; Peterson, "Examination," 252).

[k] The idiomatic use of ἀλλά as an adv particle rather than as an adversative conj occurs in literary Greek after both assertions and rhetorical questions (see *Note* s on 3:16). In such instances the original adversative quality is suppressed and the idea of assent is found. The idiom has been recognized here by AmT ("really"), Moffatt, and TEV ("as it is"). The parenthesis introduced in v 2 is continued in v 3. To treat v 3 as an adversative, as is usually done (RSV, NEB, JB, NIV), disrupts the argument and makes v 4 apply inappropriately to v 3 instead of to v 1. See Wikgren, "Some Greek Idioms," 150–51.

[l] A clue to the unexposed subject of the verb λέγει, "he says," is provided by the masc temporal ptcp εἰσερχόμενος, "when he comes." The specific reference to Christ is provided by 9:28.

[m] The citation in Hebrews reflects the text of the great uncials ℵ B A in reading σῶμα. The Rahlfs edition of the LXX reads ὠτία (with G, in conformity with the MT: "You have opened my ears"). Rather than treating the reading σῶμα as a corruption of an original ὠτία (Moffatt, 138), it is better to recognize in Ps 39:7 LXX an interpretive paraphrase of the MT. The Greek translators appear to have regarded the Heb. expression as an example of the part for the whole and translated the text in terms that express the whole for the part (cf. Stylianopoulos, *GOTR* 17 [1972] 229–30; F. F. Bruce, 232; P. E. Hughes, 386, n. 58). The translators of the OL certainly read σῶμα, not ὠτία, in their copies of the LXX.

[n] In accordance with LXX usage, περὶ ἁμαρτίας is a technical expression for the "sin offering" (cf. Moule, *Idiom-Book,* 63).

[o] In the LXX (Ps 39:7; Ezek 2:9; 3:1, 2, 3; 2 Esd 6:2) and in literature influenced by it, κεφαλίς denotes a "scroll," the form of the book that was customary prior to the time when the use of the codex became fashionable. If the qualifying term βιβλίου is understood as a gen of definition ("the book in scroll-form"), the phrase ἐν κεφαλίδι βιβλίου can be translated "in the scroll" (see Schäfer, "ΚΕΦΑΛΙΣ ΒΙΒΛΙΟΥ," 4, 8; Zerwick, *Biblical Greek* §45).

[p] The expression ἀνώτερον λέγων is the language of exegesis, in reference to the biblical citation quoted previously (cf. 2:8*b;* 8:13). The present ptcp λέγων is used to denote an action previous to the action of the main verb εἴρηκεν ("After he said . . . then he said"). Cf. Moule, *Idiom-Book,* 101.

[q] The translation of the parenthetical statement is problematical. If the pronoun αἵτινες is understood as a simple relative (as in 2:3; 10:11, 35), the proposition will be rendered "which are offered according to law" (so RSV, NASB). Alternatively, the proposition has been understood in a concessive

sense: "although the law required them to be made" (so NEB, TEV, NIV). Recently Andriessen has argued that in Hebrews the pronoun ὅστις and related forms are always used in a causative sense (cf. 8:6; 9:9; 13:7). He translates the parenthetical clause "because they were offered in a legalistic manner" (*En lisant*, 41). It seems better to recognize that αἵτινες does not appear here in a qualifying way. It serves rather to emphasize the relationship between the sacrifices and the law (so di Pinto, *Volontà di Dio*, 22).

ʳ The verb ἀναιρεῖν occurs only here in Hebrews and denotes "to suppress, to abolish, to annul." This nuance is unattested elsewhere in the NT but is amply documented in classical and hellenistic Greek, where the verb appears as a technical term in the juridical sphere. It has as its object public institutions, political regimes, commercial contracts, and wills (see di Pinto, *Volontà di Dio*, 26–27, with references). It is well suited to express a change of structures or arrangements.

ˢ The translation of τὸ πρῶτον as "the first arrangement" seeks to allow for the link between the sacrifices and the law, which is underscored by v 8b.

ᵗ The semantic value of στήσῃ reflects the usage of the LXX, where the verb ἱστάναι receives an intensification and a characteristic juridical aspect. It is a preferred word in the LXX for expressing the creative activity of God in the establishing of a covenant or the giving of an unconditional promise. It denotes "to establish, to remain valid" (e.g., Num 30:5, 6, 8, 12, 15; 1 Macc 13:38; 14:18, 24 LXX). See especially Num 30:12–16, where the paired verbs ἱστάναι, "to confirm," and περιαιρεῖν, "to invalidate, to annul," offer a close semantic parallel to the formulation in Heb 10:9b (di Pinto, *Volontà di Dio*, 27–29).

ᵘ The instrumental use of the prep ἐν can have a causal coloring: "by that will" or "because of that will" (BDF §118).

ᵛ There is a divergence of opinion on the focus of the term ἐφάπαξ, "once for all." It has been argued that the concern of 10:1–18 is the *result* of the death of Christ. Consequently, what is stressed in v 10 is not that the Lord died once for all, but that the salvation obtained for his people is eternal, one time for all. Accordingly, the term is to be attached to the expression ἡγιασμένοι ἐσμέν, "we have been consecrated": Christians are consecrated once for all by the sacrifice of Christ (cf. Westcott, 314; Michel, 339; Stählin, *TDNT* 1:384; Andriessen, *AsSeign* 8 [1972] 62). However, the periphrastic pf already has the effect of stressing a state of consecration resulting from some decisive event in the past. It is more likely that the term ἐφάπαξ defines the unique and definitive offering of the body of Jesus, as in 7:27; 9:12 (so Spicq, 2:306; P. E. Hughes, 399; Peterson, "Examination," 257).

ʷ The reading ἱερεύς is well supported by early and diverse witnesses (p¹³,⁴⁶ ℵ D K X 33 81 1739 it vg syʰ bo Ephr Chr). The variant reading ἀρχιερεύς, "high priest" (A C P 88 104 365 614 630 *al* syᵖ·ʰ sa mf arm aeth) appears to be a correction introduced by copyists under the influence of 5:1 or 8:3 (Metzger, *Textual Commentary*, 669–70).

ˣ The pf ἕστηκεν is intransitive with a present meaning (Zerwick and Grosvenor, *Grammatical Analysis*, 676).

ʸ The prep in the compound verb περιελεῖν has the perfective force, "to take away altogether," "to remove utterly." The aor tense expresses finality (A. T. Robertson, *Grammar*, 617).

ᶻ It seems more natural to relate εἰς τὸ διηνεκές to the ptcp προσενέγκας, "he offered for all time," than to treat it as the beginning of the next clause and to relate it to the verb ἐκάθισεν, "he sat down for all time" (so Moffatt, 140; Michel, 340). In Hebrews the adv expression normally follows the verb it qualifies (7:3; 10:1, 14). Cf. Stylianopoulos, *GOTR* 17 (1972) 222, n. 21.

ᵃᵃ The pass voice of τεθῶσιν implies "until his enemies are placed *by God* as a footstool under his feet."

ᵇᵇ The precise nuance in the verb τετελείωκεν is difficult to determine. The translation "decisively purged" follows Johnsson ("Defilement," 454) and has the merit of sustaining the emphasis of 9:9 and 10:1. The pf tense of the verb connotes an accomplished fact. As an alternative, Johnsson proposes to translate "he has incorporated those who are sanctified" (261–63). The notion of incorporation signifies a state rather than an act of becoming, and Johnsson argues that it is this view of τελειοῦν that is supported by the data of Heb 9–10.

ᶜᶜ The careful use of tenses in v 14 is remarkable. A suggestive contrast is involved. The pf tense of τετελείωκεν defines a work that is finished on its author's side, but that is progressively realized in the process depicted by the present ptcp. The force of τοὺς ἁγιαζομένους is purely durative, "those who are in the process of sanctification" (cf. Grothe, "Was Jesus the Priestly Messiah?" 165, n. 145). For τοὺς ἁγιαζομένους, p⁴⁶ substitutes τοὺς ἀνασῳζομένους, "those who are being saved."

ᵈᵈ These words are demanded by the context, but are left unexpressed in the early MS tradition. They are supplied by several later MSS and versions, in the form ὕστερον λέγει (69 104 323 945 1739 1881 *al* syʰᵐᵍ arm sa) or in the form τότε εἴρηκεν (1611 2495 *pc* syʰ). The dislocation in the text as transcribed in all other copies of the document may represent a primitive scribal error made when the autograph was first copied.

ᵉᵉ The double negative οὐ μή is used with the fut ind to express an emphatic negative for the fut (Zerwick, *Biblical Greek* §444).

ᶠᶠ The translation of ἄφεσις takes into account the distinctive use of the term in 9:22, where the nuance of the word must reflect the argument of the passage and its cultic setting. See Westcott, 269, who finds in ἄφεσις the broad sense of "deliverance, release," and Johnsson ("Defilement," 325–29, 454), who translates the verse "But where sins have been decisively put away, there is no longer an offering for them."

Form/Structure/Setting

It is imperative to situate 10:1–18 in its context within the homily. The writer devotes 7:1–10:18 to an exposition of distinctive features of the high priestly office of the Son. Three aspects of this subject were announced thematically in 5:9–10, and each is taken up for development (see *Introduction* to 5:11–10:39). The immediate concern of 7:1–25 is to clarify why Jesus has been designated a high priest like Melchizedek (cf. 5:10). The christological significance of Melchizedek, however, is limited because in the biblical account he has nothing to do with sacrifice. For that reason, in 7:26–28 the writer builds a bridge to the subsequent exposition in 8:1–10:18, where the sacrificial aspect of Jesus' office as high priest is elaborated. In this extended section the themes of covenant, sacrifice, and ministry are developed in concert. Jesus' singular qualification as high priest in the heavenly sanctuary is demonstrated in terms of his death and exaltation in 8:1–9:28 (cf. 5:9a). The writer then addresses the significance of designating Jesus "the source of eternal salvation for those who obey him" (5:9b) in 10:1–18. This final unit, which concludes and summarizes the exposition introduced with the thesis statement of 8:1–2, furnishes an appropriate climax to the main christological argument of Hebrews. The shift in literary genre from exposition to exhortation that occurs in 10:19–25 takes account of the perspectives developed in 8:1–10:18 and clarifies their relevance for the faith and life of the community addressed.

The integral relationship of 10:1–18 to 8:1–9:28 is established when earlier themes are recapitulated in the final segment of the exposition. In particular, the theme of the session at God's right hand, which was introduced with an allusion to Ps 110:1 in 8:1, is reiterated in 10:12–13 when the writer appeals to Ps 110:1 in reference to Christ's present status as exalted high priest. These allusions are located at the beginning and the conclusion of a development that is literarily and thematically unified. Moreover, the full citation of Jer 31:31–34 in 8:8–12 is called to mind when the salient portion of the quotation is repeated in 10:16–17. The discussion of the singular efficacy of Christ's high priestly ministry is thus framed by the allusions to Ps 110:1 and the citations of Jer 31:31–34.

There is also a degree of correspondence between the ideas elaborated in 9:1–28 and in 10:1–18. Corresponding to the exposition of the cultic provisions of the Sinai covenant in 9:1–10 is the delineation of the ineffectiveness of the repeated sacrifices in 10:1–4. The superior achievement of Christ's sacrifice as set forth in 9:11–14 is considered in its prophetic and historical aspects in 10:5–10. The presentation of the death of Christ as the sacrifice that inaugurated the new covenant in 9:15–28 finds its complement in 10:11–18. These correspondences have led at least one interpreter to insist on the literary and thematic unity of

8:1–10:18 and to argue that this unit is to be understood against the background of the Christian celebration of Pentecost as the feast of the covenant (Gourgues, *A la droite de Dieu*, 110–14; id., *RB* 83 [1976] 5–24; cf. id., *RB* 84 [1977] 26–37).

It is important not to obscure the continuity in argument in 9:1–10:18. But it is also necessary to recognize that a fundamental shift in perspective occurs in 10:1–18. In 9:11–28 the writer considers the "objective" benefits of Christ's sacrificial offering. The point of focus is the accomplishment of Christ through his death in terms of his entrance into the heavenly sanctuary in fulfillment of God's eternal plan of redemption. But in 10:1–18 the writer elaborates the "subjective" effects of Christ's offering for the community that enjoys the blessings of the new covenant. Christ's death is considered from the perspective of its efficacy for Christians. In terms of the logical structure, 9:15–28 clarifies the character of the objective salvation summarized in 9:11–12. The function of 10:1–18 is to clarify the subjective benefits of salvation reviewed in 9:13–14, where the writer referred specifically to the decisive purgation of the conscience of the worshiper (cf. Johnsson, "Defilement," 217–19, 338). The focus upon the new situation of the worshiping community achieved through the efficacy of Christ's sacrifice gives to 10:1–18 a distinctive thrust.

The reference in the final clause of 9:28 to the salvation by the eschatological high priest for those who eagerly wait for him constitutes a fresh announcement of the subject to be developed in 10:1–18. A striking contrast marks the transition to the new unit. The writer juxtaposes the single, unrepeatable nature of Christ's offering (9:28) and the perpetual repetition of the sacrifices prescribed by the law (10:1). The characteristic terms of the section are those associated with the offering of sacrifice for sins: "to offer sacrifice" ($\pi\rho o\sigma\phi\acute{\epsilon}\rho\epsilon\iota\nu$, 10:1, 2, 8, 11, 12), "offering" ($\pi\rho o\sigma\phi o\rho\acute{\alpha}$, 10:5, 8, 10, 14, 18, and not elsewhere in Hebrews), "sacrifice" ($\theta\upsilon\sigma\acute{\iota}\alpha$, 10:1, 5, 8, 11, 12), and "sins" ($\dot{\alpha}\mu\alpha\rho\tau\acute{\iota}\alpha\iota$, 10:2, 3, 6, 8, 12, 17, 18). The density of this vocabulary gives a unitary character to the section (cf. Vanhoye, *La structure*, 44, 162–63). Between the initial statement in 10:1 and the final statement of the section in 10:18 there is a correspondence by opposition. Under the law "the same sacrifices are offered continuously" (v 1); by contrast, as a result of the one offering of Christ "an offering for sins is no longer necessary" (v 18).

The argument in 10:1–18 progresses in four paragraphs arranged in concentric symmetry:

A The inadequacy of the provisions of the law for repeated sacrifices (10:1–4).
  B The repeated sacrifices have been superseded by the one sacrifice of Christ in conformity to the will of God (10:5–10).
  B' The Levitical priests have been superseded by the one priest enthroned at God's right hand (10:11–14).
A' The adequacy of the provisions of the new covenant, which render a sacrifice for sins no longer necessary (10:15–18).

The concluding paragraph responds to the situation described in the initial paragraph. The two intermediary paragraphs reflect a similar perspective. They confirm the decisive character of the purgation achieved through the one sacrifice of Christ (cf. Vanhoye, *La structure*, 162–72, whose analysis is similar, but who prefers to limit the initial paragraph to 10:1–3 and to associate v 4 with the second paragraph; the unfortunate effect is to obscure the fact that v 4 supplies the reason for the assertion made in v 1).

The literary structure of the section is sufficiently indicated by the parallel symmetry in the concluding statements to the second, third, and fourth paragraphs:

"we have been *consecrated* through the *offering*" (v 10);
"by one *offering* he has decisively purged those who are being
    consecrated" (v 14);
"where there is a decisive putting away of these, an *offering* . . .
    is no longer necessary" (v 18).

This kind of literary correspondence belongs to a strophic technique known as *responsio* and is used rhetorically to place elements of successive paragraphs in relationship (cf. Vanhoye, *La structure,* 60–61, n. 2; 169, n. 1). Its employment in 10:1–18 discloses the structure of the section more clearly and completely than the writer's customary device of *inclusio.*

Comment

The exposition in 10:1–18 brings the strictly cultic argument in Hebrews to a close. The writer's specific concern is with the purging of the conscience (cf. 9:9, 14). The sacrifices prescribed by the law were incapable of achieving decisive purgation; they could not remove the consciousness of sins (10:1–4). Their ineffectiveness in this regard exposed a fundamental weakness in the cultic provisions of the old covenant. The law was effectively precluded from becoming the organ of salvation. This realization demonstrated the necessity for the enactment of the new covenant, with its promise that God will not remember sins any longer, as the true organ of salvation (10:15–18). This entailed the repudiation of the many sacrifices prescribed by the law in favor of the one offering of the body of Jesus (10:5–10) and the rejection of the ineffective ministry of the Levitical priests in favor of the effective ministry of the eschatological priest enthroned in the presence of God (10:11–14). The argument serves to sharpen an appreciation of the ultimate character of Christ's single, personal sacrifice for sins. It also establishes a context for defining the blessings of the new covenant that were secured through his death.

1 The insufficiency of the sacrifices prescribed by the law to provide unhindered access to God is attested by the necessity of offering them continuously year after year. That the writer is recapitulating an earlier theme (8:3–5; 9:23–26) is indicated by the conjunction γάρ, "for." Previously the Levitical priests were characterized as serving a sanctuary that was a "shadowy suggestion" (ὑπόδειγμα καὶ σκιά) of the heavenly sanctuary (8:5). Now the law is described as a "foreshadowing [σκιά] of the good things which are to come." The term σκιά does not signify unreal or deceptive, as in Platonism, but rather imperfect or incomplete. Its use suggests that the function of the law was to point forward to that which was perfect or complete. The term reflects not Platonic idealism but the eschatological outlook of primitive Christianity. The contrast implied is temporal and eschatological in character; the law is a past witness to a future reality (cf.

Williamson, *Philo*, 174–75, 566–70). As a witness to the eschatological salvation that was clearly future from the vantage point of the law, the law can be described as possessing a foreshadowing quality (so Barrett, "Eschatology," 386; cf. Schulz, *TDNT* 7:398, who notes that in Hebrews σκιά occurs in this sense only in the section 8:1–10:18). The substantive participle τῶν μελλόντων ἀγαθῶν, "the good things which are to come," expresses the contrast between the preliminary and incomplete character of the law and the full salvation that was foreshadowed by its cultic provisions.

The construction of the sentence requires a sharp distinction between σκιά and εἰκών ("the actual form" which cast the shadow). The fact that the pronoun αὐτήν, "itself," is prefixed to the term εἰκών confirms this interpretation. The law possesses a foreshadowing of the future reality but οὐκ αὐτὴν τὴν εἰκόνα, "not the actual form," of the embodied realities (see *Note* b above). In this context εἰκών has the meaning "embodiment" or "actual presence" and has as its referent transcendent reality (cf. Kleinknecht, *TDNT* 2:388–89; Kittel, *TDNT* 2:395, who emphasizes that in the NT there is a strong organic connection between εἰκών and that which it represents; Nomoto, *NovT* 10 [1965] 23, who finds in the formulation evidence of a commonly confessed pattern of tradition in the hellenistic-Jewish Christian community). The most natural way to read the statement is to interpret τῶν μελλόντων ἀγαθῶν, "the good things which are to come," and τῶν πραγμάτων, "those realities," as equivalent expressions that refer to the blessings of the new age, which are here viewed from the perspective of the law (Peterson, "Examination," 250–51). The formulation of v 1 recalls 9:11, where Christ is described as "high priest of the good things which have now come" (τῶν γενομένων ἀγαθῶν). The reality only foreshadowed in the law is the actual possession of the people of God through the new covenant (so Michel, 331; cf. Schierse, *Verheissung und Heilsvollendung*, 44–45; Cody, *Heavenly Sanctuary*, 138–41).

The conclusion that the old cultus sanctioned by the law was incapable of achieving the decisive purgation of worshipers is a restatement of the argument in 7:11 and 19. As in the LXX (e.g., Exod 16:9; 34:32; Lev 9:5; Num 10:3a), the verb προσέρχεσθαι, "to draw near," is used to designate the wider circle of worshipers, on whose behalf the sacrifices have been offered, who draw near to God in solemn assembly (Riggenbach, 297; Michel, 331–34; Peterson, "Examination," 251; against Delling, *TDNT* 8:83, who takes both προσέρχεσθαι and τελειῶσαι as technical terms relating strictly to priestly ministry). As in 7:11 and 19, the concept of "perfection" occurs in a cultic context, where the object of the verb τελειῶσαι is the people of God in their role as worshipers, i.e., as those who would draw near to God. They sought through the sacrifices a decisive purgation which the Levitical cultus could not provide (see *Comment* on 9:9; 10:2). The failure of the law in this respect is underscored by expressions that convey a notion of futility: the same sacrifices are offered continually (εἰς τὸ διηνεκές) year after year (κατ᾽ ἐνιαυτόν). The reference is unmistakably to the Day of Atonement (9:25, κατ᾽ ἐνιαυτόν; cf. 9:7). The legal provision for an annual observance of the Day of Atonement was a candid acknowledgment that the sacrifices offered each year lacked ultimate efficacy (so Peterson, "Examination," 252, n. 128; cf. Stylianopoulos, *GOTR* 17 [1972] 229).

2–3 The implication of the obligation to repeat the same sort of sacrifices every year is clarified by an appeal to experience. The writer comments parenthetically that if these sacrifices had been genuinely efficacious, all sense of the collective consciousness of defilement would have been removed from the worshipers. The expression τοὺς λατρεύοντας is parallel to τοὺς προσερχομένους in v 1 and refers to worshipers in general (so Peterson, "Examination," 230–31, 251, against Strathmann, *TDNT* 4:63–64, who appeals to 8:5 and 13:10 to support his argument that λατρεύειν must be a technical term for priestly ministry here). The argument concerns the relationship of worshipers to God and the whole process of consecration to the service of God.

Under the old covenant worshipers never experienced a definitive cleansing. The participle κεκαθαρισμένους, "cleansed," is qualified by ἅπαξ, "once for all," to distinguish a cleansing with finality from an experience of purgation that will have to be repeated (cf. 9:13). Even on the occasion of the awesome ceremonies associated with the ritual of the Day of Atonement worshipers continued to have a "consciousness of sins" (συνείδησιν ἁμαρτιῶν). This expression connotes the Hebrew sense of a burdened, smitten heart, which became most pronounced on the Day of Atonement when it was necessary to confront the holiness of God (H. K. LaRondelle, *Perfection and Perfectionism* [Kampen: Kok, 1971] 240–41; cf. C. A. Pierce, *Conscience in the New Testament* [Naperville, IL: Allenson, 1955] 26, 99–102; J. Stelzenberger, *Syneidesis im Neuen Testament* [Paderborn: Schöningh, 1961] 56–61). As long as this sense of sin and transgression with respect to God remained, there could be no effective service of God. A decisive cleansing of the conscience is a prerequisite for unhindered access to God (10:22), and this has been achieved only through the sacrifice of Christ (see *Comment* on 9:14).

The Day of Atonement was designated as a day for fasting (Lev 23:26–32) and the confession of sins (Lev 16:20–22). The elaborate ritual was intended to accentuate a consciousness of sins. The solemn entrance of the high priest into the Most Holy Place dramatized the fact that sin separates the congregation from God. From this perspective, the sacrifices really provided ἀνάμνησις ἁμαρτιῶν, "a reminder of sins," which brought to the consciousness of the worshipers the reality of their sins as an obstacle to fellowship with God. This sober evaluation of the negative function of the Day of Atonement ritual stands in striking contrast to an older Jewish formulation from the time of the Maccabees: "It is written and ordained that he will show mercy to all who turn from their guilt once a year" (*Jub.* 5:18; for Philo's treatment of this theme see Williamson, *Philo,* 160–76). What impressed the writer of Hebrews was that a remembrance of sins, which constituted a barrier to worship, was confirmed and renewed κατ' ἐνιαυτόν, "year after year," by the annual Day of Atonement ritual.

4 The reason that the law is incapable of providing decisive purgation to those who approach God through the atonement sacrifices (v 1) is supplied in the axiomatic statement of v 4. The two verses are linked together by the explanatory clause ἀδύνατον γάρ, "for it is impossible," which resumes the οὐδέποτε δύναται, "can never," of v 1, and by the expression αἷμα ταύρων καὶ τράγων, "the blood of bulls and goats," which corresponds to ταῖς αὐταῖς θυσίαις, "the same sacrifices," in v 1. The argument presupposes the potency of blood for securing cleansing from defilement acknowledged in 9:22: the blood of animals cannot effect a definitive removal of sins. The issue is not whether the blood of bulls and goats sacrificed during the annual observances of the Day of Atonement (Lev 16:3, 6, 11, 14–16, 18–19) has any power to effect cleansing, but whether it has the potency to effect a *decisive* cleansing. The axiom in v 4 restates the εἰ γὰρ . . . πόσῳ μᾶλλον construction in 9:13–14 ("for if . . . how much more!"). There the writer stressed the sufficiency of the blood of Christ to effect the decisive purgation of conscience, making possible the full worship of God. Here the accent is placed on the insufficiency of the blood of sacrificial animals to remove the defilement of sins that constitutes a barrier to worship (so Johnsson, "Defilement," 340–41; cf. Stylianopoulos, *GOTR* 17 [1972] 225–26). The expression ἀφαιρεῖν ἁμαρτίας, "to take away sins," is unusual (cf. περιελεῖν ἁμαρτίας, "to remove sins," in v 11). It conveys the sense of a "burden" that needed lifting (cf. Lev 10:17; Num 14:18; Isa 1:16; 6:7; 27:9; Ezek 45:9 LXX, cited by Peterson, "Examination," 253).

5–7 In the following paragraph (vv 5–10) the writer argues that the ineffective sacrifices of the old covenant have been superseded by the sufficient sacrifice of Christ. The cultic arrangements of the Levitical law, with its annual provision for atonement, have been set aside. The basis for the consecration of the new covenant community to the service of God is the unrepeatable offering of the body of Jesus Christ in fulfillment of the will of God. In developing this point the writer makes effective use of homiletical midrash, citing an OT text and commenting upon it (see *Comment* on 2:6–9; 3:7–4:11). He appeals to Ps 40:6–8 (39:7–9 LXX) to demonstrate that it had been prophesied in Scripture that God would accord superior status to a human body as the instrument for accomplishing his will over the sacrificial offerings prescribed by the law. The text of the prophecy implied the discontinuance of the old cultus because of the arrival of the new (cf. Johnsson, "Defilement," 341–44).

The words of Ps 40:6–8 are envisaged as being in the mouth of Christ. The statement Ἰδοὺ ἥκω, "See, I have come," furnishes the basis for attributing these verses of the psalm to Jesus at the moment when he entered the world. The temporal expression εἰσερχόμενος εἰς τὸν κόσμον, "when he comes into the world," is distinctly "incarnational" language (Stylianopoulos, *GOTR* 17 [1972] 229, n. 36).

The quotation follows closely the LXX, as transmitted in the principal manuscripts ℵ B A (see *Note* m above). The most notable divergence from the MT is the translation of the second line:

MT: "but you have pierced my ears";
LXX: "but you have prepared a body for me."

The detail that God had prepared a body (σῶμα) for the speaker, who entered the world to do God's will, accounts for the writer's selection of this quotation. It not only indicated that the incarnation and active obedience of Christ had been prophesied in Scripture, but it provided biblical support for the subsequent argument that the "offering of the body (σώματος) of Jesus Christ" was qualitatively superior to the offerings prescribed by law (vv 8–10). The writer seized upon the term σῶμα and made it pivotal for his interpretation of the text. Customarily he uses the word σάρξ, "flesh," to refer to the full humanity of Jesus (2:14; 5:7). The use of the equivalent term σῶμα in v 10 to designate the human body of Jesus constituted a deliberate allusion to the text of the psalm cited in v 5 (Johnsson, "Defilement," 344–45). Elsewhere σῶμα is practically never used in the discussion of sacrifice (cf. Gen 15:11 LXX; *Apoc. Abr.* 13:3, cited by Schweizer, *TDNT* 7:1058).

In the final line of the quotation (v 7d) the writer's text differs from the LXX formulation in three respects:

LXX τοῦ ποιῆσαι τὸ θέλημά σου, ὁ θεός μου, ἐβουλήθην
"I desired to do your will, O my God";
v 7d τοῦ ποιῆσαι, ὁ θεός, τὸ θέλημά σου
"to do your will, O God."

The writer omits the personal pronoun μου, "my," transposes ὁ θεός, "O God," and deletes the final word ἐβουλήθην, "I desired." The resultant clause is made to depend upon the preceding γέγραπται, "it is written," in v 7c rather than upon the verb ἐβουλήθην as in the LXX. The effect of these changes is to make the text more directly applicable to the Son of God who entered the world in fulfillment of the prophetic Scriptures to do the will of God. The changes appear to have been made for the sake of emphasis. It is probable that the writer himself was responsible for the adaptation of the text in the light of its application to Jesus (so McCullough, *NTS* 26 [1979–80] 369; cf. Kistemaker, *Psalm Citations*, 43–44, 87–88, 124–30; Schröger, *Verfasser*, 172–77).

God's dissatisfaction with the conventional sacrificial offerings because they failed to express a corresponding desire to obey his will is a recurring motif in the prophetic Scriptures (e.g., 1 Sam 15:22; Ps 40:6; 50:8–10; 51:16–17; Isa 1:10–13; 66:2–4; Jer 7:21–24, Hos 6:6; Amos 5:21–27). The offering that God finds acceptable represents devotion from the heart. In 10:1–4 the writer had referred to animal sacrifice as a means of achieving decisive purgation. The citation of Ps 40:6–8 in vv 5–7 indicates that the focal point of concern has shifted. The point at issue here is the relative value of the prescribed sacrifices as a means of consecration to the service of God. The quotation attests that sacrifices in themselves are powerless to please God or to secure a proper relationship between God and his people. The psalm refers to a speaker who recognizes his body as the gift God has prepared to be the means by which the divine will may be accomplished. Behind that reference the writer of Hebrews recognizes the figure of the transcendent Son of God who became man in order to fulfill the divine purpose for the human family (2:10, 14, 17). Whether the parenthetical mention of the scroll which marked out the path of obedience for the Son (v 7c) has reference to the whole OT or to a single book must be left undecided (so Schäfer, "ΚΕΦΑΛΙΣ ΒΙΒΛΙΟΥ," 1). The writer understands the cited passage as a word addressed by the Son to the Father on the occasion of the incarnation, which the psalmist, as it were, overheard (Andriessen, *AsSeign* 8 [1972] 59–60; cf. Peterson, "Examination," 254–56). The attribution of the words of the psalm to Christ links the Incarnation explicitly to the accomplishment of the will of God.

8–9 The transition to the explanation of the quotation is introduced by common exegetical expressions, ἀνώτερον λέγων . . . τότε εἴρηκεν, "After he said in the former part of the quotation . . . then he said." The repetition of phrases and clauses from the citation indicates the points of emphasis in the writer's reading of the biblical text. With powerful concentration he divides his remarks on the passage into two parts. In the first he underscores the divine rejection of the conventional sacrifices. By conflating the two parallel lines of the quotation that refer to the various types of offerings, a single, emphatic contrast emerges instead of the two implied in the psalm itself. This is an important modification, for it enables the writer to distinguish sharply between "the first" and "the second" in v 9*b* (observed by Stylianopoulos, *GOTR* 17 [1972] 229). The resulting parataxis, with the four different words for sacrifice strung together ("sacrifices and offerings and whole burnt offerings and sin offerings") and the two verbal expressions of disapproval joined (v 8*a*), serves to intensify an impression of the divine disdain for the cultic provisions of the old covenant. The four terms for sacrifice in the psalm appear to include the main types of offerings prescribed in the Levitical code (so Spicq 2:306; P. E. Hughes, 397, n. 60). The alteration of the singular in the expression θυσίαν καὶ προσφοράν, "sacrifice and offering," in v 5 to the plural form when the psalm text is taken up in v 8 indicates that it is not a question of all sacrifice but of the multiplicity of the legal sacrifices that is in view. The multiplicity and repetition of the legal sacrifices unveils their fundamental inadequacy (Stylianopoulos, *GOTR* 17 [1972] 222; cf. Andriessen, *AsSeign* 8 [1972] 60).

Apart from the rearrangement of the lines and the alteration of the singular to the plural, the writer limits his interpretation of the passage to a single parenthetical remark: the unwanted and disliked sacrifices are precisely those the law prescribed (v 8*b*). This comment makes the relationship between the repetition of the sacrifices and the law explicit (cf. v 1) and relegates the sacrifices of the old cultus to the period when God's arrangement with his people was regulated by law (cf. Peterson, "Examination," 255; di Pinto, *Volontà di Dio,* 22).

The writer then draws attention to the final part of the quotation in v 7. He abridges the text to secure the pregnant formulation, "See, I have come to do your will" (v 9*a*). This represents for the writer the essential utterance of Christ attested by the psalm. It ties Christ's mission to a preoccupation with the will of God and prepares for the significant conclusion that the offering of Christ is the sacrifice God desired to be made (cf. A. B. Davidson, 193–94; Johnsson, "Defilement," 344–46). The significance of Christ's announcement to redemptive history is posited in the terse formulation of v 9*b*: "he does away with the first arrangement in order to confirm the validity of the second." That statement affirms the creation of a qualitatively new foundation for the consecration of worshipers to the service of God.

The contrast between the old and the new arrangement is accentuated by the solemn cadence and chiastic construction of v 9*b*:

ἀναιρεῖ	τὸ πρῶτον	ἵνα	τὸ δεύτερον	στήσῃ
A	B		B'	A'

The terms ἀναιρεῖν, "to suppress, abolish," and ἱστάναι, "to establish, to confirm as valid," give the declaration a strong juridical flavor (see *Notes* r and t). The content of τὸ πρῶτον, "the first," is defined by the structural link between the law and the cultic sacrifices established in v 8*b*. The old cult and the law upon which it was based are set aside on the strength of an event in which there was concentrated all the efficacy of a life fully submitted to the will of God. The content of τὸ δεύτερον, "the second," which is placed in antithesis to "the first arrangement," is defined by the will of God as realized through Jesus. In v 10 the mode of that realization is specified as "the offering of the body of Jesus Christ once for all."

Thus the second clause in v 9*b* contains a condensed reference to all the efficacy of the saving action of Christ in conformity to the will of God.

On this reading of the text, what has been set aside are the repeated sacrifices and the law which prescribed them. What has been confirmed as valid is the structural link between the will of God and the effective sacrifice of Christ (see especially, di Pinto, *Volontà di Dio,* 23–30; cf. Vanhoye, *La structure,* 166, 170). The statement in v 9*b* has rightly been characterized as one of the epochal formulations of the NT (e.g., Schierse, *Verheissung,* 66: "revolutionary principle"; 169: "the fundamental eschatological principle" of the author). The fulfillment of Ps 40:6–8 inaugurates the new arrangement. The quotation from the psalm and the event of Christ confirm that the old religious order has been abolished definitively. In the design of God, the two redemptive arrangements are irreconcilable; the one excludes the other. The suppression of the first occurs in order that (ἵνα) the validity of the new order of relationship may be confirmed (cf. 8:7, 13). Jesus Christ and the word of Scripture are agents of epochal change that introduce a radically new situation for the community of God's people (di Pinto, *Volontà di Dio,* 30–33; cf. Michel, 337–39).

10 In his application of the biblical text, the writer stresses the communal experience of consecration to the service of God. The old sacrifices were deficient because they did not entail the genuine consecration of the one who offered them. The shift from the use of the third person singular in v 9*b* to the first person plural ("we have been consecrated") lends to the formulation of v 10 a confessional quality (cf. Michel, 338; di Pinto, *Volontà di Dio,* 41–44). In a statement remarkable for its density, the writer defines the means and the ultimate source of consecration. The immediate ground of consecration is the totally new offering of the body of Jesus Christ as the inaugural act of the new covenant. The ultimate source is the will of God (cf. di Pinto, *Volontà di Dio,* 10–11; Johnsson, "Defilement," 344–45).

Certain expressions in v 10 have been borrowed from the psalm quotation, namely, the references to the divine will, the offering, and the body. The phrase ἐν ᾧ θελήματι, "by that will," interprets the expression τοῦ ποιῆσαι τὸ θέλημά σου, "to do your will," cited in vv 7 and 9*a*. The will of God that Christ came to accomplish is the will by which we are intimately transformed and consecrated to God. The word προσφορά, "offering," first occurs as a term for sacrifice in the LXX (Ps 39:7; Dan 3:38) and in writings influenced by the LXX. Its use to specify the sacrifice of Christ in vv 10 and 14 reflects this development (Weiss, *TDNT* 9:68) and makes explicit the intention of the aorist infinitive ποιῆσαι, "to do," in vv 7 and 9. The will of God involved "the offering" made by Christ. The reference to the body (σώματος) of Jesus Christ constitutes a clear allusion to the utterance in v 5, "You prepared a body [σῶμα] for me." The body of Jesus was the instrument of his solidarity with the human race (cf. 2:14). He entered the world to do the will of God; in him, intention and the commitment of the body were perfectly integrated. The term "body" shows that the contrast the writer wishes to establish is not between the sacrifice of animals and the sacrifice of obedience, but between the ineffective sacrifice of animals and the personal offering of Christ's own body as the one complete and effective sacrifice (cf. F. J. Taylor, *ExpTim* 12 [1960–61] 168–69; W. Manson, *Epistle to the Hebrews,* 144–45; di Pinto, *Volontà di Dio,* 54, 59).

The remaining terms in v 10 are among the preferred expressions of the writer. From the psalm the writer looks to Jesus and to the value of his death on the cross. The verb ἁγιάζειν denotes a definitive consecration expressed in heart-obedience toward God. The periphrastic participle ἡγιασμένοι ἐσμέν, "we have been consecrated," anticipates the description of the new people of God in v 14 as τοὺς ἁγιαζομένους, "those who are being consecrated" (cf. 2:11). The use of the term ἐφάπαξ, "once for all," to qualify the reference to the offering of the body of Christ evokes the crucifixion as the climax of a life and ministry that perfectly displayed submission to the will of God (cf. 7:27; 13:12). In the sacrifice of his body on the cross, Christ freely and fully made the will of God his own. Consequently, his sacrifice requires no repetition. It embodied the totality of obedience and eradicated the disparity between sacrifice and obedience presupposed by Ps 40:6–8. Christ's self-sacrifice fulfilled the human vocation enunciated in the psalm. By virtue of the fact that he did so under the conditions of authentic human, bodily existence and in solidarity with the human family, the new people of God have been radically transformed and consecrated to his service (cf. di Pinto, *Volontà di Dio*, 49–52; Deichgräber, *ZNW* 52 [1961] 119–22; Vanhoye, *Lectiones in Hebr. 10:1–39*, 61–64).

11 The contrast between the earthly priests who offer sacrifices that are incapable of removing sins and consequently must be repeated each day (v 11) and the priest of the new covenant (vv 12–14) sustains the comparison of the relative efficacy of the offerings of the old and new covenants respectively, which was underscored in the previous argument. The daily course of the Levitical service is described in the manner similar to v 1:

10:1	10:11
κατ᾽ ἐνιαυτόν	καθ᾽ ἡμέραν
"year by year"	"day by day"
αὐταῖς θυσίαις	αὐτὰς . . . θυσίας
"the same sacrifices"	"the same . . . sacrifices"
οὐδέποτε δύναται . . . τελειῶσαι	οὐδέποτε δύνανται περιελεῖν
"can never . . . decisively purge"	"can never remove utterly"

The posture of the priests in the performance of their functions was decreed by divine mandate: priests stand in order to sacrifice (Deut 18:5). This fact is stressed in v 11: every priest stands (ἔστηκεν) in diligent performance of his priestly duties because his work is never completed. He ministers "day after day," observing the yearly cycle of the daily sacrifices. He offers "the same sacrifices" "repeatedly" (πολλάκις), "which can never remove sins utterly." The cumulative effect of these phrases is a heightened impression of the futility that characterizes the ministry of the Levitical priests. The argument of 10:1–4 is reiterated forcefully here because it has been condensed to a single statement. Despite all the effort and the accumulated offerings of the old priesthood, there was an entrenched inability to remove sins.

12–14 Point by point the contrast in situation between the earthly priests and the heavenly priest is sharply drawn (cf. Vanhoye, *La structure*, 167, for an analysis of the concentric symmetry in the construction of v 11 and vv 12–13). Christ offered only a single sacrifice for sins (μίαν ὑπὲρ ἁμαρτιῶν . . . θυσίαν). The description of his activity provides a stark contrast to the corresponding phrase in the previous verse: the Levitical priest stands προσφέρων θυσίας, "offering sacrifices"; he προσενέγκας θυσίαν, "offered [one] sacrifice." The aorist tense of the verb indicates here that the action is past and complete. The effectiveness of his single offering extends "for all time" (εἰς τὸ διηνεκές). Even his posture declares the sharp difference between Christ and the Levitical priests. His unique sacrifice accomplished, "he sat down [ἐκάθισεν] at the right hand of God." The allusion to Ps 110:1 resumes the thesis statement in 8:1–2 and reinforces the image of Christ as the enthroned priest. The concept of Christ's session in the presence of God was first introduced in 1:3, but only now is its significance for the writer's argument clarified. Jesus sits because his sacrifice requires no repetition. His heavenly session attests that the benefits of his sacrificial death endure perpetually. The sacrificial phase of his priestly ministry is completed. Hay observes that the writer comes closer here than anywhere else in the homily to presenting Christ's death and heavenly session as a single theological event (*Glory*, 152; cf. Käsemann, *Das wandernde Gottesvolk*, 148).

The fact that Jesus waits for his enemies to be subdued beneath him (v 13) does not imply that he sits motionless (as argued by Hay, *Glory at the Right Hand*, 36–38, 87–91, 125–26). Earlier in the homily the writer associated Jesus' session with his active ministry of intercession on behalf of those who approach God through him (7:25). The session at the right hand puts Christ in a position where he may provide assistance to his people without having to offer sacrifices. The allusion to Ps 110:1 in vv 12–13 insists on the established firmness of his position. For the future he has only to wait for the complete subjugation of every power that resists the gracious redemptive purposes of God. Jesus' place in the presence of God enables him to exercise in heaven the ministry of the new covenant. This is the basis of the assurance extended to the community that they possess now full access to God (10:19–22; cf. Loader, *NTS* 24 [1977–78] 206; Gourgues, *A la droite de Dieu*, 113–14, 118–19). Although no priest of Aaron's line ever sat down in the presence of God in the earthly sanctuary, Christ has done so in the heavenly sanctuary (8:1–2).

The decisive character of Christ's finished work is underscored in v 14. The writer's statement is tied to his preceding argument by the explanatory conjunction γάρ, "for." The means by which the community has experienced definitive purging is the sacrificial death of Christ. The expression μιᾷ . . . προσφορᾷ, "by means of one offering," resumes the references to "the offering [προσφορά] of the body of Jesus Christ" in v 10 and to the "one sacrifice" (μίαν . . . θυσίαν) he offered in v 12. The stress in v 14, however, falls on the clause "he decisively purged forever," where the perfect tense of the verb τετελείωκεν in combination with the temporal expression εἰς τὸ διηνεκές emphasizes the permanent result of Christ's offering. The writer locates the decisive purging of believers in the past with respect to its accomplishment and in the present with respect to its enjoyment. Peterson rightly comments that the perfection of worshipers, which could not be achieved on the basis of the Levitical priesthood (7:11), the law, and its sacrifices (7:19; 9:9; 10:1), is announced in vv 12–14 as the accomplishment of Christ through his single offering for sins ("Examination," 259–60).

A decisive purging was the prerequisite to the consecration of the people of the new covenant. It is proper, therefore, to interpret the expression τετελείωκεν in the light of the description of the community as "the consecrated ones." If the present participle τοὺς ἁγιαζομένους is a timeless designation of the community of faith, it describes the result of Christ's sacrifice, which confers on his people definitive consecration, qualifying them for fellowship with God. Correspondingly, Christ is the consecrator (ὁ ἁγιάζων, 2:11) par excellence by virtue of his atoning death (cf. Riggenbach, 307–8; Peterson, "Examination," 260–65).

15 The writer finds confirmation of his argument in the witness of the Holy Spirit attested in Scripture (see *Comment* on 3:7*a*; cf. 9:8). The present tense of the verb in the introductory formula μαρτυρεῖ . . . καὶ τὸ πνεῦμα τὸ ἅγιον, "the Holy Spirit also bears witness," is significant; it indicates that through the quotation of the prophetic oracle the Holy Spirit is speaking now. The Spirit brings the detail of the text from the past into the present and makes it contemporary with the experience of the readers. The promises given on the occasion when God announced his intention to enact a new covenant have immediate relevance for the community addressed in the homily.

16–17 The quotation of Jer 31:31–34 in 8:7–12 served to situate the cultic argument of 8:1–10:18 in the context of a discussion of covenant. The perspective at that point was the time of Jeremiah: the reference to a new covenant implied that the old covenant was outdated and would soon disappear (8:13). The perspective in 10:15–18 is different. What was a future expectation in the time of Jeremiah has become a present reality as a result of the event of Christ's death on the cross. In consequence, the situation of the Christian community is now prominently in view.

By directing the attention of his auditors once again to the oracle in an abbreviated form in vv 16–17, the writer makes it clear that the preceding discussion of sacrifice and priesthood is to be related to the prophecy of the new covenant. The writer interprets the text in priestly and sacrificial terms because he views the old covenant in these terms. He recognized that the finished work of Christ on Calvary was the actual realization of the divine intention towards which the sacrificial cult and the prophecy were both pointing (so Peterson, *RTR* 38 [1979] 76–78). The fact that the old sacrifices had been superseded by the unique offering of Christ implied that the old covenant is indeed obsolete (8:13) and has been replaced by the promised new covenantal arrangement.

The writer selected for quotation only salient features of Jer 31:33–34. In his free repetition of the oracle, two blessings of the new covenant are underscored: God will inscribe his laws on the hearts and minds of his people, and he will no longer remember their sins and misdeeds. These verses develop the "promise" character of the new covenant that was stressed in 8:6. The first promise indicates that the people of God are no longer confronted by an exterior law. It may also suggest that God's word will no longer be carried in phylacteries upon the head and arms (Exod 13:16; Deut 6:8; Matt 23:5) precisely because it is impressed upon the center of human volition. The alternation of διάνοια, "mind," and καρδία, "heart," in the quotation of the clauses "my laws in their mind" (8:10) and "my laws upon their hearts" (10:16) shows that both words are synonymous terms related to the center of an individual's interior life (Behm, *TDNT* 4:966). The community's experience of consecration to the service of God, to which reference was made in vv 10 and 14, validates that the promise of a new relationship to God foretold in the oracle has actually been realized. The second promise is God's gracious response to the plight of Israel under the old covenant, when the observance of the Day of Atonement amounted to an annual reminder of sins for the covenant people (10:3). The assurance that God will certainly not remember the sins and transgressions of his people under the new covenant presupposes the provision of a definitive offering for sins.

18 The conclusion to the cultic argument introduced in 9:1 is expressed as an axiom: where the sins of God's people have been decisively put away, a sin offering is no longer necessary. In the light of the preceding argument, the fulfillment of Jeremiah's oracle is tied directly to the new situation introduced by the sacrificial death of Jesus. The basis for speaking about a decisive putting away of sins is the efficacy of the sacrifice offered by Christ on the cross (Peterson, *RTR* 38 [1979] 77–78). The unqualified use of ἄφεσις, "a decisive putting away," in v 18 is unusual and recalls the writer's employment of this expression as a comprehensive, powerful term for purgation with finality in 9:22 (see *Note* cc on 9:11–28 and *Comment* on 9:22 and the discussion of Johnsson, "Defilement," 349–51). Where sins have been decisively purged or put away, there is no further need for a sin offering (προσφορὰ περὶ ἁμαρτίας, where προσφορά carries the special nuance it receives in vv 10 and 14, in reference to the atoning death of Christ). Sins no longer provide an obstacle to an enduring covenantal relationship to God. The people of the new covenant enjoy unhindered access to God in worship (10:19–22). The only sacrifice required of them is a "sacrifice of praise" (13:15).

Explanation

The focus of the exposition in 9:11–28 was upon the unrepeatable action of Christ, whose single offering and entrance into the heavenly sanctuary secured eschatological redemption. The stress in that section fell upon the saving work of Christ in relationship to God rather than upon salvation realized subjectively in Christians. The suggestive reference to the potency of the blood of Christ to effect a decisive purging of the conscience of the worshiper in 9:14 was not developed. It is that strand of the argument which is picked up and elaborated in 10:1–18. The writer orients his exposition in this concluding section of the cultic argument to a consideration of the benefits of Christ's saving action for the redeemed community. The stress upon the realized aspect of salvation in 10:1–18 complements the concern for objective salvation in 9:11–28.

The new direction of the argument is announced when the plight of worshipers under the old covenant is underscored in 10:1–4. A communal perspective is consistent with the writer's tendency to consider the relative merits of the old and new covenants in terms of their respective provisions for worship (9:1, 9, 14). The law merely foreshadowed the salvation it anticipated. It was incapable of securing the decisive purgation of those who approach God year after year through the same sacrifices. This trenchant observation highlights a religious issue of the first magnitude: sin constitutes a barrier to fellowship with God. The writer focuses upon the Day of Atonement ritual, because a consciousness of sins became particularly intense on that solemn occasion. He insists that the sacrifices offered on behalf of the people really amounted to an annual reminder of their sins. The blood of bulls and goats could provide only a formal cleansing; it left the issue of the defiled conscience unaddressed. The annual observance of the solemn atonement ritual pointed to the need for a final putting away of sins as the condition for a lasting consecration of the people to God.

That need was satisfied through the efficacy of the single, personal sacrifice of Christ in fulfillment of the human vocation declared in Ps 40:6–8. The understanding of these words as the address of Christ to God, uttered on the occasion when he came into the world (10:5–7), implies a firm conviction in the personal preexistence and incarnation of the Son of God. Christ's entrance into the world is linked explicitly to the accomplishment of God's will through the bodily conditions of real human life. The emphasis upon Christ's bodily existence is pivotal in the writer's understanding of the biblical text, for it indicated Christ's solidarity with the rest of the human family. The task marked out in the psalm expressed God's design for the human family (cf. 2:6–9). Christ's assumption of that task implies that his sacrificial death was also an act of solidarity and made possible the participation of others in his own consecration to the service of God.

In his interpretation of the psalm the writer makes two essential points: (1) the multiplicity of the sacrifices of the OT cultus are precisely those prescribed by law; (2) the sacrificial offering of Christ in his death makes explicit the content of the will of God. The connections drawn between the sacrifices and the law and between the offering of Christ and the will of God are extraordinarily important. They prepare for the revolutionary statement that the old cultus and the law that prescribed it have been set aside on the strength of an event in which there was concentrated all of the efficacy of a life unconditionally submitted to the will of God (10:9b). The enunciation of the writer's fundamental eschatological principle in v 9b is not an isolated phenomenon in Hebrews. It sums up a number of prior statements in which the provisional character of the institutions of the old covenant had been indicated (cf. 8:5; 9:9; 10:1). An expert in juridical language, the writer uses a vocabulary expressive of change in reference to the old structures (cf. 7:12, 18–19), but terms of stability for the elements of the new (e.g., 6:17–18; 7:20–22). Now his point is sharply made: the old order has been disallowed with the arrival of the new. This epochal change, the writer argues, had already been anticipated in Scripture (cf. 8:13). The old covenant was a necessary, but provisional, episode in the accomplishment of redemptive history.

The significance of this interpretation for the Church is set forth in a compact formulation that may be confessional in nature (10:10). The essential factors in Christian salvation are reviewed from a communal perspective. The ultimate cause of salvation is the will of God; its determinative event was the offering of the body of Jesus Christ at his crucifixion; the result was the definitive consecration of the redeemed community to the service of God. The single, personal offering of the body of Christ on the cross reveals the nature of the sacrifice that ratified the new covenant. The sufficient sacrifice of Christ in conformity to the will of God created the new situation for the worshiping community in which every obstacle to fellowship with God has been effectively removed.

The comparison between the daily course of the Levitical ministry and the ministry of the heavenly priest has one point to make: the sacrificial phase of Christ's ministry has been completed (10:11–14). Jesus' saving action was performed in history, but it possesses a validity that transcends history. The fact that he is firmly enthroned in the presence of God provides the assurance that he is able to exercise the ministry of the new covenant on behalf of all those who approach God through him.

Throughout the course of the argument developed in 8:1–10:18, the themes of covenant, priesthood, and sacrifice have been integrated. The writer viewed the old covenant in priestly and sacrificial terms, and this accounts for the distinctive manner in which he relates the exposition of Christ's unique sacrifice to the oracle of Jeremiah concerning the new covenant in 10:15–18. Although the promises of the new covenant are not couched in cultic terms and make no reference to a new priesthood and sacrifice, the promise that God will certainly not remember sins and misdeeds any longer presupposes a definitive putting away of sins. That Christ entered the world to do the will of God shows that he is the one person in whom the intention of the new covenant was realized completely. His adherence to the will of God, even in death, indicates that God had inscribed his laws on the human heart. Christ's atoning death provided the definitive putting away of sins, which is the basis of Jeremiah's oracle. Because his one sacrifice has decisively purged the conscience of worshipers, Christ has consecrated the people of the new covenant to God in the qualitatively new relationship of heart-obedience proclaimed in the prophecy. Christ's death was the effective sin offering that removed every obstacle to the service of God. The task of the community is to appropriate this truth and to act upon it in obedience.

I. The Fourth Warning: The Peril of Disloyalty to Christ (10:19–39)

Bibliography

Adams, J. C. "The Epistle to the Hebrews with Special Reference to the Problem of Apostasy in the Church to Which It Was Addressed." Dissertation, Leeds University, 1964. **Andriessen, P.** and **Lenglet, A.** "Quelques passages difficiles de l'Épître aux Hébreux (Hb. v,7, 11; x,20; xii,2)." *Bib* 51 (1970) 207–20. **Arrington, F. L.** "Hebrews 10:19–25 New and Living Way." In *New Testament Exegesis: Examples*. Washington, D.C.: UP of America, 1977. 64–88. **Bartelink, G. J.** *Quelques observations sur παρρησία dans la littérature paléo-chrétienne.* Supplementa. Nijmegen: Dekker & Van de Vegt, 1970. **Best, E.** "Spiritual Sacrifice: General Priesthood in the New Testament." *Int* 14 (1960) 273–99. **Bornkamm, G.** "Das Bekenntnis im Hebräerbrief." *TBl* 21 (1942) 56–66. **Brownlee, W.** "The Placarded Revelation of Habakkuk." *JBL* 82 (1963) 319–25. **Cadbury, H. J.** "θεατρίζω no longer a NT hapax legomenon." *ZNW* 29 (1930) 60–63. **Campbell, A. G.** "The Problem of Apostasy in the Greek New Testament." Dissertation, Dallas Theological Seminary, 1957. **Carlston, C. E.** "Eschatology and Repentance in the Epistle to the Hebrews." *JBL* 78 (1959) 296–302. **Cavallin, H. C. C.** "'The Righteous Shall Live by Faith.'" *ST* 32 (1978) 33–43. **Costanzo, J.** "Il Peccato e la sua Remissione nella Lettera agli Ebrei." Dissertation, Pontificia Universitate Gregoriana, Rome, 1964. **Crosby, H.** "Hebrews 10:26–27." *JBL* 7

(1887) 1–2. **Cruvellier, J.** "Impossible de ramener à la repentance! À propos de deux passages difficiles de l'Épître aux Hébreux." *EEv* 12 (1952) 135–40. **Culpepper, R. A.** "A Superior Faith: Hebrews 10:19–12:2." *RevExp* 82 (1985) 375–90. **Dahl, N. A.** "A New and Living Way: The Approach to God according to Heb. 10:19–25." *Int* 5 (1951) 401–12. **Daly, R. J.** "The New Testament Concept of Christian Sacrificial Activity." *BTB* 8 (1978) 97–107. **Dibelius, M.** "Ἐπίγνωσις ἀληθείας." In *Botschaft und Geschichte.* Tübingen: Mohr, 1956. 2:1–13. **Dunham, D. A.** "An Exegetical Examination of the Warnings in the Epistle to the Hebrews." Dissertation, Grace Theological Seminary and College, 1974. **Dussaut, L.** *Synopse structurelle de l'Épître aux Hébreux.* 91–97. **Ellingworth, P.** "Jesus and the Universe." *EvQ* 58 (1986) 337–50. **Feuillet, A.** "L'attente de la Parousie et du Jugement dans l'Épître aux Hébreux." *BVC* 42 (1961) 23–31. **Fitzmyer, J. A.** "Habakkuk 2:3–4 and the New Testament." In *To Advance the Gospel: New Testament Studies.* New York: Crossroad, 1981. 236–46. **Floor, L.** "The General Priesthood of Believers in the Epistle to the Hebrews." *Neot* 5 (1971) 78–82. **Gardiner, F.** "On Heb. 10:20." *JBL* 8 (1888) 142–46. **Glombitza, O.** "Erwägungen zum kunstvollen Ansatz der Paraenese im Brief an die Hebräer—x 19–25." *NovT* 9 (1967) 132–50. **Goguel, M.** "La doctrine de l'impossibilité de la seconde conversion dans l'Épître aux Hébreux et sa place dans l'évolution du christianisme." *AEPHE* (1931) 4–38. **Grässer, E.** *Der Glaube im Hebräerbrief.* 35–45, 90–99, 102–17, 136–38, 192–98. **Hamm, D.** "Faith in the Epistle to the Hebrews: The Jesus Factor." *CBQ* 52 (1990) 270–91. **Havener, I.** "The Credal Formulae of the New Testament." Inaugural Dissertation, Münich, 1976. 455–67. **Hillmann, W.** "Glaube und Verheissung: Einführung in die Grundgedanken des Hebräerbriefes (10,32–13,25)." *BibLeb* 1 (1960) 237–52. **Hofius, O.** "Inkarnation und Opfertod Jesu nach Hebr. 10,19f." In *Der Ruf Jesu und die Antwort der Gemeinde.* FS J. Jeremias. Ed. E. Lohse. Göttingen: Vandenhoeck & Ruprecht, 1970. 132–41. ———. *Der Vorhang vor dem Thron Gottes.* 73–84. **Jeremias, J.** "Hebräer 10:20 τοῦτ' ἔστιν τῆς σαρκὸς αὐτοῦ." *ZNW* 62 (1971) 131. **Johnsson, W. G.** "Defilement and Purgation in the Book of Hebrews." Dissertation, Vanderbilt University, 1973. 224–25, 351–60, 416–17. **Katz, P.** "The Quotations from Deuteronomy in Hebrews." *ZNW* 49 (1958) 213–23. **Koch, D. A.** "Der Text von Hab 2:4b in der Septuaginta und im Neuen Testament." *ZNW* 76 (1985) 68–85. **Lacan, M. F.** "La source de l'assurance Chrétienne (Hébreux 10,1–39)." *BVC* 8 (1954–55) 89–94. **Laub, F.** *Bekenntnis und Auslegung.* 177–91. **Lewis, T. W.** "'... And if he shrinks back' (Heb X.38b)." *NTS* 22 (1975–76) 88–94. ———. "The Theological Logic in Hebrews 10:19–12:29 and the Appropriation of the Old Testament." Dissertation, Drew University, 1965. **Luck, U.** "Himmlisches und Irdisches im Hebräerbrief." *NovT* 5 (1963) 192–215. **Maasa, C. H.** "The Fearful Results of Faith (Hebrews 10:19–39)." *PSB* 61 (1968) 55–59. **MacRae, G. W.** "Heavenly Temple and Eschatology in the Letter to the Hebrews." *Semeia* 12 (1978) 179–99. **Manson, T. W.** "The Argument from Prophecy." *JTS* 46 (1945) 129–36. **Marshall, I. H.** *Kept by the Power of God.* 132–54. **McCown, W. G.** "Ὁ ΛΟΓΟΣ ΤΗΣ ΠΑΡΑΚΛΗΣΕΩΣ: The Nature and Function of the Hortatory Sections in the Epistle to the Hebrews." Dissertation, Union Theological Seminary, Richmond, 1970. 67–83, 157–59. **McCullough, J. C.** "The Impossibility of a Second Repentance in Hebrews." *BibTh* 20 (1974) 1–7. **Melbourne, B. L.** "An Examination of the Historical-Jesus Motif in the Epistle to the Hebrews." *AUSS* 26 (1988) 281–97. **Michel, O.** "Zur Auslegung des Hebräerbriefes." *NovT* 6 (1963) 189–91. **Moe, O.** "Der Gedanke des allgemeinen Priestertums im Hebräerbrief." *TZ* 5 (1949) 161–69. **Mora, G.** *La Carta a los Hebreos como Escrito Pastoral.* 48–50, 61–63, 90–106, 111, 118–30, 189–216. **Moule, C. F. D.** "Punishment and Retribution: An Attempt to Delimit Their Scope in New Testament Thought." *SEÅ* 30 (1965) 21–36. **Mugridge, A.** "Warnings in the Epistle to the Hebrews: An Exegetical and Theological Study." *RTR* 46 (1987) 74–82. **Nauck, W.** "Freude im Leiden: Zum Problem der urchristlichen Verfolgungstradition." *ZNW* 46 (1955) 68–80. **Oberholtzer, T. K.** "The Danger of Willful Sin in Hebrews 10:26–39." *BSac* 145 (1988) 410–19. **Pelser, G. M. M.** "A translation problem—Heb. 10:19–25." *Neot* 8 (1974) 43–53. **Perkins, R. L.** "Two Notes on Apostasy." *PRS* 15 (1988) 57–60.

Peterson, D. G. "An Examination of the Concept of 'Perfection' in the 'Epistle to the Hebrews.'" Dissertation, University of Manchester, 1978. 265–71. **Rice, G. E.** "Apostasy as a Motif and Its Effect on the Structure of Hebrews." *AUSS* 23 (1985) 29–35. **Richardson, A.** "Whose Architect and Maker Is God: An Exegetical Contribution to Hebrews 10,19–25." *TToday* 8 (1951) 155–56. **Rose, C.** "Verheissung und Erfüllung: Zum Verständnis von ἐπαγγελία im Hebräerbrief." *BZ* 33 (1989) 178–91. **Sabourin, L.** "Sacrificium et liturgia in Epistula ad Hebraeos." *VD* 46 (1968) 235–58. **Sailer, W. S.** "Hebrews Six: An Irony or a Continuing Embarrassment?" *EvJ* 3 (1985) 79–88. **Schröger, F.** *Der Verfasser des Hebräerbriefes.* 179–87, 204, 206. **Selby, G. S.** "The Meaning and Function of *Syneidēsis* in Hebrews 9 and 10." *RestQ* 28 (1985–86) 145–154. **Smith, D. M.** "*Ο ΔΕ ΔΙΚΑΙΟΣ ΕΚ ΠΙΣΤΕΩΣ ΖΗΣΕΤΑΙ.*" In *Studies and Documents XXIX: Studies in the History and Text of the New Testament in Honor of K. W. Clark.* Ed. B. L. Daniels and M. J. Suggs. Salt Lake City: University of Utah Press, 1967. 13–25. **Smith, R. E.** "Hebrews 10:29: By Which Was Sanctified." *Notes on Translation* 4 (1990) 32–37. **Snyder, G. F.** "Sayings on the Delay of the End." *BR* 20 (1975) 19–35. **Solari, J. K.** "The Problem of *Metanoia* in the Epistle to the Hebrews." Dissertation, Catholic University of America, 1970. 92–124. **Spicq, C.** "La penitencia impossible." *CTom* 244 (1952) 353–68. **Strobel, A.** *Untersuchungen zum eschatologischen Verzögerungsproblem auf Grund der spätjudisch-urchristlichen Geschichte von Habakuk 2,2ff.* Leiden: Brill, 1961. 79–83, 161–70. **Sullivan, K.** "Epignosis in the Epistles of St. Paul." In *Studiorum Paulinorum Congressus Internationalis Catholicus 1961.* AnBib 18. Rome: Biblical Institute, 1963. 2:405–16. **Theissen, G.** *Untersuchungen zum Hebräerbrief.* 60–67. **Thüsing, W.** "'Lasst uns hinzutreten . . .' (Hebr. 10,22): Zur Frage nach dem Sinn der Kulttheologie im Hebräerbrief." *BZ* 9 (1965) 1–17. **Tongue, D. H.** "The Concept of Apostasy in the Epistle to the Hebrews." *TynBul* 5–6 (1960) 19–26. **Toussaint, S. D.** "The Eschatology of the Warning Passages in the Book of Hebrews." *GTJ* 3 (1982) 67–80. **Vanhoye, A.** *Lectiones in Hebr. 10:1–39: De efficacia oblationis Christi et de vita christiana.* Rome: Biblical Institute, 1971–72 (*ad usum auditorum*). **Vernet, J. M.** "Cristo, él que abre el camino." *Sal* 47 (1985) 419–31. **Vorster, W. S.** "The Meaning of *ΠΑΡΡΗΣΙΑ* in the Epistle to the Hebrews." *Neot* 5 (1971) 51–59. **Weeks, N.** "Admonition and Error in Hebrews." *WTJ* 39 (1976) 72–80. **Woude, A. S. van der.** "Der Gerecht wird durch seine Treue leben: Erwägungen zu Habakuk 2:4–5." In *Studia Biblica et Semitica.* FS T. C. Vriezen. Ed. W. C. van Unnik and A. S. van der Woude. Wageningen: Veenman, 1966. 367–75. **Young, N. H.** "*τοῦτ᾽ ἔστιν τῆς σαρκὸς αὐτοῦ* (Heb. X.20): Apposition, Dependent or Explicative?" *NTS* 20 (1973) 100–104. **Zimmermann, H.** *Das Bekenntnis des Hoffnung.* 203–18.

Translation

[19] *Therefore, brothers, since we have*[a] *authorization*[b] *for free access*[c] *to the heavenly sanctuary by means of the blood of Jesus,*[d] [20] *a way*[e] *which is new*[f] *and which leads to life,*[g] *which*[h] *he made available for us through the curtain*[i] *(that is to say, by means of his flesh),*[j] [21] *and since we have*[k] *a great priest in charge of God's household,*[l] [22] *let us continue to draw near to God*[m] *with a sincere heart*[n] *in fullness*[o] *of faith, seeing that our hearts have been sprinkled clean from a burdened conscience and the body washed with clean water.*[p] [23] *Let us continue to hold fast the hope*[q] *we profess without wavering (for the One who gave the promise is faithful).* [24] *And let us keep on caring for one another*[r] *for the stimulation*[s] *of love and good works,* [25] *not discontinuing*[t] *our*[u] *meeting together as some people are regularly doing,*[v] *but rather encouraging one another, and all the more since*[w] *you see the Day of the Lord*[x] *approaching.*

[26] *For if we deliberately*[y] *persist in sin*[z] *after we have received*[aa] *the full knowledge of the truth, there is no longer any sacrifice for sins,* [27] *but only an inevitable,*[bb] *terrifying expectation*[cc] *of judgment and of raging fire ready to consume God's adversaries.*

[28] *Anyone who violates the law of Moses dies* [dd] *without pity* [ee] *on the evidence of* [ff] *two or three witnesses.* [29] *How much severer* [gg] *punishment do you suppose he will deserve who has trampled upon the Son of God and who has treated the blood of the covenant, by which he was consecrated,* [hh] *as defiled, and who has insulted the Spirit of grace?* [30] *For we know who it was who said,*

> *"Vengeance belongs to me; I will repay* [ii] *";*

and again,

> *"The Lord will judge his people."*

[31] *It is terrifying to fall* [jj] *into the hands of the living God.*

[32] *Instead, remember* [kk] *those earlier* [ll] *days, after you received the light, when you endured a hard contest with sufferings.* [33] *Sometimes* [mm] *you were publicly exposed to ridicule,* [nn] *both by insults and persecutions, and on other occasions you showed solidarity with those who were treated in this way,* [34] *for in fact you shared the sufferings of those in prison,* [oo] *and cheerfully accepted the seizure of your property,* [pp] *because you knew you yourselves* [qq] *had better and permanent possessions.* [35] *Therefore, do not throw away* [rr] *your boldness,* [ss] *seeing that it* [tt] *has a great reward.*

[36] *You need, then,* [uu] *endurance so that* [vv] *after you have done* [ww] *the will of God you may receive the promise.* [37] *For,* [xx]

> *"A little while longer,* [yy]
> the Coming One will come; he will not delay.*
[38] > *But my righteous one* [zz] *will live by faithfulness."*
> *But,* [aaa] *"if he draws back I myself* [bbb] *will reject him."* [ccc]

[39] *But we* [ddd] *are not of those who draw back, leading to destruction,* [eee] *but of those who are faithful, culminating in the acquisition of life.*

Notes

[a] The present ptcp ἔχοντες is causal, "since we have."

[b] As the obj of the ptcp ἔχοντες ("since we have παρρησίαν") and modified by the instrumental use of ἐν with the dative ("by means of the blood of Jesus"), παρρησία has "a peculiarly objective character" (Käsemann, *Das wandernde Gottesvolk*, 23). It is not the subjective attitude of "confidence" or "boldness" (as in v 35), but the "authorization" or "permission" for access to God secured through the sacrifice of Christ (cf. Schlier, *TDNT* 5:884; Vorster, *Neot* 5 [1971] 56; Pelser, *Neot* 8 [1974] 47). In Hebrews the objective element includes a subjective dimension (i.e., personal confidence arising from the God-given authorization), but the translation must not obscure the objective character of the word (so Windisch, 93; Riggenbach, 312–13; Michel, 344). Cf. JB: "we have the right to enter the sanctuary"; TEV: "we have . . . complete freedom to go into the Most Holy Place."

[c] Although most translations render the noun εἴσοδος with an inf ("to enter": RSV, NEB, JB, NIV; "to go into": TEV), this appears to be a matter of English style. The expression has reference to the act of entering, and εἴσοδος carries the nuance of "the right of entry" or "access." When used in this sense, εἴσοδος is nearly always associated with the prep εἰς (Michaelis, *TDNT* 5:76, 106). The construction with the gen τῶν ἁγίων, "the [heavenly] sanctuary," involves a loose use of the obj gen (BDF §163).

[d] In the phrase ἐν τῷ αἵματι Ἰησοῦ, the prep ἐν should be understood to be instrumental ("by means of"), as in 9:25 (Pelser, *Neot* 8 [1974] 47).

[e] Corresponding to classical usage, ὁδόν is in independent juxtaposition with εἴσοδον, "free access," as a predicate accusative dependent upon the verb ἐνεκαίνισεν, "he made available" (BDF §157[1]). It is descriptive of εἴσοδον, "free access."

[f] There is both a temporal and a qualitative aspect to the adj πρόσφατον, which occurs only here in the NT. With respect to time, the way is "new" in the sense of recent; it had not previously existed. With respect to quality, it expresses the freshness of the new revelation that will not become old (cf. Grosheide, 238; Spicq, 2:315; Maurer, *TDNT* 6:767).

8 The translation reflects the conviction that the ptcp ζῶσαν implies that "the way" leads to life (so Michel, 345), rather than that "the way" is lasting (μένουσαν, so Grosheide, 238) or that it is "living" because it is a "way" that consists in fellowship with Jesus Christ (so Westcott, 319; Riggenbach, 314; Strathmann, 319).

h The relative clause introduced by ἥν takes up again the preceding εἰς τὴν εἴσοδον, "for free access," rather than παρρησίαν, "authorization," as urged by Riggenbach, 313. See Michaelis, *TDNT* 5:76; Pelser, *Neot* 8 [1974] 47.

i The phrase διὰ τοῦ καταπετάσματος, "through the curtain," almost certainly qualifies ὁδόν, "a way." An alternative way of understanding the phrase is to link it only with ἐνεκαίνισεν, "he opened," not ὁδόν, so that the statement applies only to Jesus, and not to Christians also (so Riggenbach, 315–16).

j The relationship of the explicative clause τοῦτ' ἔστιν τῆς σαρκὸς αὐτοῦ to the rest of the sentence is a *crux interpretum*. The entire clause has been dismissed as a later epexegetical gloss (C. Hosten, *Exegetische Untersuchung über Hebräer 10:20* [Bern, 1875] 11–15, followed by Buchanan, 168). Against this radical expedient is the fact that the τοῦτ' ἔστιν construction occurs six times in Hebrews (2:14; 7:5; 9:11; 10:20; 11:16; 13:15).

A common opinion, perpetuated by most translations (RSV, JB, TEV, NASB, NIV), is that the clause stands in apposition to διὰ τοῦ καταπετάσματος (i.e., "through the curtain, that is to say, through his flesh"). The fact that the prep διά clearly governs the gen τῆς σαρκός, "the flesh," as well as the gen τοῦ καταπετάσματος, "the curtain," may appear to lend support to this interpretation; διά is certainly local in reference to the curtain. Moreover, it has been argued that apart from the questionable usage here, τοῦτ' ἔστιν is always used in Hebrews in an appositional context (N. H. Young, *NTS* 20 [1973] 103). On this understanding, "the curtain" is a metaphor for Christ's flesh (cf. Windisch, 87; Riggenbach, 315–16; Moffatt, 143; T. H. Robinson, 142; Michel, 345; W. Manson, *Epistle to the Hebrews*, 67–68; F. F. Bruce, 345; Dahl, *Int* 5 [1951] 405; P. E. Hughes, 407–10).

This interpretation, however, obscures the argument of the passage and fails to take account of the obvious parallel provided in 6:19–20, where Christ has entered the heavenly sanctuary through "the curtain." The use of καταπέτασμα, "curtain," in 10:20 seems to be clearly consistent with the local use of the term in 6:19 and 9:3, where it designates the "second curtain" separating the inner sanctuary from the holy place (cf. Hofius, *Vorhang*, 73). No metaphor is intended in 10:20.

An alternative approach finds expression in the NEB: "the new, living way which he has opened for us through the curtain, the way of his flesh." On this understanding, the τοῦτ' ἔστιν clause introduces a gen of dependence (τῆς σαρκὸς αὐτοῦ) that is to be attached to ὁδόν (i.e., "way of his flesh"). An appeal to 7:5 and 13:15 shows that word order is not decisive in determining the referent of a τοῦτ' ἔστιν clause; in these instances τοῦτ' ἔστιν refers back to a substantive other than the immediately preceding one. The value of this proposal is that the local and literal sense of διὰ τοῦ καταπετάσματος, "through the curtain," is preserved (cf. Westcott, 320–22; Seeberg, 113; Nairne, *Epistle of Priesthood*, 161, 381–82; Spicq, 2:316; Héring, 98; H. Montefiore, 173–74; Andriessen and Lenglet, *Bib* 51 [1970] 214–15; Andriessen, *En lisant*, 42–49).

It appears preferable, however, to recognize that in this instance τοῦτ' ἔστιν introduces a clause explicative of the preceding sentence as a whole (e.g., Rom 9:8; 10:7). This understanding is supported by the analogous structure of vv 19–20:

A εἰς τὴν εἴσοδον	A' ὁδὸν πρόσφατον καὶ ζῶσαν
"for free access"	"a way which is new and which leads to life"
B τῶν ἁγίων	B' διὰ τοῦ καταπετάσματος
"to the heavenly sanctuary"	"through the curtain"
C ἐν τῷ αἵματι Ἰησοῦ	C' τοῦτ' ἔστιν τῆς σαρκὸς αὐτοῦ
"by means of the blood of Jesus"	"that is, by means of his flesh"

The syntactical construction of vv 19 and 20 is similar: both verses speak of the new way, its goal, and the sacrificial death of Jesus as the basis for entrance. The difference is that the subj of v 19 is Christians, while the subj of v 20 is Christ. The two verses are closely connected to each other by the relative pronoun ἥν (i.e., free access *which* he made available). The recognition that v 20 is meant to be an elucidation of v 19 shows that the concept of ἐν τῷ αἵματι Ἰησοῦ, "by means of the blood of Jesus," is taken up again in (διά understood) τῆς σαρκὸς αὐτοῦ, "by means of his flesh." The structure of vv 19–20 calls for an interpretation of "flesh" in an *instrumental* sense. The internal logic of the sentence presupposes a shift in thought from διά taken locally with τοῦ καταπετάσματος, "the curtain," to διά (unexpressed) taken instrumentally with τῆς σαρκὸς αὐτοῦ, "his flesh." The same variation in prepositional use, which is rhetorically motivated, occurs in

9:11–12 (see *Note* c on 9:11). Both v 19 and v 20 conclude with a reference to Jesus' sacrificial death as the means by which the way into the heavenly sanctuary was provided (see Hofius, "Inkarnation und Opfertod Jesu," 136–41; id., *Vorhang*, 81–82; Jeremias, *ZNW* 62 [1971] 131; cf. Johnsson, "Defilement," 353–55; N. H. Young, *NTS* 20 [1973] 103–4).

[k] The fact that ἱερέα μέγαν, "a great priest," is dependent on the participle ἔχοντες at the beginning of v 19 is expressed in the translation by the repetition of the causal expression, "since we have" from v 19*a*.

[l] It is presupposed in the translation that the expression ἐπὶ τὸν οἶκον τοῦ θεοῦ, "over the house of God," connotes the people of God, as in 3:6. For the proposal that the reference is rather to the heavenly sanctuary, in which Christ functions as high priest, see BAGD 560. Although the use of ἱερέα μέγαν, "a great priest," in this context might favor such an interpretation, the writer nowhere else speaks of the heavenly sanctuary under the metaphor of "the house of God" (cf. Pelser, *Neot* 8 [1974] 49; Michel, *TDNT* 5:125–28).

[m] The present subjunctive προσερχώμεθα is cohortative: "let us continue to draw near." In the light of the parallel in 4:16, as well as the statements in 7:25 and 11:6, it is clear that the approach is to God. As this is the intended meaning, the reference to God should be included in the translation (so Pelser, *Neot* 8 [1974] 49, 51).

[n] In the expression μετὰ ἀληθινῆς καρδίας the term ἀληθινός has the nuance of undividedness, genuineness, sincerity (Michel, 346). It would be possible to translate the phrase "with sincere intentions."

[o] The rare word πληροφορία does not occur in classical writers or in the LXX. It may be taken to signify merely "fullness," and not necessarily "full assurance" (as Delling proposed: *TDNT* 6:310–11; see MacRae, *Semeia* 12 [1978] 193).

[p] V 19 introduces a long and involved periodic sentence that extends through v 25. It has been broken up in the translation out of consideration for English style. The decision to place a period after the first in a series of three exhortations is a natural one and is supported by the recognition that the two ptcps in v 22*b* are complementary to each other (so Riggenbach, 319). Glombitza prefers to place the period after the expression "fullness of faith" and to associate v 22*b* with v 23 (*NovT* 9 [1967] 138–40; so also Seeberg, 114–15). For an alternative proposal to acknowledge a more balanced construction in vv 22–25 and to treat the καί, "and," in v 22*b* as conjunctive, joining not only the two ptcps but the cohortatives at the beginning of v 22 and v 23 (parallel to the καί which precedes the cohortative in v 24), see Vanhoye, *La structure*, 176–77. On this reading, a full stop cannot occur before the end of v 25.

[q] The expression τῆς ἐλπίδος is a case of the obj gen. Michel correctly observes that the gen indicates the obj of the confession, not the act of hoping itself (347). It is this obj character that is stressed by the translation (so Pelser, *Neot* 8 [1974] 50–51).

[r] It is difficult to express the proper nuance of κατανοῶμεν. The lexical meanings of this verb are not helpful (BAGD 415: "fix the eyes of the spirit upon someone," "consider, notice in a spiritual sense"; cf. Behm, *TDNT* 4:975). The translation reflects a suggestion of Pelser, *Neot* 8 [1974] 50.

[s] The employment of παροξυσμός in a positive sense is unusual. In this context it can only have the sense of "incitement," "stimulation," or "encouragement" (Seesemann, *TDNT* 5:857, who directs attention to use of the verb in Jos., *Ant.* 16.125: παροξῦναι δὲ τὴν εὔνοιαν, "to stimulate good will").

[t] The two ptcps in the present tense, μὴ ἐγκαταλείποντες . . . ἀλλὰ παρακαλοῦντες, "not discontinuing . . . but rather encouraging," serve to emphasize the enduring quality of the cohortative κατανοῶμεν, "let us keep on caring for one another," in v 24 (Glombitza, *NovT* 9 [1967] 144). The verb ἐγκαταλείπειν is a singularly strong expression in Koine Gk, signifying "to desert," "to abandon," "to leave in the lurch" (2 Tim 4:10; cf. Mora, *La Carta a los Hebreos*, 50, n. 139, for references to the papyri).

[u] Reflecting a development in the LXX, NT, and non-literary papyri, the third person reflexive pronoun ἑαυτῶν is used in place of the second person ὑμῶν αὐτῶν, "of yourselves," or the first person ἡμῶν αὐτῶν, "of ourselves" (cf. Zerwick, *Biblical Greek* §209; BDF §§283[3], 284[2]). In the case of v 25, the first person is indicated since the ptcp clause is dependent upon the verb κατανοῶμεν (first person pl) in v 24 (Hanna, *Grammatical Aid*, 157).

[v] The translation of καθὼς ἔθος τισίν is idiomatic. The word ἔθος signifies "custom," "habit." The dative in τισίν may express possession ("the habit of some") or it may be a dative of reference ("the habit in reference to some").

ʷ The formula τοσούτῳ ... ὅσῳ, "all the more, since," is common in classical authors and is an example of the excellent Gk. in Hebrews (the same formula occurs in 1:4). It is used nowhere else in the NT in the precise form in which it occurs in Hebrews, but is found in the LXX (Sir 3:8; 4 Macc 15:5) and in Philo (cf. Williamson, *Philo*, 93–95). In this instance there is no comparative in the relative clause. The phrase corresponds to the English idiom, "the more ... the less," i.e., the more you see the Day of the Lord approaching, the less we should discontinue meeting together (A. T. Robertson, *Grammar*, 532, 967).

ˣ In the light of 10:36–38, the unqualified expression τὴν ἡμέραν, "the day," is clearly the Day of the Lord. This would have been understood by the recipients of the homily but needs to be expressed in translation for the sake of modern readers.

ʸ The word ἑκουσίως, meaning "deliberately," "intentionally," is found everywhere in literary Koine. As the first word in the sentence, its position is emphatic.

ᶻ The use of the present ptcp in the gen absolute construction, ἁμαρτανόντων ἡμῶν, carries the notion of continuous action: "if we persist in sin."

ᵃᵃ The expression μετὰ τό with the inf indicates time: "after we have received" (N. Turner, *Grammar*, 3:143).

ᵇᵇ The enclitic τις actually intensifies φοβερά (BDF §301[1]): the judgment is τις, "inevitable." The use of the enclitic is rhetorical (BAGD 820).

ᶜᶜ The term ἐκδοχή, which is found only here in the NT, occurs nowhere else with the meaning it must have at this point, "expectation" (BAGD 239). The nuance of the word appears to be a special one given by the writer, based on the meaning of ἐκδέχεσθαι, "to wait," "to expect," in 10:13 (Moffatt, 150).

ᵈᵈ The present tense of ἀποθνῄσκει has a frequentative idea (i.e., it refers to an action that recurs from time to time with different individuals). Cf. 7:8 (Moulton, *Grammar*, 1:114).

ᵉᵉ The word οἰκτιρμός nearly always occurs in a plural form, due to the influence of Hebraic usage. Here the expression χωρὶς οἰκτιρμῶν is used quite generally, without any differentiation from the singular (BDF §142; BAGD 561).

ᶠᶠ The prep phrase ἐπί with the dative most frequently denotes the basis for a state of being, action, or result (BDF §235[2]). Here it signifies "on the basis of" (cf. 9:10, 15). Alternatively, A. T. Robertson suggests it carries here the notion of "before," "in the presence of" two or three witnesses (*Grammar*, 604).

ᵍᵍ The construction πόσῳ ... χείρονος, "by how much ... severer," entails an "ablatival" use of the dative to express measure (Moule, *Idiom-Book*, 44). As in classical usage, a short finite verb (here: δοκεῖτε, "do you suppose") is introduced into the construction, forming a slight parenthesis for rhetorical effect (BDF §465[2]).

ʰʰ The expression ἐν ᾧ ἡγιάσθη is instrumental (Michel, 353, n. 2). Cf. 9:25; 10:10, 19.

ⁱⁱ In the compound word ἀνταποδώσω, the thought of "recompense" in ἀποδιδόναι is strengthened by the prefix ἀντί- (Büchsel, *TDNT* 1:169).

ʲʲ The articular inf τὸ ἐμπεσεῖν, "to fall," is used as the subj of the verbal adj φοβερόν, "it is terrifying" (A. T. Robertson, *Grammar*, 1059).

ᵏᵏ Not counting hortatory subjunctives, ἀναμιμνῄσκεσθε is the first real imperative since 7:4. J. Thomas has observed that the imperatives in Hebrews tend to be more specific and precise in comparison to the "hortatory" subjunctives, which tend to have a rhetorical nuance: cf. 3:1, 13; 7:4; 10:32; 12:3 ("The Use of Voice, Moods and Tenses," 64, n. 125).

ˡˡ The term πρότερος has surrendered the meaning "the first of two" to πρῶτος, and now means only "earlier" (BDF §62). Since the distinction between the comparative and superlative had been weakened in Koine, it is also possible to translate the phrase "the first days," in reference to the time when the community first responded to the message of the gospel (so P. E. Hughes, 426–27, n. 73).

ᵐᵐ The τοῦτο μέν ... τοῦτο δέ construction is characteristic of classical (Attic) and literary Koine usage to indicate a correspondence: "sometimes you were publicly exposed to ridicule ... and on other occasions you showed solidarity with," or "You not only were publicly exposed to ridicule ... but you also showed solidarity with" (BDF §290[5]; BAGD 597). It has also been suggested that the construction divides the community into two groups, one of which experienced the confiscation of their property and imprisonment, the other of which showed solidarity with the first group (cf. Vanhoye, *La structure*, 179; Riggenbach, 332; Teodorica, 177; Mora, *La Carta a los Hebreos*, 61–62, n. 183). If this is the case, the expression could be translated "in part ... in part" (BAGD 503).

ⁿⁿ For this nuance in θεατριζόμενοι, see Cadbury, ZNW 29 (1930) 62.

ᵒᵒ The correctness of the reading δεσμίοις, which enjoys the support of good representatives of both the Alexandrian and Western types of text, as well as by several Eastern witnesses (A D* H 6 33 [81] 1739 it vg syᵖ· ʰ· ᵖᵃˡ sa bo arm Ephr al), is confirmed by 13:3. For a discussion of the sources of the variants found in other MSS, see Metzger, Textual Commentary, 670.

ᵖᵖ The unusual word order of this clause seems designed to arouse the hearers' attention (N. Turner, Grammar, 4:107).

qq The third person reflexive pronoun ἑαυτούς is here used in place of the second person (see above on v 25; cf. BDF §283[3]). It occurs in the accusative case as the subj of the inf ἔχειν. In classical Gk. γινώσκοντες with the accusative and inf means "to pass judgment," and this thought can be accepted here as well (BDF §397[1]). In the context of the aor συνεπαθήσατε, "you shared the sufferings," and προσεδέξασθε, "you accepted," which are both culminative, the present γινώσκοντες suggests coincident present action. In that case one could translate: "You shared the sufferings . . . and accepted . . . knowing while doing so that you had a better and permanent possession."

ʳʳ The expression ἀποβάλλειν τὴν παρρησίαν could carry the idiomatic meaning of "lose courage" (BAGD 89). The presence of juridical vocabulary (ἀποβάλλειν/μισθαποδοσία, "reward") in v 35, however, implies that ἀποβάλλειν has a more technical meaning, "do not throw away παρρησία" (so Vorster, Neot 5 [1971] 56–57). The aor subjunctive ἀποβάλητε is used with the negative in a prohibitive sense implying that the action is not yet existent and should not occur.

ˢˢ In v 19 παρρησία has an obj nuance ("authorization, right"), but here it expresses a subj attitude ("boldness," "confidence"). In v 19 παρρησία was a gift; here it is a task (W. C. van Unnik, "The Christian's Freedom of Speech in the New Testament," BJRL 41 [1961–62] 485).

ᵗᵗ In classical Gk. the relative pronouns were frequently used in a causal sense. This appears to be the case here, where ἥτις introduces a reason for not casting away boldness. The same usage can be observed in 8:6 (so A. W. Argyle, "The Causal Use of the Relative Pronouns in the Greek New Testament," BT 6 [1955] 165–69; A. T. Robertson, Grammar, 728).

ᵘᵘ The γάρ is inferential rather than causal (T. W. Lewis, NTS 22 [1975–76] 89, n. 1).

ᵛᵛ The ἵνα . . . κομίσησθε, "so that . . . you may receive," construction is to be understood as a result clause, not a final purpose clause (cf. Burton, Moods and Tenses §219). The function of the clause is to set forth a result (conceived, not actual), of which the possession of endurance is the necessary condition.

ʷʷ The ptcp ποιήσαντες is used temporally, i.e., "after."

ˣˣ The explanatory γάρ functions as the introduction of the biblical citation (so T. W. Lewis, NTS 22 [1975–76] 90). For another example of ἔτι, "yet," "still," with the explanatory γάρ, cf. 7:10.

ʸʸ The expression μικρὸν ὅσον ὅσον, taken from Isa 26:20 LXX, means "a very little while" or "soon" (BDF §304). The correlatives ὅσον ὅσον constitute a vernacular idiom in harmony with the MT (MM 461). The idiom was strengthened by the synonym μικρόν, "little," in the LXX, and here is qualified by the adverb of time ἔτι (translated "longer"), which was undoubtedly derived from Hab 2:3 LXX (so J. A. Fitzmyer, "Habakkuk 2:3–4," 243).

ᶻᶻ The quotation in v 38 appears to follow the LXX as transmitted in Codex A and the manuscripts in Rahlfs' group C, which read δίκαιός μου ἐκ πίστεως ζήσεται, "my righteous one will live by faithfulness" (contrast manuscripts D* sy, which read ἐκ πίστεως μου, "because of my faithfulness"). By adding μου to δίκαιος, "my righteous one," it is made clear that ἐκ πίστεως modifies the verb ζήσεται, "will live by faithfulness." This is the reading of Heb 10:38 in 𝔓⁴⁶ ℵ A H* 33ᵛⁱᵈ 1739 lat sa arm Cl al (see Cavallin, ST 32 [1978] 35, n. 19; Metzger, Textual Commentary, 670–71).

ᵃᵃᵃ D. R. Goodwin pointed out a century ago that καί is a connective and not a part of the citation in v 38 ("On the use of καί in Hebrews X.38," JBL 5 [1885] 84–85). It functions as the adversative, "but." The translation seeks to reflect this fact more accurately than UBSGNT or Nestle²⁶.

ᵇᵇᵇ The expression ἡ ψυχή μου is a Sem. periphrasis for the reflexive pronoun ἐγὼ αὐτός, "I myself" (N. Turner, Grammar, 3:43).

ᶜᶜᶜ In the context of election, εὐδοκεῖν is sometimes hardened by the sense of the negative οὐκ εὐδοκεῖν to the degree that it can only imply rejection. This appears to be the case in this context (so Schrenk, TDNT 2:741).

ᵈᵈᵈ The personal pronoun ἡμεῖς, "we," is doubly emphatic, by position and by the fact that it is expressed at all (Zerwick and Grosvenor, Grammatical Analysis, 678–79).

ᵉᵉᵉ The phrases εἰς ἀπώλειαν and εἰς περιποίησιν ψυχῆς are result clauses. The translation seeks to convey this fact: "leading to destruction . . . culminating in the acquisition of life."

Form/Structure/Setting

A consideration of genre clearly indicates that 10:19–39 constitutes a distinct unit within the structural format of Hebrews. The beginning of a new section is announced by the direct address to the community in 10:19 ("Therefore, brothers") and by the intricate transition from exposition (7:1–10:18) to exhortation (10:19–39). Succinctly summarizing in 10:19–21 the argument developed in 8:1–10:18, the writer provides a firm christological basis for the series of admonitions that follow in this section. With 11:1 there is a fresh shift in genre. It is no longer appropriate to speak of exhortation, but of exposition of the character of faith as a present grasp upon unseen and future reality. The unit of exhortation introduced in 10:19 thus extends to 10:39.

Formal literary considerations substantiate this analysis based upon the alternation between exposition and exhortation throughout Hebrews. The opening and close of the unit are defined more precisely by the verbal repetition of the key term παρρησίαν, which has an objective nuance in v 19 ("authorization") and a subjective nuance in v 35 ("boldness"):

v 19   ἔχοντες οὖν . . . παρρησίαν
        "Therefore, since we have authorization"
v 35   μὴ ἀποβάλητε οὖν τὴν παρρησίαν
        "Therefore, do not throw away your boldness"

These phrases function as an *inclusio* that frames the unit. The repetition of the key term παρρησίαν with the change in nuance is purposeful. It served to alert the auditors that the final paragraph of the section (vv 36–39) was a transitional unit used to announce the subjects to be developed in the fourth major division of the sermon: steadfast endurance (v 36) and confident faith (v 39) (so Vanhoye, *La structure*, 44–46, 175–82; Spicq, 2:314; Thyen, *Stil*, 59, 106; Michel, *NovT* 6 [1963] 189–90; McCown, "Ο ΛΟΓΟΣ ΤΗΣ ΠΑΡΑΚΛΗΣΕΩΣ," 68–69; among others).

With 10:19–39 the great central division of the sermon (5:11–10:39) is drawn to a conclusion. Viewed from the perspective of the homiletical and literary structure of Hebrews, this concluding exhortation is symmetrical with the preliminary exhortation found in 5:11–6:20 (see *Introduction* to 5:11–10:39). There the writer enlisted the attention of the auditors and laid the groundwork for the extended exposition in 7:1–10:18. Here he addresses the community directly again, drawing upon the exposition of Christ's high priestly office and sacrifice as a source of motivation for the urgency of loyalty to Jesus. The great exposition of Christ as priest and sacrifice is thus framed by parallel parenetic units (cf. Vanhoye, *La structure*, 173).

A resemblance between 5:11–6:20 and 10:19–39 extends to content as well as function. McCown ("Ο ΛΟΓΟΣ ΤΗΣ ΠΑΡΑΚΛΗΣΕΩΣ," 50, 69, 158, 299) has observed that the parenetic sequence found in 5:11–6:12 can be recognized in 10:19–39 as well:

first, a reminder to the community of their privileged status, and its implications for their actual practice (5:11–6:3/10:19–25);

then, a severe warning concerning the danger of apostasy, with stress on the divine punishment apostasy deserves (6:4–8/10:26–31);

finally, pastoral encouragement based upon past performance, together with an appeal focused upon future expectations (6:9–12/10:32–39).

The pattern of stern warning followed by loving encouragement (e.g., 5:11–6:8/ 6:9–20; 10:26–31/10:32–39) was characteristic of Jewish synagogue homilies, as attested in the old rabbinic midrashim (cf. E. Stein, "Die homiletische *Peroratio* im Midrasch," *HUCA* 8–9 [1931–32] 353–71). It clearly has influenced the pastoral style of the writer of Hebrews (so Mora, *La Carta a los Hebreos*, 61, n. 182; 63, n. 192; Swetnam, *Bib* 55 [1974] 338, n. 2). The formal resemblance of 5:11–6:20 and 10:19–39, of course, must not obscure the fact that the preliminary exhortation and the concluding exhortation are distinct both in content and function (cf. A. Descamps, "La structure de l'Épître aux Hébreux," *RDT* 9 [1954] 335; Vanhoye, *La structure*, 45–46, 228–30).

The exhortation in 10:19–39 plays a central role in relationship to all of the other hortatory sections in Hebrews. It contains recognizable echoes of earlier parenetic units in its argumentation (e.g., 2:1–4/10:28–31; 6:4–8/10:26–31) and in the repetition of characteristic expressions (e.g., 3:6*b*/10:23; 3:17/10:26; other details in Vanhoye, *La structure*, 228–30, 256–57). On the other hand, the triad of Christian qualities to which the writer alludes in 10:22–25 anticipates the development of the remainder of the sermon: faith (10:22) is celebrated in 11:1–40; hope (10:23) is expressed through perseverance in 12:1–13; and love (10:24–25) furnishes the key to the conclusion of the sermon in 12:14–13:21. As a summary of the preceding parenetic sections and the announcement of the development to follow, 10:19–39 marks a major turning point in the unfolding structure of the sermon.

The writer intends 10:19–39 to be a climactic parenetic section of the sermon. Consistent with this conclusion is the concentration of rare vocabulary and expressions in 10:32–39:

10:32   ἄθλησις, "contest": nowhere else in the NT; not in Greek writers before the Christian period;

10:33   τοῦτο ... τοῦτο, "sometimes ... on other occasions": nowhere else in the NT; ὀνειδισμός, "insult": Heb 10:33; 11:26; 13:13; Rom 15:3; 1 Tim 3:7; θεατρίζεσθαι, "publicly exposed to ridicule": nowhere else in the NT; not found in the LXX or other Greek versions of the OT, including the Apocrypha; not in Greek writers before the Christian period;

10:34   ἁρπαγή, "seizure": elsewhere in the NT only Matt 23:25; Luke 11:39; but cf. Phil 2:6; ὕπαρξις, "property": elsewhere in the NT only Acts 2:35;

10:35   μισθαποδοσία, "reward": elsewhere in the NT only Heb 2:2; 11:26; not in the LXX or other Greek versions of the OT, including the Apocrypha; not in Greek writers before the Christian period;

10:37   μικρὸν ὅσον ὅσον, "a little while longer": not found elsewhere in the NT;

10:38   ὑποστέλλειν, "to draw back": elsewhere in the NT only Acts 20:20, 27; Gal 2:12;

10:39   ὑποστολή, "one who draws back": not elsewhere in the NT; not in the LXX or other Greek versions of the OT, including the Apocrypha; not in Greek writers before the Christian period; περιποίησις, "acquisition": elsewhere in the NT only Eph 1:14; 1 Thess 5:9; 2 Thess 2:14; 1 Pet 2:9.

The effect of such a concentration of unusual expressions would be the arresting of the attention of the community upon what the writer had to say (see *Form/ Structure/Setting* on 2:1–4).

Although source analysis is always difficult in Hebrews, it is possible to recognize the writer's indebtedness to a primitive Christian tradition in the formulation of 10:32–35. By means of a formal analysis of tradition in 1 Peter and elsewhere in the NT, E. G. Selwyn identified what he called a "persecution-form" (*The First Epistle of Peter* [London: Macmillan, 1947] 439–58). This refers to catechetical material that was prepared in response to the crisis of persecution. Selwyn recognized that Hebrews reflected this traditional teaching, particularly in a form that stressed persecution as a ground of rejoicing. Nauck carried this research further and identified the structure of the form on the basis of Matt 5:11–12, Luke 6:22–23, and 1 Pet 4:13–17 (*ZNW* 46 [1955] 68–80):

1*a*	Pronouncement of a blessing;
1*b*	Situation (of persecution);
2*a*	Call to rejoice;
2*b*	The reason (the promise of reward).

This formal structure remains substantially preserved in Heb 10:32–35:

1*b*	Situation (vv 32–33);
2*a*	Call to rejoice (v 34);
2*b*	Reason (the promise of reward) (vv 34–35).

In drawing upon this tradition the writer has selected and adapted those features of the form appropriate to the situation of the Christians addressed (cf. McCown, "*Ο ΛΟΓΟΣ ΤΗΣ ΠΑΡΑΚΛΗΣΕΩΣ*," 80–83). The recognition of the persecution-form behind the formulation of 10:32–35 puts the modern reader of Hebrews in touch with the harsh reality of Christian existence in the hostile environment of the first century.

Comment

This section represents a high point in the writer's message to his friends. In a climactic parenetic passage he summarizes his thematic exposition of Christ as priest and sacrifice and earnestly appeals for the community to apply the blessings of Christ's high priestly ministry to its own daily life. The preceding christological discussion motivates this powerful appeal and underscores its urgency (Dahl, *Int* 5 [1951] 401). A loyal response to Christ is the logical correlate of the magnitude of Christ's redemptive accomplishment.

The section consists of four paragraphs, each of which possesses its own distinctive characteristics. The first paragraph (vv 19–25) is cast in the form of a periodic sentence. After defining the basis for the appeal in vv 19–21, the exhortation is organized around three cohortatives: "let us continue to draw near" (v 22), "let us continue to hold fast" (v 23), and "let us keep on caring" (v 24). Each of these verbs is qualified by reference to the triad of Christian virtues: "fullness of faith" (v 22), "the hope we profess" (v 23), and "the stimulation of love" (v 24). The warning to be faithful as the Day of the Lord approaches (v 25) furnishes a transition to the next paragraph.

The elaboration of the warning explains the stern change in tone evident in the second paragraph (vv 26–31). The limits of the paragraph are indicated literarily by the verbal repetition of the key terms φοβερά/φοβερόν in v 27 and v 31, which qualify the expectation of judgment by those who despise the new covenant as "terrifying."

The return to a tone of pastoral encouragement sets off the third paragraph (vv 32–35), where the writer recalls the past fidelity of the community, which had been tested in the crucible of suffering early in its experience. The remembrance of past performance provides a powerful incentive for renewed commitment and fidelity in the present and for the future.

The final paragraph (vv 36–39) concludes the exhortation by introducing the key terms to be developed in the next major division of the sermon, "endurance" (v 36) and "faith" (v 39). The pastoral appeal to the community is rounded off as the writer picks up on some of the notes he had sounded in the initial paragraph: the need for faith (vv 22/38–39), God as the one who made the promise (vv 23/36), good works as a doing of the will of God (vv 24/36), and the nearness of the Day of the Lord (vv 25/37). In this way the climactic parenetic section is given coherence and closure (cf. Michel, 343; Vanhoye, *La structure*, 173–82).

It is instructive, finally, to observe the degree of similarity in formulation between the initial statement in the concluding exhortation (10:19–20) and the final statement in the preliminary exhortation (6:19–20). The vocabulary and conception are similar, but there is a greater degree of christological precision in 10:19–20, which reflects the detail of the exposition in 8:1–10:18. The observation that the substance of 6:19–20 is reformulated in 10:19–20 indicates the writer's purpose in 10:19–39. He intends to reiterate more forcefully his appeal for boldness expressed through uncompromising loyalty to Christ and continued support for the meetings of the house church.

19–20 These two verses are unusually difficult. The number of exegetical issues they pose has become apparent in the task of translation (see above, *Notes* g–j). Yet it is clear that the assertions in vv 19–21 are of the utmost significance to the appeal which follows for the community to affirm its fidelity to Christ. Consequently, these verses require of an interpreter patience, a careful weighing of the relative merits of an ongoing discussion, and a readiness to decide between divergent proposals.

In v 19 the focus shifts from the cultic argument the writer has been developing to the response of faith it demands. The initial phrase ἔχοντες οὖν ἀδελφοί, "Therefore, brothers, since we have," indicates that the writer is building on what has preceded. The inferential particle οὖν, "therefore," sums up the entire argument to this point, but more specifically the "crowning affirmation" in 8:1–2 and its development in 9:1–10:18 (cf. Michel, 343). The direct address of the audience as "brothers" (ἀδελφοί) is consistent with the writer's practice in earlier parenetic units where he urged the community to validate its faith by acting upon it (cf. "holy brothers" [3:1], "brothers" [3:12], "dear friends" [6:9]). This initial phrase introduces a complex periodic sentence that continues for seven verses (vv 19–25).

The present participle ἔχοντες, "since we have," has two complementary objects, παρρησία, "authorization," for access to the heavenly sanctuary (v 19) and ἱερέα μέγαν, "a great priest," in charge of God's household (v 21). These terms summarize the benefits to be appropriated by Christians, which derive from Christ's sacrificial death and exaltation. παρρησία here has an eschatological nuance. It connotes a new, objective reality obtained for the Christian community by the death of Christ, i.e., the right of free access to God (cf. Grässer, *Glaube*, 16–18, 36–37). This presupposes the objective work of Christ in purging the conscience and authorizing Christians to stand with boldness in the presence of God (9:9, 14; 10:22). Bartelink has shown that the association of παρρησία with a purged conscience was a distinctive and new development in the use of the word, which the writer shared with other hellenistic Jewish authors (*Quelques observations*, 10–11; cf. Philo, *Who is the Heir?* 5–21, discussed by Thompson, *Beginnings of Christian Philosophy*, 32–33, 93). In v 19 παρρησία implies a certainty created by Christ's definitive sacrifice. It provides the ground for the following injunction to "draw near" to God continually (v 22) (cf. Dahl, *Int* 5 [1951] 402–3). It is possible to approach God in worship at the present time because the heavenly high priest has secured εἰς τὴν εἴσοδον τῶν ἁγίων, "free access to the heavenly sanctuary." As elsewhere in Hebrews, τὰ ἅγια designates the true sanctuary in heaven where Christ appears in the presence of God on behalf of his people (cf. 6:19–20; 8:1–2; 9:11–12, 24).

The decisive factor in the authorization of the Christians that enables them to approach God is indicated in the phrase ἐν τῷ αἵματι Ἰησοῦ, "by means of the blood of Jesus." The emphasis in the use of the personal name "Jesus" is on the full humanity of Christ, and thus on the validity of his redemptive sacrifice on behalf of the human family. It is striking that whenever the writer makes his most emphatic assertions concerning the saving work of Christ, he makes an explicit reference to the blood of Jesus (9:12, 14; 10:19, 29; 12:24; 13:12, 20). This fact is indicative of the importance of the cultic argument developed in 9:1–10:18, where the blood of Jesus is a graphic expression for Jesus' death viewed in its sacrificial aspect. That cultic argument is clearly presupposed here. The association of blood with life (see *Comment* on 9:7) is here reaffirmed when the access to the presence of God achieved by Christ is defined as "a way . . . which leads to life" (v 20) (cf. Johnsson, "Defilement," 224–25, 232).

The blessing of "free access to the heavenly sanctuary" is further defined by the compressed line of thought in v 20, which is intended to elucidate v 19. The expression ὁδὸν πρόσφατον καὶ ζῶσαν, "a way which is new and which leads to life," is descriptive of εἴσοδον, "free access," in v 19. It concerns the way into the heavenly sanctuary (see *Comment* on 9:8). The way is defined as πρόσφατον, "new," a term having both a temporal and a qualitative nuance. Temporally, the community possesses a way that had not previously existed, which is the result of the definitive sacrifice of Christ. It is a recently opened way (cf. 9:8), in contrast to the old way into the earthly sanctuary that has been set aside as a mere prefiguration of what was to come (cf. 8:13; 10:1). The way is also qualitatively new because it participates in the incorruptible freshness of the new covenant, which will not become old (Maurer, *TDNT* 6:767; Pelser, *Neot* 8 [1974] 48). The way is also defined as ζῶσαν, "living," in the sense that it leads to life, as demonstrated by the powerful effect that free access to God has upon the community of faith (so also Lünemann, 327; Seeberg, 113; Michel, 345; Hofius, *Vorhang*, 80).

The access the Christian community enjoys is one that Jesus ἐνεκαίνισεν ἡμῖν
. . . διὰ τοῦ καταπετάσματος, "made available for us . . . through the curtain."
It is difficult to ascertain the precise nuance intended in the verb ἐνεκαίνισεν. In
9:18 ἐγκαινίζειν has a cultic nuance ("to consecrate"), but here, where it is associated with access, it can denote "to make a way which was not there before,"
"to use a way for the first time," "to open," or "to dedicate" a way (Behm, *TDNT*
3:454; contrast Dahl, *Int* 5 [1951] 403–4, who argues for a cultic significance for
the expression in v 20, "he consecrated"). Michel argues that the verb signifies
both consecration and "making available for use" (345). The parallel with 6:19–
20, which speaks of Jesus' entrance "through the curtain," suggests that the
primary nuance is "to make a way" or "to make available" access to God (Pelser,
Neot 8 [1974] 47).

The obvious parallel in 6:19–20 is also informative for the interpretation of
the phrase "through the curtain," which almost certainly qualifies "the way." There
has been a strong tendency to interpret the expression in a metaphorical sense
(see above, *Note* j). The use of καταπετάσματος, "curtain," here, however, seems
clearly to be consistent with the local and literal use of the term in 6:19 and 9:3.
The evident parallel with 6:19, where the term καταπέτασμα cannot be metaphorical (Christ as forerunner entered "behind the curtain . . . having become a
high priest"), is decisive. The reference to the curtain that hangs before the
heavenly sanctuary expresses the old Jewish conception of the hiddenness and
inaccessibility of God (cf. Hofius, *Vorhang*, 4–16, 73–75, who traces this conception to Merkabah mysticism). Here the writer asserts that the Christian's approach
to God has its source and parallel in Christ's approach "through the curtain"
(Johnsson, "Defilement," 353–54).

The final clause τοῦτ' ἔστιν τῆς σαρκὸς αὐτοῦ, "that is, by means of his flesh,"
is explicative of the preceding sentence as a whole (see above, *Note* j). This syntactical conclusion is supported by the analogous structure of v 19 and v 20,
which was demonstrated above (*Note* j). Both verses refer to the new access, its
goal, and the sacrificial death of Jesus as the ground for access to God. The
primary difference between the two verses is that the subject of v 19 is Christians, whereas the subject of v 20 is Christ. The structure of vv 19–20, accordingly,
calls for an interpretation of the reference to the "flesh" of Jesus in an instrumental sense; the phrase ἐν τῷ αἵματι Ἰησοῦ, "by means of the blood of Jesus,"
in v 19 is in v 20 recapitulated in the phrase (διά [understood]) τῆς σαρκὸς αὐτοῦ,
"by means of his flesh" (so Hofius, "Inkarnation und Opfertod Jesu," 136–41;
id., *Vorhang*, 81–82; Jeremias, *ZNW* 62 [1971] 131; cf. Johnsson, "Defilement,"
353–55; N. H. Young, *NTS* 20 [1973] 103–4). The term σάρξ, "flesh," in Hebrews has reference to the incarnation of Jesus (2:14; 5:7) (cf. Hofius,
"Inkarnation und Opfertod Jesu," 138–41). In this context, the term is an alternate expression for Jesus' obedient death on the cross (Jeremias, *ZNW* 62 [1971]
131, n. 3). On this understanding, both v 19 and v 20 conclude with a reference
to Jesus' sacrificial death as the means by which free access to the heavenly sanctuary was attained.

The significance of these verses was clearly appreciated in the second
century. Justin Martyr (c. A.D. 130–50) cites Heb 6:19–20 and 10:19–20 and

comments that by virtue of the sacrificial death of the crucified high priest, Jesus Christ, Christians have become "the true high priestly people of God" (ἀρχιερατικὸν τὸ ἀληθινὸν γένος τοῦ θεοῦ) (*Dialogue* 116.1.3, cited by Hofius, *Vorhang*, 96).

21 A second blessing obtained for the community through Jesus' sacrifice and enthronement is the assurance of Christ's priestly rule over the household of God. The expression ἱερέα μέγαν, "a great priest," furnishes the second complementary object to the participle ἔχοντες, "since we have," in v 19. It is evident, therefore, that v 21 is parallel in formulation to 4:14:

4:14 ἔχοντες οὖν ἀρχιερέα μέγαν
    "Therefore, since we have a great high priest"
10:19–21 ἔχοντες οὖν ... ἱερέα μέγαν
    "Therefore, since we have ... a great priest"

The phrases are equivalent. The expression ἱερέα μέγαν is simply an alternative designation for the high priest (cf. Lev. 21:10; Num. 35:25, 28 LXX, where ὁ ἱερεὺς ὁ μέγας denotes the high priest). No difference in nuance is intended by the choice of terms in v 21 (Michel, 346, n. 1; F. F. Bruce, 249, n. 97). At this point, however, the significance of the writer's assertion has been enriched by the content of exposition of Christ's high priestly office that follows 4:14.

The declaration that the community has a great priest ἐπὶ τὸν οἶκον τοῦ θεοῦ, "in charge of God's household," recapitulates the argument in 3:1–6 and the formulation in 3:6*a*:

Χριστὸς δὲ ὡς υἱὸς ἐπὶ τὸν οἶκον αὐτοῦ
"but Christ, as a son in charge of his household"

The relative clause that follows immediately (3:6*b*) identifies God's household as the community of faith, which maintains its confidence and hope. The reference in v 21, then, is to the Church and, more specifically, to the community addressed. The proposal that the expression τὸν οἶκον τοῦ θεοῦ suggests a combination of ideas (i.e., "heaven," "heavenly sanctuary," as well as the congregation: e.g., Schierse, *Verheissung und Heilsvollendung*, 171; Peterson, "Examination," 268) is improbable because the writer nowhere else refers to the heavenly sanctuary under the metaphor of "the house of God" (cf. Michel, *TDNT* 5:125–28; Pelser, *Neot* 8 [1974] 49). The assertion that Christ exercises an administration over his own household informs the congregation that the Church is the sphere of his activity as high priest enthroned in the presence of God (cf. 10:12–14). This statement enriches the conception of the relationship Christ sustains to his people and assures them that their worshipful approach to God will be welcomed (see *Comment* on 4:15–16).

22 In the rhetorical structure of 10:19–25, the parallel assertions in vv 19–21 furnish the basis for three significant cohortatives in the present tense, which follow in vv 22, 23, and 24, respectively. The fact that each of these verses begins with a different verb would seem to indicate that each verse presents a separate thought and is not necessarily to be interpreted in the light of the other two. Any other construction tends to mitigate the force of the verbs (cf. Westcott, 321–22; Riggenbach, 311–19; Havener, "Credal Formulae," 456–57).

The first of the writer's coordinated appeals calls the community to that personal and congregational "drawing near" to God through Christ which is the essence of being a Christian. This is the only appropriate response to the benefits described in vv 19–21. The formulation of v 22a recalls the earlier exhortation to prayer in 4:16:

4:16   προσερχώμεθα ... μετὰ παρρησίας τῷ θρόνῳ τῆς χάριτος
        "Let us continue to draw near to the throne of grace with frank boldness"
10:22a προσερχώμεθα μετὰ ἀληθινῆς καρδίας ἐν πληροφορίᾳ πίστεως
        "Let us continue to draw near [to God] with a sincere heart in fullness of faith"

The parallel with 4:16 is important for assessing the significance of προσερχώμεθα, "let us continue to draw near." The use of this terminology elsewhere in Hebrews (7:25; 11:6; 12:18, 22) indicates that earnest prayer is a significant expression of the new relationship between God and his people promised in the new covenant (8:10–12; 10:16; cf. Jer 31:33; Ezek 36:26–27). It is, of course, unnecessary to limit the reference in v 22a to prayer; it is undoubtedly inclusive of every expression of worship in the life of a congregation (Michel, 346; Peterson, "Examination," 268–69; cf. Thüsing, BZ 9 [1965] 5–6, 9–16, who argues that this "drawing near" takes place particularly in the celebration of the Eucharist, but acknowledges that in view of the writer's perspective throughout Hebrews the reference may be to "the whole Christian life together with faith, prayer, worship, and suffering" [12]).

A context for this admonition has been established in the preceding argument concerning the enactment of the new covenant (see *Comment* on 9:15; 10:15–18). This discussion is presupposed in the appeal to approach God μετὰ ἀληθινῆς καρδίας, "with a sincere heart." The phrase evokes the relationship of heart-obedience to God that Jeremiah envisioned in terms of the "new heart" God would create in his people (Jer 31:33). The writer is convinced that this promise has been realized for the new people of God through Christ's definitive sacrifice. As a direct result of the decisive purgation provided by the blood of Christ (see *Comment* on 9:22; 10:18), "our hearts have been sprinkled clean from a burdened conscience" (v 22b; cf. 9:13–14; 10:18). Only when the heart has been purged from the defilement of a smiting conscience can it be renewed in fullness of faith and sincerity toward God (9:9, 14; 10:1–2, 15–18). The inauguration of the new covenant and the fulfillment of its promises add a dimension of eschatological urgency to the responsibility of the community to "draw near" (Peterson, "Examination," 232–34, 270).

The encouragement to "draw near" ἐν πληροφορίᾳ πίστεως, "in fullness of faith," sounds again the note of certainty expressed in v 19 with παρρησία, "authorization." The expression "fullness of faith" in v 22a appears to be parallel to the related expression πληροφορία τῆς ἐλπίδος, "the realization of hope," in 6:11. Both phrases are descriptive of the certainty and stability that are created in Christians as a result of the work of Christ and that enable them to remain loyal to him (Thompson, *Beginnings of Christian Philosophy*, 33; cf. MacRae, *Semeia* 12 [1978] 193, who comments: "If πληροφορία τῆς ἐλπίδος is the goal of the Christian, πληροφορία πίστεως is the condition or means of it").

The solid basis for the appeal expressed in v 22a is an existing relationship with God. This is made explicit in v 22b, where the writer introduces two complementary participial clauses in the perfect tense, both of which relate to the preceding προσερχώμεθα. These clauses have reference to the application of the benefits of Christ's sacrifice to the Christian at some decisive moment in the past. The perfect tenses of the participles (ῥεραντισμένοι ... καὶ λελουσμένοι, "have been sprinkled . . . and have been washed") refer to actions which are accomplished and enduring facts; they stress conditions of approach to God which Christians already enjoy.

The most common interpretation of v 22b finds in the imagery of the sprinkled heart and the washed body an allusion to the consecration of Aaron and his sons to priestly service. When they were installed in their office, they were sprinkled with blood and their bodies were washed with water (Exod 29:4, 21; Lev 8:6, 30; cf. *Jub.* 21:16; *T. Levi* 9:11; *m. Yoma* 3:3) (so Moffatt, 144; Michel, 346; Moe, *TZ* 5 [1949] 162–63; Dahl, *Int* 5 [1951] 406–7; et al.).

It seems more satisfactory to recognize that the specific imagery of the "sprinkling of the heart from a burdened conscience" has been anticipated in 9:18–22. There the writer reminded the community of the action of Moses, who sprinkled the people with blood during the ratification of the old covenant at Sinai. The thought that Christians have been made participants in the new covenant by the blood of Christ is forcefully expressed in the immediate context (v 19). This suggests that the "sprinkling with respect to the heart" in v 22b is to be associated with Jesus' inauguration of the new covenant through his death (so Snell, 129; Peterson, "Examination," 269–70; cf. Dahl, *Int* 5 [1951] 406). The decisive purgation effected by the blood of Christ has removed the barrier of a smiting conscience, which had prevented unhindered access to God. The condition of the burdened heart belongs to the past (cf. J. Stelzenberger, *Syneidēsis im Neuen Testament* [Paderborn: Schöningh, 1961] 63–65).

The expression λελουσμένοι τὸ σῶμα ὕδατι καθαρῷ, "the body having been washed with clean water," refers to the outward sign of the inward purgation accomplished by the blood of Christ. In the LXX ὕδωρ καθαρόν, "pure water," is an expression for the water used in ritual purification (Num 5:17; Ezek 36:25; cf. *T. Levi* 8:5). Moreover, the formula for washing the body is technical (cf. Lev 14:9; 15:11, 13, 16, 27; 16:4, 24, 26; Num 19:7–8; Deut 23:12 LXX). Already in 9:13–14 the writer contrasted the cleansing that affects only the body with the decisive purgation that reaches to the conscience and makes possible the service of God.

The reference in v 22b is almost certainly to Christian baptism, which replaces all previous cleansing rites (so Windisch, 93; Moffatt, 144; Kuss, 156; Spicq 2:317; F. F. Bruce, 250–51; Strathmann, 133–34; Dahl, *Int* 5 [1951] 407; Pelser, *Neot* 8 [1974] 50; for a dissenting point of view, cf. M. Barth, *Die Taufe—Ein Sakrament?* [Zollikon/Zürich: Zwingli, 1951] 478). Christian baptism belongs to the new covenant because it is accompanied by the reality it symbolizes. Both clauses of v 22b provide complementary interpretations of the event of baptism. The washing of the body with water and the purging of the heart are complementary aspects of Christian conversion (cf. J. D. G. Dunn, *Baptism in the Holy Spirit* [Philadelphia: Westminster, 1970] 211–14). This assessment seems to be preferable to the view which regards the two clauses as merely an example of rhetorical parallelism (so Michel, 346–47; Spicq, 2:317). The emphasis upon the present possession of certain objective blessings deriving from Christ's sacrifice in vv 19–21 is sustained in v 22b with its reference to the purging of the heart and body.

23 The second appeal is for a stance of unwavering fidelity to the eschatological hope that Christians possess through Christ: κατέχωμεν τὴν ὁμολογίαν τῆς ἐλπίδος ἀκλινῆ, "let us continue to hold fast the hope we profess without wavering." The close proximity of this injunction to v 22b, where the writer speaks of Christian baptism, has encouraged interpreters to find here an allusion to a baptismal confession (e.g., Kuss, 156: "to baptism belongs the baptismal confession"; cf. A. Seeberg, *Der Katechismus der Urchristenheit* [Leipzig: Deichert, 1903] 142–47, 200–201; Bornkamm, *TBl* 21 [1942] 189–93; Dahl, *Int* 5 [1951] 410–11). This understanding rests on the assumption that v 22b and v 23 go together. The syntactical structure of the passage, however, favors the viewpoint that v 22 and v 23 express separate ideas. Moreover, it was pointed out more than sixty years ago that if a baptismal confession were intended, one would expect ὁμολογία to be qualified by τῆς πίστεως, "the confession of [our] faith," instead of by τῆς ἐλπίδος, "of [our] hope," a "correction" that is actually found in MSS 044, 1245, and 1898 (Riggenbach, 319, n. 84). It seems more satisfactory to recognize that ὁμολογία in this passage is not a technical term for an objective, traditional confession of faith, as it clearly is in 4:14 ("Let us continue to hold fast our confession"), but refers more generally to the "profession" of a definite, distinct belief (cf. Havener, "Credal Formulae," 455–60).

Rather than comparing v 23a with 4:14, it is instructive to recall 6:18, where the writer declares, "we have a strong incentive [κρατῆσαι τῆς προκειμένης ἐλπίδος] to hold fast to the hope which is placed in front of us." Both in 6:18 and 10:23a the "hope" to which the writer refers is an objective reality related to the priestly activity of Jesus. In Hebrews the term "hope" always describes the objective content of hope, consisting of present and future salvation (cf. Grässer, *Glaube*, 32–33; Mora, *La Carta a los Hebreos*, 205–6; see above, *Note* q). In fact, "the whole Christian life can be comprehended in the concept of ἐλπίς ('hope') (3:6; 6:11, 18; 7:19; 10:23; 11:1)" (Peterson, "Examination," 271). In 6:18 the term is associated with Jesus' entrance as high priest into the heavenly sanctuary (6:19–20). In 10:23a it is related to Christ's provision of access to the heavenly sanctuary (10:19–20). Accordingly, "to hold fast the hope we profess" is to maintain a firm confidence in the objective gift of salvation God has extended to the community on the basis of Christ's priesthood and sacrifice (cf. Swetnam, *Bib* 55 [1971] 336, who suggests that ἐλπὶς ἀκλινῆς, "unwavering hope," is a shorthand reference to 9:11–10:18, where Christ's cultic action and sacrifice are presented as the basis for the Christian hope). The term "hope" is a vivid reminder that the entire Christian life is "christologically and eschatologically stamped for Hebrews" (Michel, 347; cf. Havener, "Credal Formulae," 455–67).

The encouragement to "hold fast" is reinforced by the term ἀκλινής, "without wavering." This word is used by many classical authors but is found only twice in the LXX (4 Macc 6:7; 17:3) and nowhere else in the NT. It is an important word in the vocabulary of Philo, who uses it primarily to signify the immutability that belongs to God alone, but also to describe the stability of the friends of God who stand by his side (*On Giants* 49) (see Williamson, *Philo,* 31–36). It connotes "swerving neither to one side nor to the other," and so comes to mean "firm," "stable," "fixed," "steadfast." Here it qualifies the cohortative κατέχωμεν, "let us continue to hold fast," calling for the community to remain stable and to affirm its privileged status as the people who have been granted access to God through Christ. Holding fast "without wavering" is itself an act of confession, even when no words are spoken (Peterson, "Examination," 271; cf. Thompson, *Beginnings of Christian Philosophy*, 33–34).

The community possesses the strongest incentive for fidelity in the faithfulness (πιστός) of God who does what he has promised (v 23*b*). The formulation πιστὸς γὰρ ὁ ἐπαγγειλάμενος, "for he who promised is faithful," is confessional in character.

The word πιστός has the nuance of constancy (Grässer, *Glaube*, 22–23). Unchangeably, God stands behind his promise (cf. 11:11). The writer here succinctly recapitulates the emphasis upon the utter reliability of God as set forth in 6:17–18; the promise is absolutely certain because "it is impossible for God to lie" (6:18). He will keep faith with the community. The factor of uncertainty lies exclusively with the community, in their tendency to waver in their commitment to the gospel (cf. vv 25*b*, 35–36, 39). It is the responsibility of the writer's friends to act upon God's constancy by steadfastly holding on to their beliefs without wavering.

24–25 The third appeal is a summons for the continued caring for one another that finds an expression in love, good works, and the mutual encouragement that active participation in the gatherings of the community makes possible. The note of Christian love completes the triad of faith (v 22), hope (v 23), and love (vv 24–25), which is developed by means of the coordinated cohortatives in vv 22–25 (cf. 6:10–12 for this same triad).

The exhortation κατανοῶμεν ἀλλήλους εἰς παροξυσμὸν ἀγάπης καὶ καλῶν ἔργων, "let us keep on caring for one another for the stimulation of love and good works," centers on the responsibility of Christians to exhibit practical concern for one another. By considerateness and example, they are to spur one another on to the love and good works that had distinguished them as a community in the past (see *Comment* on 6:10). Exemplary service of fellow Christians had once been the hallmark of the congregation (cf. vv 33–34) and seems to have persisted in some measure. But the writer urges that the expression of love within the fellowship be deepened and extended. In this context ἀγάπη is not a technical term for the meal at which the Eucharist was celebrated (as urged by Glombitza, *NovT* 9 [1967] 143–46), but a caring response to need in the lives of other Christians. "Good works" are tangible expressions of caring love, as in 6:10. Active support and concern for the welfare of one another are matters of critical urgency in the life of a community exposed to testing and disappointment (cf. F. F. Bruce, 253; Peterson, "Examination," 271).

The appeal in v 24 is supplemented by two participial phrases in the present tense, μὴ ἐγκαταλείποντες τὴν ἐπισυναγωγὴν ἑαυτῶν, "not discontinuing our meeting together" and ἀλλὰ παρακαλοῦντες, "but rather encouraging one another" (v 25). These contrasting phrases indicate the importance of the regular gathering of the local assembly for worship and fellowship. The contrast serves to define the specific character of the term ἐπισυναγωγή, "meeting together": it is the place or occasion for mutual encouragement and exhortation (cf. P. E.

Hughes, 417–18; Mora, *La Carta a los Hebreos*, 49–50; Schrage, *TDNT* 7:841–43).
The present tense of the participles expresses the common responsibility for these
mandates (Michel, 347).

The failure of the writer to specify why some members of the community had
stopped taking an active part in the meetings of the house church has invited a
wide range of conjectures (see Schrage, *TDNT* 7:843, nn. 11–15). The reference
to "custom" or "habit" (ἔθος) implies a situation of indifference and apathy, which
is consistent with other indications throughout the sermon (2:1–3; 3:7–15; 4:1;
5:11–14; 10:23) (cf. Mora, *La Carta a los Hebreos*, 50). It is natural to think that
the neglect of the meetings was motivated by fear of recognition by outsiders in
a time of persecution, or by disappointment in the delay of the parousia, or by
some other acute concern. It is sobering to discover that in the early second
century in Rome it was simply preoccupation with business affairs that accounted
for the neglect of the meetings of a house church (*Herm. Sim.* 8.8.1; 9.20.1).
Whatever the motivation, the writer regarded the desertion of the communal
meetings as utterly serious. It threatened the corporate life of the congregation
and almost certainly was a prelude to apostasy on the part of those who were
separating themselves from the assembly (so H. Montefiore, 177–78; Williamson,
Philo, 261; Thompson, *Beginnings of Christian Philosophy*, 34). The neglect of
worship and fellowship was symptomatic of a catastrophic failure to appreciate
the significance of Christ's priestly ministry and the access to God it provided.

The reason the meetings of the assembly are not to be neglected is that they
provide a communal setting where mutual encouragement and admonition may
occur. The parallel passage in 3:13 (ἀλλὰ παρακαλεῖτε ἑαυτοὺς καθ᾽ ἑκάστην
ἡμέραν, "but encourage one another every day") may actually presuppose a daily
gathering of the house church for mutual encouragement. The verb παρακαλεῖν
includes the notions of warning and reproof as well as encouragement, with the
implication that reproof should be given in a loving way (cf. Forkman, *Limits of the
Religious Community*, 47–50). The entire community must assume responsibility
to watch that no one grows weary or becomes apostate. This is possible only when
Christians continue to exercise care for one another personally (Dahl, *Int* 5 [1951]
411–12).

The urgency for encouragement and reproof is that the community experiences an unresolved tension between peril and promise so long as it lives in the
world. The neglect of the meetings of the assembly by some of the members sufficiently attests the reality of spiritual peril. The promise is indicated by the
approaching "Day of the Lord" (v 25*b*), when God's plan for his covenant people
will be brought to realization. The sober reminder that the Day of the Lord is
drawing near offers a further incentive for continued active participation in the
life of the community. It indicates that the tension between peril and promise
will ultimately be resolved eschatologically. The description of the parousia in
9:28 as the return of the heavenly high priest with salvation to those who wait for
him is supplemented here with a complementary OT formulation implying judgment as well as salvation (cf. Marshall, *Kept by the Power*, 144; A. L. Moore, *The
Parousia in the New Testament* [Leiden: Brill, 1966] 148–49).

26–27 The explanatory γάρ, "for," with which vv 26–31 are introduced shows
that this paragraph sustains an intimate relationship to the preceding appeals
and especially to the pastoral admonitions in v 25, where the writer referred to

those who had deserted the community (so McCown, "*Ο ΛΟΓΟΣ ΤΗΣ ΠΑΡΑΚΛΗΣΕΩΣ,*" 71; H. Montefiore, 177–78; Daly, *BTB* 8 [1978] 106; among others). Attendance at worship and encouraging one another are functions of the new covenant (see Forkman, *Limits of the Religious Community,* 193, who observes that the covenant motif is connected with the limits of the community only in Hebrews). The neglect of God's gifts is almost tantamount to a decisive rejection of them. In this instance, the neglect of the meetings of the local assembly actually displayed a contemptuous disregard for the truth, which exposes hardened offenders to divine judgment. The severe warning in vv 26–31 is parallel in form and function to 6:4–8. Like that earlier passage, it exposes the gravity of apostasy (cf. Cruvellier, *EEv* 12 [1952] 137–40; Williamson, *Philo,* 247–67; Mora [*La Carta a los Hebreos,* 91–96] denies that v 26*a* can be reduced to apostasy, but includes other grave sins; for a summary of the history of the interpretation of this passage, see Grässer, *Glaube,* 192–98).

The process envisioned in 6:4–8 consisted of four stages: (1) the experience of Christian life (6:4–5); (2) the fact of apostasy (6:6); (3) the recognition that renewal is impossible (6:4, 6); and (4) the imposition of the curse sanctions of the covenant (6:8). This same process can be recognized in 10:26–29, arranged in another syntactical order but with a complementary development:

(1) the experience of Christian life ("after we have received the full knowledge of the truth," v 26);
(2) the fact of apostasy ("If we deliberately persist in sin," v 26, which is defined explicitly in v 29);
(3) the recognition that renewal is impossible ("there is no longer any sacrifice for sin," v 26);
(4) the imposition of the curse sanctions of the covenant ("only an inevitable terrifying expectation of judgment and of raging fire ready to consume God's adversaries," v 27).

The reiteration of the pattern of apostasy and its irreversible consequences demonstrates that 6:4–8 and 10:26–31 are complementary declarations (cf. P. Proulx and A. Schökel, "Heb 6,4–6: εἰς μετάνοιαν ἀνασταυροῦντας," *Bib* 56 [1975] 204–5; on the extensive terminological parallelism between 6:4–8 and 10:26–31, cf. Carlston, *JBL* 78 [1959] 296).

The real difference between 6:4–6 and 10:26–31 rests in the formulation of the argument. In 10:26–29 cultic categories provide the ground for this severe pastoral warning. The writer appeals to the necessity of a "sacrifice for sins" (v 26) and to the significance of "the blood of the covenant" by which Christians have been consecrated to the service of God (v 29). The argument in 10:26–29 clearly takes advantage of the discussion of the cultus in 9:11–10:18 (see especially, 9:26*b*, 28*a*; 10:10, 12, 14, 18). By contrast, there is no appeal to the cultus in the argument developed in 6:4–8.

That the writer appeals in 10:26–31 to the new cultic action of Christ indicates that these verses provide the counterpoint to 10:19–22. The earlier passage sets forth *the appropriate response* to the sacrifice of Christ and his entrance as high priest into the heavenly sanctuary. The provision of access to God invites sincere and earnest worship. In the present passage *the inappropriate response* of those who fail to appreciate their continuing need for Christ's redemptive action commands the writer's attention. A cultic argument underlies both paragraphs and is the determining factor whether the response warrants acceptance or judgment. It is imperative to recognize that the interpretation of vv 26–31 must be based firmly in the cultic argument of the writer (following Johnsson, "Defilement," 357–60).

The key expression in the description of the response that merits the wrath of God is ἑκουσίως . . . ἁμαρτανόντων ἡμῶν, "if we deliberately persist in sin." The word ἑκουσίως connotes a conscious expression of an attitude that displays contempt for God (cf. Forkman, *Limits of the Religious Community*, 153). The effects of this attitude are not developed until v 29. But already in v 26 it is possible to discern why the intentional persistence in sin removes a person from the sphere of grace. The writer regards sin as defilement (see *Comment* on 9:7). Sin that is committed ἑκουσίως clearly implies a rejection of the cultus itself (and of God who provided for it). People who reject the cultus can have no hope of removing the defilement of sin because their rejection expresses open, intentional and voluntary apostasy (Johnsson, "Defilement," 358–59; cf. Forkman, *Limits of the Religious Community*, 176, 193). The initial phrase in v 26a is thus equivalent to the sin of "turning away from the living God" in 3:12.

The concept of deliberate sin derives from Num 15:22–31, where a distinction is made between those who unintentionally transgress God's commandments (vv 22–29) and the person who sins "defiantly," who must be "cut off from his people" because he has despised the Lord (vv 30–31). The divine pronouncement is that "his guilt remains on him" (v 31). It is specified repeatedly in the Levitical statutes that provision for atonement is restricted to those who sin ἀκουσίως, "unintentionally" (e.g., Lev 4:1–2, 13, 22, 27; 5:14–15 LXX; cf. Heb 5:2). A deliberate and calculated violation of the commandments placed the offender beyond forgiveness. The penalty for intentional sin was extirpation, reduction to the status of one who has been cut off from every resource of the covenant community and who has ceased to be truly a person.

The heinous character of this offense resides in the fact that it occurred after the reception of τὴν ἐπίγνωσιν τῆς ἀληθείας, "the full knowledge of the truth." This technical expression refers to the acceptance of life in response to the preaching of the gospel. ἀλήθεια is saving "truth," the revelation of God's provision for the defilement of sin through Christ (cf. Mora, *La Carta a los Hebreos*, 93; Michel, 350–51); it is something to be received from God. The term ἐπίγνωσις implies "a penetrating and certain knowledge" (Riggenbach, 325), a clear perception of the truth (Michel, 351, n. 1). The phrase thus describes a dynamic assimilation of the truth of the gospel. It is an equivalent expression for the solemn description of authentic Christian experience in 6:4–5 (Mora, *La Carta a los Hebreos*, 93–94). The offensiveness of those who persist in sin is heightened by their prior experience of Christian truth (so also Marshall, *Kept by the Power*, 141–2, who calls attention to the writer's use of the plural personal pronoun ἡμῶν, "we," in v 26a ["if *we* persist in sin"]: "the word 'we' cannot refer to any other group of people than his readers and himself [cf. 2:1]").

The results of a calculated, persistent renunciation of the truth received are specified in vv 26b–27. In 10:18 the writer concluded his cultic argument by declaring οὐκέτι προσφορὰ περὶ ἁμαρτίας, "an offering for sins is no longer necessary." The reason a sin offering is no longer required is that Christ, by a single, perfect sacrifice, has decisively put away sin (cf. 9:26). In a formulation designed to recall 10:18, the writer now declares, οὐκέτι περὶ ἁμαρτιῶν ἀπολείπεται θυσία, "there is no longer any sacrifice for sins." This follows because the only sacrifice that can remove defilement has been repudiated, and the sufficient sacrifice of Christ cannot be repeated (10:10, 12, 14). What remains is an "inevitable, terrifying expectation of judgment." This describes a religious dread that reflects in anticipation upon the destruction that must follow from a display of contempt for God.

The motif of inescapable judgment is developed with an allusion to Isa 26:11. The imagery of "raging fire ready to consume God's adversaries" is vividly suggestive of the prospect awaiting the person who turns away from God's gracious provision through Christ. The apostate is regarded as the adversary of God. The description of judgment as a fire that devours and utterly destroys recalls the actual experience of the followers of Korah who were consumed by fire because they had shown contempt for God (Num 16:35; 26:10). The consequence of apostasy is terrifying, irrevocable judgment.

28–29 The form of the argument in vv 28–29 is anticipated in 2:2–3, where the law is designated as "the message spoken by angels." There the writer used a rhetorical question to drive home his point that if disregard for the Mosaic law was appropriately punished, neglect of the salvation announced in the gospel must inevitably be catastrophic. This point is taken up again here, but it is now sharpened by the allusion to Deut 17:6 in v 28 and by the delineation in v 29 of the effects of disregarding a salvation as great as Christians enjoy.

The formulation of v 28 draws on the LXX, where the verb ἀθετεῖν, "violates," signifies the willful repudiation of a divine institution. It denotes "to act unfaithfully," "to be apostate" (cf. Maurer, *TDNT* 8:158–59, who calls attention to Ezek 22:26, οἱ ἱερεῖς αὐτῆς ἠθέτησαν νόμον μου ["Her priests have violated my law"]). The declaration that anyone who violated a precept of Moses had to die "without pity on the evidence of two or three witnesses" conflates two passages from Deuteronomy. In Deut 17:2–7 the death penalty is the punishment for idolatry, provided that the commission of the act is proven by the concurrence of at least two or three witnesses (Deut 17:6; cf. Num 35:30 for the analogous crime of murder). The detail that the offender must be put to death "without pity" is drawn from Deut 13:8 ("Show him no pity. Do not spare him or shield him").

The gravity of defiance of the law of Moses under the old covenant throws into bold relief the far greater seriousness of apostasy under the new covenant. Since the blessings God has bestowed through Christ are greater than those provided through the old covenant, the rejection of those blessings entails a far more severe punishment. The impact of the *a fortiori* argument in vv 28–29 is achieved through the rhetorical question in v 29 and the dramatic switch from the inclusive "we" of vv 26–27 to the direct address in v 29: "for if *we* deliberately persist in sin . . . . How much severer punishment do *you* suppose will he deserve?" (McCown, "Ο ΛΟΓΟΣ ΤΗΣ ΠΑΡΑΚΛΗΣΕΩΣ," 71). Contempt for a privileged relationship with God through Christ in the new covenant will involve retribution more terrible than the death penalty attached to violation of the law. The πόσῳ . . . χείρονος construction ("how much severer"), which underscores the severity of the judgment to be incurred by the apostate, is the logical corollary to the πόσῳ μᾶλλον construction ("how much more") of 9:13–14: if the cleansing rites of the old covenant accomplished the purgation of the defilement of the body, *how much more* does the blood of Christ purge the defiled conscience so that we may worship God! The measure of privilege distinguishing the new covenant from the old necessarily defines the extent of the peril to which those who spurn its provisions expose themselves (cf. Johnsson, "Defilement," 357–60, 416–17).

The character of the contempt for God expressed by apostasy under the new covenant is elaborated in v 29 by three parallel participial clauses that articulate its effect. These clauses provide definition for 26a ("If we deliberately persist in sin"). In each instance the aorist tense of the participle is culminative (or constative), i.e., it summarizes a persistent attitude.

(1) The apostate "has trampled upon the Son of God" (καταπατεῖν, "to trample under," "to treat with disdain"). The designation of Jesus as "the Son of God" almost certainly has reference to the formal confession of faith which the community had openly acknowledged (see *Comment* on 4:14). The repudiation of the confession is tantamount to a scornful rejection of the Son of God. The paradoxical notion of treating with disdain one who possesses transcendent dignity commands attention.

(2) The apostate "has treated the blood of the covenant, by which he was consecrated [to the service of God], as defiled." The formulation reflects the cultic argument in 9:11–10:18, where the death of Christ is related to the enactment of the new covenant and the discussion insists on the significance of blood (cf. 9:13–22). The words "the blood of the covenant" are taken from Exod 24:8 LXX, cited in 9:20. Here they clearly refer to Christ's sacrificial death on the cross viewed from the perspective of covenant inauguration. The blood of Christ seals and activates the new, eternal covenant (cf. 13:20). The phrase ἐν ᾧ ἡγιάσθη, "by means of which he was consecrated," resumes 10:10, 14, where the subjective blessing secured by Christ's sufficient sacrifice is defined as consecration to God (cf. 13:12). This phrase in v 29 corroborates that 10:26–31 is descriptive of the Christian who has experienced the action of Christ upon his life. With biting irony, the writer envisions such a person as regarding Christ's blood as κοινόν ("defiled," "disqualified for sacrifice"). The juxtaposition of considering *defiled* blood which *consecrates* is rhetorically forceful. A deliberate rejection of the vital power of the blood of Christ to purge sins decisively is indicated (cf. Johnsson, "Defilement," 359–60).

(3) The apostate "has insulted the Spirit of grace." In 9:14 the writer declared that Christ offered himself to God as an unblemished sacrifice "through the eternal Spirit." The connection of the Spirit with sacrifice in that place may account for the reference to the Spirit of grace here. The description τὸ πνεῦμα τῆς χάριτος, "the Spirit of grace," may be an allusion to Zech 12:10 LXX, where God promised to pour forth upon the house of David πνεῦμα χάριτος καὶ οἰκτιρμοῦ, "a Spirit of grace and mercy" (so Windisch, 97; Michel, 353). If this is the intended allusion, the reference is to the Holy Spirit "poured out" at Pentecost, who offers himself to the community in free grace and effects salvation (Michel, 353). Alternatively, the presence of the Spirit in the congregation (cf. 2:4; 6:4) is the sign of the eschatological grace of God expressed through Christ (Schweizer, *TDNT* 6:446). The attitude of the apostate, however, is summarized

in the aorist participle ἐνυβρίσας, "having insulted," "having outraged," "having displayed contempt with injury" (cf. Mora, *La Carta a los Hebreos*, 99, n. 7). Here as well the juxtaposition of the contradictory notions of *insulting* a *gracious* Spirit is calculated to command attention.

Taken cumulatively, the three clauses in v 29 define persistent sin (v 26a) as an attitude of contempt for the salvation secured through the priestly sacrifice of Christ. Nothing less than a complete rejection of the Christian faith satisfies the descriptive clauses in which the effects of the offense are sketched. The magnitude of the affront displayed by apostasy clarifies why this offense is ultimate. Apostate are those who embrace worldliness in preference to the community. They have *chosen* to return to the world from which they had been separated by the blood of Christ. In their lives the sacred has been collapsed into the profane. Their denial of their need for the life of the community reflects a willful hardening of their hearts (cf. 3:12–15). Apostasy reaffirms the values of the world, which permit those who stand outside the community to regard Jesus Christ with contempt (cf. 6:6). Consequently, those who once were cleansed and consecrated to God become reinfected with a permanent defilement that cannot be purged (Johnsson, "Defilement," 416–17). They experience an absolute loss, which is deserved (cf. Moule, *SEÅ* 30 [1965] 31–32; Mora, *La Carta a los Hebreos*, 97–101).

30–31 The stern pastoral warning in vv 26–29 is summed up succinctly. Two brief scriptural texts demonstrate that the initiative for the judgment of apostates rests not with the community, but with God. In introducing the citations the writer reverts to the inclusive "we" with which he had begun in v 26a: "for *we* know who it was who said."

The first citation is taken from the Song of Moses, which was used in the liturgy of the synagogue in the Diaspora as well as in the early Church (see *Comment* on 1:6). The quotation reflects Deut 32:35a, but departs from the LXX to follow a variant Greek textual tradition that had been conformed to the MT (cf. Katz, *ZNW* 49 [1958] 219–20). The fact that Paul has the same rendering of Deut 32:35a in Rom 12:19 suggests that this particular textual tradition was the common property of the early Church. Using the emphatic first person singular, God declares that he assumes personal responsibility for taking vengeance on those who have become his adversaries.

The second quotation is introduced by the simple καὶ πάλιν formula ("and again"; cf. 1:5; 2:13). The citation is taken from the same immediate context, Deut 32:36a (= Ps 134[MT 135]:14a LXX), but has been adapted to the writer's purposes. The text follows the LXX exactly, but in the LXX the statement occurs as a clause introduced by a causal ὅτι ("because the Lord will judge his people"). By omitting the ὅτι the writer casts the quotation in the form of a declarative sentence. The thought prominent both in Deut 32:36a and in Ps 134:14a LXX is that God's judgment will result in the vindication of his people. In the context of Hebrews, it implies the certainty of the judgment of the apostates. The two quotations in v 30 serve to reinforce the reference to the inevitability of judgment in v 27a.

The sober comment in v 31 provides a climactic summation to the entire argument. The initial term φοβερόν, "it is terrifying," which is emphatic by virtue of its position, sounds again the note of terror (φοβερά) in v 27. These correlative terms evoke the numinous religious dread that the thought of the imminent judgment of God inspires in those who have forfeited the benefits of Christ's sacrifice. The final statement thus affirms the magnitude of the sin of apostasy and of the impending judgment from which there is no escape. It reflects a profound conviction of the awesome majesty and holiness of the living God (cf. F. F. Bruce, 263–64).

32 In the development of 10:19–39 the sharp warning of vv 26–31 is followed by words of reassurance and encouragement. The parenetic sequence exhibited here is anticipated in 6:4–12, where a severe warning is followed by a word of pastoral comfort (see *Comment* on 6:9–10). The degree of parallelism between these two sections can be displayed in a chart (see Figure 1).

WARNING	6:4–8	10:26–31
(1) Description of the apostate	"fallen away" (6:6) "crucifying the Son of God" (6:6) "exposing him to open shame" (6:6)	"deliberately persist in sin" (10:26) "trample upon the Son of God" (10:29) "treat the blood of the covenant as defiled" (10:29) "insult the Spirit of grace" (10:29)
(2) Prior experience	"once for all brought into the light" (6:4) "have experienced the gift from heaven" (6:4) "have received a share in the Holy Spirit" (6:4) "have experienced the goodness of God's word and the coming age" (6:5)	"have received the full knowledge of the truth" (10:26) "consecrated by means of the blood of the covenant" (10:29)
(3) Impossibility of renewal	"It is impossible . . . to restore them to repentance" (6:4/6)	"no longer any sacrifice for sins" (10:26)
(4) Expectation	"loss" (6:6) "curse" (6:8) "burning" (6:8)	"terrifying expectation of judgment" (10:27) "raging fire" (10:27) "severer punish- ment"(10:29) "dread" (10:31)
COMFORT	6:9–12	10:32–35 (36)
(1) Basis	Appeal to "better things which accompany your salvation" (6:9)	Appeal to "remember those earlier days after you had received the light" (10:32)

(2) Past experience as Christians	"work and love demonstrated" (6:10)	"endured a hard contest with sufferings" (10:32)
	"you served . . . fellow Christians" (6:10)	"showed solidarity with those who were harshly treated" (10:33)
		"shared the sufferings of those in prison" (10:34)
		"cheerfully accepted the seizure of your property" (10:34)
(3) Present responsibility	"demonstrate the same earnest concern" (6:11)	"Do not throw away your boldness" (10:35)
	"not become sluggish" (6:12)	["endurance" (10:36)]
	"become imitators of those with steadfast endurance" (6:12)	
(4) Incentive	"the realization of your hope" (6:11)	"great reward" (10:35)
	"inherit the promise" (6:12)	["receive the promise" (10:36)]

Figure 1. Parallelism between Heb 6:4–12 and Heb 10:26–36.

The structure of the warning is balanced structurally by the word of comfort. The wisdom of the pastor in addressing the house church is evident from the fact that he makes their own past experience the paradigm for the present and the immediate future. He wants them to subject their present experience as Christians to a fresh examination in the light of their past stance of firm commitment. By pointing the community to the past as well as to the future, the writer seeks to strengthen their Christian resolve for the present (cf. T. W. Lewis, *NTS* 22 [1975–76] 89, 92, n. 1, who observes that both in 6:9–12 and in 10:32–39 events in the community's past are "turned into a hortatory paradigm for its continuing existence").

The juxtaposition of 10:26–31 and 32–35 suggests that it may have been the experience of suffering, abuse, and loss in the world that motivated the desertion of the community acknowledged in v 25 and a general tendency to avoid contact with outsiders observed elsewhere in Hebrews (see *Comment* on 5:11–14). T. W. Lewis (*NTS* 22 [1975–76] 91–93) has suggested that the community found a Scriptural basis for interpreting its lifestyle in terms of withdrawal and concealment in Isa 26:20 ("Go, my people, enter your rooms and shut the doors behind you; hide yourselves for a little while until his wrath is passed"). The allusion to this text in v 37, where it is significantly modified by the citation of Hab 2:3–4, and the reference to withdrawal in vv 38–39 lend a measure of support to his proposal. In 10:32–35 the writer counters an unhealthy attitude by setting forth the community's courageous stance of commitment under adverse circumstances in the past as a model for continuing boldness now. Drawing upon a primitive Christian tradition designed to strengthen believers in the crisis of persecution, the writer applies the tradition to the experience of his audience in order to encourage them to emulate their own splendid example (see Form/Structure/Setting on 10:19–39; cf. Nauck, ZNW 46 [1955] 68–80; McCown, "Ο ΛΟΓΟΣ ΤΗΣ ΠΑΡΑΚΛΗΣΕΩΣ," 80–83).

The adversative δέ, "instead," in v 32 indicates the writer's strategy. He urges his friends to pursue a course of action opposite to that just described. The oratorical imperative ἀναμιμνῄσκεσθε, "remember," which is parallel to the cohortatives in v 22, 23, and 24, is a call for reflection. Contemplation of the events clustered around the crisis of serious persecution and loss at an earlier point in their experience as a congregation should not only revive that experience in their memories but also in their present lifestyle. That these events had been the direct result of their commitment as Christians is indicated by the participle φωτισθέντες ("after you had received the light"). The reference is not to baptism (as urged by Käsemann, Das wandernde Gottesvolk, 119, n. 4) but to the saving illumination of the heart and mind mediated through the preaching of the gospel (cf. 6:4: τοὺς ἅπαξ φωτισθέντας, "those who have once been brought into the light"; see Comment on 6:4).

The significant facet of the community's experience in that earlier period is stated in the phrase πολλὴν ἄθλησιν ὑπεμείνατε παθημάτων, "you endured a hard contest with sufferings." From the beginning, sufferings had been a constituent part of their Christian experience. The rare word ἄθλησις, "contest," was originally used of the intense efforts of athletes in the sports arena (cf. Polybius, 5.64.6; 7.10.2–4; 27.9.7; 27.9.11). Here it is used metaphorically for persecution, but there is no suggestion in the immediate context, nor elsewhere in Hebrews (cf. 12:4), of the later Christian use of the term for martyrdom (e.g., The Passion of Andrew 15, which speaks of ἡ ἡμέρα τῆς ἀθλήσεως, "[the day of the contest] of the holy apostle Andrew"; cf. 1 Clem. 5:2, ἕως θανάτου ἤθλησαν, "they contended to their death"). Although the word ἄθλησις occurs only here in the NT, the image of the athletic contest is introduced in 12:1–2 as well, and there, as in v 32, it is linked to the concept of endurance.

The use of the verb ὑπομένειν, "to endure," with ἄθλησις is indicative of the close affinity between the writer and the literature of hellenistic Judaism, where the metaphor of the contest and the notion of training through adversity is not uncommon. It is found especially in 4 Maccabees, where ὑπομένειν, "to endure," and ὑπομονή, "endurance," appear repeatedly in association with the metaphor of the contest in order to describe the endurance of suffering by the martyrs (cf. 4 Macc 1:11; 5:23–6:9; 7:9, 22; 9:6, 8, 22, 30; 13:12; 15:30–32; 17:4, 11–17, 23). Similar imagery is found in Philo (e.g., On the Unchangeableness of God 13; for the metaphorical use of ἄθλησις, On Dreams 1.170; On the Preliminary Studies 162; cf. On the Cherubim 80–81). Thompson has observed that the image of the contest for physical suffering was especially appropriate for Philo and the homilist who prepared 4 Maccabees, because these writers identified with a minority culture that was subjected to persecution and acts of violence. For them, as for the writer of Hebrews, the image of the contest was an acceptable way of giving a positive interpretation of an experience of abuse (Beginnings of Christian Philosophy, 63–64; cf. Williamson, Philo, 19–20).

33–34 The details provided in vv 33–34 clarify the character of the sufferings endured. The contrasting τοῦτο μέν . . . τοῦτο δέ statements ("sometimes . . . and other occasions" or "in part . . . and in part") introduce a chiasm having significant implications for the interpretation of the details.

> A "Sometimes you were publicly exposed to ridicule, both by insults and persecutions" (v 33a);
> B "and on other occasions you showed solidarity with those who were treated in this way" (v 33b);
> B' "for in fact you shared the sufferings of those in prison" (v 34a);
> A' "and cheerfully accepted the seizure of your property" (v 34b).

The carefully structured recital of past indignities suggests that a part of the congregation had been exposed to ridicule because they had been defenseless against the seizure of their property (A/A'). Others within the congregation had identified themselves with the hardships that those who had been imprisoned had endured from the authorities (B/B') (cf. Riggenbach, 332; Vanhoye, *La structure*, 179; Teodorico, 177; Mora, *La Carta a los Hebreos*, 61–62, n. 183). If this is a correct interpretation of the structure, the first group had experienced not only verbal and physical abuse but imprisonment as well. The other members of the house church had shown solidarity with those who had borne the brunt of these sufferings.

The public nature of the sufferings endured by members of the congregation is indicated by the rare word θεατριζόμενοι, which conveys the notion of being "exposed to ridicule" or "held up to public shame" (Cadbury, *ZNW* 29 [1930] 60–63; LSJ 787). The verb θεατρίζειν originally meant "to bring upon the stage," but it soon acquired a figurative meaning, "to make a spectacle of someone," "to hold up to derision." In v 33a it evokes the imagery of a spectacle, which is found repeatedly in descriptions of persecution and abuse (e.g., 4 Macc 17:14 ["the world and the human race were the spectators"]; Philo, *Against Flaccus* 72, 74, 84–85, 95, 173, where Jews were put on public display in the theater and were subjected to abuse during the pogrom of A.D. 38; Jos., *Ag. Ap.* 1.43; cf. 1 Cor. 4:9, θέατρον ἐγενήθημεν, "we became a spectacle"). The word vividly expresses the public abuse and shame to which members of the congregation had been exposed (cf. Thompson, *Beginnings of Christian Philosophy*, 64, 78).

The form that the abuse had taken is summed up in the phrase ὀνειδισμοῖς τε καὶ θλίψεσιν, "both by insults and persecutions." The word ὀνειδισμός, "reproach," indicates the verbal character of the abuse. Public jeering and scoffing had greeted the Christians. They had been falsely accused of crime and vice (cf. Tacitus, *Annals of Rome* 15.44; *Diogn.* 6.5; Tertullian, *Apology* 2, 4, 7, 8; *To the Nations* 1, 2, 3, 7, 15, 16; Athenagoras, *Embassy for the Christians* 31; Theophilus, *To Autolycus* 3.4). The use of ὀνειδισμός in 11:26 and 13:13 for the reproach Christ had borne from the insults of others (cf. 12:3) suggests that these Christians had shared the reproach of Christ (cf. R. Volkl, *Christ und die Welt* [Würzburg: Echter, 1961] 354). The complementary term θλίψεσιν, "afflictions," "persecutions," appears to indicate that acts of violence had accompanied verbal abuse.

The strong sense of community that had characterized the congregation in that earlier period is evident from the parallel clauses in v 33b–34a. Those who had not been affected personally by the hostility to which some members of the group had been exposed openly identified themselves with their brothers and sisters in Christ. In the periphrastic phrase κοινωνοὶ γενηθέντες, "you showed solidarity," the accent falls upon "the persistence those addressed had shown in sharing the reproach and suffering of their fellow Christians" (J. Y. Campbell, *Three New Testament Studies*, 11). They had displayed genuine empathy (συνεπαθήσατε) with those in prison by visiting them, feeding them, and undoubtedly actively seeking their release (cf. Lucian, *Peregrinus,* 12–13, for each of these activities on behalf of an imprisoned Christian). Such involvement was not without cost, as the friends and relatives of the Jews who were persecuted in the anti-Semitic riots in Alexandria in A.D. 38 discovered (Philo, *Against Flaccus* 7, 9, 10). The terminology used to describe the solidarity displayed by the community during that critical period is similar to the language expressing the profound manner in which Christ identified himself with the human situation (see *Comment* on 2:14; 4:15). The writer thus stresses that the conduct of the community exhibited a solidarity with each other that made visible in the world the solidarity Christ shares with his people (cf. P. E. Hughes, 429; Thompson, *Beginnings of Christian Philosophy,* 65).

The group that had been publicly exposed to ridicule (v 33a) had endured the seizure of their property (τὴν ἁρπαγὴν τῶν ὑπαρχόντων; v 34b). It is not certain whether this facet of their experience reflects the official judicial action of magistrates, who imposed heavy fines or confiscated property for suspected infractions (cf. Philo, *Against Flaccus* 10), or whether the reference is to the looting of houses after their owners had been imprisoned or removed (Philo, *Against Flaccus* 56: "Their enemies overran the houses now left vacant and began to loot them, dividing up the contents like spoils of war"; Lucian, *Peregrinus* 14: "Most of his possessions had been carried off during his absence"; cf. Eusebius, *Church History* 6.41, cited by P. E. Hughes, 430). Christians in Rome who had been affected by a decree of expulsion in A.D. 49 were forced to leave their property unattended (Acts 18:1–2; cf. Suetonius, *Claudius* 25.4). Whatever the precise circumstances, the Christians had cheerfully accepted their losses because they knew they had κρείττονα ὕπαρξιν καὶ μένουσαν, "better and permanent possessions" (v 34c). This knowledge was the basis of their endurance of "the hard contest with sufferings" (v 32a) (cf. T. W. Lewis, *NTS* 22 [1975–76] 89; Grässer, *Glaube,* 23).

The play on words between τῶν ὑπαρχόντων, "property," "possessions," in v 34b and ὕπαρξιν, "possessions," in v 34c is rhetorically effective in developing the contrast between possessions that can be lost through seizure and the permanent possessions Christians enjoy on the basis of their relationship to God through Christ. The source of this distinction is Jesus' teaching concerning earthly property, which cannot be protected from loss, and heavenly treasures, which remain intact and secure (Matt 6:19–20; 19:21). The adjective κρείττων, "better," is regularly used in Hebrews to express the superior quality of the reality Christians possess through Christ (cf. 6:9; 7:19; 9:23; 12:24; in 11:16 "better" [κρείττονος] is defined by an explicative clause, "that is, heavenly"). The correlative term μένουσα, "permanent," "abiding," is used to indicate the superiority and stability that characterize the heavenly world (12:27; 13:14) (cf. Cambier, "Eschatologie ou héllenisme," 31; Thompson, *Beginnings of Christian Philosophy,* 65–66, 72). The strong confidence of the early Christians that they possessed "better and permanent possessions" in the transcendent heavenly world Christ had opened to them permitted them to develop a proper perspective on the deprivation they had suffered through persecution (cf. *Herm. Sim.* 1.1–6, where this theme is developed in terms of the ownership of land, houses, and other possessions).

It must be stressed that the account in vv 32–34 describes an actual ordeal in the community's past. By a one-sided emphasis upon the homiletical aspects of the description, it has sometimes been argued that these verses have no specific reference; they are concerned solely with theoretical, typical circumstances characteristic of younger churches (so Wrede, *Das literarische Rätsel*, 25–26; Dibelius, "Der himmlische Kultus," 160–62). In vv 32–34, however, a primitive Christian tradition stressing the basis for joy in the experience of persecution has been applied to an actual occurrence. This accounts for the fusion of specific and general, typical features in the description (so Nauck, *ZNW* 46 [1955] 80; McCown, "*Ο ΛΟΓΟΣ ΤΗΣ ΠΑΡΑΚΛΗΣΕΩΣ*," 79–83). Facets of the tradition have been selected and shaped to fit the circumstances of the community addressed, but a specific course of events in the past provides the basis of the parenetic appeal made in vv 32–35. That reproach, injury, the looting of property, and imprisonment were the conditions of existence for a minority culture in the first century is sufficiently indicated by Philo's vivid description of the acts of violence that disrupted the Jewish community in Alexandria in A.D. 38, in the tractate *Against Flaccus*.

If the evidence is deemed strong enough to support a Roman destination for Hebrews (in *Introduction* see "The Social Location of the Intended Audience"), vv 32–34 shed light on the earlier history of the congregation addressed. These men and women constituted an "old guard"; they had been Christians since the Claudian period. When disturbances in the Jewish quarters in the year A.D. 49 attracted unfavorable attention from the imperial authorities, the emperor issued a decree expelling the Jews from Rome (Suetonius, *Claudius* 25.4). The size of the Jewish community in Rome made it impossible to enforce the decree completely, but certainly both Jewish and Jewish Christian leadership had been affected. Sporadic persecution of those who remained undoubtedly followed. In the case of the Jewish Christian leaders, Aquila and Priscilla (cf. Acts 18:1–2), the Claudian decree meant banishment from Rome and almost certainly the loss of property. Others in the same house church experienced various indignities, including imprisonment, injury, and deprivation for the sake of their commitment to Christ (for this reading of the evidence, see *Introduction*, "Past Stance and Present Crisis" and "The Edict of Claudius"). Throughout these experiences they had steadfastly maintained a courageous stance as Christians.

35 The continuing significance of the historical description in vv 32–34 is indicated by the pastoral directive in v 35, μὴ ἀποβάλητε οὖν τὴν παρρησίαν ὑμῶν, "Therefore, do not throw away your boldness." That this appeal is based upon the preceding verses is shown by the inferential particle, οὖν, "therefore." The community must now recapture the fervor that had characterized them. They must display in the present the same stance of steadfast commitment to Christ they had exhibited in the past.

The indignities and deprivation endured in the past are here interpreted as a display of παρρησία, "boldness." παρρησία, understood subjectively, expresses the confident attitude of the person of faith before God and the world. Precisely because he enjoys free access to God through Christ's sacrificial death and heavenly intercessory ministry (4:16; 7:24–25; 10:19, 21), he can confidently acknowledge his faith before the world. The prohibition "do not throw away your παρρησία" expresses in a negative form what was expressed positively in 3:6 in terms of "holding fast παρρησία" (Michel, 360). παρρησία is the hallmark of those who are members of God's household in the new age (3:6b). In conjunction with the strong expression μὴ ἀποβάλητε, "do not throw away," the prohibition in v 35 suggests the casting aside of a precious gift (Windisch, 97; Spicq, 2:330). It conveys both encouragement for continued fidelity and the warning that boldness for Christ must not be jettisoned.

The causal relative clause ἥτις ἔχει μεγάλην μισθαποδοσίαν, "seeing that it has a great reward," provides a strong motive for not weakly tossing aside boldness. The manifestation of Christian boldness is viewed as a "title-deed" which assures the future enjoyment of the "great reward" in the consummation of the new age. Just as the courage displayed in adversity in vv 32–34 was oriented eschatologically toward the enjoyment of "better, permanent possessions" (v 34c), so here boldness is warmly oriented toward the eschatological reward. μισθαποδοσία is an important word in the writer's vocabulary. It is found in the NT only in Hebrews, where it occurs negatively in the sense of "penalty" (2:2) and positively in the sense of "reward" (10:35; 11:26). The writer also designates God as μισθαποδότης, "the rewarder," of those who seek him in faith (11:6). The notion of reward is, of course, rooted in the OT and comes to expression in other Jewish hellenistic writers (e.g., 4 Macc 16:25; 17:12, 18; Philo, *Allegorical Interpretation of the Law* 1.80; *Who is the Heir?* 26, cited by Thompson, *Beginnings of Christian Philosophy,* 67 [Thompson observes that it is in the language of reward that the writer of Hebrews is most distinguishable from the philosophical reflection of the period.]). In v 35 the "great reward" has reference to the blessing of full salvation God has promised to those who wait for Christ (cf. 9:28; 10:23, 25). The promise of the "great reward" belongs to the category of the passionate certainty of faith (cf. Preisker, *TDNT* 4:701–2).

36 The prospect of "throwing away" boldness contemplated in v 35 underscores the need the community has for ὑπομονή, "endurance" (with the additional nuance of faithfulness). The inferential γάρ looks back not only to the preceding injunction but to vv 32–34 as well, where the cognate verb ὑπομένειν is used to celebrate the courage with which the community had responded to persecution ("you endured," v 32). With v 36 the writer anticipates the development in 12:1–13, where the summons to the endurance of hardships and disciplinary sufferings (12:1, 7) is supported by the example of Jesus who "endured" the cross and the hateful opposition of sinful persons (12:2–3). The implication is that ὑπομονή, like παρρησία, "boldness," in v 35, is the hallmark of a Christian's stance in the world.

The necessity for ὑπομονή is linked to the accomplishment of the will of God. This suggests that the measure of endurance is obedience to God. The temporal clause τὸ θέλημα τοῦ θεοῦ ποιήσαντες, "after you have done the will of God," points retrospectively to 10:5–10 where the incarnation and mission of Christ were interpreted in terms of a preoccupation with the divine will. The transcendent Son of God entered the world in fulfillment of the prophetic Scriptures to do the will of God. He regarded his body as the gift God had prepared as the instrument

for the accomplishment of the divine will. Christ's sacrificial death in conformity
to the will of God is the immediate ground of the Christian experience of renewal and consecration to the service of God (10:10). It follows from this that
Christian conduct can never be divorced from the doing of the will of God. In
the context of 10:19–39, the accomplishment of the divine will calls for a positive
response to the exhortations and directives that are developed with such pastoral
earnestness throughout this section.

The result of unwavering endurance is expressed pregnantly in the clause
ἵνα . . . κομίσησθε τὴν ἐπαγγελίαν, "so that you may receive the promise." Envisioned is the reception of what has been promised (P. E. Hughes, 433, n. 32).
The reception of the fulfillment of the promise is equivalent to receiving the
"great reward" in v 35; it stands for the final goal of the covenant people of God
(11:39–40). It is the distinctive understanding of the writer that Christians in
this life possess the realities of which God has spoken only in the form of promise
(see *Comment* on 4:1). In this sense, they experience a continuity with the faithful men and women of the old covenant who did not receive what was promised
(11:13, 39), but who conducted their lives in the light of the divine promise.
What God promised to the fathers he has repeated with strong assurance to the
people of the new covenant (cf. 8:6, "better promises"). Consequently, the believing community can be described as heirs to the divine promise (cf. 6:12, 17).
The promise is inviolable because God who gave the promise is utterly reliable
(10:23; 11:11). The confidence of the Church in that reliability provides a basis
for stability in an unstable world (cf. Thompson, *Beginnings of Christian Philosophy*, 67–68).

What God has promised is "eternal life" (9:15). In 6:12 the writer called for
the imitation of those who through faith and steadfast endurance (μακροθυμία)
inherit what is promised. That same note is sounded in v 36 with the equivalent
term ὑπομονή, which is the presupposition for the reception of the promise. God's
unalterable will to fulfill his promise finds an appropriate response from believers in the stance of endurance.

37–38 The reason the community has need for ὑπομονή, "endurance," is
clarified by the biblical citation in vv 37–38, which is formally introduced by an
explanatory γάρ, "for," in v 37. The time of patiently waiting for the consummation of God's redemptive plan is not yet over. The community of faith continues
to find itself exposed to alienation in the world. The intimate relationship between v 36 and the prophetic oracle in vv 37–38 explains why sustained boldness
and endurance are required of the congregation now as it waits for the fulfillment of the divine promise (T. W. Lewis, *NTS* 22 [1975–76] 90).

The quotation conflates Isa 26:20 LXX, a passage counseling withdrawal and
concealment μικρὸν ὅσον ὅσον, "a little while," until the wrath of God had passed,
and Hab 2:3*b*–4, a passage that contrasts faithfulness with withdrawal. The com-
posite quotation contains only a brief excerpt from the former passage ("a little
while longer"). The dominant component is a significantly modified form of the
citation from Habakkuk. The creative tension between these two OT texts furnishes the basis for calling the congregation to continued faithfulness in their
situation (cf. T. W. Lewis, *NTS* 22 [1975–76] 92–93).

Isa 26:20 belongs to "the Song of Isaiah" (Isa 26:9–20). This was one of several biblical passages that were removed from their context and appended to

the Psalter in the LXX as a collection of odes appropriate for liturgical use. As the fifth ode, the Song of Isaiah was used liturgically in the synagogue and in the morning and evening prayers of the early Church (see H. Schneider, "Die biblischen Oden im christlichen Altertum," *Bib* 30 [1949] 47). It is possible, therefore, that even a brief allusion to Isa 26:20 would be sufficient to call to mind the entire verse.

If the brief excerpt from Isa 26:20 LXX *is* intended to recall the entire verse, it may indicate that there were Christians in the house church who sought to justify a lifestyle characterized by withdrawal and concealment on the basis of this text. The writer cites enough of the verse to show that he is aware of their position but refuses to accept its validity. The mode of endurance they championed was incompatible with the courageous and joyful endurance of adversity celebrated in vv 32–36 (T. W. Lewis, *NTS* 22 [1975–76] 91–93; cf. Strobel, *Untersuchungen*, 84–86).

The posture of expectant waiting and fidelity that the members of the house church must exhibit is defined rather by Hab 2:3*b*–4 (see Fitzmyer, "Habakkuk 2:3–4," 236–41, for a discussion of this passage in the MT, lQpHab 7.5–8.3, the LXX, and other Greek translations and traditions). A comparison of the LXX text and the oracle in Hebrews will indicate the significance of the modifications the writer has made in the text.

In the LXX, the subject of v 3*a* is the vision: "the vision has its appointed time, and it will appear at length, and not to no purpose." The subject then changes: "If he is late, wait for him, because he will certainly come and will not delay. If he draws back, I will reject him. But my righteous one shall live by faithfulness." The interpretation of the text in the LXX is thoroughly messianic (cf. T. W. Manson, *JTS* 46 [1945] 134; F. F. Bruce, 273). The anonymous one who will certainly come is the expected deliverer of his people. The text implies that once he appears, his advance is certain. If he draws back, that action will provide irrefutable proof that he is not the expected one. The textual tradition then bifurcates. It declares either "the righteous one will live on the basis of my faithfulness" (B, W), the reading adopted in the critical editions of H. B. Swete, A. Rahlfs, and J. Ziegler, or "my righteous one shall live by faithfulness" (A and Group C). According to the first reading, the basis for the success of the righteous person is the reliability of God. Context, however, favors the second reading: God's righteous one shall keep faith with God and his messianic task, and so will attain life (T. W. Manson, *JTS* 46 [1945] 133–34; cf. Cavallin, *ST* 32 [1978] 35, n. 19).

The writer of Hebrews modified the LXX text in several significant ways (cf. T. W. Lewis, *NTS* 22 [1975–76] 90, n. 3).

(1) He sharpened the messianic interpretation of the text in the LXX by the addition of the masculine article to the participle ἐρχόμενος, "coming." In the LXX the participle simply serves to translate the Hebrew infinitive absolute construction ("he will certainly come"). In Hebrews the participle is personalized to create the messianic title, "the Coming One" (Matt 3:11; 11:3 [=Luke 7:19]; 21:9) (so Spicq, 2:331–32; Michel, 362). The phrase ὁ ἐρχόμενος ἥξει, "the Coming One will come," has reference to Christ at his parousia (T. W. Lewis, *NTS* 22 [1975–76] 90). In conjunction with the excerpt from Isa 26:20 LXX, the oracle affirms the absolute certainty and the imminence of the parousia:

A little while longer,
the Coming One will come;
he will not delay.

This change presupposes the apocalyptic understanding of Hab 2:3*b* LXX (Strobel, *Untersuchungen*, 127; on the meaning of the statement οὐ χρονίσει, "he will not delay," in Hab 2:3 and elsewhere, cf. Strobel, 161–70).

(2) He inverted the clauses of Hab 2:4, so that the subject of the conditional phrase ἐὰν ὑποστείληται, "if he draws back," is no longer the expected deliverer but the Christian who awaits the advent of the Coming One. The inversion is clearly the work of the writer, for it finds no support in the manuscript tradition of the LXX. It serves to fix the meaning of the "my righteous one" in v 38*a* beyond doubt. The righteous one is the Christian who demonstrates faithfulness to God as he moves toward the goal of life, eschatologically understood (i.e., "eternal life," cf. 9:15). Conversely, the one who draws back in v 38*b* is the Christian who loses sight of his goal. This means that the adversative δέ, "but," in v 38*a* introduces an important transition. In v 37 the accountability of God is at stake. He will keep his promise; the parousia of Christ is certain. In v 38, however, there is a shift in focus to the accountability of the Christian, who must demonstrate faithfulness in the face of hardships, suffering, and perhaps the unanticipated delay in the parousia of the Lord.

(3) He placed an adversative καί, "but," before the clause ἐὰν ὑποστείληται, "if he draws back," in v 38*b*. This καί is not a part of the biblical oracle but a connective effectively separating the antithetical clauses of Hab 2:4. The resultant form of the text describes alternative modes of behavior in a period marked by stress and hostility. The person whom God approves ("my righteous one") attains to life with God by faithfulness; the person whom God rejects withdraws from the covenant community (v 25!).

With these modifications the oracle was made to buttress the parenetic call to boldness and endurance in vv 35–36, corresponding to the original function of the passage in Habakkuk (Strobel, *Untersuchungen*, 127; on the interpretation of Hab 2:4 in Judaism, cf. Michel, 364–65; D. Lührmann, "Pistis im Judentum," *ZNW* 64 [1973] 35–36 [faith in Judaism was normally discussed on the basis of Deut 9:23; 1 Kgs 17:14; Hab 2:4]). It is clear that the writer has freely adapted the text of the LXX for the purposes of his argument in this section. The freedom with which he constructed this prophetic oracle, as well as its length, reflects the importance that he attached to it (cf. T. W. Manson, *JTS* 46 [1945] 135–36; Cavallin, *ST* 32 [1978] 33–43).

It is generally understood that in v 38 the reference to drawing back (ὑποστείληται) is a denotation for apostasy (Moffatt, 158; Spicq, 2:333 ["the attitude of the apostate in a time of persecution"]; cf. Michel, 363–65, who finds a gradation of possible meanings in the word ranging from withdrawal from the worshiping assembly [v 25] to defection and apostasy). This prevailing understanding has been questioned by T. W. Lewis, who finds in the term a reference to a lifestyle of withdrawal and concealment as exhorted by Isa 26:20, rather than apostasy or infidelity to God (*NTS* 22 [1975–76] 91–94). He argues that the community could have regarded this as a faithful mode of existence as they waited for the arrival of the parousia (92). At the center of vv 37–38, then, is an interpretation of faith rather than the crisis of threatened apostasy. The writer's concern was to correct a faulty understanding on the part of the community by providing in vv 32–36 a clarification of what is required of faith. The inversion of the clauses in v 38 allows the writer to address the misunderstanding on the part of the community. What is intended by the phrase ἐκ πίστεως ζήσεται, "he shall live on the basis of faithfulness," is indicated in vv 32–36, where the joyful endurance of hostility from the world is urged. What ὑποστείληται, "draws back," envisions may be inferred from the allusion to Isa 26:20 in v 37a. A mode of endurance characterized by withdrawal and concealment is shown to be displeasing to God in v 38b because it could result in the community drifting from its anchorage in the gospel (2:1), losing its way in the world, and forfeiting its ultimate goal. What is in view is not irremedial apostasy, an intentional break, but "conditions that would lead to defection if not repaired" (94).

This reinterpretation of the text, however, fails to take into account the strong terminology used for desertion of the meetings of the assembly in v 25, the sharp warning against apostasy in vv 26–31, and the apparent force of the negative construction in v 38c ("I myself will reject him"). It is necessary to recognize, in the juxtaposition of living on the ground of faithfulness and drawing back, the antithesis of fidelity leading to life and apostasy leading to rejection and death. The steadfast endurance commanded by the prophetic oracle is that demanded by the certainty of the coming of Christ (cf. Fitzmyer, "Habakkuk 2:3–4," 243).

39 The writer's understanding of the passage from Habakkuk is clear from the use he makes of it in v 39. The decisive alternatives substantiated on the basis of Hab 2:4 are sharpened in a concluding statement that summarizes the preceding argument and brings the biblical text into the experience of the congregation. The emphatic "we" (ἡμεῖς) at the beginning of the sentence identifies the writer with his friends as the company of the faithful who exhibit loyalty to Christ in the world. The writer shows no interest in the juridical question of justification that had commanded Paul's attention (cf. Rom 1:17; Gal 3:11). His focus is concentrated on two related questions: how can a Christian be assured of the enjoyment of final salvation, and on what basis can he hope to reach the goal? These questions are answered in v 39, which corroborates that the writer construed the prepositional phrase ἐκ πίστεως, "on the basis of faith," with the verb ζήσεται, "he shall live" (D. M. Smith, "Ο ΔΕ ΔΙΚΑΙΟΣ," 15). The goal of the Christian is the attainment of enduring life. In the interim before the parousia he will derive strength for movement toward that goal from faithfulness.

The interpretation of Hab 2:4 is carried forward by the dynamic tension developed between ὑποστολή ("withdrawal") and πίστις ("faithfulness"). The rare word ὑποστολή, which occurs only here in the NT, derives its meaning from the preceding ὑποστείληται ("draws back") in the quotation in v 38. It reflects a lack of steadfastness and unreliability (Rengstorf, *TDNT* 7:599). It is equivalent to turning away from the living God (3:12) and deliberate persistence in sin (10:26). The objective act of drawing back from loyalty to Christ distinguishes those who fail to attain the promised eternal life from those who through faith and steadfast endurance inherit the promise (6:12; 10:36) (cf. Carlston, *JBL* 78 [1959] 299). Conversely, πίστις connotes persistent steadfastness. It is closely allied to the stance of παρρησία, "boldness," and ὑπομονή, "endurance," commended in vv 35–36. It reflects the stability of those who maintain their firm confidence in God's word of promise, despite adversity and disappointment (cf. Grässer, *Glaube,* 23; Marshall, *Kept by the Power,* 146–47; Thompson, *Beginnings of Christian Philosophy,* 68–69). The writer's understanding of faithfulness is informed by the prophetic concept of the righteous person whose steadfastness sustains him as he waits for God's intervention (Grässer, *Glaube,* 44).

The outcome of these radically different responses is posed rigorously by means of parallel result clauses: εἰς ἀπώλειαν . . . εἰς περιποίησιν ψυχῆς, "leading to destruction . . . culminating in the acquisition of life." The concomitant event of the approaching Day of the Lord (v 25) and parousia of the Coming One (v 37) is judgment. For some this event will bring the great reward of life, but for others it will result in destruction because of the inappropriate response of withdrawal. The use of ψυχή to designate eternal life is apocalyptic (cf. G. Dautzenberg, "*Soteria Psychon,*" *BZ* 8 [1964] 267–70). It shows that the expression ζήσεται, "he shall live," in v 38 must be understood eschatologically, in the sense of "he shall attain life" (cf. Riggenbach, 337–38).

The sharp contrast between vindication and ruin occurs elsewhere in the literature of hellenistic Judaism, e.g., Wis 18:7, which juxtaposes "the vindication [σωτηρία] of the righteous, but the destruction [ἀπώλεια] of their enemies" (cf. Strobel, *Untersuchungen,* 82–83). In v 39 it demonstrates that the presupposition of the preceding argument is the structure of the covenant. Obedience to the stipulations of the covenant carries the promise of blessing and life, but disobedience invites the imposing of the curse-sanction of death (cf. Deut 30:15–20). The antithesis between destruction and the acquisition of life recapitulates the discussion in 6:4–8, where the reference to blessing and curse in 6:7–8 constitutes an allusion to the covenant.

The arrangement of the text in vv 38–39 reflects the sensitivities of a man of letters. In v 38 the writer inverted the clauses of Hab 2:4, so that the mention of the person who lives by faithfulness precedes the reference to the one who draws back. In v 39 the reference to the one who draws back precedes the mention of the one who demonstrates faithfulness. The resulting concentric symmetry (faithfulness/withdrawal::withdrawal/faithfulness) is rhetorically effective. Positioned at the beginning and at the end of the developed contrast, the expression "by faithfulness" is thrown into bold relief. It clearly enunciates the attitude of which God approves. At the same time, it announces the subject of 11:1–40, where this theme receives its major elaboration (cf. Vanhoye, *La structure,* 180–81).

Explanation

The completion of the core instruction concerning the high priestly office and sacrifice of the Son of God (8:1–10:18) called for pastoral reflection on the implications this has for Christian faith and practice. In 10:19–39 insights developed in the course of an extended exposition are taken up in a climactic parenetic section and are applied directly to the community in its situation. The stress falls upon the certainty and stability that ought to characterize a Christian presence in the world. The authorization for free access to God in the heavenly sanctuary derived from the sacrifice of Christ (10:19–20) and the knowledge that in the person of Christ Christians possess a great high priest (10:21) demonstrate the privileged relationship to God that the people of the new covenant enjoy. They enjoy the freedom for a worshipful approach to God that reflects fullness of faith (10:22). They possess a secure basis for a quality of witness in the world that reflects a firm grasp on the objective character of Christian hope (10:23). The result should be a strong communal sense demonstrated through caring love and tangible expressions of practical concern for one another (10:24–25).

The ultimate source of certainty and stability is the utter reliability of God, who acknowledges his commitment to the community through the solemn word of promise granted to it (10:23). God's covenanted promise keeps the goal of Christian pilgrimage before the congregation. The realization of the promise is surveyed under a variety of metaphors, namely, the better and permanent possession (10:34), the great reward (10:35), the fulfillment of the promise (10:36), and the acquisition of life (10:39). The constancy of God guarantees that life in pursuit of the promise cannot be in vain. The exhortation extended to the community in 10:19–39 is precisely a reminder of that fact.

The reason it was necessary for the writer to review the benefits that accrue to the community from the sacrifice of Christ and to appeal for the congregation to act responsibly was that they were exhibiting a tendency to waver in their commitment to Christ and to each other. The exhortation to approach God with sincere intentions (10:22) presupposes a lack of sincerity. The injunction to hold fast to the hope professed without wavering (10:23) implies a vacillation that undermined the integrity of Christian profession. The frank acknowledgment that some members of the house church had stopped attending the meetings of the assembly (10:25) indicated a serious defection from the community. These conditions account for the sternness of the warning concerning the spiritual peril to which a lax and calloused attitude exposed those who had experienced the reality of Christian life (10:26–31).

These developments in the life of the house church revealed a marked departure from the loyalty to Christ that had motivated the community at an earlier point in their experience. At that time they had boldly accepted the stigma of commitment to Christ and to each other (10:32–34). The stress on certainty and stability in 10:19–39 seeks to correct a dangerous tendency in the community to respond to suffering and disappointment by withdrawal and concealment (10:25, 38–39). The writer warns that continuing to react to adversity in this way could only result in the forfeiture of the benefits secured for them by Christ. His confidence is that his friends will recognize their peril and will demonstrate a quality of faithfulness and steadfast endurance consistent with their relationship with God through Christ and the goal set before them (10:39).

Throughout this extended exhortation the writer presupposes the validity of the cultic argument developed in 9:1–10:18. This is particularly clear in 10:19–20, where authorization for access to the heavenly sanctuary is grounded in Christ's death viewed in its sacrificial aspect, and in 10:26, where the consequence of apostasy is described as the forfeiture of a sufficient sacrifice for sins. It is equally evident in 10:29 when the effects of apostasy are delineated, and there is a graphic reference to the disparagement of the blood of the covenant by which a Christian is consecrated to the service of God (cf. 10:10, 14). A failure to appreciate the persistent need for the definitive sacrifice of Christ and the decisive purging of the conscience it achieved consigns apostates to a state of perpetual defilement which bars them from the presence of God and leads inevitably to destruction.

Intimately related to the cultic orientation of the writer's appeal is an understanding of Christ as the mediator of the new covenant that was inaugurated by his death (8:6; 9:18). The cultic implications of the enactment of the new covenant are drawn sharply in 10:15–18, the passage immediately preceding 10:19–39. The writer clearly assumes that the life of the persons addressed will reflect the fact that they are the people of the new covenant.

An appeal to covenant administration appears to be presupposed by the course of the development in this section. Certain objective benefits of the covenant deriving from Christ's sacrifice are first set forth. These include authorization for access to God (10:19–20), the assurance of Christ's mediatorial rule over the household of faith (10:21), the decisive purging of the heart and body of those who participate in the covenant (10:22b), and the objective hope placed in front of the community, consisting of present and future salvation (10:23a). It also embraces the firm pledge of the faithfulness of God, who stands behind his word of promise (10:23b).

The exhortations presented express the stipulations of the new covenant. The covenant community must draw near to God in worship with sincerity (10:28); they must hold fast the hope they profess without wavering (10:23); they must show loyalty to the covenant fellowship by attendance at worship and by mutual encouragement (10:24–25); they must sustain a stance of boldness (10:35) and exhibit a quality of endurance in the world which displays allegiance to God and to Christ as the mediator of the covenant (10:36). These are all functions of the new covenant.

The measure of privilege distinguishing the people of the new covenant from those who lived under the old covenant (cf. 8:6–13; 10:15–18) necessarily defines the extent of the peril to which those who spurn the benefits of the new covenant expose themselves. They not only forfeit the blessings of the new covenant, but they experience the religious dread of those who anticipate the severity of the judgment of God on those who have disparaged covenant sacrifice (10:26–31). The antithetical motifs of destruction and life (10:39) recall that in the structure of the old covenant blessing was promised to those who adhered to the stipulations of the covenant, but a curse was sanctioned for those who despised its provisions (cf. 6:7–8). This understanding is superimposed upon the structure of the new covenant in 10:35–39.

Within this conceptual framework the writer sets forth a well-developed theology of worship. The persons addressed in this sermon appear not to have recognized the implications for fellowship and Christian worship created by the high priestly ministry and sacrifice of Christ. This parenetic section, in which the writer views the whole pattern of Christian life under the aspect of worship, is offered to the community as a corrective to an impoverished point of view.

The exhortation to draw near to God on the basis of the single, unrepeatable sacrifice of Christ in 10:22 describes in a special way the proper relationship of the individual Christian and of the corporate Christian community to God. It entails a continuous approach to the holy presence of God, marked by an increasingly profound experience of the mystery of fellowship with him. Conversely, a scornful disdain for Christ and a rejection of the efficacy of his sacrifice leads to an inability to worship God (10:26-29). The argument presupposes that there can be no true worship of God apart from the sufficient sacrifice of Christ, which has replaced all other sacrifices. No other sacrifice can be anticipated. The apostates, who have spurned the sacrifice of Christ, cannot be readmitted to the worshiping community because they cannot satisfy the conditions for worship.

Behind the writer's discussion there can be discerned the language and imagery of the peace or fellowship offering. The first indication of the pattern of thought upon which his exhortation is based is provided by the concluding verses of the preceding section. The citation of Jer 31:33-34 in 10:16-17 announces the superior character of the new covenant, which covers all sins and makes superfluous any further sacrifice for sins. The summary statement in 10:18 presupposes the enactment of the new covenant and the decisive putting away of sins. According to the OT, a covenant was sealed with a fellowship offering signifying the acceptance of the arrangement by the participants (cf. Exod 20:24; 24:5). The fellowship meal, which was the distinguishing feature of the peace offering, expressed the firm covenant ties binding God and his people. In any series of offerings, mention of the peace offering invariably occurs last because it cannot be made until there has been an acceptable atonement for sin. So in 9:11-10:18 the writer directed the thinking of the community to the notion of atonement achieved through covenant sacrifice. The sin offering associated with the solemn Day of Atonement stands behind the exposition. In 10:19-25 he then contemplates Christian life under the aspect of worship because sin has been permanently and decisively put away by the sacrifice of Christ. It is this scheme that calls to mind the concept of the peace offering.

The exhortations in 10:22-25 appear to rest on a pattern of worship influenced by the peace offering. Access to God having been secured through the purging of defilement, worshipers gather for mutual exhortation to faith, hope, and love. This account faithfully reflects the experience of the old covenant people, for whom the peace or fellowship offering was an occasion for reciting God's covenant faithfulness and love (cf. Ps 26:4-9; 42:4; 69:30-33; 95:1-7; 100:1-5; 116:12-19; 147:1-20). The occasion for a peace offering was frequently a vow of allegiance to God. The vow would be repeated and kept in the assembly of the believing community gathered to share the ceremonial fellowship meal. It is characteristic of a peace offering that it can never be made alone. The writer takes up this theme in 10:22-25 and builds upon it to demonstrate the necessity and significance of Christian worship. The response of the community to God and to each other ought to declare to the world the peaceful relationship the covenant community enjoys as a result of the sacrifice of Christ.

Reflection upon the sin offering encouraged the writer to present Christ as priest and sacrifice. Reflection upon the peace offering appears to have encouraged him to view worship as the norm of Christian life in the world. As the recipients of a heavenly calling (3:1), the congregation is faced with the choice of drawing near to the heavenly world in worship or returning to the world from which they had been separated by the blood of Christ. The alternative to worship is apostasy.

The canonical shape of the pericope sheds significant light on the community addressed in this sermon. The writer reflects on the present tendency of the congregation to waver in the face of adversity and to opt for a lifestyle based on withdrawal and concealment, their past experience of indignities and deprivation in which the members demonstrated loyalty to Christ and to each other, and their future expectations of relief from suffering and vindication at the parousia of Christ. The nature of the writer's response to the men and women he addressed confirms the specifically pastoral character of the parenesis, in which he closely identifies himself with his audience. The severity with which he writes of apostasy and of the destructive lifestyle of those who have deserted the house church expresses anguish and compassionate concern that Christians should not be subverted by a form of worldliness that would separate them from the life and truth they have received from Christ and from one another.

IV. Loyalty to God through Persevering Faith (11:1–12:13)

Bibliography

Black, D. A. "The Problem of the Literary Structure of Hebrews: An Evaluation and a Proposal." *GTJ* 7 (1986) 163–77. **Bligh, J.** *Chiastic Analysis of the Epistle to the Hebrews.* 22–27. ———. "The Structure of Hebrews." *HeyJ* 5 (1964) 170–77. **Descamps, A.** "La structure de l'Épître aux Hébreux." *RDT* 9 (1954) 333–38. **Dussaut, L.** *Synopse structurelle de l'Épître aux Hébreux.* 116–28. **Gyllenberg, R.** "Die Komposition des Hebräerbriefs." *SEÅ* 22–23 (1957–58) 137–47. **Hillmann, W.** "Glaube und Verheissung: Einführung in die Grundgedanken des Hebräerbriefes (10,32–13,25)." *BibLeb* 1 (1960) 237–52. **Michel, O.** "Zur Auslegung des Hebräerbriefes." *NovT* 6 (1963) 189–91. **Nauck, W.** "Zum Aufbau des Hebräerbriefes." In *Judentum, Urchristentum, Urkirche.* FS J. Jeremias. Ed. W. Eltester. BZNW 26. Berlin: Töpelmann, 1960. 199–206. **Swetnam, J.** "Form and Content in Hebrews 7–13." *Bib* 55 (1974) 333–48. **Vanhoye, A.** "Discussions sur la structure de l'Épître aux Hébreux." *Bib* 55 (1974) 349–80. ———. "Les indices de la structure littéraire de l'Épître aux Hébreux." *SE* 2 (1964) 493–509. ———. "Literarische Struktur und theologische Botschaft des Hebräerbriefs." *SNTU* 4 (1979) 119–47; 5 (1980) 18–49. ———. *Quarta pars epistolae ad Hebraeos: De fide et patientia: Hebr. 11,1–12,13.* Rome: Pontifical Biblical Institute, 1972–73. ———. *La structure littéraire.* 45–48, 183–204. ———. "Structure littéraire et thèmes théologiques de l'Épître aux Hébreux." In *Studiorum Paulinorum Congressus Internationalis Catholicus 1961.* AnBib 18. Rome: Biblical Institute, 1963. 175–81.

Introduction

The fourth major division in Hebrews extends from 11:1 to 12:13. The writer's specific concern in this portion of the sermon is to elaborate upon the qualities of faithfulness and steadfast endurance, which were requisite if the congregation addressed were to sustain its Christian confession in the world. These traits of Christian character were formally announced in the pastoral directive of 10:36 ("You need, then, endurance") and in the summarizing declaration of 10:39 ("But we are . . . of those who are faithful").

In characteristic fashion the key terms *endurance* and *faithfulness* are taken up for development in inverted order. The fourth division in the sermon thus consists of two sections, 11:1–40, a celebration of the character of faith, and 12:1–13, a summons to steadfast endurance.

The writer addresses first the specific nature of the faith for which faithful men and women of God were attested in the biblical record (11:1–40). A kerygmatic review of redemptive history in terms of faithfulness to God establishes a confessional frame of reference for urging the community to emulate the example of those who have preceded them.

The parenetic appeal for endurance developed in 12:1–13 is based only indirectly on the antecedent exposition. Christians are to find in Jesus, whose death on the cross displayed both faithfulness and endurance (12:2–3), the supreme example of persevering faith. His exposure to hostility from those who were blind to God's redemptive design provides a paradigm for the community when they experience disciplinary suffering in the world (12:2–13).

In 11:1 the writer turns from exhortation to exposition, signaling a distinct break with the preceding discussion. A smooth transition to this new unit of thought is achieved by the introduction of the motif of faithfulness in 10:38–39. The key word πίστις, "faithfulness," supplied by the citation from Hab 2:4, furnishes a linking term to the characterization of the correlative word πίστις, "faith," in 11:1. This word then becomes the characteristic term of the first section, where it is repeated with variation twenty-four times. The opening and close of the section are indicated by an *inclusio,* which serves to bracket the exposition:

11:1–2   Ἔστιν δὲ πίστις . . . ἐν ταύτῃ γὰρ ἐμαρτυρήθησαν οἱ πρεσβύτεροι
          "Now *faith* celebrates. . . . For on this account men of the past *received attestation.*"
11:39   καὶ οὗτοι . . . μαρτυρηθέντες διὰ τῆς πίστεως
          "And all these . . . *received attestation* through *faithfulness.*"

The play on words between πίστις, "faith," and πίστις, "faithfulness," and the repetition of the verb μαρτυρεῖν in the passive, with the nuance of having "received attestation," indicate that the development begun in 11:1 extends to 11:39–40 (cf. Vanhoye, *La structure,* 46–47, 183–94; for the argument that the exposition of faith extends from 11:1 to 12:2, see Swetnam, *Bib* 55 [1974] 338–39). Christians are to recognize in those who acted upon God's promises, even though fulfillment was not in sight, a standard of persevering faith worthy of emulation.

A shift in genre, from historical recital to pastoral exhortation, serves to introduce the second section, which is much shorter in length (12:1–13). In contrast to 11:1–40, where the exposition is dominated by the use of the third person, the writer introduces the first and second person imperative and the hortatory subjunctive. A preparation for the transition is provided in the summary statement of 11:39–40. There the writer juxtaposes the attested witnesses who died without receiving what God had promised to "us," the Christian community, for whom God had planned something better. With 12:1 there is a change of tone and genre, but the same two groups are mentioned a second time: "we" Christians are to engage in our contest of faith, knowing that we are surrounded by a cloud of "attested witnesses."

The characteristic vocabulary of this section relates to the vital issue of enduring disciplinary sufferings. Anticipating the subsequent development in 12:1–13, the writer underscored the community's need for ὑπομονή, "endurance," in 10:36. That note is resumed in 12:1, when the commitment required of the Christian life is reviewed under the metaphor of an athletic contest, and the key to victory is found in "endurance." In Hebrews the noun ὑπομονή occurs in 10:36 and 12:1, but nowhere else. The cognate verb ὑπομένειν, "to endure," is found in 12:2, 3, 7, and elsewhere only in 10:32, where it is associated with the endurance of suffering at an earlier period in the history of the house church. The notion of endurance is developed by means of the noun παιδεία, "discipline" (12:5, 7, 8, 11, and not elsewhere in Hebrews), and the cognate verb παιδεύειν, "to discipline," (12:6, 7, 10, and not elsewhere in Hebrews). The concentration of this distinctive vocabulary in 12:1–13 accounts for the unitary character of this section. The subject of the second section is the necessary endurance of disciplinary suffering by the people of the new covenant, in emulation of their own earlier example (10:32–34), but especially of the example of Christ (12:2–3; cf. Vanhoye, *La structure*, 47–48, 196–204). The limits of the section are marked off primarily by the unitary concern with endurance, since this concern is not sustained in the parenetic section that follows in 12:14–29.

A. The Triumphs of Perseverance in Faith (11:1–40)

Bibliography

Bacon, B. W. "Doctrine of Faith in Hebrews, James and Clement." *JBL* 19 (1900) 12–21. **Barth, G.** "Pistis in hellenistischer Religiosität." *ZNW* 73 (1982) 110–26. **Bovon, F.** "Le Christ, la foi et la sagesse dans l'Épître aux Hébreux (Hébreux 11 et 1)." *RTP* 18 (1968) 129–44. **Brandenburger, E.** "Pistis und Soteria: Zum Verstehenshorizont vom 'Glaube' im Urchristentum." *ZNW* 85 (1988) 165–98. **Bretscher, P. M.** "Faith Triumphant—Echoes from the Epistle to the Hebrews." *CTM* 31 (1960) 728–39. **Brox, N.** *Zeuge und Märtyrer.* Munich: Beck, 1961. **Cosby, M. R.** "The Rhetorical Composition and Function of Hebrews 11 in Light of Example-lists in Antiquity." Dissertation, Emory University, 1985. ———. "The Rhetorical Composition of Hebrews 11." *JBL* 107 (1988) 257–73. **Culpepper, R. A.** "A Superior Faith: Hebrews 10:19–12:2." *RevExp* 82 (1985) 375–90. **Dautzenberg, G.** "Der Glaube im Hebräerbrief." *BZ* 17 (1973) 161–77. **Díaz, J. A.** "La estructure de la fe según la epístola a los Hebreos." *CB* 13 (1956) 244–50. **Drews, P.** *Studien zur Geschichte des Gottesdienstes und des gottesdienstlichen Leben II, und III. Untersuchungen über die sogenannte elementische Liturgie im VIII. Buch der Apostolischen Konstitutionen.* Tübingen: Mohr, 1906. 23–40. **Duplacy, J.** "La foi dans le Judaisme." *LV* 4 (1955) 443–68. **Dussaut, L.** *Synopse structurelle de l'Épître aux Hébreux.* 116–28. **Fichtner, J.** "Zum Problem Glaube und Geschichte in der israëlitisch-jüdischen Weisheitsliteratur." *TLZ* 76 (1951) 145–50. **Graber, F.** *Der Glaubensweg des Volkes Gottes: Eine Erklärung von Hebr. 11 als Beitrag zum Verständnis des Alten Testaments.* Zurich: Zwingli, 1943. **Grässer, E.** *Der Glaube im Hebräerbrief.* 45–63, 99–102, 126–36, 171–84. **Hamm, D.** "Faith in the Epistle to the Hebrews: The Jesus Factor." *CBQ* 52 (1990) 270–91. **Heigl, B.** *Verfasser und Adresse des Hebräerbriefes.* 109–18. **Hillmann, W.** "Glaube und Verheissung." *BibLeb* 1 (1960) 237–52. **Huxhold, H. N.** "Faith in the Epistle to the Hebrews." *CTM* 38 (1967) 657–61. **Jacob, E.** "L'histoire d'Israël vue par Ben Sira." In *Mélanges bibliques.* FS A. Robert. Paris: Bloud & Gay, 1955. 288–94. **Lee, T. R.** "Studies in the Form of Sirach (Ecclesiasticus) 44–50." Dissertation, Graduate Theological Union, Berkeley, 1979. **Mack, B. L.** *Wisdom and the Hebrew Epic: Ben Sira's Hymn in Praise of the Fathers.* Chicago: University of Chicago Press, 1985. **McCown, W. G.** "Ο ΛΟΓΟΣ ΤΗΣ ΠΑΡΑΚΛΗΣΕΩΣ." 84–98, 151–54. **Mercado, L. F.** "The Language of Sojourning in the Abraham Midrash in Hebrews 11:8–19." Dissertation, Harvard University, 1967. **Miller, M. R.** "What Is the Literary Form of Hebrews 11?" *JETS* 29 (1986) 411–17. **Moxnes, H.** "God and His Promise to Abraham." In *Theology in Conflict.* NovTSup 53. Leiden: Brill, 1980. 117–95. **Neudecker, R.** "Die alttestamentliche Heilsgeschichte in lehrhaftparänetischer Darstellung: Studie zu Sap ·10 und Hebr 11." Dissertation, Innsbruck, 1971. **Peake, A. S.** *The Heroes and Martyrs of Faith: Studies in the Eleventh Chapter of the Epistle to the Hebrews.* London: Hodder & Stoughton, 1910. **Peisker, M.** "Der Glaubensbegriff bei Philon." Dissertation, Breslau, 1936. **Price, B. J.** "*Paradeigma* and *Exemplum* in Ancient Rhetorical Theory." Dissertation, University of California, Berkeley,

1975. **Schille, G.** "Katechese und Taufliturgie: Erwägungen zu Hebräer 11." *ZNW* 51 (1960) 112–31. **Schlatter, A.** *Der Glaube im Neuen Testament: Eine Untersuchung zur neutestamentlichen Theologie.* Darmstadt: Echter, 1963. 520–36, 614–17. **Schmitt, A. von.** "Struktur, Herkunft und Bedeutung der Beispielreihe in Weish 10." *BZ* 21 (1977) 1–22. **Siebeneck, R. T.** "May Their Bones Return to Life!—Sirach's Praise of the Father." *CBQ* 21 (1959) 411–28. **Theissen, G.** *Untersuchungen zum Hebräerbrief.* 97–101. **Thompson, J. A.** *Beginnings of Christian Philosophy.* 53–62, 69–79. **Towner, W. S.** *The Rabbinic "Enumeration of Scriptural Examples": A Study of a Rabbinic Pattern of Discourse with Special Reference to Mekhilta d' R. Ishmael.* Leiden: Brill, 1973. **Williamson, R.** *Philo and the Epistle to the Hebrews.* 42–51, 116–17, 130, 192, 309–85, 449–56, 469–80, 483–91.

Introduction

When the writer counseled his friends to imitate "those who with faith and steadfast endurance inherit the promises" (6:12) and cited Abraham as an example for the Christian community (6:13–15), he anticipated the catalogue of attested witnesses in 11:1–40. In that earlier passage, as here, the emphasis is on the life of faith as a believing response to the promise of God. The thought of the writer at this point moves entirely on the historical plane. He brings before his audience a long series of exemplary witnesses to an enduring faith and demonstrates that faith is essentially determined by hope. The catalogue shows that throughout redemptive history attestation from God has been based upon the evidence of a living faith that acts in terms of God's promise, even when the realization of the promise is not in sight. Such a faith is able to move beyond disappointment and the sufferings of this world and to bear vibrant testimony to future generations regarding the reality of the promised blessings.

The section opens with a ringing affirmation concerning the character of faith and a précis of the catalogue of exemplars to follow (vv 1–2). The series of events and personages drawn from Scripture and presented in chronological sequence in vv 3–31 is developed in terms of the characterization of faith in v 1 and its corollary in v 6 (cf. Grässer, *Glaube*, 45–57). These first paragraphs move selectively and quickly through Gen 1 to Josh 6. The writer then alters his format. A simple enumeration of the names of those who through faith experienced triumph or deliverance from certain death (vv 32–35*a*) prepares for the frank acknowledgment of unnamed men and women of faith who were not delivered from hardship, suffering, and death (vv 35*b*–38). The section is rounded off with a summarizing conclusion, which serves to relate the experience of those who lived faithfully in terms of the promise of God to the Christian community under the old covenant.

Although much of the development is traditional in character, the writer's creative contribution is evident in the characterization of faith (vv 1–2) and in his comments upon the traditions he used (especially vv 6, 10, 13–16, and 39–40). At these points he underscores the eschatological, forward-looking character of faith, which invests the realm of objective hopes and promises with solidity (cf. Williamson, *Philo*, 366–71; Mercado, "Language of Sojourning," 76–80; Moxnes, "God and His Promise," 178, 187).

The faith celebrated in 11:1–40 is characterized by firmness, reliability, and steadfastness. It is trust in God and in his promises (cf. 4:1–3; 6:1; 11:6, 17–19, 29). The context shows that what these attested witnesses affirm is the reliability of God, who is faithful to his promise (11:11). Committing themselves to God who is steadfast, these exemplars of faith were themselves made steadfast. This concept of faith is rooted in the OT, where faith and hope are closely allied (so Grässer, *Glaube*, 85). The tension between faith and the realization of the promise of God that is developed throughout this section demonstrates that it is the nature of faith to render hope secure (vv 1, 9, 10, 13, 24–26, 39).

Faith also stands in narrow association with endurance (10:36; 12:1–3). Especially in 10:36–39, the interpretation of the oracle from Hab 2:4 gives to faith the nuance of firm, persevering faithfulness. With the seamless transition to 11:1 the writer adds to the concept of faith the eschatological dimension of an unwavering and anticipatory orientation to the future promised by God. Accordingly, the stress is on the ethical component of faith as a persevering faithfulness to God (6:1; 11:6). With this conception of faith Hebrews stands in continuity with the notion of faith in the Synoptic tradition (e.g., Mark 11:22–23 [=Matt 21:21–22]; cf. Luke 17:6; 1 Cor 13:2), especially in "Q" and the miracle narratives, where faith is often without an object ("only believe"), but the intended object is *faith in God* (Dautzenberg, *BZ* 17 [1963] 163–71, 174–75; cf. Williamson, *Philo*, 332–34, 338–43, 348, 366–71; Thompson, *Beginnings of Christian Philosophy*, 56–61).

There is a note of bold assertiveness in this celebration of faith that has been largely lost to the modern readers of Hebrews. As J. W. Thompson has observed, "a catalogue of heroes of πίστις, introduced as patterns of imitation, is unthinkable in any Greek tradition" (*Beginnings of Christian Philosophy*, 53). The reason for this is that to the formally educated person, πίστις, "faith," was regarded as a state of mind characteristic of the uneducated, who believe something on hearsay without being able to give precise reasons for their belief. The willingness of Jews and Christians to suffer for the undemonstrable astonished pagan observers (cf. E. R. Dodds, *Pagan and Christian in an Age of Anxiety* [New York: Norton, 1965] 120–22). Yet this is precisely the conduct praised in Heb 11:1–40. This fact constitutes the note of offense in this section of the homily.

Form/Structure/Setting

Both form and content serve to distinguish 11:1–40 from the remainder of the homily. The rhetorical style of this section is so distinctive that its relationship to the rest of Hebrews has been questioned. The characterization of faith is validated by a catalogue of examples selected from redemptive history. The list demonstrates that faith for the people of God under the old covenant was closely allied with hope and implied steadfast endurance supported by the promise of God. Although the section is expository in form, it is parenetic in function, inviting Christians to emulate the example of those who responded to God with active faith.

In classical antiquity lists of examples were frequently used to motivate an audience or readers to strive for virtue (for a discussion of primary sources, cf. Cosby, "Rhetorical Composition and Function," 45–106). When Judaism took its place in hellenistic society, it was influenced by hellenism to adopt and adapt this genre for its own purposes (cf. Towner, *Rabbinic "Enumeration of Scriptural Examples*," 100–16; Cosby, 114–37). Evidence for this is provided by documents emanating from the wisdom tradition. Recourse to lists of OT personages attests an interest in history that was new to the Jewish wisdom tradition (so Fichtner, *TLZ* 76 [1951] 141–50; Jacob, "L'histoire d'Israël," 288–94). This development may have been encouraged because a recital of persons and events from Israel's past occurs in Scripture both as a "sermon-form" (e.g., Josh 24:2–13; 1 Sam 12:6–15) and as a format for prayer (Neh 9:5–37).

The impact of this tendency can be traced both in the liturgy and in the preaching of the hellenistic synagogue (cf. Towner, *Rabbinic "Enumeration of Scriptural Examples,"* 95–117, 214–30). A number of older liturgical fragments, for example, now embedded in the fourth-century Christian work known as *Apostolic Constitutions,* provide lists consisting of names of exemplary figures extending from Abel to the Maccabees in historical order (cf. W. Bousset, "Eine jüdische Gebetssammlung im siebenden Buch der *apostolischen Konstitutionem," NGWG,* Philologische-historische Klasse, 1915 [1916] 435–85, who called attention to *Apost. Const.* 7.37.1–3; 7.39.2–4; 8.5.1–4; and 8.12.6–27; Bousset sought to demonstrate the hellenistic-Jewish origin of these liturgical fragments, which he felt were derived from Jewish prayers). Similar lists found in both Jewish and early Christian literature show that they constitute a distinctive literary form, the testimony list (cf. Cosby, "Rhetorical Composition," 114–61).

In one version of this form, salvation history is reviewed in terms of the action of God (or of divine Wisdom) in history (Wis 10:1–11:1; Acts 7:2–47). In another version, redemptive history is summarized in terms of God's friends and prophets who exemplified some quality worthy of emulation (Sir 44:1–49:16; 1 Macc 2:51–61; 4 Macc 16:16–23; *1 Clem.* 7:5–7; 10:1–12:8; 17:1–18:1; 31:1–4; 45:1–7; 55:1–6). A related, but different, form consists of a collection of moral *exempla* illustrated from the lives of OT figures. Philo, for example, cast two of his moral treatises in the form of exemplary anecdotes drawn from OT personages (*On the Virtues* 198–255; *On Rewards and Punishments* 7–78; abbreviated lists occur in *Allegorical Interpretation* 2.53–59; 3.228; cf. *1 Clem.* 4:1–6:4). The literary genre of a catalogue of examples was thus well established in hellenistic Judaism (cf. von Schmitt, *BZ* 21 [1977] 1–22; for an analysis of the characteristics of these lists, see Bovon, *RTP* 18 [1968] 134–36). It served defined apologetic and parenetic purposes, and was used effectively also in the missionary propaganda in which Judaism was engaged (cf. Siebeneck, *CBQ* 21 [1959] 416–19; Thyen, *Stil,* 115–16; Mercado, "Language of Sojourning," 69–75; Cosby, "Rhetorical Composition," 186–90, 260–63).

The distinctive form of Heb 11:1–40 can be determined more precisely by comparing this section with *1 Clem.* 17:1–19:3, its closest parallel. These two passages appear to be related by a common form, which is of greater significance than any supposed dependence (so D'Angelo, *Moses,* 19; for the analysis that follows I am indebted to D'Angelo's discussion, 18–26). The form is a version of the exemplary list that can be described as a *list of attested examples.* It is distinguished formally by a technical use of the verb μαρτυρεῖν in the passive to refer to the reception of attestation from God, discovered in the pages of Scripture, which validates the exemplary function of the persons listed for the edification of an audience. The verb is used in this rather special sense both in Heb 11:1–40 and in *1 Clem.* 17:1–19:3, where it serves a formal role in the structure of each of these passages.

The form consists of (1) a brief introduction to the list, which identifies it as a record of those who exemplify a quality and have been "attested" by God; (2) the series of examples, clarifying how each individual was "attested" and exemplified the quality; (3) a hortatory conclusion, encouraging the audience to recognize these models of appropriate response who received divine attestation and to persevere in their own pursuit of exemplary behavior.

The unmodified form appears more clearly in *1 Clement,* which may serve as a standard of comparison.

(1) *Introduction.* Clement opens this section of his homily with a reference to those who were "attested" (τοὺς μεμαρτυρημένους) by God:

Let us become imitators of those who . . . preached the coming of Christ . . . , even those who were *attested* [by God] (*1 Clem.* 17:1).

In a formally similar manner, the writer of Hebrews begins by characterizing faith and observing "on this account the men of the past *received attestation* [ἐμαρτυρήθησαν] [by God]" (Heb 11:2).

(2) *The Exemplars.* Clement lists four examples that exhibit a common pattern consisting of (a) the name of the example, (b) the attestation (in the first and fourth example expressed by the verb μαρτυρεῖν in the passive), and (c) the words of the individual that demonstrate his quality. With the case of Abraham, the first example, the pattern is established:

(a)   Abraham
(b)   *received* great *attestation* [ἐμαρτυρήθη] [by God] and was called the friend of God,
(c)   and, gazing upon the glory of God and humbling himself, he says, "But I am earth and ashes" (*1 Clem.* 17:2).

Although the writer of Hebrews does not follow this format, the form of the attested examples can be recognized in the first two examples, Abel and Enoch. In each case (a) the example is introduced with the formulaic πίστει, "by faith," (b) the examplar's name is given, (c) reference is made to the occasion when his faith was demonstrated, and (d) the divine attestation is asserted:

(a)   By faith
(b)   Abel
(c)   offered to God a more acceptable sacrifice than Cain
(d)   by which he *received attestation* [ἐμαρτυρήθη] [by God] (Heb 11:4).

(a)   By faith
(b)   Enoch
(c)   was translated [by God] so that he did not experience death. . . .
(d)   Now before his translation he *had been attested* [μεμαρτύρηται] [by God] as one who had been pleasing to God (Heb 11:5).

After the first two examples, however, this formal pattern is significantly modified.

(3) *Conclusion.* Clement concludes his list with a summary underscoring the significance of the examples cited:

The humility and submission through obedience of so many and of such great examples, *having been attested* [μεμαρτυρημένων] [by God] in this way, has made better not only us but also the generations before us (*1 Clem.* 19:1).

He then exhorts the Corinthians to seek peace, using the athletic metaphor for the moral life and directing their attention toward a heavenly example:

> let us race on toward the goal of peace handed down to us from the beginning, and let us fix our gaze upon the Father and Creator of the whole world. . . . Let us look upon him with the understanding and contemplate with the eyes of the soul his patient purpose (*1 Clem.* 19:2–3).

A formal similarity is evident in the conclusion to the list of attested examples in Heb 11:1–40, together with the transition to the next unit in 12:1–3:

> and although they all *had received attestation* [μαρτυρηθέντες] [from God] through faith, they did not receive what had been promised (Heb 11:39);

> let us run with endurance the race prescribed for us . . . , fixing our eyes upon Jesus, the champion and perfector of faith. . . . Consider the one who endured from sinners such opposition against themselves (Heb 12:1–3).

The reference to the attested examples, followed by the use of the athletic metaphor and the appeal to a heavenly example, exhibits the structural format preserved in *1 Clement*.

In brief, the introduction, first two examples, and conclusion of Heb 11:1–40 take the form of a list of attested exemplars who receive divine approval in the pages of Scripture. The formal similarity and the differences from the unit in *1 Clem.* 17:1–19:3 indicate the degree of freedom exercised by the writer of Hebrews in adapting the form to his own purposes.

That degree of freedom is particularly evident in the continuation of the section following Heb 11:6. As the list is developed, individual units begin to focus on redemptive events in history rather than on the person and character of the models. As M. R. D'Angelo has observed, "not each example, but each event is introduced by the words 'by faith'" (*Moses*, 25). Thus 11:8–19 is not merely a summary of Abraham's life, character, and faith. It is also a succinct history of the promise of God considered in terms of Abraham's call and migration to Canaan (11:8–10), the conception of Isaac (11:11–12), the deferment of the fulfillment of the promise (11:13–16), and the command to sacrifice Isaac (11:17–19).

This formal modification serves to situate the exemplary conduct of the several exemplars in a new perspective. There is less interest in the positive exemplary function of the models than in the understanding that their actions are informative concerning the content of *Christian* faith. The yearning of the patriarchs for a country of their own is a witness *to the Christian community* of the reality of a heavenly homeland (11:16). The heroic refusal of the martyrs to deny their confession bears witness to the better resurrection (11:35).

In this way the list of those who were attested by God has been transformed into a list of witnesses whose faith testifies to the present generation concerning the reality of the blessings for which *Christians* hope. The summation of sacred history in terms of their lives, acts, and deaths provides convincing evidence for the role that faith and faithfulness play in the history of redemption. As such, the attested exemplars of faith function as God's witnesses who seek to persuade the Christian community of the reality of the recompense upon which they secured the conduct of their lives (so D'Angelo, *Moses*, 24–26; cf. Kuss, 166, 171, 180, 185).

As a section, Heb 11:1–40 is firmly integrated within the structure of the homily. The concluding paragraph of the exhortation delivered in 10:19–39 addresses the community's need for endurance and faith (10:36–39). In a summarizing statement the writer declares, "But we are those who are of faith (πίστις), culminating in the acquisition of life" (10:39). The key word πίστις provides the verbal link with 11:1, which begins Ἔστιν δὲ πίστις, "Now faith celebrates." The transition from exhortation to the exposition of the character of faith is thus achieved naturally and smoothly (cf. Grässer, *Glaube*, 45; McCown, "Ο ΛΟΓΟΣ ΤΗΣ ΠΑΡΑΚΛΗΣΕΩΣ," 84).

The limits of the section are clearly marked by an *inclusio* that serves to bracket the exposition:

11:1–2   "Now *faith* [πίστις] celebrates. . . . For on this account men of the past *received attestation* [ἐμαρτυρήθησαν] [from God]."

11:39   "and although these all *received attestation* [μαρτυρηθέντες] [from God] *through faith* [διὰ τῆς πίστεως]."

The repetition of the decisive word πίστις and of the verb μαρτυρεῖν in the passive, which is employed in the specialized sense of "having received attestation" from God, demonstrates that the section introduced in 11:1 extends to 11:39–40 (cf. Vanhoye, *La structure*, 46–47, 183–94; Bénétreau, *ETR* 54 [1979] 625–26).

Throughout this section πίστις remains the characteristic term, which is repeated with variation twenty-four times. In vv 3–31 the development is distinguished by anaphora, the rhetorical repetition of a key word or words at the beginning of successive clauses to give unity, rhythm, and solemnity to a discourse (BDF §491; cf. Thyen, *Stil*, 50, 58–59; Cosby, "Rhetorical Composition," 171–75, 202–9; for other instances of this rhetorical figure, see the treatment of hope in Philo, *On Rewards and Punishments* 11, and of jealousy in *1 Clem.* 4:9–6:4). The use of anarthrous, anaphoric πίστει occurs eighteen times in vv 3–31, but nowhere else in the homily. The catalogue in vv 32–38 contains the word πίστις only once (v 33), but the writer was careful to introduce it again in a summary statement at the conclusion of the section (vv 39–40). The anaphora and the repetition of the characteristic word serve to unify the section literarily.

Although the literary unity of 11:1–40 is incontestable, it is more difficult to determine with precision the internal structure of the section. The striking use of anaphora in vv 1–31 separates and unifies the presentation simultaneously. Within these verses it is obvious that the introductions of Abraham (v 8) and of Moses (v 23) serve to mark off significant blocks of material. A sharp break in the format of the presentation is announced at v 32; the writer renounces any further attempt to invoke one by one the exemplary figures and events of the OT and resorts to a summarizing catalogue. It is natural to find in these three pivotal verses the openings of paragraphs. Accordingly, the section can be subdivided into four units: vv 1–7, 8–22, 23–31, 32–40 (cf. Vanhoye, *La structure*, 183–84; McCown, "*Ο ΛΟΓΟΣ ΤΗΣ ΠΑΡΑΚΛΗΣΕΩΣ*," 86–87; Moxnes, "God and His Promise," 178–80).

Certain literary features tend to confirm this analysis. The initial unit (vv 1–7) is unified by the word πίστις, which is repeated at the beginning of each statement (vv 1, 2 [ἐν ταύτῃ], 3, 4, 5, 7). The unit is framed by an *inclusio* constituted by the present participle βλεπομένων qualified by a negative:

v 1   πραγμάτων . . . οὐ βλεπομένων
       "events . . . not seen"
v 7   τῶν μηδέπω βλεπομένων
       "events as yet unseen"

Apart from the use of the present participle τὸ βλεπόμενον, "what is seen," in the singular and without the negative in v 3, it does not appear elsewhere in Hebrews. The use of the verb μαρτυρεῖν is characteristic of this first paragraph. It occurs three times in the passive with the special meaning "to have received attestation by God" (vv 2, 4, 5), and once in the active voice, where the nuance of attestation is equally evident (v 4). This verb is not reintroduced until v 39, where it functions to establish a general *inclusio* for the section. The first two verses of this paragraph furnish an introduction to the section as a whole. It is only with v 3 that the anaphoric use of πίστει begins. This verse is itself a hinge passage, linking the introduction to the exemplary witnesses in vv 4–7 by setting forth faith as a principle of interpretation for all of the examples subsequently invoked (cf. Vanhoye, *La structure*, 184–85).

The final word in v 7, κληρονόμος, "heir," is the linking term that ties the first paragraph to its sequel (vv 8–22). The second paragraph speaks of the reception of an inheritance (λαμβάνειν εἰς κληρονομίαν, v 8) and of those who are joint heirs (συγκληρονόμων, v 9). This long paragraph is unified by reference to the promise of God (vv 9, 11, 13, 17) and its corollary, the blessing (vv 20, 21; see the detailed analysis of Vanhoye, *La structure*, 186–89). The paragraph is subdivided by the commentary on the biblical record introduced by the writer in vv 13–16. By placing his most important affirmations at the center of the paragraph, he indicated the perspective from which the whole unit is to be understood (cf. Vanhoye, *La structure*, 182–91; Moxnes, "God and His Promise," 179–80).

The mention of the anticipated departure of the Israelites from Egypt in v 22 prepares literarily for the third paragraph concerning Moses and the events he set in motion with the exodus from Egypt (vv 23–31). It is possible to identify two subsections within this paragraph. The limits of the first are indicated by the repetition of several significant terms:

v 23   διότι εἶδον . . . καὶ οὐκ ἐφοβήθησαν τὸ διάταγμα τοῦ βασιλέως.
       "*because they saw* . . . and *they were not afraid* of the edict *of the king.*"
v 27   μὴ φοβηθεὶς τὸν θυμὸν τοῦ βασιλέως . . . γὰρ . . . ὁρῶν ἐκαρτέρησεν.
       "*not fearing* the rage *of the king* . . . for . . . he kept seeing continually.*"

The second subsection is marked by a rapid increase of rhythm. The initial statement in v 28 still concerns Moses, but then he recedes from view. All attention is concentrated on the events of the crossing of the Red Sea and the fall of Jericho, which furnishes the writer with the witness of Rahab, who achieved salvation by her allegiance to the faithful people of God (cf. Vanhoye, *La structure*, 189–91; Moxnes, "God and His Promise," 179).

The final paragraph constitutes an eloquent peroration to the section. The opening and closing of the paragraph are indicated by the formula διὰ [τῆς] πίστεως, "through faith" (vv 32–33/39–40), which does not appear elsewhere in the section. Within this paragraph a sharp change of tone and of subject in v 35b serves to subdivide the unit and to emphasize the contrast between those who triumphed through faith (vv 32–35a) and others who experienced humiliation and martyrdom because of steadfast faithfulness to God (vv 35b–38) (for an analysis of the varied rhythm of the paragraph, see Vanhoye, *La structure*, 192–93).

The summarizing statement in vv 39–40 serves to conclude the paragraph and the section as a whole. The new feature in these verses is the focus upon the relevance of the recital for the Christian community in v 40. There the writer speaks of God's provision for something better "with us in mind" (περὶ ἡμῶν), namely, that these attested exemplars should not reach perfection "without us" (χωρὶς ἡμῶν). The introduction of the plural pronouns in the first person provides a point of transition to the following section, which calls attention to the necessary endurance that must characterize the Christian community in its own struggle with hostility and adversity (cf. Vanhoye, *La structure*, 193–94).

The question of a source or prototype for this section has been much discussed (cf. Michel, 368–72). An early line of investigation compared Heb 11:1–40 with liturgical texts. The first scholar to do so appears to have been P. Drews, who in 1906 called attention to the lists of names of exemplary figures from the OT that are found in the seventh and eighth books of the *Apostolic Constitutions*. Although these lists are of uncertain date, they almost certainly originated in hellenistic Judaism. With the aid of one of these lists, in a prayer found in *Apost. Const.* 8.12.10, Drews posited a liturgical background for Heb 11:1–40 as well as for other early Christian texts (*Studien*, 23–40; cf. W. Bousset, "Eine jüdische Gebetssammlung im siebenden Buch der *apostolischen Konstitutionem*," *NGWG* [1916] 445–73; Eccles, "Purpose of the Hellenistic Patterns," 214–15, 221–22; for a critique of this proposal, see Bovon, *RTP* 18 [1968] 133, n. 3).

In a more recent attempt to define the source behind Heb 11:1–40 and to discover its literary genre, G. Schille pointed in a different direction. He posited that the underlying source consisted of material of an OT character cast in the form of a confession of faith. According to Schille, the confession was being used in the community addressed by the writer for the task of intensifying catechetical instruction of candidates for baptism. The source of the confession, he argued, can be traced to a pre-Christian Jewish baptistic group. Schille claimed to have found traces of the source not only in Heb 11:4–31, but also in 12:18-19a, 22–24 (*ZNW* 51 [1960] 112–31; for a critique of this proposal, see Bovon, *RTP* 18 [1968] 133–34; Mercado, "Language of Sojourning," 74–75).

These proposals are not supported by the actual form and structural format of this section. They fail to take sufficient account of the development of the wisdom tradition of hellenistic Judaism as a background for Heb 11:1–40. It is more probable that if there was a prototype for this section, it was a homily emanating from the hellenistic-Jewish synagogue (so Windisch, 98; Thyen, *Stil,* 18). But if a specific homily served as the source for this section, it is clear that it was thoroughly recast by the writer of Hebrews to serve his own pastoral purposes. Both the style and vocabulary of 11:1–40 show affinity with the rest of the homily (so Sowers, *Hermeneutics,* 132–33; Williamson, *Philo,* 310–11; Thompson, *Beginnings of Christian Philosophy,* 69). It would be more accurate to say that Heb 11:1–40 reflects a sapiential tradition rather than a precise source (so Bovon, *RTP* 18 [1968] 137–40). It is possible that this section was developed as a tractate by the writer on some prior occasion (so McCown, "*O ΛΟΓΟΣ ΤΗΣ ΠΑΡΑΚΛΗΣΕΩΣ,*" 85, 189). It bears indelibly his own literary signature. That the section originated with the writer is revealed in the careful choice of terms and in the precision and succinctness with which he expresses himself (with Mercado, "Language of Sojourning," 137, n. 1; Williamson, *Philo,* 315–16).

The Triumphs of Perseverance in Faith in the Antediluvian Era (11:1–7)

Bibliography

Adler, W. "Enoch in Early Christian Literature." In *Society of Biblical Literature 1978 Seminar Papers.* Ed. P. J. Achtemeier. Missoula: Scholars, 1978. 1:271–75. **Andel, C. P. van.** *De structuur van de Henoch-Traditie en het Nieuwe Testament.* Kampen: Kok, 1955. **Aptowitzer, V.** *Kain und Abel in der Agada, den Apokryphen, der hellenistischen, christlichen und muhammedanischen Literatur.* Vienna/Leipzig: Löwit, 1922. **Bassler, J. M.** "Cain and Abel in the Palestinian Targum: A Brief Note on an Old Controversy." *JJS* 17 (1986) 56–44. **Bauer, J. B.** "Kain und Abel." *TPQ* 103 (1955) 126–33. **Bénétreau, S.** "La foi d'Abel: Hébreux 11/4." *ETR* 54 (1979) 623–30. **Betz, O.** "Firmness in Faith: Hebrews 11,1 and Isaiah 28,16." In *Scripture: Meaning and Method.* FS A. T. Hanson. Ed. B. P. Thompson. Hull: Hull UP, 1987. 92–113. **Boman, T.** "Hebraic and Greek Thought-Forms in the New Testament." In *Current Issues in New Testament Interpretation.* FS O. A. Piper. Ed. W. Klassen and G. F. Snyder. New York: Harper and Row, 1962. 1–22. **Bover, J. M.** "La esperanza en la Epistola a los Hebreos." *Greg* 19 (1938) 110–20. **Brandenburger, E.** "Pistis und Soteria: Zum Verstehenshorizont von 'Glaube' im Urchristentum." *ZTK* 85 (1988) 165–98. **Brock, S. P.** "A Syriac Life of Abel." *Mus* 87 (1974) 467–92. **Conner, C.** "Hebrews XI.1." *ExpTim* 3 (1891–92) 373. **Cox, S.** "Enoch's Gospel: Genesis v.21–24; Hebrews xi.5, 6; Jude 14,15." *Exp* 2nd ser. 7 (1884) 321–45. **Dahl, N. A.** "Christ, Creation and the Church." In *The Background of the New Testament and Its Eschatology.* FS C. H. Dodd. Ed. W. D. Davies and D. Daube. Cambridge: Cambridge UP, 1964. 422–43. **Déaut, R. le.** "Traditions targumiques dans le corpus paulinien? (Hébr 11,4 et 12,24; Gal 4,29–30; II Cor 3,16)." *Bib* 42 (1961) 24–48. **Díez Macho, A.** "Targum y Nuevo Testamento." In *Mélanges E. Tisserant.* Studi e Testi 231. Vatican City, 1964. 153–85. **Dörrie, H.** "Zu Hebr 11,1." *ZNW* 46 (1955) 196–202. ———. " *Ὑπόστασις*: Wort- und Bedeutungsgeschichte." *NAWG* 3 (1955) 35–92. **Ehrhardt, A.** "Creatio ex Nihilo." In *The*

Framework of the New Testament Stories. Cambridge, MA: Harvard UP, 1964. 200–233. **Erdin, F.** "Das Wort Hypostasis." Dissertation, Freiburg, 1939. **Garvey, A. E.** "In Praise of Faith: A Study of Hebrews xi.1, 6; xii.1, 2." *ExpTim* 26 (1914–15) 199–202, 278–81, 328–31. **Giblet, J.** "Exegesis in Hebr. XI,1–2." *CMech* 33 (1948) 285–88. **Goldstein, J. A.** "Creatio Ex Nihilo: Recantations and Restatements." *JJS* 38 (1987) 187–94. ———. "The Origins of the Doctrine of Creatio Ex Nihilo." *JJS* 35 (1984) 127–35. **Grelot, P.** "Hénoch et ses écritures." *RB* 82 (1975) 481–88. ———. "La légende d'Hénoch dans les apocryphes et dans la Bible: Origine et signification." *RSR* 46 (1958) 5–26, 181–210. ———. "Les Targums du Pentateuque: Étude comparative d'après Genèse IV,3–16." *Sem* 9 (1959) 59–88. **Grossouw, W.** "L'espérance dans le Nouveau Testament." *RB* 61 (1954) 508–32. **Haacker, K.** "Creatio ex auditu: Zum Verständnis von Hbr 11,3." *ZNW* 60 (1969) 279–81. ———. "Der Glaube im Hebräerbrief und die hermeneutische Bedeutung des Holocaust: Bemerkungen zu eine aktuellen Kontroverse." *TZ* 39 (1983) 152–65. **Himmelfarb, M.** "A Report on Enoch in Rabbinic Literature." In *Society of Biblical Literature 1978 Seminar Papers.* Ed. P. J. Achtemeier. Missoula: Scholars, 1978. 1:259–69. **Hughes, P. E.** "The Doctrine of Creation in Hebrews 11:3." *BTB* 2 (1972) 64–77. **Jones, J. E.** "Now Faith Is . . . Hope." *RevExp* 52 (1955) 508–30. **Kendall, R. T.** *Believing God: Studies on Faith in Hebrews 11.* Grand Rapids. Zondervan, 1981. **Kilpatrick, G. D.** "The Chester Beatty Papyrus p⁴⁶ and Hebrews XI.4." *JTS* 42 (1941) 68–69. **Kraft, R. A.** "Philo (Josephus, Sirach and Wisdom of Solomon) on Enoch." In *Society of Biblical Literature 1978 Seminar Papers.* Ed. P. J. Achtemeier. Missoula: Scholars, 1978. 1:253–57. **Lampe, G. W. H.** "The New Testament Doctrine of KTISIS." *SJT* 17 (1964) 449–62. **Lewis, J. P.** "Noah and the Flood in Jewish, Christian, and Muslim Tradition." *BA* 47 (1984) 224–39. ———. *A Study of the Interpretation of Noah and the Flood in Jewish and Christian Literature.* Leiden: Brill, 1968. 3–120, 181–92. **Lührmann, D.** "Henoch und die *Metanoia.*" *ZNW* 66 (1975) 103–16. **Mathis, M. A.** *The Pauline ΠΙΣΤΙΣ-ΥΠΟΣΤΑΣΙΣ according to Heb. XI,1: An Historico-Exegetical Investigation.* Washington, DC: Catholic University of America, 1920. ——— and **Murillo, L.** "Does '*Substantia*' Mean 'Realization' or 'Foundation' in Hebr. 11,1?" *Bib* 3 (1922) 79–89. **Maynard, J. D.** "Justin Martyr and the Text of Hebrews XI.4." *Exp* 7th ser. 7 (1909) 163–71. **McNamara, M.** *The New Testament and the Palestinian Targum to the Pentatauch.* Rome: Pontifical Biblical Commission, 1966. 156–60. **Perkins, W.** *A Cloud of Witnesses: A Commentary on Hebrews 11 (1609).* Ed. J. H. Augustine. New York: Pilgrim Press, 1990. **Ross, J.** "Hebrews XI.1, ὑπόστασις." *ExpTim* 4 (1892–93) 177–78. ———. "Two Aspects of Faith (Heb. XI.1)." *ExpTim* 23 (1911–12) 182–83. **Schmitt, A.** "Die Angaben über Henoch Gen 5:21–24 in der LXX." In *Wort, Lied und Gottesspruch.* FS J. Ziegler. Ed. J. Schreiner. Würzburg: Echter, 1972. 161–69. **Schröger, F.** *Der Verfasser des Hebräerbriefes als Schriftausleger.* 204, 206, 212–15. **Schumpp, M.** "Der Glaubensbegriff des Hebräerbriefs und seine Deutung durch hl. Thomas." *DivThom* 11 (1934) 397–410. **Stewart, R. A.** "Creation and Matter in the Epistle to the Hebrews." *NTS* 12 (1965–66) 284–93. **Strong, T. B.** "The History of the Theological Term 'Substance.'" *JTS* 2 (1901) 224–35; 3 (1902) 22–40; 4 (1903) 28–45. **Tabor, J. D.** "Returning to the Divinity: Josephus's Portrayal of the Disappearances of Enoch, Elijah, and Moses." *JBL* 108 (1989) 225–38. **Taylor, R. O. P.** "A Neglected Clue in Hebrews XI.1." *ExpTim* 52 (1940–41) 256–59. **VanderKam, J. C.** "Enoch Traditions in Jubilees and Other Second Century Sources." In *Society of Biblical Literature 1978 Seminar Papers.* Ed. P. J. Achtemeier. Missoula: Scholars, 1978. 1:229–51. **Vermès, G.** "The Targumic Versions of Genesis 4,3–16." ALUOS 3 (1961–62) 81–114. **Waltke, B. K.** "Cain and His Offering." *WTJ* 48 (1986) 223–39. **Weiss, H. F.** *Untersuchungen zur Kosmologie des hellenistischen und palästinischen Judentums.* Berlin: Akademie, 1966. **White, N. J. D.** "The Doctrine of Creation according to the Epistle to the Hebrews." *Exp* 8th ser. 23 (1922) 368–75. **Widdess, A. G.** "A Note on Hebrews XI.3." *JTS* n.s. 10 (1959) 327–29. **Witt, R. E.** "ΥΠΟΣΤΑΣΙΣ." In *Amicitiae Corolla.* FS J. R. Harris. Ed. H. G. Wood. London: University of London Press, 1933. 319–43.

Translation

[1] Now faith celebrates [a] the objective reality[b] [of the blessings] for which we hope,[c] the demonstration[d] of events[e] as yet unseen.[f] [2] On this account the men of the past received attestation by God.[g]

[3] By faith[h] we understand[i] that the universe was ordered by the word of God, so that[j] what is seen was not[k] brought into being from anything observable.

[4] By faith Abel offered to God[l] a more acceptable[m] sacrifice than Cain, by which[n] he received attestation by God that he was a righteous person,[o] God himself approving of his gifts. And by faith[p] he is still speaking, although he died.[q] [5] By faith Enoch was translated[r] by God so that[s] he did not experience death, and "he could not be found because God had translated him." Now before his translation he had been approved as one who had been pleasing to God, [6] and without faith it is impossible to begin to please him,[t] for it is necessary for the one approaching God to believe that he exists and that he becomes a rewarder of those who seek him out. [7] By faith Noah, having been instructed by God concerning events as yet unseen,[u] paid attention[v] and constructed an ark for the safety[w] of his household. By faith he condemned humanity,[x] and he became an heir of the righteousness according to faith.[y]

Notes

[a] The position of ἔστιν at the beginning of the sentence is emphatic. At first sight, this appears to reflect a class of statements in Greek literature consisting of descriptions and definitions, which are commonly introduced by ἔστι (e.g., Plato, *Symposium* 186 C: ἔστι γὰρ ἰατρικὴ ὡς ἐν κεφαλαίῳ εἰπεῖν ἐπιστήμη τῶν . . . ["For medicine may be described generally as the science of . . ."]; Philo, *On the Unchangeableness of God* 87: ἔστιν δὲ εὐχὴ μὲν αἴτησις ἀγαθῶν παρὰ θεοῦ ["Now a vow is a request for good things from God"]; cf. Philo, *Allegorical Interpretations* 3.211 [a definition of groaning]; Luke 8:11; John 21:25; 1 Tim 6:6; 1 John 1:5; 5:17; and the discussion of Moffatt, 159; Williamson, *Philo*, 313–15). It has been observed, however, that Hebrews is classical and literary in its tendency to omit the copula; wherever it occurs, there is a good reason for its insertion. The presence of ἔστιν in 11:1 is either very exceptional, or it is indicative that ἔστιν does not function as a copula. That the latter is true is argued by Turner, *Grammar* 3:307, who treats 11:1 as a spontaneous phrase and translates ἔστιν by "represents." The translation adopted here seeks to render idiomatically the sense of the word in context (cf. Dörrie, *ZNW* 46 [1955] 199–200; Koester, *TDNT* 8:587, n. 142).

[b] The decisive word ὑπόστασις was used with an extensive range of connotations during the classical and hellenistic periods, and its significance in 11:1 is disputed (for a convenient survey, cf. Grässer, *Glaube*, 46–47, nn. 199–201). A review of the linguistic evidence for the meaning of the term at the time Hebrews was written demonstrates that ὑπόστασις denoted tangible reality in contrast to mere appearance (ἔμφασις) (see especially Mathis and Murillo, *Bib* 3 [1922] 79–84; Witt, "ΥΠΟΣΤΑΣΙΣ," 319, 324–25, 330–31; Dörrie, *ZNW* 46 [1955] 196–202; Koester, *TDNT* 8:572–84). The subsequent development of ὑπόστασις in Greek patristic literature, and particularly in the interpretation of Heb 11:1, confirms the obj character of the word (e.g., Chrysostom, *Hom.* 21.2, interprets ἐλπιζομένων ὑπόστασις, showing that it is the task of faith to make unseen reality as *real* as that which is seen with the human eye: "faith gives reality [ὑπόστασις] to objects of hope, which seem to be unreal, or rather does not give them reality [ὑπόστασις], but is their very essence [οὐσία]." This is the common patristic interpretation of the expression in Heb 11:1 (Matthis and Murillo, *Bib* 3 [1922] 84).

Although it is difficult to convey the range of nuances in ὑπόστασις with a single English word, it is imperative that the objective sense of the term be represented in translation: e.g., "objective guarantee" (Spicq, 2:337–38), "certainty" (Schlatter, 523, 614–17; Grässer, *Glaube*, 64–51; Dautzenberg, *BZ* 17 [1973] 169–70), "title-deed" which legally guarantees future possession (MM 659–60), "reality" (Dörrie, *ZNW* 46 [1955] 202; Koester, *TDNT* 8:586; Thompson, *Beginnings of*

Christian Philosophy, 70–71), "realization" (Mathis and Murillo, *Bib* 3 [1922] 86–87; Thompson, *Beginnings of Christian Philosophy,* 71–72), or "actualization" (Witt, "ΎΠΟΣΤΑΣΙΣ," 330–31). Translations like "confidence" or "assurance" are untenable because they give to ὑπόστασις a subj value that it does not possess (so Dörrie, *ZNW* 46 [1955] 197, n. 5; Dautzenberg, *BZ* 17 [1973] 169; Koester, *TDNT* 8:585–87).

ᶜ The present pass ptcp ἐλπιζομένων connotes the objects of hope, i.e., the totality of the expected heavenly blessings viewed in their objective certainty (cf. BAGD 282; Grässer, *Glaube,* 48–50).

ᵈ Syntactically, the second clause is in apposition to the first, with the result that ὑπόστασις, "reality," "realization," is strengthened by ἔλεγχος. This shows that ἔλεγχος has an obj rather than a subj sense: "proof," "evidence," "demonstration" (cf. MM 202; Büchsel, *TDNT* 2:476; Grässer, *Glaube,* 50–51, 126–28; Michel, 373).

ᵉ Corresponding to the normal linguistic usage, ἔλεγχος, "demonstration," "proof," takes an obj gen πραγμάτων (see the examples given by Riggenbach, 342, n. 70). R. O. P. Taylor (*ExpTim* 52 [1940–41] 256–58) has called attention to the significance of the term πραγμάτων and correctly observes that πράγματα conveys the notion of personal activity or transactions (cf. 4 Macc 1:16: "Wisdom is a knowledge of divine and human *events* and of their causes"; Luke 1:1: "an account of the *events*"; Heb 6:18: "by two irrevocable *events* in which it is impossible for God to lie"; Eusebius, *Church History* 1.1: "to recount how many and important *events* are to have occurred"). For the translation of πράγματα as "events," see Maurer, *TDNT* 6:639; Williamson, *Philo,* 354, 359, 368.

ᶠ The use of the negative οὐ with a ptcp is unusual in NT Gk. (BDF §426). The presence of οὐ with the ptcp βλεπομένων here means that the negative is decisive; it stresses the fact that the events cannot be perceived through objective sense perception (Hanna, *Grammatical Aid,* 158). The translation of οὐ βλεπομένων, "not seen," as if it read μηδέπω βλεπομένων, "not yet seen," is justified by the use of that correlative form in v 7, where it furnishes the intended sense of v 1.

ᵍ The aor tense of ἐμαρτυρήθησαν is culminative, with the summary result of the exercise of faith in view. The pass voice has been interpreted as an instance of the "theological passive," indicating that it is God who bore witness to the men of the past. Other instances of the "theological passive" are found in vv 4 ("received attestation *by God*"), 5 ("translated *by God*"/"approved *by God*"), 7 ("instructed *by God*"), 8 ("called *by God*"), 17 ("put to the test *by God*"), 39 ("received attestation *from God*"). In vv 2, 4, 5, 39 the verb μαρτυρεῖν in the pass is used in a special way to refer to the reception of attestation from God, taken from or discovered in Scripture, which is the basis of the exemplary function of the persons who are presented for the instruction of the audience (see D'Angelo, *Moses,* 19–21, who calls attention to the same specialized use of μαρτυρεῖσθαι in *1 Clem.* 17–19; cf. Ign. *Eph.* 12:2; *Phld.* 11:1; Justin, *Dialogue with Trypho* 29).

ʰ The expression πίστει, which introduces the successive examples of faith, can be read as an instrumental dative ("by means of faith"), or a dative of manner ("accordance with the modality of faith"), or a causal dative ("because of faith"). Spicq, 2:340, leans toward dative of manner; Zerwick, *Biblical Greek* §58, treats the term as a causal dative.

ⁱ The translation presupposes that πίστει modifies the main verb νοοῦμεν (it is by faith that "we understand"; so Moule, *Idiom-Book,* 168, and all major English translations). This interpretation has been challenged by Widdess, *JTS* n.s. 10 [1959] 327–29, and by Haacker, *ZNW* 60 [1969] 279–81 (who shows no awareness of Widdess' earlier article). Both scholars construe πίστει with the inf κατηρτίσθαι (it is by faith that God "formed" the universe) instead of the main verb. The resultant translation attributes πίστις to God, who exercised faith by uttering the creative word: "It was through faith, we understand, that the worlds were fashioned by the word of God" (Widdess, 327), or "Through faith, as we infer, the world was created through God's word" (Haacker, 280). This construction of the syntax, it is argued, brings the initial example of πίστις into line with the general theme of the entire passage and with the examples that follow.

The fact that πίστις elsewhere is posited only of individuals or of Jesus in his humanity calls into question this radical proposal. More importantly, it is untenable because it fails to account for the expression ῥήματι θεοῦ ("by means of the word of God"), which is clearly intended to modify the inf κατηρτίσθαι.

ʲ The εἰς τό inf construction occurs eight times in Hebrews and in the other seven instances uniformly expresses result (cf. A. T. Robertson, *Grammar,* 1003, 1090). It is most naturally taken to express a final sense here as well (Widdess, *JTS* n.s. 10 [1959] 328). Zerwick (*Biblical Greek,* §352), however, holds that it is here used in a consecutive sense and translates, "in such a way that."

ᵏ The word order in the final clause is unusual. The negative μή may be correlated either with the closest expression ἐκ φαινομένων ("*not* from anything observable"); cf. NEB: "so that the visible came forth from the invisible") or with the entire infinitival clause ("was *not* brought into being from anything observable"). The translation reflects the latter construction on the ground that the negative generally occurs before the word or phrase that is negated. In this case, μή negates the entire clause (with Haacker, *ZNW* 60 [1969] 280, n. 7; Williamson, *Philo*, 377–79; Ehrhardt, "Creatio," 217; P. E. Hughes, 443; among others).

[l] Although the textual evidence for τῷ θεῷ after προσήνεγκεν, "he offered to God," is overwhelming, the reading may be a gloss. The verb προσφέρειν, "to offer," is used twenty-one times in Hebrews, and only in 9:14, which is a special case, is the verb construed with τῷ θεῷ as the obj. The original text may be preserved by P[13] Cl (*Stromata* 2.4.12 [2.119.12, ed. Staehlin]) and in the Armenian version of Ephraem's commentary, which agree in omitting these words (so Moffatt, 164; Windisch, 100; Zuntz, *Text*, 33, 51; cf. Kilpatrick, *JTS* 42 [1941] 68–69; Metzger, *Textual Commentary*, 671).

[m] The comparative adj πλείονα usually has a quantitative value, "more abundant." Over a century ago C. G. Cobet found in this reading evidence for primitive corruption in the text of Hebrews and conjectured that in the course of transcription an original ΗΔΙΟΝΑ, "more pleasant," had been displaced by ΠΛΕΙΟΝΑ, "more abundant." This conjecture was adopted by J. M. S. Baljon and F. Blass in their critical editions of the Gk text and was accepted as "brilliant" by Zuntz, *Text*, 16. The corruption of ἥδιον into πλεῖον is attested for Demosthenes, *Prooemium* 23, and for Plutarch, *On the Cessation of Oracles* 21, 421B (see Zuntz, *Text*, 16, 285). Moreover, Maynard (*Exp* 7th ser. 7 [1909] 163–71) argued that when Justin declares that God accepts the sacrifices of believing Gentiles more agreeably (ἥδιον) than those of the Jews (*Dialogue with Trypho* 29) he had Heb 11:4 in mind and is a witness to the preservation of the original text of Hebrews into the second century. Finally, Josephus (*Ant.* 1.54) uses the cognate verb ἥδεται when he states that God "was more pleased" with Abel's sacrifice than with Cain's.

Emendation of the text, however, is unnecessary since it is clear that πλεῖον may have a qualitative rather than a quantitative significance (cf. Matt 6:25 [=Luke 12:23]; 12:41–42 [=Luke 11:31–32]; Mark 12:23). This is certainly the case here (so Tasker, *NTS* 1 [1954–55] 183; cf. F. F. Bruce, 282, n. 26; P. E. Hughes, 453, n. 1).

[n] It is necessary to relate the relative pronoun (δι' ἧς) to πίστει, "by faith," rather than to θυσίαν, "sacrifice," as do Spicq, 2:342, and Zerwick and Grosvenor, *Grammatical Analysis*, 679. In 11:2 it is said explicitly that it is faith which wins divine approval.

[o] The nom case δίκαιος, "a righteous man," occurs with the inf because it is the nominal predicate of the subj of the verb (BDF §405[1, 2]).

[p] The expression δι' αὐτῆς clearly refers back to the initial πίστει, "by faith" (cf. Zerwick and Grosvenor, *Grammatical Analysis*, 679). It is parallel in function to the phrase δι' ἧς in the preceding clause (see above, *Note* n).

[q] The participle ἀποθανών is concessive, with the usual temporal connotations (Zerwick and Grosvenor, *Grammatical Analysis*, 679).

[r] The verb μετατίθημι denotes "to remove from one place to another," and so "to translate" in the sense of to "take up to heaven" (so Moffatt; cf. ΝΙV: "taken from this life").

[s] The articular inf τοῦ μὴ ἰδεῖν introduces a consec clause (cf. Zerwick, *Biblical Greek* §352).

[t] The aor inf εὐαρεστῆσαι appears to be ingressive in character.

[u] An alternative understanding has been proposed by Andriessen, who construes the phrase "concerning events as yet unseen" with the ptcp εὐλαβηθείς, which immediately follows, rather than with the ptcp χρηματισθείς, "having been instructed," which precedes. He argues that in Hebrews the prep περί, "concerning," and its obj tend to precede the verb that they determine (2:5; 4:8; 5:3, 11; 7:14; 9:5; 10:26; 11:20, 22). Moreover, the verb χρηματίζειν, "to instruct," is used without complement in 8:5 and 12:25. Consequently, the ptcp χρηματισθείς may be understood absolutely, analogous to the ptcp καλούμενος, "having been called," in 11:8. In accordance with this rearrangement of the phrase, he assigns the notion of fear to εὐλαβηθείς and translates, "It was by faith that, having been divinely instructed, Noah, seized by fear concerning events which had not yet appeared, constructed an ark." The emphasis thus falls on Noah's state of mind, which was full of dread in the face of an imminent catastrophe, when he responded to God in faith (see "Angoisse de la mort dans l'Épître aux Hébreux," *NRT* 96 [1974] 282–84; *En lisant*, 49–50).

[v] The aor deponent εὐλαβηθείς connotes attentiveness to the divine will, as in 5:7; 12:28 (so BAGD 332; P. E. Hughes, 463, n. 25; see *Note* v on 5:7). It describes an action antecedent to the main verb ("he constructed").

[w] The noun σωτηρίαν has here the same nuance as in Acts 27:34, "well-being," "safety." For examples from the papyri, see MM 622.

ˣ In Heb 11:7, 38 τὸν κόσμον clearly designates the people who live in the world, or "humanity."

ʸ In the phrase ἡ κατὰ πίστιν δικαιοσύνη, the qualification κατὰ πίστιν, "according to faith," connotes the norm or measure of faith. BAGD 408 proposes "the righteousness of faith."

Form/Structure/Setting

See 11:1-40 above.

Comment

1 The declaration in v 1 is rhetorical and aphoristic in character. It offers not a formal definition but a recommendation and celebration of the faith that results in the acquisition of life (10:39). As the quintessence of all that the writer wished to affirm about the intensity and capacity of faith through a catalogue of attested witnesses, it is confessional in nature. It concentrates in a single, compact sentence the theme and interpretation that the following examples will substantiate (cf. Dörrie, *ZNW* 46 [1955] 198; Grässer, *Glaube,* 53, n. 233).

The opening phrase ἔστιν δὲ πίστις, "Now faith celebrates," refers retrospectively to 10:39 where the context gave to πίστις the nuance of steadfast faithfulness to God and his word of promise. The verb ἔστιν has been extracted from its normal position and placed at the beginning of the sentence for emphasis, an emphasis required in the light of the previous assertion (Williamson, *Philo,* 314–15). The characterization of faith that follows exposes the dynamic nature of the response to God which receives divine attestation in Scripture and that obtains the realization of promised blessings (cf. Käsemann, *Das wandernde Gottesvolk,* 22: "faith arises when a person lets himself be convinced by God, and so attains a certainty which is objectively grounded and which transcends all human possibilities in its reliability"). It is not intended to be exhaustive in its scope, but underscores the objective basis for the security characteristic of faith. Every word has been carefully chosen and weighed so as to draw attention to characteristics of faith that had particular relevance to the immediate situation of the persons addressed.

The object that faith celebrates is considered under two aspects: ἐλπιζομένων ὑπόστασις πραγμάτων ἔλεγχος οὐ βλεπομένων, "the reality of the blessings for which we hope, the demonstration of events not seen." Key to the interpretation of these complementary clauses is recognition of the objective character of the decisive terms ὑπόστασις and ἔλεγχος (see *Notes* b and e above).

Briefly, the word ὑπόστασις designates an objective reality that is unquestionable and securely established. Dörrie (*ZNW* 46 [1955], 197–201) contends that ὑπόστασις denotes a process of realization that takes in the beginning, middle, and completion of reality. If viewed from the perspective of the beginning, then ὑπόστασις denotes the warrant for the promised blessings that guarantees their realization (cf. Ruth 1:12; Ps 38:8; Ezek 19:6 LXX, where ὑπόστασις translates a Hebrew word for hope). But if the whole process is in view, then it is necessary to resort to paraphrase to express the intended meaning: faith celebrates *now* the reality of the *future* blessings that constitute the objective content of hope. The word ὑπόστασις thus has reference to the point of departure and the ground for a now unalterable course of events that will culminate in the realization of the promises of God.

From this perspective, πίστις, "faith," is something objective that bestows upon the objects of hope (ἐλπιζομένων) even now a substantial reality, which will unfold in God's appointed time. It gives them the force of present realities and enables the person of faith to enjoy the full certainty of future realization (Dörrie, *ZNW* 46 [1955] 201–2; Mathis and Murillo, *Bib* 3 [1922] 83–84). Faith provides the objective ground upon which others may base their subjective confidence. This capacity of faith permits Christians to exercise a present grasp upon undemonstrable truth and to exhibit stability in the presence of hostility, knowing that the blessings for which they hope are firmly secured by the promise of God (Grässer, *Glaube*, 153). The close identification of πίστις with hope underscores its forward-looking character (cf. Thompson, *Beginnings of Christian Philosophy*, 72–73, who on the basis of 9:27; 10:25, 36–39 argues that ἐλπιζομένων in 11:1 points to the expectation of a final eschatological event, the return of Christ).

The second clause, which stands in apposition to the first, is equally daring: faith demonstrates the existence of reality that cannot be perceived through objective sense perception. As the complement to ὑπόστασις, "reality," ἔλεγχος must be understood in the objective sense of "proof" or "demonstration," the evidential character that deprives uncertainty of any basis (see *Note* e above; cf. Dörrie, *ZNW* 46 [1955] 198–99, 202; Grässer, *Glaube*, 51–53, 126–28). Thus faith confers upon what we do not see the full certainty of a *proof* or *demonstration;* it furnishes *evidence* concerning that which has not been seen.

The focus of the demonstrating function of faith is defined by the objective genitival phrase πραγμάτων . . . οὐ βλεπομένων. R. O. P. Taylor's important observation that πράγματα is used of personal activity or transactions shows that it is the writer's intention to relate the characterization of faith to the realm of human *events* (*ExpTim* 52 [1940–41] 256–58; see *Note* e above). The contrast implied in the phrase is thus not between the visible, phenomenal world of sense perception below and the invisible, heavenly world of reality above, as in Platonism (so Grässer, *Glaube*, 51; Thompson, *Beginnings of Christian Philosophy*, 73–75), but between events already witnessed as part of the historical past and events as yet unseen because they belong to the eschatological future (so Williamson, *Philo*, 340).

This understanding is confirmed in v 7, where the phrase πραγμάτων . . . οὐ βλεπομένων, "events not seen," is repeated with only slight variation in the phrase περὶ τῶν μηδέπω βλεπομένων, "concerning events not yet seen." The context there indicates that the realities not seen now will be seen in the future. This temporal understanding of the participle with the negative is clearly intended in v 1 as well: faith is the demonstration of the substantial reality of events as yet undisclosed and unseen.

Faith is thus an effective power directed toward the future. It springs from a direct, personal encounter with the living God. The forward-looking capacity of faith enables an individual to venture courageously and serenely into an unseen future, supported only by the word of God. As a positive orientation of life toward God and his word, faith has the capacity to unveil the future so that the solid reality of events as yet unseen can be grasped by the believer. This is clearly an eschatological concept of faith, which the writer wishes to promote among the members of the house church for whom he was pastorally concerned. The men and women to whom he refers in the catalogue of attested witnesses that follows all directed the effective power of faith to realities that for them lay in the future (cf. vv 7, 10, 13, 27, 31, 35–38), undismayed by harsh circumstances. The writer's thoughts on faith thus move at the historical plane and find in faith a reliable guide to the future (cf. Grässer, *Glaube*, 153; Williamson, *Philo*, 334–35, 338–43, 366–71; Moxnes, "God and His Promise," 178).

2 As the immediate substantiation of v 1 and the transition to the recital of the exponents of faith in vv 4–38, v 2 is of fundamental importance. It establishes that the thesis expressed in v 1 and the examples of faith enumerated in the catalogue will be mutually verified (cf. Schlatter, 526–27). The explanatory statement that "the men of the past" (οἱ πρεσβύτεροι; cf. Ps 104[MT 105]:22 LXX) received attestation from God ἐν ταύτῃ, "on this account," clearly means within the scope of faith presupposed in v 1. Their decisions and actions reflected a stance of life that is the hallmark of faith and demonstrated the capacity of faith to sustain steadfast commitment to God.

As a result of their firm faith they "received attestation" (ἐμαρτυρήθησαν) from God himself (see *Form/Structure/Setting* on 11:1–40; cf. vv 4, 5, 7, 39). The verb μαρτυρεῖσθαι occurs seven times in Hebrews (7:8, 17; 10:15; 11:2, 4, 5, 39), and in each instance the reference is to the witness of the biblical record. The exemplars of faith to whom reference is made in the pages of the OT "enjoy the approving testimony of Scripture, and consequently of God himself, who speaks by his Spirit through the written word" (Trites, *Witness*, 221). The writer found in Scripture and in certain of the edifying books subsequently added to the Greek Bible a record of faith in action verifying the character and possibilities of faith for the Christian community.

3 The commendation of faith in vv 1–2 is supplemented by the further affirmation of v 3: faith entails knowing that the physical universe was formed in response to the dynamic, personal word of God. The logical connection of this assertion is not with the acts of faith of the attested witnesses but with v 1, for it is a statement about faith itself. The discernment of the unseen creative activity of God behind the visible universe exemplifies the capacity of faith to demonstrate the reality of that which cannot be perceived through sense perception, which is celebrated as the essence of faith in v 1*b* (so Schlatter, 527–28; Grässer, *Glaube*, 54, n. 237).

Throughout vv 3–31 the word πίστει, "by faith," is drawn forward and placed at the beginning of the sentence for emphasis. The simple dative πίστει effectively connotes the decisiveness of the faith by which faithful men and women are to live and act. The initial occurrence of πίστει, which furnishes the basis for the anaphora in vv 4–31, is distinguished from the other instances in the series by referring to the subject "we" rather than to an OT person or event. The stress in v 3 falls on the initial phrase, πίστει νοοῦμεν, "by faith we understand." It relates the characterization of faith in vv 1–3 directly to the writer and his audience: through the visible we perceive the invisible divine reality as the actual ground of all things because of the intervention of faith. The direct address of the community at this point, before the recital of the attested exponents of faith, stresses the Christian experience of the power of faith as described in the foundational statements. It is balanced in the conclusion of the section when the writer again addresses the congregation in vv 39–40, underscoring the significance *for them* of the catalogue of faith in action under the old covenant.

The formulation in v 3*a* clearly refers to Gen 1:1 and its sequel (Gen 1:3–2:1), where the creative word of God has performative power in calling forth and ordering the visible universe. The verb κατηρτίσθαι, "put into proper order," was used in the LXX in the sense of "to establish," "to order," "to create" (e.g., Ps 39[MT 40]:7 [quoted in Heb 10:5]; 73[MT 74]:16; cf. *Paris Magical Papyrus* 4.1147, ὁ θεὸς . . . ὁ τὸν κόσμον καταρτισάμενος, "God . . . who created the world," cited by Delling, *TDNT* 1:476). The detail that the universe was ordered ῥήματι θεοῦ, "by means of the word of God," alludes to the creative commands of God in Gen 1:3, 6, 9, 14, 20, 24, 26 (cf. Ps 32 [MT 33]:6, 9 LXX; *Jub.* 12:4: "the God of heaven . . . who makes everything upon the earth, and has made everything by his word, and from whom everything takes its origin").

The allusion to Scripture in v 3*a* serves to interpret the force of the words πίστει νοοῦμεν, "by faith we understand." The medium of understanding is the written word of God, which activates the capacity for religious knowledge intrinsic to faith. To understand, perceive, and acknowledge that God's will as Creator is the basis of all good things is to respond to the biblical account in terms of faith (cf. Behm, *TDNT* 4:951).

The use of the verb νοεῖν, "to understand," in the context of perceiving the magisterial activity of God in creation recalls Rom 1:20 and Wis 13:1–5. The latter passage is particularly important for exposing the conceptual background of v 3. It concerns those who were "ignorant of God" precisely because they failed to perceive the God who exists from "the good things that are seen" (Wis 13:1). Instead, they attributed the origin of the visible universe to some created entity that they invested with deity (Wis 13:2–3). This act of foolishness calls forth a vigorous protest: "And if they were amazed at their power and working, let them perceive [νοησάτωσαν] from them [created objects] how much more powerful is he who formed them. For from the greatness and beauty of created objects comes a corresponding perception of their Creator" (Wis 13:4–5). The verb νοεῖν is used in Wisdom precisely as it is in Heb 11:3. Although the assertion in v 3*a* that faith is the means through which perception occurs is unusual, it simply makes explicit the basis of the confession of God as Creator in Wis 13:1–5 and in Rom 1:20. Understanding is conferred by faith (cf. Grässer, *Glaube*, 129–30; Williamson, *Philo*, 372–85). The emphasis on knowledge and perception of unseen reality in v 3 gives to the repeated πίστει in v 3–31 the meaning "in recognition of what constitutes true reality" (so Thompson, *Beginnings of Christian Philosophy*, 72).

The statement in v 3*a* is expanded by a result clause explaining the significance of the truth that is apprehended through faith. Although v 3*a* is biblical in its formulation, the language of v 3*b* is hellenistic in its cast. The description of the visible world as τὸ βλεπόμενον is rooted in the school tradition of hellenistic Judaism (e.g., Wis 13:7, where the plural formation τὰ βλεπόμενα signifies the visible universe), while the expression ἐκ φαινομένων has a long philosophical tradition in hellenism (cf. Williamson, *Philo* , 312–13, 372–85). The interpretation of the clause is complicated by the unusual word order, in which the negative can be correlated with the closest expression, ἐκ φαινομένων, "not from anything observable," or with the entire clause ("was *not* brought into being from anything observable") (see *Note* k above). Consequently, the significance of the assertion continues to be debated.

It is commonly assumed that the writer was influenced by Platonism in his thinking about creation (e.g., Sowers, *Hermeneutics*, 134–35; Stewart, *NTS* 12 [1965–66] 284–93; cf. Thompson, *Beginnings of Christian Philosophy*, 75). In addressing this issue R. Williamson has properly stressed the importance of the writer's use of the preposition ἐκ, "out of," in the phrase μὴ ἐκ φαινομένων. What the writer affirms is that the visible world was *not* made "*out of* anything observable." On the other hand, for both Plato and Philo, "the 'material' out of which the Creator fashioned the universe was a 'visible' mass, existing at first in the state of chaotic disorder, reduced to order by the Creator using the Ideas or Forms as his patterns" (*Philo*, 378). In other words, the visible universe was made ἐκ φαινομένων, "out of visible material," in the sense that God molded φαινόμενα into the visible objects of the world we see around us (*Philo*, 377–81). That is why Philo can use the term φαινόμενον to denote the visible universe (e.g. *The Migration of Abraham* 105, 179; *On the Creation* 16, 45; *On Agriculture* 42; *On the Confusion of Tongues* 172; cf. Plato, *Timaeus* 29E). The writer's insistence in v 3b that "the visible universe was not brought into being from anything observable would seem to exclude any influence from Platonic or Philonic cosmology. It may, in fact, have been the writer's intention to correct a widespread tendency in hellenistic Judaism to read Gen 1 in the light of Plato's doctrine of creation in the *Timaeus* (e.g., Wis 11:7: God's "all-powerful hand created the world out of formless matter").

In v 3a the writer affirmed that the knowledge that the universe was ordered by the word of God is a matter of spiritual perception through faith. The result clause in v 3b adds that the physical world was not made from anything observable. It came into being because God uttered his performative word. This is the traditional Jewish understanding coming to expression, for example, in 2 Macc 7:28, when a Jewish mother encourages her son to be faithful to God in spite of torture: "I plead with you, my son, to look at the heavens and the earth and see everything that is in them, and recognize that God did not make them out of things that existed. Thus also the human family comes into being" (discussed by Ehrhardt, "Creatio," 214–15, 217, 222). The comfort derived from contemplation of God's creative power was relevant to the congregation of Christians addressed in Hebrews as well, who were experiencing adversity and testing (cf. 12:4–13).

The somewhat ambiguous wording of v 3b has made it possible to hold that the writer believed in the doctrine of *creatio ex nihilo* (creation out of nothing) (so, e.g., Widdess, *JTS* n.s. 10 [1959] 327–29; F. F. Bruce, 281; Williamson, *Philo*, 312–13, 377–85). It is better to recognize that the clause is a negative assertion; it denies that the creative universe originated from primal material or anything observable. It does not make an unambiguous affirmation of creation out of nothing (so Ehrhardt, "Creatio," 217–23, who situates the discussion of the relevant texts within the context of the protest against the political conclusions drawn from the idea of the cosmos in Hellenism; cf. Grässer, *Glaube*, 55; P. E. Hughes, *BTB* 2 [1972] 64–77).

The vital interest in creation in v 3 is itself significant for indicating that the conception of faith is rooted in the wisdom tradition of hellenistic Judaism (cf. Bovon, *RTP* 18 [1968] 142–44; Haacker, "Creatio," 281). For the writer of

Hebrews, of course, knowledge of God the Creator is grounded in and informed by faith in the God revealed in salvation history. This theological consideration is given expression in the transition from v 3 to the catalogue of attested witnesses in the remainder of the section.

4 The statement that "men of the past received attestation" from God on the ground of faith (v 2) is substantiated by a series of illustrations from the personal history of particular individuals who responded to God in faith during the centuries preceding the advent of Christ. Although there is rarely in Scripture an explicit warrant for categorizing them as exemplars of $\pi\iota\sigma\tau\iota\varsigma$, "faith," they share in common that they acted within the scope of faith as set forth in v 1 and thus demonstrated the effective power of faith. When the several illustrations are introduced with the stereotyped formula $\pi\iota\sigma\tau\epsilon\iota$, "by faith," they become exemplary figures and events, since $\pi\iota\sigma\tau\epsilon\iota$ refers to the characterization of faith in vv 1–3 (cf. Grässer, *Glaube*, 45–57).

The catalogue of attested witnesses begins with Abel, who "by faith offered to God a more acceptable sacrifice than Cain" (v 4a). The allusion is to Gen 4:3–5a, which offers the bare statement: "in the course of time Cain brought some of the fruits of the soil as an offering to the Lord. But Abel brought fat portions from some of the firstborn of his flock. The Lord looked with favor on Abel and his offering, but on Cain and his offering he did not look with favor." The reference to Abel's offerings as exemplary is traditional in character (e.g., the hellenistic-Jewish liturgical fragment in *Apost. Const.* 7.37.1: "In the first place, you respected the sacrifice of Abel and accepted it"; cf. *1 Clem.* 4:2).

The lack of detail in the biblical account invited elaboration in the subsequent Jewish tradition (see especially Aptowitzer, *Kain und Abel*, 37–55, who arranges the primary sources in terms of traditions concerning the condition of Cain's offering [37–41], the acceptance of Abel's offering [41–43], the death and burial of Abel [43–55]). Two concerns of the later tradition are relevant to the representation of the matter in v 4: (1) Why should God have shown regard for Abel's offering, while rejecting Cain's sacrifice? (2) How did the two brothers know that God had accepted Abel's sacrifice, but not Cain's?

The Jewish tradition tended to approach the first question by concentrating on the rejection of Cain's sacrifice (cf. Aptowitzer, *Kain und Abel*, 37–41). There was a deficiency of a ritual character in the presentation of the sacrifice (so Gen 4:7 LXX, "if you had offered it correctly [$\dot{o}\rho\theta\hat{\omega}\varsigma$], but you did not divide it correctly," with the implication that Abel had, in fact, cut up the pieces of his sacrifice in a ritually correct manner), or in the quality of the offering (e.g., Philo, *On the Sacrifices of Abel and Cain* 88: "But Abel brought different offerings, and in a different manner. His offering was living, Cain's was lifeless. His was first in age and quality, Cain's was second"; *On the Confusion of Tongues* 124: "Cain retained in his own possession the firstfruits of his farming and offered, as we are told, merely the harvest of a later time, although he had beside him a wholesome example," while Abel "brought to the altar the firstborn, not the later-born"). Other lines of the tradition concentrated on piety as the determining factor for the acceptance or rejection of the offerings. Cain's moral disposition was deficient (e.g., Jos., *Ant.* 1.61: Cain was depraved and his only motive was profit; cf. *Apoc. Mos.* 1:3; 2:2; 3:1–3; 40:3; 43:1, cited by le Déaut, *Bib* 42 [1961] 31) and his works were evil (1 John 3:12; Jos., *Ant.*, 1.53: "Abel was attentive to righteousness . . . but Cain was depraved").

According to the tradition preserved in the several recensions of the *Pal. Tg.*
Gen 4:8, a quarrel arose between the two brothers over God's response to their
respective offerings. The dispute between the brothers provided an occasion for
two different professions of faith, which become transformed in the successive
recensions, but the general sense remains the same: Abel was slain by his enraged brother after he affirmed his faith in God who created the world in love
and who governs it righteously. The oldest expression of the tradition appears to
be that preserved in the fragments from the Cairo Geniza (so Grelot, *RB* 82 [1975]
72–73; le Déaut, *Bib* 42 [1961] 32):

> Cain spoke and said to Abel, "I see that the world has been created by love and that it is
> governed by love. Why, then, has your offering been received from you with favor, and
> mine has not been received with favor?" Abel spoke and said to Cain, "Without doubt
> the world has been created by love and it is governed by love; but it is also governed
> according to the fruit of good works. It is because my works were better than yours that
> my offering has been received from me with favor, and yours has not been received
> from you with favor." And the two of them were disputing in the field (*Frg. Tg.* Gen 4:8).

In later recensions Cain's response is modified. He denies that the world was
created by love or that it is governed by love, and he accuses God of injustice:
"there is no judgment and there is no judge, and there is no other world; there is
no giving of a good reward to the righteous person and there is no retribution
exacted from the wicked," all of which Abel affirms (*Tg. Neof.* Gen 4:8; cf. *Tg. Ps.-
J.* Gen 4:8). These Palestinian traditions are interesting precisely because they
portray Abel as an exemplar of confessing faith, and they clearly date from a period prior to the fall of Jerusalem in A.D. 70 (see S. Isenberg, "An Anti-Sadducee
Polemic in the Palestinian Targum Tradition," *HTR* 63 [1970] 433–44).

Less attention was devoted in the tradition to the manner in which the acceptance of Abel's offering was indicated (for the primary sources, see Aptowitzer,
Kain und Abel, 41–43). The most graphic suggestion was that fire fell from heaven
and consumed Abel's offering, but Cain's offering remained untouched. This
tradition found its way into the early second-century Greek translation of the
Pentateuch by Theodotion, who added to Gen 4:4 the words καὶ ἐνεπύρισεν, "and
it was consumed by fire," and to Gen 4:5 οὐκ ἐνεπύρισεν, "it was not consumed by
fire" (F. Field, *Origenis Hexaplarum quae supersunt* [Oxford: UP, 1875] 17). The
source of this conjecture is, of course, itself biblical (cf. Lev 9:24; 2 Kgs 18:38; 2
Chr 7:1), although it finds no support in the detail of Gen 4:4–5 (see, however,
the suggestion in LSJ 549, under ἐμπυρίζω).

The reference to Abel in v 4 shows little interest in the traditional elaboration
of the biblical narrative. Taking the Scriptural account at its face value, the writer
simply notes the acceptable quality of Abel's offering, using πλείονα in its qualitative sense ("more acceptable"; see above, *Note* m), without commenting on the
basis for the acceptance of the sacrifice. The general tenor of Scripture indicates
that the superior quality of Abel's offering derived from the integrity of his heart
rather than from the nature of the offering itself. This is the clear implication of
Gen 4:7, where the Lord says to Cain, "If you do what is right, will you not be accepted?" For the writer of Hebrews, the fact that Abel offered his sacrifice πίστει, "by
faith," is sufficient explanation for the acceptance of his offering by God. His act of
worship entailed the thoughtful exposure of his self to the living and holy God.

It is possible to shed further light on the writer's understanding of the detail that God accepted Abel's sacrifice by observing that the example of Abel forms a pair with that of Enoch in v 5. The first two examples are brought together formally not only by the explicit mention of attestation received from God (see *Form/ Structure/Setting* on 11:1–40) but, more subtly, by a common interest in death. This suggests that it is the responsibility of v 6 to clarify not simply the example of Enoch, but that of Abel as well, precisely because it describes the response of faith to God without reference to the spoken word of God (as in the case of Noah) or the promise of God (as in the case of Abraham, Isaac, and Jacob). It establishes between faith and divine approval a rigorous connection, and thus furnishes an explanation for the acceptance of Abel's sacrifice (as well as of Enoch's translation). Abel approached God earnestly with a firm expectation of the reward, in the sense of the share of those who seek God himself. God was pleased with Abel and his offering because Abel fulfilled the conditions set forth in v 6. What fixed the attention of the writer on Abel was that he and his sacrifice were pleasing to God. The comparison of the fate of Abel as a martyr, and of Cain as a murderer, did not interest him in itself. Rather, it is the extraordinary fact that a person found access to God and that he received attestation of a favorable welcome (following Bénétreau, *ETR* 54 [1979] 627–29).

God's recognition of Abel's faith and acceptance of his offering is underscored by the clause δι' ἧς ἐμαρτυρήθη εἶναι δίκαιος μαρτυροῦντος ἐπὶ τοῖς δώροις αὐτοῦ τοῦ θεοῦ, "by which [faith] he received attestation [from God] that he was righteous, God himself approving of his gifts." Two terms stand out in this statement: "faith" (πίστις), the substantive of which is resumed by the prepositional phrase with the relative, δι' ἧς (see above, *Note* n), and ἐμαρτυρήθη, "he received attestation," which is explicated by the participle μαρτυροῦντος, "approving," that follows, and to which corresponds the qualitative adjective πλείονα, "more acceptable," at the beginning of the sentence. As in v 2, the writer establishes a correlation between faith and divine approval of a stance of commitment to God. The association of Abel with righteousness is found elsewhere in sources contemporary with Hebrews (Matt 23:35; 1 John 3:12; Jos., *Ant.* 1.61). For the writer of Hebrews it was axiomatic that the source of righteousness was faith (see vv 5–7).

The further statement that δι' αὐτῆς ἀποθανὼν ἔτι λαλεῖ, "through [faith] he is still speaking, although he died," is distinguished from the Jewish tradition about Abel because it reflects no interest in the act of fratricide nor in Abel as the protomartyr (in contrast to *Jub.* 4:2–3; *1 Enoch* 22:6–7; *T. Benj.* 7:3–5; 4 Macc 18:11; Matt 23:31; Luke 11:50–51; 1 John 3:12, for example; cf. Heb 12:24 below). All of the emphasis falls on the fact that it is *by his faith* (and not by his blood) that Abel continues to speak. The allusion is thus not to Gen 4:10, which speaks of the cry of Abel's blood from the ground for retribution or reconciliation (cf. Spicq, 2:343), but to the record of God's approval of his integrity and his sacrifice in Gen 4:4. It is significant that the writer does not use the verb βοᾶν, "to cry out," as in Gen 4:10 LXX, but the verb λαλεῖν, "to speak," which in Hebrews is never used of speaking to God. The writer affirms that Abel's faith continues to speak *to us* through the written record of his action in Scripture, which transmits to us the exemplary character of his offering (Moffatt, 164).

It has been proposed that the allusion in this final clause is to Abel's defense of his faith as attested by the *Pal. Tg.* tradition (so le Déaut, *Bib* 42 [1961] 34–36).

The absence of any awareness of a profession of faith by Abel in hellenistic-Jewish sources, however, makes it wholly uncertain that the writer or his audience even knew of this aspect of the Palestinian tradition. It is preferable to find in the clause the substantiation of the prophetical oracle (from Hab 2:4), cited in 10:38, that God's righteous one shall live on the ground of his faith. Although Abel died, his voice continues to speak of the faith that wins approval from God. Remembrance of the faith of Abel (as opposed to a profession of faith) harmonizes with the other examples the writer extracts from the biblical record: Enoch, Noah, Abraham, Isaac, Jacob, Joseph, and Moses (cf. le Déaut, *Bib* 42 [1961] 36).

5–6 The biblical record of Adam's line in Gen 5:1–31 consists of brief vignettes, each of which concludes with the notice of the death of the individual singled out for special mention. The phrase "and he died" (καὶ ἀπέθανεν) is repeated as the final word on the antediluvian fathers throughout the genealogy (Gen 5:5, 8, 11, 14, 17, 20, 27, 31 LXX). The only relief in this relentless chorus occurs in the account of Enoch, who "pleased God" (Gen 5:22, 24 LXX), and as a result did not experience death because God "took him away" (μετέθηκεν, Gen 5:24 LXX). As a singular individual who escaped death through translation, Enoch would inevitably become a figure around whom Jewish lore would cluster (cf. Sir 49:14: "No one like Enoch has been created on earth, for he was taken up from the earth").

The formulation of v 5 is indebted to the LXX, which exhibits a tendency to avoid anthropomorphisms. The statement in the MT that Enoch "walked with God" (Gen 5:22, 24) was translated in the LXX as "Enoch pleased God" (εὐηρέστησεν Ἐνὼχ τῷ θεῷ), and this is the basis for the wording of v 5 as well as of other references to Enoch in the hellenistic-Jewish tradition (e.g., Sir 44:16a; Wis 4:10, 14).

The writer grounds Enoch's experience of translation in faith ("by faith Enoch was translated"), and clarifies the meaning of μετετέθη, "he was translated," by the articular infinitive clause τοῦ μὴ ἰδεῖν θάνατον, "that he should not see death." The phrase "to see death," like the related expression "to taste death" (2:9), is a Semitism for the experience of death. The traditional character of this explanation is apparent from statements roughly contemporaneous with Hebrews (e.g., *1 Clem.* 9:3, "Let us take Enoch, who having been found righteous in obedience was translated, and death did not happen to him"). The statement that Enoch was translated by God is supported in v 5b by the citation of a portion of Gen 5:24 LXX, in the wording of Codex Alexandrinus (which uses the causal conjunction διότι rather than ὅτι, both meaning "because"). The primary point of interest for the writer, however, is the witness of Scripture that Enoch received divine approval as a man who pleased God prior to his experience of translation (v 5c). The attestation of Gen 5:22 LXX is repeated in Gen 5:24 LXX immediately prior to the statement that God removed Enoch from the earth. The assertion that Enoch "pleased God" provides the point of transition to the important statement about faith in v 6.

Enoch is never portrayed as an exemplar of faith in Jewish tradition. Elsewhere in hellenistic-Jewish literature he is cited as a model of repentance. For example, the brief reference to Enoch in Sir 44:16 condenses Gen 5:22–24 LXX ("Enoch pleased the Lord and was translated") and continues by asserting that "he was an example of repentance to all generations." This deduction appears to be based on the literary structure of Gen 5:21–24, where a distinction is made between the period prior to the birth of Enoch's son (v 21) and the subsequent period during which he "pleased God" (vv 22–24). The basis of the tradition is the presupposition that repentance marked Enoch's conversion to the true God, and that explains why he "pleased the Lord" (cf. Lührmann, *ZNW* 66 [1975] 106–10).

In the abundant Enoch literature emanating from apocalyptic communities in Palestine, Enoch is portrayed as a preacher of righteousness rather than as an exemplar of repentance (e.g., *1 Enoch* 91–105; *Jub.* 4:22–24). Only in the literature of hellenistic Judaism is Enoch associated with his own repentance, as in the Greek translation of Sirach (cf. Philo, *Questions and Answers on Genesis* 1.79–87: Enoch sinned prior to repentance; he went through a period of purification, and then persevered in uprightness after repentance). The firmness of the tradition that Enoch is an example of conversion to the one true God is evident from the fact that in hellenistic Judaism it was unnecessary even to specify Enoch by name in referring to that tradition. It was sufficient simply to refer to a man who "pleased God" and who was "translated" (Wis 4:10–15; Philo, *On Rewards and Punishments* 15–21; cf. the parallel passage in Philo, *On Abraham* 17–26, where Enoch is specified and personifies the virtue of repentance; for discussion of these texts, see Lührmann, *ZNW* 66 [1975] 211–14; Kraft, "Philo," 255–57).

Already in Heb 6:1 "faith toward God" and "repentance from dead works" were listed as integral aspects of conversion. On this basis, Lührmann suggests that the writer of Hebrews was fully aware of the traditional hellenistic-Jewish perspective on Enoch as an exemplar of repentance, but he purposefully chose to approach the account in Gen 5:22–24 from the vantage point of faith. The determination to present the example of Enoch under the aspect of faith explains why in v 5 the writer limits himself to reproducing the tenor of the text of Genesis, without interpreting it in any particular way. The interpretation is reserved for v 6, where Enoch is represented as a man who turned to God in terms of the confessional stance outlined there (*ZNW* 66 [1975] 103–6, 115–16).

The decisive factor in the experience of translation granted to Enoch was his faith (v 5a). The disposition of faith was also fundamental for the attestation he received prior to his translation that "he was well-pleasing to God" (v 5c). This latter fact is underscored for the Christian audience by the interpretive comment in v 6, which elaborates the simple witness of Scripture that "Enoch was well pleasing to God" (Gen 5:22, 24 LXX). The initial clause is emphatic by virtue of its position: χωρὶς δὲ πίστεως ἀδύνατον εὐαρεστῆσαι, "and without faith it is impossible to begin to be well-pleasing [to God]." The infinitive εὐαρεστῆσαι, "to be well-pleasing," resumes the expression εὐαρεστηκέναι τῷ θεῷ, "to have been well-pleasing to God," from v 5c and marks the transition from biblical text to commentary. The writer's determination to focus attention sharply upon the pleasing of God, rather than on the singular experience of translation, is indicative of his pastoral motivation. Precisely at that point Enoch can become exemplary to the Christian community. The writer's intention is intensely practical: Christians must replicate in their experience the enjoyment of the pleasure of the Lord that was the hallmark of Enoch's life.

The life that pleases God begins with the certain recognition of God and his character. This is stated explicitly in the explanatory clause that follows immediately, which clarifies two rudimentary dimensions of πίστις, "faith." The only presupposition for approaching God is the certainty that he exists and that he establishes a relationship with those who earnestly seek him.

The emphasis on believing in God's existence in v 6 is unique in the NT but is anticipated in 6:1. There, the rudimentary tenet of πίστις ἐπὶ θεόν, "faith towards God," was cited as a foundational element in the catechetical instruction to which the congregation had been exposed when they became Christians (see *Comment* on 6:1; cf. Dautzenberg, *BZ* 17 [1973] 165–66). The expression πιστεῦσαι ... ὅτι ἔστιν, "to believe that he [God] exists," is creedal in formulation and reflects missionary terminology developed in the hellenistic-Jewish synagogues.

Judaism's encounter with the polymorphic expressions of Hellenism accounts for the fact that, in addition to the traditional Jewish affirmation that God is one (εἷς), confessed in the Shema (Deut 6:4), in some circles faith in the existence of God was also given creedal status. So, for example, in the confessional statement with which Philo concluded his treatise on creation, the first article affirms ὅτι ἔστι τὸ θεῖον, "that the deity exists," followed by the traditional acknowledgment ὅτι θεὸς εἷς ἔστι, "that God is one" (*On Creation* 170–71). The biblical basis for this emphasis was Exod 3:14 LXX, ἐγώ εἰμι ὁ ὤν, "I am the one who exists" (cf. *The Worse Attacks the Better* 160; *On the Change of Names* 11–13; *On Dreams* 1.231–34).

This confessional stance distinguished Jews from pagans in the conflict with Hellenism (e.g., 4 Macc 5:24: "We worship only the God who exists"; cf. Wis 13:1: those who are ignorant of God "were unable from the good things that are seen to know him who exists"). The unwavering conviction that God exists is an elementary constituent of faith, which is the necessary presupposition for the development of other aspects of faith. In specifying in v 6 belief in the true living God as the basis of approaching him with the faith that excites his pleasure, the writer utilizes a formulation derived from his own background in the hellenistic-Jewish synagogue (Grässer, *Glaube*, 66; Mercado, "Language of Sojourning," 76–77; cf. I. Havener, "The Credal Formulae of the New Testament," Inaugural Dissertation, Munich, 1976, 327–30). The implication of the connection between v 5 and v 6 is that Enoch had an awareness that he was drawing near to the real, living God and that he regulated his conduct accordingly. For that reason he was well pleasing to God.

The second part of the ὅτι clause ("that he becomes a rewarder to those who seek him out") underscores the relational aspect of faith. A transaction occurs between God and the individual who earnestly seeks him. The description of God as a μισθαποδότης, "rewarder," employs a rare term that occurs only in Hebrews and in later ecclesiastical literature (BAGD 523; *LPGL* 873). It may have been coined by the writer to evoke the image of the paymaster who distributes the exact wage. The "wage" is the share of those who ardently seek none other than God himself. The description serves to characterize Enoch, and others (see v 26 below), as persons who relied firmly on God and found in him the source of their deepest satisfaction.

The verb ἐκζητεῖν, "to seek out," which is used here to typify those who exhibit the faith that pleases God, denotes a singular determination to devote oneself to the service of God. It implies the recognition that human action has to demonstrate its integrity before God. The firm expectation of the reward, then, is a matter of unwavering hope in the God who controls the future. It exhibits the solid faith that is the condition for receiving recompense by God (Bénétreau, *ETR* 54 [1979] 628; cf. Preisker, *TDNT* 4:701, 726). The person who puts his trust in God finds that his faith is rewarded by the transmutation of hope into present realities (cf. 11:1*a*). The particular reward granted to Enoch was the attestation of being well pleasing to God, followed by the unexpected experience of translation. In nearly all of the subsequent exemplars of faith who are paraded before the congregation, there is a direct relationship between faith and reward that is deserving of notice (cf. Williamson, *Philo*, 358–61).

7   With Noah the writer introduces the first of the attested witnesses for whom faith signified obedient response to the word of God. This emphasis thrusts forward the dimension of faith that is characteristic of most of the subsequent examples. Noah was "instructed" or "solemnly warned" (χρηματισθείς; cf. 8:5; 12:25) by God concerning "events as yet unseen" (τῶν μηδέπω βλεπομένων). The formulation is calculated to recall the similar phraseology in v1*b*, where faith is celebrated as "the demonstration of events not seen" (see *Comment* on 11:1*b*). In rounding off the first paragraph of the section, devoted to the antediluvian fathers, it is the writer's intention to clarify the quality of the faith he is promoting among the discouraged, apathetic members of the congregation. They are to find in Noah an illustration not only of the foundational statements in v 1 but of the complementary affirmation in v 6 as well.

The reference, of course, is to God's instruction concerning the building of an ark in order to preserve alive a remnant of the human family and of the animals when a cataclysmic flood destroyed civilization as Noah had known it (Gen 6:9–21; for discussion, see Lewis, *Interpretation of Noah*, 3–9). Noah's action in constructing the ark according to the specifications that God had given (Gen 6:22) reflected an attentiveness (εὐλαβηθείς, "he paid attention to") to the divine instruction. He was convinced of the certain occurrence of the events which God had disclosed, but which as yet lay in the unseen future. Faith conferred upon those events a reality so substantial that he did not hesitate to act as though they were already beginning to happen. He appears to have recognized that the word of God is performative; it sets in motion circumstances that will eventuate in the promised reality.

Noah placed his full trust in the gracious promise of God that his own household would be preserved from the threatening deluge (Gen 6:18). Yet until the time of the flood itself, that promise fell into the category of an objective hope that faith alone could invest with reality (cf. v 1*a*). What Noah's action dramatizes is the essence of faith as set forth in v 1. It also demonstrates a spiritual sensitivity to the reality of God that enabled Noah to endure the scorn of his contemporaries and the occasional doubts of his own mind, firmly persuaded that the safety of his family would be the reward that would follow a period of persevering expectation. In this manner, he embodied the confessional stance set forth in v 6 (cf. Bénétreau, *ETR* 54 [1979] 628; Williamson, *Philo*, 340, 353–54, 371).

The relative clause δι' ἧς κατέκρινεν τὸν κόσμον, "by [faith] he condemned humanity," summarizes a persistent tradition that Noah was a preacher of repentance (2 Pet 2:5; *1 Clem.* 7:6: "Noah preached repentance, and those who obeyed were preserved alive"; 9:4: "Noah . . . preached a new beginning to the world"; cf. *Sib. Or.* 1.125–29, quoted by P. E. Hughes, 464; Jos., *Ant.* 1.74; for discussion, see Lewis, *Interpretation of Noah*, 101–20). In the apocalyptic tradition of Palestinian

Judaism preserved in *Jub.* 7:20–29, the burden of Noah's preaching is supplied by the severe judgment of God upon human corruption in Gen 6:1–7 (cf. Lewis, 10–41). The writer's statement that Noah "condemned humanity" need imply no more than that the life of a person of firm faith and faithfulness to God constitutes a sharp rebuke to a godless generation. So Josephus implies that Noah shamed his contemporaries by the quality of his faith, which threw their skepticism into high relief (*Ant.* 1.99; cf. Lewis, 77–81). Construction of the ark prior to the perception of the danger was itself a prophetic act of symbolic realism announcing to the world the forthcoming judgment of God. It also proclaimed a dynamic faith in the truth of God's warning despite all appearances to the contrary (cf. T. H. Robinson, 158; Dautzenberg, *BZ* 17 [1973] 170). Ironically, the condemning of humanity and the safety of Noah's own household were concurrent events. They took place at the same time, and by the same means. The experience of Noah shows that judgment and salvation are simultaneous events (see P. E. Hughes, 465).

The correlative statement that Noah τῆς κατὰ πίστιν δικαιοσύνης ἐγένετο κληρονόμος, "became an heir of the righteousness according to faith," represents a fresh approach to the old biblical tradition that Noah was a righteous person (Gen 6:9; 7:1; Ezek 14:14, 20). That tradition is repeated in references to the flood by hellenistic-Jewish writers (e.g., Sir 44:17 LXX: "Noah was found perfect and righteous; in the time of wrath he was taken in exchange; therefore a remnant was left to the earth when the flood came"; Wis 10:4: "When the earth was flooded because of him [i.e., Cain], Wisdom again preserved it, steering the righteous man by a paltry piece of wood"). The epithet "just" or "righteous" is applied to Noah repeatedly in Philo (*On the Posterity and Exile of Cain* 48, 173, 174; *On the Migration of Abraham* 125; *On the Confusion of Tongues* 105; *On Giants* 3, 5; *On the Change of Names* 189), although Philo does not hesitate to declare that Noah's righteousness was only relative to the lack of righteousness in his own evil generation (*On Abraham* 47; cf. Lewis, *Interpretation of Noah*, 42–58). An emphasis on Noah's righteousness is pervasive in the apocalyptic tradition (e.g., *Jub.* 5:19; 4 Ezra 3:9–12; *2 Enoch* 34:3; 35:1 [text B]) and was popularized through the reading of the Targum in the synagogue service (e.g., *Tg. Neof.* Gen 6:9; 7:1; cf. Lewis, 92–100).

The writer of Hebrews correlates the tradition that Noah was a righteous person to the category of faith. By his obedient response of faith to the sober warning concerning an unperceived future, "he became an heir of the righteousness according to faith." The description of Noah as "an heir" (κληρονόμος) establishes a link between the annals of faith prior to the flood and the continuing saga of faithful response to God's word after the flood (see *Comment* on vv 8–9, where Abraham, Isaac, and Jacob are described as "joint heirs" of the divine promise). The formulation τῆς κατὰ πίστιν δικαιοσύνης, "of the righteousness according to faith," has almost a Pauline ring. The qualification of "righteousness" by κατὰ πίστιν indicates the way or the condition by which righteousness is actualized; it describes a righteousness bestowed by God according to the norm of faith. The biblical description of Noah as a righteous person is thus subsumed under the aspect of faith. Noah responded to God with a full measure of faith, and this accounts for the attestation of Scripture that he was righteous. It also anticipates the prophetic oracle that "my righteous one shall live by faith" (Hab 2:4), which was cited in 10:38 just before the catalogue of attested witnesses.

The concept of "an heir of the righteousness according to faith" implies that others who respond to God with the faith that Noah demonstrated will share with him in the righteousness God bestows upon persons of faith. The theme of the heir is a recurring motif in Hebrews, where the Son of God is acknowledged as "the heir of everything" (1:2) and Christians are described as the heirs of salvation (1:14) and of the promises of God (6:12,17; cf. 9:15).

Explanation

See 11:32–40 below.

The Triumphs of Perseverance in Faith in the Patriarchal Era (11:8–22)

Bibliography

Arowele, P. J. "The Pilgrim People of God (An African's Reflections on the Motif of Sojourn in the Epistle to the Hebrews)." *AsiaJT* 4 (1990) 438–55. **Babel, R.** *La foi d'Abraham dans le Nouveau Testament.* Paris: Gabalda, 1970. **Baird, W.** "Abraham in the New Testament: Tradition and the New Identity." *Int* 42 (1988) 367–79. **Bartina, S.** "Jacob 'adoró sobre la punta de so bastón' (Gen 47,31; Hebr 11,21)." *EE* 38 (1963) 243–47. ———. "Jesus y los saduceos: 'El, Dios de Abraham, de Isaac y de Jacob' es 'El que hace existir' (Mt 22,22–33; Mc 12,18–27; Lc 20,27–40; Hebr 11,13–16)." *EstBib* 21 (1962) 151–60. **Black, M.** "Critical and Exegetical Notes on Three New Testament Texts: Hebrews xi.11, Jude 5, James i.27." In *Apophoreta.* FS E. Haenchen. Ed. W. Eltester and F. H. Kettler. Berlin: Töpelmann, 1964. 39–45. **Braun, H.** "Das himmlische Vaterland bei Philo und im Hebräerbrief." In *Verborum Veritas.* FS G. Stählin. Ed. O. Böcher and K. Haacker. Wuppertal: Brockhaus, 1970. 319–27. **Cadbury, H. J.** "The Ancient Physiological Notions Underlying John 1:13a, Hebrews 11:11." *Exp* 9th ser. 2 (1924) 430–39. **Cambier, J.** *Eschatologie ou héllenisme dans l'Épître aux Hébreux.* 24–30. **Carmona, A. R.** *Targum y resurrección: Estudio de los textos del Targum Palestinense sobre la resurrección.* Granada: Facultad de Teologia, 1978. **Causée, A.** "De la Jérusalem terrestre à la Jérusalem céleste." *RHPR* 27 (1947) 12–36. ———. "Le mythe de la nouvelle Jérusalem du Deutero-Ésaïe à la IIIe Sibylle." *RHPR* 18 (1938) 377–414. **Collin, M.** "La tradition des 'pères' dans le Nouveau Testament." *LV* 188 (1988) 101–11. **Couffignal, R.** *L'epreuve d'Abram: Le récit de la Genèse et sa fortune littéraire.* Toulouse: Association de Publication de l'Université de Toulouse—Le Mirail, 1976. **Cox, S.** "The Conversion of Sarah: Genesis XVIII.1–15; Hebrews XI.11." *Exp* 1st ser. 12 (1880) 345–55. **Daly, R. J.** "The Soteriological Significance of the Sacrifice of Isaac." *CBQ* 39 (1977) 45–75. **Daniélou, J.** "Abraham dans la tradition chrétienne." *CSion* 5 (1951) 68–87. ———. "La typologie d'Isaac dans le christianisme primitif." *Bib* 28 (1947) 363–93. **Davies, P. R.** and **Chilton, B. D.** "The 'Aqedah: A Revised Tradition History." *CBQ* 40 (1978) 514–46. **Déaut, R. le.** "Abraham et le sacrifice d'Isaac." In *La Nuit Pascale.* Rome: Institut Biblique Pontifical, 1963. 131–212. ———. "La presentation targumique du sacrifice d'Isaac et la soteriologie paulinienne." In *Studiorum Paulinorum Congressus Internationalis Catholicis.*

AnBib 17–18. Rome: Pontifical Biblical Institute, 1963. 2:563–74. **Démann, P.** "La signification d'Abraham dans la perspective du Nouveau Testament." *CSion* 5 (1951) 44–67. **De Young, J. C.** *Jerusalem in the New Testament.* 117–45. **Ernst, J.** "Die griechische Polis—das himmlische Jerusalem—die christliche Stadt." *TGl* 67 (1977) 240–58. **Etienne, P.** "Estrangeiros e Peregrines na Terra . . . em Busca de uma Pátria: Epistola aos Hebreus 11,13–14." In *Actualidades Bíblicas-Castro.* Rio de Janeiro: Vozes, 1971. 610–15. **Feldman, L. H.** "Josephus as a Biblical Interpreter: The ʿAqedah." *JQR* 75 (1985) 212–52. **Fontecha, J. F.** "La vida cristiana como peregrinación según la Epistola a los Hebreos." In *Studium Legionense.* Léon, 1961. 2:251–306. **Greenlee, J. H.** "Hebrews 11:11: Sarah's Faith or Abraham's?" *Notes on Translation* 4 (1990) 37–42. **Harrington, D. J.** "Abraham Traditions in the Testament of Abraham and in the 'Rewritten Bible' of the Intertestamental Period." In *Studies in the Testament of Abraham.* Ed. G. W. E. Nickelsburg. SBLSCS 6. Missoula: Scholars, 1976. 165–71. **Hayward, C. T. R.** "The Sacrifice of Isaac and Jewish Polemic against Christianity." *CBQ* 52 (1990) 292–306. ———. "The Present State of Research into the Targumic Account of the Sacrifice of Isaac." *JJS* 32 (1981) 127–50. **Heller, J.** "Stabesanbetung? (Hebr. 11,21—Gen. 47,31)." *CV* 16 (1973) 257–65. **Hoare, J. N.** "Genesis XLVII.31 and Hebrews XI.21." *ExpTim* 3 (1891–92) 273. **Irwin, J.** "The Use of Hebrews 11:11 as Embryological Proof-Text." *HTR* 71 (1978) 312–16. **Jacob, E.** "Abraham et sa signification pour la foi chrétienne." *RHPR* 42 (1962) 148–56. **Johnsson, W. G.** "The Pilgrimage Motif in the Book of Hebrews." *JBL* 97 (1978) 239–51. **Jonge, M. de.** "Vreemdelingen en bijwoners: Enige opmerkingen naar aanleiding van 1 Pt. 2,11 en verwante teksten." *NedTTs* 11 (1956–57) 18–36. **Kalenkow, A. B.** "The Genre Testament and Forecasts of the Future in the Hellenistic Jewish Milieu." *JSJ* 6 (1975) 57–71. **Korvin-Krasinski, C. von.** "Die Heilige Stadt." *ZRGG* 16 (1964) 265–71. **Lerch, D.** *Isaaks Opferung christlich gedeutet: Eine auslegungschichtliche Untersuchung.* Tübingen: Mohr, 1950. 8–20, 39–43. **Lignée, H.** "La foi sur la route de Dieu (Hé 11,1–2. 8–19)." *AsSeign* 50 (1974) 59–64. **Longenecker, R. N.** "The 'Faith of Abraham' Theme in Paul, James and Hebrews: A Study in the Circumstantial Nature of New Testament Teaching." *JETS* 20 (1977) 203–12. **Lord, J. R.** "Abraham: A Study in Ancient Jewish and Christian Interpretation." Dissertation, Duke University, 1968. **Martin-Achard, R.** "La figure d'Isaac dans l'Ancien Testament et dans la tradition juive ancienne." *BFCL* 106 (1982) 5–10. **Mayer, G.** "Aspekte des Abrahambildes in der hellenistisch-jüdischen Literatur." *EvT* 32 (1972) 118–27. **McCullough, J. C.** "The Old Testament Quotations in Hebrews." *NTS* 26 (1979–80) 363–79. **Menasce, P. J. de.** "Traditions juives sur Abraham." *CSion* 5 (1951) 96–103. **Mercado, L. F.** "The Language of Sojourning in the Abraham Midrash in Hebrews 11:8–19: Its Old Testament Basis, Exegetical Traditions, and Function in the Epistle to the Hebrews." Dissertation, Harvard University, 1967. **Milgrom, J.** *The Binding of Isaac: The Akedah—A Primary Symbol in Jewish Thought and Art.* Berkeley, CA: BIBAL, 1988. **Moxnes, H.** "God and His Promise to Abraham: First Century Appropriations." In *Theology in Conflict: Studies in Paul's Understanding of God in Romans.* NovTSup 53. Leiden: Brill, 1980. 117–95. **Muntingh, L. M.** "'The City Which Has Foundations': Hebrews 11:8–10 in the Light of the Mari Texts." In *De Fructu Oris Sui.* FS A. van Selms. Ed. I. H. Eybers, F. C. Fensham, C. J. Labuschagn, W. C. van Unnik, and A. H. van Zye. Leiden: Brill, 1971. 108–20. **Rose, C.** "Verheissung und Erfüllung: Zum Verständnis von ἐπαγγελία im Hebräerbrief." *BZ* 33 (1989) 178–91. **Schmidt, K. L.** "Die Erbauung der Kirche mit ihren Gliedern als den 'Fremdlingen und Beisassen auf Erden' (Hebr 11,13)." In *Wesen und Aufgabe der Kirche in der Welt.* Zurich: Zwingli, 1947. 5–30. **Schmitz, O.** "Abraham im Spätjudentum und im Urchristentum." In *Aus Schrift und Geschichte.* FS A. Schlatter. Ed. K. Bornhäuser et al. Stuttgart: Calwer, 1922. 99–123. **Schröger, F.** *Der Verfasser des Hebräerbriefes als Schriftausleger.* 187, 206, 211–12, 215–22. **Segal, A. F.** "'He who did not spare his own son . . .': Jesus, Paul, and the Akedah." In *From Jesus to Paul.* FS F. W. Beare. Ed. P. Richardson and J. C. Hurd. Waterloo, Ontario: Wilfrid Laurier University, 1984. 169–84. **Siker, J. S.** "Abraham in Graeco-Roman Paganism." *JSJ* 18 (1987) 188–208.

Spiegel, F. *The Last Trial: On the Legends and Lore of the Command to Abraham to Offer Isaac as a Sacrifice: The Akedah.* Tr. J. Goldin. New York: Schocken, 1967. **Swetnam, J.** *Jesus and Isaac,* 1–79, 83–129, 187. **Vermès, G.** "The Life of Abraham (1): Haggadic Development: A Retrogressive Historical Study." In *Scripture and Tradition in Judaism.* Leiden: Brill, 1973. 67–95. ———. "Redemption and Genesis XXII." In *Scripture and Tradition in Judaism.* Leiden: Brill, 1973. 193–227. **Vesco, J. L.** "Abraham: Actualisation et relectures." *RSPT* 55 (1971) 33–80. **Weston, H. G.** "Jacob's Staff: Hebrews xi.21." *ExpTim* 3 (1881–82) 568. **Wilcox, M.** "The Bones of Joseph: Hebrews 11:22." In *Scripture: Meaning and Method.* FS A. T. Hanson. Ed. B. P. Thompson. Hull: Hull UP, 1987. 114–30. **Wiseman, D. J.** "They Lived in Tents." In *Biblical and Near Eastern Studies.* FS W. S. LaSor. Ed. G. A. Tuttle. Grand Rapids: Eerdmans, 1978. 195–200. **Wood, J. E.** "Isaac Typology in the New Testament." *NTS* 14 (1967–68) 583–89.

Translation

[8] *By faith Abraham, as he was being called,*[a] *obeyed by departing*[b] *for a place he was to receive as an inheritance, and he set out not knowing where he was going.* [9] *By faith he migrated to*[c] *the promised land as to a foreign land,*[d] *living*[e] *in tents, as did Isaac and Jacob, who were joint heirs with him of the same promise,* [10] *for he was looking forward with certainty*[f] *to the city which has foundations*[g] *because*[h] *its designer and creator*[i] *is God.*[j]

[11] *By faith Abraham*[k] *was enabled to become a father,*[l] *even though Sarah herself was sterile*[m] *and past the normal age of child-bearing,*[n] *because he considered the one who had made the promise faithful;*[o] [12] *so it was that from this one man,*[p] *and he already impotent,*[q] *there were born descendants as numerous as the stars of heaven and as innumerable as the grains of sand on the seashore.*

[13] *In accordance with the principle of faith*[r] *all these persons died,*[s] *not having received*[t] *the fulfillment of*[u] *the promises, but only seeing them and saluting them from a distance, and confessing*[v] *that they were strangers and sojourners in the land.*[w] [14] *Now people who say such things show plainly*[x] *that they are expecting intently*[y] *a homeland of their own.* [15] *If they had meant*[z] *that country*[aa] *from which they had set out, they would have had*[bb] *opportunity to return.*[cc] [16] *But as it is*[dd] *they were longing*[ee] *for a better homeland, in other words, a heavenly one, for which reason God is not ashamed to be called*[ff] *their God, for he has made ready a city for them.*[gg]

[17] *By faith Abraham,*[hh] *when he was put to the test by God,*[ii] *offered up in sacrifice*[jj] *Isaac; not only so,*[kk] *he who had accepted the promises*[ll] *tried to sacrifice*[mm] *his only son,* [18] *concerning whom it had been said by God, "It is through*[nn] *Isaac that you will have descendants."*[oo] [19] *He considered*[pp] *that God was able to raise him up*[qq] *even*[rr] *from the dead. Because of this conviction*[ss] *also in a foreshadowing*[tt] *he did receive him back.*[uu]

[20] *By faith Isaac blessed Jacob and Esau, even*[vv] *with respect to their future.* [21] *By faith*[ww] *Jacob, while dying,*[xx] *blessed each of Joseph's sons, and "bowed in worship,*[yy] *leaning on the top of his staff."* [22] *By faith Joseph, while coming to the end of his life,*[zz] *made mention of the departure of the Israelites from Egypt*[aaa] *and gave instruction concerning the burial of his bones.*[bbb]

Notes

[a] The coupling of the present pass ptcp καλούμενος with the aor of the main verb ὑπήκουσεν, "he obeyed," emphasizes Abraham's immediate response of obedience (so Moffatt, 169).

[b] The inf ἐξελθεῖν is used to explain the result of the obedience (so BAGD 837; cf. BDF §391; Andriessen, *En lisant,* 50, who insists on the absolute use of the ptcp καλούμενος). Among current

translations, this understanding is reflected in the NASB ("By faith Abraham, when he was called obeyed by going out") and the TEV ("it was faith that made Abraham obey when God called him, and go out"). All other major translations construe the inf ἐξελθεῖν with the ptcp καλούμενος (i.e., "called to depart"): so RSV, NEB, JB, NIV.

ᶜ The expression παρῴκησεν εἰς is an idiom meaning "he migrated to," followed by the accusative of destination (here "the land") (so BAGD 628). The idiom appears to have been missed in the major translations, which speak of Abraham's sojourn in the promised land.

ᵈ The adj ἀλλοτρίαν modifies γῆν, "land," not Abraham (see BAGD 40). This fact is obscured in NEB ("he settled as an alien"), TEV ("as though he were a foreigner"), and NIV ("like a stranger").

ᵉ The coincidental aor ptcp κατοικήσας modifies the main verb παρῴκησεν, "he migrated"; it describes the circumstances under which the action of the verb occurred. The aor tense is culminative in quality.

ᶠ The main verb ἐξεδέχετο is intensive in force (so Spicq, 2:347, who understands the verb to mean "he expected with an absolute confidence"; cf. P. E. Hughes, 469, n. 31). The impf tense emphasizes continuous expectation (so Grosheide, 264; Moffatt, 170).

ᵍ The definite article in τοὺς θεμελίους is emphatic, connoting presumably the eternal foundations appropriate to a city designed and created by God.

ʰ In accordance with classical usage, the relative pronoun ἧς is used in a causal sense ("because its designer" or "seeing that its designer") (see A. W. Argyle, "The Causal Use of the Relative Pronouns in the Greek New Testament," BT 6 [1955] 168–69, who finds another instance of this usage in 9:14).

ⁱ By the first century, when Hebrews was written, δημιουργός was the generally accepted word in literary language for God the Creator (see the review of the evidence in Williamson, Philo, 42–51).

ʲ By virtue of its final position in the sentence, ὁ θεός is emphatic.

ᵏ This verse is unusually difficult, presenting questions of a textual, grammatical, and lexical character. Consequently, any translation must remain tentative. The primary question concerns the grammatical subj of the principal clause: Is Abraham or Sarah the subject of the main verb ἔλαβεν, "he/she received"? Two considerations have been decisive in the determination of the grammatical subj of the sentence for this translation: (1) the expression εἰς καταβολὴν σπέρματος is a fixed hellenistic idiom for the specifically male function in procreation; (2) the subj of v 12, which stands in the closest relationship to v 11, is clearly Abraham, since both the pronoun ἑνός, "one," and the qualifying ptcp νενεκρωμένου, "already impotent," are masc in gender. Accordingly, Abraham appears to remain the subj understood from v 8 (so also TEV, NIV).

In the text as printed in the UBSGNT³, the subject appears to be καὶ αὐτὴ Σάρρα [στεῖρα], "By faith even sterile Sarah received power." This reading, which is supported by P⁴⁶ D* ψ 81 88 1739 it vg syᵖ·ʰ, receives only a "D" rating (i.e., the committee expresses a very high degree of doubt concerning the reading selected for the text). One consideration which may account for this caution is that the descriptive adj στεῖρα, "sterile," is absent from several important witnesses (P¹³ᵛⁱᵈ א A D² K 33 181 326 330 451 614 629 630 1877 249 Byz Lect Chr Thret John of Damascus Aug). Although στεῖρα has been labelled an "obvious gloss" by Beare (JBL 63 [1944] 396; cf. Moffatt, 171; Michel, 396; Swetnam, Jesus and Isaac, 98), other textual critics contend that it is more likely that στεῖρα was omitted through transcriptional oversight in the copying of uncial MSS (ΣΑΡΡΑΣΤΕΙΡΑ) (so Hoskier, Text of the Epistle to the Hebrews, 51; Metzger, Textual Commentary, 672–73).

One proposal is to treat the entire clause that mentions Sarah (with or without στεῖρα) as the intrusion of a marginal gloss (so Field, Notes, 232; Windisch, 101; Zuntz, Text, 15–16, 34). The resultant assertion is then parallel to the statements in vv 8–10. This radical expedient, however, finds no support in the MS tradition. Moreover, this conjecture fails to explain how a reading was introduced into v 11 that was inconsistent with the tenor of the text (with its reference to a masc function in its sexual imagery) and nevertheless was able to prevail to the point that it succeeded in erasing any trace of the original text (so Swetnam, Jesus and Isaac, 99–100).

A more acceptable proposal is to treat the reference to Sarah as a Hebraic circumstantial clause and to translate, "By faith, even though Sarah was sterile, he [Abraham] received strength for procreation" (so M. Black, "Critical and Exegetical Notes," 41–44; cf. P. E. Hughes, 472, n. 40; Metzger, Textual Commentary, 672–73; Moxnes, "God and His Promise," 182–83). On this understanding καὶ αὐτὴ Σάρρα στεῖρα is a concessive clause, subordinate to the principal clause where Abraham is the subj of the main verb. The translation reflects this proposal.

It is also possible to construe the words ΑΥΤΗ ΣΑΡΡΑ ΣΤΕΙΡΑ as a dative of accompaniment or association rather than a nom, since in the uncial script iota subscript was not normally indicated. The text would then be translated, "By faith he [Abraham] also, together with sterile Sarah, received power for procreation" (so Riggenbach, 356–59; Michel, 396; F. F. Bruce, 302; cf. BDF §194[1]; Turner, *Grammar,* 3:220). A similar proposal is to treat *ΑΥΤΗ ΣΑΡΡΑ* as a dative of advantage, and to translate, "It is by faith that, *to the benefit of Sarah herself,* he [Abraham] received strength for procreation" (so Andriessen, *En lisant,* 50–52). Although this construction is classical, the use of a dative for a person (αὐτῇ Σάρρα, "together with Sarah") immediately following a dative for a quality (πίστει, "by faith") would be stylistically awkward and inconsistent with the literary refinement exhibited by the writer elsewhere in the homily (so Swetnam, *Jesus and Isaac,* 99).

Those who are convinced that the most natural construction is to accept Sarah as the subject of the sentence generally understand the hellenistic idiom εἰς καταβολὴν σπέρματος to mean that Sarah received power "to conceive" (so RSV, NEB, JB, NASB). This presupposes that the idiom used by the writer actually stands for εἰς σύλληψιν καταβεβλημένου σπέρματος, "for the reception of the semen which has been deposited," (cf. Moffatt, 171; Spicq, 2:349). The function of the female in conception, however, was normally expressed by the noun ὑποδοχή ("reception" of semen at conception) or the cognate verb ὑποδέχεσθαι ("to receive" semen) (cf. LSJ, ὑποδοχή, IV. 2 [1880]; *LPGL,* ὑποδοχή 1*a* [1448]). This proposal thus fails to explain why a writer with such a skillful command of the language would wish to deviate from standard Gk. usage. If his intention had been to describe Sarah as having power to conceive, he almost certainly would have written εἰς ὑποδοχήν, not εἰς καταβολήν (M. Black, "Critical and Exegetical Notes," 40).

A different approach to explaining the formulation εἰς καταβολὴν σπέρματος contends that καταβολή means "establishment" or "foundation" (as elsewhere in the NT) and σπέρμα signifies "posterity." Accordingly, the key phrase signifies that Sarah received power for the establishment of a posterity (so P. E. Hughes, 473, "by faith Sarah herself received power for the founding of a posterity, even though she was [sterile and] past the age of child-bearing"; similarly, Buchanan, 170). This proposal, however, attributes to the writer a misleading use of a fixed hellenistic idiom. Moreover, it reduces v 12 to a tautology (so Swetnam, *Jesus and Isaac,* 99).

Finally, Swetnam has recently proposed that the word σπέρμα be understood in a "spiritual sense": Sarah assumed the function of the male with regard to Abraham's spiritual offspring and thus assumed a certain parity with her husband. He translates, "By faith even Sarah herself received power for the production of seed [i.e., that offspring which is constituted by all who, like Abraham at the offering of Isaac, individually must place their faith in God in the face of death] even beyond the suitable time of life" (*Jesus and Isaac,* 100–101). The objections urged against the previous proposal would seem to be equally valid for this interpretation as well. Moreover, this proposal reads v 11 in the light of vv 17–19, which appears to be unwarranted.

¹ Behind this idiomatic translation stands the fixed hellenistic idiom for the specifically male role in procreation, εἰς καταβολὴν σπέρματος. The text could also be translated "he received strength for procreation."

ᵐ The translation adopts the reading of P⁴⁶ and its allies, and treats the text as a concessive, circumstantial clause, as proposed by M. Black, "Critical and Exegetical Notes," 41–44.

ⁿ The phrase καὶ παρὰ καιρὸν ἡλικίας, "and past the normal age," could conceivably be descriptive of Abraham (so TEV, NIV) as of Sarah. It applies, however, more appropriately to Sarah than to Abraham because it describes the condition of a woman who had reached the menopause. Josephus uses similar terminology in describing a woman as having "passed the age" of child-bearing (τὴν ἡλικίαν ἤδη προβεβηκός, *Ant.* 7.182). Cf. Augustine, *City of God* 16.28: both Abraham and Sarah were old, "but she . . . had ceased to menstruate, so that she could no longer bear children even if she had not been barren" (cited by P. E. Hughes, 474).

ᵒ In the syntax of the final clause, the position of πιστόν, "faithful," is emphatic.

ᵖ In the expression ἀφ' ἑνός, "from one person," the gender of the pronoun is masc.

ᑫ The qualifying pf pass ptcp νενεκρωμένου is usually translated "as good as dead" (so RSV, NEB, JB, NIV, TEV: "practically dead"), but in the context of v 11 it must here signify "he had become impotent" (so Zerwick and Grosvenor, *Grammatical Analysis,* 680). The expression καὶ ταῦτα is classical; it here introduces the adv ptcp, which is used concessively (Turner, *Grammar,* 4:157; cf. BDF §425[1]). The clause could be translated, "and he, moreover, had become impotent," or "and that even when he had become impotent."

ʳ The position of κατὰ πίστιν at the beginning of the sentence is emphatic. The change from the simple dative πίστει, "by faith," to the phrase κατὰ πίστιν is remarkable. The fact that the dative πίστει occurs eighteen times in 11:3–31, while κατὰ πίστιν occurs only here, indicates that more than literary variation is intended. The expression κατὰ πίστιν indicates that it was "in accordance with the principle of faith" that the patriarchs faced the moment of death (cf. P. E. Hughes, 477; MM 323).

ˢ The tense of ἀπέθανον is a striking instance of the constative aor, occurring in a summary state-ment (cf. A. T. Robertson, *Grammar*, 833).

ᵗ The reading λαβόντες, supported by P⁴⁶ D Ψ 1739, has a strong claim to being original (cf. 9:15: τὴν ἐπαγγελίαν λάβωσιν, "may receive the promise"). It was displaced in ℵ I P 326 et al. by κομισάμενοι, which is the standard verb for receiving divine reward, apparently under the influence of 10:36 and 11:39 (so Zuntz, *Text*, 52–53; Beare, *JBL* 63 [1944] 394; F. F. Bruce, 303). The translation of the phrase is unaffected by the textual variation.

ᵘ Although the patriarchs received "the promises," they did not receive "what was promised." It was clearly the intention of the text to refer to the fulfillment of "the promises."

ᵛ The aorists ἰδόντες, "seeing," ἀσπασάμενοι, "greeting," and ὁμολογήσαντες, "admitting," are culminative in force, as indeed this cataloguing of them suggests. As such, the switch to the present tense of the copula εἰσίν in the clause that follows is significant. It implies the identity between the writer's audience and the patriarchs, as do the verbs in the present tense in v 14 (so J. Thomas, "The Use of Voice, Moods and Tenses," 37).

ʷ The prep phrase ἐπὶ τῆς γῆς could be translated "on the earth" (so RSV, NEB, JB, NIV, TEV). The close proximity of v 9, however, which speaks of Abraham migrating to "the land of the promise" (γῆν τῆς ἐπαγγελίας), indicates that the experience of being only a temporary settler in *the land* of Canaan is in view in v 13 (with Buchanan, 194).

ˣ The present tense of ἐμφανίζουσιν is significant: "show plainly"—now.

ʸ The present tense of ἐπιζητοῦσιν indicates a continual, habitual attitude of life.

ᶻ Here, and in v 22, the verb μνημονεύειν, which ordinarily denotes "to remember," means "to re-fer to," "to think of," "to keep in mind," "to make mention of" (BAGD 525; Zuntz, *Text*, 119).

ᵃᵃ The demonstrative pronoun ἐκείνης has its antecedent in πατρίδα, "homeland," "country" (v 14). The verb μνημονεύειν takes the gen.

ᵇᵇ The presence of εἰ, "if," with a past tense and ἄν in the apodosis is characteristic of a 2nd class conditional (i.e., contrary-to-fact) sentence. Here the impf εἶχον is used for an "unreal" past and is descriptive of continuous action: "they would have kept on having opportunity" (cf. Zerwick, *Biblical Greek* §§313–14, 316; BDF §360[4]).

ᶜᶜ The inf ἀνακάμψαι is used to complement or to further define the noun καιρόν, "opportunity." As such it can be translated "for returning" (cf. Moulton, *Grammar*, 1:204).

ᵈᵈ Following a sentence expressing an unfulfilled condition, the expression νῦν δέ is used in a logical, rather than a temporal, sense and can be translated "but as it is," "but as the case now stands" (cf. Thrall, *Greek Particles*, 31).

ᵉᵉ The present tense of ὀρέγονται is significant for indicating a continual, habitual perspective; it is "timeless" and paradigmatic of the faith of the patriarchs, and, as such, should speak to the audi-ence addressed (cf. P. E. Hughes, 480).

ᶠᶠ The translation reflects the judgment that ἐπικαλεῖσθαι is a pass inf. If the verb is read as a middle, translate: "God is not ashamed *to call himself* their God."

ᵍᵍ The personal pronoun αὐτοῖς is a particularly clear example of the dative of advantage.

ʰʰ The name "Abraham" is omitted by P⁴⁶ Ψ 330 2005 syʰ Chr, and this may represent the original text, for in the remainder of the textual tradition the position of the name "Abraham" fluctuates curiously (for details see Metzger, *Textual Commentary*, 673). The varying positions of the name suggest that it is secondary, although the mass of evidence supports its inclusion in the text.

ⁱⁱ The circumstantial ptcp πειραζόμενος is coincident with the main verb προσενήνοχεν, "offered up in sacrifice." It offers another instance of the "theological passive" ("put to the test *by God*").

ʲʲ The pf tense of προσενήνοχεν, "offered up in sacrifice," should be noted, because it contrasts with the use of the impf tense in the complementary clause that follows immediately (see *Note* mm below). The significance of the tense can be interpreted in one of two ways: (1) with reference to an OT event, it can mean that this event still retains its exemplary meaning (so Moulton, *Grammar*, 1:142, 143–44 ; BDF §342[5]); or (2) it may indicate that as far as Abraham's intention was con-cerned, the sacrifice was a completed act with lasting consequences (so Spicq, 2:353; Swetnam, *Jesus and Isaac*, 122).

ᵏᵏ The καί is epexegetical, introducing a complementary clause that explains more precisely the prior assertion (Riggenbach, 363; Moffatt, 176; Spicq, 2:352; Swetnam, *Jesus and Isaac*, 121). For the translation, see Zerwick and Grosvenor, *Grammatical Analysis*, 681.

ˡˡ The predominant meaning of ἀναδέχεσθαι in the papyri is "to undertake," "to assume responsi-bility for," and this notion is appropriate here (MM 32). An alternative proposal is to view the verb as an intensive compound meaning "to receive with confidence" (P. E. Hughes, 483, n. 52).

[mm] The conative impf προσέφερεν is used of attempted, incomplete, or interrupted action. It is used here to soften the harshness of the previous statement that Abraham had actually sacrificed Isaac (cf. Moule, *Idiom-Book,* 9; Turner, *Grammar,* 3:65; Swetnam, *Jesus and Isaac,* 122).

[nn] It is possible that, influenced by the LXX, the prep ἐν has a causal sense, i.e., "By reason of Isaac" (so Moulton and Howard, *Grammar,* 2:463).

[oo] The translation of Gen 21:12 LXX is idiomatic, following the lead of TEV. The syntax is Sem., employing the "ethical" dative σοι with the suggestion of "for you," or "in your interests": "it is through Isaac that offspring will be reckoned for you" (cf. Zerwick and Grosvenor, *Grammatical Analysis,* 681).

[pp] The middle voice of λογισάμενος places the stress on the subj: *Abraham* "considered."

[qq] The present tense of the inf ἐγείρειν is gnomic; it expresses a self-evident truth for the person of faith. This context dictates the addition of "him" (Isaac) in the translation.

[rr] The force of the καί is emphatic (Zuntz, *Text,* 211, who recommends the translation "even").

[ss] Consistent with the five other places where ὅθεν occurs in Hebrews (2:17; 3:1; 7:25; 8:3; 9:18), the term has been translated as a causal conj (cf. RSV; Spicq, 2:354; Swetnam, *Jesus and Isaac,* 119). The decision to treat ὅθεν here as a relative adv accounts for those translations which refer to Abraham recovering Isaac "from the dead" (NEB, JB, TEV, NIV; cf. Seeberg, 124; Westcott, 368).

[tt] The expression ἐν παραβολῇ is often understood adverbially, "figuratively speaking," or "as it were," but more seems to be involved. Abraham received Isaac back "in a foreshadowing" or "type" of resurrection (so BAGD 612; Swetnam, *Jesus and Isaac,* 122–23; cf. Riggenbach, 365–66; Hauck, *TDNT* 5:752; Moule, *Idiom-Book,* 78; and the use of παραβολή in 9:9 ["an illustration pointing to"]).

[uu] The verb ἐκομίσατο could also be translated "he did recover him," since in the middle voice κομίζεσθαι is used of getting back what belongs to you (e.g., Gen 38:20 LXX; Philo, *Concerning Joseph* 35, cited by Moffatt, 177).

[vv] The force of the καί is emphatic; it functions as an intensive element (cf. Zuntz, *Text,* 211).

[ww] Every other occurrence of πίστει in 11:3–31 is instrumental or dative of manner, but here the sense is almost locative, "in faith Jacob . . . blessed."

[xx] The translation seeks to express the temporal nuance of ἀποθνῄσκων. The present tense denotes the process leading up to an attained goal (so A. T. Robertson, *Grammar,* 827).

[yy] The expression προσκυνεῖν ἐπί with the accusative means to worship on or over something. The implied obj of the verb ("bowed in worship") is God, as in NEB, TEV. A misunderstanding of the idiom is evident in the vg ("he worshiped the top of his staff") and has been perpetuated in the translation of R. Knox ("Jacob made reverence to the top of Joseph's staff") and in the *New Confraternity Verson* ("Jacob . . . bowed in worship towards the top of his staff").

[zz] The present ptcp τελευτῶν has the same temporal nuance as ἀποθνῄσκων in v 21 (see *Note* xx above).

[aaa] The translation is idiomatic; the text says that Joseph mentioned "the exodus of the sons of Israel."

[bbb] Translating according to the sense, it is necessary to speak of the burial of "his bones."

Form/Structure/Setting

See 11:1–40 above.

Comment

8 The writer devotes more space to Abraham as an exemplar of faith than to any other OT figure (vv 8–12, 17–19). The insertion of his own commentary on the biblical account in v 10 and in vv 13–16 makes it more difficult to discern the structure of the unit, but similarity between the various components in the story of Abraham clearly suggests that vv 8–12 and vv 17–19 form a literary unity (so Vanhoye, *La structure,* 182–191; Moxnes, "God and His Promise," 178–80). When these two separated sections are viewed as one unit, it becomes apparent that both in content and in actual outline there is a correspondence to the reference to Abraham in the speech of Stephen in Acts 7:2–8. Although each version of the narrative contains material that is not duplicated in the other (e.g., the reception of

the covenant of circumcision in Acts 7:8, and the sacrifice of Isaac in Heb 11:17–19), the two accounts share major themes of the Abraham story, which derive from a Greek-speaking Jewish homiletical tradition, probably from the Diaspora (cf. Moxnes, 130–64, 169–77). The primary difference between the two accounts is found in the actual presentation of the material. Acts 7:2–8 tends to emulate the simple style of the biblical narrative, whereas the writer of Hebrews develops the tradition by means of interpretive comments (Moxnes, 180).

Evidence for the importance of Abraham in the Jewish exemplary tradition is provided in *1 Clement* as well (10:1–7; 17:2; 31:2). In *1 Clem.* 10:1–7 Clement mentions the same episodes from Abraham's life that were selected by the writer of Hebrews, namely, his call and departure from Mesopotamia, the birth of a son, and the offering of Isaac as a sacrifice. D. A. Hagner has suggested that there was direct literary influence of Heb 11:8–19 upon *1 Clem.* 10:1–7 (*The Use of the Old and New Testament in Clement of Rome* [Leiden: Brill, 1973] 184–86). In the presentation of the episodes, however, the differences between the two accounts are more striking than the similarities (cf. Moxnes, "God and His Promise," 190–95). The heavy stress upon God and his faithfulness to his promises, for example, which was so important to the writer of Hebrews, is missing from Clement (cf. *1 Clem.* 10:1–2, 7). The significance of *1 Clem.* 10:1–7 lies in the independent witness it bears to the structure of the hellenistic-Jewish tradition concerning Abraham, which is attested in Heb 11:8–19 as well (so Drews, *Studien*, 23–40; Mercado, "Language of Sojourning," 87–91; Moxnes, 190).

The closest parallels between these independent witnesses to a fixed homiletical tradition concerning Abraham are found in the first episode recorded: Abraham's departure from Canaan and his life as a resident alien in the promised land (cf. Acts 7:2–5; Heb 11:8–10; *1 Clem.* 10:1–3).

The writer's presentation of Abraham's call and departure from Mesopotamia is anchored in Gen 12:1 LXX, but the only term reproduced from the biblical text is the verb ἐξελθεῖν, "to depart," which is used twice in v 8 (for details, see Mercado, "Language of Sojourning," 83). The emphasis in Gen 12:1 falls upon the divine initiative; God called Abram to leave his country, his people, and his father's household and to go to a land he would be shown. In v 8 the account is recast in the form of a statement about Abraham, who exemplified faith by responding immediately with obedience even as he was being called: καλούμενος Ἀβραὰμ ὑπήκουσεν ἐξελθεῖν, "as he was being called, Abraham obeyed by departing" (see above, *Note* a). The emphasis falls upon the correlation between faith and obedience in the response of Abraham.

The use of the verb ὑπακούειν, "to obey," in the context of the call of Abraham is striking because it finds no support in the detail of Gen 12 or elsewhere in Scripture. In fact, ὑπακούειν is used only twice in the OT to describe Abraham's response to God (Gen 22:18; 26:5 LXX); both instances denote Abraham's readiness to sacrifice his son in obedience to the divine command. Reference is made to Abraham's faithful (πιστός) heart in response to the call to leave Ur (Neh 9:7–8 LXX) but not to his obedience.

The detail that Abraham "obeyed" God by departing from Ur is rooted in the exegetical tradition of hellenistic Judaism. Philo, for example, uses the language of obedience to describe Abraham's response to God's command, employing the verb πείθεσθαι, "to obey," and the predicate adjective καταπειθής, "obedient" (*On*

Abraham 60, 85, 88). Philo finds in the immediateness of Abraham's response an indication of his eagerness to obey God (*On Abraham* 62). This is precisely the impression conveyed in v 8 with the expression καλούμενος . . . ὑπήκουσεν ("as he was being called . . . he obeyed"). Although Philo does not use the verb ὑπακούειν, he is an independent witness to the exegetical tradition that stands behind the formulation of v 8. Another independent witness to this tradition is provided in *1 Clem.* 10:1–2, which states that Abraham "was found faithful [πιστός] by being obedient [ὑπήκοον] to the words of God. Through obedience [δι᾽ ὑπακοῆς] he departed from his country." The writer of Hebrews thus shares with others a common exegetical tradition stressing Abraham's obedience to God's call and the immediateness of his response (cf. Mercado, "Language of Sojourning," 83–92).

The stress on obedience in v 8 serves to underscore a dimension of the πίστις, "faith," that wins divine approval (v 2), which Abraham demonstrated when he departed from Ur πίστει, "by faith": faith is active response to the spoken word of God. It reinforces the emphasis on obedience found elsewhere in Hebrews (see above on 5:8–9; cf. R. Leivestad, "Jesus som forbillede ifølge Hebreerbrevet," *NorTT* 74 [1973] 195–206). The portrayal of Abraham as an exemplar of obedience shows that he is not merely an attested example of faith but an exemplary witness to the Christian community as well (cf. D'Angelo, *Moses*, 18, 25).

The goal of Abraham's migration is described as τόπον ὃν ἤμελλεν λαμβάνειν εἰς κληρονομίαν, "a place he was to receive as an inheritance." The κληρονομία, "inheritance," does not appear in the terms of the divine call in Gen 12:1–3. Nevertheless, the theme of inheritance is closely associated with the enduring and certain possession of the land of Canaan in the biblical tradition (Gen 15:7; 22:17; 28:4; 1 Chr 16:18; Ps 104[MT 105]:11 LXX; cf. *Jub.* 22:17; Acts 7:5–6). The call of God is directed toward an inheritance. The subsequent development of this motif, however, in vv 9–10 and vv 13–16 shows that the content of the inheritance in Hebrews is not the land of Canaan (4:8; cf. 9:15) but the city that God has prepared for his people.

This suggests that the substitution of the term τόπος, "a place," for the corresponding expression ἡ γῆ, "the land," in Gen 12:1 LXX is purposeful. It implies that the goal was not sharply defined (cf. Michel, 342). Moreover, τόπος can refer in popular usage to a city, a district of a city, or a home (cf. Koester, *TDNT* 8:188). It is thus an appropriate term to anticipate the reference to the city whose designer and creator is God (v 10) as the final goal of Abraham's migration. The reference points beyond historical geography to an inheritance transcendent in character. The conception is apocalyptic to the extent that the city remains a future reality (see *Comment* on v 10; cf. Mercado, "Language of Sojourning," 93–98, 105, 113).

The assertion that Abraham set out μὴ ἐπιστάμενος ποῦ ἔρχεται, "not knowing where he was going," which amplifies the thought of v 8*a*, is an exegetical comment on the phrase ἣν ἄν σοι δείξω, "which I will show you," in Gen 12:1 LXX (cf. Philo, *On the Migration of Abraham* 43–44). Abraham went out courageously into the unknown, to "a strange land and an uncertain future" (J. Schneider, 108). He responded to uncertainty with trust in the word of God. His faith rested, ultimately, in the promise of a future that was assured because it had been guaranteed by God's promise. In setting out, "not knowing where he was going," Abraham exemplified the faith that invests events not seen with the substantial reality of a demonstration or proof (v 1*b*).

9–10 The description of pilgrimage in v 9*a* summarizes succinctly and graphically the tenor of the biblical narrative; Abraham was a nomadic wanderer, sojourning in Egypt (Gen 12:10) and in various districts in Canaan (Gen 20:1; 21:23, 34; 35:27). Wherever he went he incurred the stigma of a stranger and a foreigner. This impression is accurately conveyed in v 9*a* with the idiomatic statement παρῴκησεν εἰς γῆν τῆς ἐπαγγελίας ὡς ἀλλοτρίαν, "he migrated to the promised land as to a foreign country." In the LXX the verb παροικεῖν and its cognates are used to characterize Abraham's status and experience as an alien who resides in a foreign country without native and civil rights (see Mercado, "Language of Sojourning," 32–41). The biblical basis for the depiction of Abraham in v 9 is Gen 23:4 LXX, where Abraham describes himself as "an alien and a stranger" (πάροικος καὶ παρεπίδημος) among the resident citizens of Hebron.

The idea of the promise is prominent in v 9, where it is mentioned twice. In the first instance it is used to describe the land to which Abraham migrated. The expression γῆν τῆς ἐπαγγελίας, "the promised land," does not come from the OT, which speaks of "the land which God swore" to give to the fathers (cf. Gen 50:24; Exod 13:5; 31:1; Num 11:12; 14:16, 23; 32:11; Deut 1:8, 35; 6:10, 18, 23; 7:8). The specific formulation in v 9 does not occur elsewhere in the NT and is equally rare in Jewish sources (*T. Jos.* 20:1 [MS *d*]; *T. Abr.* [Recension A] 8:5; 20:11; cf. *T. Abr.* 3:6, where ἐπαγγελία, "promise," refers to the land). Although the motif of the promise of God in reference to the land has no preliminary history in the OT, it is found occasionally in Jewish sources (e.g. *T. Jos.* 20:1 [MSS]; *T. Abr.* 3:6; cf. Acts 7:5) and appears to be traditional.

The description of the land of Canaan as ἀλλοτρία, "a foreign land," however, is without parallel elsewhere (Mercado, "Language of Sojourning," 119). The sharp contrast between "the promised land" and "a foreign country" serves to throw into bold relief the writer's portrayal of the unsettled life of Abraham. Entrance into the promised land had brought no settlement. On the contrary, the new situation required renewed faith and a fresh commitment of obedience (Michel, 393). The expression ἐν σκηναῖς κατοικήσας, "living in tents," corresponds to the picture that Genesis offers of Abraham, constantly pitching his tents for a shorter or longer period as a migrant nomad residing in a foreign land (Gen 12:8; 13:3, 5, 12, 18; 18:1, 2, 6, 9, 10 LXX; cf. Muntingh, "The City," 108–10; Wiseman, "They Lived in Tents," 195–200). Tents and tent-encampments were normative for both nomadic and semi-nomadic people throughout the patriarchal period. The detail that Abraham lived in tents, as did Isaac (Gen 26:17, 25) and Jacob (Gen 25:27; 32:25, 33–34; 33:18–19; 35:21), bears vivid witness to their status as aliens (Michaelis, *TDNT* 7:377). It also suggests that they refused to establish a permanent settlement in a culture devoid of the presence of God. "Living in tents" is the sign that believers are pilgrims and strangers whose goal is yet before them.

The description of Isaac and Jacob as τῶν συγκληρονόμων τῆς ἐπαγγελίας τῆς αὐτῆς, "joint heirs [with Abraham] of the same promise," resumes the note of the utter reliability of the promise of God so prominent in this section. The rare term συγκληρονόμος, "joint heir," which does not appear in the LXX, is not used elsewhere of the patriarchs. It is entirely appropriate, however, for emphasizing the important concept of inheritance (cf. vv 7–8) and the renewal of the promise to each successive generation through its representatives who were called to orient themselves toward the future rather than to the present (cf. Longenecker, *JETS* 20 [1977] 209–10).

This understanding is made explicit in v 10, which must be considered the writer's own interpretation of the biblical tradition summarized in vv 8–9. His account of the story differs sharply from the version in Acts 7:2–5 or *1 Clem.* 10:1–4, where assured possession of the land is the goal of Abraham's migration. According to the writer of Hebrews, Abraham's status as an immigrant and alien in the land had the positive effect of indicating that Canaan was not, in the final sense, the promised inheritance. It served to direct his attention beyond Canaan to the established city of God as the ultimate goal of his pilgrimage. As a commentary on the traditional account of Abraham's migration, v 10 is closely related to the eschatological perspective developed in vv 13–16. The emphasis falls upon the forward orientation of faith and the eclipsing of present incompleteness by the overshadowing objective reality of the transcendent blessings for which we hope (v 1*a*) (cf. Vanhoye, *La structure*, 186–87; Moxnes, "God and His Promise," 181). This is, of course, a perspective informed by primitive Christian eschatology.

The commentary introduced by the explanatory γάρ, "for," in v 10 explains the fact that, at the end of his migration, Abraham continued to accept an unsettled mode of existence in the promised land, living in tents: ἐξεδέχετο γὰρ τὴν τοὺς θεμελίους ἔχουσαν πόλιν, "for he was looking forward with certainty to the city which has foundations." Both the nuance and the tense of the main verb ἐξεδέχετο, "to wait for," "to look forward to," are significant. The verb is intensive in force, connoting "to expect with absolute confidence" (Spicq, 2:347), while the imperfect tense expresses continuous expectation (Grosheide, 264; Moffatt, 170). Accordingly, Abraham did not migrate to Canaan and reside there as a stranger in a foreign country, because Canaan was an intermediate station on a journey toward heaven. He migrated to Canaan because it was "the promised land," that is to say, the country in which Abraham was to receive the promised inheritance. For that reason he was continuously waiting *there* for the appearance of the city of God, of which he was already a citizen by virtue of the divine call and promise (with Hofius, *Katapausis*, 147–49).

Abraham's true status as a citizen of an established city is juxtaposed ironically in vv 9–10 with his apparent status as a tent-dweller in the promised land, which assumed for him the character of a foreign country. The certainty with which he looked forward to the city of God identifies Abraham as a witness to that eschatological faith characterized in v 1 as "standing firmly with the reality for which one is hoping" on the basis of the promise given by God. From the writer's distinctly Christian perspective, the promise involved for Abraham a share in the transcendent eternal inheritance that has been secured for all the people of God by the death of Christ as the mediator of the new covenant (see *Comment* on 9:15).

The focus of Abraham's expectation was τὴν τοὺς θεμελίους ἔχουσαν πόλιν, "the city which has foundations." This description is without precise parallel elsewhere but is occasioned by the reference to Abraham's "tents" in v 9. A tent-encampment was a city without foundations. In contrast to the impermanent existence of a tent-encampment, moved from place to place in response to the demands of the situation, a city with foundations offered a fixed and settled home (cf. de Young,

Jerusalem, 138). The description is based upon the biblical representation of Zion as the city firmly established by God (e.g., Ps 47:9 [MT 48:8]; 86[MT 87]:1–3, 5; Isa 14:32 LXX; cf. Ps 122[MT 121]:3; Isa 33:20 LXX). The strength of its foundations indicates that the city is firmly founded (e.g., Ps 86[MT 87]:1 LXX).

In v 10 "the city with foundations" is the transcendent heavenly city, which possesses an unshakable and abiding quality (12:28; 13:14). It is unlikely that the writer was aware that in the patriarchal period the expression "a city with foundations" was idiomatic for a city in which the king had firmly established its organization and administration, as proposed by Muntingh ("The City," 116–20). Muntingh suggests that Abraham saw in the establishment of the authority of Melchizedek, the royal priest of Salem, a prototype of the city of God. Allusion to the city recurs under a variety of metaphors: "the heavenly homeland" (v 16), "the city of the living God, heavenly Jerusalem" (12:22), "the unshakable kingdom" (12:28), and "the abiding city that is to come" (13:14). The biblical realism in the reference to the established city shows that there is nothing abstract or contingent about the promised "inheritance" (v 8; on the difference between Philo and Hebrews in this regard, see Braun, "Das himmlische Vaterland," 319–27, especially 323; de Young, *Jerusalem*, 121–22).

The reason the city has eternal foundations is supplied in v 10*b*: ἧς τεχνίτης καὶ δημιουργὸς ὁ θεός, "because its designer and creator is God." The description of God serves as a guarantee for the hope in a heavenly city. The biblical concept that God laid the foundations of the city of Jerusalem (Ps 86[MT 87]:1, 5 LXX) was extended to the foundations of the glorified, heavenly city as well (Isa 28:16; 54:11 LXX), and this motif is echoed in later Jewish and Christian apocalyptic literature (e.g., 4 Ezra 10:27; Rev 21:10–14, 19–20). The well-founded city of God furnishes a fixed metaphor for the kingdom of God or the reign of God in its totality (e.g., Ezek 48:35; Tob 13:7–18; Heb 12:22; 13:14; Rev 3:12; 4 Ezra 7:26; 8:52; see *Comment* on Heb 11:16; 12:22; 13:14). An interesting strand of the tradition in post-biblical Jewish apocalyptic affirms that God had shown the pre-existent heavenly city to Abraham during the incident reported in Gen 15:9–21 (*2 Apoc. Bar.* 4:2–5; cf. 4 Ezra 3:13–14; *T. Abr.* 2:6 [Recension A]). There is no influence from this tradition on the formulation of v 10, or elsewhere in Hebrews.

The terms τεχνίτης, "designer," "craftsman," and δημιουργός, "creator," "builder," are not found elsewhere in the NT. The use of these terms in v 10 is rooted in hellenistic Judaism, which adopted this literary terminology for referring to God as Creator of the physical universe (for τεχνίτης of God, see Wis 13:1; Philo, *Who is the Heir?* 133, 225; *On Dreams* 1.123, 136, 206; 2.27; *On the Change of Names* 31; for δημιουργός of God, see Philo, *On the Creation of the World* 10, 13, 36, 68, 138, 139, 146, 171, and elsewhere; Jos., *Ant.* 1.155, 272; 7.38; cf. *1 Clem.* 20:11; 26:1; 33:2; 35:3; 59:12). Philo frequently brings together δημιουργός and τεχνίτης in reference to God as Creator, without any noticeable differentiation between the two terms (*On the Eternity of the World* 41, 43; *On the Cherubim* 27–28; *On the Unchangeableness of God* 21, 25, 30–31).

Philo's use of the term δημιουργός was clearly influenced by Plato and by the doctrine of creation set forth in the *Timaeus* (28E-30A, 30C, 32C, 41A, 42E; for δημιουργός elsewhere in Plato, cf. *Republic* 530A, 596A-597A; *Politics* 273B; *Laws* 270A, 273B). A passage from the *Timaeus* 41A is quoted by Philo in his treatise *On the Eternity of the World* (13) and is incorporated into his argument (for discussion of these texts, see Williamson, *Philo*, 44–48). It is, therefore, not surprising that the use of the term δημιουργός in v 10 has commonly been read as an indication of Platonism in Hebrews, perhaps mediated to the writer through Philo (cf. Spicq, 1:41–46; Stewart, *NTS* 12 [1965–66] 284–93; Cambier, *Eschatologie*, 24–26; Mercado, "Language of Sojourning," 130–36). That Josephus could use δημιουργός of God with none of the philosophical associations of the word found in Plato or Philo shows that the mere presence of a term is an insufficient basis for determining its significance. Williamson has observed a significant difference in context for δημιουργός in Philo and in Hebrews. Philo consistently uses δημιουργός and τεχνίτης of God to refer to the creation of the physical universe. In v 10, however, the context established for the use of these terms is distinctly eschatological; the city is unquestionably the heavenly city of God. The context in which the combination of the two words occurs in Hebrews suggests that it is no more than a rhetorical flourish, appropriate to the literary language of the homily (*Philo*, 48–51; cf. Moffatt, 170).

If a differentiation in nuance is to be made between the two terms, τεχνίτης connotes God's creative wisdom in planning the heavenly city and δημιουργός connotes God's creative power in executing his plan (so Westcott, 362; Riggenbach, 355; Grosheide, 265). For the community of faith, the description signifies that the city has been prepared (see *Comment* on 11:16) and is ready to be revealed at the appropriate time. The city furnishes the objective ground of God's promise as the focus of faith, both for Abraham and for Christians. The picture of Abraham in v 10, therefore, is not of a person engaged in pilgrimage toward heaven but of a man of eschatological faith continuously waiting for the consummation of redemption (cf. de Young, *Jerusalem*, 138; Hofius, *Katapausis*, 149).

11–12 Perhaps nowhere in Hebrews is the axiom that translation implies interpretation more evident than in v 11. The decisions reached in translating this verse inevitably determine to a significant extent the direction the commentary must pursue (see the full discussion above, *Note* k). It becomes necessary only to supply the detail that tends to corroborate the accuracy of the translation and to set vv 11–12 in the larger context of this section.

The third illustration of Abraham's active faith concerns the fathering of a child in old age, even though his wife was sterile and past the normal age for child-bearing (Gen 15:1–6; 17:15–22; 18:9–15) and his own body had ceased to function sexually (cf. Gen 18:11–12; Rom 4:19; Heb 11:12). Unquestionably, both Abraham and Sarah were called to ignore the circumstances of their past experience and their current age because of a greater trust in God's promise that they would have a son. In spite of initial incredulity, in which they both shared (Gen 17:17; 18:10–12), both achieved the ability to believe that parenthood was possible. But in vv 11–12, attention is focused narrowly on the faith of Abraham, as in vv 8–10. The same perspective is reflected elsewhere in the tradition, which speaks of the conception of Isaac from the vantage-point of Abraham (Acts 7:8*b*: "And Abraham became the father of Isaac"; *1 Clem.* 10:7*a*: "Because of his faith . . . a son was given to him in his old age"; cf. the old Palestinian tradition in *Tg. Neof.* Exod 12:42: "Is Abraham, at 100 years of age, going to be able to become a father, and is Sarah his wife, at 90 years of age, going to be able to conceive?").

The declaration πίστει . . . δύναμιν εἰς καταβολὴν σπέρματος ἔλαβεν, "by faith he was enabled to become a father," indicates that Abraham's physical powers were renewed by faith. The expression δύναμιν ἔλαβεν, "he received power," implies that faith cooperated with his aged body to produce the strength to father a child. The phrase εἰς καταβολὴν σπέρματος is a fixed hellenistic idiom for the specifically male function of producing sperm (Lucian, *Love Affairs* 19; Galen, *On the Natural Faculties* 1.6; *On the Use of the Parts of the Body of Man* 14.7; Epictetus, *Discourses* 1.13.3; Philo, *On Drunkenness* 211; *On the Cherubim* 49; *On the Creation* 132; Greek *Apoc. Ezra* 5:12; cited by Swetnam, *Jesus and Isaac,* 98; cf. Michel, 396). The sexual expression must be understood in its normal active sense of Abraham's part in the generation of Isaac (M. Black, "Critical and Exegetical Notes," 40; Moxnes, "God and His Promise," 182–83).

The circumstantial clause concerning Sarah throws Abraham's faith into bold relief. The concession καὶ αὐτὴ Σάρρα στεῖρα . . . καὶ παρὰ καιρὸν ἡλικίας, "even though Sarah herself was sterile . . . and past the normal age of child bearing," summarizes the situation sketched by Genesis. Sarah had been unable to conceive a child (Gen 15:2–3; 16:1–2). At the time that God promised that she would become pregnant with a son (Gen 17:16, 19, 21; 18:9–10, 13–14), Sarah was close to ninety years of age. She was "past the age of child-bearing" (Gen 18:11). Her incredulous laughter is thoroughly understandable (Gen 18:12 LXX: "This has not yet happened to me, even until now, and my husband is old"; cf. MT: "after I am worn out and my husband is old, will I now have sexual pleasure?"). The sharing of physical intimacy had apparently ceased for the couple, and menopause had occurred long ago. The writer shows no interest in explaining the laughter of Abraham or of Sarah. He concentrates all attention on the active faith through which they became capable of resuming normal sexual relations, in the course of which Abraham was enabled to become a father.

The reason given for this unexpected capability is πιστὸν ἡγήσατο τὸν ἐπαγγειλάμενον, "he considered the one who had made the promise faithful." This deduction from the biblical narrative places at the center of the account the utter reliability of God, rather than the faith of Abraham. The reference to the exemplary faith of Abraham in vv 11–12 thus becomes transformed into a statement about God who is faithful to his promises (Moxnes, "God and His Promises," 183–84). The verb ἐπαγγέλλεσθαι, "to promise," is used four times in Hebrews (6:13; 10:23; 11:11; 12:27), and in each case the one who promises is God. The verb is used here, as in 6:13 and 10:23, to highlight the trustworthiness of God who accomplishes what he has said he will do. In the light of 10:23, the assertion is confessional in nature. Philo ascribes a similar confession to Sarah in the course of his exposition of Gen 18:12 (cf. *On the Change of Names* 166; *Allegorical Interpretation* 3.128; *Questions and Answers on Genesis* 4.17; see Moxnes, 161–62).

The consequence of confessing faith is set forth in v 12, where the connecting particle διό, "so it was that," shows the relationship between v 11 and v 12 to be that of cause and effect (Swetnam, *Jesus and Isaac,* 99). The conception of a son is now set within the larger context of the fulfillment of the promise of innumerable posterity (cf. Gen 12:2; 15:5; 22:17). The reliability of God is underscored in the contrast between the singularity of Abraham (ἀφ' ἑνός, "from this one man") and the unimaginable plurality of his physical descendants, in accordance with the divine promise. The reference to the condition of Abraham's body, acknowledged in the concessive clause καὶ . . . νενεκρωμένου, "and he already impotent," describes Abraham as dead as far as the natural possibility of fathering a child was concerned. This serves to stress that it is the performative power of God's spoken word alone that accounts for "descendants as numerous as the stars of heaven and as innumerable as the grains of sand on the seashore" (cf. Rom 4:19–21).

The allusion to Abraham's large posterity is not a direct quotation of any single passage but a conflation of expressions drawn from several texts (cf. Gen 15:5; 22:17; Exod 32:13 LXX). The comparison with grains of sand on the seashore is found in Gen 22:17 LXX, while Exod 32:13 LXX contains the expression $\tau\tilde{\omega}$ $\pi\lambda\dot{\eta}\theta\epsilon\iota$, "as the stars of heaven *for number*" (cf. also Deut 1:10; 10:22; 28:62 LXX). It is probable that the writer was quoting from memory at this point (so Moxnes, "God and His Promise," 184–85; McCullough, *NTS* 26 [1979–80] 374, finds the primary reference to be Gen 22:17*b* LXX but suggests the situation was influenced by Dan 3:3*b* LXX as well as by stylistic considerations).

The related statements in vv 11–12 belong thematically with the exposition presented in 6:13–15. Both passages focus attention upon God as the giver of the promise and identify the content of the promise as a large posterity. In 6:13–15 Abraham was cited as an illustration of those who through faith and steadfast endurance inherit the promises (6:12). Emphasis was placed especially on the necessity of steadfast endurance (6:15). The tenor of the argument is restated in vv 11–12 in a more direct way, but here the emphasis is placed upon the role that faith plays in acting upon the promise (cf. Moxnes, "God and His Promise," 183–85; unfortunately, Moxnes fails to give sufficient weight to the fact that what Abraham received, according to 6:13–15, was *the promise*, not the fulfillment of the promise; it is precisely the element of *fulfillment*, however, which is dominant in v 11–12).

13 In vv 13–16 the writer suddenly interrupts his recital of Abraham's acts of faith in order to analyze the strands of the tradition he has woven together. The insertion of his own comments at this point is surprising. A restrospective glance over the patriarchal period at the conclusion of the unit in order to summarize the significance of the development might have been expected. On the other hand, the commentary introduced is related thematically to vv 8–9, and actually elaborates the eschatological perspective set forth in v 10. If vv 13–16 had been appended to v 10, the logical sequence in the unit would have been apparent.

As the paragraph now stands, the writer's comments separate vv 11–12 and vv 17–19, which are stylistically and thematically allied. Both of those brief units consist of sentences that begin with the anaphoric use of $\pi\iota\sigma\tau\iota$, "by faith," followed by an example in which Abraham acted by faith, and both celebrate the power of God to overcome death (vv 12, 19). When vv 13–16 are removed, the unity of form and content becomes evident (Michel, 390–91; Buchanan, 195; cf. Moxnes, "God and His Promise," 178–80, 185–86). Why, then, did the writer introduce his interpretation of the tradition precisely where he did, with v 13? Although no certain answer can be given, the arrangement of the catalogue appears to be rhetorical. The writer placed at the center of the paragraph his most important affirmations, in order to emphasize the eschatological perspective from which the entire unit (vv 8–22) is to be understood (cf. Swetnam, *Jesus and Isaac*, 91–92, who recognizes the problem but offers a different solution, based on the formulation of v 19).

The reference in v 12 to the eventual fulfillment of the promise to Abraham of an innumerable posterity presupposes an advanced point in time, far beyond the life-span of the patriarch or his immediate family line. This point is acknowledged in the reflective comment of v 13 *a*: "all these people died, not having received the fulfillment of the promises." The reference to the reception of τὰς ἐπαγγελίας, "the promises," keeps before the audience the terminology of promise, which plays so significant a role in this section (vv 9 [twice], 13, 17, 33, 39; cf. 4:1; 6:12, 17; 7:6; 8:6; 9:15; 10:23, 36). The promises in view were those concerning possession of the land, the foundation of a great nation, and the blessing of the people of the earth through Abraham and his descendants (Gen 12:2–3, 7). The tension between the reception of the promises and their realization was unresolved throughout the course of their lives. Yet these early exemplars of faith did not allow even the event of death to call into question the validity of the promises. This point is stressed for the Christian community in the comment κατὰ πίστιν ἀπέθανον οὗτοι πάντες, "all these persons died in accordance with the principle of faith." The phrase κατὰ πίστιν, which is emphatic by virtue of its position at the beginning of the sentence, signifies that their lives were regulated by faith. They were firmly persuaded that God would fulfill the promises he had made to them (cf. F. F. Bruce, 303–4).

The fact that the individuals included in the expression οὗτοι πάντες, "all these persons," are unspecified has encouraged some interpreters to refer the designation to all of the persons mentioned up to this point, with the exception of Enoch in v 5, who is explicitly excluded from the experience of death (e.g., Windisch, 101; Mercado, "Language of Sojourning," 62–63). The detail of v 13*b*, however, that these individuals confessed that they were "strangers and sojourners in the land" and the development of this thought in vv 14–16 show that this interpretation is untenable. The reference must be to those who engaged in pilgrimage in response to the divine mandate, namely, Abraham and Sarah, and with them Isaac and Jacob (vv 8–9, 11; so Westcott, 394; Moffatt, 173; Spicq, 2:350; Michel, 397). Although they were promised "a place" they were to receive as an inheritance (v 8), they remained resident aliens in "the promised land" throughout their lives (v 9).

The deferment of the fulfillment did not obscure the objective character of the promise, which faith invested with a substantial reality (cf. v 1*a*). In advancing this thought, the writer associates faith with the concept of sight: ἀλλὰ πόρρωθεν αὐτὰς ἰδόντες καὶ ἀσπασάμενοι, "but only *seeing* them and saluting them from a distance." Regulated by the principle of faith, the patriarchs were able to "see" as certain to happen events that were "as yet unseen" (vv 1*b*, 7: cf. vv 26, 27). Faith conferred "*fore*-sight" (so Williamson, *Philo*, 363–66). The nuance in πόρρωθεν, "from a distance," accordingly, is temporal rather than spatial, and the perspective is eschatological (cf. Mercado, "Language of Sojourning," 168). The correctness of this understanding is confirmed by what the writer says about faith in relationship to hope and the fulfillment of the promises throughout this section.

The metaphorical expression πόρρωθεν . . . ἀσπασάμενοι, "saluting from a distance," has classical analogies (e.g., Euripides, *Ion* 585–87; Plato, *Charmenides* 153B; cf. Windisch, *TDNT* 1:497; LSJ 258), where usually it is a person, or one's homeland or native city, which is saluted from afar. Philo at one point comments on the plight of slaves who were sold into a foreign country and as a result were unable to "dream again of saluting the soil of their native land" (*On the Special Laws* 4.17, cited by Spicq, 1:84). The presence of the term πατρίς, "homeland," in v 14 suggests that the writer was thinking of the metaphorical salute given by the returning traveler to his homeland when he penned the phrase in v 13*b*. In point of fact, however, the object of the salute is the fulfillment of the promises, which was yet deferred in time.

The phrase καὶ ὁμολογήσαντες ὅτι ξένοι καὶ παρεπίδημοί εἰσιν ἐπὶ τῆς γῆς, "and confessing that they were strangers and sojourners in the land," stands in opposition to the previous clause and describes an action concomitant with the saluting of the fulfilled promises from a distance in time. The participle ὁμολογήσαντες should be understood as a technical term signifying a public profession of faith (so Michel, 398; Swetnam, *Jesus and Isaac*, 91). It serves to align the patriarch's response of faith with that of the members of the Christian community, who were being urged to hold fast their confession (see *Comment* on 4:14; 10:23). The content of the confession ("strangers and sojourners in the land") shows that the perspective expressed in v 10 was characteristic not only of Abraham but of the other patriarchs as well.

The formulation ξένοι καὶ παρεπίδημοι, "strangers and sojourners," is a hendiadys, the expression of an idea by two nouns joined by the conjunction "and." It is equivalent to "sojourning strangers." The source of the expression is almost certainly Gen 23:4 LXX, where Abraham described himself as a temporary resident in the district of Kiriath Arba, without native or civil rights: πάροικος καὶ παρεπίδημος μεθ᾽ ὑμῶν, "I am an alien and sojourner among you." That description, which refers strictly to civic status, was subsequently generalized and applied to specifically religious alienation from God: πάροικος ἐγώ εἰμι ἐν τῇ γῇ καὶ παρεπίδημος καθὼς πάντες οἱ πατέρες μου, "I am an alien in the land and a sojourner, as were all my fathers" (Ps 38:13 LXX, Codex B [MT 39:12]; *v.l.* Codex A, πάροικος ἐγώ εἰμι παρὰ σοί, "I am an alien with you and a sojourner, as were all my fathers"). The confession in v 13*c* reflects elements from both of these quotations. It has been cast into the plural to make its reference inclusive of all of the patriarchs who have been named (v 9).

The substitution of ξένος, "stranger," for πάροικος, "alien," is little more than a stylistic variation sanctioned in the tradition, where Abraham is described as "a stranger" (e.g., *T. Levi* 6:9; "and they persecuted Abraham our father when he was a stranger [ξένον ὄντα]). The correlative word παρεπίδημος, "sojourner," was widely used in the papyri to indicate a person who settled in a district only temporarily (as in Gen 23:4 LXX; cf. 1 Pet 1:1–2) (MM 493). The reference to the patriarchs' status ἐπὶ τῆς γῆς, "in the land," harks back to v 9, where they were described as nomadic tent-dwellers. The unwarranted assumption that the reference is to alien status "upon the earth" (see above, *Note* w) has encouraged interpreters to find in v 13 an expression of Platonic dualism, affirmed in the spatial contrast between "the earth down here" and "the heavenly homeland above" (so, for example, Mercado, "Language of Sojourning," 145–47, with a recognition of significant differences in emphasis between Philo and Hebrews in this regard, 147–56; cf. Braun, "Der himmlische Vaterland," 319–27; Thompson, *Beginnings of Christian Philosophy*, 73–76). It is imperative to take into account the immediate context, which speaks of the alien status of the patriarchs in "the promised land," which was to them no more than "a foreign country" (v 9). Their citizenship was in the city of God, which was for them, as for Christians, a reality as yet unseen (cf. v 1). There is no evidence of Platonism in v 13.

14   The implications of the stance of faith assumed by the patriarchs, according to v 13, are drawn sharply for the congregation in vv 14–16. The present tense
of ἐμφανίζουσιν, "they show plainly," in v 14 serves to bring the confession of
v 13c into the current experience of the house church. It *shows* Christians *plainly*
what the habitual stance of their lives had become. The fact that the patriarchs
regarded themselves as "strangers and sojourners in the land" made explicit ὅτι
πατρίδα ἐπιζητοῦσιν, "that they are expecting intently a homeland." The metaphorical representation of the promised inheritance as a πατρίς, "homeland," is
governed by the confession in v 13c. The "homeland" is, of course, identical with
"the city which has foundations" of v 10 and "the better country, that is, a heavenly one" of v 16. This is the only case in the Bible where πατρίς has a religious
meaning. A close parallel in expression occurs in Philo's treatise *On Agriculture*
(65), where he contrasts "the heavenly homeland" (πατρίδα μὲν οὐράνον) with
earth as "a foreign country" (ξένην δὲ γῆν). There is a profound difference in
thought, however, between Philo and Hebrews. According to Philo, heaven is the
homeland of the pre-existent soul of the wise man, who experiences alienation
on earth (cf. *On the Confusion of Tongues* 77). For that reason also he disparages
material possessions. The conception of the pre-existence of the soul and the
ethical dualism of Philo are without parallel in Hebrews. The writer describes
the heavenly city of God as the homeland of the exemplars of faith because God
conferred upon them citizenship in this city when he called them (cf. Williamson,
Philo, 268–76, 326–28).

The thought of migration is appropriate to v 8, but it has no place in v 14.
Linguistically, the verb ἐπιζητοῦν does not denote "to try to reach (by migration)"
but "to desire," "to wish" (i.e., "to believe"), "to long for," "to expect intently" (cf.
BAGD 292). It corresponds in thought to ἐκδέχεσθαι, "to wait for," "to look forward to," in v 10 and to ὀρέγεσθαι, "to long for," in v 16, both of which express
the fervent expectation of the appearance of the city of God. Accordingly, v 14
does not speak of Abraham and his family line traveling toward the "homeland"
prepared in heaven, but as waiting for it with keen anticipation. The analogous
thought is expressed in v 16, where the patriarchs are portrayed as "longing for
the heavenly city which God has prepared for them."

The city of God does not represent a goal for migration toward heaven (as
urged by Westcott, 364; Käsemann, *Das wandernde Gottesvolk*, 16–19, 27–32, and
often; Mercado, "Language of Sojourning," 156–59; Johnsson, *JBL* 97 [1978] 245;
among others), for in that case the writer would have asserted that with their
death their migration was completed and the goal was attained. This understanding is excluded by the formulation of vv 13 and 39. The city is rather a reality that
is to appear concurrently with the consummation of redemption (cf. 13:14, where
ἐπιζητοῦν is used again). The patriarchs expressed their faith by being persistent
in their expectation, even though they died before the city had appeared (with
Hofius, *Katapausis*, 147–48).

15–16   The deduction in v 15 is based on Gen 12:1, the call of Abraham to
depart from his homeland. His thoughts, and those of his son and grandson after him, were oriented not toward Ur or even Haran but toward God (cf. Michel,
TDNT 4:583). They could have sought for roots in the great city that had been
their ancestral home. Their unsettled existence in Canaan offered them abundant "opportunity for returning." If they had not regulated their lives in

accordance with faith, the experience of alienation in the promised land would have provided an incentive for turning back. That they showed no inclination to do so is indicative of the orientation of faith toward the promise.

Resuming the thought of vv 10 and 14, in v 16 the writer describes the attitude of the patriarchs with the verb ὀρέγεσθαι, "to aspire to," "to long for." They were molded by a clear and concentrated will that took into account the objective reality of the promise. Their response to the divine promise dictated that the direction of their longing must be the better, heavenly homeland. Their attitude was informed not by reason nor experience but by faith. In the same obedience of faith that Abraham exemplified when he left Ur (v 8), they oriented their lives to the city that is to come, which is qualitatively superior to every other place. An eschatological perspective thus became pervasive of their whole lives (cf. Heidland, *TDNT* 5:448).

That explains why God is not ashamed to be called "the God of Abraham, of Isaac, and of Jacob" (cf. Exod 3:6, 15, 16; and often) or "the God of the fathers" (cf. Exod 3:13, 15, 16; and often). These designations of God were familiar to the audience from Scripture and from the prayers of the synagogue liturgy. The affirmation that God οὐχ ἐπαισχύνεται, "is not ashamed," of them is the appropriate response to the confessional stance of faith in the promise expressed by the patriarchs, according to v 13c. The expression, like ὁμολογήσαντες, "confessing" (v 13c), is technical for public acknowledgment (e.g., Mark 8:38; Luke 9:26; Rom 1:16; 2 Tim 1:8, 12, 16; Heb 2:11; cf. Michel, "Zum Sprachgebrauch von ἐπαισχύνεται in Rom 1,16," in *Glaube und Ethos*, FS G. Wehrung [Stuttgart: Kohlhammer, 1940] 36–53). To acknowledge that he is their God is to act on their behalf. Only one aspect of that action is delineated, the preparation of the heavenly city for them.

The concept of the preparation of a place of sanctuary is an important theme in apocalyptic literature (e.g., Rev 12:6; 21:2; *2 Apoc. Bar.* 4:3; cf. John 14:2). It was popularized through the Targum that was read during the synagogue services (e.g., *Tg.* 1 Chr 17:9: "And I will appoint for my people *a prepared place*, and they shall dwell in their places, and they shall not tremble any more"). The point of the statement in v 16b is that the fervent longing of the exemplars of faith was not misguided. It was fully justified by the objective reality of the city that God had already prepared as the reward of faith (v 6) and that would appear at the appointed time (cf. Grosheide, 268; de Young, *Jerusalem*, 137–38).

The perspective set forth for the Christian community in vv 15–16 was one that was easily lost. In the early second century in Rome, the anonymous writer of the *Shepherd of Hermas* found it necessary to shame the Christians of his day, who no longer made the city of God the object of their longing: "You know that you, who are servants of God, are dwellers in a foreign land; for your City is far from this city [i.e., Rome]. If then you recognize your City, in which you shall dwell, why do you prepare here fields and expensive displays and buildings and dwellings, which are superfluous? The person who prepares these things for this city does not intend to return to his own City" (Herm., *Sim.* 1.1; cf. 1.6).

The attitude of expectant faith commended by the writer of Hebrews is appreciated in the depiction of Christians as those engaged in pilgrimage in the *Epistle of Diognetus*, an apology for Christianity written not long after the *Shepherd of Hermas* had appeared: "[Christians] dwell in their own countries, but only as sojourners; they bear their share of all responsibilities as citizens, and they endure all hardships as strangers. Every foreign country is a homeland to them, and every homeland is foreign. . . . Their existence is on earth, but their citizenship is in heaven" (*Diogn.* 5.5–9; cf. 5.1–9). It was precisely this perspective that the writer of Hebrews was concerned to cultivate among his apathetic friends in Rome in vv 13–16, which are programmatic for Christian faith in every generation.

17–19 The final episode in the sequence concerning Abraham to which the writer directs the attention of the house church was the patriarch's readiness to comply with the terrifying command to offer his son Isaac to God in sacrifice (Gen 22:1–18). When Abraham obeyed God's mandate to leave Ur, he simply gave up his past. But when he was summoned to Mount Moriah to deliver his own son to God, he was asked to surrender his future as well. The fulfillment of the promise of an innumerable posterity was tied securely to the life of Isaac. The demand for the life of Isaac was a fierce challenge to the faith of Abraham, for it threatened the integrity of the promise. It also seemed to contradict both the character of God and the depth of human affection. Abraham accepted what he could not understand on the basis of his own rich experience with God. He appears to have understood intuitively that the obedience of faith called for an allegiance to God that extended beyond even the most intimate of family ties (cf. Spicq, 2:353, who comments on the cruel nature of the conflict between apparently irreconcilable demands of conscience).

This dramatic trial of faith was accorded a central place in the Jewish tradition. On the basis of Gen 22:9, which states that Abraham "bound" (ויעקד) Isaac, this episode was designated as the *Aqedah*, that is to say, the *Binding* (of Isaac). In postbiblical Judaism the *Aqedah* became the subject of an extraordinary homiletical development that went far beyond the detail of Gen 22. The incident was regarded as programmatic for the true character of acceptable sacrifice and as efficacious in its redemptive significance (cf. Lerch, *Isaaks Opferung*, 8–20; le Déaut, "Abraham," 131–212; Daly, *CBQ* 39 [1977] 47–63; Vermès, "Redemption and Genesis XXII," 193–227; Davies and Chilton, *CBQ* 40 [1978] 514–46). A moving prayer attributed to Abraham in very old Palestinian tradition may be cited as typical of this development: "Now I pray for mercy before you, O Lord God, that when the children of Isaac come to a time of distress, you may remember in their behalf the Binding [*Aqedah*] of Isaac their father, and loose and forgive their sins and deliver them from all distress" (*Pal. Tg.* Gen 22:14).

The impact of Gen 22 upon the tradition can be estimated from the prominence of the treatment of the *Aqedah* throughout Jewish literature (e.g., *Jub.* 17:15–18:19; Philo, *On Abraham* 167–297, especially 167–77 where the incident is treated in its historical dimension; 4 Macc 7:11–14; 13:12; 16:18–20; Jos., *Ant.* 1.222–36; Ps.-Philo, *Bib. Ant.* 18.5; 23.8; 32.1–4; 40.2–3). Abraham's action was constantly celebrated in the exemplary tradition of Judaism as a model of faithfulness and obedience to God (e.g., Sir 44:20; Jdt 8:25–26; 1 Macc 2:52; 4 Macc 16:20; cf. Jas 2:21–24; *1 Clem.* 10:7). The clearest and most complete reference to the *Aqedah* in the NT is found in vv 17–19 (cf. Daly, *CBQ* 39 [1977] 63–74; Swetnam, *Jesus and Isaac*, 189), where the writer presents Abraham as an exemplar of those who express faith in God in the face of death. Although the source of the example is Gen 22:1–18 LXX, details in the presentation appear to justify the assumption that the writer has been influenced by the rich Jewish *Aqedah* tradition (so Swetnam, *Jesus and Isaac*, 83–84).

Among the exemplars of faith, Abraham is the only one who is described as having been tested (πειραζόμενος) by God. This a common motif in the *Aqedah* tradition (e.g., Sir 44:20: "when he was tested [by God], he was found faithful"; 1 Macc 2:52: "was not Abraham found faithful when tested [by God]?"). Its source is the detail of the biblical account (Gen 22:1 LXX: "Sometime later God tested [ἐπείραζεν] Abraham with these words"). The trial to which Abraham's faith was subjected was the command to take Isaac and go to the region of Moriah, and there sacrifice him as a burnt offering on a mountain designated by God (Gen 22:2). The account of Abraham's compliance with this incomprehensible mandate, which threatened his faith as well as the promise, was well known and is simply presupposed in the statement of v 17a: πίστει προσενήνοχεν Ἀβραὰμ τὸν Ἰσαὰκ πειραζόμενος, "by faith Abraham, when he was tested [by God], offered in sacrifice Isaac."

The nuance of προσφέρειν, "to offer," which is used twice in v 17, is sacrificial. The verb has been used with a precise concern for tenses in each of the complementary clauses of v 17, which are arranged on the model of OT poetic sense-parallelism. In v 17a the sacrifice is considered from the perspective of Abraham's intention to comply with the solemn command and its effect; the perfect tense (προσενήνοχεν, "offered") views the sacrifice as an accomplished and perfectly accepted event (so also Philo, *On Abraham* 177: Abraham's sacrifice was complete because of his intention; cf. Ps. Philo, *Bib. Ant.* 32.4, where the perfect tense is used). In the complementary clause, v 17b, however, the sacrifice is considered in terms of its execution; the conative imperfect tense (προσέφερεν, "tried to offer") indicates that the sacrifice was not actually made but was interrupted by the intervention of God (cf. Michel, 401–2; Spicq, 2:253; Daly, *CBQ* 39 [1977] 67; Swetnam, *Jesus and Isaac*, 122).

The larger implications of Abraham's attempt to sacrifice his own son are drawn in vv 17b–18, where the episode is related to the significant theme of the reception of the promises. The reference to Abraham as ὁ τὰς ἐπαγγελίας ἀναδεξάμενος, "he who had accepted responsibility for the promises," recalls 7:6, where the descriptive phrase τὸν ἔχοντα τὰς ἐπαγγελίας, "the one possessing the promises," is sufficient to identify the subject as Abraham. The assumption of the responsibility to be the human instrument for the fulfillment of the promises naturally entailed an awareness of the indispensability of Isaac, the one person upon whom the future realization of the promise now depended. This fact is stressed when the writer designates Isaac as τὸν μονογενῆ, Abraham's "only son." The detail is rooted in Gen 22:2 ("Take your son, *your only son* Isaac"). The expression of v 17b, however, was not contributed by the LXX, which refers to Isaac as the "beloved son" (ἀγαπητός) rather than Abraham's only son. It appears to have been borrowed from the *Aqedah* tradition, which emphasized the motif of the "only son" (cf. Jos., *Ant.* 1.222; Gen 22:2 Aq. for μονογενῆς; for the motif, cf. *Gen. Rab.* 22:4; *Lev. Rab.* 23:4; *Pesiq. Rab Kah.* 23). The concentration of the promise in Isaac is emphasized with the quotation of the divine promise to Abraham (Gen 21:12 LXX) in v 18: "It is *through Isaac* that you will have descendants," or possibly, "It is *because of Isaac* that you will have descendants") (see *Note* nn above; cf. Rom 9:7, 10; Gal 4:28). The quotation indicates the heightened tension between the command and the promise, which was of profound theological significance not only to Abraham but ultimately to all of those who were involved in the promises made to him (cf. Swetnam, *Jesus and Isaac*, 88–89, 91–93).

It may actually have been the promise in Gen 21:12 that motivated Abraham to offer his son as a gift to God. Abraham believed against all natural probability that God would be able to accomplish his promise of descendants through Isaac, despite the seemingly contradictory command to sacrifice his life as a burnt offering. This seems to be the connection between the biblical quotation and the deduction that follows immediately in v 19a: λογισάμενος ὅτι καὶ ἐκ νεκρῶν ἐγείρειν δυνατὸς ὁ θεός, "he considered that God was able to raise up even from the dead" (so Windisch, 103; Michel, 402; Spicq, 2:352; Swetnam, *Jesus and Isaac*, 88, n. 15; 92–93; 94, n. 41; 100). Abraham was so certain that God would perform what he had promised that by faith he attempted to offer Isaac, in the conviction that God could revive the dead. The word λογισάμενος denotes inward conviction, persuasion, and not simply a considered opinion (stressed by Lerch, *Isaaks Opferung*, 39; Teodorico, 196); the temporal force of the aorist tense is that Abraham's conclusion was made once and finally (Westcott, 366).

On the other hand, the thematic connection between vv 11–12 and vv 17–19 (see *Comment* on 11:13; cf. Swetnam, *Jesus and Isaac*, 100, n. 71, where the parallelism between these units is set out in a chart; Moxnes, "God and His Promises," 185–86) may indicate that in the writer's view Abraham was influenced by his own experience of being empowered to become a father to Isaac (vv 11–12). As a direct result of his experience of the power of God to overcome death with respect to his own body (v 12a), he considered that God was able to vanquish death in the case of his son (Teodorico, 196; cf. Swetnam, *Jesus and Isaac*, 89, who finds in 2 Macc 7:22–23 an antecedent to this line of reasoning: the mother of seven martyrs reasons from the power of God in producing life in the womb to the ability of God to restore life to the dead). In any event, Abraham placed his full confidence in the power of God, before which even death cannot erect any barrier. The ὅτι clause of v 19a is firmly embedded in its context, but the reference to God who is able to revive the dead is confessional in form and may have its source in a primitive Christian creedal formulation (so I. Havener, "The Credal Formulae of the New Testament," Inaugural Dissertation, Munich, 1976, 378–79).

The meaning of the final comment in v 19b is debated, and no consensus has been reached among interpreters. The translation of ὅθεν αὐτὸν καὶ ἐν παραβολῇ ἐκομίσατο as a causal clause ("because of this conviction also in a foreshadowing he did receive him back") reflects several important exegetical decisions that must ultimately be validated by the writer's practice elsewhere in the homily and by the excellent sense that this rendering brings to the context (see above, *Note* ss).

Elsewhere in Hebrews ὅθεν is an inferential conjunction, with reference to what immediately precedes (cf. 2:17; 3:1; 7:25; 8:3; 9:18). On this understanding, the writer affirmed in v 19b that the direct result of Abraham's firm conviction concerning God's ability to raise the dead was that he received back Isaac ἐν παραβολῇ, "in a foreshadowing." The restoring of Isaac by the unanticipated reprieve at the last moment was a specific instance of God's power to raise up from the dead. The sacrifice is seen as a gift that God returns, guaranteeing the reception of what was promised according to Gen 21:12 (cited in v 18).

What precisely is meant, however, by the problematic expression ἐν παραβολῇ, "in a foreshadowing"? The interpretation of this expression must take into account both the reference to the God who raises the dead in the immediate context (v 19a) and the writer's previous use of the term παραβολή (9:9). In 9:8–9 he argued that the front compartment of the tabernacle provides a spatial metaphor for the time when the former covenant, with its daily and annual cultic ritual, was in force. As such, it was a παραβολή, "a foreshadowing," of the present age (see above, *Note* tt). In that context, παραβολή connotes a past institution that foreshadows in some way a reality that is yet to come. This would appear to be appropriate for the meaning of ἐν παραβολῇ in v 19*b*: when Abraham received Isaac from the altar of sacrifice there was a foreshadowing of the future resurrection from the dead (cf. Swetnam, *Jesus and Isaac,* 119–21).

This understanding appreciates the causal relationship between the inference drawn in v 19*b* and the reference to the resurrection in v 19*a* (cf. Windisch, 103; Moffatt, 177; Riggenbach, 365; Michel, 402–3). The expression ἐν παραβολῇ implies that the "foreshadowing" was veiled. It is not necessary to believe that Abraham recognized the connection between the receiving of Isaac from the altar and resurrection from the dead. But the Christian community *is* capable of recognizing the deeper import of the event.

That the reference is specifically to the violent death and resurrection of Jesus (as urged by BAGD 612; Sowers, *Hermeneutics,* 96; Swetnam, *Jesus and Isaac,* 121–23, 128; among others) finds no support in the immediate context. For the writer the sacrifice of Isaac is not a type of the sacrificial death of Christ (as it is already in the early second century; cf. *Barn.* 7.3). There is no evidence for this early period that the narrative of Gen 22 had been related to the cross and resurrection of Jesus (so also Lerch, *Isaaks Opferung,* 41–42; Moxnes, "God and His Promise," 187–88).

It is more natural to read v 19*b* in the light of the conceptual background shared by the writer and his audience through the Diaspora synagogues. The recitation of the first three of the Eighteen Benedictions was an integral part of the synagogue liturgy by the first century. In Jewish tradition the second of these prayers, which pronounces a blessing upon God "who makes the dead alive," was linked with the *Aqedah.* When Isaac was restored to Abraham, he exclaimed together with his father: "Blessed be God who raises the dead" (*Pirqe R. El.* 31 [16b], cited by Kuss, 175; cf. 4 Macc 7:19; 13:17; *Pal. Tg.* Lev 22:27; and for later traditions Spiegel, *Last Trial,* 28–37; for discussion of sources and their date, le Déaut, "Abraham," 205–6; Swetnam, *Jesus and Isaac,* 46, n. 187; 53, n. 231; 122–23, n. 208). In drawing a connection between the resurrection and the *Aqedah* in v 19, the writer of Hebrews is probably influenced by a Jewish tradition with which the members of the house church were also familiar (so Mercado, "Language of Sojourning," 150–51; cf. Rom 4:17).

Abraham offered his son to God because he took account of the power of God to make alive (v 19*a*). What was foreshadowed to Abraham when God returned his son to him (v 19*a*) was the great resurrection at the end of history (cf. Lerch, *Isaaks Opferung,* 39–43; Michel, 402–3; Moxnes, "God and His Promise," 187–88; as opposed to Spicq, 2:354–55, who draws upon early patristic interpretation to support a christological reference in v 19*b*). In presenting this prototypical example of faith in God who raises the dead to his brothers and sisters, the intention of the writer is to call them from apathy and despair to a fresh experience of faith in the power of God, which stands behind his solemn pledge to fulfill his unalterable word of promise to them. It is the faithfulness of God to his promises, more than the faith and obedience of Abraham, that is the primary thrust of the writer in vv 17–19 (cf. Lerch, 40–41; Moxnes, 186–87).

20 The story of Abraham is rounded off by tracing the family line from Abraham through Isaac and Jacob to the twelve patriarchs, represented by Joseph (vv 20–22; similarly, Acts 7:8). In a summary fashion the writer comments briefly on the faith of these later representative figures. Like Abraham, they possessed the visionary perspective of faith, which permitted them to see beyond the limit of their own lives to the future guaranteed by the objective reality of the promise. The reference to the actions of Isaac and Jacob in blessing their sons and grandsons when the prospect of death was imminent may be rooted in the hellenistic-Jewish testamentary tradition (for a helpful discussion of the literature, see Kalenkow, *JSJ* 6 [1975] 57–71). The conferring of a final blessing shows that even when dying they continued to look forward to the fulfillment of the promises. The same eschatological perspective is evident in the provision Joseph made for the disposal of his remains. The final three exemplars of faith from the patriarchal period illustrate concretely the truth set forth programmatically in v 13, that although they all died without having experienced the fulfillment of the promises, they "saw" their realization with the eyes of faith and saluted them from a distance.

In faith Isaac blessed Jacob and Esau (v 20). In Hebrews the act of blessing is intimately related to the theme of the promise (cf. 6:14; 12:17). The formulation of v 20 accentuates Isaac's unqualified adherence to whatever God had planned καὶ περὶ μελλόντων, "even with respect to the future." The force of καί, "even," is intensive; it functions to place the phrase περὶ μελλόντων in high relief. The absence of the article with μελλόντων, "future," indicates that Isaac's faith was not expressed in reference to the known future but in reference to a future "as yet unseen" (cf. v 1*b*; so Westcott, 370; Swetnam, *Jesus and Isaac*, 93–94). The association of Isaac with a concern for the future may be simply a deduction from Gen 27:1–40, which reports the episode concerning the blessing of the two sons. On the other hand, it may be a traditional motif, for it finds an interesting parallel in reference to the *Aqedah*: "Isaac, *with confident knowledge of the future* [μετὰ πεποιθήσεως γινώσκων τὸ μέλλον], was gladly led as a sacrifice" (*1 Clem.* 31:3). The future aspect of the blessing of Jacob is stressed in Gen 27:29, 37 and is clear in the blessing of Esau as well (Gen 27:39–40). When Isaac pronounced the blessing upon Jacob, the promises made to Abraham were activated with respect to the future, so that an emphasis upon the future in v 20 is fully warranted (so Michel, 404).

In the sequel to Gen 27:1–40, a second blessing was conferred upon Jacob, which expresses Isaac's concern for the realization of the promises given to Abraham concerning numerous descendants and possession of the land (Gen 28:1–4). Isaac's readiness to bestow upon Jacob "the blessing of Abraham" (Gen 28:4) was indicative of his faith. Isaac's faith consists in the sanctioning of an arrangement which, humanly speaking, posed a threat to the attainment of what had been promised because of the reversal of the normal order, with the younger son usurping the place of the elder (Gen 27:30–33) (Michel, 404: "It is an act of faith when Isaac blesses and prefers the younger son before the elder"; cf. Spicq, 2:355; Swetnam, *Jesus and Isaac*, 93–94).

21 The blessing of Ephraim and Manasseh, the two sons of Joseph, is reported in Gen 48:1–22. The detail that Jacob blessed his grandsons ἀποθνῄσκων, "while dying," is drawn from Gen 48:21 (cf. Gen 47:29; 48:1). It has been considered remarkable that the writer should select this example, rather than the subsequent account of the blessing of the twelve patriarchs, reported in Gen 49, which received such extensive elaboration in post-biblical Jewish tradition (see H. C. Kee, "Testaments of the Twelve Patriarchs [Second Century B.C.] New Translation and Introduction," in *The Old Testament Pseudepigrapha*, ed. J. H. Charlesworth [Garden City, NY: Doubleday, 1983] 1:775–828; cf. Spicq, 2:355: "It is astonishing that the blessing of the twelve patriarchs [Gen 49] should be omitted"; similarly, Michel, 404). The writer's primary interest, however, is in the response of faith in the promises on the part of Abraham, Isaac, and Jacob, and the incident reported in Gen 48 is highly informative in this regard. As in the case of the blessing of Jacob and Esau introduced in v 20, the normal order of genealogical descent was reversed in the blessing of Ephraim and Manasseh. Jacob's right hand rested in blessing upon the head of Ephraim, the younger son, while his left hand was placed on the head of Manasseh, the firstborn. When Joseph attempted to correct what he perceived as a serious mistake, Jacob resisted, in faith preferring Ephraim before Manasseh (Gen 48:12–20). Jacob's faith consisted in the conviction that God's designs were invincible and that the promises were being worked out under God's care (cf. Swetnam, *Jesus and Isaac*, 95).

The conferring of the blessing documents the orientation to the future that was characteristic of the faith of the patriarchs (cf. vv 10, 13, 16, 20, 22). The writer's interest in this dimension of faith is apparent in the quotation of Gen 47:31 LXX: προσεκύνησεν ἐπὶ τὸ ἄκρον τῆς ῥάβδου αὐτοῦ, "he bowed in worship, leaning on the top of his staff." The citation emphasizes Jacob's submission to God's will (Michel, 405). It also furnishes a transition to v 22, which speaks of Joseph's faith, for the allusion is not associated with the conferring of a blessing but with burial in the promised land. When Jacob recognized that he would soon die, he made Joseph promise that he would not bury his father in Egypt but in the cave Abraham had purchased from Ephron the Hittite in Canaan (Gen 47:28–31; cf. Gen 49:29–32; 50:4–13). Burial in Canaan was an expression of faith in the promise of possession of the land. Jacob's final act of worship, leaning upon the top of his staff, was characteristic for one who lived his life as a stranger and a sojourner (vv 9, 13; cf. Michel, 405: "The staff is for Hebrews the sign of pilgrimage").

The quotation reflects exactly the LXX of Gen 47:31, which differs from the MT in stating that Israel "worshiped as he leaned on the top of his staff" rather than Israel "bowed down at the head of his bed" (NIV marg). The variation in translation arose from the interpretation of the unpointed Hebrew text; the radicals מטה (*mth*) could be read *matteh*, "staff," or *mittâh*, "bed." Although the latter translation is supported by Bartina (*EE* 38 [1963] 243–47), it is clear that the writer read his Bible in Greek and carefully selected the quotation for its description of Jacob as a sojourner who, in the face of death, lays claim to the future through the exercise of faith in the realization of the promises of God (cf. Heller, *CV* 16 [1973] 260–63, whose helpful presentation is weakened when he invests the quotation with an unwarranted messianic interpretation of the staff on the basis of Num 24:17; Ps 110:2 [263]).

22 The faith of Jacob in requiring Joseph to exercise oversight of his burial in Canaan (Gen 47:28–31) undoubtedly influenced Joseph's determination that his remains would be transported from Egypt to Canaan as well. Although he had achieved great prominence in Egypt, Joseph's home was not in the land of the Nile. With the foresight that faith confers, he saw "events as yet unseen" (v 1*b*) as clearly as the events occurring at the time and responded to them with firm faith. In faith he recognized that the prospect of the departure of the Israelites from Egypt was assured because it was intrinsic to the realization of the promise of possession of the land (Gen 50:24–25). His temporal orientation to the future, which is the factor that links him to the other patriarchs, finds expression in complementary clauses:

περὶ τῆς ἐξόδου τῶν υἱῶν Ἰσραὴλ ἐμνημόνευσεν
"concerning the departure of the sons of Israel he made mention"
περὶ τῶν ὀστέων αὐτοῦ ἐνετείλατο
"concerning his bones he gave instruction"

The form of the expressions recalls v 20, where Isaac pronounced a blessing upon Jacob and Esau περὶ μελλόντων, "concerning the future." Joseph's concern for burial in the land of Canaan expressed a desire informed by faith to be associated with those who through faith became the heirs of the promises (cf. 6:12).

Jewish tradition tended to focus upon the fidelity of Joseph in the context of the trials he had endured (e.g., Wis 10:13–14; 1 Macc 2:53; 4 Macc 18:11; *1 Clem.* 4:9; cf. Ps 105:17–19). The instruction that he had given his brothers concerning the final disposal of his remains received far less attention (Sir 49:15: "And no man like Joseph has been born, and his bones are cared for"; *T. Jos.* 20:2: "But you should carry up my bones with you"). The writer of Hebrews singled out this example because it illustrates an act of faith in the face of death (cf. vv 12, 13, 17–19, 20, 21). He refused to recognize in death any threat to the fulfillment of the promise (cf. Michel, 405; Spicq, 2:356). When the Exodus did occur, the Israelites remembered Joseph's instruction and carried the coffin containing his mortal remains with them when they left Egypt (Exod 13:19). Joseph's bones were finally interred at Shechem, after the settlement of Canaan (Josh 24:32).

Explanation

See 11:32–40 below.

The Triumphs of Perseverance in Faith in the Mosaic Era (11: 23–31)

Bibliography

Barber, C. J. "Moses: A Study of Hebrews 11:23–29a." *GJ* 14 (1973) 14–28. **Bittner, W.** "Der Umgang mit Gott, dem Unsichtbaren (Hebr 11,27)." *TBei* 16 (1985) 1–4. **Bloch, R.** "Quelques aspects de la figure de Moïse dans les traditions rabbinique." *CSion* 2 (1955) 93–

167. **Botte, B.** "La vie de Moïse par Philon." *CSion* 2 (1955) 55–62. **Brooks, C. L.** "The Choice of Moses (Heb. 11:24)." *MQR* 3rd ser. 55 (1929) 463–72. **D'Angelo, M. R.** *Moses in the Letter to the Hebrews.* 17–64. **Descamps, A.** "Moïse dans les évangiles et la tradition apostolique." *CSion* 2 (1955) 171–87. **Feather, J.** "The Princess Who Rescued Moses: Who Was She? With a Note on Heb. XI.24–26." *ExpTim* 43 (1931–32) 423–25. **Hanson, A. T.** "Rahab the Harlot in Early Christian Theology." *JSNT* 1 (1978) 53–60. ———. "The Reproach of the Messiah in the Epistle to the Hebrews." *SE* 7 (1982) 231–40. **Harris, J. R.** "Two Remarkable Glosses in the Text of Hebrews." *ExpTim* 39 (1927–28) 550–53. **Hay, D. M.** "Moses through New Testament Spectacles." *Int* 44 (1990) 240–52. **Hruby, K.** "Moïse dans la liturgie synagogale." *CSion* 2 (1955) 317–43. **Jones, P. R.** "The Figure of Moses as a Heuristic Device for Understanding the Pastoral Intent of Hebrews." *RevExp* 76 (1979) 95–105. **Kilpatrick, G. D.** "The Text of the Epistles: The Contribution of Western Witnesses." In *Text-Wort-Glaube: Studien zu Überlieferung, Interpretation und Autorisierung biblischer Text.* FS K. Aland. Ed. M. Becht. Berlin: de Gruyter, 1980. 46–68. **Moran, W. L.** "The Repose of Rahab's Israelite Guests." In *Studi sull' Oriente e la Bibbia.* FS P. G. Rinaldi. Ed. G. Buccellat. Genova: Studio e Vita, 1967. 273–84. **Riesenfeld, H.** "The Meaning of the Verb ἀρνεῖσθαι." *ConNT* 11 (1947) 207–19. **Saito, T.** *Die Mosevorstellungen im Neuen Testament.* Bern/Frankfurt/Mainz: Lang, 1977. 103–8. **Schröger, F.** *Der Verfasser des Hebräerbriefes als Schriftausleger.* 204, 206, 222–25. **Vermès, G.** "La figure de Moïse au tournant des deux testaments." *CSion* 2 (1955) 63–92. **Whitaker, G. H.** "Hebrews XI.27." *ExpTim* 27 (1915–16) 186. **Wiseman, D. J.** "Rahab of Jericho." *TynBul* 14 (1964) 8–11.

Translation

[23] *By faith when Moses was born he was hidden*[a] *for three months*[b] *by his parents, because they saw that the child was uncommonly striking,*[c] *and they did not become afraid*[d] *of the king's edict.*[e] [24] *By faith Moses, when he had grown up,*[f] *disdained*[g] *to be called the son of Pharaoh's daughter,* [25] *having chosen*[h] *to endure hardship with the people of God rather than*[i] *to enjoy the temporary pleasure of sin.* [26] *He regarded*[j] *abuse incurred for the sake of the Christ*[k] *greater wealth than the treasures of Egypt, because he was looking ahead to*[l] *the reward.*[m] [27] *By faith he left Egypt, not fearing*[n] *the king's rage, for he kept the one who is invisible continually before his eyes,*[o] *as it were.*[p]

[28] *By faith he kept*[q] *the Passover and the spreading of the blood, so that the destroying angel*[r] *might not touch*[s] *their firstborn.*[t] [29] *By faith the people crossed the Red Sea as if on dry land; but when the Egyptians attempted to do so,*[u] *they were drowned.*[v] [30] *By faith the walls of Jericho fell, when they had been encircled for seven days.*[w] [31] *By faith Rahab the prostitute*[x] *did not perish with the unbelievers, because she had welcomed*[y] *the spies.*

Notes

[a] The verb ἐκρύβη is used as a constative aor, which sums up a period of time (A. T. Robertson, *Grammar*, 833).

[b] The adj τρίμηνον should be regarded as an accusative of duration (cf. Zerwick and Grosvenor, *Grammatical Analysis*, 682).

[c] The predicate adj ἀστεῖος can mean "beautiful" or "fine" but here must carry the overtones of "extraordinary" (cf. P. E. Hughes, 492, n. 75).

[d] The aor deponent ἐφοβήθησαν appears clearly to be ingressive in character.

[e] After v 23 certain witnesses, which are primarily Western, add the equivalent of a whole verse: "By faith Moses, when he had grown up, destroyed the Egyptian when he observed the humiliation of his brothers." The interpolation almost certainly originated in a marginal comment inspired by Acts 7:24 and/or Exod 2:11–12 (so Harris, *ExpTim* 39 [1927–28] 550–53; Metzger, *Textual Commentary*, 674). The

addition, which is found in D* 1827 it^d vg^{mss}, is accepted as original by Kilpatrick, "The Text of the Epistles," 65–66. He points out that v 24 begins with the same words as this passage, and that would invite omission. Moreover, the scarcity of evidence for the reading should not be surprising since there are so few Western witnesses to the text of Hebrews. He concludes that a paleographical mistake resulted in the omission of a substantial piece of text. It is more probable, however, that a corrector felt that the incident reported in Exod 2:11 preceded or explained Moses' rejection of his royal title in v 24 (so D'Angelo, *Moses*, 43).

^{f} The term μέγας is used figuratively to express measure of age (BAGD 497). The sense is expressed in the notion of reaching maturity.

^{g} It is customary to translate ἠρνήσατο in its classical sense: Moses "*refused* to be called" (RSV, NEB, JB, TEV, NIV). The context, however, shows that the verb here has a subj gradation, as a personal decision between two choices is in question (so Riesenfeld, *ConNT* 11 [1947] 209–10, 218, who proceeds from a passage in Plato, *Republic* 437B, which has ἀρνεῖσθαι followed by an inf [as in Heb 11:24] with the somewhat more subj sense of "despising," "disdaining").

^{h} The aor middle ἑλόμενος is a true middle, placing emphasis on Moses' decision.

^{i} The μᾶλλον . . . ἤ construction implies forthright contradiction; its sense may really be "not . . . but" (cf. H. Kruse, "Dialektische Negation als semitisches Idiom," *VT* 4 [1954] 385–400; Zerwick, *Biblical Greek* §445).

^{j} The aor tense in ἡγησάμενος seems to be culminative.

^{k} The expression τὸν ὀνειδισμὸν τοῦ Χριστοῦ is open to more than one interpretation. The translation considers the abuse as that attached to the cause of Christ (BAGD 674). Alternatively, it may signify the abuse that Christ himself suffered (so NEB: "the stigma that rests on God's Anointed"; cf. Zerwick and Grosvenor, *Grammatical Analysis*, 682). The basis for the choice expressed in the translation is set forth in the *Comment* below.

^{l} The verb ἀπέβλεπεν implies that Moses "looked away" *from* the present experience of suffering *to* the reward. The impf tense emphasizes the continuous disposition displayed in the past time.

^{m} For a temporal interpretation of the noun τὴν μισθαποδοσίαν, see the paraphrase in NEB: "for his eyes were fixed on *the coming day of recompense.*"

^{n} When the verb precedes the aor ptcp, the ptcp nearly always expresses coincident action (Moulton, *Grammar*, 1:131). This is the case here.

^{o} It is customary to treat the ptcp with ἐκαρτέρησεν as circumstantial (e.g., A. T. Robertson, *Grammar*, 1121; Grundmann, *TDNT* 3:617; D'Angelo, *Moses*, 17, 27, 30–33, 58–59). The stress then falls on the fact that Moses "persevered" or "was steadfast," while the ptcp is descriptive of the circumstance: "as if he saw the one who is invisible" (cf. RSV, NEB, JB, NASB, NIV). Unfortunately, the idiom ὁρῶν ἐκαρτέρησεν has been missed in these translations. Hellenistic usage demonstrates that "the participle with καρτερεῖν does not denote an accompanying circumstance, but rather the quality in which someone endures or is steadfast" (BAGD 405 with examples from Diodorus Siculus, Arrian, and Pseudo-Dicaerrchus). The key thought is contributed by the ptcp, while the function of καρτερεῖν is to stress the continuation of the quality expressed by the ptcp.

^{p} The particle ὡς serves to soften the statement (cf. Turner, *Grammar*, 3:320). Contrast the NIV: "he persevered because he saw him who is invisible" (which presupposes ὡς ὁρῶν in the sense "as in fact seeing").

^{q} The pf tense of the verb πεποίηκεν is appropriate in reference to a permanent institution. It indicates the inauguration of a rite still observed (BDF §342[4]). There are examples from the papyri of the use of this verb with the nuance "celebrate" (MM 523).

^{r} The expression ὁ ὀλοθρεύων could equally be translated "the Destroyer" (cf. BAGD 564).

^{s} The force of the aor θίγῃ is ingressive: "would not begin to touch."

^{t} The neuter pl τὰ πρωτότοκα is appropriate, signifying the firstborn of persons and animals. It is impossible to duplicate in translation the alliteration achieved by five words beginning with the letter π (πίστει, πεποίηκεν, πάσχα, πρόσχυσιν, πρωτότοκα) (cf. Turner, *Grammar*, 4:107).

^{u} The phrase πεῖραν λαβόντες τινός is an idiom meaning "to attempt something," "to have experience of something." Although there are few examples from the papyri, its use is fully illustrated from late Gk. writers (cf. Field, *Notes*, 232–33; MM 501).

^{v} The prep in the compound verb κατεπόθησαν is intensive: "they were totally engulfed," "overwhelmed" (P. E. Hughes, 501, n. 83).

^{w} The prep ἐπί with the accusative is equivalent to the simple accusative of duration (Zerwick, *Biblical Greek* §80).

ˣ The textual variant in אּ syʰ Cl R (*v.l.* [*1 Clem.* 12]), Ῥαάβ ἡ ἐπιλεγομένη πόρνη ("Rahab, the so-called prostitute"), indicates an acquaintance with a Jewish tradition attested in Josephus (*Ant.* 5.7–8) that Rahab was not a prostitute but a respectable innkeeper (cf. *Tg. Ps.-J.* to Josh 2:1). For a defense of the translation "innkeeper" (with an admission of much hesitation), see G. Verkuyl, "The Berkeley Version of the New Testament," *BT* 2 (1951) 84–85. For background on the innkeeper of Old Babylonian times, see Wiseman, *TynBul* 14 [1964] 8–11.

ʸ The aor ptcp δεξαμένη introduces a causal clause. The expression δεξαμένη . . . μετ᾽ εἰρήνης could be translated "because she received . . . peaceably" (BAGD 227).

Form/Structure/Setting

See 11:1–40 above.

Comment

23 The third division of this catalogue of exemplary witnesses is devoted to Moses and to certain events he set in motion (vv 23–31). An analysis of form and of the OT texts that stand behind the recital show that vv 23–27 constitute one complete unit, while vv 28–31 belong to another formal unit (cf. D'Angelo, *Moses*, 17–18, 27–28, 54). The initial unit constitutes a brief chronological narrative, detailing moments in the early career of Moses. D'Angelo has aptly described this unit as a very condensed "life of Moses" or "portrait of the prophet as a young man" (17). The first phase of the life of Moses is reviewed in three parallel statements in vv 23–27, each of which (a) is introduced by the anaphoric use of πίστει, "by faith," (b) directs attention to an event in the life of Moses in which active faith was demonstrated, and (c) is rounded off with an explanatory comment upon the role of faith in the event. The vocabulary and development reflect the influence of hellenistic Jewish moral teaching upon the characterization first of Moses' parents, and then of Moses himself; the emphasis in these verses is placed on the element of moral choice (cf. D'Angelo, 27–28).

The courageous action of Moses' parents in preserving alive their newly born child is celebrated in v 23. In flagrant disobedience of the royal edict of the pharaoh that all male babies were to be thrown into the Nile, they hid their child for three months (Exod 1:15–22; 2:1–2). The text behind the account in v 23 is Exod 2:2 LXX: "and seeing that he was uncommonly striking [ἀστεῖον], they hid him for three months." This version differs from the MT in assigning responsibility for the decision to defy the royal edict to both parents, rather than to Moses' mother alone. The writer follows the LXX, as did other hellenistic-Jewish authors (Philo, *Moses* 1.7 ["his father and mother"], 9, 10 ["his parents"]; Jos., *Ant.* 2.218; Ps.-Philo, *Bib. Ant.* 9.5). As an indication of the motivation of the parental action, the explanatory phrase διότι εἶδον ἀστεῖον τὸ παιδίον, "because they saw the child was uncommonly striking," is surprising. Parental pride appears to be remote from the writer's characterization of faith (vv 1, 6). The modality of faith is nevertheless respected, for the sovereign design and promises of God are combined perfectly with a pattern of human behavior that looks to the future, despite adverse circumstances and extreme risk (cf. F. F. Bruce, 217–18).

The only term reproduced from Exod 2:2 LXX is the distinctive word ἀστεῖον, which describes the striking attractiveness of the infant. In calling attention to this detail, the writer reflects a common tradition of interpretation in hellenistic

Judaism. Philo, for example, also saw a causal connection between the child's extraordinary appearance and the parental decision to preserve his life (*Moses* 1.2; cf. 1.9: the child possessed "a more beautiful appearance [ἀστειοτέραν] than ordinary"; on these, and related texts, see Williamson, *Philo*, 469–79). Josephus also comments on the extraordinary appearance of the baby (*Ant.* 2.230–31) and finds in Moses' beauty a visible sign of God's favor, which explains why his parents did not fear the royal edict (*Ant.* 2.225). In the version of the tradition preserved in Stephen's speech, a causal connection is not drawn between Moses' appearance and the three-month period in which he remained in his parents' home, but it is stated that he was ἀστεῖος τῷ θεῷ, "beautiful in the sight of God," or "well-pleasing to God" (Acts 7:20).

The evidence indicates a well-established tradition of interpretation that found in the word ἀστεῖος an indication that the infant possessed a visible sign of God's elective favor. According to v 23, Moses' parents found in the extraordinary appearance of their son a basis for faith in the as yet unseen purposes of God; his unusual attractiveness was to them a visible sign that he enjoyed God's favor and protection. Their readiness to risk their own lives to preserve the life of their son was the response of faith to a sense of vocation (cf. D'Angelo, *Moses*, 38–41).

A second explanation for the response of faith by Moses' parents is also given: καὶ οὐκ ἐφοβήθησαν τὸ διάταγμα τοῦ βασιλέως, "and they did not become afraid of the king's edict." They chose to fear God rather than the might of the pharaoh (cf. Ps.-Philo, *Bib. Ant.* 9.5: Moses' father Amram chose to respect the commandment of God rather than the decree of the king). Their confidence in God's power to accomplish his sovereign purposes more than outweighed their fear of reprisals because they had defied the royal decree. Of the two motivations for concealing the child for a three-month period, parental pride and absence of fear, only parental pride is specified in Exod 2:2. The second explanation is a deduction from the text, which finds considerable support in the action of the Hebrew midwives, whose fearless response to the cruel mandate of the pharaoh is reported in Exod 1:17–21. The writer's insistence on the fearlessness of the parents introduces a motif that is stressed in the portrait of Moses as well (see *Comment* on v 27 below) and is indicative of his own interest in this example of faith in action. He found in the conduct of Moses' parents a paradigm for the capacity of faith to overcome fear, and this was of immediate pastoral significance to the community he addressed (correctly perceived by P. R. Jones, *RevExp* 76 [1979] 98–99).

24–26 Moses himself is presented as an exemplar of faith for an apathetic and discouraged congregation in vv 24–27. The first episode directs attention to his decisive renunciation of privilege and power in the determination to identify himself with his own people who were enslaved in Egypt. The event of faith celebrated in vv 24–26 is not recorded directly in Scripture (cf. Exod 2:11–15) but reflects a complex exegetical tradition that can be reconstructed through hellenistic-Jewish sources roughly contemporary with Hebrews (see D'Angelo, *Moses*, 36, 42–53).

The declaration that Moses acted in faith μέγας γενόμενος, "when he had grown up," constitutes an allusion to Exod 2:11 LXX, where these words occur. What is described there, however, is not a formal renunciation of Moses' privileged status as the son of the pharaoh's daughter, but his experience with an Egyptian who was striking a Hebrew. This connection is made explicitly in the marginal gloss now found in certain Western witnesses to the text of Hebrews (discussed above, *Note* e; cf. Acts 7:23–24). Exod 2:11 states that "when Moses grew up he went out to his brothers, the sons of Israel." The expression "he went out to his brothers" was understood traditionally to mean that Moses chose to dissociate himself from the Egyptian court (e.g., Ezekiel the Tragedian, cited by Eusebuis, *Preparation for the Gospel* 9.28: "When I reached full maturity I went out of the royal house, for anger and the cunning projects of the king drove me to works"; cf. Philo, *Moses* 1.33, 40: the forced labor that the pharaoh exacted from the Hebrew slaves angered Moses and alienated him from his prior allegiance to his adoptive parents). This appears to be the tradition behind the formulation of vv 24–26, which refers to Moses' moral choice of the experience of hardship with the Hebrews rather than the enjoyment of the Egyptian court (following D'Angelo, *Moses*, 43–45).

The statement that Moses was called υἱὸς θυγατρὸς Φαραώ, "the son of Pharaoh's daughter," is a deduction from Exod 2:10 ("became her son"; cf. Philo, *Moses* 1.19, 32, 45). For Philo, this clearly signified not only formal adoption but that Moses had been designated the heir apparent (*Moses* 1.49–51; cf. Jos., *Ant.* 2.232; *Jub.* 47:9). This assumption may reflect the Roman practice of adoption, which conferred upon the adopted son the legal status of a natural son of the family; this would indeed have made Moses the pharaoh's heir. If this is the legal background presupposed in v 24, a moral choice was clearly forced upon Moses, for the Roman practice of adoption also abolished the status of the adopted son in his natural family. The stage would then be set for Moses' exemplary renunciation of power and status (so D'Angelo, *Moses*, 42–43, with reservations). It is clear from v 24 that Moses enjoyed every advantage privileged status could procure.

It has been argued that the formulation of v 24, ἠρνήσατο λέγεσθαι υἱὸς θυγατρὸς Φαραώ, "he disdained to be called the son of Pharaoh's daughter," denotes a *legal* renunciation (Feather, *ExpTim* 43 [1931–32] 424–25). It is preferable, however, to recognize in v 24 an interpretation of Exod 2:11–12. By his forceful intervention on behalf of a Hebrew slave, Moses confessed himself to be a Hebrew, and thus effectively denied that he was the "son of Pharaoh's daughter." To have acquiesced in that honorific designation inevitably would have demanded that he dissociate himself from his own people, who were the people of God (D'Angelo, *Moses*, 45–46, who overinterprets the evidence when she adds, "Thus his denial [ἠρνήσατο] is the martyr's confession [ὁμολογία] for he must flee in peril of his life"). What is described is a personal moral decision between two alternatives, rather than a formal legal renunciation (so Riesenfeld, *ConNT* 11 [1947] 218; Trites, *Witness*, 219; see above, *Note* g).

The deliberate choice Moses made is defined in vv 25–26. The key expressions are informed by a larger context in hellenistic-Jewish moral teaching, where the vocabulary of choice was developed and refined. The phrases μᾶλλον ἑλόμενος, "he chose rather," and πρόσκαιρον . . . ἁμαρτίας ἀπόλαυσιν, "temporary pleasure of sin," help to situate the choice of Moses in the perspective of a moral decision between a greater and lesser advantage.

In the LXX the term πρόσκαιρος, "temporary," "momentary," is used exclusively in 4 Macc 15:2, 8, 23, where the context concerns the dilemma within which a supreme moral choice must be made. A mother must choose whether to set aside the "momentary safety" (πρόσκαιρον σωτηρίαν) of her seven children and her own "temporary maternal love" (πρόσκαιρον φιλοτεκνίαν) for the sake of "a piety which saves to eternal life" (4 Macc 15:8, 23). The character of her choice is expressed sharply: "the mother, when two choices were proposed to her, piety and the momentary safety of her sons, loved rather [μᾶλλον ἠγάπησεν] piety" (4 Macc 15:2–3). Her choice was between an eternal and a temporary benefit, as in vv 25–26.

In retelling the story of Joseph and Potiphar's wife, Josephus uses similar expressions. Joseph "chose rather [εἵλετο μᾶλλον] to suffer unjustly, even to endure the supreme penalty, than to seize the pleasure of the present [τῶν παρόντων ἀπολαύειν], upon which indulgence he knew he would be condemned by his conscience justly" (*Ant.* 2.50). As the drama unfolds, the vocabulary of moral choice recurs in the contrast drawn between the "momentary" (πρόσκαιρον) enjoyment of lust and the secure "pleasure" (ἀπόλαυσις) that marriage brings. These examples (cited by D'Angelo, *Moses*, 28–29) serve to illustrate the vocabulary of v 25, where the moral choice is between the present enjoyment of pleasure and present mistreatment for doing what is right. (For the portrait of Moses as moral hero who abandons "pleasure" [ἀπόλαυσις] in favor of devoting himself to suffering on behalf of the people of God, see Jos., *Ant.* 4.495, cited by Windisch, 103.)

The phrase συγκακουχεῖσθαι τῷ λαῷ τοῦ θεοῦ, "to endure hardship with the people of God," defines the choice of Moses. It recalls the formulation of Exod 1:11 LXX, which reports that slave masters were appointed over the Hebrews ἵνα κακώσωσιν αὐτοὺς ἐν τοῖς ἔργοις, "in order to oppress them with [forced] labors." Moses chose present suffering and identification with the people of God in preference "to enjoying the temporary advantage of alliance with a sinful nation" (Phillips). When Moses joined his brothers, he rejected the benefits of his royal station. Philo reflects a similar understanding: Moses renounced his natural inheritance, since he could enjoy it only at the cost of complicity in the impiety of the king (*Moses* 1.32–33, 148–49). He recognized that the advantages that accrued to him as the son of the pharaoh's daughter were obtained through the oppressive enslavement of the Hebrew nation. That is why they are designated "the temporary enjoyment *of* [the benefits of] sin" in v 25 (so D'Angelo, *Moses*, 42, 45–46; cf. Moffatt, 180; Feather, *ExpTim* 43 [1931–32] 424–25; Williamson, *Philo*, 471–72, who argue that the "sin" Moses renounced was apostasy, which Moses would have committed had he united himself with the royal court rather than with the oppressed people of God). Moses' decisive action in choosing hardship with God's people distinguishes him sharply from certain members of the house church, whose decision to abandon the community of faith is sadly acknowledged in 10:25.

The surprising contrast developed in v 26a serves to clarify the implications of Moses' choice: "he considered abuse incurred for the sake of the Christ greater wealth than the treasures of Egypt." The suggestive expression "the treasures of Egypt" evokes an impression of limitless wealth, which Moses rejected when he joined himself to his fellow Hebrews (Spicq, 2:358–59, prefers to speak of "the treasuries of Egypt," which he identifies with granaries). Philo makes much of the motif of the renunciation of wealth and luxurious living (*Moses* 1.29, 47, 135, 149, 152, 154), but shows his indebtedness to the hellenistic-Jewish moral tradition when he summarizes "the wealth" that Moses preferred to the "treasure-gathering of former rulers" with a virtues list headed by endurance and self-control (*Moses* 1.154). Moses thus proves to be the ideal philosopher-king. The writer to the Hebrews breaks with this moral tradition when he identifies "the greater wealth" that Moses preferred with τὸν ὀνειδισμὸν τοῦ Χριστοῦ, "the reproach of the Christ."

The interpretation of this phrase is difficult and uncertain (see D'Angelo, *Moses*, 48–53, 64). It is not an exact quotation from the LXX. The phrase may have originated in Ps 68(MT 69) LXX, where the term ὀνειδισμός, "reproach," occurs in vv 8, 10, 11, 20, and 21. The writer may have applied the words of the psalmist to Moses, who shared the mistreatment of his brothers. Because he, like Christ, chose to share the suffering of the people of God, the reproach he bore is "the reproach of Christ" (see the discussion in D'Angelo, 48–50). More probably the phrase is an elliptical summary of Ps 88(MT 89):51–52 LXX:

> Remember, O Lord, the reproach [τοῦ ὀνειδισμοῦ] of your servants which I have borne in my breast from many nations, with which your enemies, O Lord, have reproached [ὠνείδισαν] [me (?)], with which they have reproached [ὠνείδισαν] your anointed one by way of recompense [το ἀντάλλαγμα τοῦ χριστοῦ σου].

The Greek is difficult, and its translation somewhat problematical (see F. F. Bruce, 320). If these verses were in the writer's mind, he appears to have read them as indicative of Moses' response of faith to God in the situation described in Exod 2:11–12: "I have borne in my breast the reproach with which your enemies [the Egyptians] reproached your servants [my brothers, the Hebrews] because of the exchange-price of the Christ" (so D'Angelo, *Moses*, 50; cf. Buchanan, 197). Like Christ, Moses exchanged the joy he could have had for the endurance of hardship with the people of God (cf. 12:2–3). The reproach he incurred was abuse endured for the cause of Christ, in the specific sense that he identified himself with God's people, sharing their hardship and contempt (H. Montefiore, 203, argues that the phrase "the reproach of the Anointed" is used in v 26 precisely as it is in Ps 88:51 LXX, where the chosen people are considered collectively as "the Anointed"; cf. Williamson, *Philo*, 363, 473; D'Angelo, 63–64).

Moses had been motivated to make his choice in faith, ἀπέβλεπεν γὰρ εἰς τὴν μισθαποδοσίαν, "because he was looking ahead to the reward." The expression ἀπέβλεπεν εἰς, "looking ahead to," suggests concentrated attention, while the imperfect tense denotes the habitual stance of Moses. The use of the verb with "the reward" as its object is similar to its use in the LXX and the papyri (cf. Williamson, *Philo*, 116–17). In content, the statement is parallel to 10:35. Moses deliberately turned his attention away *from* the present suffering to the future reward. His faith consisted in an emphatic refusal of the present, visible rewards of status and privilege in the certain expectation of the as yet unseen, but enduring, reward bestowed by God, to which he could look ahead (cf. Braun, *TLZ* 96 [1971] 330).

This orientation to the future expresses a wholly different perspective on Moses' choice from that embraced by Philo, who stresses that God rewarded Moses *presently* with "the kingship of a nation more populous and mightier [than Egypt], a nation destined to be consecrated above all others" (*Moses* 1.149, cited by Moffatt, 180). The explanation for Moses' response of faith in v 26*b* illustrates the earlier characterizations of faith in vv 1 and 6*b*. Moses' action was regulated by a perspective on the future which found its ground in a vibrant faith in God and in the reward he confers upon those who please him. His faith thus bears witness to the reality of God as the rewarder of those who earnestly seek him. The perspective of faith enabled Moses to make the appropriate moral choice and freed him from a debilitating fear of identifying himself with the people of God (cf. P. R. Jones, *RevExp* 76 [1979] 99, 104, who analyzes the account from the perspective of Moses' rejection of worldliness).

The portrait of Moses as an exemplar of faith who endured reproach on behalf of the Christ has been accommodated to the description of the early experience of the community addressed. In the past they had publicly endured "reproaches" (ὀνειδισμοί) and loss because they were identified with Christ and with the new people of God, who had been subjected to insult, persecution, and imprisonment (10:33–34). They had been motivated by the certainty that they enjoyed a better and abiding possession, which is contemplated under the metaphor of a "great reward" (10:35). With vocabulary recalling that report, Moses is described as choosing to suffer hardship with the people of God, a choice that entails loss and abuse for the sake of the Christ. The congregation could identify with the experience of a suffering Moses because he had endured what they had experienced.

The continuity in experience between Moses and the house church functions to reinforce a pattern of fidelity to God and the community that the writer wishes to promote in the congregation as belonging to the very nature of Christian faith (Descamps, *CSion* 2 [1955] 187, who links vv 24–26 with 13:13; cf. P. R. Jones, *RevExp* 76 [1979] 99; D'Angelo, *Moses*, 33–36).

27 In the context of vv 24–26, it is natural to refer v 27 to the departure from Egypt reported in Exod 2:14–15. When the fact that Moses had killed an Egyptian taskmaster became public knowledge, he was forced to flee for his life to Midian. On this understanding, v 27 is a midrashic paraphrase of Exod 2:14. What makes this conclusion questionable is that Exod 2:14 LXX states explicitly ἐφοβήθη δὲ Μωυσῆς, "and Moses was afraid," when he learned that his act of violence had become known. Although there is no reference to fear of the pharaoh's wrath in Exod 2:15 LXX, the pharaoh's intention of demanding Moses' life and his departure from Egypt appear to be directly related. The tenor of the account would seem to be contradicted by the statement in v 27 that "by faith he left Egypt, μὴ φοβηθεὶς τὸν θυμὸν τοῦ βασιλέως, "not fearing the king's rage."

For this reason, some interpreters refer v 27 to Moses' departure from Egypt as the head of the people at the time of the Exodus (e.g., Westcott, 373; H. Montefiore, 204; Spicq, 2:359, refers this verse to Moses' courageous conversations with pharaoh during the period covered by Exod 5:1–15:21). It is argued that the statement in v 27*a* harmonizes well with the description of events in Exod 10–12. Moreover, if the reference is to the departure of the Exodus, the three episodes reported in vv 23–27 mark the beginning of three forty-year periods in Moses' life: Moses' birth to his maturity in Egypt (v 23), Moses' departure from the royal court, his slaying of the Egyptian, and forty-year sojourn in Midian (vv 24–26), and Moses' departure from Egypt through the forty years of wandering to his death (v 27). This pattern, which occurs also in Acts 7:20, 23, 36, is a standard one (see Str-B 2:679–80; cf. D'Angelo, *Moses*, 53–54).

The conclusion, however, is open to serious objections. It requires some explanation for the disarrangement in sequence between v 27 and v 28, for the institution of the Passover (v 28) should logically have been mentioned prior to the exodus from Egypt (v 27). The pattern discerned in vv 23–27 is at best implicit in the text and is not clearly specified, as it is in Acts 7. More significant than these two considerations is a final observation. The detail that Moses was not afraid of the king's rage seems superfluous in v 27 if the reference is to the Exodus, for at the time of this departure both the pharaoh and the Egyptian people were urging Moses and the Hebrews to leave as rapidly as they could (Exod 12:31–33) (cf. F. F. Bruce, 322–23; P. E. Hughes, 497–500; D'Angelo, *Moses*, 54–56).

It seems preferable, therefore, to recognize that Exod 2:11–14 stands behind vv 24–27 and to seek to interpret the reference to Moses' lack of fear in the context of the tradition as well as the larger pastoral concerns of the writer. Philo (*Moses* 1.49–50; *Allegorical Interpretation* 3.14) and Josephus (*Ant.* 2.254–56) agree in eliminating the motive of fear from the account of Moses' departure from Egypt, as reported in Exod 2:14–15. They bear independent witness to a tradition of interpretation that stressed Moses' fearlessness with respect to the pharaoh, a tradition to which the writer of Hebrews may also have been an heir. More significantly, in v 23 the writer went beyond the detail of Exod 2:2 LXX in emphasizing the lack of fear of the royal edict in Moses' parents. The deduction "and they did not fear the decree of the king" (v 23) is virtually parallel in form and content with the factual statement of v 27 that Moses left Egypt "not fearing the rage of the king." Both at the beginning and at the conclusion of the unit on Moses as a young man, the writer emphasizes the role of faith in overcoming any fear of the king. This is the key to the interpretation of v 27*a*: Moses did express fear when he knew his violent action had become public knowledge (Exod 2:14), but by faith he overcame his fear of reprisals and left Egypt, finding in faith a substantiation of hopes as yet unrealized and events as yet unseen (v 1). The emphasis upon faith overcoming fear is indicative of the pastoral intention of the writer in bringing this example before the community he addressed (P. R. Jones, *RevExp* 76 [1979] 98–99, 104; cf. D'Angelo, *Moses*, 56–63, 190).

The manner in which Moses overcame his fear is delineated in the explanation clause of v 27*b*: τὸν γὰρ ἀόρατον ὡς ὁρῶν ἐκαρτέρησεν, "for he kept the one who is invisible continually before his eyes, as it were." Although the assumption that God cannot be seen, and that it is unsafe to attempt to see him, is pervasive in Scripture (e.g., Exod 33:18–23; Deut 4:12; Ps 97:2; cf. Jos., *Ant.* 4.346), God is never described in the LXX as ὁ ἀόρατος, "the invisible One." In educated circles in Judaism and early Christianity, however, the adjective ἀόρατος, "invisible," was broadly applied to God as one of his attributes (e.g., Philo, *On Abraham* 183; cf. Rom 1:20; Col 1:15; 1 Tim 1:17); Philo, for example, uses it more than a hundred times (Spicq, 1:85, n. 2). It was the fact that Moses kept the invisible God continually before him that explains how he succeeded in overcoming his fear through faith (for the unwarranted suggestion that the reference is to Jesus, "the seeable of the Unseen" God, see D'Angelo, *Moses*, 187–88).

The key to the proper interpretation of v 27*b* is the fixed hellenistic idiom ὁρῶν ἐκαρτέρησεν, "he kept seeing continually." The idiom has frequently been missed (see above, *Note* o), with the result that v 27*b* is translated "for as seeing the invisible one, he endured" (e.g. D'Angelo, *Moses*, 30, 33, 35). The verb ἐκαρτέρησεν (now rendered "he endured") then becomes the basis for finding in v 27 the example of faith as endurance (e.g., Grundmann, *TDNT* 3:617; Williamson, *Philo*, 363, 473–75; Dautzenberg, *BZ* 17 [1973] 171; and especially D'Angelo, 11–12, 17–18, 27–33, 62–63, who finds in vv 24–27 the portrait of Moses the martyr, who exemplifies the martyr's endurance). The fact that Philo (*Moses* 1.154; *Allegorical Interpretation* 3.11–14) and Josephus (*Ant.* 2.256–57) interpret Moses' departure from Egypt as an example of the hellenistic moral virtue of καρτερία, "endurance," may have misled interpreters of v 27b.

The emphasis, however, falls not on endurance but on continually seeing, as it were, the unseen God (BAGD 405). The reference is not to the awesome event at the burning bush (as urged by Spicq, 2:359; Héring, 105; F. F. Bruce, 320; among others), as if to say that Moses saw one who is invisible, but to a fixed habit of spiritual perception. Once that is recognized, it is clear that the explanatory clause in v 27b is a parallel comment to v 26b and must be interpreted in the light of that earlier statement. Moses' departure was an act of faith motivated by the vision of God, which faith invested with a substantial reality. In conjunction with v 26b, the explanation of Moses' lack of fear in v 27b testifies to an eschatological faith oriented to the future because it seized upon the reality of God and of the reward he bestows in response to active faith (v 6; cf. Barrett, "Eschatology," 380–81; Williamson, *Philo*, 475–77).

In the context of Exod 2:11–15, the reward must ultimately be related to the deliverance of the oppressed people of God. Moses looked beyond the events of the present to the yet unseen events of the future. From the pastoral perspective of the writer, the firmly entrenched habit of Moses in keeping God continually in view establishes a standard for imitation by the community in its experience of fear and governmental oppression.

28 The catalogue of exemplary witnesses to faith turns suddenly from the early phase of Moses' career to the final act in the dramatic sequence of events that were the prelude to the Exodus. Although Moses remains the subject of the main verb ("by faith he celebrated the Passover"), there is a subtle transition in v 28 from exemplary persons to exemplary events, and this shift in emphasis is reflected in vv 29–30 as well as in the enumeration of the accomplishments of faith in vv 33–38.

The writer makes no reference to the forty years that Moses spent in Midian, climaxed by the awesome event of the burning bush when Moses was summoned to return to Egypt to demand the release of the Hebrews (Exod 3:1–4:18). He passes in silence the fierce contest of will between the pharaoh and Moses that ensued (Exod 4:29; 10:29). All attention is concentrated upon Moses' celebration of the Passover in response to God's command (Exod 11:1–12:28) as the critical event in the deliverance of the people from enslavement. Moses' careful attention to the detailed instruction of God was evidence of faith; it demonstrated how firmly he believed God's promise that he would spare the firstborn of Israel when the angel of death executed the sentence of judgment upon Egypt. The specific reference to τὴν πρόσχυσιν τοῦ αἵματος, "the spreading of the blood," alludes to the marking of the top and sides of the doorframe of a house with the blood of the paschal lamb (Exod 12:7, 22) in response to the divine promise: "When I see the blood, I will pass over you. No destructive plague will touch you when I strike Egypt" (Exod 12:13).

It has been argued that the phrase πρόσχυσις τοῦ αἵματος is inappropriate for the smearing of the doorposts and lintel but reflects the later practice of sprinkling the paschal blood upon the altar of burnt offering (2 Chr 35:11; Jub. 49:20; m. Pesaḥ. 5:6; so Riggenbach, 374, n. 68; Jeremias, TDNT 5:898, n. 21). The action of sprinkling the blood with a sprig of hyssop, however, is prescribed explicitly in Exod 12:22. The reference to "blood" in v 28 is wholly casual, yet it conforms precisely to the function of blood as a life-affirming medium, as elsewhere in Hebrews (see Comment on 9:7; cf. Johnsson, "Defilement," 362).

The reference to the destroying angel (ὁ ὀλοθρεύων) as the agent who executes the sentence of judgment is taken directly from Exod 12:23 LXX (cf. Wis 18:25). God promised that when he saw the blood on the top and sides of the doorframe he would himself pass over the threshold of the home, and prevent the destroyer from entering the house. In faith Moses and the Israelites complied with the divine directive. Guarded by God, their firstborn children and livestock were spared from the plague of death that ravaged the Egyptians (Exod 11:4–5; 12:12, 27, 29–30).

29 The subject of v 29 is no longer Moses, although his role in the incident at the Sea of Reeds was crucial to the action of the people (Exod 14:13–28; cf. Acts 7:36). The subject is the people of Israel, whom God had led to an encampment at the edge of the sea (Exod 13:17–14:4). The writer had prepared for the change in subject in v 28, when he referred to "their [αὐτῶν] firstborn." The vocabulary of v 29 is illustrated in a second century B.C. account concerning Alexander the Great, who experienced the same miracle at the Pamphylian Sea (History of Alexander 151, cited by BAGD 181; cf. Lives of the Prophets 3.8–9 [ed. C. C. Torrey, 23, 37]).

The action of the people in crossing the sea indicates that they shared the faith of Moses. The biblical record is explicit that they had been terrified by the approach of the Egyptian army and had begun to complain bitterly. As in the case of Moses (v 27), faith in the reality and presence of God entailed an overcoming of an initial fear that could have paralyzed them (Exod 17:13–14). At the critical moment they demonstrated that they were prepared to attempt the impossible at the command of God (Exod 14:15–22, 29; 15:19). The declaration that they acted πίστει, "by faith," has specific reference to the command of God to "go forward" (Exod 14:15). The deliverance that had been procured for them could be appropriated only through the response of faith.

The formulation of v 29 constitutes an allusion to Exod 14:22 LXX, which states that "the people went into the midst of the sea on dry ground [κατὰ τὸ ξηρόν]." A strong east wind, which blew all night, caused the sea to recede before them, and they were able to walk across the mud flats "as if on dry ground" (Exod 14:21–22). The Egyptian chariot corps attempted to duplicate this feat, but when they were halfway across and the chariot wheels had become mired in the mud, the waters returned to their normal place and the Egyptians were drowned (Exod 14:23–28). Philo, elaborating on the experience of the Israelites, declares that "the waters dried up and became a broad highway capable of carrying a host of people" (Moses 1.177; cf. 2.254: the Israelites marched safely through the sea "as on a dry path or a stone-paved causeway"). The phrase used in v 29, ὡς διὰ ξηρᾶς, "as if on dry land," is dictated by the compound verb διαβαίνειν, "to go through," "to cross," which is resumed in the preposition διά, "through" (so Williamson, Philo, 479–80).

The incident at the Sea of Reeds is celebrated in Scripture as an awesome disclosure of the sovereign power of God and a firm pledge of his unfailing love (cf. Exod 15:1–21; Ps 106:9–12; Isa 43:16–17; 44:27; 51:10). It possesses a secure place in the wisdom tradition of hellenistic Judaism, which attributed the triumph to divine Wisdom:

> She [Wisdom] brought them over the Red Sea
>   and led them through deep waters,
> but she drowned their enemies
>   and cast them up from the depth of the sea (Wis 10:18–19).

The striking similarity in formulation between this encomium and v 29 may reflect the writer's own indebtedness to the wisdom tradition (cf. Bovon, *RTP* 18 [1968] 138, who argues for a literary relationship between Wis 10:18–19 and Heb 11:29).

30 The writer had earlier referred to the faithlessness of the wilderness generation in 3:16–19. It is not surprising that in a catalogue of exemplary persons and events he passes over in silence the forty-year period during which those who had experienced the celebration of the Passover, the exodus from Egypt, and the miraculous crossing of the Red Sea wandered aimlessly in the wilderness. Not until the entrance into Canaan can a recital of the acts of faith be resumed. The exemplary function of an event is illustrated in the example of the fall of the virtually impregnable fortress city of Jericho (cf. Josh 2:1). No reference is made to Joshua, although he had been mentioned by name in 4:8, and his faith is implied in 4:2. In the Wisdom of Joshua ben Sira, Joshua is exalted as one of "the fathers" who is worthy of praise (Sir 46:1–6; cf. 46:2; "How glorious he was when he lifted his hands and stretched out his sword against the cities," but without specific reference to Jericho). A different perspective is evident in v 30, which focuses upon the role of faith in a sequence of events climaxed by the collapse of the walls of the city (Josh 6:1–21).

Faith in this instance consisted in the readiness to act in accordance with God's mandate. It was expressed by Joshua, the priests, and the company of fighting men. From a military standpoint the assurance that a great walled city could be taken simply by encircling it for seven days, the silence broken only by the muffled tramp of feet, the sounding of rams' horns, and a loud shout on the seventh day, must have seemed remote from reality. But the people complied with the instructions God had given, and their faith was rewarded. After they had marched around the city seven times, on the seventh day at the pre-arranged signal the people shouted, "and when the people gave a loud shout, the wall collapsed; so every man charged straight in, and they took the city" (Josh 6:20). The incident was recalled in the conflict with the Seleucid forces at the time of Judas Maccabaeus: "But Judas and his men, calling upon the great Sovereign of the world, who without battering-rams or engines of war overthrew Jericho in the days of Joshua, rushed furiously upon the walls. They took the city by the will of God" (2 Macc 12:15–16). For the community of faith addressed in the homily, the message of this example is clear: obedient faith achieves its objective because God intervenes for its vindication (Spicq, 2:361; cf. F. F. Bruce, 327–28).

31 The catalogue of exemplary witnesses introduced with the reference to Abel in v 4 ends abruptly with the example of Rahab. Apart from Sarah, who was mentioned as the wife of Abraham in v 11, Rahab is the only woman who is listed in the catalogue. An interest in Rahab as an exemplar of faith and good works is traditional (cf. Jas 2:25; *1 Clem.* 12:1–8; for discussion, cf. F. W. Young, "The Relation of 1 Clement to the Epistle of James," *JBL* 67 [1948] 339–45; A. T. Hanson, *JSNT* 1 [1978] 55–59]. The reference to Rahab in v 31, with allusion to Joshua 6:17–25, follows logically as the sequel to the episode cited in v 30.

The traditional description of Rahab as ἡ πόρνη, "the prostitute," has its source in Scripture (Josh 2:1; 6:17, 22, 25). She was, nevertheless, a recognized member of her family group (Josh 2:12–13, 18; 6:23), and this was a status not normally enjoyed by a prostitute (so Wiseman, *TynBul* 14 [1964] 8, who suggests that the Hebrew word זוֹנָה [*zônâ*], which identifies Rahab in Josh 2:1, denotes "to act in a friendly way to an enemy"; he adds: "The original need carry no more stigma than that Rahab was in a limited way a friend of those owing allegiance to an alien power" [11]).

The account of Rahab's assistance to the spies whom Joshua had sent out to gather intelligence concerning the military and economic potential of the Jericho area is recorded in Josh 2:1–15. Her profession of faith is epitomized in the words, "I know that the Lord has given this land to you" (Josh 2:9–11). The knowledge that motivated her to preserve the life of the spies was "a recognition which engages the whole person and commits one to action" (Moran, "Repose," 283). What she knew and acknowledged and professed by her action was informed by the events of the crossing of the Red Sea and the overthrow of the Amorite kings, Sihon and Og, which had become public knowledge (Josh 2:10). Although a foreigner to the covenant people, she manifested a faith that was oriented toward the future and that found specific content in the acts of the God of Israel (Josh 2:11). She was prepared to assume present peril for the sake of future preservation (Josh 2:12–16).

This biblical background is presupposed in the contrast implied in the statement that "by faith Rahab οὐ συναπώλετο τοῖς ἀπειθήσασιν [did not perish with the unbelievers]." The "unbelievers" are the residents of Jericho who perished when the city and its people were devoted to destruction (Josh 6:17, 21). The descriptive expression τοῖς ἀπειθήσασιν, "the unbelievers," serves to distinguish them sharply from Rahab, who acted in faith. It recalls the earlier use of the same expression to designate unbelieving Israel during the wilderness period (3:18). The fundamental distinction recognized by the writer is the division between those who believe and those who do not (cf. A. T. Hanson, *JSNT* 1 [1978] 54). The critical importance of this distinction has already been emphasized for the Christian community in 10:39. It is now reinforced by the reference to Rahab and the consequence of her decisive stance of faith.

Explanation

See 11:32–40 below.

The Triumphs of Perseverance in Faith in Subsequent Eras (11:32–40)

Bibliography

Caquot, A. "Bref commentaire du 'Martyre d'Isaïe.'" *Sem* 23 (1973) 65–93. Debrunner, A. "Über einige Lesarten der Chester Beatty Papyro des Neuen Testaments." *ConNT* 11 (1947) 33–49. Downing, J. "Jesus and Martyrdom." *JTS* 14 (1963) 279–93. Esbroeck, M. van. "Hébreux 11,33–38 dans l'ancienne version géorgienne." *Bib* 53 (1972) 43–64. Fischel, H. A. "Martyr and Prophet." *JQR* 37 (1946–47) 265–80, 363–86. Gaster, M., and Heller, B. "Der Prophet Jesaja und der Baum: Beiträge zur vergleichenden Sagen- und Märchenkunde." *MGWJ* 80 (1936) 32–52. Grässer, E. "Exegese nach Auschwitz? Kritische Anmerkungen zur hermeneutischen Bedeutung des Holocaust am Beispiel von Hebr. 11." *KD* 27 (1981) 152–63. Henten, J. W. van, Dehandschutter, B. A. G. M., and Klaauw, H. J. W. van der, eds. *Die Entstehung der jüdischen Martyrologie.* Studia Post-Biblica 38. Leiden: Brill, 1989. Hofius, O. "Στόματα μαχαίρης, Hebr 11,34." *ZNW* 62 (1971) 129–30. Loftus, F. "The Martyrdom of the Galilean Troglodytes (*B. J.* i 312–13; *A* xiv 429–30): A Suggested *Traditionsgeschichte.*" *JQR* 66 (1966) 212–23. Maas, M. "Die Maccabäer als christliche Heilige." *MGWJ* 44 (1900) 145–56. Manson, T. W. "Martyrs and Martyrdom." *BJRL* 39 (1956–57) 463–84. Mora, G. *La Carta a los Hebreos como Escrito Pastoral.* 172–75. O'Hagan, A. P. "The Martyr in the Fourth Book of Maccabees." *Liber Annuus: Studii biblici Fransiscani* 24 (1974) 94–120. Owen, E. C. E. "ἀποτυμπανίζω, ἀποτυμπανισμός (τυμπανισμός), τυμπανίζω, τύμπανον (τύπανον)." *JTS* 30 (1929) 259–66. Peterson, D. G. "An Examination of the Concept of 'Perfection' in the 'Epistle to the Hebrews.'" Dissertation, University of Manchester, 1978. 271–78. Rose, C. "Verheissung und Erfüllung: Zum Verständnis von ἐπαγγελία im Hebräerbrief." *BZ* 33 (1989) 178–91. Schatkin, M. "The Maccabean Martyrs." *VC* 28 (1974) 97–113. Schoeps, H. J. *Die jüdischen Prophetenmorde.* Uppsala: Symbolae Biblicae Upsalienses, 1943. Simon, M. "Les saints d'Israel." *RHPR* 34 (1954) 98–127. Torrey, C. C. *The Lives of the Prophets: Greek Text and Translation.* SBLMS 1. Philadelphia: Society of Biblical Literature and Exegesis, 1946. Willcock, J. "1 Samuel xii.11; Hebrews xi.32." *ExpTim* 28 (1916–17) 41–42. Williams, S. K. *Jesus' Death as Saving Event.* 59–202, 233–54. Winslow, D. F. "The Maccabean Martyrs: Early Christian Attitudes." *Jud* 23 (1974) 78–86.

Translation

[32] And[a] *what more shall I say? For time would fail me if I told[b] about Gideon, Barak, Samson, Jephthah, of both David and[c] Samuel and the prophets,* [33] *who through faith conquered[d] kingdoms, practiced justice,[e] and attained the promised blessings;[f] who shut the mouths of lions,* [34] *extinguished the fury of the flames, and escaped[g] the edge of the sword; who after weakness[h] became strong;[i] who became mighty in war and routed[j] foreign armies.* [35] *Women received their dead by resurrection. But others[k] were tortured,[l] after refusing to accept[m] the offered release in order that they might attain a better resurrection.* [36] *And others experienced[n] jeering and lashing, and even[o] chains and prison.* [37] *They were stoned; they were sawn in two;[p] they were murdered by the sword.[q] They went about in sheepskins and goatskins, destitute, oppressed, and mistreated[r]* [38] *(humanity[s] was not worthy of them). They wandered aimlessly in uninhabited regions and on mountains, and in caves and crevices in the ground,* [39] *and although they all[t]*

had received attestation from God [u] *through faith,* [v] *they did not receive* [w] *what had been promised.* [40] *God had provided* [x] *something better with us in mind,* [y] *so that they should not reach perfection except with us.* [z]

Notes

[a] The conj καί frequently precedes an interrogative statement (Zerwick, *Biblical Greek* §459). It is a rhetorical and literary feature that could be omitted from translation.

[b] The adv ptcp διηγούμενον has a conditional sense (Turner, *Grammar*, 3:157). The masc ending of the ptcp is adverse to the proposal that Hebrews was composed by Priscilla or by some other woman.

[c] The force of the τε καί . . . καί construction is to distinguish as well as to connect. The second καί connects Samuel with the prophets, as the first of the regular prophetic line (cf. Acts 3:24). The construction serves to distinguish "Samuel and the prophets" from David, who was not a prophet (cf. BDF §444[4]).

[d] The series of aorists in v 33 is best understood as culminative in force. For the force of the prep in the compound κατηγωνίσαντο, see Moulton and Howard, *Grammar*, 2:316.

[e] For the idiom ἐργάζεσθαι δικαιοσύνην in the sense of "to practice justice," see Ps 14[MT 15]:2 LXX. An alternative translation is "to enforce justice," (BAGD 196).

[f] The translation seeks to stress the pl in ἐπαγγελιῶν.

[g] The translation presupposes the aor tense of ἔφυγον is perfective, indicating the success of the fleeing. For the suggestion that the force of the tense is actually ingressive, denoting the first and decisive step away from danger, see Moulton, *Grammar*, 1:116.

[h] The prep phrase ἀπὸ ἀσθενείας has a temporal sense (BDF §209[4]). It is equivalent to the classical use of ἐκ in the sense "out of a former state of [weakness]."

[i] The force of the aor tense of ἐδυναμώθησαν is ingressive. It is difficult to determine whether the pass voice has the nuance of a "theological passive."

[j] The verb ἔκλιναν in context has the nuance of breaking a military formation (so Zerwick and Grosvenor, *Grammatical Analysis*, 683).

[k] The expression ἄλλοι δέ marks a change of subj in the long sentence that extends from v 32 to v 40.

[l] On the significance of the expressive word ἐτυμπανίσθησαν, see especially Owen, *JTS* 30 [1929] 259–66.

[m] The action of the ptcp προσδεξάμενοι is antecedent to ἐτυμπανίσθησαν. The negative οὐ is used with the ptcp in order to emphasize strongly that these persons of faith did not accept the opportunity to gain freedom so as to avoid torture (Hanna, *Grammatical Aid*, 160; cf. BAGD 590).

[n] The expression πεῖραν ἔλαβον could be translated "received a trial (consisting of)."

[o] For ἔτι in the sense of "even," cf. Zerwick and Grosvenor, *Grammatical Analysis*, 683.

[p] The presence of the colorless word ἐπειράσθησαν, "they were put to the test," in most MSS containing v 37 is surprising. It is inappropriate in an enumeration of the kinds of violent death suffered by the martyrs. On the supposition that the term is a primitive corruption of some other word more suitable to the context, commentators have proposed a broad range of conjectural emendations (conveniently reviewed by Metzger, *Textual Commentary*, 674–75, to which add ἐνεπρήσθησαν, "they were burned," proposed by Michel, 461). Moreover, the position of ἐπειράσθησαν is uncertain: it occurs before ἐπρίσθησαν, "they were sawn in two," in א L P 33 81 326 2495 syp,h boms Euthalius, but after this verbal form in p13vid A D² K X 88 104 181 330 436 451 614 629 630 1739 1877 1881 1962 2127 2492 *Byz Lect* it vg bo arm Orgr 5/7 lat Ephr Ambr Chr Thret John of Damascus. It is almost certainly a gloss or an inadvertent scribal dittogr of ἐπρίσθησαν (D*, which reads ἐπιράσθησαν ἐπιράσθησαν, is a clear case of dittogr).

The short reading ἐπρίσθησαν, "they were sawn in two," is supported by p46 1241 1984 Lect44,53 syp sa (which transposes the order: "they were sawn in two, they were stoned") aethro,pp Orgr 2/7 lat Eus Acac Ephr Hier Socrates Pseudo-Augustine Theophylact. Although this reading is given only a "D" classification in UBSGNT³ (i.e., the committee expresses a very high degree of doubt concerning the reading selected for the text), it has received the support of a number of distinguished textual critics (cf. Debrunner, *ConNT* 11 [1947] 44–45; Zuntz, *Text*, 47–48; Tasker, *NTS* 1 [1954–55] 184–85; Hoskier, *Commentary*, 56–57; Metzger, *Textual Commentary*, 674–75). The longer reading, which is adopted by the NASB and the Berkeley Version, has recently been defended as original by Swetnam, *Jesus and Isaac*, 88, n. 14; 89, n. 18.

�q The prep phrase ἐν φόνῳ μαχαίρης has an instrumental sense: "they died by being murdered by the sword" (cf. A. T. Robertson, *Grammar*, 590).

ʳ The shift to the three present ptcps (ὑστερούμενοι, θλιβόμενοι, κακουχούμενοι) is striking after so many aorists. The present tense serves to circumscribe the class of persons described (so J. Thomas, "The Use of Voice, Moods and Tenses," 38).

ˢ The expression ὁ κόσμος has been translated to stress the human dimension of "the world," as in v 7.

ᵗ The demonstrative pronoun οὗτοι, "these persons," is absent from P⁴⁶ 1739 Cl Aug. All other witnesses add it, on the model of v 13. Zuntz, *Text*, 33–34, points out that in v 13, after ἀπέθανον, "they died," οὗτοι is necessary; but in v 39, after the conj καί, it is intolerable because it encourages a full stop before this clause and ruins the context.

ᵘ The aor ptcp μαρτυρηθέντες is used concessively (Zerwick and Grosvenor, *Grammatical Analysis*, 683). The pass voice is a further instance of the "theological passive," expressed in translation with the qualification "from God."

ᵛ It is natural to construe the expression διὰ τῆς πίστεως, "through faith," with the aor pass ptcp; the statement that the men and women to whom reference has been made received attestation through faith recapitulates v 2. It is also possible, however, to construe the phrase with the main clause: "they did not receive what had been promised *through their faith*" (so D'Angelo, *Moses*, 23, who suggests that this shifting perspective is intentional).

ʷ The aor tense of ἐκομίσαντο is used constatively, summarizing the action of a number of persons (A. T. Robertson, *Grammar*, 833).

ˣ Although the verb προβλέπειν in the active voice means "to foresee" (Ps 36:13 LXX, cf. Michaelis, *TDNT* 5:381), in the middle voice it denotes "to provide something for someone" (MM 538; BAGD 703; Moffatt, 190; F. F. Bruce, 343, n. 298; Michel, 421).

ʸ The prep phrase περὶ ἡμῶν, "for us," has been translated idiomatically.

ᶻ There has been a tendency in translation to transpose the negative final clause (ἵνα μὴ . . . τελειωθῶσιν) into a positive formulation: "so that only together with us should they reach perfection" (cf. NEB, TEV, NIV). It seems preferable to preserve the actual tenor of the text (cf. RSV, JB, NASB).

Form/Structure/Setting

See 11:1–40 above.

Comment

32　The catalogue of exemplary persons and events, each introduced by the anaphoric use of πίστει, "by faith," in vv 4–31, now gives place to an enumeration of names in rapid succession, followed by an abstract of the accomplishments of faith that extends the historical survey into the Maccabean period. The swift and eloquent summary of the acts of triumphant and supportive faith provides an effective peroration to the discourse (BDF §491).

The transition from one version of the exemplary list to another is achieved with a rhetorical question, καὶ τί ἔτι λέγω, "And what more shall I say?" This is a common homiletical and literary idiom for indicating that time and space are limited (cf. Jos., *Ant.* 20.256; τί δεῖ πλείω λέγειν, "Is it necessary for me to say anything more?"). The response, ἐπιλείψει με γὰρ διηγούμενον ὁ χρόνος περί, "for time would fail me if I tell about," is one form of a common rhetorical phrase, with parallels in classical authors and in Philo (e.g., Isocrates 1.11; 6.81; 8.56; Ps.-Isocrates, *Demonicus* 11; Demosthenes 18.296; Lysias 12.1; Dionysius of Halicarnassus, *Concerning the Composition of Words* 4.30; Plutarch, *Cicero* 42; Philo, *On the Sacrifices of Abel and Cain* 27; *On the Embassy to Gaius* 323; *On the Special Laws* 4.328; *Moses* 1.213; cf. Williamson, *Philo*, 316–17). The rhetorical flourish commonly announces an intention of abbreviating the matter under discussion. In v

32, which exhibits "an elegant, genuinely oratorical word order" (BDF §473[2]), the rhetorical future ἐπιλείψει describes time as going off and leaving the writer engaged in an animated discourse about Gideon and other exemplars of faith.

The six men who are named represent a random sampling permitting the writer to enumerate in summary fashion some of the achievements of faith. He resorts to paraleipsis, a rhetorical device in which an orator pretends to pass over something which he in fact mentions. The brief mention serves to emphasize the suggestiveness of what has been omitted (BDF §495[1]). The individuals named span the interval from the period of the judges to the early monarchy. The random character of the list is evident from the fact that the order of the names as given is not chronological. In the OT, Barak (Judg 4–5) is introduced before Gideon (Judg 6–8), Jephthah (Judg 11–12) before Samson (Judg 12–16), and Samuel (1 Sam 1–15) before David (1 Sam 16–2 Sam 24). A sampling of other exemplary lists indicates that they often exhibit little concern for historical sequence (e.g., 1 Sam 12:11 LXX, where the order is Gideon, Barak, Jephthah, Samuel; *Apost. Const.* 7.37.1, where the order is Gideon, Samson, Jephthah, Barak; *Tg. Ps.-J.* Deut 34:1, where the order is Jephthah, Samson, Barak, Gideon).

The names of the four judges in v 32b may have been suggested by 1 Sam 12:11 LXX, where Samuel refers to God's provision of deliverance for Israel through "Jerubbaal [i.e., Gideon, cf. Judg 6:32; 7:1], Barak, Jephthah, and Samuel." The Syriac Peshitta replaces "Jerubbaal" by the more familiar name "Gideon," and for the fourth name, "Samuel," substitutes "Samson," a reading which is intrinsically probable (cf. NEB). This reading is also found in certain LXX manuscripts, so that the text speaks of Jerubbaal, Barak, Jephthah, and Samson. If the writer of Hebrews was aware of this variant, he could have found in 1 Sam 12:11 LXX the names of the four judges and an indifference to chronology, since Gideon appears before Barak, as in v 32 (first proposed by Willcock, *ExpTim* 28 [1916–17] 42; cf. F. F. Bruce, 331; P. E. Hughes, 506, n. 90). On the other hand, the names of the four judges may simply be traditional. They are included in an early hellenistic-Jewish liturgical fragment now embedded in *Apost. Const.* 7.37.1, which indicates that they had achieved a special significance that made their inclusion in a catalogue of exemplary witnesses appropriate. That particular fragment of Jewish liturgical tradition includes all the names listed by the writer in Hebrews 11, with the exception of Enoch and Rahab (cf. Eccles, "Hellenistic Patterns," 221–22).

Gideon's crushing victory over the Midianite coalition (Judg 6:33–8:21) was so well entrenched in the tradition it could be recalled without reference to Gideon (cf. Ps 83:11; Isa 9:3–4; 10:26). It had required a profound exercise in faith when God instructed him to reduce his army of 32,000 fighting men to a small band of 300, equipped with torches in clay jars and trumpets. Yet the strategy he employed threw into confusion the vastly superior numbers of the Midianites, and Gideon's tiny force was swept to victory (Judg 7:1–25; cf. 1 Sam 12:11). Later tradition spoke of "the redemption of Gideon the son of Joash" (e.g., *Tg. Neof.* Gen 49:18), and pronounced a blessing upon God who "accepted the sacrifice . . . of Gideon at the rock and the fleeces" (*Apost. Const.* 7.37.1; cf. Judg 6:11–24, 36–39).

Barak was the military commander of the Israelite army who led them to victory over Sisera, commander of the confederate Canaanite army supported by a force of nine hundred iron chariots. When commanded to take the field against Sisera, Barak refused to do so unless supported by the presence of Deborah, a

prophetess. Nevertheless, at the critical moment he acted in faith, for when told
to advance against a vastly superior military machine at the head of his infantry,
he did so (Judg 4:4–16). His exploits were celebrated in the Song of Deborah
(Judg 5:1–31) and in the exemplary tradition (e.g., *Tg. Ps.-J.* Deut 34:1–2: "And the
word of the Lord showed [Moses] all of the heroes of the land, and the mighty
deeds that would be done. . . . And the thousand princes of the house of Naphtali
who gather with Barak"; cf. *Apost. Const.* 7.37.2: "You accepted the sacrifice . . . of
Barak and Deborah in the days of Sisera").

Samson championed Israel's cause against the Philistines (Judg 13:1–16:31).
Although he frequently acted rashly, he is described in Scripture as a man who
was deeply conscious of being empowered by the Spirit of the Lord (Judg 13:24;
14:6, 19; 15:14) and who acknowledged that his victories over the Philistines were
the gift of God (Judg 15:18; cf. 16:17, 28). The later exemplary tradition spoke of
"the redemption of Samson, the son of Manoah" (e.g., *Tg. Neof.* Gen 49:18; cf. *Tg.
Ps.-J.* Deut 34:1: the Lord showed Moses "the mighty victories of Samson, the son
of Manoah of the tribe of Dan") and remembered Samson's prayerful dependence
upon God at a critical point in his life (*Apost. Const.* 7.37.1: "You accepted the sacrifice . . . of Samson in his thirst before the transgression"; cf. Judg 15:18–19).

Jephthah the Gileadite is celebrated in Scripture as a great warrior, who was
summoned to be the commander of the Transjordanian tribes against the Ammonites (Judg 10:6–11:32). His faith consisted in the firm conviction that God,
who had guided Israel during the period of the Exodus and entrance into the
wilderness, would decide the dispute between the Israelites and the Ammonites
(Judg 11:14–27). Even his rash vow (Judg 11:29–39) is an indication of the depth
of his devotion to the God of Israel. His triumphs, recalled by Samuel (1 Sam
12:11), were subsequently incorporated into the exemplary tradition (e.g., *Tg. Ps.-
J.* Deut 34:1: "And the word of the Lord showed [Moses] all the heroes of the
land, and the mighty deeds that would be done by Jephthah of Gilead"; *Apost.
Const.* 7.37.2: "You respected the sacrifice . . . of Jephthah in the war before his
rash vow"; cf. Judg 11:11).

The reference to David is not surprising since he holds such a firm place in
the exemplary tradition (e.g., Sir 45:25; 47:2–11; 1 Macc 2:15; *1 Clem.* 18:1–17; cf.
Apost. Const. 7.37.2: "You accepted the sacrifice . . . of David on the threshing
floor of Ornan the Jebusite"). Especially interesting in the light of v 2, which
speaks of all of the exemplars of faith as having "received attestation" from God,
is the formulation in *1 Clem.* 18:1: "What shall we say concerning David, who received attestation [μεμαρτυρημένῳ] [from God]?" A strong reliance upon God
and an intense faith distinguished David, even as a young man (1 Sam 17:26, 32,
34–37, 45–47; cf. Sir 47:4–5). It is not necessary to think of a particular episode in
which David demonstrated the response of faith. It is sufficient to refer to the
depth and scope of the tradition of praise to God which is attributed to David in
Scripture and in the later exemplary tradition (e.g., Sir 47:8–11).

Samuel was the last of the charismatic judges (1 Sam 7:15–17) and the first of
the regular prophetic line (1 Sam 3:19–20; cf. Sir 46:13–20; Acts 3:24). He is listed
after David and before the prophets in v 32 because he enjoyed the prophetic
office (see above, *Note* c). Prophetic guilds are mentioned for the first time during the period he served as a judge (1 Sam 10:5, 10–11), and he is identified as
the leader of such a guild (1 Sam 19:20). He is remembered particularly for his

powerful intercession on behalf of Israel at Mizpah, where God intervened in response to his stance of faith and the Philistine strong hold upon Israel was broken (1 Sam 7:5–14; Sir 46:16–18; cf. *Apost. Const.* 7.37.2: "You accepted the sacrifice . . . of Samuel at Mizpah"). His long life was distinguished by the integrity and intensity of an active faith (cf. 1 Sam 12:3–5; Sir 46:19).

The prophets are mentioned in a general way, without the differentiation common in the exemplary tradition (e.g. Sir 48:1–49:10, with specific reference to Elijah, Elisha, Isaiah, Jeremiah, Ezekiel, and the twelve prophets). It was sufficient simply to refer to "the prophets" to evoke a clear impression of men who were exemplars of faith to their own generations. Faith informed both their word and their actions. The generalized reference provided a transition to the nameless enumeration of the accomplishments of faith in the abstract that follows.

33–35a The digest of the deeds of men and women of faith during the biblical and post-biblical periods that is presented in vv 33–38 appears to be "spontaneous and unstudied" (P. E. Hughes, 508). It presupposes a rather detailed knowledge of the OT and of Jewish history on the part of the writer and the congregation addressed. The move from the particular to the general invited audience response, and evidence of this response can be traced in very early primary source material (see *Comment* on v 34). By the fourth Christian century, there is clear evidence of a move from the general to the particular as names, which had been entered as marginal illustrations of the several clauses of vv 33–38, were progressively blended into the text itself (see van Esbroeck, *Bib* 53 [1972] 43–64, who traces this phenomenon in the old Georgian version, the Great Lectionary of the Church of Jerusalem, the Armenian version of Ephraem's commentary on the epistles, and the Greek patristic tradition).

The resolution of the sentence into terse clauses joined with asyndeton (see BDF §494) produces a powerful effect as the writer enumerates the accomplishments of faith. In vv 33–35a the recital progresses from one glorious achievement or deliverance to another, each achieved διὰ πίστεως, "through faith." In v 35b, however, the tone changes, as attention is focused upon those who exercised faith but were granted no immunity from humiliation, suffering, and death (vv 35b–38). The initial phrase in v 33, οἱ διὰ πίστεως, "who through faith," has an immediate antecedent in those individuals named in v 32b, and it is appropriate to seek to illustrate the consequences of vibrant faith from their experiences. Nevertheless, it is evident already in v 33 that the writer had in mind others who through faith experienced a remarkable deliverance, and this broader perspective is mandated by the detail of the text through v 38.

Of the nine short clauses in vv 33–34, the first three appear to form a group prompted by the antecedent reference to those named in v 32b. They concern the impact of acts of faith upon the theocratic nation. The first clause summarized the martial prowess of the judges and of David, who through faith κατηγωνίσαντο βασιλείας, "conquered kingdoms." It is natural to think of the military exploits for which Gideon, Barak, Jephthah, and Samuel are remembered (see *Comment* on v 32). These courageous acts brought relief from oppression but no enduring peace, until David expanded the borders of Israel from the Egyptian frontier to the Euphrates River (cf. 1 Kgs 4:20–21). Although the verb καταγωνίζεσθαι does not occur in the LXX or elsewhere in the NT, it is used by Josephus in reference to David's conquest of the Philistines (*Ant.* 7.53).

The second clause, εἰργάσαντο δικαιοσύνην, "they practiced justice," has specific reference to the establishment and administration of just government. The idiom is used in Scripture of doing what is right in the sense of personal integrity (Ps 14[MT 15]:2 LXX; Acts 10:35). In the context of v 33a, however, it is appropriate to recall the valedictory address of Samuel, in which he was able to review a lengthy tenure of judging Israel with absolute integrity (1 Sam 12:3–5, 23). A synonymous expression is used with reference to David, who ruled over Israel, καὶ ἦν Δαυὶδ ποιῶν κρίμα καὶ δικαιοσύνην ἐπὶ πάντα τὸν λαὸν αὐτοῦ, "and David was administering judgment and justice for all his people" (2 Sam 8:15; 1 Chr 18:14 LXX; cf. 1 Kgs 10:19).

These exemplars acted "through faith," and as a result ἐπέτυχον ἐπαγγελιῶν, "they attained the promised blessings." Their faith was vindicated with respect to particular promises. As the immediate sequel to v 32b, it is possible to specify Gideon (Judg 6:12–16; 7:7), Barak (Judg 4:6–7, 14), Samson (Judg 13:5), and David (2 Sam 7:11) as those who obtained specific blessings that had been promised by God.

The next three clauses (vv 33d–34b) allude to remarkable deliverances from certain death. The assertion ἔφραξαν στόματα λεόντων, "they shut the mouth of lions," referred to Samson (Judg 14:5–6) and to David (1 Sam 17:34–37; cf. Sir 47:3: "[David] played with lions as with young goats") in certain strands of the Greek and Syriac patristic tradition (cf. van Esbroeck, Bib 53 [1972] 47; Riggenbach, 377, n. 87). The allusion, however, is almost certainly to Daniel; he was cast into the lions' den because he had been faithful to God and yet was preserved alive ὅτι ἐπίστευσεν ἐν τῷ θεῷ αὐτοῦ, "because he exercised faith in his God" (Dan 6:24 Theod.). The formulation in v 33d is an allusion to Dan 6:23 (Theod.): "My God sent his angel and he shut the mouths of the lions" (ἐνέφραξεν τὰ στόματα τῶν λεόντων). As an example of a proto-Theodotion reading, it may represent a local text-type used by the extensive Jewish communities in Asia minor, which later became the basis of Theodotion's translation (so J. Jellicoe, The Septuagint and Modern Study [Oxford: Clarendon, 1968] 87–92). The importance of Daniel's experience to the exemplary tradition is richly attested (1 Macc 2:60; 3 Macc 16:3, 21; 18:13; 1 Clem. 45:6; Apost. Const. 7.37.2; cf. Jos., Ant. 10.262).

The allusion to Daniel brought to the writer's mind the remarkable experience of Daniel's three friends, Hananiah, Azariah, and Mishael, who through faith ἔσβεσαν δύναμιν πυρός, "extinguished the fury of the flames" (Dan 3:19–28, 49–50 LXX, Theod.). The two accounts of deliverance through divine intervention reported in the Book of Daniel are often mentioned side by side in the Jewish exemplary tradition (1 Macc 2:59–60; 3 Macc 6:6–7; 4 Macc 16:3, 21; 18:12–13; cf. 1 Clem. 45:6–7; Apost. Const. 7.37.2–3). Hananiah and his companions were confident that God was able to deliver them from the blazing furnace, but they had received no assurance that he would do so (Dan 3:17–18). Their allegiance to God and unwavering determination to serve him were predicated on firm commitment, not on the promise of deliverance.

Escape from the edge of the sword brandished by enemies or a tyrant marked the experience of David (e.g., 1 Sam 17:45–47; cf. Ps 144:10) and of the prophets: Elijah escaped from Jezebel (1 Kgs 19:1–3), Elisha from Jehoram (2 Kgs 6:26–32), and Jeremiah from Johoiakim (Jer 26:7–24, where his experience is contrasted with that of the prophet Uriah, who was murdered by the sword

[Jer 26:20–23]; cf. Jer 36:1–26). The threat of death by the sword hung over all Jews under Artaxerxes (Add Esth 13:6: "all, with their wives and their children, shall be utterly destroyed by the sword . . . without pity or mercy"; cf. Esth 3:13; 4:13; 7:3–4) and was averted only through the courageous action of Esther (Esth 8:1–9:10, 16–17; cf. *1 Clem.* 55:6; cf. J. R. Harris, "Side-lights," 172–73). The unusual plural in στόματα, "the edge," reproduces a Semitic idiom for the edge of the sword, for which there are several parallels in Hebrew and Aramaic (but not in Greek; cf. Hofius, *ZNW* 62 [1971] 129–30).

The clause ἐδυναμώθησαν ἀπὸ ἀσθενείας, "who after weakness became strong," is parallel in sense with the praise of Hannah, ἀσθενοῦντες περιεζώσαντο δύναμιν, "those who were weak were girded with strength" (1 Sam 2:4 LXX). The precise sense in which the writer defined "weakness" is unclear, but in the context of the exemplars named in v 32*b* it is natural to think of Samson, who after the humiliating experience of weakness literally became strong for one final assault upon the Philistines, which proved to be more effective than all of his earlier exploits (Judg 16:17–21, 25–30; cf. Judg 15:19). The principle, however, is illustrated repeatedly in Scripture; as P. E. Hughes has remarked, "faith is the response of all who are conscious of their own weakness and accordingly look to God for strength" (510). Clement of Rome was thoroughly familiar with this section of Hebrews (cf. *1 Clem.* 17:1, where he quotes and comments on Heb 11:37). At one point he appears to allude to the phrase in v 34*c*: "Many women became strong [ἐδυναμωθεῖσαι] through the grace of God and have performed many acts of courage" (*1 Clem.* 55:3, with reference to Judith [55:4–5] and Esther [55:6], who risked peril to rescue their own people from grave danger). The reference to Judith (cf. Jdt 8:1–15:7) suggests that Clement interpreted the clause in conjunction with the following phrases, which speak of those "who became mighty in war and routed foreign armies."

The two final clauses of v 34 belong together: "they became mighty in war, and routed foreign armies." These general affirmations were validated in the experience of Gideon, Barak, Jephthah, David, and even Samuel (cf. 1 Sam 7:5–14), not to speak of others who gave faithful leadership to Judah in times of national crisis. They were also richly illustrated in the early Maccabean resistance to Seleucid repression at the time of Antiochus IV Epiphanes (cf. 1 Macc 3:17–25; 4:6–22, 34–36). In 1 Maccabees the Seleucid troops are repeatedly designated as "the foreigners" (ἀλλόριοι; e.g., 1:38; 2:7; 4:12, 26), and the phrase παρεμβολὰς ἔκλιναν ἀλλοτρίων, "they routed foreign armies," provides an apt summary of such passages as 1 Macc 3:17–25; 4:6–22, 30–33. The verb is used in the sense of breaking a military formation, a nuance that is never given in the LXX or elsewhere in the NT, but which is found in classical Greek from the time of Homer (*Iliad* 5.37; 17.7–24, cited by Spicq, 2.364).

The present series of terse clauses is broken in vv 35–36 by a piece of connected speech that brings the chronicle of the triumphs of faith to a conclusion and effects the transition to the martyrology in vv 35*b*–38. The reference to women who "received their dead by resurrection" (v 35*a*) belongs to the initial series as a final proof of the benefits of faith. The allusion is to the widow at Zarephath of Sidon, who received from God, as a result of the dynamic faith of Elijah, her son who had died (1 Kgs 17:17–24; cf. Sir 48:5; *Lives of the Prophets* 10.5–6 [ed. C. C. Torrey, 27, 42]), and to the Shunemite woman, whose son was restored to her as a result of the indomitable faith of Elisha (2 Kgs 4:18–37). In the latter case, the mother's haste in going to Elisha on Mount Carmel despite her own deep distress, and her quiet response to inquiry, "Everything is all right" (2 Kgs 4:22–26), were expressions of her own firm faith that she would indeed receive her son from the dead "by resurrection." The formulation of v 35a, ἔλαβον γυναῖκες ἐξ ἀναστάσεως τοὺς νεκροὺς αὐτῶν, "women received their dead by resurrection," appears to be influenced by 2 Kgs 4:37 LXX, ἡ γυνὴ . . . ἔλαβεν τὸν υἱὸν αὐτῆς, "The woman . . . received her son."

35b–36 The catalogue of those who enjoyed the rich benefits of faith after difficult trials (vv 32–35a) now gives place to a recital of the experience of others, for whom deliverance came ultimately only through suffering and martyrdom. The transition is effected by a change of subject in vv 35b–36, ἄλλοι δὲ . . . ἕτεροι δέ ("but others . . . and others"), followed by the frank acknowledgment that the demonstration of invincible faith did not imply an immunity from persecution, humiliation, and violent death.

The statement ἐτυμπανίσθησαν οὐ προσδεξάμενοι τὴν ἀπολύτρωσον, "they were tortured, after refusing to accept the offered release," evokes a graphic impression of suffering without relief. The noun τύμπανον denotes the "rack" or stake to which those who were beaten were fastened (2 Macc 6:19, 28), or the cudgel with which a beating was administered (Aristophanes, *Plutus* 476). The cognate verb τυμπανίζειν signifies "to beat to death," and then generally "to torture" (e.g., Plutarch, *Moralia* 60A). There is no singular usage, but the reference may be to a form of torture in which a person was stretched out on a rack, and then his taut stomach was beaten as one beats a drum (τύμπανον; cf. LSJ 1834), until the muscle-walls collapsed and death occurred from internal injuries. From this practice the verb came to mean "to break on a wheel" (cf. 3 Macc 3:27; Jos., *Ag. Ap.* 1.20, 148; Plutarch, *Dio* 28.2, where the compound ἀποτυμπανίζειν is used, as it is in Codex D* at this point; for reference to the "wheel" [τροχός], see 4 Macc 5:32; 8:13; 9:12, 17, 19, 20; 10:7; 11:10, 17; 15:22; Philo, *Against Flaccus* 10, 85; see further Owen, *JTS* 30 [1929] 259–66). On the other hand, the reference may be to death by brutal scourging (4 Macc 5:32; 6:3–6, 10; cf. Tacitus, *Annals of Rome* 2.35.5; Suetonius, *Nero* 49; *Claudius* 34). The experience of such humiliation was one of recent memory for the Jewish community in Alexandria when the Roman prefect Flaccus (appointed A.D. 32) arranged a spectacle in a theater that consisted of Jews "being scourged, hung up, bound to a wheel, brutally mauled and hauled off for their death march through the middle of the orchestra" (Philo, *Against Flaccus* 85).

Those who were so tortured had refused the opportunity to gain their freedom at the cost of renouncing their faith. They could have avoided torture and death had they been prepared to comply with the demands of their tormentors, but they resolutely refused to do so (see above, *Note* m). The word ἀπολύτρωσις, "the offered release," is used in the common Greek sense of setting a slave or captive free for a ransom (e.g., *Ep. Arist.* 12, 33; Philo, *Every Good Man Is Free* 114; Jos., *Ant.* 12.27); the elements of "cost" and "price" are present in v 35b, although the use of the word is clearly metaphorical. The deliverance not accepted reflects a ransom refused because the price was the renunciation of commitment to God (cf. Büchsel, *TDNT* 4:354). The statement is amply illustrated by the behavior of the ninety-year-old scribe, Eleazar, who refused the pretense of renouncing commitment to God so that he might ἀπολυθῇ τοῦ θανάτου, "be released from death" (2 Macc 6:22). He willingly chose the rack (τύμπανον) and endured a brutal beating: "When he was about to die under the blows, he groaned aloud and said: 'It is clear to the Lord in his holy knowledge that, though I might have been released from death, I am enduring terrible sufferings in my body through this beating, but in my soul I am glad to suffer these things because I fear him'" (2 Macc 6:30; cf. 2 Macc. 7:24).

The resoluteness expressed in the refusal of release was purposeful: ἵνα κρείττονος ἀναστάσεως τύχωσιν, "in order that they might obtain a better resurrection." The reception of those who had died ἐξ ἀναστάσεως, "by resurrection," in v 35a had reference to a temporary gift of life, as young sons were restored to their mothers. The vanquishing of death, however, was only anticipated in their experience; it was not definitive. They would experience mortality again. It is the final defeat of death in the experience of eschatological resurrection that is contemplated in the phrase κρείττονος ἀναστάσεως, "the better resurrection," where the adjective "better" expresses a qualitative distinction. The contrast implied is between a temporary return to mortal life after having come so close to death and the experience of authentic, endless life (so Spicq, 2:365, 369–71), or between resuscitation (v 35a) and final resurrection to life (so Mercado, "Language of Sojourning," 151–52; F. F. Bruce, 338).

The reference to the refusal of release and the enduring of torment in the context of a firm expectation of attaining the resurrection shows unmistakably that the allusion in v 35b is to 2 Macc 6:18–7:42, where the Jewish historian recounts the martyrdom of Eleazar and of a mother and her seven sons at the hands of Antiochus IV Epiphanes and his officers. Specific reference is made to the hope of the resurrection in the account of the sufferings endured by three of the seven brothers, as well as in the encouragement offered to them by their mother (2 Macc 7:9, 11, 14, 22–23, 29). The defiant words of the fourth brother to Antiochus capture the spirit in which they all met their death: "One cannot but choose to die at the hands of men and to cherish the hope that God gives of being raised again [ἀναστήσεσθαι] by him. But for you there will be no ἀνάστασις εἰς ζωήν [resurrection to life]!" (2 Macc 7:14). The example of the Maccabean martyrs demonstrates the ability of faith to sustain a resilient spirit even while being subjected to dehumanizing abuse. Faith proves to be the source of endurance in suffering and of moral courage in the face of death.

Others had escaped martyrdom, but they had endured contempt and personal injury because they were faithful to God (v 36). Their ordeal consisted of being the objects of cruelly directed verbal abuse (ἐμπαιγμῶν) and flogging (μαστίγων), and even of "chains and imprisonment," a hendiadys for captivity, with the deprivation and exposure to inhumane treatment that imprisonment in antiquity entailed. An account of the infliction of such indignities upon servants of God could be marshalled from almost every generation in which fidelity to God became a matter of costly commitment (cf. 2 Chr 36:23). Jeremiah had been beaten and placed in the stocks and complained bitterly that he had been made an object of ridicule and mockery, whose ministry brought only insult and reproach (Jer 20:2, 7–8). On another occasion he had been beaten and imprisoned in a dungeon, where he remained for a lengthy period (Jer 37:15–16, 18–20). When he was subsequently lowered into a mud-filled cistern, he would have starved to death had not a Cushite official of the royal palace secured permission to remove him from the cistern (Jer 38:6–13). In summarizing a long history of abuse, Joshua ben Sira said of Jeremiah, "they had afflicted him" (Sir 49:7). Other prophets were similarly mistreated (e.g., 1 Kgs 22:26–27 [Micaiah]; 2 Chr 16:10 [Hanani]). The price of fidelity to God was often intense suffering. The community addressed could identify with this sober reminder, for it had been confirmed in their own earlier experience (10:32–34).

37–38 The long chain of asyndeta in v 37 is rhetorically effective. The writer strings together a series of terse statements, without the conjunctions that normally join coordinate clauses, just as he had done in vv 33–34, in order to create an aural and sensory impression upon his audience. The enumeration of acts of violence and deprivation is indicative of a martyr-catalogue, which brings the exemplary commitment of the martyrs before the Christian congregation.

Jerusalem had earned a reputation for killing the prophets and stoning those whom God had sent to deliver his word (Matt 23:27; Luke 13:34). Only one specific incident of such a stoning is reported in the OT. Zechariah, son of Jehoiada the priest, had been stoned to death in the Temple courtyard by order of King Joash (2 Chr 24:20–21; cf. *Lives of the Prophets* 23.1 [ed. C. C. Torrey, 31, 47]; Matt 23:35; Luke 11:50–51). The plural form of ἐλιθάσθησαν, "they were stoned," presupposes an appeal to Jewish tradition concerning others who were stoned, including Jeremiah, who purportedly met death by stoning at the hands of Egyptian Jews who were enraged because he had denounced their idolatrous practices (*Lives of the Prophets* 2.1 [ed. C. C. Torrey, 21, 35]; cf. Tertullian, *Scorpion Antidote* 8; Hippolytus, *Concerning Christ and Antichrist* 31; Jerome, *Against Jovinian* 2.37). Summarizing the witness of Scripture concerning the fate of the righteous, Clement of Rome declared, "They were stoned by law-breakers" (*1 Clem.* 45:4; cf. Acts 7:57–60; 14:5, 9).

Suggested by the euphonic similarity in sound, ἐπρίσθησαν, "they were sawn in two," presupposes a familiarity with the tradition concerning the death of Isaiah (cf. *Lives of the Prophets* 1.1 [ed. C. C. Torrey, 20, 34]: "He met his death at the hands of Manasseh, sawn in two"). The source of the tradition appears to have been an old genealogical book found in Jerusalem (*b. Yebam.* 49*b* [baraitha: Tanna R. Simeon b. Azzai]; cf. *y. Sanh.* 10.2.28*c*, *b. Sanh.* 103*b*, *Pesiq. R.* 4.3). According to these mutually complementary rabbinic sources, Manasseh, enraged because Isaiah had prophesied the destruction of the Temple, ordered his arrest. Isaiah fled to the hill country and hid in the trunk of a cedar tree. He was discovered when the king ordered the tree cut down. Isaiah was tortured with a saw because he had taken refuge in the trunk of a tree (cf. Caquot, *Sem* 23 [1973] 65, 83–91; Gaster and Heller, *MGWJ* 80 [1936] 32–52). A Christian source, the *Ascension of Isaiah*, contains the vestiges of an older Jewish writing relating to the martyrdom of Isaiah, but the tradition is reported in an elliptical fashion (*Mart. Isa.* 5:1–4, 11–14; cf. Justin, *Dialogue with Trypho* 120.5; Tertullian, *On Patience* 14; Origen, *Epistle to Africanus* 9; Hippolytus, *Concerning Christ and Antichrist* 30). The practice of sawing men in two was perpetuated by the Romans at the time of the Jewish War (*Gen. Rab.* 65.22: a certain Jose Meshita was sawn by the Romans on a sawhorse) and by certain Cyrenian Jews during the insurrection of A.D. 115 (Cassius Dio 68.32).

Although some exemplars of faith had "escaped the edge of the sword" (v 34), others had been murdered by the sword for the boldness with which they delivered the word of the Lord. Elijah escaped the wrath of Jezebel, but other prophets had not been so fortunate (1 Kgs 18:4, 13; 19:10). The prophet Uriah, a contemporary of Jeremiah, fled to Egypt to escape Jehoiakim, but the king had him brought back forcibly. When he was brought before the monarch, he was "struck down with the sword," and his body was cast into a commoner's grave (Jer 26:20–23). In a vision Daniel was shown a time when the Temple would be desecrated, the daily sacrifice abolished, and faithful men and women would "fall by the sword or be burned or captured or plundered" (Dan 11:31–33). The fate of being murdered by the sword was certainly not an isolated experience in the OT or in the post-biblical period (cf. 1 Macc 1:30; 2:9, 38; 5:13; 7:15–17, 19; 2 Macc 5:24–26).

Although the call to the prophetic office did not always entail a violent death, it often meant a life of severe privation. This aspect of faith is exposed in v 37b: "they went about in sheepskins and goatskins, destitute, oppressed, and mistreated." The terms μηλωτή, "sheepskin," and αἴγειος, "goatskin," denote undressed skins, with their wool or hairs (cf. Num 31:10; 3 Kgdms 19:13, 19 LXX). The allusion is primarily to Elijah and Elisha, although other prophets may also have been in the writer's thought. In the LXX Elijah is identified as a man with a garment of skins with hair (δασύς, 4 Kgdms 1:8), and the word μηλωτή, "sheepskin," is used exclusively of Elijah's coarse cloak (3 Kgdms 19:13, 19; 4 Kgdms 2:8, 13–14), which was subsequently passed on to Elisha. The "hairy cloak" appears to have become the standard uniform of the prophets (Zech 13:4; *Mart. Isa.* 2:10). The writer finds in the characteristic garb of the prophets a symbol of their distinctiveness from the world and of their impoverished condition (Michel, *TDNT* 4:637; cf. Matt 11:8–9). Alluding to v 37b, Clement of Rome urged Christians at Corinth to emulate "those who went about in goatskins and sheepskins, heralding the coming of Christ; we mean Elijah and Elisha, and moreover Ezekiel, the prophets" (*1 Clem.* 17:1).

The portrayal of the rudely dressed prophets as homeless wanderers, "destitute, afflicted and mistreated," is an apt summarization of the itinerant ministries of Elijah and Elisha (cf. 1 Kgs 17:2–16; 19:1–19; 2 Kgs 1:3–15; 2:23; 4:1–2, 8–12, 38–43; 8:1–2). It is equally appropriate for others who chose to endure severe hardships rather than to compromise their convictions. Following the seizing of Jerusalem by the troops of Antiochus IV Epiphanes, earnest Jews fled, only to find themselves destitute and hunted: "Judas Maccabaeus, with about nine others, got away to the wilderness, and kept himself and his companions alive in the mountains as wild animals do; they continued to live on what grew wild, so that they might not share in the defilement" (2 Macc 5:27; cf. *Mart. Isa.* 2:9–11: Isaiah and his company remained in the mountains for two years, subsisting on herbs gathered on the mountains).

The continuation of the statement refers to a large company of faithful men and women who sought refuge in remote areas in preference to disloyalty to God and to the law: "they wandered aimlessly in uninhabited regions [ἐπὶ ἐρημίαις πλανώμενοι] and on mountains [ὄρεσιν] and in caves [σπηλαίοις] and crevices [ὀπαῖς] in the ground" (v 38). A flight to the desert or hill country was a normal response to persecution in Palestine (cf. 1 Kgs 18:4, 13; 19:1–3, 9; *2 Apoc. Bar.* 2; *Mart. Isa.* 2:9–11; *As. Mos.* 9:1–7). The formulation in v 38 is patterned after Ps 106[MT 107]:4 LXX: "They wandered in uninhabited, waterless regions" (ἐπλανήθησαν ἐν τῇ ἐρήμῳ ἐν ἀνύδρῳ). A close parallel occurs in a reference to those who fled from Jerusalem after the city had been sacked by Pompey in 63 B.C.: "They wandered in uninhabited regions [ἐπλανῶντο ἐν ἐρήμοις] so that their lives might be preserved from harm" (*Pss. Sol.* 17:17). In point of fact, however, the vocabulary and detail of v 38 can be richly illustrated from many periods during which pious Jews found a refuge from persecution only in remote areas where they could hide (e.g., 1 Macc 2:29–38; 2 Macc 5:27; 6:11; 10:6 for the period 169 B.C.; Jos., *Ant.* 14.421, 429–30, for the period 40–37 B.C.; cf. Loftus, *JQR* 66 [1966] 212–21).

The parenthetical comment ὧν οὐκ ἦν ἄξιος ὁ κόσμος, "humanity was not worthy of them," means that society did not deserve to possess them (BAGD 78; contrast Westcott, 381: although they were deprived of everything, they were worth more than the whole world). As an aide to the Christians addressed, the pronouncement effectively sums up the worth of those courageous Jews who freely embraced a homeless and wretched existence in order to remain loyal to God.

39–40 The epilogue to the section brings the catalogue of exemplary witnesses to an appropriate conclusion and provides a transition to the argument of 12:1–13. It achieves this by summarizing the chapter succinctly and by tying the audience's experience to that of the attested witnesses who have preceded them. Recapitulating the substance and vocabulary of v 2, the writer declares that all those whose response to God has been celebrated in the preceding verses received attestation from God because of their faith (μαρτυρηθέντες διὰ τῆς πίστεως). As such, they serve as examples for later generations of believers, especially for Christians, who have been called to face "the last great hour of testing" (Michel, 421, with reference to 12:9–13). The parallel with v 2 suggests that πάντες, "all," in v 39 has reference to the entire list, and not simply to the exemplars of faith to whom the writer referred in vv 32–38 (as urged by Michel, 421; cf. Vanhoye, *La structure*, 193–94, who is influenced by the formula διὰ πίστεως, "through faith," in v 33, which is resumed in διὰ τῆς πίστεως, "through faith," in v 39).

Although "all" had received attestation in Scripture, οὐκ ἐκομίσαντο τὴν ἐπαγγελίαν, "they did not receive what had been promised." The realization of particular promises (e.g., vv 11, 33) is not to be confused with the definitive fulfillment of the promise. The exemplars of the past did not obtain the promised eternal inheritance (cf. 9:15). The writer's emphasis in v 39 resumes v 13, where the expectation of the patriarchs was considered in terms of "promises" that they only saw and saluted from a distance (cf. Peterson, "Examination," 271–72). Living in terms of the promises of God without experiencing the eschatological reward became characteristic of faith itself. The emphasis in v 39 shows that the writer has not simply compiled a list of examples. He has compiled a list of examples ordered toward a historical goal marked by the fulfillment of God's ultimate promises (Swetnam, *Jesus and Isaac*, 87).

The failure of the exemplars of faith to obtain the promised eternal inheritance can be traced to no fault of their own. It was because of the gracious providence of God who περὶ ἡμῶν κρεῖττόν τι προβλεψαμένου, "provided something better with us in mind" (v 40a). The key expression κρεῖττόν τι, "something better," is given definition by the final ἵνα clause in v 40b: ἵνα μὴ χωρὶς ἡμῶν τελειωθῶσιν, "so that they should not reach perfection except with us." The final clause is epexegetical and indicates that κρεῖττόν τι should be understood absolutely: the better plan was that the attested witnesses should not experience perfection without "us" (cf. Riggenbach, 382). They were denied the historical experience of the messianic perfection until Christians could share in it. In short, God in his providence deferred the bestowal of the final reward until the advent of Christ and the enactment of the new covenant (so Moffatt, 191; du Plessis, *Teleios*, 224–25). That the attested exemplars of faith died without having received the ultimate promise simply indicated God's special graciousness toward those living under the conditions of the new covenant (so Peterson, "Examination," 273). Emphasis is placed on the sovereignty and grace of God.

This interpretation presupposes that the expression ἵνα . . . τελειωθῶσιν, "in order that . . . they should reach perfection," builds upon the writer's prior use of the verb τελειοῦν, "to make perfect," "to bring to perfection." In Hebrews, the verb bears a distinctive religious sense. Perfection entails the accomplishment of a decisive purging of sin with the consequence that believers are consecrated to the service of God (10:14, cf. 9:9; 10:1). The terminology of perfection is used by the writer to stress the realized aspect of salvation, viewed from the perspective of the Christian era. The advantage that Christians enjoy over the exemplars of faith under the old covenant is that they have been "perfected" already by Christ's sacrificial death (see *Comment* on 10:14; cf. Peterson, "Examination," 259–65, 272). The context emphasizes the social dimension of salvation. In v 40 the attaining of perfection is clearly an eschatological event experienced in fellowship with the people of the new covenant (cf. Michel, 421, n. 4: "each individual Christian must acquire it, but he receives the gift in association with the whole Church").

If the reference to the reception of "what was promised" in v 39*b* indicates the sense in which the perfection of v 40*b* is to be understood, τελειοῦν should be interpreted in terms of entrance into the promised eternal inheritance (so Kögel, "Der Begriff τελειοῦν im Hebräerbrief," 55–56; cf. Riggenbach, 383, who correctly suggests that the promise in v 39 has reference to the eschatological salvation as a whole, viewed from the perspective of OT prophecy; it is unnecessary to distinguish here between the achievement of Christ at his first coming and the full realization of God's promises at the second coming). In Hebrews the concept of perfection, as related to the believing community, consistently has in view the totality of Christ's ministry on their behalf, in his death and heavenly exaltation. His high priestly work secures for them in the present unrestricted access to God, which fulfills the promises of the new covenant (cf. 10:16–20). This advantage, in turn, is the pledge of their ultimate transfer to the actual presence of God in the heavenly sanctuary.

In its context, v 40 places the emphasis on the final realization of the relationship with God. The writer has argued that the sacrifice of Christ secured all that is necessary for the enjoyment of the eschatological blessing of τελείωσις, "perfection": a definitive putting away of sin, consecration to the service of God, and glorification. It is therefore clear that the perfecting of faithful men and women under the old covenant depended upon the sacrificial death of Jesus; the promised eternal inheritance that was offered to them has become attainable only by virtue of Christ's sacrifice (cf. 9:15). The exemplary witnesses of the old covenant were denied the historical experience of the messianic perfection as a totality. But now that Christ has accomplished his high priestly ministry, they too will share in its blessings (so Peterson, "Examination," 274–77, who cautions that the formulation in v 40 does not resolve the question as to the present status of these men and women of faith; F. F. Bruce, 344, argues that they now enjoy the same privileged status as Christians; Spicq, 2:368, argues that they are still not perfected, but must await "the better resurrection" [v 35*b*] to experience perfection).

In summary, in vv 39–40 the writer contrasts all of the attested witnesses with "us" and uses the verb "to be perfected" to refer back to the concept of eschatological salvation effected completely by the high priestly ministry of Christ (10:14). His intention is to impress the Christians he addressed with a particular instance of the grace of God: "the coming of the messianic τελείωσις ['perfection'] was actually deferred to allow *them* to share in it!" (Peterson, "Examination," 277). The privileged status of Christians as those who have shared in the fulfillment of God's promise should motivate them to be more willing and equipped to endure the testing of faith than were their predecessors, all of whom received attestation from God through their faith.

Explanation

The recommendation and celebration of faith in 11:1–40 are firmly embedded in its context. Confronted with the fact that there had been defections from the house church (10:25) and an apparent loss of confidence in the promise of God (10:35), the writer had stressed the utter reliability of God. His faithfulness to his promise guarantees the assurance that the reward for doing the will of God is reception of what he has promised (10:23, 36). The will of God, however, is defined by the prophetic oracle, "my righteous one will live by faith" (10:38), while the context gives to faith the nuance of steadfast faithfulness to God and to his word of promise. The categorization of Christians as those who have faith and so acquire life (10:39) invited clarification of the dynamic nature of biblical faith. In the exposition that follows, faith is characterized as a quality of response to God that celebrates the reality of promised blessings and the objective certainty of events announced but as yet unseen (11:1). This understanding is substantiated by a catalogue of persons and events viewed from the perspective of faith in action. The demonstration of the effective power of faith under the old covenant verifies the character and possibilities of faith for the Christian community.

Faith is shown to be a temporal orientation to the future. The eschatological, forward-looking character of faith invests the realm of objective hopes and promises with solidity. It is the property of faith to render hope secure. The writer finds in faith a substantiation of hopes as yet unrealized and events as yet unseen. Faith celebrates now the reality of the future blessings that are secured by the promise of God. It recognizes that it is the future, and not the past, that molds the present. By conferring upon objects of hope the force of present realities, faith enables the people of God to enjoy the full certainty of their future realization.

From this perspective, it is proper to speak of a demonstrating function of faith. Faith demonstrates the existence of substantial reality, which cannot be perceived through empirical sense perception. It furnishes evidence concerning events as yet undisclosed because they belong to the eschatological future. When faith has its source in a direct, personal encounter with the living God, life is given a positive orientation toward God and his word. The men and women celebrated in the catalogue of attested exemplars all directed the capacity of faith to realities which for them lay in the future (cf. 11:7, 10, 13, 27, 31, 35–38). They found in faith a reliable guide to the future, even though they died without experiencing the fulfillment of God's promise (11:23, 39). The writer confesses and promotes the intensity of faith as a predicating force for Christian life that is directed to the future. For the person of faith, the future is no longer insecure.

The motifs of pilgrimage, sighting the goal but not attaining it, and the disavowal of a worldly goal permit the writer to explore the dialectic between faith and hope. He intuits that a mind is capable of hoping precisely because its consciousness can be shaped by a non-present, or invisible, heavenly world. This intuition stands behind the recital of actions regulated by a perspective on the future that finds its ground in a dynamic faith in God and in the reward he confers upon those who please him (11:6). The reward is the portion of those who seek God himself. The firm expectation of the reward is a matter of unwavering hope in God who has disclosed the future through the word of his promise. Faith holds onto the promise, even when the evidence of harsh reality impugns its integrity, because the one who promised is himself faithful.

The most distinctive aspect of the exposition is the development of the relation of faith to suffering and martyrdom. It is striking that the individuals mentioned in this celebrated digest of the history of Israel are those who exercised faith in the face of death. Almost without exception, the context links each exemplar in some way or other to death, either his own or one of his family (11:4, 5, 7, 11–12, 13, 17–19, 20, 21, 22, 23, 25–26, 29, 30, 31, 33–34, 35–38). Those for whom death is not specified in the context were exposed to severe trial or peril for fidelity to God. The capacity to endure suffering and death presupposes a relationship to the unseen world. This dimension of the recital of faith in action displays the practical and pastoral orientation of the catalogue. It has been carefully crafted to address a crisis of faith in the life of the Christian community. They had already experienced adversity, humiliation, loss of property, and imprisonment (10:32–34). The list of attested witnesses, composed of those who were their forebearers, was designed to strengthen Christians in their resolve to be faithful to God, even in the event of martyrdom (cf. 12:1–4).

B. The Display of the Necessary Endurance (12:1–13)

Bibliography

Andriessen, P. "La communauté des 'Hébreux' était-elle tombée dans le relâchement?" *NRT* 96 (1974) 1054–66. ———. "Renonçant à la joie qui lui revenait." *NRT* 97 (1975) 424–38. ———. and **Lenglet, A.** "Quelques passages difficiles de l'Épître aux Hébreux (5,7.11; 10, 20; 12, 2)." *Bib* 51 (1970) 207–20. **Ballarini, T.** "ARCHEGOS (Atti 3, 15; 5, 31; Ebr 2, 10; 12, 2): autore o condottiero?" *SacDoc* 16 (1971) 535–51. **Bartlett, R. E.** "The Cloud of Witnesses: Heb. xii.l." *Exp* 1st ser. 5 (1877) 149–53. **Bertram, G.** "Der Begriff der Erziehung in der griechischen Bibel." In *Imago Dei*. FS G. Krüger. Leipzig: Hinrichs, 1932. 33–51. **Black, D. A.** "A Note on the Structure of Hebrews 12:1–2." *Bib* 68 (1987) 543–51. **Bonnard, P. E.** "La traduction de Hébreux 12, 2: 'C'est en vue de la joie que Jésus endura la croix.'" *NRT* 97 (1975) 415–23. **Bornkamm, G.** "Sohnshaft und Leiden." In *Judentum, Urchristentum, Kirche*. FS J. Jeremias. Ed. W. Eltester. BZNW 26. Berlin: Akademie, 1960. 188–98. **Bream, N.** "More on Hebrews xii. 1." *ExpTim* 80 (1968–69) 150–51. **Caird, G. B.** "Just Men Made Perfect." *LQHR* 35 (1966) 89–98. **Campos, J.** "Concepto de la 'Disciplina' biblica." *RevistCal* 6 (1960) 47–73. **Clark, K. W.** "The Meaning of APA." In *Festschrift to Honor F. Wilbur Gingrich*. Ed. E. H. Barth and R. E. Cocroft. Leiden: Brill, 1972. 70–84. **Costé, J.** "Notion grecque et notion biblique de la 'souffrance educatrice.'" *RSR* 43 (1955) 497–508. **Dodd, C. H.** "Some Problems in NT Translation." *ExpTim* 72 (1961) 268–74. **Dussaut, L.** *Synopse structurelle de l'Épître aux Hébreux*, 122–28. **Dyck, T. L.** "Jesus our Pioneer: *APXHΓOΣ* in Heb. 2:5–18; 12:1–3." Dissertation, Northwest Baptist Theological Seminary, 1980. 124–51, 165–67. **Ellingworth, P.** "New Testament Text and Old Testament Context in Heb. 12.3." In *Studia Biblica* 3. Ed. E. A. Livingston. JSNTSup 3. Sheffield: JSOT Press, 1980. 89–96. **Fiorenza, E. S.** "Der Anführer und Vollender unseres Glaubens: Zum theologischen Verständnis des Hebräerbriefs." In *Gestalt und Anspruch des Neuen Testaments*. Ed. J. Schreiner. Würzburg: Echter, 1969. 262–81. **Galitis, G. A.** "'Αρχηγός—'Αρχηγέτης ἐν τῇ ἑλληνικῇ γραμματείᾳ καὶ θρησκείᾳ." *Athena* 64 (1960) 17–138. ———. Ἡ χρῆσις τοῦ ὅρου "ἀρχηγός" ἐν τῇ Καινῇ Διαθήμῃ. Athens: Athinon, 1960. **Gambiza, F. K. M.** "*Teleiosis* and *Paideia* as Interpretation of Sufferings: The Perfecting of Jesus and the Disciplining of Christians in the Letter to the Hebrews." Dissertation, Christ Seminary-Seminex, 1981. **Garvie, A. E.** "The Pioneer of Faith and of Salvation." *ExpTim* 26 (1914–15) 502–4, 546–50. **Gourgues, M.** *A la droite de Dieu*. 120–25. **Grässer, E.** "Exegese nach Auschwitz? Kritische Anmerkungen zur hermeneutischen Bedeutung des Holocaust am Beispiel von Heb 11." *KD* 27 (1981) 152–63. ———. *Der Glaube im Hebräerbrief*. 57–62, 102–5, 153. **Hamm, D.** "Faith in the Epistle to the Hebrew: The Jesus Factor." *CBQ* 52 (1990) 270–91. **Harris, J. R.** "Base-born and True-born." *Exp* 49 (1923) 155–60. ———. "Some Notes on 4 Maccabees. " *ExpTim* 32 (1920–21) 183–85. **Hayes, D. A.** "Jesus the Perfecter of Faith (Hebr 12,2)." *BW* 20 (1902) 278–87. **Healon, F. A.** "Hebrews XII,2." *Th* 2 (1930) 43–44. **Hengel, M.** *Crucifixion in the Ancient World and the Folly of the Message of the Cross*. Philadelphia: Fortress, 1977. 1–10, 22–32, 39–45, 51–63, 69–90. **Horning, E. B.** "Chiasmus, Creedal Structure, and Christology in Hebrews 12:1–2." *PCSBR* 23 (1978) 37–48. **Jaeger, W.** *Early Christianity and Greek Paideia*. Cambridge: Belknap, 1961. 3–26, 105–118. ———. "Paideia Christi." *ZNW* 50 (1959) 1–14. **Jentsch, W.** *Urchristliches Erziehungsdenken: Die Paideia Kyriou in Rahmen des hellenistisch-jüdischen Umwelt*. BFCT 45.3. Gütersloh: Bertelsmann, 1951. **Johnston, G.** "Christ as Archegos." *NTS* 27 (1980–81) 381–85. **Jones, P. R.** "A Superior Life: Hebrews 12:3–13:25." *RevExp* 82 (1985) 391–405. **Jonge, M. de.** "Vreemedelingen en bijwoners: Einige opmerkingen narr aanleiding van I Pt 2:11 en verwante teksten." *NedTTs* 11 (1956–57) 11–36. **Käsemann, E.** "Hebräer 12, 12–17." In *Exegetische Versuche und Besinnungen*. Göttingen: Vandenhoeck & Ruprecht, 1970. 1.307–12. **Köberle, A.** "Die Wolke den Zeugen (Hebr. 12, 1–3): Wortverkündigung zum Reformationsfest." In *Gestalten und Wege den Kirche im Osten*. Ed. H. Kimiska. Leipzig: Hinrichs, 1958. 13–18. **Kraus, H.** "*Paedagogia Dei* als theologischer Geschichtsbegriff." *EvT* 8 (1948–49) 517–97. **Kudasiewicz, J.** "Circumstans peccatum (Hbr 12, 1)." *CollTh* 46 (1976) 127–40. **Kuhn, H.-W.** "Jesus als Gekreuzigter in der frühchristlicher Verkündigung bis zur Mitte des 2. Jahrhunderts." *ZTK* 72 (1975) 1–46. **Laub, F.** *Bekenntnis und Auslegung*. 154–65. **Leivestad, R.** "Jesus som forbillede ifølge Hebreerbrevet." *NorTT* 74 (1973) 195–206. **Lenglet, A.** "A la suite de l'initiateur (He 12, 1–4)." *AsSeign* 51 (1972) 56–61. **Loader, W. R. G.** "Christ at the Right Hand—Ps. CX.1 in the New Testament." *NTS* 24 (1977–78) 199–217. **Logan, S. P.** "The Background of *Paideia* in Hebrews." Dissertation, Southern Baptist Theological Seminary, 1986. **Matthews, J.** "Hebrews XII.2" *ExpTim* 8 (1896–97) 238. **McCown, W. G.** "Holiness in Hebrews." *WesThJ* 16 (1981) 58–78. ———. Ό ΛΟΓΟΣ ΤΗΣ ΠΑΡΑΚΛΗΣΕΩΣ: The Nature and Function of the Horatory Sections in the Epistle to the

Hebrews." Dissertation, Union Theological Seminary, Richmond, 1970. 98–119, 149–51, 185, 205–6, 225. **Melbourne, B. L.** "An Examination of the Historical-Jesus Motif in the Epistle to the Hebrews." *AUSS* 26 (1988) 281–97. **Michel, O.** "Zur Auslegung des Hebräerbriefes." *NovT* 6 (1963) 189–91. **Mora, G.** *La Carta a los Hebreos como Escrito Pastoral.* 63–66, 80–83, 171–91. **Moulton, W. J.** "The Relay Race." *ExpTim* 33 (1921–22) 73–74. **Müller, P. G.** ΧΡΙΣΤΟΣ ΑΡΧΗΓΟΣ: *Der religionsgeschichtliche und theologische Hintergrund einer neutestamentlichen Christusprädikation.* Bern: Lang, 1973. 302–12, 353–93. **Nauck, W.** "Freude im Leiden: Zum Problem der urchristlichen Verfolgungstradition." *ZNW* 46 (1955) 68–80. **Niederstrasser, H.** *Kerygma und Paideia: Zum Problem den erziehenden Gnade.* Stuttgart: Evangelisches Verlagswerk, 1967. 397–406. **Nisius, J. B.** "Zur Erklärung von Hebr. 12, 2." *BZ* 14 (1916–17) 44–61. **Peterson, D. G.** "An Examination of the Concept of 'Perfection' in the 'Epistle to the Hebrews.'" Dissertation, Universtiy of Manchester, 1978. 291–305, 325 (cf. *Hebrews and Perfection.* SNTSMS 47. Cambridge: University Press, 1982). **Pfitzner, V. C.** *Paul and the Agon Motif: Traditional Athletic Imagery in the Pauline Literature.* Leiden: Brill, 1967. 1–15, 23–72, 134–56. **Robb, J. D.** "Hebrews xii.1." *ExpTim* 79 (1967–68) 254. **Ross, G. A. J.** "Enduring for Education." *ExpTim* 14 (1902–3) 272–74. **Rusche, H.** "Glauben und Leben nach dem Hebräerbrief." *BibLeb* 12 (1971) 94–104. **Sanders, J. A.** *Suffering as Divine Discipline in the Old Testament and Post-Biblical Judaism.* Rochester, NY: Colgate Rochester Divinity School, 1955. **Scott, J. J.** "*Archēgos* in the Salvation History of the Epistle to the Hebrews." *JETS* 29 (1986) 47–54. **Trilling, W.** "Jesus der Urheber und Vollender des Glaubens (Hebr. 12, 2)." In *Das Evangelium auf dem Weg zum Menschen.* Ed. O. Knoch. Frankfurt am Main: Knecht, 1973. 3–23. **Turner, N.** "To Purchase Joy? (Heb, 12:2)." In *Grammatical Insights into the New Testament.* Edinburgh: Clark, 1965. 172–73. **Vaccari, A.** "Hebr. 12.1: lectio emendatior." *Bib* 39 (1958) 471–77. ———. "Per meglio comprendere Ebrei 12,1." *RevistB* 6 (1958) 235–41. **Vanhoye, A.** "La souffrance éducatrice: Hé 12, 5–7. 11–13." *AsSeign* 52 (1974) 61–66. **Vitti, A. M.** "Proposito sibi gaudio (Hebr. 12,2)." *VD* 13 (1933) 154–59. **Watson, J. K.** "L'épître aux Hébreux et l'historicité." *CCER* 20 (1972) 1–13. **Weeks, W. R.** "More on Hebrews xii.1." *ExpTim* 80 (1968–69) 151. **Williams, S. K.** *Jesus' Death as Saving Event.* 165–70, 239–40. **Williamson, R.** *Philo and the Epistle to the Hebrews.* 250–51, 302–8, 483–91, 572–75.

Translation

[1] *Consequently, since we ourselves[a] have so great[b] a host[c] of witnesses about us, let us lay aside[d] all excess weight and the sin[e] that so easily distracts, [f]and let us run with endurance the race[g] prescribed[h] for us,* [2] *fixing our eyes upon[i] Jesus,[j] the champion in the exercise of faith and the one who brought faith to complete expression,[k] who rather than the joy[l] set before him[m] endured a cross,[n] disregarding the disgrace,[o] and has now taken his seat[p] at the right hand of the throne of God.* [3] *By all means[q] consider the one who endured[r] from sinners[s] such opposition[t] against themselves,[u] so that you may not become weary[v] and lose heart.[w]*

[4] *You have not yet resisted[x] to the point of bloodshed[y] while struggling[z] against sin.* [5] *And have you forgotten completely[aa] the encouragement[bb] which[cc] speaks to you as sons?[dd]*

"My son, do not regard lightly the discipline of the Lord,
    and do not lose heart when corrected by him;
[6] for the Lord disciplines the one whom he loves,
    and[ee] bestows corrective[ff] punishment upon every son whom he receives
    favorably."[gg]

[7] *You must endure[hh] [your trials[ii]] as [divine] discipline;[jj] God is treating[kk] you as sons.[ll] For what son is there whom a father, in his capacity as a father,[mm] does not*

discipline? [8]*But if you are left without [divine] discipline,*[nn] *in which all [sons] share,*[oo] *then you are illegitimate children rather than true sons, are you not?* [pp] [9]*Then again,*[qq] *we used to have* [rr] *our natural fathers* [ss] *as those who disciplined us, and we respected them.*[tt] *Should we not* [uu] *much more* [vv] *submit ourselves to the Father of spirits* [ww] *so that* [xx] *we shall live?* [10]*For our fathers* [yy] *continually disciplined* [zz] *us for a short time at their discretion,*[aaa] *but he [disciplines us] to our advantage*[bbb] *in order that we may share*[ccc] *in his holy character.* [ddd] [11]*All discipline at the actual time* [eee] *seems not to be pleasant but painful,*[fff] *but later it yields the fruit which consists of peace* [ggg] *and of righteousness for those who have been trained*[hhh] *by it.* [iii] [12]*Therefore, strengthen your drooping*[jjj] *hands and weakened knees,* [13]*and move in a straight direction*[kkk] *with your feet,* [lll]*so that what is lame might not be dislocated,*[mmm] *but rather healed.*[nnn]

Notes

[a] The expression καὶ ἡμεῖς is emphatic. Cf. NEB: "And what of ourselves?"

[b] It is impossible in translation to reflect the genuinely oratorical word order of the text. In ordinary speech, closely related elements are normally placed together. Vivid, impassioned discourse gives rise to the dislocation of closely related words for rhetorical effect. When a word is torn out of its natural context and made more independent it becomes emphatic. This occurs twice in verse 1: τοσοῦτον ἔχοντες περικείμενον (where τοσοῦτον modifies περικείμενον) and ὄγκον ἀποθέμενοι πάντα (where πάντα modifies ὄγκον). The expressions τοσοῦτον, "so great," and ὄγκον, "excess weight," are emphatic [BDF §473[2]]. Other examples of oratorical word order occur in vv 3, 8, and 11. Cf. Turner, *Grammar,* 4:106.

[c] The translation reflects the metaphorical use of the term νέφος, "cloud." For parallels from literary Gk. see LSJ 1171.

[d] The ptcp ἀποθέμενοι can be read as an ind, with the usual temporal suggestions ("having set aside all excess weight"), or it can be understood as having a hortatory nuance ("set aside all excess weight!"). In the context of the hortatory subjunctive, which follows as the main verb of the sentence, it is better to recognize the imperative force of the participle (so J. Thomas, "The Use of Voice, Moods and Tenses," 38–39, 46; cf. BAGD 553; A. P. Salom, "The Imperatival Use of the Participle in the New Testament," *AusBR* 11 (1963) 41–49).

[e] New arguments in support of the conjecture ἀπαρτίαν, "baggage," "equipment," in place of the reading of the text ἁμαρτίαν, "sin," have been put forth by Vaccari, *Bib* 39 (1958) 473–77, and *RevistB* 6 (1958) 235–41. He translates: "Let us also . . . set aside every encumbrance and *superfluous equipment,* and run the race." Although this proposal has been accepted by Vanhoye (*La structure,* 197, n. 1), the unbroken witness of the textual tradition, considerations of context, and problems associated with the conjecture indicate that ἁμαρτίαν must be the genuine reading (see Kudasiewicz, *CollTh* 46 [1976] 127–36).

[f] The determination of the original text at this point is unusually difficult but must ultimately be based on the suitability of alternative readings. For the translation the reading εὐπερίσπαστον, found in P46 and 1739, has been adopted. It is to be understood in its active sense, "liable to distract," "easily distracting," "readily diverting" (cf. NEB[mg]: "the sin which all too readily distracts us"). This reading has been dismissed as "a paleographical error or a deliberate modification of εὐπερίστατον, 'easily entangling,' 'easily clinging' which is unsupported by all the other known witnesses" (Metzger, *Textual Commentary,* 675; cf. P. Benoit, "Le codex paulinien Chester Beatty," *RB* 46 [1937] 66). Nevertheless, it has the decided advantage of removing the difficulties associated with the traditional reading, which has never been fully explained, and it makes good sense of the exhortation not to be distracted or diverted from the course, which is entirely appropriate to the metaphor of the race.

A serious problem with the dominant reading, εὐπερίστατος, is that the term is found nowhere else in the Gk. Bible nor in secular Gk., but only in Christian writings, most of which are dependent upon this place (Kudasiewicz, *CollTh* 46 [1976] 136; cf. Vaccari *Bib* 39 [1958] 472; Zuntz, *Text,* 25, denies that it is a *hap leg.,* but does not list any occurrences of the word in secular Gk., and none are noted by LSJ 726, MM 264, or BAGD 324). The verbal adj may be construed actively or passively and is therefore susceptible to different translations. There is still no general agreement concerning the meaning of the term (e.g., LSJ 726: "easily besetting," perhaps "leading to distress"; BAGD 324: "easily ensnaring"; MM 264: "easily avoided," "admired," "dangerous"; RSV: "clings so closely"; NIV: "so easily entangles"; E. K. Simpson, *Words Worth Weighing in the Greek New Testament* [London: Tyndale, 1946] 26–27: "so prone to hamper"; for the range of interpretation in the Patristic tradition, see *LPGL* 573).

The difference in text could have arisen from an error of the eye in transcribing from a copy or of the ear in the case of transcription from dictation. The corruption must have occurred in those early copies from which the extant MS tradition derives. For a full discussion of the issue and a defense of the reading εὐπερίσπαστον, see Beare, *JBL* 63 (1944) 390–91; Zuntz, *Text*, 25–29; Tasker, *NTS* 1 (1954–55) 184; Vaccari, *RevistB* 6 (1958) 235–41; Kudasiewicz, *CollTh* 46 (1976) 137–40; cf. Vaccari, *Bib* 39 (1958) 472–73, 476. The argument has been accepted by J. H. Davies, *SE* 4 (1968) 118–19; Snell, 148; and F. F. Bruce, 345.

ᵍ J. D. Robb attempted to argue on lexical grounds that there is no basis for translating ἀγών as "race." He maintained that the notion is rather of a "fight" or "struggle" (*ExpTim* 79 [1967–68] 254; cf. Kudasiewicz, *CollTh* 46 [1976] 130, who holds that τρέχειν ἀγῶνα is a technical expression signifying "to engage in a contest" (see Herodotus 8.102). In fact, the classical expression τρέχειν ἀγῶνα was used metaphorically for the endurance of peril by both prose writers and poets (cf. LSJ 1814 [II]; Bleek, 2.2:860–61; Moffatt, 195–96; Spicq, 2:382–83, 385; Grässer, *Glaube*, 57, n. 263).

Strictly speaking, ἀγών does not mean "race." It denoted a place of assembly for athletic events, and by derivation an athletic event. Only secondarily, and by natural transference did it come to signify a fight against an opponent (Dodd, *ExpTim* 72 [1961] 269–70; cf. LSJ 18). In the context of the metaphor of the footrace, τρέχειν ἀγῶνα is analogous to τρέχειν δρόμον (cf. 1 Cor 9:24; Gal 2:2; Phil 2:16), and "run the race" is the best translation (so BAGD 15, 825; LSJ 1814 [II, τρέχω with cognate accusative ἀγῶνα, "to run a course, a heat"]; Bream, *ExpTim* 80 [1968–69] 150–51; Weeks, *ExpTim* 80 [1968–69] 151).

ʰ Linguistically the ptcp προκείμενον may be understood to define the race as "laid out," "prescribed," "appointed," or alternatively as "lying before," "ahead." For the phrase τὸν προκείμενον ἡμῖν ἀγῶνα, the former understanding is preferable in the light of numerous parallels for a course being set or assigned (e.g., Herodotus 9.60: ἀγῶνος μεγίστου προκειμένου, "a great course laid out"; similar phrasing in Plato, *Laches* 182A; 4 Macc 15:2; Philo, *On Agriculture* 112; Epictetus, *Enchiridion* 3.25; *Testament of Forty Martyrs* 1). For a defense of the latter understanding see Dyck, "Jesus our Pioneer," 137.

ⁱ The expression ἀφορᾶν εἰς signifies "to look away from [the immediate surroundings] to" (MM 98). It is typically hellenistic (e.g., 4 Macc 17:10: εἰς θεὸν ἀφορῶντες, "looking to God"; Epictetus, *Enchiridion* 2.19: εἰς τὸν θεὸν ἀφορῶντες ἐν παντί, "looking to God in everything"; cf. Jos., *Ant.* 8.290). The present ptcp ἀφορῶντες is temporally concomitant with the main verb τρέχωμεν, i.e., while running let us fix our eyes upon Jesus. The present tense of the ptcp expresses duration.

ʲ By virtue of its deferred position, the personal name Ἰησοῦν is emphatic, as elsewhere in Hebrews (see *Comment* on 2:9).

ᵏ The dense expression τὸν τῆς πίστεως ἀρχηγὸν καὶ τελειωτήν is extraordinarily concise and resists facile translation. It must be given precision in the light of the larger development in Hebrews. The basis of the translation adopted for the commentary is set forth in *Comment* on v 2 below.

The syntactical position of the gen τῆς πίστεως indicates that it relates equally to both of the following nouns, and not simply to ἀρχηγόν. In the context of 11:1–40, "faith" must be understood absolutely, and not as the subjective act of Jesus in the individual, as if to say that *our* faith finds its point of origination and final development in Christ (so RSV: "the pioneer and perfecter of our faith"; or JB: "Jesus, who leads us in our faith and brings it to completion"; similar constructions in NEB, TEV, NIV, Phillips, Berkeley, Beck).

ˡ There are two competing translations of the expression ἀντὶ τῆς προκειμένης αὐτῷ χαρᾶς: (1) "in view of the joy set before him" (i.e., to obtain the joy as a prize, giving to ἀντί a final sense) or (2) "rather than [instead of] the joy that was set before him" (i.e., renouncing the joy that could have been his, giving ἀντί a substitutionary sense). A careful review of the uses of ἀντί leads Turner to conclude that "the sole significance of the preposition in each New Testament context is that of substitution and exchange" ("To Purchase Joy?" 173). Although a majority of exegetes and all modern English translations adopt the first alternative (defended by Bonnard, *NRT* 97 [1975] 415–23; cf. Hanna, *Grammatical Aid*, 160–61), considerations of context support the translation of ἀντί as "instead of," "in place of," "rather than." For a full discussion of the grammatical question and a defense of the translation adopted for the commentary, see Nisius, *BZ* 14 [1916–17] 44–61; Vitti, *VD* 13 [1933] 154–59; Turner, "To Purchase Joy?" 172–73; Andriessen and Lenglet, *Bib* 51 [1970] 215–20; and Andriessen, *NRT* 97 [1975] 424–38. The second alternative is favored by BAGD 73(1), 707(2);

J. Schneider, *TDNT* 7:577; Riggenbach, 390; Michel, 425, 435; Vanhoye, *La structure*, 197–98; Mora, *La Carta a los Hebreos*, 176, n. 112; Gourgues, *A la droite de Dieu*, 120, 122, n. 109; among others. See also the next note.

[m] Elsewhere in Hebrews *προκείμενος* does not relate to something future but to a present possibility (6:18; 12:1). Accordingly, the expression *προκειμένης αὐτῷ* implies "was within his grasp" (see BAGD 707 [2]).

[n] The expression is made definite in P$^{13, 46}$ D* co sa arm by the insertion of the article: *ὑπέμεινεν τὸν σταυρόν*, "he endured the cross." The anarthrous expression is idiomatic, signifying "submit to the cross" (see BAGD 764, 846).

[o] In this context the word *αἰσχύνη* carries the nuance of disgrace, together with the shame associated with it (see Bultmann, *TDNT* 1:190; Gourgues, *A la droite de Dieu,* 121, n. 108; Horning, *PCSBR* 23 [1978] 43; cf. BAGD 25).

[p] The verb *κεκάθικεν* is a normal durative pf. That which occurred in the past remains valid for the present and the future.

[q] In self-evident conclusions, especially exclamations and strong affirmations, *γάρ* is to be translated as inferential (BAGD 152: "certainly, by all means") or corroborative (Mora, *La Carta a los Hebreos*, 64, n. 194: "Yes, consider"). An alternative proposal is to regard the *γάρ* clause as supplying the motive for the writer's previous sentence (so Thrall, *Greek Particles*, 45: "I say this because I want you to consider . . . , so that you may not grow weary").

[r] The pf tense of the ptcp *ὑπομεμενηκότα* suggests initially the durative effect of Christ's redemptive sufferings, which were evoked in v 2 with the idiom *ὑπέμεινεν σταυρόν*, "he submitted to the cross." On the other hand, the pf can mean that this event still retains its exemplary significance. Jesus' voluntary submission to suffering offers an abiding example to the community (see BDF §342 [5]).

[s] In the phrase *ὑπὸ τῶν ἁμαρτωλῶν*, the prep functions as an equivalent to the classical *παρά* with the gen ("from sinners") (so Zerwick and Grosvenor, *Grammatical Analysis,* 684).

[t] It is impossible in translation to capture the euphonic word play between the main verb *ἀναλογίσασθε*, "consider," and *ἀντιλογίαν,* "hostility," "antagonism," "active opposition."

[u] The pl expression *εἰς ἑαυτούς* (or *αὐτούς*) is shown to be the correct reading by the quality of the support it enjoys in the MS tradition. All early Gk. witnesses and most versions lend the weight of their testimony to the pl (P$^{13, 46}$ ℵ* D* Ψ^{c} 048 33 1739* *al* it vg^{A,C} sy^{p} bo aeth Or). In spite of that fact there has been almost a consensus in favor of adopting the sg *εἰς ἑαυτόν* (or *αὐτόν*), supported primarily by Byzantine witnesses (A D^{c} K P Ψ Byz it^{ar,c,dem,div,f} vg^{B,D} sy^{h} Chr John of Damascus), on the ground that only the sg is suitable to the context. E. Riggenbach's statement that the pl reading is "very strongly attested, but utterly meaningless" (391) has been echoed numerous times (e.g., Zuntz, *Text,* 120; F. F. Bruce, 346, n. 5; Michel, 437, n. 1; P. E. Hughes, 126, n. 122). Zuntz regards the pl reading as evidence of "primitive corruption" in the text of Hebrews and considers the sg to be a "correct conjecture" (120). Alternatively, both the sg and pl readings have been rejected as competing glosses entered in the margin of an archetype (so Moffatt, 198; W. Manson, 83; Spicq, 1:429–30).

The UBSGNT^{3} adopts the sg for the printed text but assigns it only a "D" rating, indicating a very high degree of doubt concerning the correctness of the reading. Although the committee acknowledged that the external evidence "strongly favors" the pl, the difficulty of making sense of the pl led the majority to prefer the sg reading. Only A. Wikgren was prepared to adopt the pl, arguing that it is "the qualitatively best supported and the more difficult (though meaningful) reading, and the one more likely to be altered" (Metzger, *Textual Commentary,* 675).

Apart from the marginal readings, the plural is adopted by RV and AmT, following the Westcott-Hort edition of the text, and by the Jehovah's Witnesses' New World Translation. It is accepted as original by Westcott, 397–98; H. Montefiore, 216; and is defended on exegetical grounds by P. Ellingworth, "New Testament Text," 89–96. See the exegetical *Comment* on the reading below.

[v] The aor tense of *κάμητε* is ingressive: "become weary."

[w] The expression *ταῖς ψυχαῖς*, as a dative of respect, is to be construed with the ptcp *ἐκλυόμενοι* as elsewhere in hellenistic Gk. (Schweizer, *TDNT* 9:650, n. 209; Kistemaker, 372).

[x] On the basis of P^{46} Beare has proposed a radically different understanding of the text; he holds that the scribe wrote *ὅπου*, "where" (in the sense of occasion [see LSJ 1242 (II)]), at the beginning of the clause rather than *οὔπω*, "not yet," and the third sg form of the verb, *ἀντικατέστηκεν*, "he resisted," rather than the usual second pl form *ἀντικατέστητε*, "you have resisted." Beare argues that the thought of the previous sentence is continued in v 4. It conveys a warning against the danger of falling short of the steadfast endurance displayed by Jesus, "lest you become weary and lose heart, where he has resisted unto blood, in your strife against sin" (*JBL* 63

[1944] 391; cf. Hoskier, *Commentary*, 58). The unique reading of P⁴⁶ is without support elsewhere in the MS tradition.

ʸ The phrase μέχρις αἵματος is a case of the prep with the gen of degree or measure ("to the point of bloodshed"). Αἷμα, "blood," occurs here for "bloodshed" (so Zerwick and Grosvenor, *Grammatical Analysis*, 684). For the suggestion that the expression μέχρις αἵματος ἀντικατέστητε is an idiom meaning "resist unto death," see BAGD 74.

ᶻ This translation fails to reflect the word play between the compounds ἀντικατέστητε, "you have resisted," and ἀνταγωνιζόμενοι, "while struggling," which is rhetorically effective in the Gk. text.

ᵃᵃ In the middle voice, the compound verb ἐκλανθάνειν denotes "to forget altogether" or "completely" (BAGD 242).

ᵇᵇ The expression τῆς παρακλήσεως combines the notions of exhortation and comfort (cf. Riggenbach, 394; BAGD 618). In this context the note of encouragement appears to be dominant (cf. 6:18)

ᶜᶜ The relative pronoun ἥτις is used classically to refer to an antecedent, in this instance τῆς παρακλήσεως. Zerwick suggests that it may be concessive in this verse: "though it is such as addresses you as sons" (*Biblical Greek* §§215, 219).

ᵈᵈ The introductory statement may be construed as a question (RSV, JB, TEV) or as an assertion (NEB, NASB, NIV). The stylistically rhetorical character of the statement favors reading v 5a as an interrogative (so, for example, McCown, "Ο ΛΟΓΟΣ ΤΗΣ ΠΑΡΑΚΛΗΣΕΩΣ," 203–5; Peterson, "Examination," 300; cf. Thyen, *Stil*, 60). Vanhoye suggests that the intention of the text is expressed better by translating the ind as an imperative: "Do not forget completely" (*AsSeign* 52 [1974] 62).

ᵉᵉ The conj δέ is not adversative but continuative (Hanna, *Grammatical Aid*, 161).

ᶠᶠ It seems necessary in this context to stress the positive notion in the verb μαστιγοῦν; the punishment is "corrective" in character. Cf. C. Schneider, *TDNT* 4:518; BAGD 495.

ᵍᵍ The synonymous parallelism in v 6 (= Prov 3:12) shows that "receives favorably" implies "loves" (BAGD 614; cf. MM 482, who translate "welcomes," but who also call attention to the meaning "approve," "commend" in *Ep. Arist.* 190).

ʰʰ The verbal form ὑπομένετε may be construed as a present ind or a present imperative. Vanhoye, for example, translates the statement as an ind: "It is an educative suffering that you endure" (*AsSeign* 52 [1974] 63; cf. Westcott, 402; Moffatt, 201). The parenetic character of the context, however, seems to favor the imperative (so Michel, 440–41; Zerwick and Grosvenor, *Grammatical Analysis*, 685; BAGD 603, among others). The ind interpretation tends to weaken the force of ὑπομένειν somewhat (Michel, 441).

ⁱⁱ Although there is no linguistic equivalent in the text for the words in brackets, they are required to bring out the sense of the clause, which is a striking example of a compressed statement.

ʲʲ The translation presupposes the correctness of the reading εἰς παιδείαν, which is attested by the better witnesses. The variant reading εἰ παιδείαν [ὑπομένετε] (i.e., "if you endure correction God is treating you as sons"), found in Ψ⁴⁶ and the late cursives 104 326 365 630 945 *al*, has been defended as preferable by Jentsch, *Urchristliches Erziehungsdenken*, 169, Riggenbach, 395; Bornkamm, "Sohnshaft und Leiden," 189, n. 3; 197; and Bertram, *TDNT* 5:622. Yet it almost certainly represents a case of assimilation to the conditional construction found in v 8 (so Michel, 440; F. F. Bruce, 356, n. 58).

The uses of the prep εἰς are so varied that there has been no common agreement concerning the translation of εἰς παιδείαν. J. R. Mantey treated the clause as ind and argued that the context seemed to demand a causal translation of εἰς: "It is because of discipline that you are enduring" ("The Causal Use of ΕΙΣ in the New Testament," *JBL* 70 [1951] 47; so also Kistemaker, 380). In reply, R. Marcus denied the presence of the causal εἰς in the NT and argued for a purposive use of the preposition: "It is for discipline that you endure" ("On Causal ΕΙΣ," *JBL* 70 [1951] 129–30, and "The Elusive Causal ΕΙΣ," *JBL* 71 [1952] 44; so also Zerwick and Grosvenor, *Grammatical Analysis*, 685; BAGD 846). Turner conceded that the context would suit a causal sense but affirms that "as a discipline" is sufficient (*Grammar*, 3:266–67). On the other hand, if the construction is influenced by the LXX, where the expression ὑπομένειν εἰς means "wait for," "look eagerly for," "endure for" (e.g., Ps 129[130]:5; Jer 14:19), v 7a, could be translated "Wait patiently for discipline" (cf. Turner, *Grammar*, 4:112). This last proposal, however, seems least suitable to the context, which develops the thought that the endurance of disciplinary sufferings is a prerequisite for godly living.

ᵏᵏ Elsewhere in Hebrews the verb προσφέρειν means "to offer" in the technical sense of presenting a sacrifice. Here it occurs in the middle voice with the dative and is used with a nonbiblical nuance attested in the papyri: "to deal with," "to treat" (MM 552; cf. Swetnam, *Jesus and Isaac*, 121–22).

ll In the expression ὡς υἱοῖς the anarthrous υἱοῖς, "sons," has a qualitative nuance.

mm The omission of the article with both υἱός, "son," and πατήρ, "father," serves to emphasize the qualitative aspect of these concrete nouns (cf. Moulton, *Grammar*, 1:82–83; Zerwick, *Biblical Greek*, §179; BDF §257 [3]).

nn It is impossible to reflect in translation the elegant, genuinely oratorical word order of the phrase (see *Note* b above and BDF §473[2]).

oo The periphrastic construction ἐστὲ . . . γεγόνασιν highlights the present tense nature of the verb παιδεύει, "he disciplines," in v 7c. The pf tense of γεγόνασιν stresses the general truth of the clause.

pp The particle ἄρα at the beginning of the apodosis is commonly treated as an inferential connecting particle ("in that case"), as in classical literature (so Thrall, *Greek Particles*, 36). The inferential idea, however, is expressed by the context itself. In such cases the function of ἄρα is to express a sense of the tentative, of the suspense between opposing alternatives that at the moment are unresolved. The ἄρα acknowledges that an opposing response is considered equally eligible (so K. W. Clark, "The Meaning of APA," 77–79, 81–84).

qq The adv εἶτα functions as a transitional word to introduce a new argument in a demonstration (BAGD 234).

rr The verb εἴχομεν has been treated as a customary impf. An alternative proposal is to translate the tense as perfective: "we have had" (so Kistemaker, 380).

ss In the expression τοὺς μὲν τῆς σαρκὸς ἡμῶν πατέρας, the term σάρξ is simply a designation for the sphere of humanity (cf. 2:14; 5:7). It is used without special theological significance. The phrase could be translated "our earthly fathers" (so Schweizer, *TDNT* 7:141–42).

tt In the middle voice the verb signifies "to have regard for," "to respect," with the complement αὐτούς, "them," to be supplied from the context (so BAGD 269). This usual understanding has been challenged by Vanhoye, who argues that the result clause καὶ ἐνετρεπόμεθα in v 8a corresponds structurally to the result clause καὶ ζήσομεν, "so that we shall live," in v 8b. As parallel clauses, the verb in the initial clause should be construed as without complement. In that case it focuses not on the attitude of the child in response to correction (i.e., respect) but on the results obtained by correction. The sense will be "we acquired good manners" (*La structure*, 201–2).

uu The negative particle οὐ with the interrogative expects an affirmative answer, "yes."

vv The comparative form πολὺ μᾶλλον functions to draw a contrast with the clause introduced by the particle μέν in v 9a. The combination of the accusative sg πολύ with the adv μᾶλλον is equivalent to the expression πολλῷ μᾶλλον, where the dative expresses the degree of difference (so Kistemaker, 380).

ww The translation seeks to preserve the note of transcendence that seems to be integral to the designation (cf. Num 16:22; 27:16 LXX; 2 Macc 3:24). For the suggestion that the reference is to the "Father of *our* spirits" (so Moffatt, NIV), see Zerwick and Grosvenor, *Grammatical Analysis*, 685. The contrast with "our natural fathers" (v 9a) accounts for the translation "our spiritual Father" (NEB, JB, TEV), which is defended by P. E. Hughes, 530–31.

xx The καί is final, expressing result (Zerwick, *Biblical Greek*, §455γ).

yy The contrast expressed in οἱ μὲν γάρ . . . ὁ δέ is sharp and refers to definitely designated persons, as in 7:20–21 (BDF §250). Although the contrast could be expressed adequately by translating "for they . . . but he," it seems better to specify the reference from v 9a.

zz The tense of the verb ἐπαίδευον is significant; as a descriptive impf it calls to mind repeated action in the past, perhaps iteratively.

aaa The expression κατὰ τὸ δοκοῦν αὐτοῖς is idiomatic (BAGD 202).

bbb The expression ἐπὶ τὸ συμφέρον is idiomatic and conveys a legal notion of advantage (BAGD 289, 780). The prep expresses purpose or result. For the counterproposal that ἐπί with the accusative has been used here not to specify result but to specify the measure of an intervention, see Vanhoye, *La structure*, 203. He holds that κατά with the accusative is used to suggest the margin of uncertainty in all human training, while ἐπί with the accusative indicates the objective certainty that is characteristic of the divine discipline. God's discipline is based directly on (ἐπί) real usefulness.

ccc The prep εἰς with the articular inf introduces a classic purpose clause.

ddd The rare term ἁγιότητος denotes the holiness that is the essential attribute of God (cf. Procksch, *TDNT* 1:114). For the translation, see BAGD 10.

eee The temporal expression πρὸς . . . τὸ παρόν is classical, referring to the present time or "for the moment" (BAGD 624). It is impossible in translation to reflect the use of alliteration based on the letter π, which is rhetorically effective (πᾶσα δὲ παιδεία πρὸς μὲν τὸ παρόν or the unusual word order, which is calculated to arouse attention (cf. Turner, *Grammar*, 4:107).

ᶠᶠᶠ In the phrase χαρᾶς εἶναι ἀλλὰ λύπης, the genitives are qualitative (BAGD 875).

ᵍᵍᵍ Translating according to the sense, it seems necessary to understand εἰρηνικόν, "that which relates to peace," as a substitute for the gen, and thus as parallel in construction with δικαιοσύνης, which is a gen of apposition (so K. Weiss, *TDNT* 9:77, n. 18): "the fruit which consists of peace" (following Michel, 445; cf. Foerster, *TDNT* 2:419). See the *Comment* below on the full expression. The alternative is to translate εἰρηνικόν as an adj qualifying καρπόν: "the peaceful fruit of righteousness" (so BAGD 228, 404–5).

ʰʰʰ The ptcp γεγυμνασμένοις is a true pf; the temporal element is to be heavily accented.

ⁱⁱⁱ The antecedent of δι᾽ αὐτῆς is παιδεία, "discipline," "correction," not λύπης, "painful sorrow."

ʲʲʲ The pf pass ptcps παρείμενας, "indolent," "drooping," "listless," and παραλελυμένα, "weakened," "disabled," are entirely adjectival (BDF §97[3]).

ᵏᵏᵏ In the larger context of 12:1–2 the biblical expression τροχιὰς ὀρθὰς ποιεῖτε does not signify "make straight paths" (as in Prov 4:26) but "pursue ways that are directed straight to the goal" (so Preisker, *TDNT* 5:449–50; cf. Stauffer, *TDNT* 1:137; BAGD 580, 828).

ˡˡˡ The translation treats τοῖς ποσίν as a dative of instrument (with Zerwick and Grosvenor, *Grammatical Analysis*, 685).

ᵐᵐᵐ The clause ἵνα μὴ τὸ χωλὸν ἐκτραπῇ is difficult. The dominant meaning of ἐκτρέπειν is "to turn aside." It is, therefore, possible to translate the clause "that the lame should not be turned from the way" (so Oepke, *TDNT* 3:214). The presence of ἰαθῇ, "be healed," in the immediate context, however, suggests that ἐκτραπῇ is to be understood with the nuance it bears as a medical technical term, "be dislocated" (cf. Käsemann, "Hebräer 12:12–17," 312). Linguistically, still another possibility is "that what is lame might not be avoided" (see BAGD 246, with references to parallels in hellenistic texts).

ⁿⁿⁿ The ἵνα construction is continued with the clause ἰαθῇ δὲ μᾶλλον: "so that . . . not . . . but rather be healed" (Hanna, *Grammatical Aid*, 161).

Form/Structure/Setting

The introduction of a new section is indicated by a shift in genre and mood. In 12:1 the writer turns from historical recital (11:1–40) to pastoral exhortation. The previous section was composed entirely in the indicative mood; this unit is marked by the use of the imperative and the hortatory subjunctive. In striking contrast to 11:1–40, where the exposition was carried forward almost exclusively by the use of the third person, the verbs in this section are expressed in the first (12:1, 9) or the second person (12:3, 4, 5, 7, 8, 12, 13). The subject is no longer the attested witnesses of Israel's remote or more recent past but the struggle in which Christians are currently engaged (12:1, 3, 5, 7, 9, 12–13).

The ground is laid for the transition from historical exposition to exhortation in the epilogue to the celebration of faith under the old covenant. In 11:39–40 the writer comments upon the recital of past faithfulness, bringing the catalogue of chap. 11 into direct relationship with his audience. The "attested witnesses" who died without receiving the ultimate fulfillment of the promise are juxtaposed to "us," the Christian community for whom God had planned something better. In 12:1 the same two groups are mentioned for a second time: "we" Christians are to demonstrate our faithfulness, knowing that we are surrounded by the host of attested "witnesses" surveyed in 11:4–38.

The connection between the two sections is underscored by the effective use of linking terms:

11:39	μαρτυρηθέντες, "attested witnesses"	12:1	μαρτύρων, "witnesses"
11:40	ἡμῶν, "us," . . . ἡμῶν, "us"	12:1	καὶ ἡμεῖς, "we ourselves"

The climactic comment in 11:39–40 provides the basis for the moving appeal addressed to the community in 12:1–13. The conclusive particle at the beginning of 12:1, τοιγαροῦν, "consequently," marks the point of transition (cf. Mora, *La Carta*, 172; Gourgues, *A la droite de Dieu*, 120–21; Vanhoye, *La structure*, 46–47).

There is no consensus on the limits of the new section. McCown, for example, insists on the parenetic and literary unity of 12:1–29. He holds that the distinctive literary form of 11:1–40 on the one hand, and of 13:1–25 on the other, combine to set off chap. 12 as an identifiable entity within the larger concluding division of Hebrews. Although the unit actually consists of a number of component parts, McCown subdivides the chapter into three major segments, corresponding to the parenetic sequence he identified in 5:11–6:12 and 10:19–39:

A   Reminder of the situation of the community (12:1–11);
B   Warning against apostasy (12:12–17);
C   Encouraging appeal (12:18–29).

The proposed limits for the initial section, then, will be 12:1–11 (McCown, "*O ΛΟΓΟΣ ΤΗΣ ΠΑΡΑΚΛΗΣΕΩΣ*," 98–99, 103, 109–10, 225; cf. Moffatt, 206; Michel, 425–26; Käsemann, "Hebräer 12,12–17," 307).

An alternate proposal, put forth by Vanhoye, identifies the section as 12:1–13. Vanhoye asserts that the limits of the section are indicated by "a sort of *inclusio*." The unit is bracketed at its beginning in 12:1 by the main verb τρέχωμεν, "let us run," and at its conclusion in 12:12–13 by the rare cognate term τροχιάς, "track," "path," which occurs only here in the NT. The latter expression is derived from Prov 4:26 LXX, which the writer has adapted for his own purposes, inverting the order of the biblical clause so as to assign to τροχιά the first place. Its emphatic position, Vanhoye argues, is intended to call to mind τρέχωμεν at the beginning of the section (*La structure*, 47–48, 203; cf. Buchanan, 210).

In response, it must be observed that a single verb and its euphonic echo are an insufficient basis for determining the limits of a section. Vanhoye appears to recognize this when he describes the basis for his determination as "a sort of *inclusio*" (*La structure*, 47). It is preferable to acknowledge that the limits of this unit must be determined thematically.

Although "faith" continues to be the underlying theme (cf. 12:2), it is faith as it is actualized in endurance and submission under discipline (Michel, 426). The section elaborates the exhortation in 10:32–39, and specifically the pastoral directive in 10:36: ὑπομονῆς γὰρ ἔχετε χρείαν, "for you have need of endurance." The parenetic appeal for steadfast endurance extends from 12:1 to 12:13. Pastoral exhortation extends beyond 12:13, but it no longer has any direct bearing upon the theme of endurance (so Gourgues, *A la droite de Dieu*, 120–21; Peterson, "Examination," 291–92 cf. Dussaut, *Synopse structurelle*, 116, 122–28).

The note of endurance is present in each verse of 12:1–3. This initial paragraph sets forth the tenor of the exhortation and its basis in Jesus' own endurance of hostile opposition in the world. A second unit, 12:4–11, is integrally connected to 12:1–3. It clarifies the meaning of the sufferings that Christians experience, in which steadfast endurance must be manifested (note especially 12:7, "You must endure [your trials] as [divine] discipline"). The necessity for endurance is clearly implied as well in the concluding exhortation of 12:12–13, which appeals to the community to endure in the struggle, while showing a genuine concern for the weakest of their number. A thematic concern with the necessity for endurance identifies the limits of the section as 12:1–13 (cf. Vanhoye, *La structure,* 196–294; Spicq, 2:391–414; UBSGNT³, 774; although Dussaut, *Synopse Structuralle,* 122–28, locates the beginning of the section in 11:32, he agrees that it extends to 12:13).

The characteristic vocabulary of this section relates to the vital factor of enduring disciplinary sufferings. In Hebrews the noun ὑπομονή, "endurance," is used in the formal announcement of the subject in 10:36, and in 12:1, but not elsewhere. The cognate verb ὑπομένειν ("to endure," with a range of nuances) is found in 12:2, 3, 7, and elsewhere only in 10:32, where it connotes the endurance of sufferings by the audience early in their experience as Christians. The notion of endurance is developed by means of the noun παιδεία, "discipline," "correction" (12:5, 7, 8, 11, and not elsewhere in Hebrews), the derivative noun παιδευτής, "one who administers discipline" (12:9, but not elsewhere in the homily), and the cognate verb παιδεύειν, "to discipline," "to correct" (12:6, 7, 10, but nowhere else in Hebrews). The concentration of this distinctive vocabulary serves to unify the section (Vanhoye, *La structure,* 196–204).

The section falls naturally into three small units, 12:1–3, 4–11, 12–13. The central paragraph clarifies the meaning and purpose of disciplinary sufferings in the life of the people of God. It is framed by shorter paragraphs that develop a common metaphor, the running of a race to the appointed goal:

A   Exhortation to run with endurance (12:1–3);
  B   The meaning of the sufferings to be endured (12:4–11);
A' Exhortation to renewed commitment to complete the race (12:12–13).

The hinge between 12:1–3 and 12:4–11 is found in v 4, when the attention of the audience is drawn to its own experience of hostile opposition in the world. A change both in metaphor (from the footrace to the boxing match) and in focus (from Christ to the community itself) serves to signal the introduction of the new paragraph-unit (cf. Michel, 425–26). Moreover, the conjunction καί, "and," that joins vv 5–11 to v 4 gives to v 4 a transitional character. (For the argument that v 4 must be taken with 12:1–3 rather than with 12:5–11 see McCown, "Ο ΛΟΓΟΣ ΤΗΣ ΠΑΡΑΚΛΗΣΕΩΣ," 98–100; Mora, *La Carta,* 63; 66, n. 200; 174–79.) The reference to "losing heart" (ἐκλυόμενοι) in v 3 appears to have called to the writer's mind Prov 3:11–12, with its pastoral directive, "Do not lose heart" (μηδὲ ἐκλύου), for that text is cited in v 5. The second paragraph is firmly linked to the first by key-word association. The transition from the central paragraph to the concluding exhortation in 12:12–13 is indicated by the explanatory particile διό, "therefore," in v 12.

The use of εἶτα, "then again," "furthermore," as a transitional word in v 9 shows that the central paragraph may be subdivided into two smaller units, 12:4–8 and 12:9–11. The first unit is integrated thematically around the issue of sonship; the term "son" or "sons" occurs six times in vv 4–8. Genuine sonship is attested in the experience of disciplinary sufferings. By way of contrast, there is no reference to sonship in the second unit. In vv 9–11 balanced clauses develop the distinction between paternal and divine discipline in terms of their respective character, intention, and results (for a more detailed literary analysis see Vanhoye, *La structure,* 196–201).

The form of 12:5–11 may be classified as parenetic midrash (cf. 3:7–4:13). Midrash entails the actualization of the authority of a biblical text for the present situation. In this instance, Prov 3:11–12 furnishes the point of departure for the exposition. The parenetic midrash supports the appeal not to grow weary in a period marked by stress and suffering. The unit is structured in terms of the citation and is presented for the sake of the biblical text. Three issues bearing on divine discipline receive an expository explanation: the necessity of paternal discipline for true sonship (vv 7–8), the appropriate response to discipline (v 9), and the benefits that accrue to those who are disciplined (vv 10–11). The designation of the form as parenetic midrash recognizes that the purpose of the exposition is explicitly hortatory, as distinct from an exposition structured upon an exegetical or narrative basis (so A. G. Wright, *The Literary Genre Midrash* [Staten Island: Alba House, 1968] 52–59, 64–67; cf. McCown, "Ο ΛΟΓΟΣ," 102, 149–51, 185).

McCown has argued that 12:5–11 was an existing literary unit, which the writer simply incorporated without modification from some hellenistic-Jewish source (100–102, 114, 189). He points to the formulaic introduction in v 5*a*, which suggests that the material was familiar to the audience, the absence of anything distinctively Christian in the exposition, the concentration in vv 7–11 of terminology that has a background in hellenistic Judaism, the designation of God in v 9 as "the Father of spirits," and the fact that the exposition exhibits a strong affinity with several passages in the literature of hellenistic Judaism. All of these factors, however, may be explained by an educational background in hellenistic Judaism, which the writer shared with others. It seems wiser to attribute the midrashic development of Prov 3:11–12 to the writer himself, as McCown has done with the prior example of parenetic midrash in 3:7–4:13 ("Ο ΛΟΓΟΣ," 190).

One of the most striking features of 12:1–13 as a section is the writer's cultivation of an eloquent, rhetorical style. The Greek text exhibits elegant, genuinely oratorical word order, sonorous instances of effective word play, the use of alliteration, and carefully balanced clauses (see above *Notes* b, t, z, nn, q, qq, eee). Density of expression (*Note* k) and the repeated use of significant terminology with altered nuances, (ὑπομονή/ὑπομένειν in 12:1, 2, 3, 7) were rhetorical devices calculated to arouse and engage the attention of the audience as the section was read aloud. These stylistic and linguistic features display a concern for rhetorical effect appropriate to the concluding section of a larger division within the homily (11:1–12:13). The result is lively and animated discourse.

Comment

The parenetic intention of the catalogue of faithful men and women in 11:1–40 becomes transparent in 12:1–13. The writer resumes the more direct mode of appeal he had used in 10:35–39 and urges patient and trusting perseverance in spite of hardship as the proper response of Christian faith. There is both a logical and dramatic connection between the reference to the martyrs in 11:35*b*–38 and the formulation of 12:1. The writer recognizes, however, that an earnest appeal for Christian endurance cannot finally be based upon the antecedent exposition of faithfulness to God under the old covenant. There can be an appropriate response to the appeal only in the light of the struggle and triumph of Christ.

Christians are to find in Jesus, whose death on the cross displayed both faithfulness and endurance (12:2–3), the supreme example of persevering faith. His endurance of hostility from those who were blind to God's redemptive design and their own welfare provides a paradigm for the community of faith whenever it encounters hostility from society (cf. Mora, *La Carta*, 172).

Jesus' own experience of triumph through suffering provides perspective on the purpose of suffering in the experience of Christians (12:4–11). The trials of the community are described as disciplinary in character. They have been assigned by God to those who are his children. There is a necessary and integral relationship between disciplinary sufferings and sonship. Although Jesus enjoyed a unique sonship (5:8), he himself came to share God's throne only after he had experienced the disgrace of the cross rather than joy (12:2). Christians should be prepared through faith to share in his exposure to active opposition and suffering. The recognition of the fruitful role played by suffering in the maturing of the relationship with God (12:10–11) undergirds the appeal for endurance in pursuing the goal marked out for the community (12:12–13). The section summons the members of the house church to persevere in faith in view of the encouragements offered to them through attested witnesses from the past, through Jesus himself, and through the testimony of Scripture (cf. P. G. Müller, *ΧΡΙΣΤΟΣ ΑΡΧΗΓΟΣ*, 302–12; Michel, 426, 430).

1–2 In 12:1–3 the writer's intention is to apply to his audience the parenetic appeal implicit in the previous section. The theme of perseverance in faith is sustained. In 12:1, however, the emphasis is placed on καὶ ἡμεῖς, "we ourselves," in contrast with καὶ οὗτοι πάντες, "and all of these [attested witnesses]," in 11:39, which looks retrospectively at the preceding recital of those who were commended by God as faithful under the old covenant.

The intensified conjunction τοιγαροῦν, "consequently," is found elsewhere in the NT only in 1 Thess 4:8 but is common in literary Koine. It functions as a coordinating particle introducing an inference. By its consecutive position at the beginning of the sentence, it links 12:1–3 firmly to 11:1–40 and shows that the admonition that follows is the consequence of the preceding exposition (BDF §415[3]). The particle refers specifically to 11:39–40 and alerts the community to find in v 1 a distillation of the prior section.

The extended period in vv 1–2 develops the metaphor of an athletic contest in a stadium or arena. It offers two encouragements for Christian perseverance in faith and obedience toward the prescribed goal. The first encouragement is the certainty of being surrounded by "a host of witnesses." These "witnesses" are the men and women of chap. 11 who have received acknowledgment from God because of the constancy of their faith (11:2, 4, 5, 39). They figure in Scripture as witnesses to the character and validity of committed faithfulness, whose lives provide evidence for subsequent generations of the possibilities of faith. With the explicit reference to the presence of the host of witnesses, "the writer indirectly asserts again that Scripture speaks with a living voice to believers in all ages" (Peterson, "Examination," 293–94; cf. Trites, *Witness*, 220–21). Among these earlier exemplars of faith are those who exhibited the endurance of faith (11:35*b*–38).

In the phrase τοσοῦτον ἔχοντες περικείμενον ἡμῖν νέφος μαρτύρων, "since we are surrounded with so great a host of witnesses," the position of τοσοῦτον, "so great," is emphatic, and the qualitative aspect is pronounced (see above, *Note* b; cf.

BDF §473[2]). The metaphorical use of the term νέφος, "cloud," to describe a crowded group of people is a common classical figure (e.g., Homer, *Iliad* 4.274; 16.66; 17.755; Herodotus 8.109; Timo Phlasius 39 [=Timon in Diogenes Laertius, 8.16]; Diodorus Siculus 3.29.2; Pseudo-Callisthenes, *History of Alexander the Great* 1.2, 2; Virgil, *Aeneid* 7.793). The description νέφος μαρτύρων, "a host of witnesses," connotes not only the great number of persons but also the unity of the crowd in their witness to the integrity of faith (Michel, 424).

In the context of the athletic metaphor, it is perhaps natural to think of an amphitheater, with its ascending rows of spectators who gather to watch the games (so LB: "since we have such a huge crowd of men of faith watching us from the grandstands"; cf. Westcott, 393; Strathmann, *TDNT* 4:491; Pfitzner, *Paul and the Agon Motif,* 196; Horning, *PCSBR* 23 [1978] 37–38). The participle περικείμενον, "surrounded by," particularly suggests that they are witnesses to our efforts (so P. G. Müller, *ΧΡΙΣΤΟΣ ΑΡΧΗΓΟΣ,* 304; Dyck, "Jesus our Pioneer," 136).

In the NT, however, a witness is never merely a passive spectator but an active participant who confirms and attests the truth as a confessing witness (cf. Riggenbach, 385; Michel, 427, n. 3, 428; Peterson, "Examination," 294). The tendency to associate "witness" with martyrdom is strengthened by the account of the martyred and persecuted exemplars of faith in 11:35*b*–38 (cf. Michel, 427–28, who develops the parallel between Heb 12:1 and 4 Macc 17:10–24). The emphasis in v 1 thus falls on what Christians see in *the host of witnesses* rather than on what *they* see in Christians. The appeal to their example is designed to inspire heroic Christian discipleship (so F. F. Bruce, 346; cf. Trites, *Witness,* 220–21, who remarks, "the context rules out the thought of spectators in an amphitheatre who watch the contemporary Christian race, and instead speaks of God's testimony to the heroes of faith in the pages of the OT"). Christians can benefit from the testimony of these OT witnesses to the validity of faith as they exert themselves in the race of faith prescribed for them.

The comparison of life to engagement in an athletic contest was the common property of preachers of moral philosophy, whose sermons could be heard in the streets of every hellenistic town in the first century. The agonistic metaphor is one of the most frequently occurring images in the Cynic-Stoic diatribe (see Pfitzner, *Paul and the Agon Motif,* 28–35). The frequency with which it occurs in hellenistic-Jewish sources, especially Philo and 4 Maccabees, suggests that it was a commonplace in synagogue preaching throughout the Greek-speaking Diaspora as well (see especially Pfitzner, 38–72; H. A. Harris, *Greek Athletics and the Jews* [Cardiff: University of Wales Press, 1976] 24–95, for a full discussion of primary sources). The imagery was well suited to typify moral struggle in the form of a metaphor and was readily extended to the contest of martyrdom. The terms ἀγών, "contest," and ἀγωνίζεσθαι, "to strive," "to engage in a contest," evoked thoughts of tense exertion, maximum effort, and a constantly renewed concentration of energy on the attainment of the goal (see especially Pfitzner, 1–10, 23–72). An appeal to athletic imagery to dramatize the character of Christian experience in 12:1 and elsewhere in Hebrews (see 5:14; 10:32, 33; 11:33; 12:4, 11) is simply traditional.

Christians are called to participate in an ἀγών, "an athletic contest," and to do all that is necessary in order to complete the event. The metaphor of running a race is taken from the stadium (see above *Note* g), and reflects the recognized preeminence of the footrace in the Greek games. (On the imagery of the race, see Michel, 425–26; P. G. Müller, *ΧΡΙΣΤΟΣ ΑΡΧΗΓΟΣ*, 302, 305; for the characterization of the Christian calling as a race, see Pfitzner, *Paul and the Agon Motif*, 134–38.) The footrace was one of the five contests of the pentathalon in the great panhellenic games and always came first. At the Olympic Games the footrace was the only athletic contest for an extended period (Bream, *ExpTim* 80 [1968–69] 150–51). The exhortation to run δι' ὑπομονῆς, "with endurance," identifies the race not as a contest of speed but of stamina. The allusion is to a distance race requiring disciplined commitment and endurance (cf. Grässer, *Glaube*, 58: "not the sprinter but the marathon runner!"; so also H. Montefiore, 214; Dyck, "Jesus our Pioneer," 137–38).

Giving to the participle ἀποθέμενοι a hortatory nuance (see above, *Note* d), the writer directs his intended audience to "lay aside all excess weight and the sin that so easily distracts us." The formulation recalls the usual preparation of stripping for a race. Contestants removed all of their clothing before running so that nothing could impede them during the race. In the phrase ὄγκον ἀποθέμενοι πάντα the emphasis falls upon the initial term ὄγκον, "excess weight." The term occurs only here in biblical Greek but had been used metaphorically of vices since the time of Demosthenes (8.46; cf. *Ep. Arist.* 122: Lucian, *Dialogues of the Dead* 10.8–9). Here it refers most naturally to the weight of a long heavy robe, which would hamper running (cf. Bleek, 458; Kuss, 110; Michel, 429); it may apply equally to superfluous bodily weight (F. F. Bruce, 349). The qualifying adjective πάτνα, "all," indicates that the writer did not have any particular consideration explicitly in mind (Seesemann, *TDNT* 5:41). The combined expression covers any encumbrance that would handicap a runner, and by analogy anything that would interfere with responsible commitment to Jesus Christ. This might have reference to the love of wealth, attachment to the world, preoccupation with earthly interests, or self-importance. Christians are to divest themselves of every association or concern that would limit their freedom for Christian confession (Mora, *La Carta*, 82, n. 49; cf. Spicq, 2:385).

The participle is complemented by the challenge to rid ourselves of τὴν εὐπερίσπαστον ἁμαρτίαν, "the sin that so easily distracts." The characterizing of sin as "distracting" or "diverting" vividly sustains the athletic metaphor (see above, *Note* f). The use of the singular (τὴν ἁμαρτίαν) shows that the writer is concerned with *sin itself*, rather than with specific sins (Michel, 428–29; Peterson, "Examination," 293).

It is unwarranted to interpret the reference to sin in terms of apostasy (as does Käsemann, *Das wandernde Gottesvolk*, 25–27: "for the people of God, sin can only be apostasy" [26]). As H. Montefiore has observed, apostasy would disqualify a Christian from running at all (214). Christians are always capable of being subverted by "the deceitful attractiveness of sin" (3:13b). One has only to reflect upon everyday compromises of faith in an effort to avoid conflict or to conform to the norms of the society at large. The writer warns his audience to guard against sin in any form because it will distract them, causing them to look away when they should be fixing their gaze upon Jesus (12:2). In the light of the further appeal not to become weary and lose heart in 12:3 (cf. 3:12–13), it is appropriate to give to ἁμαρτία, "sin," the nuance of "discouragement." It contemplates the weariness experienced by the distance runner, which can deter him from continuing the race (so Spicq, 2:385; Teodorico, 210; Mora, *La Carta*, 82–83). Christian faith finds its essential expression in persevering devotion to Christ and in a lifestyle that reflects consecration to the service of God.

The term ὑπομονή, "endurance," which is the linking word throughout the paragraph, is accented in v 1 by its literary position at the beginning of a long phrase (Michel, 430; Mora, *La Carta*, 81). The writer calls for a diaplay of endurance through faith. The admonition to run the prescribed race δι᾽ ὑπομονῆς, "with endurance," makes explicit the element of struggle that is integral to mature commitment (cf. 4 Macc 17:13). There must be firm resolve not to drop out of the contest but to exert every effort to cross the finish line despite hardship, exhaustion, and pain (cf. Philo, *On the Unchangeableness of God* 13, who speaks of those who "through courage and endurance persevere to the finish of the contest"; similarly, *On the Preliminary Studies* 164, where Philo contrasts those who faint early in the contest of life with those who carry it through to completion). The audience is summoned to an intense perseverance in faith in view of the example of those who have preceded them. Their unwavering fidelity should encourage and inspire Christians to emulate them, enduring trials similar to their own (cf. P. G. Müller, *ΧΡΙΣΤΟΣ ΑΡΧΗΓΟΣ*, 302–12; Michel, 411, n. l). Because the race has been prescribed for us (τὸν προκείμενον ἡμῖν ἀγῶνα; on which see above, *Note* h), we can be assured that it will bring us to the desired goal (cf. F. F. Bruce, 347–48, Michel, 430).

Contemplation of Jesus offers paramount encouragement to Christians in their struggle. The appeal in v 2 is for a concentrated attention that turns away from all distractions, with eyes only for the person of Jesus. The phrase ἀφορῶντες εἰς ... Ἰησοῦν, "looking away from [other considerations] to Jesus," commands the same focused attention for which Moses was commended in 11:26 (ἀπέβλεπεν ... εἰς: "he fixed his attention upon [the reward]"; for the idiom cf. 4 Macc 17:10: "[the Maccabean martyrs] vindicated their nation, concentrating their attention upon God [εἰς θεὸν ἀφορῶντες] and enduring torture even to death"). The use of the simple personal name "Jesus" shows that the accent is upon his humanity, and especially his endurance of pain, humiliation, and the disgrace of the cross (cf. Michel, 436; P. G. Müller, *ΧΡΙΣΤΟΣ ΑΡΧΗΓΟΣ*, 302–3). Concentrated attention upon the person of Jesus and his redemptive accomplishment on behalf of the new people of God typifies "the fundamental challenge of Hebrews" (Peterson, "Examination," 294).

The instruction to look to Jesus sustains the metaphor of the runner, who must keep his eyes fixed on the conclusion of the prescribed course. The members of the house church are in the final and decisive stages of the race. Jesus is positioned at the finish line; like a runner, the Christian must intently focus on the goal of Jesus. In 6:20 the designation of Jesus as πρόδρομος, "forerunner," brought before the congregation an athletic term entirely appropriate to the metaphor of the race (cf. Julius Pollux, *Onomasticon* 3.30, 148, who defines πρόδρομος as the swiftest runner who breaks away from the pack to cross the finish line first; see *Comment* on 6:19–20). Πρόδρομος is a relative term implying a sequence of other runners who must follow the pace setter to the completion of the course (Bauernfeind, *TDNT* 8:235, argues that πρόδρομος draws attention to the race itself as well as to its conclusion).

Here, however, the writer places in apposition to "Jesus" a descriptive phrase remarkable for its conciseness and rich suggestiveness: τὸν τῆς πίστεως ἀρχηγὸν καὶ τελειωτήν, "the champion in the exercise of faith and the one who brought faith to complete expression." The fact that the two predicates are firmly linked by the single article τόν and the common genitive attribute τῆς πίστεως, "of faith," suggests that ἀρχηγός and τελειωτής are parallel christological titles (G. Johnston, *NTS* 27 [1980–81] 385, n. 1, prefers to treat τελειωτής as adjectival and thus epexegetic; he translates "the Prince of our faith who is also its perfect example"; see, however, the formal parallel in Aelius Aristides, *Orations* 43.41: "Zeus, who has power over all things," is "the only originator and finisher of all things" [ἀρχηγετήν καὶ τέλειον μόνον . . . τῶν πάντων]). Michel suggestively describes the expression as a liturgical "messianic redeemer designation" that the writer adopted to describe Christ's triumphant work of perfection on behalf of the Church (431–34; cf. Vanhoye, *Situation du Christ*, 314–28; P. G. Müller, *ΧΡΙΣΤΟΣ ΑΡΧΗΓΟΣ*, 72–102).

In the light of the athletic metaphor, it is proper to recognize in ἀρχηγός the nuance of "champion" demonstrated for the term in its first occurrence in 2:10 (see *Comment* on 2:10; cf. Snell, 148–49: Jesus is "the exemplar, the champion of faith"). In 2:10–16 Jesus' solidarity with the family of faith was presented under the aspect of cosmic struggle with the devil (2:14–15). In 12:2–3 his struggle is recalled in its personal aspect as the enduring of shame and of hostility from sinful men. The comparison of Jesus' experience with that of believers in 12:1–4 also suggests a leadership motif: Christ's conduct has exemplary value for his people in their own engagement with the demands of persevering faith (P. G. Müller, *ΧΡΙΣΤΟΣ ΑΡΧΗΓΟΣ*, 110–11, 147–48, 171, 187, 376, 379; cf. Mora, *La Carta*, 177, who suggests that in this context ἀρχηγός signifies "trainer or chief of the games" [*entrenador o gimnasiarca*]; for a different understanding see Ballarini, *SacDoc* 16 [1971] 541–43). The theme of Jesus as a model for imitation is peculiar to this passage in Hebrews (so Leivestad, *NorTT* 74 [1973] 195–97).

It is necessary to be alert to other nuance in ἀρχηγός as well. The formulation τὸν . . . ἀρχηγὸν καὶ τελειωτής recalls prior instances in Hebrews where the writer juxtaposed the roots ἀρχη- and τελ- for rhetorical effect (3:14*b*: τὴν ἀρχὴν . . . μέχρι τέλους, "beginning . . . to the end"; 7:3: ἀρχὴν ἡμερῶν . . . ζωῆς τέλος, "beginning of days . . . end of life"). Taking a clue from the writer's interest in the notions of origin and completion, beginning and end, the predicates ἀρχηγός and τελειωτής suggest that Jesus is the initiator and head of the rank and file in the order of faith, just as he is the one who brought faith to its ultimate expression. He was the first who expressed unqualified obedience to the will of God in a fallen world consigned to death, and so displayed the goal of faith as well as its paramount power (5:8; 10:5–10). The predicates express the conviction that from first to last Jesus exercised faith in an essential sense and brought it to its triumphant completion (cf. Dautzenberg, *BZ* 17 [1963] 167–68).

The descriptive term τελειωτής not found elsewhere in the Greek Bible and is unknown from other literature of the period. As a noun of agency, it was almost certainly formed from the verb τελειοῦν, and bears the nuance of "accomplisher," "finisher," "perfecter" (LSJ 1770; BAGD 810; *LPGL* 1384). The importance of the idea of perfection and the prominence of the verb τελειοῦν in Hebrews suggest that the writer may have coined the term to form a christological complement for ἀρχηγός (so Moulton and Howard, *Grammar*, 2:365). The expression should be interpreted formally: "as the 'perfecter of faith' Jesus is the one in whom faith has reached its perfection" (Peterson, "Examination," 298; cf. P. G. Müller, *ΧΡΙΣΤΟΣ ΑΡΧΗΓΟΣ*, 310: "He strode ahead of all believers in faith and led faith to its definitive end"). This understanding helps to clarify the significance of ἀρχηγός. ἀρχηγός implies priority or preeminence in the exercise of faith precisely because of Jesus' supremacy in bringing faith to complete realization and giving it a perfect basis through his suffering (cf. Westcott, 395; Riggenbach, 390; Schlatter, *Glaube*, 531–32; Peterson, 298). In relationship to ἀρχηγός, the predicate τελειωτής reinforces the significant consequence of Jesus' achievement as the champion of salvation who by the exercise of faith and his ensuing exaltation ushered in the age of fulfillment (Dyck, "Jesus our Pioneer," 142–43).

The syntactical position of τῆς πίστεως, "of faith," indicates that it relates equally to both of the following nouns, and not simply to ἀρχηγός. In the context of 11:1–40, "faith" must be understood absolutely, as the believing response to God demonstrated by the host of witnesses and preeminently by Jesus himself (cf. Riggenbach, 389–90; P. E. Hughes, 522–23; P. G. Müller, *ΧΡΙΣΤΟΣ ΑΡΧΗΓΟΣ*, 308–9). The poignant description as a whole points to Jesus as the perfect embodiment of faith, who exercised faith heroically. By bringing faith to complete expression, he enabled others to follow his example. The phrase reiterates and makes explicit what was affirmed with a quotation of Scripture in 2:13, that Jesus in his earthly life was the perfect exemplar of trust in God (so Moffatt, 196; cf. Westcott, 387; F. F. Bruce, 351).

The primary reference in 12:2a is to the exercise of faith by Christ himself. Jesus, however, is not simply the crowning example of steadfast faithfulness, whose response to God is cited to encourage the community to persevere in faith. His attainment of exaltation glory by way of faithful obedience in suffering was unprecedented and determinative, and not merely exemplary. The unique character of his personal sacrifice and achievement is not forgotten. There is between the response of Jesus to God and that of the attested exemplars of faith in chap. 11 a qualitative distinction.

In 12:2b the writer reminds his audience that Jesus passed through humiliation and shame to the glory of the Father's right hand. He himself was perfected and obtained perfection for all who believe in him and obey him by the unique offering of himself to God (2:10; 5:7–9; 7:28; 9:14; 10:5–10, 14). In this specific manner faith in God attained its full expression in Jesus. His high priestly sacrifice created a new dimension and possibility for faith, so that it can be said that with Jesus we have entered a new age of faith. The "host of witnesses" who preceded the Christian community in faith (l2:1) demonstrated their faith in exemplary fashion and received divine approval (11:2, 39). Nevertheless, they died without having received the promises (11:13, 39). Since the time of Jesus, however, Christians have gained entrance into the possession of the promise (10:36; 11:40). Jesus' own exercise of the endurance of faith in submitting to a cross thus offers Christians a greater incentive for persevering faith than does the faith exercised by men and women under the old covenant. His faith was "qualitatively" and not simply "quantitatively" greater than theirs (following Peterson, "Examination," 298–300, cf. Grässer, *Glaube*, 58–59; du Plessis, *TELEIOS*, 224–28; Gourgues, *A la droite de Dieu*, 123).

The pregnant formulation in 12:2b recalls the process by which Jesus endured in faith and attained its reward. The clause exhibits many of the characteristics of a creedal formula, notably the introductory relative pronoun ὅς, "he who," simplicity of syntax, rhythm and formal structure, the stylistic juxtaposition of antithetic notions, and explicit reference to the cross and the session at God's right hand (cf. Horning, *PCSBR* 23 [1978] 40). A material correspondence between 12:2*b* and Phil 2:6–8 has often been observed. In both passages "the way of the Incarnate One is described as the way to the cross, and the death on the cross is understood from the perspective of humiliation, as the expression of shame and disgrace"; moreover, in both formulations "the public display of the eschatological glory of God in the exaltation of the crucified Jesus Christ" is celebrated (Hofius, *Der Christushymnus Philipper 2:6–11* [WUNT 17; Tübingen: Mohr, 1976] 15, 65; cf. Andriessen, *NRT* 97 [1975] 435–36].

In v 2*b* the exaltation is expressed typically with the notion of enthronement based upon Ps 110:1. This constitutes a restatement of a theme formally announced in 1:3 and elaborated in 2:5–9; 8:1–2; and 10:12–13. The "right hand of the throne of God" simply repeats with slight variation the formulation found in 8:1 ("the right hand of the throne of Majesty") (cf. Peterson, "Examination," 294–95; Gourgues, *A la droite de Dieu*, 124–25; Cody, *Heavenly Sanctuary*, 21–25).

The accent in v 2*b* is placed on Jesus' attitude toward suffering entailing shame and disgrace. Renouncing the joy that could have been his, he endured a cross, disregarding the shame associated with crucifixion. In the phrase ἀντὶ τῆς προκειμένης αὐτῷ χαρᾶς, "rather than the joy that was set before him," ἀντί should be given a substitutionary sense ("instead of," "in place of"; see above, *Note* l). Underscored is the fortitude of faith demonstrated in the choice that Jesus made (so Mora, *La Carta*, 176, n. 112; cf. Andriessen and Lenglet, *Bib* 51 [1970] 219–20). An undeniable parallelism exists between τὸν προκείμενον ἡμῖν ἀγῶνα, "the race set before us," of v 1 and τῆς προκειμένης αὐτῷ χαρᾶς, "the joy set before him," in v 2. In both phrases προκείμενος relates not to something future but to a present possibility (as in 6:18): the joy was within Jesus' grasp.

Understood in this way, the joy to which reference is made cannot be the eternal felicity that Jesus shared with the Father, of which he voluntarily divested himself in his incarnation (as urged, for example, by Vitti, *VD* 13 [1933] 154–59; Andriessen, *NRT* 97 [1975] 424, 434–36; H. Montefiore, 215; Mora, *La Carta*, 176, n. 112; with an appeal to Phil 2:6–7 for a parallelism of ideas). It has reference to a precise historical circumstance in which Jesus was confronted with a supreme moral choice. He could embrace the joy that was available to him or a humiliating death upon a Roman cross (for the use of προκείμενος in relationship to the martyr's choice, cf. 4 Macc 15:2–3). He deliberately chose to renounce the joy proposed to him in order to share in the contest proposed for us. This necessarily meant a commitment to tread the path of obedience and suffering.

This interpretation is supported by the appellation "Jesus" (which demands a reference to an experience contingent upon his humanity), by the fact that "joy" is placed in opposition with the very particular experience of the cross, and by the prior treatment of the Passion. The clause should be considered as a comment on Heb 5:7–9. There Jesus' prayers and supplications were described as a priestly offering to "the one who was able to save him from death" (5:7). The "joy that was within his grasp" was that of being delivered from an impending and degrading death. Having learned obedience through the suffering of death (5:8), Jesus was "perfected" (5:9), not by being removed provisionally from death but by removal from the power of death definitively through vindication and enthronement at the Father's right hand. The pregnant expression in v 2*b* is parallel in force to Rom 15:3 ("for even Christ did not please himself," followed by the citation of Ps 68:10 LXX with reference to the Passion). Submitting to the cross, Jesus did not pursue his own pleasure (so Gourgues, *A la droite de Dieu*, 122–23; cf. Nisius, *BZ* 14 [1916–17] 44–61; J. Schneider, *TDNT* 7:577; Spicq, 2:357, prefers to find an allusion to the earthly felicity offered to Jesus by the Tempter in the wilderness).

The pregnant expression ὑπέμεινεν σταυρόν, "he endured a cross," is not used elsewhere to designate crucifixion (cf. Mora, *La Carta*, 65, n. 197). The writer chose it to emphasize that Jesus demonstrated the endurance of faith to which Christians are called. The same root is used in vv 1 and 2 with differing nuances. In v 1 ὑπομονή carries the nuance of "endurance" in the active sense of exertion against all weariness; in v 2 the cognate verb has the more passive nuance of "to endure" in the sense of "to bear" or tolerate a degrading experience (noted by Michel, 430). The phrase treats the death of Jesus not so much as a redemptive event (as in 1:3) but as an ordeal inflicted through the active opposition of sinners (12:3). It places his death under the specific modality of the harsh reality of crucifixion in antiquity. This is the only explicit reference to the cross of Christ in the homily, although the writer clearly presupposed that Jesus' death on the cross was the objective event through which salvation was achieved for the people of God.

The circumstantial clause αἰσχύνης καταφρονήσας, "disdaining the shame," recalls the ancient formula of execution, "Lictor, go bind his hands, veil his head, hang him on the tree of shame [*arbori infelici suspendito*]" (Cicero, *Pro Rabirio* 13; Livy, 1.26.6–7). It reflects the universal response of antiquity toward the horrific nature of crucifixion and underscores Christ's utter humiliation in dying ignominiously like a slave or common criminal, in torment, on the cross. (On the shameful disgrace associated with the cross see especially Hengel, *Crucifixion*, 1–10; 22–32; 43, n. 9; 62–63; 83; 88–89; cf. S. K. Williams, *Jesus' Death as Saving Event*, 165–70.) In the death of Jesus of Nazareth, God identified himself with an extreme expression of human wretchedness, which Jesus endured as the representative of fallen humanity. As a matter of fact, the attitude denoted by καταφρονεῖν, "to scorn," acquires in this context a positive nuance: "to brave" or "to be unafraid" of an experience in spite of its painful character (cf. C. Schneider, *TDNT* 3:632). The note of "shame" in v 2 prepares the congregation for the pastoral appeal in 13:12–13 to identify ourselves with Jesus, "bearing his shame" (for a close verbal parallel cf. 4 Macc 6:9: Eleazar "endured the pains and despised the compulsion" [ὁ δὲ ὑπέμενε τοὺς πόνους καὶ περιεφρόνει τῆς ἀνάγκης]).

The regal session at God's right hand is thrown into sharp contrast with the humiliating death, marking a striking reversal of the situation of rejection and animosity endured by Jesus. The enthronement constitutes the rewarding, fulfilling status obtained in recompense for the acceptance of the ordeal. The permanence of the satisfaction experienced in the session, underscored by the use of the durative perfect κεκάθικεν, "he sat down," stands in sharp contrast to the ephemeral joy that Christ rejected with his free decision to submit to the cross. The ascension and enthronement of Jesus was an event of enduring significance (cf. Michel, 436).

Elsewhere in Hebrews the motif of exaltation based upon Ps 110:1 is introduced as part of a christological development (cf. 1:3, 13; 2:5–9; 8:1–2; 10:12–13).

Here alone it occurs in a parenetic development and has a hortatory significance (cf. Hay, *Glory*, 88–89; Gourgues, *A la droite de Dieu*, 120–21). The crucified Jesus is the exalted Son. The exemplary fidelity of Jesus and its consequence is stressed to encourage the community, undergoing its own ordeal, in a resolve to persevere in faithfulness. The session at the right hand is the guarantee of the absoluteness of Christ's exaltation and the utter security of those who have placed their hope in him (cf. Grässer, *Glaube*, 153; Hay, *Glory*, 103; Gourgues, *A la droite de Dieu*, 123–24; Spicq, 2:388 notes that in this context Jesus' session suggests an athlete's rest after the exertion of the contest).

3 The parenetic purpose in evoking the endurance of Jesus in his Passion is made explicit in v 3. The writer was well aware of the disheartened condition of his audience and was genuinely concerned that they might abandon their faith in the face of the struggles confronting them (cf. 10:32–35). He invites the congregation to compare their experience with that of Jesus and in v 3*a* specifies a further consideration in the endurance of suffering by Jesus. He endured the hostile opposition of sinners.

The element of the endurance of suffering is carried forward from v 2, but no further attention is devoted to Jesus' free and generous choice of the cross in place of joy or to his subsequent enthronement. By concentrating his focus upon the endurance of Jesus, the writer provides the ground for the pastoral exhortation in v 3*b*, which corresponds perfectly to the appeal in v 1 δι' ὑπομονῆς τρέχωμεν, "let us run with endurance" (Mora, *La Carta*, 176). That Jesus endured from sinners such hostility had pointed relevance for the members of the house church. In the past they had experienced hostile opposition (10:32–34), and it was reasonable to expect that they would encounter opposition again (10:35–39; 13:13). Indeed, v 3 sets the exhortative tone for the verses that follow.

In contrast to τρέχωμεν, "let us run," in v 1, the aorist imperative ἀναλογίσασθε, "consider," is rather blunt and direct in its address to the community. The verb, which occurs only here in the NT (cf. 3 Macc 7:7; *1 Clem.* 38:3), contemplates a process of comparison and reflection. Its import can be conveyed in the appeal, "Allow Jesus to be an example to you." Grässer comments, "calculating, they should make a rough estimate of what Jesus endured as active opposition in order that they may find and renew their own energy" (*Glaube*, 62, cf. Michel, 436, who notes that ἀναλογίζεσθαι is more meditative than ἀφορᾶν, "to look to," in v 2). Similar to the writer's appeal in 3:1–2 (where κατανοήσατε, "observe," is used), the emphasis is placed upon the exemplary conduct of Jesus. He did not allow weariness, despair, or discouragement to deter him from obedience. His endurance of opposition has exemplary value for the congregation (cf. Seesemann, *TDNT* 6:33–34).

The reference to hostile opposition (ἀντιλογία) endured from sinners is a sober reminder that "crucifixion was a punishment in which the caprice and sadism of the executioners was given full rein" (Hengel, *Crucifixion*, 25; cf. Jos., *J. W.* 5.449–51, for the treatment of those condemned to crucifixion as a cruel jest). The term ἀντιλογία sums up the total opposition toward Jesus, which found its supreme documentation in the crucifixion (Riggenbach, 391). The indignities that Jesus suffered satisfied a primitive lust for revenge and exposed the sadistic cruelty of those involved. Christian revulsion toward this aspect of Jesus' sacrifice finds expression in the designation of those who were the source of his sufferings as "sinners" (ἁμαρτωλοί) (cf. Michel, 436). In the expression τοιαύτην... ἀτιλογίαν, "such active opposition," the qualifying term underscores the depth of the hostility Jesus endured. It may also imply an allusion to the immediate situation confronting the audience (cf. Kuss, 111; Spicq, 2:389; Michel, 436–37).

Adopting the best supported and more difficult reading (see above, Note u), the antagonism was expressed εἰς ἑαυτούς, "against themselves." The attributive position of the phrase εἰς ἑαυτούς indicates that it is to be taken closely with ἀντιλογίαν, "antagonism," "active opposition." The significance of the phrase has been considered problematical, if not nonsensical.

Ellingworth has argued that "sense can be made of the plural if, and only if, it is seen as a verbal allusion to the LXX of Num 17:3 (16:38 in EVV). . . . Arguments for a plural reading unsupported by a reference to Num 17:3 are so strained as to be self-defeating" ("New Testament Text," 90–91). According to Ellingworth, the passage in question refers to the apostasy of Korah, Dathan, Abiram and their 250 supporters. Num 17:2-3 LXX reads ἡγίασαν τὰ πυρεῖα τῶν ἁμαρτωλῶν τούτων ἐν ταῖς ψυχαῖς αὐτῶν, "they [Korah, Dathan, Abiram] have sanctified the censers of these [250] sinners at the cost of their [i.e., the sinners] lives." Ellingworth argues that the author of Hebrews intends an allusion to the rebellion reported in Num 16–17, since even before his incarnation Christ was the Lord against whom Korah's rebellion was directed. The reference is thus specifically to the sinners who spoke and acted against the Lord in Israel's distant past as in recent times. Ellingworth's understanding is sufficiently indicated in his expanded translation of v 3a: "Compare, then, your situation with that of Christ, who throughout our people's history endured opposition similar to what you endure; notably when 'the sinners,' led astray by Korah and his friends, brought about their own destruction" (92–94).

This line of exegesis, however, is unconvincing. It is by no means clear that the writer intended an allusion to Num 17:3 LXX (cf. J. Moffatt, 198). F. F. Bruce observes soberly that the formulation of the LXX (τῶν ἁμαρτωλῶν τούτων ἐν ταῖς ψυχαῖς αὐτῶν) "would scarcely have suggested to our author the locution τῶν ἁμαρτωλῶν εἰς ἑαυτούς" (345–46, n. 5).

More to the point, the argument advanced by Ellingworth fails to appreciate sufficiently the close parallel offered by Hebrews itself. In Heb 6:6 apostates are described as "crucifying to themselves the Son of God" (ἀνασταυροῦντας ἑαυτοῖς τὸν υἱὸν τοῦ θεοῦ, where ἑαυτοῖς is to be understood as a dative of disadvantage, i.e., "to their own hurt"). The formulation of 6:6 lends support to the plural reading εἰς ἑαυτούς, "against themselves," in v 3a and sheds light on its meaning. It suggests that one of the more sobering features of the crucifixion was the riot of self-contradiction that was expressed in the sadism with which Jesus was treated. The statement that Jesus endured from sinners "such opposition against themselves" is biting irony.

The concept that an evil doer really injures himself is, of course, a commonplace in antiquity (e.g., Prov 8:36 LXX: "Those who sin against me harm themselves" [οἱ δὲ εἰς ἐμὲ ἁμαρτάνοντες ἀσεβοῦσιν τὰς ἑαυτῶν ψυχάς]; M. Aurelius, Meditations 9.4: "he who sins sins against himself; he who acts unjustly acts unjustly against himself"; cf. Aristotle, Magna Moralia 1196A; Xenophon, History of Greece 1.7, 19; Philo, The Worse Attacks the Better, 15, 16). The clear implication for the audience is that if they were to relinquish their commitment to Christ under the pressure of persistent opposition they would express active opposition against themselves (as in 6:6!), just as did Jesus' tormentors.

The parenetic intention of the exhortation in v 3a is made explicit with the purpose clause of 3b. ἵνα μὴ κάμητε ταῖς ψυχαῖς ὑμῶν ἐκλυόμενοι, "so that you may not become weary and lose heart." The formulation is consistent with the athletic metaphor. Aristotle had used both verbal expressions to describe the condition of runners who collapsed from exhaustion once the goal line had been crossed (*Rhetoric* 3.9.1409B. 1, cited by Spicq, 2:389; Mora, *La Carta* 82, n. 54). The writer was concerned pastorally that the men and women he addressed might "become weary and lose heart" prior to completing their course. Jesus had not allowed the hostile opposition of sinful men to wear him down but had triumphed over it. The tendency of the community, however, was to become fatigued. Their courage and readiness to identify themselves with Jesus faltered. Seeking to avoid suffering, they could fall. Consideration of the disposition and attainment of Jesus points out the element of struggle and the endurance required. What is called for is stamina and the determination to "go the distance" in order to attain the goal.

The link between 12:1–3, where the focus is upon Jesus' endurance of redemptive suffering, and 12:4–13, where Christians are called to endure disciplinary sufferings, is the appeal "not to lose heart." The formulation μὴ . . . ἐκλυόμενοι in v 3b anticipates the Scriptural mandate, "Do not lose heart" (μηδὲ ἐκλυόυ), in v 5 as well as the challenge expressed metaphorically in vv 12–13. These formulations extend the sober warning in 10:38–39 that God is displeased with those who "draw back" to their own destruction. Such passages address a weakening of resolve and a failure of nerve on the part of some of the persons addressed in the homily (so also Peterson, "Examination," 296).

4 In a transitional sentence the writer directs his audience to reflect upon their own experience of hostile opposition in the world. Jesus' experience of triumph through suffering provides perspective on the suffering actually endured by the community (cf. 10:32–34; 13:3). The athletic metaphor is sustained by the use of agonistic vocabulary: ἀντικαθίστημι, "to resist" (cf. Deut 31:21 LXX) and ἀνταγωνίζεσθαι, "to struggle" (cf. 4 Macc 17:14) occur only here in the NT. They are terms appropriate to athletic language (Teodorico, 210). The image in v 4, however, is decidedly more combative. It is no longer the footrace that is in view but the boxing arena, involving bloodshed and even death (for a similar shift in metaphor, see 1 Cor 9:24, 26). The sudden change in metaphor together with the shift in focus from Christ to the community signals the introduction of a new paragraph (12:4–11), in which the writer will clarify the meaning and purpose of disciplinary sufferings in the life of the new people of God.

The pointed observation οὔπω μέχρις αἵματος ἀντικατέστητε, "you have not yet resisted to the point of bloodshed," can be understood figuratively to mean, "You still have not done your utmost." The expression is drawn from the games, in which the most dangerous contest was the armed boxing match. Boxing was the supreme test of the pentathalon, and bloody wounds were commonplace (cf. Spicq, 2:390; Kudasiewicz, *CollTh* 46 [1976] 130–31; Mora, *La Carta*, 65–66, n. 200, and especially R. Brophy and M. Brophy, "Death in the Pan-Hellenic Games II: All Combative Sports," *AJPh* 106 [1985] 171–198). According to the writer's contemporary, the Stoic philosopher Seneca, the true athlete was the man who "saw his own blood" (Letter 13 in *L. Annaei Senecae ad Lucillum epistula moral,* ed. O. Heuse [Lipsiae: Teubner, 1914] 24). In the immediate context the allusion is to the violent death of Jesus, who endured crucifixion (12:2; cf. Phil 2:8 μέχρι θανάτου [="to the point of death"]). Jesus had to suffer more degrading shame and deeper hostility than anything yet experienced by the congregation. On this understanding the writer's intention is to say that the community had not yet given the fullest measure in their struggle against sin. The sustaining of an athletic metaphor throughout vv 1–4 lends support to this interpretation.

An alternative proposal is to find a reference to bloody persecution. The writer's declaration amounts to a statement of fact. Although members of the community had endured persecution in the form of insults, imprisonment, banishment, and loss of property (10:32–34), they had not yet been exposed to the ignominy of martyrdom. Some of their leaders may, in fact, have borne witness to their faith through martyrdom (13:7), but this at least had not been their lot. As one house church within a larger Christian community (13:17, 24), they had escaped an ordeal involving bloodshed. The text then reflects upon the relationship between the church and public authorities. No one has yet died a martyr's death (cf. Andriessen, *NRT* 96 [1974] 1061–62; Peterson, "Examination," 295–96; Thompson, *Beginnings of Christian Philosophy,* 29, n. 47; among others).

The strongest argument in favor of this alternative explanation is the parallel use of the expression "to resist to the point of death" with clear reference to martyrdom in accounts of those who endured torture and death at the time of the Maccabees (2 Macc 13:14: ἀγωνίσασθαι μέχρι θανάτου [="to contend to the point of death"]; cf. 4 Macc 17:9–10; "they avenged their race by looking unto God, and by enduring tortures, even unto death [εἰς θεὸν ἀφορῶντες καὶ μέχρι θανάτου τὰς βασάνους ὑπομείναντες]). The suggestion of an antagonist and of a conflict involving bloodshed in v 4 calls to mind the extensive use of athletic imagery in 4 Maccabees to portray the Jewish martyrs as athletes who were exemplars of endurance in the contest of faith (e.g., ἀγών, "contest," in 11:20; 13:15; 15:29; 16:16; 17:11; ἀγωνίζεσθαι, "to contend in an athletic contest," in 17:13; see the discussion of this theme in Harris, *ExpTim* 32 [1920–21] 183–85; Thompson, *Beginnings of Christian Philosophy,* 63–64). The fact that the writer of Hebrews commonly compares the situation of his audience with that of Christ strongly favors the second interpretation.

The concluding phrase πρὸς τὴν ἁμαρτίαν ἀνταγωνιζόμενοι, "while struggling against sin," suggests conflict with "a hostile power standing against the church" (Michel, 437). The reference to ἁμαρτία, "sin," has commonly been interpreted as the unfaithfulness that is always possible and against which it is necessary to contend (e.g., Teodorico, 210; Mora, *La Carta,* 82–83). It is necessary, however, to allow the progression of the writer's statement within a section to determine the nuance of his vocabulary.

In v 1 the writer identified as a hindrance to Christian life "the sin that so easily distracts." In that context ἁμαρτία suggests the weariness that overtakes the distance runner, which can subvert his determination to complete the race. The primary reference in v 1 is to the subjective, inward struggle against sin. With the change of image in v 4, however, there is a change of nuance in ἁμαρτία. The personification of "sin" as an enemy who must be overcome, even by bloodshed, shows that the reference is more objective. The distinctive coloration of ἁμαρτία in v 4 is determined by the reference to ἁμαρτωλοί, "sinners," in v 3, where the term refers to those who were "hostile to the representative of faith in the concrete situation and who were the cause of his suffering" (Michel, 436). The expression ἁμαρτία in v 4 is a periphrasis for ἁμαρτωλοί in v 3. It refers objectively to any source of hostile opposition to the Church (Michel, 437; Peterson, "Examination," 296; cf. Vanhoye, *La structure*, 199).

In the light of the context established by vv 2–3, the writer's observation in v 4 as a whole has a shaming function. The sufferings of the community were insignificant in comparison with those endured by Jesus. His sufferings were both quantitatively and qualitatively greater than theirs. Yet the members of the house church appeared to be on the verge of becoming weary and disheartened. They are summoned to a firm resolve to contend for faith, regardless of the cost. Christians are, to a certain extent, engaged in the same struggle that Jesus was. They must not regard themselves as exempt from the ordeal of faith endured by the attested witnesses who preceded them (11:35b–38; 12:1) and by Jesus himself (12:2–3).

5–6 In vv 5–11 the writer seeks to justify the experience of hostility and abuse that the community has encountered because they identified themselves with Christ. He fully recognized that suffering has the ability to disturb faith or to provoke uncertainty and despair. The consideration of these harsh experiences as exposure to the παιδεία, "instructive discipline," "correction," of God, which attests a filial relationship with the Father, brings a fresh perspective on these aspects of Christian experience. The sufferings of the community were actually disciplinary in character and expressed the love that God has for his children. As proof of sonship they reflected God's grace and forgiveness.

Bornkamm has denied that the issue of theodicy plays any role in this context ("Sohnschaft und Leiden," 195–98). He contends that 12:5–11 develops the theme of "the Son and the sons," and that sonship is to be understood only from the perspective of christology. Sonship is grounded and procured through the Son, through whose sufferings God is leading many sons to glory (2:10). According to Bornkamm, the writer's christological understanding of sonship, especially in 2:5–18, has opened up "a new horizon on the question of the divine παιδεία and gives to the sonship of believers a new meaning" (cf. 5:8; 12:1–11). Consequently, the theodicy problem that does lie behind Prov 3:11–12 "in our context generally plays no further role" (195, 196, 198; cf. Bertram, *TDNT* 5:622).

The significance of the sonship of believers certainly explains in part how the writer responds to the problem of theodicy, but it is erroneous to suggest that he did not face it. More of the perspective of Prov 3:11–12 on this matter is made than Bornkamm is prepared to allow. The writer questions whether his audience had forgotten altogether the sort of encouragement with which God addresses his children in Prov 3:11–12 (v 5a). Moreover, as Michel has observed, 12:1–3 is constructed christologically but does not use the motif of sonship. Conversely, 12:4–11 is not structured christologically and cannot be understood as such. The problem of theodicy finds in christology the eschatological beginning of a solution, but no more than a beginning. It is the full realization of God's redemptive plan that will finally remove the need for theodicy (Michel, 439–40; id., *NovT* 6 [1963] 190–91).

The stylistically rhetorical character of v 5a favors taking the introductory statement as an interrogative: καὶ ἐκλέλησθε τῆς παρακλήσεως, ἥτις ὑμῖν ὡς υἱοῖς διαλέγεται, "And have you forgotten completely the encouragement which speaks to you as sons?" The question represents a firm, but gentle, rebuke. The members of the house church appear to have forgotten completely the biblical concept of disciplinary or educative sufferings (cf. Costé, RSR 43 [1955] 499–503; J. A. Sanders, Suffering, 33–34, 39–40, 92). The sufferings the community had endured were actually disciplinary in character. Properly understood, they were a means of training them for the life of committed obedience appropriate to members of God's family.

The expression τῆς παρακλήσεως combines the notions of exhortation and comfort (BAGD 618), but in this context the notes of comfort and encourgement appear to be dominant (as in 6:18). The point of encouragement is found in God's acknowledgment of the community as his sons and daughters. The positive role that disciplinary sufferings play in the molding of Christian character furnishes the writer with the basis of his argument. Far from being an occasion for discouragement, the imposition of the discipline of suffering must stimulate confidence and a renewed sense of dignity, since it attests the filial relationship with God that Christians enjoy. The choice of the verb διαλέγεται, "speaks," underscores the relational dimension that the writer intends to develop, since it views the utterance of the text of Scripture as the voice of God in conversation with his child (cf. Schrenk, TDNT 2:94: Kilpatrick, "Διαλέγεσθαι and διαλογίζεσθαι in the New Testament," JTS n.s. 11 [1960] 338–40; Michel, 438).

Scripture sheds light on the meaning and purpose of disciplinary sufferings in the experience of the people of God. The authoritative word in Prov 3:11–12 directs attention toward the action of God and invites his people to recognize that God disciplines his people, collectively and individually, to draw them closer to himself. The citation brings together the concepts of divine discipline and sonship.

The biblical concept of discipline (παιδεία) combines the nuances of training, instruction, and firm guidance with those of reproof, correction, and punishment. The notion of God as disciplinarian was derived from the parent-child relationship: "As a man disciplines his son, so the Lord your God disciplines you" (Deut 8:5). God is the loving Father who desires only good for his children, but who knows that obedience to his revealed will is the condition for realizing this goal. The imposition of divine discipline is an evidence of God's responsible love and commitment. Adversity and hardships are to be recognized as means designed by God to call his people to faithful and obedient sonship. The proper framework for understanding the character of divine discipline is the covenant, which binds God and his children together in a familial relationship.

Citing Prov 3:11–12 LXX[A] with only slight modification, the writer reminds the community that the presence of discipline is a sign and proof of sonship. The addition of the personal pronoun μου, "my," to the conventional wisdom formula υἱέ, "son," in v 5b makes the citation more intimate. The vocative υἱέ without the addition is used when a teacher is addressing a pupil, and as such is appropriate in Proverbs (see E. Ahlborn, "Die Septugainta-Vorlage der Hebräerbriefes," 132; McCullough, NTS 26 [1979–80] 377–78). In this context, however, it is God who addresses the Christian as his son. The addition of the personal pronoun, together with the phrase "the encouragement which speaks to you as sons" in the formulaic introduction to the text (v 5*a*), shows that the writer regards Prov 3:11–12 as God's personal word to those who enjoy sonship through the mediation of Jesus, who inaugurated the new covenant. This perspective gives to the παιδεία of God in this context an eschatological orientation (cf. Bertram, *TDNT* 5:621–22; Bornkamm, "Sohnschaft und Leiden," 196–98). The function of the citation is to demonstrate that there is a necessary and integral relationship between sufferings and a filial relationship with the Lord. Adversity and hardships are to be understood as firm correction attesting God's love for his child (cf. J. A. Sanders, *Suffering*, 4–5).

The directives not to regard lightly (μὴ ὀλιγώρει) the discipline of the Lord and not to lose heart (μηδὲ ἐκλύου) when corrected by him (v 5*b*) are parallel in intention. They invite reflection upon the divine purpose that informs the experience of God's people; sufferings and testing are disciplinary and educative in character (cf. Vanhoye, *AsSeign* 52 [1974] 62–63). When regarded rightly, they provide assurance that God is maturing his children through responsible, corrective love.

The paradox that suffering and abuse are positive in character is thrown into bold relief by the chiastic form of Prov 3:12, cited in verse 6:

ὃν γὰρ ἀγαπᾷ	κύριος παιδεύει
"the one whom he loves"	"the Lord disciplines"
μαστιγοῖ δὲ	πάντα υἱόν ὃν παραδέχεται
"and scourges"	"every son whom he receives favorably."

The essentially negative theme of painful suffering is subsumed in the positive notions of love and sonship (Vanhoye, *AsSeign* 52 [1974] 63). The positive character of divine discipline affirmed in Prov 3:12 demonstrates that corrective suffering is motivated by God's love and grace.

The citation of Prov 3:11–12 in vv 5*b*–6 summons the members of the community to persevere in faith in view of the encouragement extended to them through the testimony of Scripture. They are to recognize in the hardships and abuse they experience an intervention of the fatherly love of God for his children.

7–8 The quotation of Prov 3:11–12 furnishes the point of departure for an exposition of the text in vv 7–11. This unit is structured in terms of the citation and serves to actualize the authority of the biblical text for the community in its situation. In this context παιδεία, "corrective discipline," signifies the suffering that may have to be endured because of fidelity to God (cf. 10:32–34; 11:35*b*–12:4). Three considerations based on the concept of divine discipline receive a midrashic explanation: the necessity of paternal discipline (vv 7–8), the appropriate response to discipline (v 9), and the benefits that result from nurture through discipline (vv 10–11). The exposition is explicitly hortatory and parenetic in character.

The initial clause is a striking example of compressed statement: εἰς παιδείαν ὑπομένετε (v 7*a*). Its meaning can be conveyed only through paraphrastic expansion in the light of the immediate context: "Endure your trials as an expression of divine discipline." Although ὑπομένετε may be construed as a present indicative ("You are enduring") or as a present imperative ("Endure!"), the parenetic character of the context supports the decision to read the verb as an imperative (so Michel, 440–41; BAGD 603). Although the precise significance of the phrase εἰς παιδείαν continues to be debated (see above, Note jj), the sense is sufficiently clear from the reference to divine discipline in the citation of Prov 3:11–12. The trials of the community are seen as disciplinary in nature. The pastoral directive develops the thought that the endurance of disciplinary sufferings (παιδεία) is an essential aspect of Christian experience. Bearing their trials with patient and trusting endurance will have the effect of demonstrating their sonship and will strengthen their resolve to persevere further (Peterson, "Examination," 301–2).

The presence of hardships is proof that God is dealing with the community ὡς υἱοῖς, "as sons" (v 7b). Adverse circumstances have been assigned by God to those who are his children. The phrase ὡς υἱοῖς ὑμῖν προσφέρεται, "he is treating you as sons," balances a similar phrase in v 5a, in the formula introducing the biblical citation.

v 5a   τῆς παρακλήσεως, ἥτις ὑμῖν ὡς υἱοῖς διαλέγεται
          "the encouragement which speaks to you as sons"
v 7b   ὡς υἱοῖς ὑμῖν προσφέρεται ὁ θεός
          "God is treating you as sons."

Prov 3:11–12 employs the singular forms υἱέ μου, "my son," and πάντα υἱόν, "every son." The repetition of the phrase ὡς υἱοῖς, "as sons," in the two statements that frame the citation serves to generalize the text and apply it to the experience of the community as a whole.

The anarthrous form of the noun υἱοῖς has a qualitative nuance: the members of the community are "real sons." The same qualitative nuance is to be recognized in the anarthrous nouns υἱός, "son," and πατήρ, "father," in the rhetorical question that follows in v 7c: τίς γὰρ υἱὸς ὃν οὐ παιδεύει πατήρ, "for what son is there whom a father does not discipline?" The absence of the article, which normally would be expected with concrete nouns, calls attention to the nature and quality of what is expressed by the nouns. Here the stress falls upon a "son" in his character as a true son and upon a "father" in his capacity as a responsible father (cf. Zerwick, Biblical Greek, §179; BDF §257[3]).

The point that genuine sonship is attested in the experience of disciplinary sufferings is driven home by means of an analogy drawn from the household. Paternal discipline is an integral aspect of family life. All legitimate children are sharers (μέτοχοι) in this experience (v 8a). An absence of discipline, then, would actually be an indication of a father's rejection.

The background to the argument is furnished by the OT. Among the Hebrews, primary responsibility for the establishment of discipline belonged to the father, whom God held accountable for the instruction and correction of his children (e.g., Exod 12:26; 13:14; Deut 6:7). The experience of redemption from Egypt and the subsequent gift of the Law at Sinai demonstrated God's commitment to Israel and established his claim for filial obedience. It was the father's task to make his children aware of this claim and to enforce it with integrity, in the knowledge that blessing from God depended upon compliance with the revealed will of God. The authority of God is presupposed in all biblical statements concerning parental discipline. A father disciplines his child precisely because he loves him and desires him to experience life as approved by God (cf. Prov 13:24; 19:18; 22:15; 23:13–14; 29:17).

The members of the house church must recognize that exemption from the corrective discipline that is experienced by all genuine sons would imply the unwelcome inference ἄρα νόθοι καὶ οὐχ υἱοί ἐστε, "then you are illegitimate children rather than true sons, are you not?" (v 8*b*). The term νόθοι, which occurs only here in the NT, must be understood in its ancient legal sense as descriptive of those who do not enjoy the privileges of the family nor the protection of the father. They are also denied by law the rights of inheritance, which belong exclusively to those who are υἱοί, "legitimate sons," (see Spicq, 2:393–94; cf. P. E. Hughes, 528–29). God's imposition of corrective discipline is both intentional and necessary.

9 Vv 9–11 constitute a new unit. Vv 4–8 were integrated thematically around the issue of sonship. The point was made that genuine sonship is attested in the experience of disciplinary sufferings. There is no reference to sonship in vv 9–11. In this unit, balanced clauses develop the parallel and contrast between paternal and divine discipline in terms of its character, intention, and results.

The transitional term εἶτα, "then again," "furthermore," serves to alert the audience in the house church that a new argument is being introduced in the demonstration that submission to divine discipline is essential. From our natural fathers we learned respect as the appropriate response to correction. The writer argues in a pastoral vein that divine discipline is more necessary than ordinary paternal discipline, because God is training his children for the enjoyment of life in its fullest sense. The appeal to the common experience of corrective discipline in the sphere of the home points to the greater significance of submission to divine discipline.

Although the argument is cast in the form of a rhetorical question, it has a specifically hortatory purpose. An initial assertion concerning paternal discipline in v 9*a* furnishes the basis for applying an *a fortiori* argument concerning divine discipline in v 9*b* (cf. 2:2–3; 10:28–29). Such complex statements (consisting of an assertion followed by a rhetorical question calling for an affirmitive response) are designed to make a strong impact upon the emotions and the imagination. The immediacy with which the hortatory force of the appeal can be felt make this class of statements rhetorically effective (see McCown, "Ο ΛΟΓΟΣ ΤΗΣ ΠΑΡΑΚΛΗΣΕΩΣ," 205–6).

In v 7–8 the argument was advanced that paternal discipline was purposeful. It provided a demonstration of sonship. An absence of discipline would have been an expression of abandonment by a father. A second purpose for discipline at the hands of "our natural fathers" is specified in v 9*a*: paternal discipline was necessary to teach us due respect. In the designation of human fathers as παιδευταί, "those who instruct, especially by discipline," the idea of correcting through discipline is prominent (BAGD 603). Although this noun of agency occurs only here in the homily (cf. Hos 5:2 LXX; *Ps. Sol.* 8:29; Rom 2:20), it is entirely at home in a context where the cognates παιδεύειν, "to discipline," "to correct," and παιδεία, "discipline," "correction," recur with frequency. The pointed observation καὶ ἐνετρεπόμεθα, "and we respected [them]," calls attention to the attitude that resulted appropriately from submission to paternal correction.

The result clause at the end of v 9*a* provides the point of transition to the rhetorical question in v 9*b*, where the negative particle οὐ, "not," with the interrogative calls for an affirmative answer, "Yes." The comparative form πολὺ μᾶλλον, "much more," in v 9*b* serves to underscore a contrast with the previous clause, introduced by the particle μέν, "on the one hand." The much greater degree of respect owed to God as Father makes submission to the imposition of divine discipline all the more necessary than was true in the case of ordinary paternal discipline.

The designation of God as ὁ πατὴρ τῶν πνευμάτων, "the Father of spirits," reflects the influence of the Septuagint, where the notion of transcendence is integral to the expression (Num 16:22; 27:16 LXX: "the Father of spirits and of all flesh"; cf. 2 Macc 3:24: "Sovereign of spirits and all authority"). The divine title is to be interpreted in terms of the two-sphere thinking characteristic of Hebrews. "The Father of spirits" is the transcendent God to whom the heavenly world is also subject (cf. Kuss, 112; Schweizer, *TDNT* 7:141). As the sovereign Lord of heaven and earth, God's right to discipline us and to demand our devotion proceeds from the highest authority.

The importance of willing submission to God is stressed in a final clause, expressing result, καὶ ζήσομεν, "so that we shall live." The formulation recalls the summons to life issued in the framework of covenant obedience in Deut 30:11–20. Submission to divine discipline is integrally related to the enjoyment of eschatological salvation (cf. 10:38; see Peterson, "Examination," 301–2).

10–11 These verses, which elaborate the benefits that accrue to those who are nurtured through divine discipline, bring the central paragraph (vv 4–11) to a conclusion. The analogy between paternal correction and divine discipline is developed in v 10 through a series of contrasts that serve to distinguish the discipline imposed by our natural fathers from the disciplinary sufferings imposed by God. The contrast expressed in the formulation οἱ μὲν γὰρ . . . ὁ δέ, "for they . . . but he," is sharp. The personal pronouns find their antecedent in the persons designated definitely in v 9, "our natural fathers" and "the Father of spirits."

The temporal restriction of paternal discipline and the motivating consideration behind it is observed in v 10*a*: οἱ μὲν γὰρ πρὸς ὀλίγας ἡμέρας κατὰ τὸ δοκοῦν αὐτοῖς ἐπαίδευον, "for they continually disciplined us for a short time at their discretion." The tense of the verb ἐπαίδευον is significant; as a descriptive imperfect it calls to mind repeated action in the past ("they continually disciplined [us]"). Unfortunately, the judgment of parents is imperfect. The discipline imposed κατὰ τὸ δοκοῦν αὐτοῖς, "at their discretion," may or may not have been beneficial to a child. There is a margin of uncertainty in all human training. Paternal discipline originated often in anger. At times it was unjust. Furthermore, it was imposed only πρὸς ὀλίγας ἡμέρας, "for a short time."

In contradistinction to this, God's paternal discipline is determined by his perfect wisdom and is motivated by an intrinsic concern for our welfare (v 10*b*). It is adjusted directly upon (ἐπί) real usefulness (Vanhoye, *La structure*, 203; cf. F. F. Bruce, 361: "The man who accepts discipline at the hand of God as something designed by his heavenly Father for his good will cease to feel resentful and rebellious; he has 'stilled and quieted' his soul, which thus provides fertile soil for the cultivation of a righteous life"). The idiomatic expression ἐπὶ τὸ συμφέρον, "for our benefit," stands in sharp contrast to the idiom used in reference to our natural fathers, κατὰ τὸ δοκοῦν αὐτοῖς, "at their discretion." It conveys a legal notion of advantage that is relevant to the Christian throughout his earthly life. The goal of divine discipline is to bring God's children to spiritual maturity and to prepare them to share in his holiness.

The divine intention is expressed in a classic purpose clause: εἰς τὸ μεταλαβεῖν τῆς ἁγιότητος αὐτοῦ, "in order that we may share in his holiness." The rare term ἁγιότητος denotes the holiness that is the essential attribute of God's character, which Christians are to share (Procksch, *TDNT* 1:114). The expression came into use only late in hellenistic Judaism (e.g., 2 Macc 15:2; *T. Levi* 3:4); it occurs only here in the NT. In v 10 the stress is placed not on human endeavor (as in v 14) but upon the fact that God bestows as a gift a share in his holiness through divine discipline. The clear implication is that it is impossible to share in God's holiness apart from the correction administered through disciplinary sufferings. Such sufferings have the salutary effect of maturing Christians as men and women of God. The concept of correction through discipline is thus related to the formation of godly character.

The time when the gift of sharing in God's holiness is bestowed is not conveyed by the aorist infinitive, but the reference is almost certainly to a future conformity to God's character through persevering faith. Disciplinary sufferings are the prelude to participation ultimately in the divine life. The experience of redemption is the pledge of the final experience of holiness as yet another blessing of eschatological salvation (cf. Michel, 446–7; P. E. Hughes, 531; K. Weiss, *TDNT* 9:77, n. 18; Peterson, "Examination," 262, n. 155). It is instructive to recall that it is God's intention to lead many sons and daughters to glory (2:10). It is also his intention that they shall participate in his holiness (12:10). The two experiences are presumably concurrent.

Appealing to the human analogy again, the writer acknowledges in v 11 that all discipline, however brief in duration, at the actual time seems painful rather than pleasant. It is only after the fact, when the results of that discipline emerge, that its relative value can be determined. The basis of the argument is ordinary human experience, which permits a distinction to be made between two successive phases of correction: πρὸς τὸ παρόν, "for the moment," and ὕστερον, "later." *At the moment* all discipline seems to entail λύπη, "painful sorrow." The use of the verb δοκεῖ, "seems," serves to stress that this initial impression is superficial. *Later* the profound impact of the discipline imposed becomes apparent: ὕστερον δὲ καρπὸν . . . ἀποδίδωσιν, "but later it produces fruit." In the case of Christians who are disciplined by God, the result is substantial and pleasant: καρπὸν εἰρηνικὸν τοῖς δι᾿ αὐτῆς γεγυμνασμένοις ἀποδίδωσιν δικαιοσύνης, "it yields a harvest which consists of peace and of righteousness for those who are trained by it" (cf. Vanhoye, *AsSeign* 52 [1974] 64–66).

The expression καρπὸν εἰρηνικὸν . . . δικαιοσύνης is unusually dense. It seems necessary to understand εἰρηνικόν, "that which relates to peace," as a substitute for the genitive, and thus as parallel in construction with δικαιοσύνης, a genitive of apposition qualifying καρπόν, "harvest," "fruit." The expression refers to "the harvest which consists of peace and of righteousness" (following Michel, 445; K. Weiss, *TDNT* 9:77, n. 18). The harvest enjoyed in peace (cf. Isa 32:17; James 3:18) is also the fruit that consists of righteousness. "Peace" and "righteousness" are gifts of eschatological salvation that "point to the new age and to the future perfection" (Michel, 446). There is no need to restrict the enjoyment of these benefits to the future (as does, for example, Wilckens, *TDNT* 8:595, who interprets ὕστερος with reference to the eschatological future). They are present possessions that anticipate the prospect of sharing in the holiness of God (so Peterson, "Examination," 302–3). The period of discipline is followed by a period of joy (χαρά),

which in this instance is linked to the immediate enjoyment of peace and righteousness and the ultimate enjoyment of God's character and presence.

The exposition of Prov 3:11–12, which began in v 5, extends through v 11.
Motifs rooted in the OT wisdom tradition are sharpened by an appreciation of
the eschatological salvation that Christians enjoy. In rounding off his parenetic
midrash, the writer again introduces an image borrowed from athletics: the benefits of divine discipline belong τοῖς δι' αὐτῆς γεγυμνασμένοις, "to those who have
been trained by it." As athletes engaged in a contest, for whom discipline is the
key to their training and perseverance, the members of the house church are
challenged to respond appropriately to the abuse and hardships they were experiencing and to remain steadfast. Their sufferings were disciplinary in character
and were assigned by God for their benefit. They hold the prospect of joy and
rest following painful suffering (cf. Moffatt, 205; P. E. Hughes, 533).

12–13 A transition from the central paragraph (vv 4–11) to the concluding
exhortation of the section (vv 12–13) is signaled by the explanatory particle διό,
"therefore." The thought of training through disciplinary sufferings in v 11 suggested the metaphor of an athletic contest requiring flexed arms and strong knees.
The members of the house church, however, are characterized by listless arms
and weakened knees. The appropriate response to divine discipline is a renewed
resolve to engage in a demanding contest. The necessity for endurance is clearly
implied in the pastoral directive to ready themselves for the contest, bracing their
drooping hands and weakened knees. They must keep on running, moving straight
toward the goal without wavering. The appeal is ultimately for the community to
endure in the struggle, with a genuine concern for the weakest of their number.

The source for the exhortation is to be located in two directives drawn from
Scripture, Isa 35:3 and Prov 4:26. The text of v 12 reflects an oracle in Isaiah that
announces the decisive intervention of God:

> Say to those with fearful hearts,
> "Be strong, do not fear;
> your God will come,
>   he will come with vengeance;
> with divine retribution
>   he will come to save you." (Isa 35:4)

It is this assurance that furnishes the ground for the directive to "strengthen the
feeble hands, steady the knees that give way" (Isa 35:3).

The quotation in v 12 does not correspond exactly to the LXX or to the MT; it
appears to represent an independent translation, in which the adjectival participles were placed before the nouns they qualify, a word order supported only in
the Heb. text of Sir 25:23 recovered in the Cairo Genizah (G. Howard, *NovT* 10
[1968] 213–14). The quotation is adopted appropriately to the situation of the
members of the house church. The descriptive phrases τὰς παρειμένας χεῖρας
καὶ τὰ παραλελυμένα γόνατα, "drooping hands and weakened knees," evoke the
picture of the person who is thoroughly exhausted and discouraged (e.g., Sir
2:12: "Woe to timid hearts and drooping hands [χερσὶν παρειμέναις]"; 25:23:
"Drooping hands and weak knees are caused by the wife who does not make her
husband happy"; cf. Job 4:3–5). The figure of the athlete (the wearied and beaten

boxer?) who drops his hands in weakness was a commonplace in antiquity (e.g., Philo, *On the Preliminary Studies* 164: "Some faint before the struggle has begun, and lose heart altogether, counting toil a formidable antagonist, and like weary athletes drop their hands in weakness . . . But there are others who . . . with patience and stoutness of heart carry through to its finish the contest of life, keeping it safe from defeat and taking a strong stand against the forces of nature"). The allusion to Isa 35:3 in v 12 thus resumes the reference to weariness and loss of heart developed in the larger context (12:3, 5). The endurance of faith demands heart, a fact recognized by the writer in his thematic concern with the loss of heart within the community addressed. (For an attempt to restrict the reference in v 12 only to certain members of the community who were faltering, see Andriessen, *NRT* 96 [1974] 1062–63.)

The directive of v 12 is not followed up with the assurance that God is coming to rescue the community, as in Isa 35:4. That almost certainly would have encouraged a false attitude of triumphalism. Instead, the imagery of v 12 is enriched from another passage from Proverbs which the writer evidently recalled:

> My child . . . let your eyes look straight ahead;
>   fix your gaze directly before you.
> make level paths for your feet
>   and take only ways that are firm.
> Do not swerve to the right or to the left;
>   keep your feet from evil. (Prov 4:25–27)

The instruction is appropriate for a person who is to compete in a race that will be long and arduous. He must move straight toward the goal, not swerving from the track that will lead him to his determined destination. Normally, those whose limbs are lame cannot compete in the race. Christians who are prepared to heed the writer's pastoral instruction, however, have the prospect that even the lame will not be disabled but will experience the healing that God provides to those whose purpose is narrowly determined by Christ.

The formulation of v 13 is adapted from Prov 4:26 LXX. In this instance the directive is cast in the plural to make it relevant to the entire community, and the word order of the biblical clause is altered so as to assign to τροχιάς, "track," "direction," the place of emphasis. In the context of Proverbs, the mandate to "make level paths for your feet, and keep your ways straight" refers to proper conduct under the direction of divine wisdom. The meaning of ὀρθάς, "level," "straight," is fundamentally ethical. In the larger context of Heb 12:1–12, however, the biblical expression τροχιὰς ὀρθὰς ποιεῖτε τοῖς ποσίν does not mean "make straight paths for your feet" but "pursue ways that are directed straight to the goal" or "move in a straight direction with your feet" (see Preisker, *TDNT* 5:449–50). The term ὀρθάς is not used ethically, as in classical Greek, Stoicism, and Jewish Wisdom literature, but has a distinctive nuance informed by the eschatology of primitive Christianity. Its point of reference in this context is the ultimate goal of faith, which can be reached only through the endurance of stringent tests of faith. Encouraged by the example of the attested witnesses (v 1) and especially of Jesus (v 2), men and women of faith cannot waver but move in a straight direction, certain of their goal. The mandate of v 13a indicates an eschatological orientation of life toward the final goal and implies the pledge

of attaining the goal. On this understanding, v 13 rounds off the unit by resuming the thought of reaching the goal implied prominently by the formulation of
vv 1–3 at the beginning of the section (so Michel, 447–48; cf. Stauffer, *TDNT*
1:137; BAGD 580, 828).

The determination of the precise meaning of the final clause (v 13*b*) is difficult because the clause is open to more than one translation (see above,
Note mmm). Käsemann, for example, prefers to give to the verb ἐκτρέπεσθαι the
meaning "to fall away from the true path," as in 1 Tim 1:6; 5:15; 2 Tim 4:14
("Hebräer 12:12–17," 312; cf. P. E. Hughes, 535, n. 138). This decision is consistent with his argument that the context exposes the danger of apostasy; the "lame"
can stray on to the crooked paths and be lost to God's people in their pilgrimage.
It seems necessary, however, to take into account the reference to the prospect of
healing (ἰαθῇ δὲ μᾶλλον, "but rather be healed"), which suggests that ἐκτραπῇ is
to be understood with the nuance it bears as a medical term, "be dislocated"
(following Vanhoye, *AsSeign* 52 [1974] 66; Andriessen, *NRT* 96 [1974] 1063; cf.
BAGD 368, 889). This understanding is reflected in the translation adopted for
the commentary: "so that what is lame might not be dislocated, but rather be
healed." The reference is to persons within the house church who have been
severely weakened by fatigue, for whom the others are to be genuinely concerned.
If those who are stronger will move in a straight direction toward the goal, the
brother or sister who is lame will follow more easily and will be healed of his hurt
(cf. Moffatt, 207; McCown, "Ο ΛΟΓΟΣ ΤΗΣ ΠΑΡΑΚΛΗΣΕΩΣ," 118). The prospect of healing for the weakest of their number adds a word of encouragement
to the clear directive to the community. The section is thus brought to a conclusion on the note of redemptive comfort.

Explanation

In 12:1–13 the community addressed is called to display a quality of endurance, which is the essential corollary of committed faith. Their attention is directed
from models of faithfulness in Israel's remote or more recent past under the old
covenant to Jesus, whose death on a cross displayed both faithfulness and endurance (12:1–3). Jesus' deliberate disregard for disgrace and his endurance of hostile
opposition from those who understood neither the depth of God's redemptive
love nor the extremity of their own plight provide a pattern for emulation whenever Christians experience an antagonistic response from the world. The audience
is summoned to concentrate their attention upon Jesus and to recognize that he
was not exempt from the conflicts that were integral to their own experience in a
hostile environment.

A depth of pastoral concern is evident throughout this section. The writer
understood that faith can be eroded by constant exposure to harsh circumstances.
He responds by presenting Jesus as the supreme witness to the life of committed
faith expressed through endurance and submission to the will of God. His renunciation of joy and endurance of the abject humiliation of crucifixion were
vindicated by his enthronement in God's presence. Christians must fix their gaze
upon Jesus and draw from his example the courage to display responsible commitment in their situation. *Jesus humiliated* offers Christians the supreme example

of endurance whenever they experience humiliation. *Jesus vindicated and enthroned* provides certainty that Christians will also be vindicated when they demonstrate the necessary endurance, which validates the life of committed faithfulness.

The writer appreciates that his audience, at least to some extent, shared the same struggle in which Jesus was engaged. His endurance of unjustified antagonism and his voluntary submission to shame displayed the profound trust in God to which Christians are called. As such, Jesus offers a model for Christians whenever they are tempted to become disheartened with the intensity of the opposition they encounter from society. There was, of course, both a qualitative and a quantitative difference between the sufferings endured by Jesus and those experienced by the Christians addressed in the homily (12:4). He had endured the excruciating pain and shame of the cross; they had not been subjected to such treatment. But the difference was one of degree. They had experienced contempt, abuse, and loss as a result of their open identification with Jesus (10:32–34). Their immediate prospect was for sufferings that were more severe in character. The development of the meaningful category of "disciplinary sufferings" in 12:4–11 is designed to assist the members of the house church to perceive the significance of the hardships they were experiencing.

The writer presupposes that the concept of disciplinary sufferings was already familiar to the community. Firmly entrenched in the Jewish wisdom and martyrological traditions, the notion would have been expounded in the course of synagogue preaching. It was necessary only to remind the community that their trials were disciplinary in character. Grounding his argument in the witness of Scripture, the writer cites a passage that was significant in the passion theology of both Judaism and early Christianity, Prov 3:11–12. That text demonstrates that there is an essential and integral relationship between sufferings and a filial relationship with God. Sufferings are corrective in character. Consequently, they are purposeful.

Responsibility for the infliction of suffering may be traced to those who are hostile to God, who find in the people of God a target for their hostility. Such sufferings become "disciplinary" in character when God makes them a means for maturing his children spiritually. The goal of divine discipline is Christian maturity and, ultimately, participation in the holiness of God. It is God's ability to transform an expression of hostility into a measure for spiritual nurture that is emphasized in 12:5–11.

The writer wanted his audience to draw from his exposition of the biblical text the implication that those who are prepared to submit to disciplinary sufferings participate in the triumph of the cross of Christ. That is the connection between 12:2–3 and 4–11. Those who show contempt for the people of God by inflicting painful sufferings cannot frustrate the divine purpose, which is motivated by God's pastoral love for his children. Conversely, whenever the community of faith experiences unpleasantness, pain, and adversity because they are Christians, they should recognize in these sufferings the pledge of the Father's love. They should also firm up their resolve to persevere in faith and to complete the course prescribed for them by God (12:12–13). The clarification of the significance of sufferings in the maturing of a relationship with God provides the basis for the sustained appeal for endurance in pursuing the goal marked out for the community.

As a section, 12:1–13 is important for the clues it provides concerning the audience addressed and for its demonstration of the dominant pastoral dimension of the homily. Indeed, these two aspects are inextricably bound together. The passsage speaks directly to the situation of the community and to the point of their need for solid encouragement. By doing so, it suggests a partial profile of the group addressed. Wearied from the constant need to maintain their Christian stance in a social setting that is no longer simply unreceptive to their message and life style but has become increasingly hostile toward their presence, they are thoroughly disheartened. A weakening of resolve and a failure of nerve are clearly presupposed for at least some of the persons addressed in the homily. The writer's conviction was that they urgently needed the encouragement offered to them through attested witnesses from the past, through Jesus himself, and through the testimony of Scripture.

V. Orientation for Life as Christians in a Hostile World (12:14–13:25)

Bibliography

Black, D. A. "The Problem of the Literary Structure of Hebrews: An Evaluation and a Proposal." *GTJ* 7 (1986) 163–77. **Bligh, J.** *Chiastic Analysis of the Epistle to the Hebrews.* 28–33. ———. "The Structure of Hebrews." *HeyJ* 5 (1964) 170–77. **Descamps, A.** "La structure de l'Épître aux Hébreux." *RDT* 9 (1954) 333–38. **Dussaut, L.** *Synopse structurelle de l'Épître aux Hébreux.* 128–37. **Gyllenberg, R.** "Die Komposition des Hebräerbriefs." *SEÅ* 22–23 (1957–58) 137–47. **Hillmann, W.** "Glaube und Verheissung: Einführung in die Grundgedanken des Hebräerbriefes (10,32–13,25)." *BibLeb* 1 (1960) 237–52. **Nauck, W.** "Zum Aufbau des Hebräerbriefes." In *Judentum, Urchristentum, Kirche.* FS J. Jeremias. Ed. W. Eltester. BZNW 26. Berlin: Töpelmann, 1960. 199–206. **Rice, G. E.** "Apostasy as a Motif and Its Effect on the Structure of Hebrews." *AUSS* 23 (1985) 29–35. **Swetnam, J.** "Form and Content in Hebrews 7–13." *Bib* 55 (1974) 333–48. **Thien, F.** "Analyse de l'Épître aux Hébreux." *RB* 11 (1902) 74–86. **Thurén, J.** *Das Lobopfer der Hebräer: Studien zum Aufbau und Anliegen von Hebräerbrief* 13. Åbo: Acedemiae Aboensis, 1973. 25–49. **Vaganay, L.** "Le Plan de l'Épître aux Hébreux." In *Mémorial Lagrange.* Ed. L. H. Vincent. Paris: Gabalda, 1940. 269–77. **Vanhoye, A.** "Discussions sur la structure de l'Épître aux Hébreux." *Bib* 55 (1974) 349–80. ———. "Les indices de la structure littéraire de l'Épître aux Hébreux." *SE* 2 (1964) 493–509. ———. "Literarische Struktur und theologische Botschaft des Hebräerbriefs." *SNTU* 4 (1979) 119–47; 5 (1980) 18–49. ———. *"Retti cammini."* In *L'ultima parte dell' Epistola agli Ebrei: Ebr 12,14–13,25.* Rome: Pontifical Biblical Institute, 1974. ———. *La structure littéraire.* 46–49, 205–235. ———. "Structure littéraire et themes théologiques de l'Épître aux Hébreux." In *Studiorum Paulinorum Congressus Internationalis Catholicus 1961.* AnBib 18. Rome: Biblical Institute, 1963. 175–81.

Introduction

In the fifth major division in Hebrews, extending from 12:14 to 13:21, the sermon is brought to a close. The concluding segment of the homily consists primarily of a series of pastoral directives. Whenever exposition is introduced, it is integrated with the parenetic instruction that precedes and follows. Its sole purpose is to provide a sound basis for the directives and an incentive for compliance with the writer's appeal to his audience (12:18–24; 13:11–12). The instruction in this section is frequently supported by brief clarifying statements (12:14*b*, 17, 26–27; 13:2*b*, 5*b*–6, 8, 10, 18; the unit 13:11–12 appears to fall into this category as well). The range and general character of the directives, the appeal to previous instruction ("For you know," 12:17), the use of example (12:16–17; 25–26), and the call to imitation of those who were models of committed faithfulness (13:7, 12–13) identify the concluding portion of the sermon as parenesis, or practical instruction.

The major characteristics of parenesis can be succinctly summarized.

(1) Parenesis is traditional, unoriginal, and axiomatic. It is instruction that will be recognized as familiar by those who receive it. Since what is being urged is

not new, no extended treatment of a particular topic is necessary. A brief reminder is sufficient.

(2) Parenetic precepts are applicable generally to a wider audience. This is true to such an extent that it has been questioned whether the pastoral directives addressed shed any light on the actual situation of the audience.

(3) Parenesis presupposes that the hearers or readers already know what is being stated. Repetition of what is already known serves only to jog the memory (cf. 12:17). The task of parenetic instruction is not to teach but to arouse and focus the attention. It is to concentrate the memory and keep it from losing its grip. In the light of a fundamental failure to act on the basis of what is already known, it is necessary to bring significant instruction to remembrance. This is true even when that instruction consists of traditional wisdom.

(4) A common element in parenetic instruction is the appeal to example (12:16–17, 19–21, 25; 13:2, 8). What is called for is the imitation or emulation of the qualities of life and conduct exhibited in those who were Christians in an earlier generation (13:7). In order to be a true disciple, one must imitate the model. The call to remembrance (13:7) is, in fact, a summons to conduct oneself as an imitator of the model.

(5) The form that parenetic instruction takes is exhortation, advising the audience to pursue some course of action, or to abstain from some form of behavior.

It is evident that the instruction in 12:14–13:21 exhibits these characteristics and is parenetic in character.

The transition from 12:1–13 to 12:14–13:21 is not signaled by a shift in genre, as elsewhere in the homily. The writer continues in the mode of exhortation. The appeal for endurance, however, which characterizes the parenesis in 12:1–13, is not sustained beyond v 13. The exhortation assumes a new direction in the section that immediately follows with the abrupt summons to "pursue peace along with everyone" (12:14). The introduction of a new focus for pastoral concern marks the transition to the fifth and final division of the sermon.

The limits of the concluding division are sufficiently designated by the presence of a new key word, εἰρήνη, "peace." Assigned a position of emphasis at the beginning of the section (εἰρήνην διώκετε, "Pursue peace" [12:14]), it is invoked again as descriptive of God in the homiletical benediction that formally concludes the sermon (ὁ δὲ θεὸς τῆς εἰρήνης "the God of peace" [13:20]). The emphatic position of εἰρήνη in the initial directive of the division and its striking repetition at the end serve to bracket 12:14–13:21 as an integrated unit within the larger structure of the sermon (so Vanhoye, Bib 55 [1974] 361–63, 373–74, 379).

The new direction pursued by the writer in 12:14–13:21 appears to have been prompted by extended reflection upon the Greek text of Proverbs 4:26–27b. In 12:13 he concluded his exhortation to endurance in a hostile society by appealing for his auditors to pursue ways that are directed straight to the goal. The distinctive formulation καὶ τροχιὰς ὀρθὰς ποιεῖτε τοῖς ποσὶν ὑμῶν, "move in a straight direction with your feet," was adapted from Prov 4:26 LXX, where the reference is to the proper conduct of life:

Make straight paths for your feet [ὀρθὰς τροχιὰς ποίει σοῖς ποσίν],
    and guide your ways.

Deviate neither to the right nor to the left,
and turn away your feet from the evil way. (Prov 4:26–27 LXX)

The instruction is as general as it is conventional, inviting the specification provided in Heb 12:14–13:21.

In Proverbs the admonition to move in a straight direction is supported in the immediate context by the certainty that God will act to make the path of his servant straight and will direct him "in peace":

[God] himself will make your paths straight,
and he will lead your ways forth in peace.
αὐτὸς δὲ ὀρθὰς ποιήσει τὰς τροχιάς σου,
τὰς δὲ πορείας σου ἐν εἰρήνῃ προάξει (Prov 4:27b LXX)

The formulation furnishes an example of Semitic synonymous parallelism. The declaration that God will make the paths of his servant straight furnishes the basis for the assurance that his servant will be led forth ἐν εἰρήνῃ, "in peace." The immediate sequel to Prov 4:26 thus introduced the new thought of the pursuit of peace, which is taken up in Heb 12:14a.

The formal connection between Prov 4:26 and 4:27b LXX appears to account for the transition from Heb 12:1–13 to 12:14–13:21, where the implications of the biblical text are developed in terms of traditional wisdom. Here the writer specifies what the life of pilgrimage under the direction of God entails. Moreover the substance of Prov 4:27b may have influenced the formulation of the homiletical benediction in 13:20–21, with its assurance that "the God of peace . . . will equip you with everything good for doing his will, doing in us what is pleasing to him."

On this understanding, the announcement of the subject for 12:14–13:21 is provided in 12:13, with its call to responsible action on the part of the congregation. The writer admonishes his audience to "make straight paths for your feet" and proceeds in 12:14–13:18 by specifying ways by which this can be done. The concern with Christian behavior implied in 12:13 is elaborated in the series of directives for the Christian life in the final part of the sermon (see Vanhoye, *Bib* 55 [1974] 361–63, modifying and correcting an earlier proposal that the announcement of the subject was to be found in the expression καρπὸν εἰρηνικὸν . . . δικαιοσύνης, "the peaceful fruit . . . which consists of righteousness," in Heb 12:11, as argued in *La structure,* 48, 57, 205; cf. now id., *SNTU* 4 [1979] 130–31; D. A. Black, *GTJ* 7 [1986] 168–69. For an older approach to literary structure similar to that of Vanhoye, but identifying the limits of the final division as 12:14–13:17, see M. dal Medico, *L'auteur de l'épître aux Hébreux* [Rome: Pontifical Biblical Institute, 1914] 187–89).

In the final division of the homily the writer provides the members of the house church with a fresh orientation for life as Christians in a hostile society. The new people of God are engaged in pilgrimage to the city of God. This world is not their home; their goal is "a kingdom that cannot be shaken" (12:28) or "the city that is to come" (13:14). The metaphor of the journey to the city of God characterizes men and women of committed faith as pilgrims and implies an understanding of Christian life as commitment to pilgrimage. It also implies fidelity to the covenant. The instructions that constitute the major portion of the concluding section of the address are appropriate to this theme.

This perspective sheds light on the structure of the final division of the homily. The development can be outlined as follows:

A. Pilgrimage and covenant obligation (12:14–29);
B. Life within the confessing community (13:1–19);
C. Concluding prayer-wish for the covenant people (13:20–21);
D. An appended personal note (13:22–25).

The several sections in this unit are integrated thematically in terms of the concept of committed pilgrimage and of covenant privilege and obligation.

There is a striking correspondence between the first and fifth divisions of the sermon. The sermon began with the characterization of God as the one who has intervened decisively in human history through his spoken word (1:1). The transcendent dignity of the Son, through whom he spoke his definitive word (1:2a), underscores the necessity of paying the closest attention to the message declared to the community by those who stood in direct relationship to the word declared by the Lord. The severity of the judgment imposed upon those who chose to ignore God's word under the old covenant demonstrates the peril of all who willfully neglect the word of salvation delivered through Jesus (2:1–4).

The significant motifs of God speaking and of the importance of listening to his voice appear again in the conclusion of the sermon. The enumeration of the awesome circumstances that attended the giving of the law when God spoke at Sinai (12:18–21) is balanced by reference to the gracious character of the word spoken at the inauguration of the new covenant (12:24). The dramatic juxtaposition of the terrifying experience of Israel at Sinai with the privileged status of the Christian community is presented not for its own sake, but to sharpen the appeal, "See that you do not refuse the one who is speaking" (12:25). The urgency of this solemn warning is consistent with the awesome character of the God who speaks.

Corresponding to the form of the argument in 2:2–3 ("For since what was once spoken by God through the angels proved to be valid, and every infringement and disobedience received the appropriate punishment, how shall we escape if we disregard a salvation as great as this?"), the writer reasons persuasively, "If they did not escape when they refused him who warned them on earth, how much less will we, if we turn away from him who warns us from heaven?" (12:25b). The members of the congregation must understand how much is at stake in their response to the gospel. The failure to heed the warning would be catastrophic. It is here, and in the elaboration of the point in 12:26–29, that the writer brings his sermon to its pastoral and theological climax.

What follows in 13:1–19 amounts to concluding exhortations that further clarify the life of pilgrimage in the confessing community. The development of godly character (13:1–6) and the call for identification with Jesus and the life of the church (13:7–19) are appropriate to the pilgrim people of God. The recurrence of cultic terminology and of themes familiar from earlier sections of the homily serve to integrate the parenesis of chap. 13 with the sermon as a whole. The homiletical benediction in 13:20-21 brings the division and the homily to a solemn conclusion.

In the closing lines (13:22–25) the writer adds an appeal for his audience to listen willingly to the sermon, announces his travel plans, and conveys his greetings. These final verses have the character of a personal note appended to the homily.

A. The Final Warning: The Peril of Refusing God's Gracious Word (12:14–29)

Bibliography

Anderson, J. C. "Repentance in the Greek New Testament." Dissertation, Dallas Theological Seminary, 1959. Andriessen, P. *En lisant l'Épître aux Hébreux.* 52–56. ———. "Angoisse de la mort dans l'Épître aux Hébreux." *NRT* 96 (1974) 282–92. ——— and Lenglet, A. "Quelques passages difficiles de l'Épître aux Hébreux." *Bib* 51 (1970) 207–20. Aptowitzer, V. *Kain und Abel in der Agada, den Apokryphen, den hellenistischen, christlichen und muhammedanischen Literatur.* Vienne/Leipzig: Löwit, 1922. Arowele, P. J. "The Pilgrim People of God (An African's Reflections on the Motif of Sojourn in the Epistle to the Hebrews)." *AsiaJT* 4 (1990) 438–55. Auffret, P. "Note sur la structure littéraire d'Hb ii.1–4." *NTS* 25 (1979) 166–79. Baarlink, H. "De stem van het bloed: De betekenis van Hebr. 12,24 voor de leer der vorzoening." *GTT* 74 (1974) 73–86. Ballarini, T. "Il peccato nell' epistola agli Ebrei." *ScC* 106 (1978) 358–71. Bauckham, R. "The Eschatological Earthquake in the Apocalypse of John." *NovT* 19 (1977) 224–33. Bennett, E. N. "Hebrews XII.18." *ClRev* 6 (1892) 263. Betz, O. "The Eschatological Interpretation of the Sinai-Tradition in Qumran and in the NT." *RevQ* 6 (1961) 89–108. Bonsirven, J. " 'Nisi fornicationis causa': Comment résoudre cette 'Crux Interpretum'?" *RSR* 35 (1948) 442–64. Braun, H. "Das himmlische Vaterland bei Philo und im Hebräerbrief." In *Verborum Veritas.* FS G. Stählin. Ed. O. Bocher and K. Haacker. Wuppertal: Brockhaus, 1970. 319–27. Caird, G. B. "Just Men Made Perfect." *LQHR* 191 (1966) 89–98. Carlston, C. E. "Eschatology and Repentance in the Epistle to the Hebrews." *JBL* 78 (1959) 296–302. Casey, J. M. "Christian Assembly in Hebrews: A fantasy island?" *TD* 30 (1982) 323–35. ———. "Eschatology in Heb 12:14–29: An Exegetical Study." Dissertation, Catholic University of Leuven, 1977. Causée, A. "De la Jérusalem terrestre à la Jérusalem céleste." *RHPR* 27 (1947) 12–36. Costanzo, J. "Il Peccato e la sua Remissione nella Lettera agli Ebrei." Dissertation, Gregorian Pontifical University, Rome, 1964. Daly, R. J. "The New Testament Concept of Christian Sacrificial Activity." *BTB* 8 (1978) 99–107. Déaut, R. le. "Traditions targumiques dans le corpus paulinien? (Hebr 11,4 et 12,24; Gal 4,29–30; II Cor 3:16)." *Bib* 42 (1961) 26–48. Delville, J. P. "L'Épître aux Hébreux à la lumière du proselytisme juif." *RevistCatT* 10 (1985) 323–68. De Young, J. C. *Jerusalem in the New Testament.* 117–21, 138–45. Dibelius, M. "Der himmlische Kultus nach dem Hebräerbrief." *TBl* 21 (1942) 1–11. Dumbrell, W. J. " 'The Spirits of Just Men Made Perfect.'" *EvQ* 48 (1976) 154–59. Dussaut, L. *Synopse structurelle de l'Épître aux Hébreux.* 128–46. Elliott, E. "Esau." *ExpTim* 29 (1917–18) 44–45. Enger, A. R. *The City of the Living God: A Note on Hebrews XII.22–24.* London: SPCK, 1895. Ernst, J. "Die griechische Polis—das himmlische Jerusalem—die christliche Stadt." *TGl* 67 (1977) 240–58. Fontecha, J. F. "La vida cristiana como peregrinación según la Epistola a los Hebreos." In *Studium Legionense.* Léon, 1961. 2:251–306. Frey, J. B. "La Signification du terme ΠΡΩΤΟΤΟΚΟΣ d'après une inscription Juive." *Bib* 11 (1930) 373–90. **Gärtner, B.** *The Temple and the Community in Qumran and the New Testament.* Cambridge: Cambridge UP, 1965. 88–99. **Goguel, M.** "La doctrine de l'impossibilité de la seconde conversion dans l'Épître aux Hébreux et sa place dans l'evolution du Christianisme." *AEPHE* (1931) 4–38. **Gray, W. A.** "The Great Convocation." *ExpTim* 14 (1902–3) 222–27. **Grelot, P.** "Les Targums du Pentateuque: Étude comparative d'après Genèse IV.3–16." *Sem* 9 (1959) 59–88. **Hanson, A. T.** "Christ in the Old Testament according to Hebrews." *SE* 2 (1964) 393–407. **Harrisville, R. A.** *The Concept of Newness in the New Testament.* Minneapolis: Augsburg, 1960. 48–53. ———. "The Concept of Newness in the New Testament." *JBL* 74 (1955) 69–79. **Helyer, L. R.** "The Prōtotokos Title in Hebrews." *StudBibTh* 6 (1976) 3–28. **Hillmann, W.** "Glaube und Verheissung." *BibLeb* 1 (1960) 237–52. **Hurst, L. D.** "The Background and Interpretation of the Epistle to the Hebrews." Dissertation, Oxford University, 1981. 61–67 [cf. id. *The Epistle to the Hebrews: Its Background and Thought.* SNTSMS 65. Cambridge: Cambridge UP, 1990]. **Johnsson, W. G.** "The Pilgrimage Motif in the Book of Hebrews." *JBL* 97 (1978) 239–51. **Johnston, G.** "*OIKOYMENH* and *KOΣMOΣ* in the New Testament." *NTS* 10 (1963–64) 353–60. **Jones, P. R.** "The Figure of Moses as a Heuristic Device for Understanding the Pastoral Intent of Hebrews." *RevExp* 76 (1979) 95–105. ———. "A Superior Life: Hebrews 12:3–13:25." *RevExp* 82 (1985) 391–405. **Jonge, M. de.** "Vreemdelingen en bijwoners: Einige opmerkingen narr aanleiding van I Pt 2:11 en verwamte teksten." *NedTTs* 11 (1956–57) 18–36. **Käsemann, E.** "Hebräer 12,12–17." In *Exegetische Versuche und Besinnungen.* Göttingen: Vandenhoeck & Ruprecht, 1960. 1:307–12. **Katz, P.** "The quotations from Deuteronomy in Hebrews." *ZNW* 49 (1958) 213–23. **Koenig, J.** "Le Sinai, montagne de feu dans un désert de ténèbres." *RHR* 167 (1965) 129–55. **Koester, W.** "Platonische Ideenwelt und Gnosis im Hebräerbrief." *Schol* 4 (1956) 545–55. **Korvin-Krasinski, C. von.** "Die heilige Stadt." *ZRGG* 16 (1964) 265–71. **Lang, W.** "L'Appel à la pénitence dans le christianisme primitif." *CMech* n.s. 29 (1959) 380–90. **Laub, F.** *Bekenntnis und Auslegung.* 253–57. **Lécuyer, J.** "Ecclesia Primitivorum (Hébr 12,23)." In *Studiorum Paulinorum Congressus Internationalis Catholicus 1961.* AnBib 17–18. Rome: Pontifical Biblical Institute, 1963. 2:161–68. **Leeuwen, W. S. van.** *EIRENE in het Nieuwe Testament: Een Semasiologische, Exegetische Bijdrage op Grond van de Septuaginta en de Joodsche Literatuur.* Wageningen: H. Veenman & Zonen, 1940. 214–17, 220–28. **Luck, U.** "Himmlisches und irdisches Geschehen im Hebräerbrief." *NovT* 6 (1963) 192–215. **MacRae, G.** "A Kingdom that Cannot Be Shaken: The Heavenly Jerusalem in the Letter to the Hebrews." *TY* (1979–80) 27–40. **Marshall, I. H.** *Kept By the Power of God.* 143–54. ———. "The Problem of Apostasy in New Testament Theology." *PrsRS* 14 (1987) 65–80. **McCown, W. G.** "Holiness in Hebrews." *WesThJ* 16 (1981) 58–78. ———. "*Ο ΛΟΓΟΣ ΤΗΣ ΠΑΡΑΚΛΗΣΕΩΣ*: The Nature and Function of the Hortatory Sections in the Epistle to the Hebrews." Dissertation, Union Theological Seminary, Richmond, VA, 1970. 104–10, 116–19. **McCullough, J. C.** "The Impossibility of a Second Repentance in Hebrews." *BibTh* 20 (1974) 1–7. ———. "The Old Testament Quotations in Hebrews." *NTS* 26 (1979–80) 367–79. **Mendelssohn, I.** "On the Preferential Status of the Eldest Son." *BASOR* 156 (1959) 38–40. **Michaelis, W.** "Der Beitrag des LXX zur Bedeutungsgeschichte von πρωτότοκος." *ZST* 23 (1954) 137–57. **Minear, P. S.** *New Testament Apocalyptic.* 144–52. **Mora, G.** *La Carta a los Hebreos como Escrito Pastoral.* 51–54, 100–107, 111–30, 180–89. **Mugridge, A.** "Warnings in the Epistle to the Hebrews: An Exegetical and Theological Study." *RTR* 46 (1978) 74–82. **Nestle, E.** "Hebrews xii,24." *ExpTim* 17 (1905–6) 566. **Nicolau, M.** "El 'Reino de Dios' en la carta a los Hebreos." *Burg* 20 (1979) 393–405. **Nötscher, F.** "Himmlische Bücher und Schicksalsglaube in Qumran." *RevQ* 1 (1958–59) 405–11. **Oberholtzer, T. K.** "The Failure to Heed His Speaking in Hebrews 12:25–29." *BSac* 146 (1989) 67–75. **Oepke, A.** *Das neue Gottesvolk im Schriftum, Schauspiel, bildender Kunst und Weltgestatung,* 57–73. **Perkins, R. L.** "Two Notes on Apostasy." *PRS* 15 (1988) 57–60. **Peterson, D. G.** "An Examination of the Concept of 'Perfection' in the 'Epistle to the Hebrews.'" Dissertation, University of Manchester, 1978. 278–90. ———. "The Prophecy of the New Covenant in the Argument of Hebrews." *RTR* 38 (1979) 74–81. **Porteous, N. W.** "Jerusalem-Sion: The Growth of a Symbol." In *Verbannung und Heimkehr.*

Ed. A. Kuschke. Tübingen: Mohr, 1961. 235–52. **Rice, G. E.** "Apostasy as a Motif and Its Effect on the Structure of Hebrews." *AUSS* 23 (1985) 29–35. **Schlosser, J.** "La Médiation du Christ d'après l'épître aux Hébreux." *RevScRel* 63 (1989) 169–81. **Schmidgall, P.** "The Influence of Jewish Apocalyptic Literature on the Book of Hebrews." Dissertation, Western Kentucky University, 1980. 24–70. **Schmidt, K. L.** "Jerusalem als Urbild und Abbild." *ErJb* 18 (1950) 207–48. **Schnackenburg, R.** "Typen der 'Metanoia' Predigt im Neuen Testament." *MTZ* 1 (1950) 1–13. **Schröger, F.** *Der Verfasser des Hebräerbriefes als Schriftausleger.* 190–94, 205–11, 220. **Selwyn, E. C.** "On ΨΗΛΑΦΩΜΕΝΩ in Heb. XII.18." *JTS* 11 (1910–11) 133–34. **Smith, G. A.** "Esau." In *The Forgiveness of Sins.* New York: Hodder & Stoughton, 1904. 174–91. **Solari, J. K.** "The Problem of *Metanoia* in the Epistle to the Hebrews." Dissertation, Catholic University of America, 1970. 143–50. **Spicq, C.** "La Panégyrie de Hébr. xii,22." *ST* 6 (1952) 30–38. ———. "La pénitencia impossible." *CTom* 224 (1952) 353–68. **Swetnam, J.** "Sacrifice and Revelation in the Epistle to the Hebrews." *CBQ* 30 (1968) 227–34. **Teodorico, P.** "Un antica esegesi di Ebrei 12,23: 'Chiesa di primogeniti.'" *RevistB* 6 (1958) 166–73. **Theissen, G.** *Untersuchungen zum Hebräerbrief.* 62–67. **Thompson, J. W.** *The Beginnings of Christian Philosophy: The Epistle to the Hebrews.* 41–52. ———. "'That Which Abides': Some Metaphysical Assumptions in the Epistle to the Hebrews." Dissertation, Vanderbilt University. 1974. 5–6, 230–52. ———. "'That Which Cannot Be Shaken': Some Metaphysical Assumptions in Hebrews 12:27." *JBL* 94 (1975) 580–87. **Toussaint, S. D.** "The Eschatology of the Warning Passages in the Book of Hebrews." *GTS* 3 (1982) 67–80. **Vagaggini, L.** "La XIV Settimana Biblica." *DivThom* 60 (1957) 91–98. **Vanhoye, A.** "Le Dieu de la nouvelle alliance dans l'Épître aux Hébreux." In *La Notion biblique de Dieu.* Ed. J. Coppens. Louvain: Leuven University Press, 1976. 315–30. ———. "L'οἰκουμένη dans l'épître aux Hébreux." *Bib* 45 (1964) 248–53. ———. "*Retti cammini.*" In *L'ultima parte dell' Epistola agli Ebrei (Ebr. 12,14–13,25).* Rome: Biblical Institute, 1974. **Vögtle, A.** "Das Neue Testament und die Zukunft des Kosmos: Hebr. 12,26f. und das Endschicksal des Kosmos." *BibLeb* 10 (1969) 239–53. ———. *Das Neue Testament und die Zukunft des Kosmos.* Dusseldorf: Patmos. 1970. **Waal, C. van der.** "'The People of God' in the Epistle to the Hebrews." *Neot* 5 (1971) 83–92. **Watkins, R. T.** "The New English Bible and the Translation of Hebrews xii.17." *ExpTim* 73 (1961–62) 29–30. **Williamson, R.** *Philo and the Epistle to the Hebrews.* 41–42, 64–70, 192–93, 251–52, 263–67, 324–25.

Translation

[14]*Pursue peace*[a] *along with everyone,*[b] *and the holiness without which*[c] *no one will see the Lord.*[d] [15]*Watch*[e] *that no one forfeits*[f] *the grace of God, and that no bitter root*[g] *grows up to cause trouble*[h] *and the whole community*[i] *be defiled through it.* [16]*Watch*[j] *that no one becomes apostate*[k] *or secular like Esau, who gave up his inheritance rights as the older son*[l] *rather than*[m] *one*[n] *dish of food.* [17]*For you know*[o] *that later on*[p] *when he wished to inherit the blessing, he was rejected,*[q] *for he found no opportunity for repentance,*[r] *even though he had diligently sought*[s] *the blessing*[t] *with tears.*

[18]*For*[u] *you have not*[v] *come*[w] *to what may be touched*[x]
and blazing fire,
and to darkness
and gloom[y]
and whirlwind,
[19]   *and to a trumpet blast*
and a sound of words[z]
that made the hearers beg
that no[aa] *further message be given to them,*[bb] .

20   *for they were unable to bear*[cc] *the command,*
    "If even an animal
    touches the mountain,
    it shall be stoned";[dd]

21   *and the spectacle*[ee] *was so*[ff] *awesome*
    that Moses said,
    "I am terrified and trembling."

    22 *On the contrary, you have come to Mount Zion,*
    even[gg] *to the city of the living God,*
      heavenly Jerusalem,[hh]
    and to innumerable companies[ii] *of angels,*
      a festal gathering,[jj]

23   *and to the assembly of the firstborn*
      inscribed permanently[kk] *in heaven,*
    and to a Judge who is God of all,[ll]
    and to the spirits[mm] *of righteous persons made perfect,*

24   *and to Jesus,*[nn] *mediator of a new*[oo] *covenant,*
    and to sprinkled blood speaking[pp] *more effectively than the blood of Abel.*[qq]

25 *Be careful that you do not disregard*[rr] *the one who is speaking.*[ss] *For since those did not escape*[tt] *when they disregarded*[uu] *the one who warned them on earth,*[vv] *how much less will we, if we reject*[ww] *the one who warns*[xx] *us from heaven?* 26 *At that time his voice shook the earth, but now he has promised,*[yy] *"Once again I will shake*[zz] *not only the earth but also the heavens."* 27 *The phrase,*[aaa] *"once more," points to the removal*[bbb] *of what can be shaken, as of these things having been made,*[ccc] *so that what cannot be shaken may remain.* 28 *Therefore, since we are receiving*[ddd] *a kingdom*[eee] *that cannot be shaken, let us be thankful,*[fff] *and through*[ggg] *thanksgiving*[hhh] *let us worship God in an acceptable manner,*[iii] *with fear*[jjj] *and awe,* 29 *for*[kkk] *our God is a consuming fire.*

Notes

[a] By virtue of its initial position in the sentence, εἰρήνην, "peace," is emphatic.

[b] It is commonly understood that εἰρήνην διώκετε μετὰ πάντων signifies "pursue peace with everyone" (RSV, NEB, NASB, JB, TEV, NIV, BAGD 227). What has not been appreciated is that the writer avoids the prep σύν, but uses μετά with the gen in the sense of "along with" (11:9; 13:23), while πάντων means "all the other believers" (as in 13:24). See Moffatt, 208; BDF §227(3), where this admonition is translated "Seek peace in company with everyone"; cf. Foerster, *TDNT* 2:412, 415, who points out that if the idiom meant to seek concord with others, the prep πρός would be demanded, as in Rom 5:1.

[c] Here χωρίς follows the word it governs (οὗ χωρίς). This is the only occurrence of this word order in the NT. See Moule, *Idiom-Book*, 87; BDF §§216(2), 487.

[d] The clause οὗ χωρὶς οὐδεὶς ὄψεται τὸν κύριον provides a perhaps unintentional instance of iambic poetic meter (Moule, *Idiom-Book*, 199). For a study of the rhythms in Hebrews, cf. Moffatt, lvi–lix.

[e] In the Gk. text vv 14–16 form a single sentence. V 15 is introduced not with a main verb but with the ptcp ἐπισκοποῦντες, which is dependent upon the main verb in v 14, διώκετε, "pursue." This structure is reflected in the KJV: "Pursue peace . . . and holiness . . . looking diligently lest." It is due to considerations of English style that a new sentence is begun in v 15 in the translation prepared for the commentary.

The present active ptcp ἐπισκοποῦντες stresses continual effort. It derives its function from the imperative διώκετε, "pursue"; the ptcp governs the three subordinate final clauses of warning that follow in vv 15–16, each of which is introduced by μή τις: "Watch that no one is excluded from . . .

that no bitter root grows up . . . that no one is apostate or irreligious." In each instance these negative purpose clauses have the same force as an ἵνα clause ("so that").

ᶠ The idiom ὑστερεῖν ἀπό followed by the gen of separation suggests the notion of being excluded from some benefit (i.e., the grace of God) through one's own fault (so BAGD 849; cf. BDF §180[5]). Cf. NEB: "that there is no one among you who forfeits the grace of God."

ᵍ In the expression ῥίζα πικρίας, the gen case functions in place of an adj of quality; the gen of quality describes the root as "bitter," i.e., a root that bears bitter fruit (BDF §165; BAGD 657; Michel, 454–55).

ʰ One important difference between prohibition and warning is that warning may be expressed either through the use of the present or aor subjunctive. The construction μή τις . . . ἐνοχλῇ is an example of the present subjunctive (Moulton, *Grammar* 1:178).

The attestation of ἐνοχλῇ, "cause trouble," is virtually unanimous in the MS tradition. Nevertheless, Katz (*ZNW* 49 [1958] 213–17) has argued that it is a corruption that arose through metathesis from ἐν χολῇ, "in gall." The corruption, according to Katz, originated during the course of the transmission of Hebrews at a date early enough to influence the best MSS of Deut 29:17*b* LXX as well (B* A F*). In these MSS the combination ἐστὶν . . . ἐνοχλῇ in the same sentence is "syntactically impossible" (cf. Michel, 454, n. 1).

There may be a measure of support for this conjecture in P⁴⁶, which appears to read ευχ[•]λη (see Hoskier, *Commentary*, 58; Nestle²⁶ 584). This conjectural emendation is accepted by BDF §165; Michaelis, *TDNT* 6:124–25, n. 73; and P. E. Hughes, 539, n. 143, who translates "that there be no root of bitterness springing up in anger."

If the emendation of the text is adopted, there are in Heb 12:15–16 three anaphoric clauses, each of which begins with μή τις and then continues without a verb or a copula. If, on the other hand, ἐνοχλῇ is read with the MS tradition, the symmetry of three anaphoric clauses without verbs is destroyed. The emendation remains, however, only an attractive alternative to the attested text. For a full discussion of the critical issues and a cautious response to Katz's proposals, see Casey, "Eschatology in Heb 12:14–29," 105–9.

ⁱ The superior textual reading is the anarthrous πολλοί (P⁴⁶ D H Ψ 1739 Byz), which in context has an inclusive nuance in the sense of "the many," "the whole community" (cf. Jeremias, *TDNT* 6:541–42). This understanding is made explicit in the variant οἱ πολλοί, "the many," found in ℵ A 048 33 81 104 326 1241ᶜ 2495. Cf. BAGD 688: "the majority," "most."

ʲ The expression μή τις is governed by the preceding ptcp ἐπισκοποῦντες, "watching," in v 15 and is continuous with the sentence begun in v 14. Considerations of English style dictate the sentence structure in the translation of vv 14–16.

ᵏ It is commonly understood that the adj πόρνος is to be understood literally (e.g., NIV: "sexually immoral"). The context, however, points to a metaphorical understanding of the term; it is roughly equivalent to "apostate" (so W. Manson, 85; Williamson, *Philo*, 265–66). For a metaphorical use of πόρνος in the pl, see Philo, *Allegorical Interpretation* 3.8: "deserters [πόρνοι] from the rule of the One, to whom entrance into the assembly of God is absolutely forbidden."

ˡ The translation "inheritance rights as the older son" seeks to bring out the pl form of τὰ πρωτοτόκια (similarly TEV, NIV).

ᵐ The phrase ἀντὶ βρώσεως μιᾶς ἀπέδετο is commonly understood to mean "he sold [his birthrights] for [i.e., in exchange for] one dish of food," finding in ἀντὶ βρώσεως an expression replacing the classical gen of price (RSV, NEB, NASB, JB, TEV, NIV, BAGD 74, 726, among others). A related alternative proposal is that Esau "sold [his birthrights] for the sake of one meal," finding in ἀντὶ βρώσεως a similarly classical use of ἀντί with the gen meaning "for the sake of" (cf. Epictetus, *Discourses* 1:29.21, ἀντὶ λύχνου κλέπτης ἐγένετο ["for the sake of a lamp he became a thief"], cited by BDF §208[2]; Atkinson, *Theology of Prepositions*, 6; cf. Moule, *Idiom-Book*, 71, 204). The verb ἀποδίδοσθαι in the middle voice can have the sense of "to sell," but the gen of price which accompanies it is never preceded by the prep ἀντί. Consequently, it is better to translate ἀπέδετο "he gave up" or "he handed over" (cf. A. S. Way, *The Letters of St. Paul* [New York: Macmillan, 1901]: "he bartered away his rights"; J. W. C. Wand, *The New Testament Letters* [London: Oxford UP, 1944]: "who surrendered his birthright for a single plate of food"), and to find in the prep ἀντί the nuance of "in place of," "rather than" (so Andriessen and Lenglet, *Bib* 51 [1970] 219–20; BAGD 90 [4b]). The idiom is found in *T. Iss.* 2:2. For ἀντί with this nuance in the near context, see Heb 12:2, ἀντὶ . . . χαρᾶς, "rather than the joy," and the extended discussion of the idiom in *Note* 1 on 12:2 above.

ⁿ The qualifying term, μιᾶς, "one," is emphatic.

° According to the classical form, ἴστε may be ind or imperative. The context favors the ind (so Moffatt, 211–12; F. F. Bruce, 362; Michel, 457). On the assumption that it is ind, it is a purely literary term, corresponding to the usual Koine οἴδατε, "you know" (cf. Moulton, *Grammar*, 1:245 (who favors the imperative); BDF §99[2]; Solari, "The Problem of *Metanoia*," 147).

ᴾ The adv μετέπειτα is unique to Heb 12:17 in the NT but is well attested in classical and hellenistic Gk. See *NewDocs* 2:91 (no. 59).

ᑫ The verb ἀπεδοκιμάσθη is an example of the theological pass: "he was rejected *by God*" (so BAGD 91; Michel, 457; Andriessen and Lenglet, *Bib* 51 [1970] 228; cf. BDF §130[1]). F. F. Bruce, 368, suggests the translation "disqualified."

ʳ The expression μετανοίας τόπον εὑρεῖν is an idiom "to find a possibility [or, opportunity] for repentance" (cf. BAGD 512, 823[2c]). Although linguistically it would be possible to translate μετάνοια as "a change of mind," the phrase is a stereotyped one in Jewish circles and always has reference to repentance in a religious sense (e.g., Wis 12:10; 4 Ezra 7:82; 9:12; *2 Apoc. Bar.* 85:12; *2 Enoch* 62:2; cf. *1 Clem.* 7:5; *2 Clem.* 8:2; Tatian. *To The Greeks* 15). It is unlikely, therefore, to mean that Esau found no chance of making Isaac change his mind (as argued by Spicq. 2:401–3; cf. JB: "he was unable to elicit a change of heart"; NIV: "he could bring about no change of mind"). Spicq appeals to the Latin juridical expression *locus poenitentiae* signifying "an opportunity to change a decision *or* to overturn a decision." But this always occurs in the sense of modifying one's own conception and never in the sense of eliciting a change of mind in others (so Andriessen, *En lisant*, 53–54, citing Livy 44.10; Pliny, *Letters* 10.97, as well as the texts for the fixed idiom cited above). The pastoral concern with the significance of repentance in Hebrews (cf. 6:1, 4–6) is decisive in determining the nuance of μετάνοια here. The position of μετανοίας in the phrase is emphatic.

ˢ The compound verb ἐκζητεῖν seems to denote that the seeker has sought to the utmost (Moulton and Howard, *Grammar*, 3:310). It translates as a past pf: "he had diligently sought," "he had begged for."

ᵗ The antecedent for the fem pronoun αὐτήν has been found in the nearest fem term, the gen μετανοίας (RSV, NEB, NASB, TEV; Windisch, 113; Spicq, 2:402; Michel, 457; Carlston, *JBL* 78 [1959] 299, n. 10; Casey, "Eschatology in Heb 12:14–29," 135–46; among others). It is argued in support of this understanding that the contrast between the verb "to seek" (17*c*) and the verb "to find" (17*b*) demands logically that they have the same obj, i.e., μετανοίας (so Moffatt, 212; Riggenbach, 408; Médebielle, 363).

This seems unlikely, because the gen μετανοίας in this instance is dependent upon the anarthrous masc noun τόπος, "opportunity." The two terms constitute a fixed idiom, to which antecedent reference would presumably be made with the masc pronoun αὐτόν, referring to τόπος. The antecedent must be the more remote independent articular noun τὴν εὐλογίαν, "the blessing," in 17*a*. This accords with the narrative of Gen 27:34, 38, to which the writer alludes. What Esau sought with tears was the blessing, which Jacob had secured from Isaac with a ruse. For the writer's habit of separating words that logically belong together (in this instance 17*a* and 17*c*), see 2:14; 7:11; 9:2–5; 10:20. As in 7:11, a parenthesis (17*b*) interrupts the course of the thought being developed: "for you know that later on when he wished to inherit the blessing, he was rejected, even though he had begged for *it* with tears." The logical link is not between the verbs "to seek" and "to find" but rather between "to beg for" and "to be rejected" (cf. RV; Way; Basic; Knox; Berkeley; NIV: Westcott, 409; Lenski, 449; Watkins, *ExpTim* 73 [1961–62] 29–30; F. F. Bruce, 368, Marshall, *Kept By The Power*, 144; McCullough, *BibTh* 20 [1974] 4; Kistemaker, 387; Andriessen, *En lisant*, 52–53.

ᵘ The periodic sentence in vv 18–24 is characteristic of artistically developed prose (BDF §§458, 464). Moule has called attention to the striking series of omissions of the article, which is typical of classical Gk. composed in the large tragic style (*Idiom-Book*, 114). For a fresh translation and poetic arrangements of vv 18–24 see P. R. Jones, *RevExp* 76 [1979] 100. He suggests that the passage should be read "as a poem to be experienced for imagery and feeling tones and atmospherics."

The importance of the inferential γάρ, which serves to link vv 18–24 with the preceding unit, must be recognized. It marks the transition to a unit that provides grounding for the exhortation and warning in vv 14–17. It also establishes that the development of a judgment motif in vv 15–17 is foundational to a proper understanding of vv 18–24 (so Moffatt, 213–14; Schierse, *Verheissung*, 173–75; Thompson, *JBL* 94 [1975] 580; Laub, *Bekenntnis*, 253).

ᵛ As the initial word in the sentence, the negative particle οὐ is emphatic. Its significance is underscored by the contrast drawn in v 22 with the particle ἀλλά, "on the contrary."

ʷ It is important to recognize in the verbal form προσεληλύθατε in vv 18 and 22 the cultic nuance of προσέρχεσθαι, which is found throughout the homily (4:16; 7:25; 10:1, 22; 11:6), a nuance that is well established outside of Hebrews (cf. J. Schneider, *TDNT* 2:683–84; Johnsson, "Defilement," 332, n. 207, who calls attention to the inadequacy of the translation "you have drawn near," adopted by H. Montefiore, 229). The pf tense of the verb underscores lasting results (cf. Zerwick, *Biblical Greek* §285).

ˣ External evidence strongly supports the reading ψηλαφωμένῳ without ὄρει, "mountain" (P⁴⁶ ℵ A C 048 33 81 1175 vg syʳ co aeth). Among the witnesses that include ὄρει, it stands before ψηλαφωμένῳ in 69 255 462 syʰ, and after it in D K P Ψ 88 614 1739 *Byz Lect*). The absence of a fixed position suggests that ὄρει is "a scribal gloss derived from verse 22" (Metzger, *Textual Commentary*, 675).

The form ψηλαφωμένῳ is a dative present ptcp functioning as a verbal adj (BDF §651[3]). For the translation of ψηλαφώμενος, see Thompson, *Beginnings of Christian Philosophy*, 45. The conjectural emendation πεφεψαλωμένῳ (a "calcined," "oxidized" volcano; cf. Aeschylus, *Prometheus Vinctus*, 364) proposed by Selwyn (*JTS* 11 [1910–11] 33–34) is unnecessary. This is equally true of the earlier conjecture offered by Bennett (*ClRev* 6 [1892] 263); ὕψει νενεφωμένῳ, "to a height enveloped in dense cloud" (cf. Exod 19:16). The NEB chose to ignore the copula καί and associates ψηλαφωμένῳ with the phrase that follows: "the palpable, blazing fire of Sinai," following the vg and Westcott, 409.

ʸ The variant reading καὶ σκότει (P⁴⁶) or σκότῳ, "and darkness," found in ℵᶜ Dᵇᶜ 4 Byz is clearly spurious. It apparently originated as a gloss on the reading καὶ ζόφῳ (ℵ* A C D* P 048 33 81 326 365 1175 1241ˢ). The source of the gloss will have been Exod 10:22; 14:22; Deut. 4:11; 5:22 LXX, where the synonymous words for darkness, σκότος and γνόφος, are juxtaposed. It is impossible in translation to capture the euphonic word play between γνόφῳ, "darkness," and ζόφῳ, "gloom."

ᶻ The expression καὶ φωνῇ ῥημάτων might be translated "a sound of words" or "a voice whose words" (BAGD 735, 870). The former was chosen as being more parallel in conception to the preceding expression καὶ σάλπιγγος ἤχῳ, "and a blast of a trumpet." The parallelism is demonstrated by the chiastic order in which the four nouns are placed: σάλπιγγος ἤχῳ καὶ φωνῇ ῥημάτων (i.e., ABBA).

ᵃᵃ The negative particle μή seems to be pleonastic here, since the verb παρῃτήσαντο, "to beg that something not be done," already carries a negative sense (BDF §429).

ᵇᵇ For the idiom προστιθέναι λόγον τινί in the sense of "speak a further message to someone," see BAGD 616, 719.

ᶜᶜ For this nuance in the verb ἔφερον see MM 666; K. Weiss, *TDNT* 9:59; cf. Heb 13:13. The impf is descriptive; it lucidly describes the response of the people to the divine command: "they were unable to bear the command." There is no justification for the translation proposed by Andriessen and Lenglet, "they *would* not bear the command" (*Bib* 51 [1970] 230).

ᵈᵈ A few witnesses extend the quotation from Exod 19:13 LXX with, ἤ βολίδι κατατοξευθήσεται, "or shot down with a javelin." Cf. AV: "or thrust through with a dart."

ᵉᵉ The expression τὸ φανταζόμενον, which occurs only here in the NT, means "the sight," "the spectacle," but clearly has reference to the theophany (for parallels, see Ps.-Aristotle, *Mirabilia* 108, of Athena; Herodian 8.3.9, cited by BAGD 853). It is emphatic in the sentence structure.

ᶠᶠ In this instance the adv οὕτω does not signify "in the same way" (so P. R. Jones, *RevExp* 76 [1979] 100) but is used classically before the adj φοβερόν to denote, "so terrible" (BAGD 598).

ᵍᵍ The Gk. copula καί introduces the explanation of what is meant by "Mount Zion"; it calls for the translation "even" rather than "and," which would suggest a separate entity (with P. E. Hughes, 545). It is impossible in translation to capture the euphonic word play between the datives of place ὄρει καὶ πόλει, in which the noun πόλει, "city," stands in apposition to ὄρει, "Mount [Zion]."

ʰʰ The expression "heavenly Jerusalem" stands in apposition to "city of the living God."

ⁱⁱ The term μυρίας refers to a number that cannot be counted. Cf. the expressions in Deut 33:2; Dan 7:10; *1 Enoch* 40:1; 71:8.

ʲʲ The term πανήγυρις, which occurs only here in the NT, is used of joyful festivities in both pagan and Jewish sources (see Spicq, *ST* 6 [1952] 30–38; Williamson, *Philo*, 65–69). The translation adopted by the RV, "solemn assemblies," conveys the wrong impression. The thought is of a joyous worship assembly. Cf. Theophylact's comment: Ἔνθα πανήγυρις ἐκεῖ χαρά, "where there is a festal gathering there is joy," (cited by Moffatt, 216).

The question has been debated whether in the syntax of the sentence πανηγύρει is to be related to the preceding phrase, "to innumerable companies of angels" (RSV; JB; NIV; Westcott, 413–14; Moffatt, 216; Michel, 463; F. F. Bruce, 310, n. 131; Buchanan, 222–23; P. E. Hughes, 552–53), or to the following phrase, "to the assembly of the firstborn" (AV; ASV; NASB; NEB: "the full concourse and the assembly of the firstborn citizens of heaven"; UBSGNT³; Grosheide, 301; de Young, *Jerusalem*, 139, n. 69; Dumbrell, *EvQ* 48 [1976] 155–56). The first alternative is preferable on the basis of the syntax in v 22*a*, where "heavenly Jerusalem" clearly stands in apposition to the phrase "and to the city of the living God." The connective καί, "and," then introduces the next phrase. The same syntactical structure is visible in v 22*b*, where πανηγύρει stands in apposition to the preceding phrase, while καὶ ἐκκλησίᾳ πρωτοτόκων, "and to the assembly of the firstborn," introduces the next phrase. Alternatively, πανηγύρει can be understood as a circumstantial dative qualifying the preceding phrase ("myriads of angels in festal gathering"). For a full discussion of the interpretations that have been proposed, see Spicq, 2:406–8; Casey, "Eschatology in Heb 12:14–29," 356–58; P. E. Hughes, 552–55.

ᵏᵏ The force of the pf ptcp ἀπογεγραμμένων emphasizes the indelible permanance of the registration or enrollment. Cf. the use of the Gk. pf in parallel expressions elsewhere in the NT: Luke 10:20; Rev 13:8; 17:8; 20:12; 21:27.

ˡˡ It is difficult to decide whether the word order in the phrase κριτῇ θεῷ πάντων is deliberate or oratorical. As it stands, the phrase is ambiguous. It can be translated "to a Judge, who is God of all" (RSV; i.e., the word order is deliberate), or "to God, the judge of all" (NEB, NIV; i.e., the conventional word order was inverted for oratorical effect). The former alternative has been preferred in view of the word order and because usually a gen (in this case πάντων) immediately follows the noun that it modifies (cf. Moule, *Idiom-Book*, 170; Hanna, *Grammatical Aid*, 161). Dumbrell, *EvQ* 48 [1976] 158, prefers the rendering "to God who is judge of all."

ᵐᵐ An early attempt to clarify the unusual phrase, "to the spirits of just persons made perfect," is preserved in the text of D*, which substitutes the sg πνεύματι for the dominant pl πνεύμασι (i.e., "to the Spirit of righteous persons made perfect"). Construed in this way, the text contains a reference to the Trinity: Christians have come "to a Judge who is God of all, and to the Spirit . . . and to Jesus, mediator of a new covenant" (vv 23*b*–24*a*). The variant is of interest for indicating how unusual and difficult the actual phrase appeared.

ⁿⁿ In the initial phrase καὶ διαθήκης νέας μεσίτῃ Ἰησοῦ, the personal name "Jesus" is emphatic. For the writer's distinctive practice of deferring the position of the name "Jesus" to the end of a phrase for emphasis, see 2:9; 3:1; 6:20; 7:22; 10:19; 12:2; 13:20.

ᵒᵒ The descriptive term νέα is interchangeable with the word καινή which appears in 8:8, 13; 9:15. Cf. Harrisville, *Newness*, 70, who shows that καινός and νέος are synonymous in the NT, in the papyri, and in the early church fathers.

ᵖᵖ It is imperative to appreciate the significance of the present act ptcps λαλοῦντι in v 24 and τὸν λαλοῦντα in v 25. The "speaking" is occurring now.

ᑫᑫ It is preferable to read παρὰ τὸ Ἅβελ, "than that of Abel," with P⁴⁶ L and a few other MSS. The reading adopted in the Nestle²⁶ and UBSGNT³ text, παρὰ τὸν Ἅβελ, "in comparison with Abel," enjoys massive support but is improbable since the writer places the article before proper names only when needed for the sake of clarity (e.g., 11:4; so Hunzinger, *TDNT* 6:981). In the comparison, the prep παρά has the notion of "beyond" or "than" (Hanna, *Grammatical Aid*, 162). See further Baarlink, *GTT* 74 [1974] 73–75.

ʳʳ The negative particle μή with a subjunctive verb generally occurs with an imperative form of βλέπειν ("to see") to denote the content of that imperative (cf. Luke 21:8; Acts 13:40; 1 Cor 8:9; 10:12; Gal 5:15). Thus, in essence, it has a prohibitory sense, "See that you do not disregard" (so Hanna, *Grammatical Aid*, 162). For the idiom παραιτεῖσθαι τινά, with the meaning to "refuse or disregard one," see Zerwick and Grosvenor, *Grammatical Analysis*, 687.

ˢˢ The translation seeks to emphasize the present tense of the ptcp in the expression τὸν λαλοῦντα. The article functions as a pronoun: "the one who is speaking."

ᵗᵗ In a third-class conditional clause (εἰ with the verb in the ind), the negative adv οὐκ is used instead of μή, since emphasis is laid on the fact that they did not escape. The sense is: "if they failed to escape" (as they did). The impf tense of the verb ἐξέφυγον is descriptive; it intimates that attempts were made to escape (cf. Moulton, *Grammar*, 1:200).

ᵘᵘ The aor tense of the verb παραιτησάμενοι is culminative, indicating that the disregarding was antecedent to the action expressed by ἐξέφυγον. The sense is: "they did not escape, only after they had disregarded."

ᵛᵛ In the phrase ἐπὶ γῆς παραιτησάμενοι τὸν χρηματίζοντα, the prep expression ἐπὶ γῆς, "on earth," modifies the present substantive ptcp χρηματίζοντα, "warns." It is thrown back to the beginning of the phrase for emphasis, in anticipation of the following contrasting expression ἀπ' οὐρανῶν, "from heaven." The attempt to make this understanding explicit can be traced in the MS tradition, which attests three different word orders. The word order adopted for the critical editions of the Gk. text is found in P⁴⁶ᶜ ℵ* A C D I 048 0121b 33 81 1241ˢ 1739 1881 co Cyp, and is defended as correct by Moffatt, 220; Zuntz, *Text*, 258; and Michel, 471–72. Any possible ambiguity as to the reference of ἐπὶ γῆς is removed in the word order τὸν ἐπὶ γῆς παραιτησάμενοι χρηματίζοντα (P⁴⁶ ℵᶜ K L P Ψ Chr) or the variant tradition παραιτησάμενοι τὸν ἐπὶ γῆς χρηματίζοντα (69 256 263 436 1837 2005 vg), both of which would be translated "when they disregarded the one who warned them on earth." In each instance the concern of the variant textual traditions was to clarify that the expression ἐπὶ γῆς modifies the one who warns, not those who failed to escape.

ᵂᵂ Adopting the sg reading of P⁴⁶, which omits οἱ in v 25c, the Gk. text ἡμεῖς . . . ἀποστρεφόμενοι, "if we reject," is parallel to the expression in 2:3: ἡμεῖς . . . ἀμελήσαντες, "if we disregard." A conditional ptcp, "if we reject," is more consistent with the writer's attitude toward his audience than is the relative "we who are rejecting," as the better attested text would have to be translated. For a recommendation of the text of P⁴⁶ at this point, and a defense of the translation adopted, see Beare, *JBL* 63 (1944) 385, 391–92; cf. Moffatt, 219.

ˣˣ The translation presupposes an ellipsis; the article τὸν functions as a pronoun and resumes the full expression from the protasis τὸν χρηματίζοντα, "the one who warns."

ʸʸ The form ἐπήγγελται is not pass, but a middle whose meaning is act. The pf tense does not imply that what has been promised has already occurred (as argued by Spicq, 2:412: "the perfect indicates the actuality of the result"). It is the making of the promise that stands in the past with ramifications for the present, rather than the realization of the promise (Casey, "Eschatology in Heb 12:14–29," 521–22).

ᶻᶻ An explanation for the substitution of the present tense σείω, "I shake," for the future tense in D K L P Ψ can be found in the fact that a close parallel to Hag 2:6 is found in Hag 2:21b, which contains the present tense of the verb: Ἐγὼ σείω τὸν οὐρανὸν καὶ τὴν γῆν, "I shake heaven and earth." This formulation appears to account for the variant textual tradition.

ᵃᵃᵃ The expression τὸ δέ is used to introduce the quotation of the phrase, as in Eph 4:9 (Turner, *Grammar*, 3:182).

ᵇᵇᵇ The MS tradition is divided concerning the presence or absence of the article τήν in the phrase [τὴν] τῶν σαλευομένων μετάθεσιν, "[the] removal of what can be shaken." The article is omitted by P⁴⁶ D* 048 0121b 323 1739, and this reading is preferred by Zuntz, *Text*, 117–18, who argues that word exegesis (in this case of ἔτι ἅπαξ, "once more") was normally given without the article, according to the Gk. grammarians. Moreover, the addition of the article impairs the sense of the phrase: "the writer indicates the 'removal of the things shaken' as a fresh and additional inference from his interpretation of the psalm [*sic*]. This reasoning . . . requires the absence of the article. 'τὴν μετάθεσιν would imply reference to a fact previously mentioned" (118). The presence of the article is supported by ℵ* A C 33 326 1175 1241ˢ and a few others.

For a review of the various proposals for translating μετάθεσιν in v 27 (e.g., "transformation," "renovation," "destruction," "disappearance," "displacement") and the argument that the word means simply "change", see A. Vögtle, *BibLeb* 10 (1969) 241–53. The term means either "change" (cf. Heb 7:12) or "removal" (cf. Heb 11:5). The translation adopted recognizes that the conceptual idea certainly includes "removal." See further, Casey, "Eschatology in Heb 12:14–29," 540–47, 550–51, 553–54.

ᶜᶜᶜ The phrase ὡς πεποιημένων stands in apposition to τῶν σαλευομένων, "of what can be shaken." The expression may be parenthetical (so Moffatt, 222). The pf pass ptcp πεποιημένων has a present force: "what has been and remains made." Thompson clearly slants the interpretation of the text when he translates the ptcp as "what is merely made" in the conviction that the phrase reflects the writer's dualistic world view (*JBL* 94 [1975] 585).

ᵈᵈᵈ The force of the present ptcp παραλαμβάνοντες is that Christians are in the process of receiving the unshakeable kingdom and that this process will continue into the future (BDF §323; Zerwick, *Biblical Greek* §278).

ᵉᵉᵉ In the syntax of the sentence, the position of βασιλείαν, "kingdom," is emphatic. For the translation "receive a kingship which cannot be shaken" see BAGD 619 (with reference to Herodotus 2.120; *OGI* 1.54.5–7; 56.6; 90.1; Dan 6:1 LXX, Theod.; 6:29 LXX; 2 Macc 10:11; Jos., *Ant.* 15.16; *Ag. Ap.* 1.145; but cf. BAGD 114, where βασιλείαν ἀσάλευτον is translated "a kingdom that cannot be shaken").

ᶠᶠᶠ The MS tradition is divided between the ind ἔχομεν χάριν, "we are thankful" (P⁴⁶* ℵ K P Ψ 6 33 69 104 326 365 629 1881 2495 lat syʰ), and the subjunctive ἔχωμεν χάριν, "let us be thankful" (P⁴⁶ᶜ A C D 0121b Byz *a b* syʳ co vg³ᵐˢˢ). This variation between the ind and the subjunctive is a common textual phenomenon, since the pronunciation of the two forms was practically identical. The context demands the subjunctive (so Spicq, 2:413; F. F. Bruce, 380, n. 186). For the idiom ἔχειν χάριν τινί see BAGD 878(5); MM 684–85. Here it clearly means, "Let us be thankful [to God]" (cf. Luke 17:9; 1 Tim 1:12; 2 Tim 1:3).

An alternative proposal is to recognize that the absence of a dative complement to ἔχωμεν χάριν and the continuation of the phrase with δι' ἧς signal that the writer is not using the common idiom for the expression of thanksgiving. His intention is to refer specifically to that divine grace to which reference was made in 12:15, so that the phrase would be translated "let us maintain grace, through which we worship God in an acceptable manner" (so Spicq, 2:413, who finds evidence of *inclusio* between τῆς χάριτος τοῦ θεοῦ, "the grace of God," in v 15 and χάρις in v 28 and translates "let us conserve grace"; and Casey, "Eschatology in Heb 12:14–29," 562–65, who translated "let us have grace").

In reviewing this proposal Vanhoye has properly observed that there is little basis for speaking of an *inclusio* between v 15 and v 28. In 12:15 the reference to "grace" is preceded by the article and completed by a gen (τῆς χάριτος τοῦ θεοῦ); in 12:28, however, χάρις is anarthrous and is part of a verbal phrase (ἔχωμεν χάρις). The most suitable sense of the expression in 12:28 is that of gratitude, which is a different nuance from that of the polyvalent term χάρις in 12:15 (*La structure*, 109).

ggg The fact that the relative pronoun in the phrase δι᾽ ἧς has its antecedent in χάριν is made explicit by translating "through thanksgiving."

hhh In the phrase δι᾽ ἧς λατρεύωμεν, it is important to recognize the present hortatory subjunctive, "through which let us worship" (BDF §337[3]).

iii The adv εὐαρέστως is found only here in the NT, but is well attested in classical and hellenistic Gk. (BAGD 318–19). For cognate forms of this word, see 11:5, 6; 13:16, 21.

jjj The translation of εὐλάβεια takes account of the fact that it occurs here in company with δέος, a term that connotes fear and anguish (cf. 2 Macc 3:17, 30; 15:23), and is completed by the sobering warning of v 29. In context, it signifies the fear of the Christian "before an imminent peril, namely, before the judgment of God" (Andriessen, *NRT* 96 [1974] 284, with a reference to the significance of εὐλάβεια in Heb 11:7). Cf. Casey, "Eschatology in Heb 12:14–29," 566–68.

kkk In the expression καὶ γάρ, καί has completely lost its force. It simply means "for," as in 5:12 (BDF §452[3]).

Form/Structure/Setting

The extended exhortation to steadfast endurance of disciplinary sufferings in 12:1–13 reaches its closure when the community is summoned to prepare for a demanding contest in a manner that will strengthen the weakest of their number (see *Comment* on 12:13). The directive to pursue peace and holiness in 12:14 appears to initiate an unrelated train of thought. It is only in the continuation of the pastoral instruction in vv 15–17 that a logical connection can be discerned with the new factor of congregational life that was introduced metaphorically in v 13b. Among the members of the house church are those who are experiencing serious spiritual and emotional fatigue, for whom the others are to be pastorally concerned. The responsibility of the community for this group of persons is elaborated in vv 15–17. The prospect of the forfeiture of God's grace through personal carelessness, of the defilement of the community through apostasy, and of the irrevocable loss of covenant status through thoughtlessness underscores the urgent need for vigilance. It is apparent that earnest concern for the spiritual peril to which some of the weaker members of the church were exposed motivated the formulation of 12:14–17 as the introduction to 12:18–29. It is appropriate, then, to locate in v 13 the announcement of the subject to be developed in 12:14–29.

Although there is common agreement that vv 18–29 form a single literary unit and that v 29 marks the end of a section, the precise limits of the units of thought in this portion of the homily continue to be debated. The absence of explicit literary indices pointing to the introduction of a new section in vv 14–17 accounts for the fact that many commentators treat 12:12–17 as a cohesive unit of thought. They regard vv 14–17 as simply a continuation of the exhortation addressed to the community in vv 12–13 rather than a new development. For these scholars the decisive consideration is that vv 12–13 and 14–17 share in common the form of parenetic instruction. On this understanding, 12:12–17 furnishes the conclusion to the section 12:1–17 (e.g., Windisch, 111; Moffatt, 206; Riggenbach, 401; Käsemann, "Hebräer 12:12–17," 307–12; Michel, 451; F. F. Bruce, 362–64) or, alternatively, serves to introduce the final exhortation of the homily (e.g., Schierse, *Verheissung*, 105; Thompson, *Beginnings of Christian Philosophy*, 43–44).

It is preferable, however, to recognize that in the absence of clear literary indices, the limits of a section must be determined thematically. A thematic concern with the necessity of steadfast endurance identifies 12:1–13 as an integrated unit of thought (see *Form/Structure/Setting* on 12:1–13). Parenetic instruction does extend beyond 12:13, but it no longer has any direct bearing upon the theme of enduring corrective suffering. The inferential conjunction διό, "therefore," in v 12 indicates that the response demanded by the preceding argument is provided in vv 12–13, furnishing an appropriate conclusion to the section (cf. Spicq, 9:396).

In 12:14–29 the appeal is broader in scope than the exhortation that preceded it. The focus shifts from the response of the community as it experiences suffering to the peril of rejecting the God who continues to speak to the church through his Son and through the Scriptures. A basis for sensitivity to this peril is provided in the initial paragraph, 12:14–17, which makes explicit the responsibility of the community for any of their number prone to apostasy. These concerns were not expressed in 12:1–13, but they are determinative for the development in 12:14–29.

The introductory character of 12:14–17 becomes clear when it is observed that motifs introduced in these verses are developed in the two paragraphs that follow. The call to holiness, for example, is motivated by the prospect of seeing the Lord (v 14). The motif of the vision of God is then elaborated in vv 18–24, where the terrifying aspects of that vision at Sinai (vv 18–21) serve only to underscore the festive joy of the vision under the new covenant (vv 22–24). The privileged status of those who enjoy the blessings of the new covenant accounts for the sternness of the warning in vv 25–29 that Christians who show contempt for God will not escape his judgement. The concluding paragraph resumes the motifs of forfeiting the grace of God, of contempt for birthrights secured through the covenant, and of the consequent rejection by God, all of which were introduced in vv 15–17.

There are, then, weighty considerations for identifying the limits of the new section as 12:14–29 (with Thien, *RB* 11 [1902] 85–86; Vaganay, "Le Plan," 269–77; Vanhoye, *La structure*, 205–10; H. Montefiore, 223; Andriessen and Lenglet, *Bib* 51 [1970] 224; Buchanan, 216; Casey, "Eschatology in Heb 12:14–29," 70–79; Dussaut, *Synopse structurelle*, 128–46).

The section consists of three paragraphs that are tightly laced together. The point of transition from 12:14–17 to the arresting period that follows in vv 18–24 is indicated by the conjunction γάρ, "for," at the beginning of v 18. The inferential γάρ serves to tie the two paragraphs together and suggests that the paragraphs that follow are intended to provide support for the exhortation and warning in vv 14–17. The intermediate unit, vv 18–24, is joined to the concluding paragraph, vv 25–29, by catch word association. The writer makes uses of the device of a hook word in vv 24 and 25, consisting of a participial forms of the verb λαλεῖν, "to speak":

καὶ αἵματι ῥαντισμοῦ κρεῖττον λαλοῦντι παρὰ τὸ Ἄβελ.
"and to sprinkled blood *speaking* more effectively than the blood of Abel."
βλέπετε μὴ παραιτήσησθε τὸν λαλοῦντα
"Be careful that you do not disregard *the one who is speaking.*"

The purpose of linking the constituent units together in this manner is to exhibit their internal coherence and unity.

Once the limits of this section have been defined as 12:14–29, it may be observed that this thematic unit is parallel in composition to 12:1–13. A structural pattern emerges in which a central paragraph of exposition is framed by exhortation:

12:1–13	12:14–29
A Exhortation (12:1–3)	A Exhortation (12:14–17)
B Exposition (12:4–11)	B Exposition (12:18–24)
A' Exhortation (12:12–13)	A' Exhortation (12:25–29)

Both sections begin with exhortation. The exposition constitutes a supporting argument for the advice advanced. The writer then reiterates, in even stronger terms, his original admonition. In 12:1–13, the conclusion to be drawn from the preceding exposition is introduced in v 12 by the inferential conjunction διό, "therefore." Corresponding to this procedure, in 12:14–29 the conclusion to be drawn from the preceding exposition is indicated by the same inferential conjunction διό in v 28.

In 12:14–29 all three paragraphs are unified by a hortatory appeal to material drawn from the OT to warn the recipients of the awful consequences of showing contempt for God. That uniform concern is highlighted by the use of direct address in the form of the second person plural at the beginning of each of the paragraphs (Dussaut, *Synopse structurelle,* 131). In the use made of the OT, however, two distinct forms may be recognized. The form of 12:16–17 and 12:18–24 may be classified as descriptive analogy. As the name implies, descriptions derived from Scripture are applied to Christ or to the Christian community on the basis of redemptive analogy (cf. 3:1–6; 6:13–20; 13:10–16). In this form the primary interest is in the descriptive language of the biblical text, from which the writer derives authority for his own parenetic appeal (cf. R. Bultmann, "Ursprung und Sinn der Typologie als hermeneutischer Methode," *TLZ* 75 [1950], 212; McCown, "Ο ΛΟΓΟΣ ΤΗΣ ΠΑΡΑΚΛΗΣΕΩΣ," 106–7, 154–56).

In 12:16–17 the form is only incompletely developed. The writer alludes to Esau, whose secular orientation is evident in the contempt he displayed for his birthrights and the covenant by which they were secured. It is left to the auditors, however, to draw the analogy and apply it to themselves: if they emulate Esau's apostate disposition, they too will find no opportunity for repentance. Like him, they will be rejected by God.

In 12:18–24 the form is employed more freely. Initially, the description of Israel's terrifying experience on the occasion of the fiery epiphany at Sinai throws into bold relief the degree to which the experience of Christians is *not* analogous to that of Israel. Nevertheless, in 12:28–29 descriptive language drawn from the Sinai event recurs with direct reference to Christian worship. Formal analysis suggests the complex character of this mode of reading Scripture in the light of its pointed relevance to the current situation of Christians. From the point of view of form, the parenetic appeal is shaped by the detail of the biblical text and is expressed in terms of redemptive analogy.

The form of 12:25–29 may be classified as parenetic midrash (cf. 3:7–4:13; 12:5–11). The basic purpose of midrash, or exposition of Scripture, is to actualize the authority of the biblical text for the present situation. In this instance, the point of departure for the exposition is Hag 2:6 LXX. The citation in v 26 identifies the one who is speaking to the community as he who warned of a future shaking that would remove all that can be shaken. It supports the appeal to respond with grateful worship to the God who was revealed in the fiery epiphany of Sinai. The designation of the form as parenetic midrash asserts that the purpose of the exposition is explicitly hortatory, as distinct from an exposition that has merely an exegetical or narrative basis (so A. G. Wright, *The Literary Genre Midrash* [Staten Island: Alba House, 1968] 52–59; cf. McCown, "*Ο ΛΟΓΟΣ ΤΗΣ ΠΑΡΑΚΛΗΣΕΩΣ*," 102, 149–51, 185).

It has often been supposed that in 12:18–24, or 12:18–29, the writer made use of an older tradition, which he adopted for his own purposes (cf. Käsemann, "Hebräer 12,12–17," 27–29; Schille, "Katechese und Taufliturgie: Erwägungen zu Hebräer 11," *ZNW* 51 [1960] 130; Michel, 469; McCown, "*Ο ΛΟΓΟΣ ΤΗΣ ΠΑΡΑΚΛΗΣΕΩΣ*," 107–9, 189–90; J. W. Thompson, *JBL* 94 [1975] 581–84; among others). The basic structure of the tradition, consisting of the comparison of Mount Sinai and the eschatological Zion, is exhibited as early as *Jubilees* (4:26: "this mountain which you are upon today, Mount Sinai, and Mount Zion, which will be sanctified in the new creation for the sanctification of the earth"); it was subsequently given a distinctively Christian interpretation by Paul in Gal 4:24–26. In a late collection of traditional Jewish homiletical material, *Midr. Tanḥuma B* (דברים 1, beginning), it is said that in the messianic age God will perform all the signs accomplished in the wilderness. Two of these signs, the hearing of the divine voice (Exod 20:18) and the shaking of the earth, have significance for the development of Heb 12:18–29. The existence of such literary parallels lends a measure of plausibility to the proposal that the writer took over an older eschatological tradition that compared the events relating to Sinai with the hope for the eschatological Zion.

Additional support for this proposal has been found in certain details in the description of Zion in 12:22–23 that are common in apocalyptic literature but are not mentioned elsewhere in Hebrews. Thus it has been supposed that the references to "innumerable companies of angels," to the heavenly register in which the names to "the firstborn" are permanently inscribed, and to the departed "spirits" of righteous persons were derived from an older apocalyptic tradition. The reference in the concluding paragraph to the reception of the βασιλεία, "kingdom" (12:28), also appears to be traditional in character. It is unattested elsewhere in Hebrews and appears to reflect a primitive Christian tradition. (For an attempt to distinguish the tradition from its redaction by identifying recurring motifs within Hebrews that furnish evaluative and interpretive comments on the tradition, see Thompson, *JBL* 94 [1975] 581–84).

The writer certainly made use of a variety of traditions in composing his sermon. It is unnecessary, however, to assign to an earlier tradition the rhetorically balanced description of Sinai (12:18–21) and of Zion (12:22–24), as Thompson,

for example, has done (*Beginnings of Christian Philosophy*, 44; id., *JBL* 94 [1975] 581).
The skillful composition of artistic prose is an identifying characteristic of the
writer's literary signature. He is a master of the intricate, and yet lucid, periodic
sentence (see above on 1:1–4; 2:2–4, 14–15; 3:12–15; 4:12–13; 5:1–3, 7–10; 6:4–6;
7:1–3, 26–28; 9:24–26; 10:19–25). The formulation of 12:18–24, with its distinctive cadence achieved through measured phrases, the striking series of omissions
of the article, balanced conceptions, euphonic word plays and polished expression, is harmonious with the demonstrated individuality and stylistic creativity of
the writer. He alone is responsible for the disciplined, continuous flow of 12:14–
29. Within that flow, 12:18–24 constitutes a brilliant rhetorical achievement (so
Vögtle, *BibLeb* 10 [1969] 240; Schierse, *Verheissung*, 171–72).

The significance of 12:18–29 to the pastoral strategy of the writer has been
broadly recognized. The passage furnishes a magisterial résumé of themes and
motifs introduced throughout the homily (correctly observed by Cambier,
"Eschatologie," 62; cf. Spicq, 2:199). Taking into account the introductory paragraph, 12:14–17, as well, the writer once more appeals for the assembly to share
his sharp concern that no member of the house church forfeit the blessings of
the gospel through carelessness (12:15; cf. 2:1–4; 3:12–15; 4:1, 11; 10:24–25). He
repeats the stern warning that apostasy will entail irreversible loss (12:16–17; cf.
3:12, 16–4:2; 6:4–8; 10:26–31, 38–39). He juxtaposes Sinai and Zion in order to
contrast the old and the new covenants, with their respective mediators (12:18–
24; cf. 3:1–6; 8:5–13; 9:15–23; 10:28–31). Simultaneously, he stresses once more
the distance that separated worshipers from God under the old covenant (12:20–
21; cf. 9:1–10; 10:1–3, 11), in striking contrast to the unrestricted access to God
through worship that is the hallmark of life under the new covenant (12:22–24;
cf. 4:15–16; 9:11–14; 10:10, 12–14, 19–22). The resumption of these important
themes is foundational to the restatement of the recurring motifs of the God
who speaks and of the urgency that qualifies listening to his voice (12:25–29; cf.
1:1–2*a*; 2:1–4; 3:7–4:14; 5:11–14; 8:8–13; 10:36–39). The synthesis of so many significant themes and motifs within a single section identifies 12:14–29 as the pastoral
and theological climax of the sermon (cf. Spicq, 2:412; P. R. Jones, *RevExp* 76
[1979] 100; among others).

Comment

In 12:14–29 the writer once more directs his attention to the peril to which
members of the house church were exposed through careless disregard of the
blessings of the new covenant. The introductory paragraph, consisting of exhortation and stern warning (12:14–17), sets the tone for the section as a whole.
These verses summarize what has been said previously concerning irrevocable
loss through disobedience, unbelief, apostasy, and contempt for the covenant
privilege (2:1–4; 3:7–19; 6:4–8; 10:26–31). Earlier warnings culminate in the example of Esau, who sought in vain to recover the blessing he had forfeited through
his preoccupation with personal gratification (12:16–17). An impression of the
awesome certainty of judgment pervades the entire section. Evoking the threat
of catastrophic loss, these verses possess a sense of urgency that compels insight.

The writer turns in 12:18–24 from admonition to exposition, from concern
with the threat of loss to the recital of what the Christian stands to lose through

spiritual indifference or carelessness. He does so by contrasting Israel's encounter with God at Sinai and the new covenant encounter that takes place at Zion, the city of the living God. Resorting to rhythmic, dense construction, the writer depicts the Sinai event as an occasion for stark terror, so that even Moses, mediator of the covenant, acknowledges his alarm (12:18–21). The awesome description of the tangible and menacing aspects of the scene builds in intensity until a vivid sense is conveyed of the majestic presence of the God who is unapproachable. So frightening is the experience that the people turn away from this awesome revelation of God.

This is not the foundational experience of Christians; they order their lives in accordance with another, different revelation. They have come to Mount Zion to participate in a heavenly, festive gathering of angels and of persons who enjoy unlimited access to the God who is approachable and to Jesus, the mediator of the new covenant (12:22–24). The scene is marked by joy rather than fear. The accent falls on the accessibility of God rather than on his unapproachability. Thus in one grand finale the writer graphically illustrates the difference between the old covenant and the new, and between Moses and Jesus, respectively, as mediators of the encounter with God. These verses are the climax toward which the writer has been building throughout the homily (see further Casey, "Eschatology in Heb 12:14–29," 303–6, 333–34; P. R. Jones, *RevExp* 76 [1979] 100).

As a result of Jesus' sacrificial death, the people of the new covenant have both greater privilege and greater obligation than Israel under the old covenant. The ramifications of this fact are developed in the final paragraph (12:25–29) in the demand that they respond appropriately to the God who is addressing them through the gospel and through Scripture.

14 Christians must not become indifferent to the gifts they possess through the gospel. The members of the house church are to pursue "peace" and "the holiness without which no one will see the Lord." The verb διώκειν, "to pursue," which is a stronger term than the more usual ζητεῖν, "to seek," connotes an earnest pursuance. The implied intensity underscores the urgency with which this pastoral directive is addressed to the community (Oepke, *TDNT* 2:119–30; Michel, 451). The stress falls on active Christian effort in response to divine gifts.

The linking of "peace" and "holiness" as direct objects of the main verb διώκετε, "pursue," is remarkable. It indicates that εἰρήνη, "peace," like ἁγιασμός, "holiness," is not to be interpreted subjectively. "Peace" is not simply harmony within the community or in personal relationships (as argued by van Leeuwen, *Eirene*, 214–17; cf. also Spicq, 2:398; F. F. Bruce, 362; H. Montefiore, 223; Andriessen and Lenglet, *Bib* 51 [1970] 226; among others). In this context "peace" is an objective reality that results from the redemptive accomplishment of Christ in his sacrificial death on the cross. It is a gift of eschatological salvation as well as a sign that points to the presence of the new age and to the future perfection (see above on 12:11; cf. Foerster, *TDNT* 2:400; van Leeuwen, *Eirene*, 222; Käsemann, "Hebräer 12,12–17," 310–11). "Peace" denotes the objective basis of the solidarity of the community. It is an expression of the reality of Christ's accomplishment. "Peace" is to be actively pursued because this gift of Christ is given visibility in the solidarity of the community. It also is exhibited in the solidarity of responsibility for the welfare of one another (cf. Rom 14:9; 1 Pet 3:11 in the context of 3:8–12 for similar emphasis). That is why vv 15–16 flow from the pastoral directive in v 14 (correctly observed by Käsemann, "Hebräer 12,12–17," 311). Those verses define the manner in which the pursuit of peace and holiness is to be given practical expression.

It follows from these observations that the qualifying phrase in v 14a μετά πάντων, "along with everyone," has reference only to persons within the community of faith. It signifies "together with all the other believers" (see above, Note b). The expression πάντων is the linguistic equivalent to the term πολλοί in v 15, which in accordance with Jewish usage is to be understood inclusively and translated "the whole community" (see above, Note i). The house church is the demonstration in society of the presence of the new age. Consequently, it must be a dynamic reflection of the peace that is characteristic of God's reign. (Cf. Käsemann, "Hebräer 12,12–17," 311: "Peace . . . is an eschatological possibility, a gift and an indication of the divine presence—indeed, the expression of the heavenly kingdom itself.") Those who enjoy the blessings of the new covenant are to be united in earnestly pursuing the peace that is both sign and gift from God.

Within the community of faith, there is to be no separation of peace and holiness. If "peace" binds the community together as the achievement of Christ, "holiness" is that quality which identifies the community as the possession of Christ.

In Koine Greek, nouns ending in -μος describe action. Consequently, it is commonly asserted that τὸν ἁγιασμόν, "the holiness," in v 14b, as the direct object of the main verb διώκετε, "pursue," expresses the process of sanctification, not the positional state or fact of sanctification (so, e.g., Westcott, 347–48; Windisch, 112; Procksch, TDNT 1:113; McCown, WesThJ 16 [1981] 58–59; Kistemaker, 388; among others).

It is imperative, however, to interpret the term in v 14 in the context of the cultic argument in Hebrews. In Hebrews human endeavor is never the subject of sanctification. Christ alone is the one who consecrates others to God through his sacrificial death. Holiness is a gift, to which it is necessary to respond with our personal "Yes" (Michel, 451). Christians are those who have been made holy through Christ (10:10, 14). They are consecrated to God as those who belong to the one who makes men and women holy (2:11). In Hebrews ἁγιασμός, "holiness," does not possess an ethical significance. It draws its distinctive nuance from the cultic argument concerning the efficacy of Jesus' high priestly ministry. It is eschatological in character as the objective gift of Christ achieved through his sacrificial death on the cross (10:29; 13:12). The directive διώκετε . . . τὸν ἁγιασμόν, "pursue . . . the holiness," then, means earnestly to hold firmly the gift of Christ through which believers have been made holy (with Käsemann, "Hebräer 12,12–17," 310; Michel, 451, n. 3; Casey, "Eschatology in Heb 12:14–29," 90–91).

Holiness is an essential attribute of God. As those who enjoy the prospect of sharing in the holiness of God (see above on 12:10, where ἁγιότης is a quality), Christians must themselves be holy. They are to make the pursuit of holiness their great quest in life. The basis for a practical holiness of life is τὸν ἁγιασμόν, "the holiness," which is the gift of Christ (cf. Michel, 451; F. F. Bruce, 364–65; McCown, WesThJ 16 [1981] 61, 69).

The crucial importance of the pursuit of holiness is underscored by the qualifying phrase οὗ χωρὶς οὐδεὶς ὄψεται τὸν κύριον, "without which no one will see the Lord." The phrase is a sober reminder that "holiness" is that provision which alone allows one to come into the presence of God. Only those consecrated to

God through the objective gift of Christ have access to God. Only the pure (οἱ καθαροί) will see God (Matt 5:8). In Hebrews "pure" and "holy" are interchangeable terms because those who have been made holy are those for whom Christ has made purification (see above on 1:3; 9:14, 22–26; 10:10, 14). They possess as a gift τὸν ἁγιασμόν, "the holiness," which is required for the vision of the Lord. In this instance τὸν κύριον, "the Lord," is not Christ, but God, as in 8:2 (see also Riggenbach, 402; Windisch, 112; Spicq, 2:399; Grosheide, 295; Michel, 452–53; among others). Christians have within their reach the holiness that is indispensable for seeing God.

The admonition to "pursue holiness" in v 14*b* anticipates the further development of the sentence in vv 15–16. It prepares for the subsequent reference to those who are prepared to forfeit the grace of God through spiritual carelessness, and to defile the holy character of the community through apostasy. In the context of vv 15–16 "holiness" has social as well as personal ramifications (so McCown, *WesThJ* 16 [1981] 70). It is foundational especially for the reference in v 16 to Esau, who spurned ἁγιασμός for something secular and became himself the archetype of the secular person. He relinquished that provision which alone would have allowed him to draw near to God. In this context ἁγιασμός is the objective provision of Christ that actively opposes itself to the life style described by the adjectives πόρνος, "apostate," and βέβηλος, "irreligious," in v 16 (so also Käsemann, "Hebräer 12,12–17," 310).

15–16 The command to exercise vigilant concern for each member of the house church flows from the directive of v 14. The solidarity experienced by the fellowship was the direct result of the gifts of peace and holiness secured by Christ for his people. That solidarity implied a mutual responsibility for one another from which no one is released (cf. Casey, "Eschatology in Heb 12:14–29," 99: "As all must strive for peace and holiness, so too all must be concerned for the members of the community"; similarly Spicq, 2:399). The admonition earnestly to pursue peace and holiness is given concreteness and a specifically communal dimension with the call to vigilance in vv 15–16 (cf. Forkman, *Limits*, 176–77).

The structure of these verses exhibits the depth of pastoral concern expressed by the writer. The present active participle ἐπισκοποῦντες, "watching continually," derives its function and imperatival force from the main verb, the present imperative διώκετε, "pursue." The participle governs the three subordinate clauses of warning that follow, each of which is introduced by the construction μή τις:

Watch   *that no one* forfeits . . .
        that no bitter root grows up . . .
        that no one is apostate or irreligious.

Each of the μή τις clauses becomes progressively longer and more complex. The construction ἐπισκοποῦντες μή, "watch that not," should be recognized as an expression of apprehension (cf. Michel, 453: "a verb of dread"; BDF 370[1], where μή is identified as an expression of apprehension which, if combined with the subjunctive, as in vv 15–16, indicates an anxiety directed toward the prevention of some development that is still dependent upon the human will).

The call to vigilance expressed in ἐπισκοποῦντες refers not to some official expression of ministry but rather to the engagement of the community as a whole in the extension of mutual care (cf. 3:12–13; 4:1; 10:24–25). Christian vigilance is the proper response to a peril that poses an imminent threat to the entire community. The danger is first envisioned as the forfeiture of the grace of God through carelessness. It is then presented as the peril of defilement that would alter the character of the community. It is finally identified as apostasy, resulting in the irrevocable loss of inheritance rights. In view of this very real danger, the members of the house church are urged to vigilant concern for one another (so Käsemann, "Hebräer 12,12–17," 311; Casey, "Eschatology in Heb 12:14–29," 97–98).

The writer is initially concerned lest anyone (the indefinite τις) should be excluded from the grace of God through personal carelessness (v 15a). The idiom ὑστερεῖν ἀπό, followed by the genitive of separation, suggests the notion of *exclusion from* some benefit through one's own fault [BAGD 849; cf. BDF §180[5]). The writer used a form of the verb ὑστερεῖν in 4:1 when he warned his audience to be concerned lest anyone should seem to *fall short* of the promised entrance into God's rest. There is a distinct difference, however, between the force of ὑστερεῖν in 4:1 and its significance here. In 4:1 ὑστερεῖν connotes a failure to attain to what has been promised; in v 15a it denotes a more active "disregard of the grace of God made available in the gospel which issues from unbelief, carelessness, and a willful renunciation of grace" (Riggenbach, 403; similarly Spicq, 2:400). It is thus descriptive of apostasy. It connotes the objective act of "drawing back" (10:39) that distinguishes those who forfeit the grace of God from those who through faith and steadfast endurance inherit the promised blessing (cf. Tasker, *The Gospel*, 50; Marshall, *Kept by the Power of God*, 153, n. 44; Carlston, *JBL* 78 [1959] 299).

The term χάρις is used eight times in the homily (2:9; 4:16 [twice]; 10:29; 12:15, 28; 13:9, 25), and apart from the idiom in 12:28, ἔχειν χάριν, "to give thanks," it consistently denotes "grace" viewed from its divine aspect. It is the ground of God's saving action on behalf of humanity (2:9; 10:29; 13:9), or of his provision for those who turn to him for help (4:16; 13:25). Accordingly, in v 15a the writer expresses concern that no one be excluded from the grace of God expressed in Jesus' death on behalf of the human family (2:9) through spiritual indifference or carelessness (so also Michel, 453; H. Montefiore, 223; Casey, "Eschatology in Heb 12:14–29," 102–4; for the variant point of view that the expression refers to the concrete reality of the assembled community, where grace is dispensed, see Schierse, *Verheissung*, 105–6).

The source of the μή τις clause in v 15a has been identified by Katz as Deut 29:17a LXX, which warns that idolatry and apostasy invoke the curse sanctions of the covenant. The μή τις clause in Deut 29:17a reads:

μή τίς ἐστιν ἐν ὑμῖν ἀνὴρ . . . τίνος ἡ διάνοια ἐξέκλινεν ἀπὸ κυρίου τοῦ θεοῦ ὑμῶν
"lest there be among you a man . . . whose heart turns away from the Lord your God."

Katz suggests that the distinctive formulation in Hebrews appears to take into account the following verse as well. Deut 29:18 LXX refers to the person who, hearing the curse, "blesses himself in his heart," convinced that he may act as he pleases with impunity. So calloused and falsely secure is he that he can say to himself, "I shall be safe, even though I walk in the stubbornness of my heart."

That is the person who forfeits the grace of God (*ZNW* 49 [1958] 214; so also Marshall, *Kept by the Power*, 143).

The correctness of Katz's proposal becomes evident when in v 15*b* the danger is addressed in a different way: ἐπισκοποῦντες . . . μή τις ῥίζα πικρίας ἄνω φύουσα ἐνοχλῇ καὶ δι᾽ αὐτῆς μιανθῶσιν πολλοί, "watch . . . . that no bitter root grows up to cause trouble and the whole community be defiled through it." The formulation appears to be adapted from Deut 29:17*b* LXX as represented in MSS A and F*:

μή τίς ἐστιν ἐν ὑμῖν ῥίζα πικρίας ἄνω φύουσα ἐνοχλῇ καὶ πικρίᾳ
"lest there be among you a bitter root growing up and causing trouble and bitter fruit."

The writer of Hebrews customarily follows the A text in the LXX (see Spicq, 1:330–50, esp. 336). If he has done so in this instance, he omitted the phrase ἐστὶν ἐν ὑμῖν, "there is among you," because the combination ἐστὶν . . . ἐνοχλῇ is "syntactically impossible" (Michel, 451, n. 1). He also omitted the final πικρία, "bitter," because it was repetitive. By shortening and correcting the A text of Deut 29:17*b* LXX, the writer disturbed the parallelism between his own three μή τις clauses. (For a different proposal, see Katz, *ZNW* 49 [1958] 213–17, summarized above in *Note* h; for a convenient listing of the variations in the manuscript tradition of Deut 29:17*b* LXX, see Michel, 454–55, n. 1; for a survey of several proposals concerning the relationship of Heb 12:15*b* to Deut 29:17*b* LXX, see Casey, "Eschatology in Heb 12:14–29," 105–9.)

The two μή τις clauses in v 15 are adaptations of the two μή τις clauses found in Deut 29:17 LXX: v 15*a* corresponds to the clause in Deut 29:17*a* LXX; v 15*b* corresponds to Deut 29:17*b* LXX. The fact that the writer of Hebrews has been reflecting on Deut 29:17 LXX indicates that the directives of vv 15–16 are to be interpreted within the conceptual framework of the covenant. (For allusions to this same passage [=Deut 29:18 MT] in the course of developing a covenantal perspective at Qumran, see 1QS 2:11–17; 1QH 4:14 and the discussion of Forkman, *Limits*, 41–42, 176–77, 193.) The writer consistently interprets apostasy with expressions and OT texts that are covenantal in character (see above on 6:4–8; 10:26–31; and now 12:15–17).

In the metaphorical expression ῥίζα πικρίας, "bitter root," the genitive of quality describes the root as one that produces bitter or poisonous fruit (BDF §165; BAGD 657; Michel, 454–55). The phrase ἄνω φύουσα, "growing up," describes the root as living; it sprouts and produces noxious fruit (cf. 6:8). The citation of Deut 29:17*b* LXX shows that the metaphor refers to a stubborn disposition that expresses itself in unbelief and apostasy. The clause in v 15*b* is thus parallel with the clause in v 15*a*: both clauses refer to arrogant unbelief and apostasy. Stubbornness, when it grows, produces the noxious fruit of apostasy, which is equivalent to excluding oneself from the grace of God. The urgent warning recalls 3:7–19, and especially 3:12, which refers to an evil heart of unbelief that leads one to turn away from the living God (cf. F. F. Bruce, 366; Andriessen and Lenglet, *Bib* 51 [1970] 266; Casey, "Eschatology in Heb 12:14–29," 110–12; the interpretation of Michel [455], who identifies the bitter sprout as a metaphor for an anti-Christ who opposes himself to the "Sprout of Jesse," the Christ, fails to restrict the interpretation of the text to the context established by the citation of Deut 29:17*b* LXX).

The warning concerning apostasy in v 15*b* focuses upon the trouble it will cause (ἐνοχλῇ), namely, the defilement of the whole community. The sin of one individual can corrupt the entire community when that sin is apostasy, because defilement is contagious. One who is defiled by unbelief and apostasy becomes a defiler of others.

There is no reference to defilement in Deut 29:17–18 LXX, but only to a turning away from the Lord, with the result that the curse sanctions of the covenant are invoked upon the arrogant individual, resulting in suffering for the community. The writer's introduction of the term μιανθῶσιν, "be defiled," brings to v 15*b* a distinctly cultic perspective. Sin is that which defiles. Apostasy is cultic impurity.

The verb μιαίνειν possesses both cultic and moral overtones (cf. John 18:28; Titus 1:5; Jude 8). The writer previously used the cognate term ἀμίαντος, "undefiled," "unstained," in its cultic nuance to describe the character of Jesus as high priest (7:26). It is used again with a distinctly moral nuance to describe the intimacy of marriage (13:4). This dual aspect of cultic and moral overtones in μιανθῶσιν in 15*b* is sharpened by the prior reference to ἀγιασμός, "holiness," in v 14 and to the qualities πόρνος, "apostate," and βέβηλος, "irreligious," "secular," in v 16. Apostasy within the house church would pose the threat of defiling the entire assembly because it would obscure its character as the holy community within a society devoid of the knowledge of God. It would disparage peace and holiness because it springs from a root that is alien to Christ. Viewed in the perspective of Deut 29:17*b*, the second μή τις clause contains an explicit warning against apostasy (Johnsson, "Defilement," 367; Käsemann, "Hebräer 12,12–17," 311).

The third μή τις clause in v 16 does not draw its inspiration from Deut 29:17 LXX but from Gen 25:29–34. The Genesis text describes the transaction in which Esau freely gave up his inheritance rights as the eldest son in exchange for a plate of lentil stew. With reference to this account, the writer dramatizes his appeal for vigilance μή τις πόρνος ἤ βέβηλος ὡς Ἠσαῦ, "that no one become apostate or secular like Esau."

The term πόρνος, "immoral," can be used of sexual immorality, as in 13:4, where it is said that God will judge those who are sexually immoral and adulterers. There is no basis, however, for the use of πόρνος in this literal sense in the OT tradition concerning Esau. The emphasis in the biblical account falls on the fact that Esau despised his birth rights as the elder son, and, by implication, the covenant by which they were secured (Gen 25:34). This fact encouraged Elliott to argue that πόρνος in v 16 is not descriptive of Esau. According to Elliott, the particle ἤ in v 16 must be understood in a separating sense. It serves to distinguish between two types of individuals, i.e., those who are sexually immoral (πόρνος) and others who are secular or irreligious like Esau (*ExpTim* 29 [1917–18] 44–45, with a reference to Westcott, 407; cf. Riggenbach, 404–5; F. F. Bruce, 367). The proposal fails to be convincing, however, because ἤ is never strictly disjunctive; in fact, it frequently has the force of a copulative conjunction in negative clauses that include synonyms like πόρνος, "immoral," "apostate," and βέβηλος, "irreligious," "secular" (so BDF §446; Spicq, 2:400; Bonsirven, *RSR* 35 [1948] 505).

A broad spectrum of late Jewish tradition clearly did associate Esau with sexual immorality (e.g., *Jub.* 25:1, 7–8; 26:34; 35:13–14; Philo, *On the Virtues* 208–10,

Questions and Answers on Genesis 4.201, *Allegorical Interpretation* 3.2; *Gen. Rab.* 65 on Gen 26). It has often been argued that the writer of Hebrews drew upon this tradition, which becomes increasingly virulent against Esau (so Schröger, *Verfasser,* 220; Michel, 456; H. Montefiore, 224–25; among others). It seems necessary in this instance, however, to give strict regard to the immediate context in which πόρνος occurs. Consistent with the writer's appeal to Deut 29:17 LXX in v 15 is the more figurative sense of πόρνος in the OT as one who breaks covenant with God (e.g., Exod 34:15–17; Deut 31:16 LXX; cf. Hauck, *TDNT* 6:587). The word conveys the nuance "unfaithful to God." The context of v 16 clearly points to a metaphorical understanding of the term in the figurative sense of "apostate" (see above, *Note* k). In support of this proposal are the general symmetry of the three clauses introduced by μή τις in vv 15–16, the repetition with variations of the warning against apostasy, and the symbolic significance of Esau for the members of the house church (so also W. Manson, 85; Williamson, *Philo,* 265–66; Andriessen and Lenglet, *Bib* 51 [1970] 227–28; Casey, "Eschatology in Heb 12:14–19," 123–24).

The synonym βέβηλος, "irreligious," "secular," describes Esau as a man who was preoccupied only with personal gratification. For such a person there are only the self and the present moment (cf. Gen 25:32: "'Look, I am about to die,' Esau said. 'What good are the inheritance rights to me?'"). In the LXX βέβηλος functions as the antonym of ἅγιος, "holy" (Hauck, *TDNT* 1:604, citing Lev 10:10; Ezek 22:26; 44:23 LXX). It describes the persons who are prepared to turn their backs on that which is holy in order to focus their attention on that which is immediately present. Esau thus typifies the godless person who relinquishes the rights conferred upon him by the covenant for the sake of momentary relief. He is "the prototype of all who throw away the heavenly reality for the sake of the earthly one" (Thompson, *Beginning of Christian Philosophy,* 43).

The incident in Gen 25:29–34 is recalled with a brief, pregnant phrase: ὃς ἀντὶ βρώσεως μιᾶς ἀπέδετο τὰ πρωτοτόκια ἑαυτοῦ, "who gave up his inheritance rights as the older son rather than one dish of food." The idiom ἀντὶ . . . ἀπέδοτο, with the meaning "he gave up . . . rather than" (see above, *Note* m), sharply expresses the unthinkable exchange. The emphatic position of μιᾶς, "one," heightens the impression of the thoughtlessness and perversity of Esau's action. Esau chose a meager meal rather than the inheritance rights conferred upon him as the older of two sons. The expression τὰ πρωτοτόκια, "the inheritance rights" (which are the prerogative of the firstborn son; cf. Gen 27:36), which occurs only here in the NT, alludes to Esau's status as heir to the material possessions of his father. More significantly, it included the blessing of Isaac, conferring the blessings promised in the covenant God made with Abraham (cf. Gen 12:2–3; 15:18–20; 17:3–8, 16, 19–21; 25:5; 27:28–29). Esau despised blessings that ultimately affected a whole posterity rather than (ἀντί) endure an empty stomach.

The expression τὰ πρωτοτόκια serves to situate the action of Esau in a redemptive-historical perspective. Esau's willingness to give up all that was his as the firstborn son reflected a contempt for the covenant by which his rights were warranted. By descriptive analogy, he is representative of apostate persons who are ready to turn their backs on God and the divine promises, in reckless disregard of the covenant blessings secured by the sacrificial death of Jesus. The immediate reference is to the objective blessings of "peace" and "holiness," specified in v 14. With the example of Esau, apostasy is further defined as a decisive rejection of God's gifts.

17 In commenting on Esau's frivolous behavior, the writer does not stress the disparity between the meagerness of that which Esau chose over the magnitude of the blessing. He places the accent on the irretrievable loss that Esau suffered. He assumes that his audience is familiar not only with the account in Gen 25:29–34 but with its sequel in Gen 27:1–40. Esau came before Isaac fully expecting he would receive the blessing of his father. His father had spoken to him specifically regarding the bestowal of his blessing (Gen 27:2–4). Isaac apparently knew nothing of the transaction between Jacob and Esau. When Esau requested the blessing (Gen 27:31), he discovered that it had already been bestowed, through a ruse, upon his brother. Although he begged for the blessing with tears (Gen 27:34, 36, 38), Isaac responded, "I blessed him—and indeed he will be blessed! . . . So what can I possibly do for you, my son?" (Gen 27:33, 37). The words finally pronounced over Esau were not a blessing, but prophecy that Esau would live under the curse sanctions attached to the covenant (Gen 27:39–40). The expression ἴστε γάρ, "for you know," in Heb 12:17a indicates that the writer had only to allude to this course of events for the entire scenario to be recalled.

The substantiating γάρ refers initially to the preceding verse; the subsequent experience of Esau is the ground of the concern expressed in v 16. At the same time it follows from the structure of the sentence in vv 14–16 that v 17 is also the ground of the directive in v 14 and the injunctions of v 15. The entire paragraph stands under the aspect of judgment implied in the writer's observations in v 17.

The writer's interpretation of Gen 27:30–40 focuses on the detail that Esau later desired to receive his father's blessing (Gen. 27:31, 32b, 34, 36, 38): καὶ μετέπειτα θέλων κληρονομῆσαι τὴν εὐλογίαν, "and later on, when he wished to inherit the blessing." The formulation incorporates two expressions of vital theological significance to the writer, "to inherit," and "the blessing." Both expressions reflect on the relationship of God to his people.

The verb κληρονομῆσαι, "to inherit," was undoubtedly suggested by the expression τὰ πρωτοτόκια, "the inheritance rights of the firstborn son," in v 16. It derives its significance from the patriarchal narratives, where the call of God is directed toward an inheritance. It was specifically Gen 15:7–8 that determined the concept of inheritance in the OT. Inheritance signified the enduring and certain possession of the land, in accordance with the promise of God to his people (Gen 15:7; 22:17; 28:4; cf. J. Herrmann, TDNT 3:769–70). From that primary significance, "inheritance" came to connote that which was allotted by God and was possessed only on that basis. "Inheritance" implied "gift," and specifically "gift from God."

The writer of Hebrews draws upon this tradition (6:13–17; 11:8), even when he develops a distinctly Christian and eschatological perspective on inheritance. In Hebrews, inheritance is associated with sonship. Jesus is the essential Son who has been appointed heir of all things (1:2, 4); Christians are those who enjoy the status of "sons" through him (2:10) and so inherit the divine promises (1:4; 6:12, 17–18; 9:15).

The notion of "blessing" is closely associated with that of "inheritance." The narrative in Gen 27:27–40 concerns the blessing bestowed by Isaac, reflecting the patriarchal practice of a father blessing his oldest son. The "blessing," however, is in reality God's blessing (cf. Heb. 6:14). The father simply acted as God's agent when he passed on to his eldest son the blessing bestowed by God in his covenant with Abraham. That is why the blessing is expressed as prayer: "May God give you of heaven's dew and of earth's richness" (Gen. 27:28). "Blessing," like "inheritance," is the gift of God (cf. Heb 6:7, 14; 11:20). It is this gift that Esau wished to inherit and that was denied to him because he had despised the gifts of God (cf. Westcott, 408; Kuss, 198; Andriessen and Lenglet, *Bib* 51 [1970] 228). Esau sought the blessing that was the prerogative of the oldest son but was rejected.

Using the theological passive ἀπεδοκιμάσθη, "he was rejected *by God*" (see above, *Note* q), the writer places the account in Gen 27:30–40 within a redemptive-historical perspective. What transpired ultimately has reference to God. The moment of judgment arrives when God bestows blessing or pronounces rejection (Schierse, *Verheissung*, 150). It was not simply Jacob's ruse that defrauded Esau of the promised blessing. His rash action had displayed contempt for the gifts of God and for the covenant by which they were secured. For that reason he was rejected by God. The sense of ἀπεδοκιμάσθη is informed by the expression ἀδόκιμος, "rejected," in 6:8. There the writer places instruction concerning apostasy (6:4–6) in the context of covenant blessing (6:7) and curses (6:8): ἀδόκιμος καὶ κατάρας ἐγγύς, "it is rejected and in danger of being cursed." The statement that Esau was "rejected by God" signifies that he was placed under God's irrevocable curse (so Käsemann, "Hebräer 12,12–17," 308).

The writer juxtaposes the action of Esau with the action of God in a rhetorically effective way:

v 16 Esau ἀπέδετο, "gave up," his inheritance rights;
v 17 When he wished to inherit the blessing he was ἀπεδοκιμάσθη, "rejected by God."

Esau's thoughtless action in relinquishing his birthrights in order to secure a meal for which he hungered demonstrated his character as πόρνος, "apostate," and βέβηλος, "secular." The drastic consequence was the permanent loss of the blessing and the awesome reality of divine rejection.

The interpretation of v 17*bc* depends upon the resolving of critical questions that have to be faced when translating the text. These concern the significance of the fixed idiom μετανοίας τόπον εὑρεῖν in v 17*b* and the determination of the antecedent for the ambiguous feminine pronoun αὐτήν in v 17*c*, which in turn has bearing upon the complex sentence structure of v 17. The decisions that stand behind the translation may be briefly reviewed, with reference to the *Notes* for discussion and supporting evidence.

The determination that the fixed idiom in v 17*b* should be translated "to find a possibility [or, opportunity] for repentance" (see above, *Note* r) brings v 17 within the perspective of the pastoral concern with repentance in the homily (cf. 6:1, 4–6). It indicates that the example of Esau has been cited because it has direct bearing on the question whether repentance is possible after willful apostasy. The idiom τόπος μετανοίας is strongly attested as a technical expression in teaching on repentance. It signifies an objective possibility for repentance granted by God. In v 17*b* the substantive μετανοίας, "repentance," has been placed emphatically at the beginning of the clause because it is of vital pastoral significance to the writer.

The identification of the antecedent of αὐτήν, "it," in v 17c as the independent articular noun τὴν εὐλογίαν, "the blessing," in v 17a (see above, Note t) demonstrates that the writer has conformed his statement to the detail of the account in Gen 27:30–40. There, it is the blessing, not repentance, that Esau sought with tears. The structure of v 17 is complex, consisting of three separate phrases. Consistent with his practice elsewhere in the homily, the writer has separated for oratorical effect words that logically belong together (cf. 2:14; 7:11; 9:2–5; 10:20). As in 7:11, a parenthesis (v 17b) interrupts the course of the thought being developed in v 17a and c: "for you know that later on, when he wished to inherit the blessing, he was rejected . . . even though he had begged for it (i.e., the blessing) with tears." The logical link in the statement is between the verbs "to beg for" and "to be rejected." Esau begged for the blessing, but he was rejected by God.

The parenthetical phrase in v 17b, μετανοίας γὰρ τόπον οὐχ εὗρεν, "for he found no opportunity for repentance," serves to underscore the ultimate seriousness of a rash and thoughtless rejection of the gifts of God. The objective possibility of repentance is created only by the action of God and is conditioned by a time limit determined by him. It does not depend upon human will. God alone determines its beginning and its end (Schierse, *Verheissung*, 150; cf. Käsemann, "Hebräer 12,12–17, 309: "It is important to observe that in the entire NT repentance is the sign of the eschatological age. Repentance is the other side of faith in the gospel (cf. 6:1); it is the "no" spoken to the old age, which results from the "yes" addressed to the new age of God's sovereignty. Within this perspective, one can repent only as long as God's grace is available. This means something definite: today, while God's voice can be heard"). The deduction that repentance was denied to Esau follows from the fact that he had been rejected by God (v 17a).

The concern with repentance in v 17 is not derived from the account in Gen 27:30–40 but from the writer's meditation upon that account. There is no indication in the narrative that Esau recognized his responsibility for what had transpired (cf. Gen 27:36) or the depth of his guilt. He thought only of the extent of his loss and sought to reclaim the blessing he had forfeited, even with tears (Gen 27:34, 38; rightly emphasized by Riggenbach, 406–10; Michel, 458; Spicq, 2:402). It is characteristic of the person who is πόρνος ἢ βέβηλος ὡς Ἠσαῦ, "apostate and secular like Esau," that he does *not* think in terms of repentance. But the writer of Hebrews does think in these terms. For him the biblical text has prophetic significance for the community; it foreshadows the future for the community that has inherited the blessings Esau frivolously lost. For that reason the writer is prepared to go beyond the detail of the biblical text in order to place the account in Gen 27:30–40 in the perspective of the gospel and of the catechetical teaching in which the members of the house church have been grounded (6:1). It is for their sake that he inserts the parenthetical clause concerning repentance, concentrating this motif in the example of Esau (so correctly, Solari, "The Problem of *Metanoia*," 148).

The clause concerning repentance in v 17b reiterates with inexorable sharpness the point already asserted emphatically in 6:4–6: δύνατον . . . πάλιν ἀνακαινίζειν εἰς μετάνοιαν, "for it is impossible to renew [them] again to repentance." Esau is brought to the attention of the assembled house church as the person in whom the apostasy addressed in 6:4–8 and 10:26–31 is realized. A reckless disregard for God and his gifts is reprehensible, because it entails a willful rejection of a divine vocation. This is the essence of apostasy. By descriptive analogy, there can be no opportunity for repentance for the Christian who renounces his "heavenly calling" (3:1) or who shows contempt for the blessings of the new covenant secured by Jesus' sacrificial death upon the cross. There remains only the certainty of an inescapable judgment and of rejection by God.

18–19a The arresting periodic sentence in vv 18–24 develops an extended comparison between Israel's experience at Mount Sinai and the new covenant encounter with God that takes place at Mount Zion, the city of the living God. The terrifying atmosphere that characterized the theophany at Sinai (vv 18–21) throws into bold relief the festive joy of Zion (vv 22–24). Addressing the members of the house church, the writer states emphatically: οὐ γὰρ προσεληλύθατε ψηλαφωμένῳ ... ἀλλὰ προσεληλύθατε Σιὼν ὄρει, "for you have not come to what may be touched ... on the contrary, you have come to Mount Zion," (vv 18, 22). The initial emphatic position of the negative particle οὐ, "not," in v 18 is underscored by the correlative negative particle ἀλλά, "on the contrary," in v 22 and by the parallel construction of the two parts of the sentence. The foundational experiences of Christians have been qualitatively different from those of Israel at Sinai. The sharp contrast, brilliantly drawn in rhythmic, measured phrases and balanced conceptions, exhibits the fundamental differences between the old and new covenants and between Moses and Jesus, respectively, as mediators of the encounter with God.

The writer carefully links the unit as a whole with the preceding paragraph by the inferential γάρ, "for," at the beginning of v 18 (cf. Schierse, *Verheissung*, 171–72, who argues that the conjunction γάρ provides the key to the interpretation of vv 18–24). In v 17 the substantiating γάρ served to introduce the ground for the pastoral directives of vv 14–16. In a similar manner, the inferential γάρ in v 18 marks the transition to the balanced statement in vv 18–24, which provides additional grounding for vv 14–17 (so Casey, "Eschatology in Heb 12:14–29," 308–9, who describes the function of γάρ as connecting "two passages which stand together as warning and ground for warning"). The privileged experience of Christians indicates why they must hold fast to the objective gifts of peace and holiness (v 14) and why they must guard against apostasy in their midst (vv 15–17). The γάρ also indicates that the motif of judgment developed in vv 14–17 informs the formulation of vv 18–24, lending to this unit the urgent tone of pastoral concern that characterizes the prior warning (so Schierse, *Verheissung*, 171–72, who argues that both vv 18–21 and vv 22–24 refer to judgment revelations).

The developed contrast between vv 18–21 and vv 22–24 is governed by the initial verb προσέρχεσθαι, "to come to," in v 18, which is repeated in v 22. This verb reflects the writer's source, Deut 4:11 LXX, where Moses recalls Israel's experience at Sinai: "You came [προσήλθετε] and stood at the foot of the mountain while it blazed with fire . . . with black clouds and deep darkness." The verb προσήλθετε in Deut 4:11 LXX has a cultic nuance since the Sinai event was understood in terms of a solemn covenant ceremony (cf. Deut 4:10–14). The writer of Hebrews substituted the perfect tense of the verb for the aorist he found in Deut 4:11 LXX, because he was concerned with the enduring result of the encounter with God.

It is important to recognize in the verbal form προσεληλύθατε in v 18 the cultic and liturgical nuance of προσέρχεσθαι that is found throughout the homily (4:16; 7:25; 10:1, 22; 11:6). The verb is used exclusively of an approach to God. The writer compares Israel's approach to God in cultic ceremony to the Christian's experience in worship (cf. J. Schneider, *TDNT* 2:683–84; Michel, 461; Thompson, *JBL* 94 [1975] 582, n. 11; and for a dissenting point of view, Peterson, "Examination," 279–80). The foundational experience of the people of God under the old and the new covenants is described in terms of a coming into the divine presence. In the two cases where an approach to God under the old covenant is described, however, the reference is negative in its import (10:1; 12:18). Apart from the generalized statement in 11:6, the remaining references describe a coming to God that is mediated through the high priestly ministry of Jesus (see 4:15–16; 7:24–25; 10:21–22; 12:22–24).

Drawing selectively on the accounts of the Sinai event in the Pentateuch (Exod 19:16–22; 20:18–21; Deut 4:11–12; 5:22–27 LXX), the writer recreates in vv 18–19 the event of Israel's frightening experience in coming to Sinai, where they encountered God in a fiery epiphany. The scene consists of seven elements, each connected by the copulative καί, "and," which build in intensity toward the climactic final element, καὶ φωνῇ ῥημάτων, "and to a sound of words." The cumulative effect from the awesome description of the tangible and threatening aspects of the scene is an indelible impression of the majestic presence of the God who is unapproachable.

Although the description in vv 18–21 leaves no doubt that the writer has Sinai in mind, he makes no explicit reference to the mountain of revelation. He chooses instead to emphasize the tangible and sensory aspects of the theophany described in his sources. He uses his sources creatively. He adds the expression ψηλαφωμένῳ, "to that which can be touched," as the first term descriptive of the event and then selects from his sources only those external elements that explain the atmosphere of dread and confusion at Sinai. He omits significant elements from the Pentateuchal accounts. Vanhoye has observed that although the divine name appears six times in Deut 5:23–27 LXX, it is completely absent from Heb 12:18–21 ("Le Dieu," 320–21). The impression is conveyed that God was not unambiguously present at Sinai. There was only "a sound of words" (v 19). The term ὄρει ("mountain") appears four times in Deut 4:11–12; 5:22–27 LXX. Its omission in v 18 serves to generalize the representation of the event. Casey observes, "It is the whole old covenant which our author describes under the guise of the Sinai theophany. It is not simply the mountain of Sinai which is the scene of a less than perfect encounter" ("Eschatology in Heb 12:14–29," 318). The writer presents in vv 18–21 a purposeful theological recasting of the event in order to sharpen the contrast to be developed in vv 22–24.

In recreating the scene at Sinai, the writer cites as the first of seven descriptive terms an expression he did not find in the biblical accounts, ψηλαφωμένῳ, "to what may be touched" (see above, *Note* x). The term may be a reflection of Exod 19:12–13, which decreed death to anyone who *touched* the mountain, as Thompson has suggested (*JBL* 94 [1975] 582). More likely, it was suggested by the cognate verbal adjective ψηλαφητός, which is used in Exod 10:21 LXX of the darkness "which may be felt." What is certain is that the choice of this term is determinative for the developed contrast between Sinai and Zion. It indicates that the writer was guided by a theological point of view and appraisal: Sinai was physical and tangible; it consisted of a combination of external visual and auditory phenomena (cf. Windisch, 112; BAGD 892; Casey, "Eschatology in Heb 12:14–29," 322).

It is unwarranted to find in the use of ψηλαφώμενος a pejorative code word for "earthly" or "sense-perceptible" in a Platonic metaphysical sense, as proposed by Thompson (*JBL* 94 [1975] 582–84; id., *Beginnings of Christian Philosophy*, 45–47). He is convinced that ψηλαφώμενος indicates that the Sinai event is evaluated and interpreted with assumptions that indicate the writer's cosmological dualism. According to Thompson, the writer opposes "tangible" to "intangible," "earthly" to "heavenly," and "sense-perceptible" to "true" in the sense of the "intelligible world" of the Platonic tradition. For Thompson, the writer no longer thinks typologically in terms of old event and new event. His purpose is to describe Sinai as merely an event in the created order, in which "material objects can only be inferior agents for the expression of the nature of God" (*Beginnings of Christian Philosophy*, 46).

The mere presence of a term is an insufficient basis for determining its significance. Thompson's argument imports a philosophical tradition as the key to an exegetical tradition. It should be recognized that the writer compares two covenants under the imagery of two mountains in order to contrast the distance that separated the worshiper from God under the old covenant with the unrestricted access to God under the new covenant. It is this primary contrast that underscores the responsibility of those who enjoy the blessings of the new covenant to listen to God's voice (12:25–29). Sinai and Zion are extended metaphors that exhibit the difference in quality between the relationship to God under the old and new covenants, respectively (see Peterson, *RTR* 38 [1979] 79–80). The Sinai theophany should make clear to Christians the significance of the new covenant and of their eschatological encounter with God. The Sinai event was ψηλαφώμενος, "tangible," "palpable," in the sense of being perceptible to the senses. The writer's re-creation of the event conveys an impression of an overwhelming of the senses by the presence of the God who is unapproachable in his holiness. The term ψηλαφώμενος is not informed by a philosophical tradition but by the exegetical tradition that led the translators of the LXX to describe the darkness of the ninth plague as that "which could be felt" (ψηλαφητός, Exod 10:21 LXX). When the writer says that Christians have not come "to what may be touched" (ψηλαφωμένῳ) in v 18 it is not because of the noumenal concern of the philosopher. It reflects the fact that the city of God is essentially *future* (13:14). In making this point, Hurst writes, "Christians have certainly 'come' to it (12:22) and 'received' it (12:28), but only through faith, a faith which grasps the future as though it were the present (11:1)" ("Background," 63, in the context of an extended interaction [61–67] with Thompson's article; cf. O. Betz, *TDNT* 9:297; Casey, "Eschatology in Heb 12:14–29," 503).

The writer found the series of sensory terms that follow in his sources: "blazing fire," "darkness," "gloom" (the more euphonic word ζόφῳ is substituted for σκότος; see above, *Note* y), and "whirlwind" occur in Deut 4:11; 5:22–23 LXX. Reference to a "trumphet blast" is taken from Exod 19:16, 19; 20:18 LXX (where the substantive ἦχος, "a blast," was suggested by the cognate verb ἤχει, "blasted," in Exod 19:16 LXX, to distinguish φωνὴ τῆς σάλπιγγος, "a sound of the trumphet," from φωνὴ ῥημάτων, "a sound of words") and to "a sound of words"

from Deut 4:12 LXX. These are the external visual and auditory phenomena
that accompany theophany. The writer has been highly selective in the use of
his sources, however. At Sinai the mountain blazed with fire, and God spoke to
the Israelites from out of the fire (Deut 4:11–12; 5:22, 24, 26). No mention of
the fact that God spoke from the fire disrupts the flow of v 18. For the writer,
"blazing fire" is simply one of the terrifying external aspects of the event (Casey,
"Eschatology in Heb 12:14–29," 319; cf. Schierse, *Verheissung*, 176; Thompson,
Beginnings of Christian Philosophy, 46–47).

The full impact of the recital of these terms in measured cadence would have
been conveyed to the gathered house church only when the homily was read
aloud. They combine to create a verbal impression of the awesome majesty of
the God who made his presence known at Sinai. The external phenomena were
certain to provoke fear and to intensify the ambiguity of the encounter with
God. The visual images ("blazing fire," "darkness," "gloom") suggest that which
obscures rather than reveals. There is, as Casey observes, "no clear vision of God
here—the Israelites do not see *him*, but only the violent effects of his presence"
("Eschatology in Heb 12:14–29," 320). Similarly, the auditory terms ("whirlwind,"
"a trumpet-blast," "a sound of words") combine to create an impression of great
noise that effectively interfered with any distinct hearing.

The final expression assumes particular importance because it is descriptive
of the form of the divine revelation at Sinai: καὶ φωνῇ ῥημάτων, "and to a sound of
words." The figure is derived from Deut 4:12 LXX, which states that the Israelites
did not see God; they only heard φωνὴν ῥημάτων, "a sound of words." The
writer's expression underscores the equivocal character of the Sinai event. Israel
heard a sound of words, but it is left unclear whether they experienced the encounter with God (Casey, "Eschatology in Heb 12:14–29," 320, argues that the
writer denies that the Sinai event was a true encounter with God). Just as they
heard a trumpet blast, so too they heard the noise of a voice, but it evoked fear
rather than understanding. The Israelites were incapable of enduring it. Sinai
was not an occasion for revelation so much as for dread.

19b–20 The Israelites were terrified by the experience. They responded to
"a sound of words" by pleading that no further message be given to them
(v 19b). The writer's statement summarizes Deut 5:23–27; it particularly reflects
on Deut 5:25 LXX, where the people express the fear that they will be consumed
by the fire if they continue to listen to the voice (cf. Exod 20:18–19). According
to the Deuteronomic account, God approved of their request that he should
speak to them through Moses (Deut 5:28). There is no suggestion of guilt in the
text.

It has often been suggested that the writer's choice of the verb παρῃτήσαντο
("they begged" that something not be done) actually carries the nuance of "they
refused," or "they rejected," as in v 25. Israel turned away from the revelation of
God's holiness and refused to listen to his voice (so Windisch, 113; Spicq, 2:404;
Schierse, *Verheissung*, 177; Andriessen and Lenglet, *Bib* 51 [1970] 230; among
others). It is important, however, to observe that when the verb signifies "to disregard" or "to reject," it is followed by the accusative (BAGD 616), as in v 25,
where Christians are warned μὴ παραιτήσησθε τὸν λαλοῦντα, "do not disregard
the one speaking," even as at a later point in time the Israelites παραιτησάμενοι
τὸν χρηματίζοντα, "disregard the one who warned [them]." In v 19b, however, the

verb is followed by the negative particle μή and an infinitive and conveys the sense of pleading that something not be done. The emphasis in vv 19–21 is wholly on the element of fear that the experience provoked in those who heard the frightening "sound of words" and not on their guilt. At this point, the writer continues to follow his source (so also Casey, "Eschatology in Heb 12:14–29," 324–25).

This understanding is supported by v 20, which is tied to v 19b by the explanatory γάρ: "*for* they were unable to bear the command." The reference is to Exod 19:12–13, which speaks of placing a limit for the people around the mountain beyond which they can not go on penalty of death: "whoever touches the mountain will surely be put to death" (Exod 19:12b). The prohibition extended to "person or animal" (Exod 19:13). The writer focuses upon the most stringent aspect of the command, κἂν θηρίον θίγῃ τοῦ ὄρους λιθοβοληθήσεται, "if even an animal touches the mountain, it shall be stoned," in order to emphasize the gravity of the injunction and the peril of coming before the annihilating holiness of the divine appearing (K. Weiss, *TDNT* 9:59; cf. K. J. Thomas, *NTS* 11 [1964–65] 317; Schröger, *Verfasser,* 209–11). Judgment for anyone who ignores the holiness of God is swift and terrible. The injunction served to reinforce the emotion of terror Israel experienced at the prospect of encountering God and accounts for their action in begging that Moses mediate God's word to them (v 19b). In the context of vv 18–21, it emphasizes the unapproachability of God under the old covenant (K. J. Thomas, *NTS* 11 [1964–65] 317; Casey, "Eschatology in Heb 12:14–29," 327).

21 The climactic reference to the reaction of Moses, the mediator of the covenant, to the awesome event heightens the impression of the terror that was evoked by the theophany at Sinai: καὶ οὕτω φοβερὸν ἦν τὸ φανταζόμενον Μωϋσῆς εἶπεν, Ἔκφοβός εἰμι καὶ ἔντρομος, "and the spectacle was so awesome that Moses said, 'I am terrified and trembling.'" The term φοβερόν conveys the connotation of profound dread at the prospect of an encounter with the living God. It is informed by its prior use in 10:27 and 31 in the context of divine judgment. In the conclusion to 10:26–31 the writer comments, φοβερὸν τὸ ἐμπεσεῖν εἰς χεῖρας θεοῦ ζῶντος, "it is terrifying to fall into the hands of the living God." The revelation of Sinai, which is summed up in the rare expression τὸ φανταζόμενον, "the spectacle" (only here in early Christian literature), was "terrifying," or "awesome." The encounter with God is presented under the aspect of a judgment scene, even for Moses, mediator of the covenant (cf. Schierse, *Verheissung,* 171–72; Vögtle, *BibLeb* 10 [1969] 240).

At this point, however, the writer deviates sharply from his sources. According to the Pentateuch, Moses alone was allowed to come into the presence of God (Exod 19:16–25; 20:21; Deut 5:5, 31), and he appears to have done so in complete safety. There are no references to the emotions he experienced in the divine presence. When the people saw the sights and heard the sounds that accompanied the theophany, "they trembled with fear" (Exod 19:16; 20:18a). They pleaded for Moses to mediate to them God's word, convinced that if God spoke to them directly they would die (Exod 20:18b–19). Moses reassured them with the comforting words, "Do not be afraid" (Exod 20:20). Yet, according to v 21, it is Moses who openly acknowledged, "I am terrified and trembling."

Three proposals have been made concerning the source of v 21.

(1) The initial expression was borrowed from Deut 9:19*a* LXX, where Moses exclaimed, "and *I am terrified* (ἔκφοβός εἰμι) on account of the anger and the wrath [of the Lord], because the Lord was sufficiently angry with you to destroy you." The last two words, καὶ ἔντρομος, "and trembling," were then apparently added to strengthen Moses' statement, since ἔντρομος is commonly used to express trembling associated with fear (cf. Pss 17:18; 76:19 LXX; Dan 10:11 (Theod.); Wis 17:10; 1 Macc 13:2). Although this cry of horror was uttered over the idolatrous action of Israel in worshiping the golden calf, and not in response to the frightening spectacle of Sinai, it has been identified as the source of the writer's statement in v 21 (Moffatt, 216; Kuss, 198; K. J. Thomas, *NTS* 11 [1964–65] 317–18; Buchanan, 222; UBSGNT³, 775).

(2) The key to v 21 is to be located in its second expression, καὶ ἔντρομος, "and trembling." In Acts 7:32 Stephen describes Moses as trembling in the presence of the burning bush from which God spoke to him: ἔντρομος δὲ γενόμενος Μωϋσῆς οὐκ ἐτόλμα κατανοῆσαι ("*and trembling*, Moses did not dare to look" (cf. Exod 3:6: "Moses hid his face for he was afraid to look at God"). The event took place at Sinai (Acts 7:30) and is described as a τὸ ὅραμα τὸ μέγα, "a great sight," (Exod 3:3), which is roughly equivalent to τὸ φανταζόμενον, "the spectacle." The writer of Hebrews, it is argued, found in the reaction of Moses at the burning bush a basis for attributing to him the response reported in v 21 (P. E. Hughes, 533; R. W. Thurston, "Midrash and 'Magnet Words' in the New Testament," *EvQ* 51 [1979] 30–31; Andreissen and Lenglet, *Bib* 51 [1970] 231).

(3) The writer drew upon a Jewish homiletical tradition that ascribed fear and trembling to Moses at Sinai. For example, according to a haggadic tradition in *b. Šabb.* 88*b*, Moses at Sinai declared, "I was afraid that the angels could consume me with the breath of their mouths" (cited by Riggenbach, 414; Spicq, 2:405; Michel, 462; cf. Westcott, 412; Windisch, 113; F. F. Bruce, 371–72).

In the absence of sufficient evidence, it is clear only that the writer reinforced the notion of fear by expanding it to include Moses as well as the people. The result is to associate the Sinai dispensation with fear. The description of the visual and auditory aspects of the theophany as φοβερός, "frightening," "awesome," was itself sufficient to suggest that *all* the human participants in the event experienced the frightening manifestations as an occasion for dread. The emphasis falls on the sense of immense distance that separates the worshiper from God under the Sinai covenant. There was a numinous awareness of the God who was unapproachable, an experience of blazing fire, black clouds, gloom, whirlwind, loud noise, and a frightening "sound of words" (cf. P. R. Jones, *RevExp* 76 [1979] 101).

22a Christians order their lives in accordance with a different revelation. Corresponding structurally to the seven features descriptive of the encounter with God at Sinai are seven images, each connected by the copulative καί, "and," which create a vision of the heavenly city of God (cf. Dumbrell, *EvQ* 48 [1976] 158, who notes that the description in vv 22–24 is modeled to some extent on the pattern at Sinai, with its "angels, assembled participants, a presiding Deity, scrutiny, and a mediator"). In sharp contradistinction from the scene at Sinai, every aspect of this vision provides encouragement for coming boldly into the presence of God (cf. 4:16). The atmosphere at Mount Zion is festive. The frightening visual imagery of blazing fire, darkness, and gloom fades before the reality of the city of the living God, heavenly Jerusalem. The cacophony of whirlwind, trumpet blast, and a sound of words is muted and replaced by the joyful praise of angels in a festal gathering. The trembling congregation of Israel, gathered solemnly at the base of the mountain, is superseded by the assembly of those whose names are permanently inscribed in the heavenly archives. An overwhelming impression of the unapproachability of God is eclipsed in the experience of full access to the presence of God and of Jesus, the mediator of the new covenant (for a different construction of the contrasts, see O. Betz, *TDNT* 9:297, n. 91).

The images chosen by the writer in vv 22–24 have apocalyptic overtones; they are expressions rich in tradition and significance, descriptive of the realization of the eschatological hopes of the people of God. They announce the objective blessings that are the result of the conclusion of the new covenant.

The sentence begun in v 18 is continued in v 22a: οὐ γὰρ προσεληλύθατε ψηλαφωμένῳ . . . ἀλλὰ προσεληλύθατε Σιὼν ὄρει, "For you have not come to what can be touched . . . on the contrary, you have come to Mount Zion." The adversative particle ἀλλά, "on the contrary," which is correlative to the emphatic negative particle οὐ, "not," at the beginning of the sentence, indicates that this mountain must be appreciated as decisively different from Sinai.

The structural parallelism between the two parts of the sentence is emphasized by the repetition of the verb προσεληλύθατε, "you have come." The writer represents vividly the experience of encountering God through Christ in the metaphor of a journey or pilgrimage to the city of God. What he describes is essentially an act of faith and personal commitment (cf. Michel, 460, n. 2: "One draws near to the good things of salvation by first grasping the word of God, which receives through the new covenant a particular urgency. This 'drawing near' is on the one hand eschatological: we stand directly before the final perfection. On the other hand, it is present: we are bound in faith to the word"). Through faith that grasps the future as though it were the present (11:1), Christians in their pilgrimage come to that future reality that is not palpable to the senses, Mount Zion, the city of the living God. Just as eschatological faith stands firmly with the unseen reality for which one hopes on the basis of God's promise (11:1), it grasps hold of those things as yet "untouched" (Hurst, "Background," 63). The emphasis in προσεληλύθατε falls upon the forward orientation of faith in the light of an objective goal, the transcendent blessings secured for Christians by the death of Jesus as mediator of the new covenant (v 24). "Mount Zion, even the city of the living God, heavenly Jerusalem," is a reality in which the community already has a share (cf. Hillmann, *BibLeb* 1 [1960] 247; Michel, 461; F. F. Bruce, 372; P. E. Hughes, 544). This is, of course, a perspective informed by primitive Christian eschatology.

The first of seven images that enumerate suggestively the blessings of the new covenant is "Mount Zion, even the city of the living God, heavenly Jerusalem." The three designations are synonymous and should be treated as a unit (so Spicq, 2:404–5; Kuss, 202; Michel, 462–63; F. F. Bruce, 372–75; Andriessen and Lenglet, *Bib* 51 [1970] 232–33; among others; for attempts to appreciate a distinction between the three designations, see Westcott, 413; Riggenbach, 415; Casey, "Eschatology in Heb 12:14–29," 337–46). In the structure of the sentence, the qualifying phrase πόλει θεοῦ ζῶντος, "to the city of the living God," which is introduced by an appositional καί, "even," clarifies what is meant conceptually by

"Mount Zion" (see above, *Note* gg). The phrase Ἱερουσαλὴμ ἐπουρανίῳ, "to heavenly Jerusalem," stands in apposition to the preceding phrase, "to the city of the living God," strengthening the identification.

Behind the image evoked by the three designations there stands a rich biblical and apocalyptical tradition of the heavenly city. The biblical declaration that God laid the foundations of the city of Jerusalem on Mount Zion (e.g., Ps 47:9 [MT 48:8]; Ps 86[MT 87]:1–7; Isa 14:32 LXX) was extended to the foundations of the glorified heavenly city as well (e.g., Isa 28:16; 54:11–14 LXX), and this theological motif is echoed in later Jewish and Christian apocalyptic literature (e.g., Tob 13:7–18; 4 Ezra 10:27; *2 Apoc. Bar.* 4:1–6; Rev 21:10–14, 19–20). The city of God, "heavenly Jerusalem," furnished the writer with a fixed metaphor for the kingdom of God or the reign of God viewed comprehensively (see below on 12:28; cf. Ezek 48:35; Rev 3:12; 4 Ezra 7:26; 8:52; 10:60). The concept is distinctly eschatological (see further, K. L. Schmidt, *ErJb* 18 [1950] 207–48; de Young, *Jerusalem,* 28–57, 117–21, 138–45; Casey, "Eschatology in Heb 12:14–29," 338–46).

In Hebrews the motif of the city of God recurs under a variety of metaphors and is developed as a major theme. The writer refers to "the place" (11:8), "the heavenly homeland" (11:16), "the unshakable kingdom" (12:28), and "the abiding city which is to come" (13:14). The motif is elaborated through the related themes of pilgrimage and promise. The description of the city in 11:10, 16 indicates an objective reality prepared by God and ready to be revealed at an appropriate future time. Men and women of faith under both covenants are citizens of this city by virtue of the divine call and promise. The eschatological perspective introduced in 11:10, 13–16 is elaborated in 12:22*a.* "The city of the living God" is the transcendent "heavenly Jerusalem" that God creates (cf. Isa 65:17–25). The new covenant people of God are described in v 22*a* as the eschatological community that has already arrived at the gates of the heavenly Jerusalem and who are only waiting for the revelation of the "unshakable kingdom" (v 28) they are about to receive. Their characterization as pilgrims who have come to Mount Zion is made from the perspective of eschatological faith (cf. de Young, *Jerusalem,* 137–38, 141; Hofius, *Katapausis,* 147–49; Williamson, *Philo,* 268–76, 326–38).

The designation "city of the living God, heavenly Jerusalem" evokes the thought of the heavenly sanctuary or temple as well. Cody has observed that in the NT, when the idea of God present and meeting with his people is stressed, there is a strong tendency to prefer the temple symbolism. When the allusion is to the goal of pilgrimage in its social significance (the fellowship of the elect and the angels), writers prefer to use the symbol of the city, as in v 22*a* (*Heavenly Sanctuary,* 115, n. 65). The dignity of the city is enhanced by designating it "the city *of the living God.*" The genitive θεοῦ ζῶντος recalls the use of this terminology earlier in the homily when the writer warned of the peril of apostasy from "the living God" (3:12; 10:31). The God whom the apathetic members of the house church serve is alive and powerful and is accessible to them. It is to his city they have come.

The expression "heavenly Jerusalem" does not occur elsewhere in the NT (cf. Gal 4:26; Rev 21:2) nor in Jewish apocalyptic literature. Nevertheless, there can be no doubt that the metaphor was derived from the apocalyptic tradition (cf. Bietenhard, *Die himmlische Welt,* 192–204; Lohse. *TDNT,* 7:337, especially n. 287).

There has been a strong tendency to interpret the notion of the heavenly city in Hebrews from the perspective of the Platonic tradition as mediated by Philo (e.g., Cambier, *"Eschatologie,"* 24–27; Cody, *Heavenly Sanctuary,* 78–83; Schierse, *Verheissung,* 121–26; Thompson, *JBL* 94 [1975] 584; among others). In Philo, however, there is no concept of a heavenly city prepared by God that will be made visible in the new age. Philo concentrates on the etymology and the symbolism of the name "Jerusalem" rather than speaking of the city itself (cf. *On Dreams* 2.250; *Allegorical Interpretation* 3.83–84; for the key passage on the ideal city in Plato see *Republic* 9.592A, B). This is the decisive difference between the Greek philosophical treatment of the heavenly city and the biblical realism that informs the formulation of this theme in Hebrews (so K. L. Schmidt, *ErJb* 18 [1950] 217; de Young, *Jerusalem,* 121–22; Braun, "Das himmlischen Vaterland," 319–27, especially 323). In Hebrews the heavenly city is a transcendent reality that faithfully reflects the realism of the Jewish apocalyptic tradition as represented in 4 Ezra and 2 *Apocalypse of Baruch.* There is nothing abstract or contingent about the heavenly city in v 22*a*, which differs fundamentally from the philosophical concept in Philo (so also Windisch, 113; Barrett, "Eschatology," 375–76; Michel, 394; Casey, "Eschatology of Heb 12:14–29," 343–54).

22b–23a In the heavenly city a vast array of angels surrounds God, just as they did at Mount Sinai (see above on 2:2, which draws on Deut 33:2 LXX; cf. Acts 7:38, 53; Gal 3:19). Elaborating the vision of Mount Zion the writer declares: "you have come . . . καὶ μυριάσιν ἀγγέλων πανηγύρει [and to innumerable companies of angels, a festal gathering]." In the syntax of the sentence, πανηγύρει stands in apposition to the preceding phrase in v 22*b*, or is to be treated as a circumstantial dative relating to the preceding phrase ("and to innumerable companies of angels in festal gathering"; see the discussion of the syntactical question above, *Note* jj). The accent in the full expression falls on the density of the angelic population, as innumerable multitudes gather in plenary assembly for an exultant celebration of worship.

The term πανήγυρις, which occurs only here in the NT, has reference to a joyful gathering in order to celebrate a festival (see Spicq, *ST* 6 [1952] 30–38; Williamson *Philo,* 64–70). In the LXX the cognate verb, πανηγυρίζειν, is synonymous with ἑορτάζειν, "to celebrate a religious festival" (Isa 66:10 LXX; for close association with ἑορτή, "festival", see Amos 5:21; Hos 2:13; 9:5; Ezek 46:11 LXX). The gathering of the angels has a distinctively festive character to it. Drawing on the rich associations of the noun πανήγυρις with the celebrating of a great triumph, Spicq envisions the angels as engaged in "a joyful celebration of the victory achieved by Christ, a victory over sin (1:3) achieved by no other angelic being and by no other high priest" (2:407). The fervent joy in the gathering distinguishes the atmosphere of Zion from the terror that dispersed the Israelites at the foot of Sinai. This aspect of the vision of heavenly Jerusalem recalls the use in 4:9 of the rare term σαββατισμός, which refers to the festivity and praise of a sabbath celebration, to describe the future heavenly rest of the people of God. Heavenly Jerusalem is a place of blessing, where the redeemed can join with "angels and archangels, and with all the company of heaven" in celebratory worship of God.

Gathered with the angels are a company who are described as ἐκκλησία πρωτοτόκων ἀπογεγραμμένων ἐν οὐρανοῖς, "the assembly of the firstborn inscribed permanently in heaven." The use of ἐκκλησία to describe those gathered for celebratory worship was anticipated in 2:12, where the writer cited Ps 21:23 LXX in reference to those whom Jesus came to consecrate to the service of God: "I will declare your name to my brothers, in the midst of *the assembly* [ἐκκλησίας] I will sing praises to you." The term is thus used in v 23a in the nontechnical sense of "a gathering" or "an assembly" of the redeemed people of God (Michel, 463–64). The reference sustains the note of joy and fellowship in worship introduced with v 22b and indicates that the redeemed take their place in the festive assembly at Zion. What is striking, as Westcott already noted, is that here angels and the people of God are "no longer separated as at Sinai, by signs of great terror, but united in one vast assembly" (415; cf. Michel, 463–64; P. E. Hughes, 552–54).

This union of angels and the people of the covenant in a liturgical fellowship has led some interpreters to refer to Qumran, where there was an awareness of the presence of angels with the community and a vital interest in the angelic liturgy (e.g., Spicq, 2:406; F. F. Bruce, 375; Gärtner, *Temple*, 89–94; cf. J. Strugnell, "The Angelic Liturgy at Qumrân—4Q Serek Šîrôt 'Ôlat Haššabāt," In *Congress Volume, Oxford, 1959*, VTSup 7 [Leiden: Brill, 1960] 318–45). There are, however, between the texts at Qumran (e.g., 1QS 11:8–9; and especially 1QM 12:1–9) and vv 22b–23a important distinctions that need to be observed (see further, G. Klinzing, *Die Umdeutung des Kultus in der Qumrangemeinde und im Neven Testament*, SUNT 7 [Göttingen: Vandenhoeck & Ruprecht, 1971] 201–2, who argues that both Qumran and the writer of Hebrews have adopted, with differences, a common Jewish apocalyptic tradition).

The identification of the "assembly" as the company of the redeemed has not gone unchallenged. Appeal has been made to isolated texts in the OT (Ps 82:1; 88:6 LXX) and early Christian literature (*Herm. Vis.* 3.4.1; Clement of Alexandria, *Extracts of Theodotus* 27.3–5) to argue that the phrase ἐκκλησία πρωτοτόκων, "assembly of the firstborn," is actually a title of majesty referring to the highest angels as the "first-created" (πρωτόκτιστοι) of God's creative activity. Corresponding to the threefold characterization of Mount Zion, it is argued, is a threefold reference to the hosts of heaven: "innumerable companies of angels, a festal gathering, and an assembly of the firstborn" (so Käsemann, *Das wandernde Gottesvolk*, 28, 126; Spicq, 2:407–8; H. Montefiore, 231). The qualifying phrase ἀπογεγραμμένων ἐν οὐρανοῖς, "permanently inscribed in heaven," however, is a strong indication that the reference is to the redeemed, since this expression is never used of angels.

Lécuyer has shown that the entire formulation in v 23a is rooted in the description of Israel in the Pentateuch. The Israelites are designated the ἐκκλησία, "congregation," in Deut 4:10; 18:16 LXX (cf. Acts 7:38), while the occasion when God addressed the people at Sinai is called ἡμέρα ἐκκλησίας, "the day of the gathering," in Deut 4:10; 9:10; 18:16 LXX. The title πρωτότοκοι, "firstborn," was given to the Israelites when God brought them out of Egypt in order to lead them to Sinai (Exod 4:22–23 LXX; cf. Jer 31:9; Sir 36:11 LXX). Moreover, their names were written in the heavenly register (Exod 32:32–33 LXX; cf. Ps 69:29; Isa 4:3; Dan 12:1 LXX) (Lécuyer, "Ecclesia Primitivorum (Hébr. 12,23)," 161–68; so also Westcott, 415; Riggenbach, 416–17; Michel, 464; F. F. Bruce, 376–77; P. E. Hughes, 554–55; Andriessen and Lenglet, *Bib* 51 [1970] 233–34; among others). "Firstborn" in the plural is an apocalyptic title applied to the redeemed community (e.g., *Jub.* 2:20; 4 Ezra

6:58; cf. Michel, 464–65; Helyer, *StudBibTheol* 6 [1976] 15–16, 20; Marshall, *Kept by the Power of God*, 148, recognized in v 23*a* an allusion to Ps 87:5–6; the identification, unfortunately, depends upon the formulation of the MT, which at this point differs considerably from the LXX, the version customarily used by the writer).

The fixed metaphor of a heavenly book or register into which the names of people are inscribed or blotted out is rooted in the OT (Exod 32:33; Ps 68[MT 69]:29; Isa 4:13; Dan 12:1 LXX) and is common in apocalyptic literature (e.g., *Jub.* 2:20; *1 Enoch* 47:3–4; 104:1; 108:3) and in the NT (Luke 10:20; Phil 4:3; Rev 3:5; 13:8; 17:8; 20:12) (cf. Nötscher, *RevQ* 1 [1958–59] 405–11). The phrase occurs in the context of judgment (e.g., Dan 12:1; Rev 3:5; 20:12). The detail that the names of the firstborn are permanently inscribed (stressing the perfect tense of ἀπογεγραμμένων) has reference to those who in some sense have stood in judgment and have experienced acquittal or vindication. As Helyer observes, "the vindication and sovereignty of the one who for a little while was made lower than the angels, but now is exalted at God's right hand, is shared by his church" (*StudBibTheol* 6 [1976] 22; cf. de Young, *Jerusalem*, 140).

The expression in v 23*a* can be used in regard to those who are still on earth (Luke 10:20). Consequently, it has been suggested that the reference in v 23*a* is to men and women of faith whose names are inscribed in the heavenly archives but who are not themselves in heaven, in distinction from the company of the redeemed who have died who are mentioned in v 23*c* (so Michel, 464–65; Michaelis, *TDNT* 6:881; Buchanan, 223; Casey, "Eschatology in Heb 12:14–29," 363–65). The assembly in view, however, is an eschatological or heavenly gathering. It is better, therefore, to recognize that the vision has reference to "the ultimate, completed company of the people of God, membership of which is now enjoyed by faith" (Peterson, "A Examination'," 282).

In 1:6 Jesus was designated by the honorific title ὁ πρωτότοκος, "the Firstborn." It is through their relationship to him who is "the Firstborn par excellence" that the redeemed have become the "firstborn" heirs of God (so F. F. Bruce, 377; cf. Michel, 464, Helyer, *StudBibTheol* 6 [1976] 13). Those who have become ἀδελφοί, "brothers [and sisters]," (2:11, 17) or μέτοχοι, "partners" (3:14) with him share in the blessings he secured. In contrast to Esau, who disparaged his legacy, τὰ πρωτοτόκια, "the inheritance rights of the firstborn," and forfeited his right to the blessing (12:16–17), this company consists of those who persevere in faith and so secure the inheritance and the objective blessings associated with it (so Helyer, 16, who insists that the reference to Esau in 12:16–17 should not be overlooked in the interpretation of v 23*a*).

The assembly of the firstborn is constituted of all those who ultimately will enjoy the privileges of the πρωτότοκα, i.e., faithful men and women of both the old and new covenants who will comprise "the first-born citizens of heaven" (NEB). By virtue of their faith, the members of the community addressed have come to the heavenly Jerusalem in the company of a vast multitude of believers from all ages. This conforms to the perspective of Hebrews that the Church is historically and intentionally rooted in a relationship to men and women of faith under the old covenant (11:13–16, 39–12:2; so F. F. Bruce, 376–77; P. E. Hughes, 547–49, 554–55; Helyer, *StudBibTheol* 6 [1976] 13–17).

23b In the enumeration of seven images that create a vision of the heavenly city to which Christians have come, the writer places in the center the phrase καὶ κριτῇ θεῷ πάντων, "and to a Judge who is God of all." On the assumption that the word order is deliberate (see above, *Note* ll), the initial term, "to a Judge," is in the emphatic position. The formula is confessional in character. It acknowledges God as Judge and Creator. The initial expression evokes an eschatological perspective, namely, the prospect of standing in the immediate presence of God as Judge. As such, it provides a powerful motivation for responding to the stern warning to be addressed in v 25: "See that you do not disregard the one who is speaking." The qualifying phrase θεῷ πάντων, "to the one who is God of all," vindicates his rights as Creator (2:10; 11:3) over the whole human family. This confession is informed by the biblical revelation where there is no separation between God who creates, governs, and scrutinizes as Judge. These mighty acts of God complement each other (Michel, 466; cf. Spicq, 2:408).

The writer views this heavenly convocation as in some sense convened for scrutiny or judgment. Throughout the homily he has focused the attention of the house church on the prospect of such an encounter with God (2:2–3; 4:13; 6:8; 9:27; 10:26–31; 11:6; 13:4). For the Christian who has "trampled upon the Son of God and who has treated the blood of the covenant, by which he was consecrated, as defiled, and who has insulted the Spirit of grace" there exists "only an inevitable, terrifying expectation of judgment" (10:26–29). The writer had warned the recipients of his sermon that "it is terrifying to fall into the hands of the living God" (10:31). However, for those who have been "decisively purged" and "consecrated" to God by the sacrificial death of Jesus (10:10, 14) and who "hold firm to the end the basic position" they had at the beginning (3:14), there remains the certainty of eschatological acceptance. The festive associations of πανηγύρει, "to a festal gathering," in the immediate context are reassuring; they imply an approving judgment for the assembled multitude (Dumbrell, *EvQ* 48 [1976] 158–59).

In an early strand of the Jewish apocalyptic tradition, Sinai was interpreted eschatologically as the site of God's future judgement (*1 Enoch* 1:3–9). In 4 Ezra, however, a source more nearly contemporary with Hebrews, the mountain of judgment is Zion, although the judge is identified by God as "my son" (4 Ezra 13:1–39, especially vv 6–7, 25–39). The elaborate apocalyptic description of the judgment in 4 Ezra 13 throws into bold relief the restraint in the writer's reference to the supreme Judge who is God of all.

An intimate relationship exists between the reference to the presence of God in his office as Judge and the allusion to καὶ πνεύμασι δικαίων τετελειωμένων, "and to the spirits of the righteous persons made perfect." The juxtaposition of the two phrases in v 23*b* implies God's powerful intervention in his fallen creation. Between the description of God as Judge and Creator and of Jesus as mediator of the new covenant, the writer inserts a reference to those who enjoy the presence of God in the heavenly city. In Jewish apocalyptic literature the expression "spirits [or souls] of righteous persons" is an idiom for the godly dead (e.g., *Jub.* 23:30–31; *1 Enoch* 22:9; 102:4; 103:3–4; *2 Apoc. Bar.* 30:2). In v 23*b* the expression πνεύμασι δικαίων, "the spirits of righteous persons," refers to those who have died (BAGD 810) but who now inhabit the heavenly city that is the goal of the pilgrimage of godly men and women under both covenants (11:10, 13–16; 13:14). The choice of this designation for those righteous persons who have died and who now enjoy the divine presence is consistent with the writer's use of the old biblical expression ὁ πατὴρ τῶν πνευμάτων, "the Father of spirits," in 12:9 (cf. Num 16:22; 27:16 LXX). That description contemplates God in his character as the one to whom the heavenly realm is subject (cf. Kuss, 112; Schweizer, *TDNT* 6:445–46; 7:141). The formulation in v 23*b* has a distant parallel in *1 Enoch* 39:4–8, which speaks of the dwelling of the righteous in the heavenly world together with the righteous angels under the protection of "the Lord of spirits."

The fact that these persons are described as τετελειωμένων, "made perfect," indicates that they lack nothing in their relationship with God. The use of the perfect participle implies the stable and definitive character of their condition (Spicq, 2:408–9). The participle can be understood eschatologically, in reference to those who have already passed through judgment (cf. 9:27) and have obtained the verdict that they are righteous, or soteriologically, in reference to those who have been decisively purged and consecrated to God by the sacrificial death of Jesus (so Michel, 466–68, who argues that both perspectives must be maintained).

The key to the interpretation of the participle, however, must be supplied by the writer's prior use of the verb τελειοῦσθαι. The verb is used specifically with reference to all who have been "perfected" by the sacrifice of Jesus in 10:14. The description of the righteous dead in v 23*b* as τετελειωμένων reinforces the declaration in 10:14 that Jesus "by means of one sacrifice perfected [τετελείωκεν] forever those who are being consecrated to God." That the participle is used in v 23*b* rather than the adjective "perfect" (τελείων) decisively favors the soteriological interpretation of the expression (following Peterson, "Examination," 284–86).

It is equally important to interpret the descriptive term δίκαιοι, "righteous," from the perspective of Hebrews. The citation of Hab 2:4 LXX in Heb 10:38*a* makes explicit that those in this group are δίκαιοι, "righteous," because their lives reflected the faith of which God approves (cf. also 11:4). This qualification pertains to Christians (10:39) as well as to faithful men and women of the old covenant. The expression πνεύμασι δικαίων in v 23*b* is inclusive of all who have died exhibiting true faith. It is unnecessary to restrict their number to those valiant for faith in the period prior to Christ (F. F. Bruce, 378; cf. Delling, *TDNT* 8:83) or to Christians who have died (Michel, 467). It embraces all those attested by God as faithful under both covenants who have been "perfected" on the basis of Jesus' sacrifice. The formulation takes account of the declaration in 11:40 that attested witnesses to the vitality of faith under the old covenant should experience the realization of their hope in fellowship with Christians (P. E. Hughes, 516; cf. also Spicq, 2:408–9; Casey, "Eschatology in Heb 12:14–29," 372–73; Peterson, "Examination," 286–88).

Christians enjoy the objective blessings of the new covenant already in this life. It was necessary, however, for the people under the old covenant to wait until their transfer to the heavenly city, which is the direct result of the accomplished sacrifice of Jesus in his office as high priest. It is probable that this transfer to the heavenly city is what is described in the expression "the better resurrection" in 11:35 (cf. Peterson, "Examination," 287–88). They take their place in the heavenly Jerusalem as those whose faith was oriented toward the work of Christ (so Grässer, *Glaube*, 47).

The relationship between the vast multitude designated in v 22*b* as "the assembly of the firstborn inscribed permanently in heaven" and this company can now be clarified. The earlier description alludes to the whole people of God, the eschatological assembly in its ultimate and complete state, gathered for the encounter with God, while those to whom reference is made in v 23b are the aggregate of faithful men and women who have already died and faced their judgment (9:27), having been "perfected" on the ground of Jesus' high priestly offering (10:14). The intervening reference to "a Judge who is God of all" clarifies why the same group of people needed to be described from a different point of view. It is the fact of death and vindication by the supreme Judge that is stressed in the distinctive formulation of v 23b (so Peterson, "Examination," 283, 286–88; cf. Dumbrell, *EvQ* 48 [1976] 158, who refers to a "staged progression" in vv 22–24, and suggests that the formal approval for which the assembly of v 22b convenes is expressed in the subsequent phrase, "the spirits of righteous persons made perfect").

24 In two parallel clauses the writer finally presents the ground and the reason for this festal gathering on Mount Zion. He introduces Jesus, mediator of the new covenant, and alludes graphically to his sacrificial death by which the eschatological, final covenant was sealed and eternal redemption was secured for his people (cf. 9:11–15). By pointing to Jesus in his office as mediator of a better, more effective covenant (8:6) the writer provides the balancing contrast to Moses, mediator of the old covenant, terrified and trembling in the presence of God (v 21). The use of the personal name "Jesus" is significant. It places the emphasis upon the full humanity of Jesus, who in his historical existence was qualified for his mediatorial office through the suffering of death on behalf of the redeemed community (2:9–10; 9:28). The final two images furnish the climax to vv 22–24 and serve to situate the entire vision of the heavenly city in a salvation-historical and covenantal perspective. It is essential to integrate all of the images in terms of the explicit reference to the new covenant in v 24a (rightly stressed by Dumbrell, *EvQ* 48 [1976] 157).

The members of the house church have come διαθήκης νέας μεσίτη Ἰησοῦ, "and to Jesus, mediator of a new covenant." Consistent with his practice throughout the homily, the writer builds suspense in his statement by deferring the name of the mediator to the end of the phrase for emphasis: "to the mediator of the new covenant—Jesus" (cf. 2:9; 3:1; 6:20; 7:22; 10:19; 12:2; 13:20). In Hebrews the term μεσίτης, "mediator," is always used in association with the new covenant of Jer 31:31–34 (8:6; 9:15; 12:24). As the mediator of the new covenant, Jesus is its guarantor. The identification of Jesus as the mediator of the new covenant resumes the significant theme of Jesus' death as covenant sacrifice in 9:14–26, and more specifically in 9:14–15:

> seeing that he offered himself through the eternal Spirit as an unblemished sacrifice to God. And for this reason he is the mediator of a new covenant.

Jesus' office as mediator is predicated upon the efficacy of his redemptive death. He is the mediator of a new covenant because he entered the heavenly sanctuary and obtained eternal redemption (9:11–14). This theme is introduced in 9:11–15, is elaborated in 10:15–18, and comes to expression once more in the parallel clauses of v 24.

The description of Jesus as mediator of the new covenant in v 24a and the figurative allusion to his death as covenant sacrifice in v 24b presuppose the necessary connection between sacrifice and covenant ratification (9:15–22). The cultic metaphor in the expression καὶ αἵματι ραντισμοῦ, "and to sprinkled blood," is based formally on the Pentateuchal expression ὕδωρ ραντισμοῦ, "sprinkled water," in Num 19:9, 13, 20, 21 LXX (cf. Heb 9:13–14). The phrase in v 24*b* recalls the account in Exod 24:8, where the sprinkling of the blood of the sacrifice sealed the covenant between God and his people. Just as Moses inaugurated the covenant concluded at Sinai in the blood of the sacrifice, so also was the new covenant activated through the blood of sacrifice (Casey, "Eschatology in Heb 12:14–29," 375–77).

The cultic metaphor in v 24*b* must be interpreted in the light of the explicit reference to the new covenant in v 24*a*; the reference is to the blood of the covenant that is applied ("sprinkled") for the purgation of defilement. The expression recalls 9:19–21, where reference is made to the ritual sprinkling of blood at the ratification of the old covenant. It also evokes 10:22 where the effect of the new covenant in the lives of Christians is described metaphorically as ρεραντισμένοι τὰς καρδίας ἀπὸ συνειδήσεως πονηρᾶς, "seeing that our hearts have been sprinkled clean from a burdened conscience." The writer found in the ritual of sprinkling blood, which accompanied covenant ratification, a powerful metaphor. The death of Christ, which secured for the community the objective blessings of the covenant, was a covenant sacrifice.

Resorting to personification for rhetorical affect, the writer declares that Christians have come αἵματι ραντισμοῦ κρεῖττον λαλοῦντι παρὰ τὸν Ἄβελ, "to sprinkled blood speaking more effectively than the blood of Abel." The personification of blood is striking because it serves to recall the writer's view of blood as a highly potent medium of purgation in chaps. 9–10. In that context, reference to the blood of Christ was a fixed metaphor for Jesus' sacrificial death on the cross (cf. Johnsson, "Defilement," 363). As the community reflects on the significance of the vision of the heavenly city to which they have come, they must begin to appreciate the import of the witness of Christ's death *to them.*

The comparison in the latter half of v 24*b* presupposes the factor of the violent death of an innocent person. The allusion to "the blood of Abel" is recognizably a reference to his death. "Cain attacked his brother and killed him" (Gen 4:8 LXX). According to Gen 4:10–12, the blood of Abel cries out to God for the avenging of his murder, and this motif was frequently echoed in the later Jewish tradition (e.g., *Jub.* 4:3; *1 Enoch* 22:6–7; *T. Benj.* 7:3–5; 4 Macc 18:11; Ps.-Philo, *Bib. Ant.* 16.2; *Tg. Neof. 1* Gen 4:10; *m. Sanh.* 4:5; *b. Sanh.* 37b). The shedding of Abel's blood is associated with the imposing of a curse (Gen 4:11–12). The death of Jesus was also a violent affair (12:2–3) despite the innocence of the victim (4:15; 7:26). In this instance, however, it is associated with the securing of blessing. The ratification of the new covenant on the ground of Jesus' death secured for the Church the promised blessings attached to that covenant (8:6, 10–12; 10:15–18). It is to this gracious provision of God for his people in the present time that the "sprinkled blood continues to speak more effectively than the blood of Abel."

The notion of Abel "speaking" was introduced in 11:4 in reference to his faith: "and by faith he is still speaking, although he died." In that context all of the emphasis falls on the fact that it is *by his faith,* and not by his blood, that Abel continues to speak. The allusion is not to Gen 4:10, which speaks of the cry of Abel's blood from the ground for retribution, or even reconciliation (cf. Spicq,

2:343), but to the record of God's approval of his integrity and his sacrifice in Gen 4:4. It is significant that in 11:4 and 12:24 the writer does not use the verb βοᾶν, "to cry out," as in Gen 4:10 LXX, but the verb λαλεῖν, "to speak," which in Hebrews is never used of speaking to God. What the writer affirms in 11:4 is that Abel's faith continues to speak *to us* through the written record of his action in Scripture, which exhibits the exemplary character of his offering. Similarly, in 12:24b the reference is to what the blood of Abel has to say *to us* through the written record concerning his death in Scripture, which declares that it was unable to effect reconciliation (cf. Baarlink, *GTT* 74 [1974] 75–78).

On the basis of an analysis of κρείττων, "better," "more effective," in Heb 7:19; 8:6; 9:23, Baarlink has shown that the idiom κρείττων παρά in v 24b denotes an opposition ("more effectively than"). Christ's blood accomplishes what Abel's blood could not achieve. It is in this sense that it "speaks more effectively" of accomplished redemption and reconciliation (*GTT* 74 [1974] 83–86; cf. Casey, "Eschatology in Heb 12:14–29," 377–79, who shows that κρείττων is used in Hebrews characteristically of the new order and of all that is entailed in the new covenant). It "speaks" in the idiom of grace rather than of vengeance (2:9). It "speaks" of Jesus' adequacy in securing full salvation for all who draw near to God through him (7:25; 9:15). It declares that the way into the heavenly sanctuary is open so that God may be approached now through faith (4:16; 10:19–21); ultimately the people of God will enter his immediate presence (12:22–23). The voice that "speaks" at Zion, in sharp contrast to the frightening "sound of words" at Sinai (12:19b), provides a strong incentive for Christians to hold fast their confession "without wavering" (3:6) (following Peterson, "Examination," 289–90).

It must be acknowledged that the reference to Abel in v 24b is unexpected, because it does not belong to the developed comparison between Sinai and Zion. It may have been suggested by the reference in v 23b to the presence of πνεύμασι δικαίων, "the spirits of righteous persons," in the heavenly city, since the writer had specified in 11:4 that Abel was attested by God as δίκαιος, "righteous." It may also have been the writer's intention to evoke the whole history of redemption, from the righteous Abel to the redemptive sacrifice of Jesus, mediator of the new covenant (cf. Casey, "Eschatology in Heb 12:14–29," 380–82).

The emphasis in v 24 falls on the realization of the eschatological covenant through the death and exaltation of Jesus. The presence in the heavenly city of Jesus, the mediator of the new covenant whose blood speaks more effectively than the blood of Abel, provides assurance that those who pursue peace and holiness (v 14) will be welcomed. Entrance into the city, however, is conditioned on the acknowledgment of covenant obligation. It calls for allegiance and obedience as the response of gratitude to the objective blessings secured by Jesus.

25 The transition from exposition in vv 18–24 to exhortation in vv 25–29 is abrupt. It is achieved by the literary device of a "hook word." The participle λαλοῦντι, "speaking," in v 24b is repeated with only slight variation in v 25a, τὸν λαλοῦντα, "the one speaking." There is a sharp change in tone as the writer resumes the expression of urgent concern that characterizes vv 14–17. In this instance, however, the sternness of the parenetic warning is justified by the detailing of the privileged status of Christians in the preceding paragraph. They have a qualitatively greater responsibility than Israel did to listen attentively to the voice of God. Those who deliberately ignore the eschatological revelation of

God through his Son and who show contempt for the blessings of the new covenant cannot possibly escape judgment. The concluding paragraph consists of a sober caution to listen to what God is saying, a concentration of his word in the form of prophecy, and a final admonition to respond appropriately with gratitude and worship.

A tendency toward apathy or complacency is sharply rebuked with the oratorical imperative βλέπετε μὴ παραιτήσησθε τὸν λαλοῦντα, "Be careful that you do not disregard the one who is speaking." The form of the statement recalls 3:12, where the imperative βλέπετε, "Be careful," followed by a negative particle, introduced a trenchant warning against apostasy. Here the imperative is followed by the negative particle with the verb in the subjunctive mood and functions as a cautionary prohibition: "See that you do not disregard." The content of the injunction is supplied by the idiom παραιτεῖσθαι τινά, "to refuse or disregard someone." In distinction from the use of the verb παραιτεῖσθαι in v 19b, where the syntax of the clause shows that it signifies "to beg" that something not be done (see *Comment* on 12:19), the idiom carries a pronounced negative nuance (BAGD 616). It connotes a deliberate and culpable refusal to listen to the one speaking (Casey, "Eschatology in Heb 12:14–29," 510–11).

The motif of "speaking" that was introduced in v 24b is carried forward rhetorically in v 25 with references to τὸν λαλοῦντα, "the one who is speaking," in v 25a, and to τὸν χρηματίζοντα, "the one who warns," in v 25bc. The obliqueness of these expressions demands that careful attention be given to the detail of the text. Although it has been inferred that reference is given to at least two speakers, i.e., one who warned "on earth" and the other who warned "from heaven," the writer himself makes it clear in v 26a that only a single speaker is in view. The structure of the complex sentence in vv 25–26 supports this understanding.

Reference to the Present	*Reference to the Past*
25a μὴ παραιτήσησθε τὸν λαλοῦντα "Do not disregard the one who is speaking"	
25b	ἐπὶ γῆς παραιτησάμενοι τὸν χρηματίζοντα "they disregarded the one who warned them on earth"
25c τὸν ἀπ᾽ οὐρανῶν "the one who warns us from heaven"	
26a	οὗ ἡ φωνὴ τὴν γῆν ἐσάλευσεν τότε, νῦν δὲ ἐπήγγελται "whose voice shook the earth at that time, but now has promised"

The one who is speaking now to the members of the house church, whose warning originates from heaven, is the one who in the past issued his warning from earth and whose voice shook the earth "at that time" (so also Andriessen, *En lisant,* 55).

Reference is made in vv 25–26a to two different revelational events, the speaking that took place at Sinai (cf. v 19a: "a sound of words"; v 19b: "no further

message") and that which is intrinsic to Christian experience. The antithesis in
v 25bc between the spatial categories of earth ("warned on earth") and heaven
("warned from heaven") is complemented by the temporal perspective of "then"
and "now" in v 26a. The first event of speaking is clearly to be identified with the
old covenant, the second with the new (cf. Casey, "Eschatology in Heb 12:14–29,"
511, 515, 518). The writer's intention is to draw the consequence of the contrast
he has developed in vv 18–24 between the old covenant and the new in terms of
the effect of the two distinct events of speaking. The expressions "on earth" and
"from heaven" are used in a local.sense to indicate the sphere of the old covenant and the new covenant, respectively (so Spicq, 2:411; Michel, 471–72; F. F.
Bruce, 381; P. E. Hughes, 536).

Although the speaker who warned (τὸν χρηματίζοντα) Israel on earth (v 25b)
has commonly been identified as Moses (e.g., Moffatt, 220; W. Manson, 159;
Vanhoye, La structure, 208; Sowers, Hermeneutics, 129; Buchanan, 224), there is
little warrant for that opinion. The verb χρηματίζειν, "to warn" (in the sense of
uttering an oracle or a royal decree [see Reicke, TDNT 9:482]), is never used in
the NT of any human being. It is used on two other occasions in Hebrews, and
in each instance the reference is to a divine message delivered by God: Moses was
warned (κεχρημάτισται) to construct the tabernacle according to the pattern God
showed him on Mount Sinai (8:5); similarly, Noah was warned (by God)
(χρηματισθείς [a theological passive]) of the impending flood (11:7). According
to Deut 5:23–24 LXX, it was God who spoke to Israel, not Moses. The same impression is conveyed by Exod 20:18–20 LXX (A. T. Hanson, SE 2 [1964] 403–4).
The writer has already insisted that it was God's voice that Israel subsequently
chose to disregard in the wilderness (3:7–11, 16–18); it was his voice (καὶ φωνῇ
ῥημάτων, "and to a voice speaking words") that warned the terrified Israelites of
covenant obligation (12:19a). Moreover, the voice (ἡ φωνή) that shook the earth
"at that time" (v 26a) was clearly the divine voice that was heard at Sinai (cf. Casey,
"Eschatology in Heb 12:4–29," 512–13).

An alternative proposal has been to identify the speaker with Jesus, on the
basis of the reference in v 24b to "sprinkled blood speaking more effectively than
that of Abel" (A. T. Hanson, SE 2 [1964] 403–5; A. Feuillet, SE 2 [1964] 377; cf.
Kosmala, Hebräer, Essener, Christen, 124; Sowers, Hermeneutics, 129). A. T. Hanson,
for example, argues that Christ is the one who spoke on earth at Sinai as well
as the one speaking now from heaven (403–5). This conclusion fails to appreciate the sharp delineation the writer has drawn between the encounter with God
under the old covenant and that which occurs as a result of Jesus' unique
sacrifice through which he became the mediator and guarantor of the new covenant.

It is necessary to recognize that the text gains in clarity when the speaker is
identified as God, whose voice shook the earth at Sinai, who swore that those
who broke covenant would not enter his rest (3:7–11), who promised that he
would establish a new covenant with the house of Israel (8:6–12), and who now
continues to speak to the new covenant community through his Son (1:1–2a) (so
Westcott, 418; Moffatt, 220; Riggenbach, 424; Windisch, 114–15; Spicq, 2:410–
11; F. F. Bruce, 381, n. 193; Andriessen and Lenglet, Bib 51 [1970] 236; among
others). The sermon prepared for the house church began with a majestic sentence declaring that God has spoken (ἐλάλησεν) his final word through his Son

(1:1–2*a*). This significant theological motif is elaborated in 3:7–4:13, where the fact of God's speaking *at the present time* is driven home by the recurring refrain, "Today, if you hear his voice, do not harden your heart" (3:7–8*a*, 15; 4:7, citing Ps 94[MT 95]:7 LXX). The sermon is brought to its pastoral climax with the cautionary admonition in v 25*a*, "Be careful you do not disregard the one who is speaking."

This understanding is confirmed when it is observed that the reasoning in v 25*bc* is formally similar to the first of the several warning passages in the homily, 2:1–4. The argument presupposes as axiomatic that the response to any message must take into account the dignity and competence of the one who is speaking. In response to the declaration that God has spoken through his Son, the writer deduces, "We must pay the closest attention, therefore, to what we have heard" (2:1). What follows is an appeal based on a comparison (*syncrisis*): since the word spoken at Sinai proved to be valid, and every infringement and disobedience was appropriately punished, a disregard for the word preached to the community must inevitably be catastrophic (2:2–3*a*). The argument reflects a recurring theme in the homily, namely, the superior basis for responsible commitment to God under the new covenant as compared to the old and the appropriately greater certainty that those who disregard their covenantal relationship with God will be severely punished. This argument is developed in 10:28–31, is reinforced in 12:18–24, and is presupposed in the formulation of v 25*bc* (cf. Riggenbach, 421; Swetnam, *CBQ* 30 [1968] 233–34; Casey, "Eschatology in Heb 12:14–29," 517–18).

The formulation of v 25*b*, εἰ γὰρ ἐκεῖνοι οὐκ ἐξέφυγον ἐπὶ γῆς παραιτησάμενοι τὸν χρηματίζοντα, "Since those did not escape when they disregarded the one who warned them on earth," is informed by 3:16–18. In 3:16 the writer alludes to those who "heard and rebelled" (ἀκούσαντες παρεπίκραναν), who are identified as "all those whom Moses led out of Egypt." They are further described in 3:18 as "those who refused to obey" (τοῖς ἀπειθήσασιν). It is clear from the context that it was subsequent to Sinai and the issuing of the warning concerning covenant obligation that Israel rebelled against God and refused to obey him. They discovered that the curse sanctions attached to the covenant were effective when they died in the wilderness (3:19).

That scenario is resumed in v 25*b* and fortifies the rhetorical question in v 25*c*, πολὺ μᾶλλον ἡμεῖς οἱ τὸν ἀπ᾽ οὐρανῶν ἀποστρεφόμενοι, "how much less will we, if we reject the one who warns us from heaven?" The article τόν resumes the full expression from the protasis, τὸν χρηματίζοντα, "the one who warns," and indicates that Christians also face covenant obligation. In their case it is the whole eschatological scene in vv 22–24 that provides the basis for warning. The nature of the salvation offered to the community poses both a greater responsibility and danger. If properly understood, the warning from heaven is more ominous than any comparable warning from earth. The warning presupposes the qualitatively superior character of the Christian message, recalling 1:1–2*a* and 2:1–4. This makes the comparison with the solemn warning at Sinai judicious (cf. Hillmann, *BibLeb* 1 [1960] 249; Braun, *TLZ* 96 [1971] 325).

The form of the argument is precisely that of 2:2–3*a*, with only slight variation. Adopting the singular reading of P⁴⁶, which omits the relative pronoun οἱ in v 25*c* (see above, *Note* ww), the phrasing is parallel:

2:3a   ἡμεῖς ... ἀμελήσαντες
        "if we disregard"
12:25c ἡμεῖς ... ἀποστρεφόμενοι
        "if we reject"

The use of the first person plural ἡμεῖς, "we," in v 25c is consistent with the writer's practice when applying exposition to his audience. Here, however, the argument is strengthened by the use of ἀποστρέφειν to denote the rejection of the covenant relationship. A stronger term than παραιτεῖσθαι, "to disregard," that is used to express Israel's foolish neglect of covenant obligation, it is descriptive of a catastrophic turning away from God and a rejection of his salvation (cf. Riggenbach, 423; Casey, "Eschatology in Heb 12:14–29," 518). The use of the present tense in the participle implies a real and pressing danger. The writer does not say that the rejection of God is an accomplished fact (as argued by Westcott, 419) but that it is a possibility that threatens the existence of the community. In v 25 the writer addresses an urgent final warning to the members of the house church not to reject God's word, which is being spoken to them now from heaven.

26 The temporal perspective from which the writer addressed his audience is sharply defined in v 26 in the contrast established by the adjacent terms τότε, νῦν δέ, "at that time, but now." The earth was shaken *then*, but *now* the heavenly voice has promised a dynamic future event. The contrast juxtaposes the time of Sinai (τότε) with an eschatological shaking, which is promised now (νῦν) as a result of the inauguration of the new covenant (see P. Tachau, *"Einst" und "Jetzt" im Neuen Testament*, FRLANT 105 [Göttingen: Vandenhoeck & Ruprecht, 1972] 91). It is actually necessary to distinguish in v 26 three distinct moments: the past event of Sinai, the present moment of the promise, and the announcement of a future shaking that will affect not only the earth but heaven as well.

With reference to the past it is said, ἡ φωνὴ τὴν γῆν ἐσάλευσεν τότε, "at that time his voice shook the earth." The statement looks retrospectively at vv 18–21, and it is natural to recall the description of a volcanic eruption in Exod 19:18 MT that the "the whole mountain trembled violently." According to Exod 19:18 LXX, however, which presumably was the text the writer had before him, "all the people trembled." It is better, therefore, to recognize an allusion to Judg 5:4–5 LXX: "the earth trembled [ἐσείσθη] ... the mountain shook [ἐσαλεύθησον] before the Lord, the One of Sinai, before the Lord, the God of Israel" (cf. also Ps 67[MT 68:8]:9; 76[MT 77:18]:19; 113[MT 114]:7 LXX). Michel has observed that a NT writer will often prefer the paraphrases of the Psalms to the more sober report of past events in the Pentateuch (472). It is the poetic accounts of Sinai in the Song of Deborah in Judg 5 or in the Psalter that appear to have contributed the significant term σαλεύειν, "to shake," in vv 26a, 27, and which suggested the cognate term ἀσάλευτον, "unshakable," in v 28 (see especially Vanhoye, *Bib* 45 [1964] 250–53, who calls attention to Ps 95[MT 96]:9–11). The restraint in v 26a distinguishes the writer from the contemporary apocalyptic tradition, where the Sinai earthquake has become a cosmic event: "There you bent the sky, shook the earth, moved the round world, made the depths shudder, and turned creation upside down" (4 Ezra 3:18).

The present is conditioned by the promise of God: νῦν δὲ ἐπήγγελται, "but now he has promised." It is the distinctive understanding of the writer that Christians on earth possess the realities of which God has spoken in the form of promise (see above 4:1; 9:15). In Hebrews the subject of the verb ἐπαγγελίζεσθαι is exclusively God (6:13; 10:23; 11:11); the writer grounds the certainty of the realization of the promise in the reliability of God (10:23; 11:11). What God promised to the fathers he has repeated with assurance to the people of the new covenant.

In v 26*b* the perfect tense of the verb indicates that the act of promising stood in the past, but the promise has been brought into the present by the event of God's speaking now (see above, *Note* yy). In this context the concept of promise assumes the nuanced aspect of warning, for the content of the promise concerns the certainty of a future shaking of heaven and earth. The temporal aspect of v 26*b* is to be stressed; the promise impinges upon the present (cf. Theissen, *Untersuchungen*, 93, who acknowledges the temporal aspect in the text and argues that the spatial categories in v 25 serve as grounding for the urgent expectation announced in v 26).

The future is informed by what God has promised to do: ἔτι ἅπαξ ἐγὼ σείσω οὐ μόνον τὴν γῆν ἀλλὰ καὶ τὸν οὐρανόν, "Once again I will shake not only the earth but also the heaven." The writer found in the shaking of the earth at Sinai (v 26*a*) a proleptic event anticipating an eschatological shaking that will affect both heaven and earth (v 26*b*). The temporal contrast between "then" and "now" is extended to include the future as well. The spatial contrast between "earth" and "heaven" in v 25 is reaffirmed but transformed with the promise that οὐ μόνον τὴν γῆν ἀλλὰ καὶ τὸν οὐρανόν, "not only the earth but also the heaven," will be subject to the divine shaking.

The theological motif of a shaking of heaven and earth is a recurring feature in the prophetic announcement of the Day of the Lord that throws nations into confusion and heralds their destruction (e.g., Isa 13:13 in the context of Isa 13:1–22 [of the destruction of Babylon]; Joel 2:10 in the context of Joel 2:1–11; Hag 2:6–7, 21–22; cf. Bornkamm, *TDNT* 7:198; Bietenhard, *Himmlische Welt*, 49–50). The "shaking" is a metaphor for the judgment of God executed in history, as in the case of the fall of Babylon announced in Isa 13:1–22. In the Jewish apocalyptic tradition, which was particularly indebted to Hag 2:6, the "shaking" was understood eschatologically with reference to a cataclysmic final shaking of heaven and earth (e.g., *Jub.* 1:29; *1 Enoch* 45:1; *Sib. Or.* 3.675–80; Ps.-Philo, *Bib. Ant.* 19.5; *2 Apoc. Bar.* 32:1; 59:3; cf. *b. Sanh.* 97b; *Exod. Rab.* 18 [81a]; *Midr. Tanhuma B* (דברים §1, beginning).

Within the historical context of Haggai's prophetic ministry, the prophecy of another shaking was a message of encouragement and hope (Hag 2:6–9). Addressing the future glory of the temple, Haggai announced that the fall of Babylon (cf. Isa 13:1–22), which had made possible the return from exile, was not the great shaking. That event lay in the near future. In a short while God will once again shake heaven and earth and overthrow the nations. This future shaking will be the means by which he will fill his temple with glory. He himself will rule over his people from that place (see Schröger, *Verfasser*, 190–94).

The writer appeals to Hag 2:6 LXX as a summary of what God has promised. In v 26*b* he cited an abbreviated form of the text, freely adapting it so as to emphasize what he felt was most important in the prophecy. He made three changes: (1) he omitted the reference to the sea and the dry land, with the result that the focus of the shaking is concentrated on the heaven and the earth; (2) he added the expression οὐ μόνον ... ἀλλὰ καί, "not only ... but also," which accentuated the contrast between the two spheres; and (3) he altered the word order, transposing the phrases τὴν γῆν, "the earth," and τὸν οὐρανόν, "the heaven," assigning "the heaven" to the final emphatic position at the end of the citation. These modifications of the text indicate that his intention was to stress the shaking of the heaven. In contrast to Sinai, where the earth alone was shaken, the future shaking will extend to heaven as well (cf. Casey, "Eschatology in Heb 12:14–29," 527–30).

It is commonly assumed that the referent in the expression τὸν οὐρανόν, "the heaven," in v 26b is to the visible, created, cosmological heaven. Michel, for example, calls attention to the citation of Ps 101:25–27 LXX in 1:10–12, which asserts that the heavens and earth will perish. He finds in the citation a suggestion of the actual future eschatological drama which is fully described in 12:26–27 (121, 473; cf. Riggenbach, 424; van der Ploeg, RB 54 [1947] 226; Stählin, TDNT 1:382; Hillmann, BibLeb 1 [1960] 249–50; Andriessen and Lenglet, Bib 51 [1970] 237; among others).

It seems preferable, however, to interpret the nuance of "the heaven" in v 26b from the immediate context. The writer modified the text he found in his source, Hag 2:6 LXX, in order to intensify the contrast between a past and future shaking and between earth and heaven. In the past only the earth was affected. The future shaking will make an impact not only on the earth but on heaven as well. The explicit association of "the earth" with Sinai and the old covenant (vv 25b, 26a) implies that "the heaven" is to be associated with the new covenant (v 25ac). "Earth" and "heaven" are symbols of the revelation at Sinai and of the new covenant revelation to the writer's generation, respectively (K. J. Thomas, NTS 11 [1964–65] 318).

The writer found in the text of Hag 2:6 LXX the powerful metaphor of "shaking." The shaking promised in v 26b must be interpreted in relationship to the shaking of the earth at Sinai in v 26a. The Sinai revelation is defined in v 26a as one of judgment, and the future shaking will entail an intensification of the event of judgment. The "shaking" of heaven and earth is not intended to describe a coming historical event, namely the future transformation of the world or its ultimate destruction. It is descriptive of God's eschatological judgment, which is the corollary of the reception of the fullness of salvation through the new covenant. The quality of that salvation explains why the threat of ruin is brought to bear upon those who reject the God who warns from heaven in vv 25–26. Just as elsewhere in the OT the "shaking" of heaven and earth exhibits God's destructive power and wrath toward Israel or the nations, so too here the "shaking" of earth and heaven should be read as a fixed metaphor for divine judgment. The new covenant community lives now, in the present time, under the threat of the divine promise ἔτι ἅπαξ ἐγὼ σείσω, "once more I will shake," which implies an eschatological sifting that proceeds from the Judge who is God of all (cf. Vögtle, BibLeb 10 [1969] 240–41; K. J. Thomas, NTS 11 [1964–65] 318; Casey, "Eschatology in Heb 12:14–29," 530–32, 548–50).

The modifications of Hag 2:6 LXX indicate that the writer found in the text a prophecy of a "shaking" that signified a searching judgment for the members of the new covenant community. Those who have been "warned from heaven" will be held as accountable as those who were "warned on earth." The promise expressed through the citation of the biblical text is that those who reject the new covenant revelation will receive the same summary judgment as those who disregarded the revelation given at Sinai. The citation of the text expresses the pastoral concern for the threat of apostasy within the community in 12:14–29.

27 The writer's interpretation of the prophetic text is offered in v 27, while the implication he drew from it is set forth in v 28 a. His exposition, which hinges on the adverbial phrase ἔτι ἅπαξ, "once more," is an example of parenetic midrash. Its purpose is to actualize the authority of the biblical text and to apply it to the situation he felt compelled to address. The designation "parenetic midrash" takes into account that the exposition of Scripture is intended to serve a hortatory purpose (see *Form/Structure/Setting* above). The interpretation of the text is subservient to the parenetic concern expressed in vv 25–29 as a unit. That explains why the writer provides the community with a terse, condensed, even cryptic statement in v 27. It is meant to be suggestive and provocative rather than exegetical and exhaustive (cf. 8:13).

The repetition in v 27 a of the initial phrase of the quotation serves to direct attention to the formulation of the prophecy, calling the members of the house church to active reflection. The thought progresses from the pending promise of the future shaking in v 26 b to the effect that event will have on all that can be shaken and on what is incapable of being shaken in v 27. The antithesis between "earth" and "heaven" in v 26 is replaced in v 27 by the difference between the shakable and the unshakable.

The writer focuses upon the adverbial phrase ἔτι ἅπαξ, "once more," because it is the detail in the prophecy that calls for a comparison between the past shaking at Sinai (v 26 a), which affected the old covenant community, and the yet pending, greater shaking promised by God (v 26 b), which impinges upon the new covenant community. He declares that the phrase indicates, or points suggestively (δηλοῖ) to τῶν σαλευομένων μετάθεσιν ὡς πεποιημένων, "a removal of all that can be shaken as of things having been made." The substitution of the synonym σαλεύειν, "to shake," for the verb σείειν, which was used in expressing the promised shaking in the quotation, is striking. It is reasonable to believe that the change was deliberate and that it served the writer's parenetic purpose. A basis for the substitution was provided in v 26 a when reference was made to the divine voice that shook (ἐσάλευσεν) the earth at Sinai. In each of the clauses of v 27, the verb is repeated in the contrast between τῶν σαλευομένων, "what can be shaken," and τὰ μὴ σαλευόμενα "what cannot be shaken."

A theological reason for the writer's preference for σαλεύειν may be found in the LXX, which was so frequently the source for his significant vocabulary. The translators of the LXX used the verb σαλεύειν metaphorically as an expression for the effect of divine judgment. Those who experience God's judgment are "shaken" (e.g., 2 Kgs 17:20; Pss 30[MT 31:22]:23; 47[MT 48]:6; 115[MT 116:3]:2; Lam 1:8 LXX). The translators used σαλεύειν with the negative, especially in the Psalms, as a fixed idiom for unshakableness. The idiom is applied to the righteous as those who share in the unshakable character of God. They enjoy the confidence that they will not be "shaken" (e.g., Ps 14[MT 15]:5; 15[MT 16]:8; 54[MT 55:22]:23; 61[MT 62:2]:3; 65[MT 66]:9; 111[MT 112]:6; 120[MT 121]:3; 124[MT 125]:1 LXX). Familiarity with the figurative use of σαλεύειν in passages referring to eschatological judgment in the Psalms accounts sufficiently for the writer's preference for this verbal expression in his interpretation of Hag 2:6 LXX (cf. Vögtle, *BibLeb* 10 [1969]

252–53; Bertram, *TDNT* 7:66–67; for an alternative proposal, see Vanhoye, *Bib* 45 [1964] 250–53, discussed below on v 28*a*). A distinction between "what can be shaken," which is subject to removal as created reality (see above, *Note* ccc), and "what cannot be shaken" provided the writer with a pregnant judgment/salvation metaphor.

As created reality (ὡς πεποιημένων), what is shakable is subject to the scrutiny of the Creator and is incapable of escaping the divine shaking. However, the essential difference between the shakable and the unshakable lies not in their natural status as "created" as opposed to "uncreated" but in their relationship to God (with G. B. Caird, *The Basis of Christian Hope* [London: Duckworth, 1970] 23).

The result of the promised testing is a μετάθεσις of what is shakable. The term μετάθεσις has invited a broad spectrum of interpretation (see especially Vögtle, *BibLeb* 10 [1969] 241–53; Casey, "Eschatology in Heb 12:14–29," 540–47, 550–51, 553–54; for an interpretation of v 27 from the perspective of Greek metaphysics, see Thompson, *JBL* 94 [1975] 580–87; id., *Beginnings of Christian Philosophy*, 48–51). It has been possible to fill the term with conceptions brought to the text from outside its parameters, appealing either to the Jewish apocalyptic or to the Greek metaphysical traditions, because the word μετάθεσις is found relatively rarely. It occurs only once in the LXX (2 Macc 11:24). In the NT it is found in Heb 7:12 and 12:27, but not elsewhere. Its basic sense is a local one ("removal" from one location to another; cf. Vögtle, *BibLeb* 10 [1969] 247), but it can be used figuratively with the nuance of a change or alteration in condition or status, as 7:12 demonstrates (Vögtle, 249–50, finds this nuance in 12:27 as well). The use of the cognate verb in 7:12 and 11:5 shows that the conceptual meaning ranges from "change" to "removal." In the case of v 27, with its contrast between what is shakable and subject to μετάθεσις as opposed to what is unshakable, which "remains," μετάθεσις must mean "removal." The precise sense in which the thought of "removal" is used is clarified by reference to the result clause in v 27*b*.

The result of the shaking promised in v 26*b* is ἵνα μείνῃ τὰ μὴ σαλευόμενα, "so that what cannot be shaken may remain." This clause indicates that the judgment that the writer found promised in Hag 2:6 LXX will have a discriminating function. It will remove some ("all that can be shaken") and allow others to endure ("what cannot be shaken"). This interpretation was fostered by the text of Haggai. The promise of a shaking of heaven and earth is repeated in Hag 2:21. The result will be the removal of thrones, kings, and powerful armies, and the establishment of God's chosen servant (Hag 2:22–23). Although the term μετάθεσις, "removal," is not found in the text of Hag 2:22 LXX, the promise of divine intervention entails the decisive removal of all those who would oppose God's announced plan. Hurst has observed that the writer is "fond of explaining OT texts with illustrative words not properly found within the text" ("Background," 272, n. 414, with an appeal to 8:13 as an example). It is highly probable that it was reflection on the larger context of Hag 2:6–9, notably Hag 2:21–23 LXX, that suggested the use of the significant term μετάθεσις.

The result of the removal of that which can be shaken is that what is unshakable "remains." The term μένειν appears in the LXX with the meaning "to be lasting," "to endure." It is used frequently in reference to the enduring, unchangeable character of God, of reality like the new heaven and earth, and of persons who are rightly related to God (e.g., Ps 102:25; Isa 66:22; Zech 14:10 LXX; cf. Hauck,

TDNT 4:574–76; Hurst, "Background," 66–67). In v 27*b* the verb is used in reference to the stability and unchangeableness of God and his kingdom (note v 28*a*). It is not primarily a temporal concept reflecting on durability and futurity but a qualitative concept stressing the reality and stability of that which "remains" (so Grässer, *Glaube,* 144).

The juxtaposition of the theologically significant verb μένειν, "to remain," with the fixed idiom from the LXX to describe the stability and security of those who share in God's unshakableness is striking. It indicates that the reference to what cannot be shaken includes those faithful members of the community who will not be removed when God's threatened intervention occurs. However, all opposition to God's sovereign rule will be shaken and removed. That event will result in the decisive removal from the community of those who have disregarded God's speaking and rejected his solemn warning (v 25). They will experience not only the loss of their birthrights (cf. vv 16–17) and the blessings of the new covenant reviewed in the vision of vv 22–24 but also the invoking of the curse sanctions of the covenant (cf. v 25*b*). Among that which "remains" are all those who share in the unshakableness of the Judge who is God of all (v 23*b*). Their fidelity to the new covenant is the ground of the assurance that they will enjoy an eternal salvation, receiving as their legacy an unshakable kingdom (v 28*a*) (cf. Vögtle, *BibLeb* 10 [1969] 251–52).

The citation of Hag 2:6 LXX and its interpretation in vv 26–27 are an integral part of a severe warning that there is no escape for those who disregard God or reject his word (vv 25–29). The midrashic approach to the text occurs within a paragraph that reiterates the pattern of old covenant example, *a fortiori* argument, and menacing threat introduced in 2:2–3*a*. It is informed by the carefully structured comparison drawn between the old covenant and the new in vv 18–24 and by the explicit concern with apostasy in vv 14–17. Casey has observed that the cautions against apostasy in vv 16–17 and in vv 25–26*a* are both based upon comparisons with old covenant sin. The writer stressed the shaking of "the heaven" in v 26*b* because for him "heaven" was a symbol of the new covenant relationship to God. In vv 26*b*–27 he asserts that everyone will be shaken and tested yet once more, especially those who enjoy the blessings of the new covenant ("Eschatology in Heb 12:14–29," 548–50).

The complex of statements in vv 25–27 indicates that the writer was passionately concerned for the members of the house church. They face a yet pending final test that will expose either sensitivity or insensitivity to the one who is speaking on the basis of fidelity or infidelity to the gift of the new covenant. He concentrates his concern not on the future of the cosmos but on the future of the new covenant community, which stands before the threat of divine shaking and the promise of divinely given unshakability (cf. also Hurst, "Background," 62–64).

28–29 The severity of vv 25–27 is momentarily softened when the writer announces that Christians are in the process of receiving an unshakable kingdom. This gift, secured on the ground of the new covenant, calls for gratitude expressed in thankful worship of the God whose awesome and holy character was disclosed in the fiery epiphany of Sinai. The pattern of stern warning followed by pastoral encouragement (e.g., 5:11–6:8/6:9–20; 10:26–31/10:32–39) was characteristic of Jewish synagogue homilies, as attested in the old rabbinic midrashim (cf. E. Stein, "Die homiletische *Peroratio* im Midrasch," *HUCA* 8–9 [1931–32] 353–71). It clearly has influenced the pastoral style of the writer of Hebrews as he brings his own homily to its theological and pastoral climax (so Mora, *La Carta*, 61, n.181; 63, n. 192; Swetnam, *Bib* 55 [1974] 33, n. 2).

In v 28a the writer applies the biblical quotation and its interpretation to the members of the house church: διὸ βασιλείαν ἀσάλευτον παραλαμβάνοντες ἔχωμεν χάριν, "Since we are receiving a kingdom that cannot be shaken, let us be thankful." Although the future is qualified by the divine promise of a searching judgment, the present is enriched by the prospect of the reception of a divine gift. The participle παραλαμβάνοντες, "we are receiving," does not express possession (cf. Cody, *Heavenly Sanctuary*, 141: "we have already received our unshakable kingdom") but acceptance of a gift or office that is being bestowed (Spicq, 2,413; cf. Delling, *TDNT* 4:13). The present tense of the participle emphasizes that Christians are now only in the process of receiving this gift and that this process will continue into the future (see above, *Note* ddd; cf. Michel, 475–76; F. F. Bruce, 383, n. 199; and especially Laub, *Bekenntnis*, 253, who emphasizes that the "already/not yet" character of salvation is expressed in the formulation of v 28a). It is the prospect of the ultimate enjoyment of the gift in its fullness that provides the motivation for the exhortation to thanksgiving.

The expression βασιλείαν ἀσάλευτον, "a kingdom which cannot be shaken," which defines the content of the gift, occurs only here in the NT. The formulation reflects the writer's interpretation of Hag 2:6 LXX in v 27 by means of the categories of shakability and unshakability. The adjective ἀσάλευτος, "unshakable," is equivalent in linguistic value to the idiom in v 27b τὰ μὴ σαλευόμενα, "what cannot be shaken." It is common, therefore, to find a more precise identification of the writer's oblique reference to what cannot be shaken in the expression βασιλείαν ἀσάλευτον (e.g. Bertram, *TDNT* 7:70; Michel, 475; Buchanan, 225; P. E. Hughes, 559; Braun, 445). It is important, however, to recognize in the expression in v 27b both the neuter plural and a formal similarity to the use in the LXX of σαλεύειν, "to shake," with the negative particle as a technical expression for God and all that is properly related to him (see *Comment* on 7:27b). It is preferable, therefore, to find in the plural expression in v 27b a more global reference, which is inclusive of the unshakable kingdom and of those who share in the unshakable character of God.

It is not immediately apparent to a modern reader that there is an allusion to the reception of "an unshakable kingdom" in the quotation of Hag 2:6 LXX or its interpretation in v 27. It has often been suggested that the source of the conception is Dan 7:14, 18 LXX (e.g. Westcott, 442; Grosheide, 306; Michel, 475–76; Andriessen and Lenglet, *Bib* 51 [1970] 238). Dan 7:14 LXX refers to a "kingdom that will never be destroyed" (ἡ βασιλεία ... ἥτις οὐ μὴ φθαρῇ). Moreover, Dan 7:18 LXX contains the idiom παραλαμβάνειν τὴν βασιλείαν, "to receive the kingdom." The saints of the Most High "will receive the kingdom" (παραλήψονται τὴν βασιλείαν) and "possess it forever." The fact that the promise of a shaking of heaven and earth is repeated in Hag 2:21, so that foreign kingdoms are removed (Hag 2:22), implied the establishment of an unshakable kingdom, according to Michel. The text of Dan 7:14, 18 LXX was then called to mind (475). However, if there is an allusion to Dan 7:14, 18 LXX in v 28a, it certainly is not an obvious one. Moreover, it remains unclear why the writer should have thought of Dan 7 at the time he was interpreting Haggai.

These difficulties are overcome by Vanhoye's proposal that the source of the verb σαλεύειν, "to shake," which the writer used to interpret Hag 2:6 LXX, is actually Ps 95[MT 96]:9–11 LXX. The LXX translators assigned to the psalm a superscription not found in the MT: "When they constructed the House [of the Lord] after the exile." The focus of Haggai's prophetic ministry was this same event. It is this correlation established in his Bible which clarifies why the writer would have brought together in his mind the detail of Ps 95 LXX when he was, in fact, interpreting the prophecy of Hag 2:6 LXX. An important principle in Jewish hermeneutics was that two passages which concern the same event or contain the same phrase are mutually interpretive *(gĕzêrâh šāwâ)*. What the writer recalled in Ps 95:9–10 LXX was a call to worship:

προσκυνήσατε τῷ κυρίῳ ἐν αὐλῇ ἁγίᾳ αὐτοῦ
"Worship the Lord in his holy court,"
σαλευθήτω ἀπὸ προσώπου αὐτοῦ πᾶσα ἡ γῆ
"let all the earth be shaken before him."
εἴπατε ἐν τοῖς ἔθνεσιν ὁ κύριος ἐβασίλευσεν
"Say to the nations, 'The Lord has inaugurated his reign,'"
καὶ γὰρ κατώρθωσεν τὴν οἰκουμένην ἥτις οὐ σαλευθήσεται
"for he will complete the [heavenly] world, which will not be shaken."

The prophecy of Haggai indicated that the divine shaking would affect not only the earth but heaven as well. It was Ps 95:10 LXX, however, which clarified what would not be shaken because God has inaugurated (ingressive aorist) his reign. It is the eschatological heavenly world (ἡ οἰκουμένη) established by God as his trophy (Vanhoye, *Bib* 45 [1964] 250–51).

The focus of Vanhoye's interest is not the "unshakable kingdom" of v 28a. It is the term οἰκουμένη in Heb 1:6, and 2:5, which he properly interprets in terms of the heavenly world into which the divine Son entered at his exaltation. He identifies the content of the expression τὰ μὴ σαλευόμενα in v 27 as the world of the definitive eschatological realities, and casually refers to Dan 7:18 LXX as the source of the expression "to receive a kingdom" (*Bib* 45 [1964] 251). His suggestion concerning σαλεύειν is made incidentally by way of identifying the source of the formulation in v 27b. It is, nevertheless, incisive, because it directs attention to the inner connection in Ps 95:10 LXX between the declaration "the Lord has inaugurated his reign" (ὁ κύριος ἐβασίλευσεν) and its result, "he will complete the heavenly world which will not be shaken" (τὴν οἰκουμένην ἥτις οὐ σαλευθήσεται). The conception of the royal heavenly world which is "unshakable" is clearly the source of "the unshakable kingdom" in v 28a.

One other detail is significant. Although Vanhoye has no interest in the introductory statement in Ps 95:9 LXX ("Worship the Lord in his holy court") and does not quote it in his article, it is precisely this command that explains why the writer appeals for the grateful worship of God, with fear and awe, as the appropriate response to the reception of an unshakable kingdom. Fear and awe are appropriate to the holy court of the sovereign Lord. The unstated link between Hag 2:6 LXX and the formulation of Heb 12:28 is Ps 95:9–10 LXX.

The connection between the kingship of God and the establishing of an unshakable realm is found in Ps 92[MT 93]:1 LXX as well: "The Lord has inaugurated his reign . . . for he has established the heavenly realm which will not be shaken" (καὶ γὰρ ἐστερέωσεν τὴν οἰκουμένην ἥτις οὐ σαλευθήσεται). There is in this instance, however, no reference to a prior "shaking" that would call to mind the promise of Hag 2:6 LXX. The statement is interesting primarily because it is parallel to Ps 95:10 LXX and illustrates the fixed idiom for unshakability in the LXX. A closer parallel is Ps 45[MT 46:5–6]:6–7 LXX, which speaks of the unshakableness of the city of God, in contrast to the confusion of the nations, the fall of kingdoms, and the shaking of the earth because God has uttered his voice: ἔδωκεν φωνὴν αὐτοῦ, ἐσαλεύθη ἡ γῆ, "he uttered his voice, the earth was shaken." Elsewhere in the LXX it is said that Mount Zion "will not be shaken" (Ps 124[MT 125]:1; Isa 33:20 LXX). The royal "city of the living God," which is firmly established because it shares in God's unshakable character (cf. Heb 11:10), is, in fact, the "unshakable kingdom" of v 28a. The content of the pregnant expression in v 28a is thus clarified by the vision of the heavenly Jerusalem in vv 22–24 (cf. Nicolau, *Burg* 20 [1979] 393–405). It describes the realm of relationships among those who share the quality of the unshakableness of their God who is present with them.

The appropriate response to this gift is a grateful disposition toward God. "Since we are receiving a kingdom which cannot be shaken," the writer urges, ἔχωμεν χάριν, "let us be thankful." The idiom ἔχειν χάριν τινί, "to be grateful to someone," is well attested (BAGD 878 [5]) and in this context clearly means "Let us be grateful to God" (for alternative proposals, see above, *Note* fff). The ground for Christian gratitude was elaborated in vv 22–24 and is summarized in the reference to the reception of an unshakable kingdom in v 28a. Recognizing that thankfulness is a strong support to obedience and fidelity, the writer calls for the response of gratitude that will prepare the heirs to the unshakable kingdom for the future "shaking" of earth and heaven. That is the connection between vv 26–27 and v 28a.

A channel for the expression of thanksgiving is provided in worship. Having called the community to thankfulness, the writer continues δι' ἧς λατρεύωμεν εὐαρέστως τῷ θεῷ μετὰ εὐλαβείας καὶ δέους, "through which let us worship God in an acceptable manner, with fear and awe." The writer transposes the summons to worship in Ps 95:9 LXX into his own distinctive idiom when he uses the verb λατρεύειν, "to worship, to serve." This verb has cultic associations that are enriched by its prior use in the homily in reference to the sacrificial arrangement under the old covenant (8:5; 9:9; 10:2; 13:10), which was inadequate to remove the impediments to worship. It was also used in 9:14 of Christians. They are now capable of the worship and service of God because their consciences have been purged of defilement; every impediment to worship has been removed by the sacrificial action of Christ in offering himself to God as an unblemished sacrifice. A fully adequate basis for the response of grateful worship has therefore been provided.

The concept of worship is almost certainly to be expanded in v 28b to include "a manner of life which is pleasing to God and which is sustained both by gratitude and by a serious sense of responsibility" (Strathmann, *TDNT* 4:64; cf. Michel, 477). The members of the house church are to regard every aspect of their lives as an expression of devotion to God. This is to serve God acceptably (εὐαρέστως; cf. BAGD 318–19), as each Christian offers to him the "acceptable" (εὐαρεστεῖται) sacrifices of pleasing him through practical obedience (13:16) and conformity to his will (cf. εὐάρεστον, 13:21). Under the old covenant it was only the Levitical priests who "served" (λατρεύειν). With the actualizing of the new covenant, all of God's people are summoned to the worship of God in an acceptable manner (cf. Michel, 477, who calls attention to the correspondence between 9:14 and 12:28*b*).

The qualification of λατρεύωμεν, "let us worship," by the phrase μετὰ εὐλαβείας καὶ δέους, "with fear and awe," constitutes a sober reminder of the holy character of God. It is common to attribute a religious sense to εὐλαβεία here and to find in the word the nuance of reverent awe or piety (e.g., Westcott, 422; Grosheide, 307; Vögtle, *BibLeb* 10 [1969] 253–54). It is preferable, however, to recognize that the meaning of εὐλαβεία is qualified by the term δέος, which occurs only here in the NT, but always connotes fear, terror, or dread (2 Macc 3:17, 30; 15:23; cf. Kosmala, *Hebräer, Essener, Christen*, 297–98, who translates the expression "with fear and dread"). In the context of vv 25–29, εὐλαβεία signifies the fear that is appropriate "before an imminent peril, namely, before the judgment of God" (Andriessen, *NRT* 96 [1974] 284, with a reference to εὐλαβεία in 11:7; cf. R. Bultmann, *TDNT* 2:753; Casey, "Eschatology in Heb 12:14–29," 566–68). The reference to "consuming fire" in v 29 supports this understanding. Blazing fire provokes fear, as it did at Sinai (v 18*a*); it serves to recall 10:27, where the "terrifying expectation of judgment" is an expectation of "raging fire ready to consume God's adversaries" (cf. Andriessen, *NRT* 96 [1974] 284–86). The life that is appropriate worship expresses fear and awe, because it recognizes the certainty of the promised eschatological shaking.

The climactic statement in the writer's peroration is the austere reminder καὶ γὰρ ὁ θεὸς ἡμῶν πῦρ καταναλίσκον, "for our God is a consuming fire." McCown describes this pronouncement as an apothegm. In such sentences the mood is indicative (ἐστίν understood), the style rhetorical, the motif judgmental, and the function hortatory ("Ο ΛΟΓΟΣ ΤΗΣ ΠΑΡΑΚΛΗΣΕΩΣ," 213). The expression καὶ γάρ, "for," indicates that it is God's essential character that provides the reason for the fear and awe that are appropriate to his worship. The predicate used to describe God evokes the one whose holiness was displayed in the fiery epiphany of Sinai. There is a clear allusion to Deut 4:24 LXX, where Moses reminded the Israelites that κύριος ὁ θεός σου πῦρ καταναλίσκον ἐστίν, θεὸς ζηλωτής, "the Lord your God is a consuming fire, a jealous God" (cf. Deut 9:3 LXX). In adapting the Mosaic statement for his purpose, the writer abbreviated it and substituted the first personal pronoun ἡμῶν, "our," for the singular σου, "your," in order to actualize the text for his Christian audience. It was appropriate in this context to recall the Sinai revelation, since God's holy character remains unaltered under the new covenant (cf. Riggenbach, 427–28; Moffatt, 223; Michel, 477–78).

The reference to fire evokes the theme of the judgment of God which is expressed through the symbol of fire in each of the prior warnings concerning apostasy (6:8; 10:27). In these texts, consignment to the flames is a metaphor for the completeness and severity of the judgment the apostate can anticipate. As such, the concluding statement in 12:14–29 furnishes a sharp caution against the rejection of the divine voice, complementing the sharpness of the cautionary imperative in v 25*a*, "Be careful that you do not disregard the one who is speaking." (Cf. Casey, "Eschatology in Heb 12:14–29," 570–71, who argues that the allusion to Deut 4:24 LXX provides a fitting conclusion for Hebrews in the light of the larger context in Deuteronomy, since the people are on the verge of entering the promised land [Deut 4:21] and are at the end of their pilgrimage.)

Explanation

In 12:14–29 the writer once more directs his attention to the pastoral situation that made his homily necessary. It is the threat of apostasy to which members of the house church were exposed through careless disregard for the blessings of the new covenant. Spiritual and emotional fatigue combined to create a climate of apathy and insensitivity to the voice of God heard through preaching and Scripture. Earnest concern for the spiritual peril to which that condition exposed the weaker members of the congregation motivated the call to the pursuit of peace and holiness in 12:14 as an expression of Christian maturity. It also accounts for the elaboration of the responsibility of the community for any of their members prone to apostasy in 12:15–17. The frightening prospect of the forfeiture of God's grace as a result of personal or corporate carelessness, of the defilement of the character of the community through apostasy, and of the irrevocable loss of covenant status through a thoughtless disregard for God's voice demonstrated the urgency for vigilance.

Although the threat envisioned is addressed in three parallel clauses in 12:15–16, there is in view not three dangers but one. All three clauses refer to apostasy. The formulation of the clauses in v 15 shows the influence of Deut 29:17 LXX, whereas that in v 16 is informed by Gen 25:29–34 LXX. This is significant, because both OT texts serve to situate the directives in 12:14–17 within the conceptual framework of the covenant.

The writer consistently interprets apostasy with expressions and OT texts that are covenantal in character (3:7–19; 6:4–8; 10:26–31). With the example of Esau, apostasy is defined as a decisive contempt for the gifts of God secured on the basis of covenant and as a rejection of a significant vocation defined through covenant. Esau is the person who breaks covenant with God and who experiences divine rejection and the irretrievable loss of covenant blessing. The presence of covenantal motifs in the initial paragraph announces the salvation-historical and covenantal perspective that is sustained throughout the section as a whole.

The example of Esau identifies the cost of an apostate disposition as covenantal exclusion. It also summarizes the stern warnings concerning the seriousness of unbelief and apostasy in 3:7–19; 6:4–8; and 10:26–31. Esau's experience of irreversible exclusion and loss recalls the inability of the exodus generation to enter God's rest in 3:19, the impossibility of renewal to repentance in 6:4, 6, and the invalidation of a sacrifice for sin in 10:26. The members of the house church are to recognize, on the principle of dynamic analogy, the dire consequences of showing contempt for God and for covenantal relationship that are so vividly illustrated in Esau.

The grounding for the pastoral directives in 12:14–17 is provided in 12:18–24. The privileged experience of Christians indicates why they must hold fast to the objective gifts of peace and holiness (v 14) and why they must guard against apostasy (vv 15–17). The integral connection between the two paragraphs also indicates that the motif of inexorable judgment introduced in 12:14–17 informs the brilliantly developed comparison between Mount Sinai and Mount Zion in 12:18–24 and the sharp parenetic warning in 12:25–29.

The significance of 12:18–29 to the writer's pastoral strategy must be appreciated. This unit furnishes a magisterial résumé of themes and motifs that have been introduced throughout the homily. These include the theme of the distance that separated worshipers from God under the old covenant (9:1–10; 10:1–3, 11; 12:18–21) as opposed to the unrestricted access to God in worship that is the hallmark of the life of faith under the new covenant (4:15–16; 9:11–14; 10:10, 12–14, 19–22; 12:22–24). Related to this contrast is the declaration that God has spoken and continues to speak (1:1–2a; 3:7–4:5; 8:8–12; 12:25–26), with the consequences that close attention to what he is saying is an urgent concern (2:1–4; 3:7–4:13; 5:11–14; 10:36–39; 12:25–29). The synthesis of these significant themes and motifs in a single section serves to identify 12:18–29 as the pastoral and theological climax of the homily.

In 12:18–24 the writer compares two covenants under the imagery of two mountains in order to illustrate their fundamental differences. Sinai and Zion are extended metaphors for the qualitatively different encounters with God under the old covenant and the new covenant, respectively. They also serve to exhibit the essential contrast between Moses and Jesus, respectively, as mediators of the encounter with God. Throughout this unit the writer is guided by a theological point of view and appraisal informed by extended reflection on the new covenant (cf. 8:8–13; 9:11–15; 10:15–18; 12:24). Presented in 12:18–21 is a powerful theological recasting of the Sinai event in order to emphasize its intrinsic inadequacy. It also serves to sharpen the contrast developed in 12:22–24 in the vision of Zion, the heavenly city of God.

In re-creating the scene at Sinai, the writer emphasized the tangible and sensory aspects of the theophany in order to convey an indelible impression of the ambiguity in the encounter with God under the old covenant. He stressed the threatening aspects of the Sinai epiphany, which created an atmosphere of dread and confusion. God was not unambiguously present at Sinai. The form of the divine revelation was a frightening sound of words mixed with the cacophany of whirlwind and trumpet blasts. The writer also stresses the immense distance that separated the worshipers from God under the old covenant. God is there, but he is unapproachable (vv 19–20). The equivocal nature of the entire event is accentuated when the writer goes beyond the detail of the Pentateuch and emphasizes that Moses, the mediator of the old covenant, was terrified (v 21). According to the writer, all of the human participants experienced the frightening manifestation of God's presence as an occasion for dread. It is left unclear in what sense it can be said that Israel experienced the encounter with God under the old covenant. Under the aspect of Sinai, the writer summarizes his convictions concerning the inadequacy of the old covenant as a whole.

It is apparent that the writer believed that the Sinai theophany should make clear to Christians the significance of the eschatological encounter with God in the new covenant. The images selected to create the vision of Mount Zion are rich in tradition and meaning. They describe the realization of the eschatological hopes of God's people under both the old and the new covenants. They give form and substance to the transcendent objective blessings secured for the Christian community as a result of the inauguration of the new covenant. Zion is decisively different from Sinai.

The experience of encountering God through Jesus is presented by means of the metaphor of a journey or pilgrimage to the heavenly city of God. This description of the new covenant encounter with God is almost certainly informed by extended reflection on Jer 38[MT 31]:2–14 LXX. There the return of the exiles is represented as a glorious new exodus. Their journey is hastened by ease and festive joy, in marked contrast to the hardships and sufferings of the first exodus. The goal of the new exodus is specified as Mount Zion (Jer 38:6, 12 LXX). The return of the exiles resembles the triumphant procession that accompanied the transfer of the ark of the covenant to Jerusalem under David (2 Sam 6:1–15; cf. Jer 38:4, 12–13 LXX) more than it does the wanderings of the wilderness generation. They are to be party to the oracle of the new covenant God will conclude with his people (Jer 38:31–34 LXX). The metaphor of the new people of God in pilgrimage to the heavenly Jerusalem, where they encounter God and Jesus, the mediator of the new covenant, reflects the writer's reinterpretation of Jer 38 in terms of his vision of covenantal conclusion.

Described in 12:22–24 is a genuine encounter with God through an act of faith and personal commitment. Through new covenant faith, which grasps the future as though it were present reality (11:1), Christians have come to a reality that is not perceptible to the senses because it is essentially future, the city of the living God. The fundamental difference between the old and the new covenants that emerges from the contrasting images in 12:18–24 is that God can be approached in the new covenant, as opposed to the restrictions on approaching God under the old covenant (cf. 9:1–10; 10:1–3, 11; 12:19–20). Although in 12:18–21 all mention of God, or any indication of communication between him and the people, has been eliminated from the description of Sinai, he is strikingly present in Zion (12:23).

The new covenant encounter with God signifies access to God in the presence of those who gather for the festive acclamation of his "worthship." Christians come to God, the Judge who is the God of all, the one from whom Israel felt estranged at Sinai and fled. They meet him in joyful assembly, together with angels, the faithful men and women of God under both covenants, and Jesus himself. It is the writer's firm conviction that the high priestly work of Jesus in his death and heavenly exaltation has secured for Christians in the present time a living relationship with God, which fulfills the promises of the new covenant. Expressed in terms of the vision of vv 22–24, the Christian's experience with God now is the pledge of his ultimate transfer to the actual presence of God in the heavenly city.

The final two images in the writer's vision (v 24), which focus upon Jesus, the mediator of the new covenant, and the efficacy of his sacrificial death, serve to situate the entire vision of the heavenly city in a salvation-historical and covenantal perspective. The eschatological encounter with God is mediated through the encounter with Jesus and with the message of salvation that he proclaimed (2:3–4). The emphasis in v 24 falls on the activating of the final covenant through the death and exaltation of Jesus. It demonstrates that Jesus' death, which secured for the community the objective blessings of the new covenant, is to be interpreted as covenant sacrifice.

This pervasive emphasis upon the covenant is not incidental to the writer's pastoral strategy. Covenant privilege calls for allegiance and obedience. The clear implication of the central paragraph in this section is that entrance into the city of God is conditioned ultimately on the acknowledgment of covenantal obligation. Loyalty and compliance with covenantal stipulations are grateful responses to the objective blessings secured by Jesus. The privileged status of the Christian community as the people of the new covenant has as its consequence the greater obligation to remain sensitive to the voice of the covenant-God.

The sharpness of the warning addressed to the community in 12:25–29 is thus fully justified in the light of the promised blessings by which Christians are to regulate their lives. Those promises, reviewed in vv 22–24, are fully warranted by the new covenant. However, life under the new covenant is conditioned not only by promise in the sense of future blessings but by promise in the sense of future scrutiny. That aspect of the present and future is explored in terms of the promise in Hag 2:6 LXX that a divine "shaking" will profoundly affect the new covenant community. Those who carelessly ignore the revelation of the eschatological salvation of God through his Son and who show contempt for the blessings of the new covenant cannot possibly escape detection. A discriminating judgment will remove from the community those who through apostasy have denied their character as men and women consecrated to the service of God.

In the final paragraph of the section the developed contrast between the old and the new covenants, which is elaborated in the distinction between warning on earth and warning from heaven, is transformed into the opposition of shakable and unshakable, the removed and that which remains (vv 26–27). This subtle change is significant. It serves to shift the emphasis in the section from the essential difference between the old and new covenants to the crucial distinction between those who are faithful and those who are not within the new covenantal community. The repeated exhortations to faithfulness and warnings against apostasy that have appeared throughout the homily find their culmination in vv 25–29, which express a final, urgent warning based on the proximate nearness of a definitive judgment.

Christians under the new covenant are to enter into an experience of maturity in which all of life becomes an expression of worship. Authentic worship is a grateful response to covenantal blessings already experienced and to the certainty of the reception of the unshakable kingdom (v 28). It is deepened by the frank awareness of the awesome character of God's holiness, which was disclosed in the fiery epiphany of Sinai (v 29). A failure to listen attentively to what God is saying to the community now, at this present time, can only be catastrophic.

B. Life within the Confessing Community (13:1–25)

Bibliography

Aalen, S. "Das Abendmahl als Opfermahl im Neuen Testament." *NovT* 6 (1963) 128–52. **Andriessen, P.** *En lisant l'Épître aux Hébreux.* 56–60. ———. "La communauté des 'Hebreux' était-elle tombée dans le relachement?" *NRT* 96 (1974) 1054–66. ———. "L'Eucharist dans l'Épître aux Hébreux." *NRT* 94 (1972) 269–77. **Arowele, P. J.** "The Pilgrim People of God (An African's Reflections on the Motif of Sojourn in the Epistle to the Hebrews)." *AsiaJT* 4 (1990) 438–55. **Attridge, H. W.** "Paraenesis in a Homily (λόγος παρακλήσεως): The Possible Location of, and Socialization in, the 'Epistle to the Hebrew.'" *Semeia* 50 (1990) 211–26. **Baldwin, C. E.** "The Form and Function of the ΑΣΠΑΖΟΜΑΙ Formula: A Study in Greek Epistolography." Dissertation, Vanderbilt University, 1973. **Barton, G. A.** "The Date of the Epistle to the Hebrews." *JBL* 57 (1938) 195–207. **Best, E.** "Spiritual Sacrifice: General Priesthood in the New Testament." *Int* 14 (1960) 273–99. **Betz, J.** *Die Eucharistie in der Zeit der griechischen Väter.* II/1: *Die Realpräsenz des Leibes und Blutes Jesu im Abendmahl nach dem Neuen Testament.* 2nd ed. Freiburg: Herder & Herder, 1964. 144–66. **Bischoff, A.** "Exegetische Randbemerkungen. *ZNW* 9 (1908) 168–72. **Black, C. C. II.** "The Rhetorical Form of the Hellenistic Jewish and Early Christian Sermon: A Response to Lawrence Wills." *HTR* 81 (1988) 1–8. **Bornkamm, G.** "Das Anathema in der urchristliche Abendmahlsliturgie." In *Das Ende des Gesetz.* Munich: Kaiser, 1952. 123–32. ———. "Das Bekenntnis im Hebräerbrief." *TBl* 21 (1942) 52–66. ———. "Lobpreis, Bekenntnis und Opfer." In *Apophoreta.* FS E. Haenchen. BZNW 30. Berlin: Töpelmann, 1964. 46–63. **Bracewell, R. E.** "Shepherd Imagery in the Synoptic Gospels." Dissertation, Southern Baptist Theological Seminary, Louisville, 1983. 13–89. **Braun H.** "Das himmlische Vaterland bei Philo und im Hebäerbrief." In *Verborum Veritas.* FS G. Stählin, ed. O. Bocher and K. Haacker. Wuppertal: Brockhaus, 1970. 319–27. **Broschi, D. G.** "Fondamenti biblici per una teologia del laicato." *SacDoc* 26 (1981) 133–48. **Bruce, F. F.** "'To the Hebrews': A Document of Roman Christianity?" *ANRW* 25.4 (1987) 3496–3521. **Brunner, P.** "Die Bedeutung des Altars für den Gottesdienst der christlichen Kirche." *KD* 20 (1974) 218–44. **Burggaller, E.** "Das literarische Problem des Hebräerbriefes." *ZNW* 9 (1908) 110–31. **Cambier, J.** "Eschatologie ou héllenisme dans l'Épître aux Hébreux." *Sal* 11 (1949) 62–96. **Campbell, J. Y.** "ΚΟΙΝΩΝΙΑ and Its Cognates in the New Testament." In *Three New Testament Studies.* Leiden: Brill, 1965. 1–28. **Casson, L.** *Travel in the Ancient World.* Toronto: Hakkert, 1974. 115–225. **Causée, A.** "De la Jérusalem terrestre à la Jérusalem céleste." *RHPR* 27 (1947) 12–36. **Champion, L. G.** *Benedictions and Doxologies in the Epistles of Paul.* Oxford: Kemp Hall, 1934. 90–116. **Clavier, H.** "Ο ΛΟΓΟΣ ΤΟΥ ΘΕΟΥ dans l'Épître aux Hébreux." In *New Testament Essays.* FS T. W. Manson. Ed. A. J. B. Higgins. Manchester: University of Manchester Press, 1959. 81–93. **Cody, A.** *Heavenly Sanctuary and Liturgy in the Epistle to the Hebrews.* 133–34, 141–44. **Countryman, L. W.** *Dirt, Greed & Sex: Sexual Ethics in the New Testament and Their Implications for Today.* London: SCM, 1989. 129–31, 147–234. **Cranfield, C. E. B.** "Hebrews 13:20–21." *SJT* 20 (1967) 437–41. **Creed, J. M.** "Great Texts Reconsidered: Hebrews XIII.10." *ExpTim* 50 (1938) 13–15. **Cuming, G. M.** "Service-Endings in the Epistles." *NTS* 22 (1975–76) 110–13. **Dacquino, P.** *Storia del matrimonio cristiano alla luce della bibbia.* Leumann/Torino: Elle Di Ci, 1984. **Daly R. J.** "The New Testament Concept of Christian Sacrificial Activity." *BTB* 8 (1978) 99–107. **Danesi, G.,** and **Garofalo, S.** *Migrazioni e accoglienza nella Sacra Scrittura.* Padua: Messaggero, 1987. 131–290. **Delling, G.** "Partizipiale Gottesprädikationen in den Briefen des Neuen Testaments." *ST* 17 (1963) 1–59. **De Young, J. C.** *Jerusalem in the New Testament.* 107–9, 117–45. **Dussaut, L.** *Synopse structurelle de l'Épître a Hébreux.* 131–35. **Dyck, T. L.** "Jesus Our Pioneer." Dissertation, Northwest Baptist Theological Seminary, 1980. 152–64. **Elliott, E. B.** *We Have an Altar: An Exposition of Hebrews 13:10.* London: Seeley, 1903. **Elliott, J. H.** *A Home for the Homeless: A Sociological Exegesis of 1 Peter.* Philadelphia: Fortress, 1981. 145–50, 165–200. **Exler, F. X. J.** *The Form of the Ancient Greek Letter: A Study in Greek Epistolography.* Washington, DC: Catholic University of America, 1923. 101–16. **Fascher, E.** "Zum Begriff des Fremden." *TLZ* 96 (1971) 161–68. **Ferguson, E.** "Spiritual Sacrifice in Early Christianity and Its Environment." *ANRW* 23.2 (1980) 1151–89. **Filson, F. V.** "The Significance of the Early House Church." *JBL* 58 (1939) 105–12. ———. *'Yesterday': A Study of Hebrews in the Light of Chapter 13.* SBT 2:4. Naperville: Allenson, 1967. **Finkelstein, L.** "The *Birkat ha-Mazon.*" *JQR* n.s. 19 (1928–29) 211–62. **Fischer, J.** "Covenant, Fulfilment and Judaism in Hebrews." *ERT* 13 (1989) 175–87. **Fontecha J. F.** "La vida cristiana como peregrinación según la Epistola a los Hebreos." In *Studium Legionense.* Léon, 1961. 2:251–306. **Galot, J.** "Le sacerdoce catholique: III. Le sacerdoce du Christ selon l'épître aux Hébreux." *EE* 91 (1981) 689–96. **Gordis, R.** "The Text and Meaning of Hosea xiv 3." *VT* 5 (1955) 88–90. **Grässer, E.** "Die Gemeindevorsteher im Hebräerbrief." In *Vom Amt des Laien in Kirche und Theologie.* FS G. Krause. Ed. H. Schröer and G. Müller. Berlin: de Gruyter, 1982. 67–84. ———. "Der historische Jesus im Hebräerbrief." *ZNW* 56 (1965) 63–91. **Gyllenberg, R.** "Die Christologie des Hebräerbriefes." *ZST* 11 (1934) 662–90. ———. "Die Komposition des Hebräerbriefes." *SEÅ* 22–23 (1957–58) 137–47. **Haensler, B.** "Zu Hebr 13,10." *BZ* 11 (1913) 403–9. **Hamm, D.** "Faith in the Epistle to the Hebrews: The Jesus Factor." *CBQ* 52 (1990) 270–91. **Harnack, A.** "Probabilia über die Adresse und den Verfasser des Hebräerbriefs." *ZNW* 1 (1900) 16–41. **Herrmann, L.** "L'Épître aux (Laodicéens et l'apologie aux) Hébreux." *CCER* 15 (1968) 1–9. **Hillmann, W.** "Glaube und Verheissung: Einführung in die Grundgedanken des Hebräerbriefes (10,32–13,25)." *BibLeb* 1 (1960) 237–52. **Holtzmann, O.** "Der Hebräerbrief und das Abendmahl." *ZNW* 10 (1909) 251–60. **Hunt, B. P. W. S.** "The 'Epistle to the Hebrews': An Anti-Judaic Treatise?" *SE* 2 (1964) 408–10. **Hurst, L. D.** "The Background and Interpretation of the Epistle to the Hebrews." Dissertation, Oxford University, 1981. 60–61, 212–13, 229–35, 241–43 [cf. id., *The Epistle to the Hebrews: Its Background of Thought.* SNTSMS 65. Cambridge: UP, 1990]. **Jeremias, J.** "Zwischen Karfreitag und Ostern: Descensus und Ascensus in der Karfreitags theologie des Neuen Testaments." *ZNW* 42 (1949) 194–201. **Jewett, R.** "The Form and Function of the Homiletical Benediction." *ATR* 51 (1969) 18–34. **Johnsson, W. G.** "The Pilgrimage Motif in The Book of Hebrews." *JBL* 97 (1978) 239–51. **Jones, E. D.** "The Authorship of Hebrews xiii." *ExpTim* 46 (1934–35) 562–67. **Jones, P. R.** "The Figure of Moses as a Heuristic Device for Understanding the Pastoral Intent of Hebrews." *RevExp* 76 (1979) 95–107. ———. "A Superior Life: Hebrews 12:3–13:25." *RevExp* 82 (1985) 391–405. **Katz, P.** "οὐ μή σε ἀνῶ, οὐδ' οὐ μή σε ἐγκαταλίπω (Hebr xiii 5): The Biblical Source of the Quotation." *Bib* 33 (1952) 523–25. ———. "The Quotations from Deuteronomy in Hebrews." *ZNW* 49 (1958) 213–23. **Kirschläger, W.** *Ehe und Ehescheidung im Neuen Testament: Überlegungen und Anfragen zur Praxis der Kirche.* Vienna: Herold, 1987. **Kistemaker, S.** *The Psalm Citations in Hebrews.* 54–57, 88. **Klauck, H. J.** *Hausgemeinde und Hauskirche im frühen Christentum.* Stuttgart: Katholisches Bibelwerk, 1981. ———. "θυσιαστήριον—eine Berichtigung." *ZNW* 71 (1980) 247–77. ———. "θυσιαστήριον in Hebr 13,10 und bei Ignatius von Antiochien." In *Studia Hierosolymitana III.* Ed. G. C. Bottini. Jerusalem: Franciscan, 1987. 147–58. **Koenig, J.** *New Testament Hospitality: Partnership with Strangers as Promise and Mission.* Philadelphia: Fortress, 1985. **Koester, H.** "'Outside the Camp': Hebrews 13:9–14." *HTR* 55 (1962) 299–315. **Koester, W.** "Platonische Ideenwelt und Gnosis im Hebräerbrief." *Schol* 4 (1956) 545–55. **Korošak, B.** "'Gesù Cristo è lo stesso ieri, oggi e sempre' (Eb 13,8)." *Anton* 60 (1985) 279–308. **Korvin-Krasinski, C. von.** "Die heilige Stadt." *ZRGG* 16 (1964) 265–71. **Kosmala, H.** "The Three Nets of Belial." *ASTI* 4 (1965) 91–113. **Kuss, O.** "Der theologische Grundgedanke des Hebräerbriefes: Zur Deutung des Todes Jesu im Neuen Testament." *MTZ* 7 (1956) 233–71. **Lampe, G. W. H.** "The Evidence in the New Testament for Early Creeds, Catechisms, and Liturgy." *ExpTim* 71 (1959–60) 359–63. **Lane, W. L.** "Hebrews: A Sermon in Search of a Setting." *SWJT* 28 (1985) 13–18. ———. "Unexpected Light on Hebrews 13:1–6 from a Second Century Source." *PRS* 9 (1982) 267–74. **Laub, F.** *Bekenntnis und Auslegung.* 143–65, 265–72. ———. "Verkündigung und Gemeindeamt: Die Autorität der ἡγούμενοι Hebr 13,7. 17. 24." *SNTU* 6–7 (1981–82) 169–90. **Lea, T. D.** "The Priesthood of All Christians according to the New Testament." *SWJT* 30 (1988) 15–21. **Legg, J. D.** "Our Brother Timothy: A Suggested Solution to the Problem of the Authorship of the Epistle to the Hebrews." *EvQ* 40 (1968) 220–23. **Lemcio, E. E.** "The Unifying Kerygma of the New Testament." *JSNT* 33 (1988) 3–17. **Loader, W. R. G.** *Sohn und Hoherpriester.* 49–54, 178–81. **Lo Bue, F.** "The Historical Background to the Epistle to the Hebrews." *JBL* 75 (1956) 52–57. **Luck U.** "Himmlisches und irdisches Geschehen im Hebräerbrief." *NovT* 6 (1963) 192–215. **Lührmann D.** "Der Hohepriester ausserhalb des Lagers (Hebr 13:12)." *ZNW* 69 (1978)

178–86. **Lyonnet, S.** "De natura peccati quid doceat Novum Teatamentum—de epistulis Paulinis." *VD* 35 (1957) 332–43. **Malherbe A.** *Social Aspects of Early Christianity.* 2nd ed. Philadelphia: Fortress 1983. 60–112. **Mathews, J. B.** "Hospitality and the New Testament Church: An Historical and Exegetical Study." Dissertation, Princeton Theological Seminary, 1965. **McCown, W. G.** "*Ο ΛΟΓΟΣ ΤΗΣ ΠΑΡΑΚΛΗΣΕΩΣ.*" 120–49, 154–56, 177–81, 197–201. **McCullough, J. C.** "The Old Testament Quotations in Hebrews." *NTS* 26 (1979–80) 367–79. **McDermott, M.** "The Biblical Doctrine of *KOINΩNIA.*" *BZ* 19 (1975) 64–77, 219–33. **Melbourne B. L.** "An Examination of the Historical-Jesus Motif in the Epistle to the Hebrews." *AUSS* 26 (1988) 281–97. **Minear, P.** *New Testament Apocalyptic.* 144–52. **Moe, O.** "Das Abendmahl im Hebräerbrief: Zum Auslegung von Hebr 13,9–16." *ST* 4 (1950) 102–8. **Moffatt, J.** "Exegetica—Hebrews xiii. 22." *Exp* 9th ser. 7 (1914) 192. **Mora G.** *La Carta a los Hebreos como Escrito Pastoral.* 50–54, 66–67, 213–15. **Morrice, W. G.** "The Imperatival *ἵνα.*" *BT* 23 (1972) 326–30. **Moule, C. F. D.** "Sanctuary and Sacrifice in the Church of the New Testament." *JST* n.s. 1 (1950) 29–41. **Mullins, T. Y.** "Greeting as a New Testament Form." *JBL* 87 (1968) 418–26. **Munier, C.** *Mariage et virginité dans l'Église ancienne (Iᵉʳ–IIIᵉ siècles).* Paris: Lang, 1987. **Newton, B. W.** "Note on Hebrews 13:10." In *Thoughts on Scriptural Subjects.* London: Houlston, 1871. 66–79. **Nikiprowetzky, V.** "La Spiritualisation des sacrifices et le culte sacrificiel au temple de Jérusalem chez Philon d'Alexandrie." *Sem* 17 (1967) 98–114. **Nitschke, H.** "Das Ethos des wandernden Gottesvolkes: Erwägung zu Hebr 13 und zu den Möglichkeiten evangelischer Ethik." *MPTh* 46(1957) 179–83. **Oepke, A.** *Das neue Gottesvolk.* 17–24, 57–75. **Old, H. O.** "The Psalm of Praise in the Worship of the New Testament Church." *Int* 39 (1985) 20–33. **Oulton, J. E. L.** "Great Texts Reconsidered: Hebrews 13.10." *ExpTim* 55 (1943–44) 303–5. **Perdelwitz, R.** "Das literarische Problem des Hebräerbriefs." *ZNW* 11 (1910) 59–78. **Ploeg, J. van der.** "L'exégèse de l'Ancien Testament dans l'épître aux Hébreux." *RB* 54 (1947) 187–228. **Ramsay, W. M.** "Roads and Travel (in the New Testament)." *HDB* 5 (1904) 375–402. **Randall E. L.** "The Altar of Hebrews 13:10." *ACR* 46 (1969) 197–208. **Reicke, B.** *Diakonie, Festfreude und Zelos in Verbindung mit der altchristlichen Agapenfeier.* Uppsala: Lundquistska, 1951. 35–37, 167–200. **Reissner, H.** "'Wir haben hier keine bleibende Stadt, sondern die zukünftige suchen wir' (Hebr 13,14): Erwägungen über das Wallfahren." *GL* 35 (1962) 96–103. **Riddle, D. W.** "Early Christian Hospitality: A Factor in the Gospel Transmission." *JBL* 57 (1938) 141–54. **Robertson, O. P.** "The People of the Wilderness: The Concept of the Church in Hebrews." Dissertation, Union Theological Seminary, Richmond, 1966. 144–45, 151–66. **Robinson, W. C.** "Jesus Christ the Same Yesterday, and Today, and Forever (Heb. 13:8)." *EvQ* 16 (1944) 228–35. **Rose, A.** "Jésus-Christ, Pasteur de l'Église." *VSpir* 110 (1964) 501–15. **Rousselle, A.** *Porneia: On Desire and the Body in Antiquity.* Tr. F. Pheasant. Family, Sexuality, and Social Relations in Past Times. Oxford: Blackwell, 1988. **Ruager, S.** "'Wir haben einem Altar' (Hebr 13,10): Einige Überlegungen zum Thema: Gottesdienst/Abendmahl im Hebräerbrief." *KD* 36 (1990) 72–77. **Rusche, H.** *Gastfreundschaft in der Verkündigung des Neuen Testaments und ihr Verhältnis zur Mission.* Münster: Aschendorff, 1959. 37–40. **Sahlin, H.** "Die drei Kardinalsünden und das Neue Testament." *ST* 24 (1970) 93–112. **Saito, T.** *Die Mosevorstellungen im Neuen Testament.* 101–3. **Salom, A. P.** "*Ta Hagia* in the Epistle to the Hebrews." *AUSS* 5 (1967) 59–70. ———. "The Imperatival Use of *ἵνα* in the New Testament." *AusBR* 6 (1958) 123–41. **Sanders, J. A.** "Outside the Camp." *USQR* 24 (1969) 239–46. **Sandvik, B.** *Das Kommen des Herrn beim Abendmahl im Neuen Testament.* Zurich: Zwingli, 1970. 108–13. **Saunders, L.** "'Outside the Camp': Hebrews 13." *RestQ* 22 (1979) 19–24. **Schenk, W.** "Die Paränese Hebr 13:16 im Kontext des Hebräerbriefes—Einer Fallstudie semiotisch-orientierter Textinterpretation und Sachkritik." *ST* 39 (1985) 73–106. **Schick, E. A.** "Priestly Pilgrims: Mission outside the Camp in Hebrews." *CurrThMiss* 16 (1989) 372–76. **Schmidgall, P.** "The Influence of Jewish Apocalyptic Literature on the Book of Hebrews." Dissertation, Western Kentucky University, 1980. 50–55. **Schröger, F.** "Der Gottesdienst der Hebräerbriefgemeinde." *MTZ* 19 (1968) 161–81. ———. *Der Verfasser des Hebräerbriefes als Schriftausleger.* 194–97, 205–6, 239–43, 258. **Sedlaczek, H.** "*φιλαδελφία* nach den Schriften des heiliges Apostels Paulus." *ThQ* 76 (1894) 272–95. **Seesemann, H.** *Der Begriff KOINΩNIA im Neuen Testament.* Giessen: Töpelmann, 1933. 18–27, 99–100. **Shalders, E. W.** "'In a Few Words': A Note on Hebrews xiii. 22." *Exp* 1st ser. 7 (1878) 155–57. **Simcox, G. A.** "Heb. xiii; 2 Tim. iv." *ExpTim* 10 (1898–99) 430–32. **Slot, W.** *De Letterkundige Vorm van de Brief aan de Hebreeën.* Groningen: J. B. Wolters, 1912. 94–103. **Smith, T. C.** "An Exegesis of Hebrews 13:1–17." *FM* 7 (1989) 70–78. **Snell, A.** "We Have an Altar." *RTR* 23 (1964) 16–23. **Spencer, W. H.** "Hebrews xiii.10." *ExpTim* 50 (1938–39) 284. **Spicq, C.** "L'authenticité du chapitre XIII de l'Épître aux Hébreux." *ConNT* 11 (1947) 226–36. **Stelzenberger, J.** *Syneidēsis im Neuen Testament.* Paderborn: Schöningh, 1961. 56–65. **Stott, W.** "The Conception of 'Offering' in the Epistle to the Hebrews." *NTS* 9 (1962) 62–67. **Swetnam, J.** "Christology and the Eucharist in the Epistle to the Hebrews." *Bib* 70 (1989) 74–95. ———. "Form and Content in Hebrews 7–13." *Bib* 55 (1974) 333–48. **Tasker, R. V. G.** "The Integrity of the Epistle to the Hebrews." *ExpTim* 47 (1935–36) 136–38. **Theissen, G.** *Untersuchungen zum Hebräerbrief.* 15, 76–79, 103–5. **Theobald, M.** "'Wir haben hier keine bliebende Stadt sonden suchen die zukünftige' (Hebr 13,14): Die Stadt als Ort der frühen christlichen Gemeinde." *TGl* 78 (1988) 16–40. **Thompson, J. G. S. S.** "The Shepherd-Ruler Concept in the OT and Its Application in the NT." *SJT* 8 (1955) 406–18. **Thompson, J. W.** *The Beginnings of Christian Philosophy.* 141–50. ———. "Outside the Camp: A Study of Heb 13:9–14." *CBQ* 40 (1978) 53–63. **Thurén, J.** *Das Lobopfer der Hebräer: Studien zum Aufbau und Anliegen von Hebräerbrief 13.* Åbo: Åbo Akademi, 1973. 49–247. **Thüsing, W.** "'Lasst uns hinzutreten . . .' (Hebr 10,22): Zur Frage nach der Sinn der kulttheologie im Hebräerbrief." *BZ* n.s. 9 (1965) 1–17. **Torrence T. F.** "The Last of the Hallel Psalms." *EvQ* 28 (1956) 101–8. **Torrey, C. C.** "The Authorship and Character of the so-called 'Epistle to the Hebrews.'" *JBL* 30 (1911) 137–56. **Trudinger, L. P.** "The Gospel Meaning of the Secular: Reflections on Hebrews 13:10–13." *EvQ* 54 (1982) 235–37. ———. "ΚΑΙ ΓΑΡ ΔΙΑ ΒΡΑΧΕΩΝ ΕΠΕΣΤΕΙΛΑ ΥΜΙΝ: A Note on Hebrews XIII.22." *JTS* n.s. 23 (1972) 128–30. **Übelacker, W. G.** *Der Hebräerbrief als Appell: Untersuchungen zu exordium, narratio und postscriptum (Hebr 1–2 und 13,22–25).* Stockholm: Almquist & Wiksell, 1989. 197–223. **Vanhoye, A.** "Discussions sur la structure de l'Épître aux Hébreux." *Bib* 55 (1974) 349–80. ———. "La question littéraire de Hébreux xiii.1–6." *NTS* 23 (1976–77) 121–39. ———. "*Retti cammini*": *L'ultima parte dell'Epistola agli Ebrei (Ebr. 12,14–13,25).* Rome: Biblical Institute, 1974. **Vitalini, A.** *La nozione d'accoglienza nel Nuovo Testamento.* Fribourg: Herder, 1963. **Watson, J. K.** "L'Épître aux Hébreux." *CCER* 15 (1968) 10–16. **Watson, R. A.** "The Shepherd, God and Man, Heb. xiii.20–21." *Exp* 4th ser. 9 (1894) 239–40. **Williams, C. R.** "A Word-Study of Hebrews 13." *JBL* 30 (1911) 129–36. **Williamson, R.** "The Eucharist and the Epistle to the Hebrews." *NTS* 21 (1975) 300–312. ———. *Philo and the Epistle to the Hebrews.* 176–78, 180–81, 193–95, 200, 230–32, 275–76, 301–2, 480–83, 570–72. **Wills, L.** "The Form of the Sermon in Hellenistic Judaism and Early Christianity." *HTR* 77 (1984) 277–99. **Wilson J. P.** "The Interpretation of Hebrews xiii.10." *ExpTim* 50 (1938–39) 380–81. **Wrede, W.** *Das literarische Rätsel des Hebräerbriefs.* 3–5, 39–73. **Young, F. M.** "The Use of Sacrificial Ideas in Greek Christian Writers from the New Testament to John Chrysostom." Dissertation, Cambridge University, 1967. 103–4, 129, 217. [cf. id., *The Use of Sacrificial Ideas in Greek Christian Writers from the New Testament to John Chrysostom.* Patristic Monograph Series 5. Cambridge, Mass.: Philadelphia Patristic Foundation, 1979.]

Form/Structure/Setting

The homily reaches its pastoral and theological climax in 12:14–29. That fact has encouraged some scholars to regard the final chapter as an appendix or supplement that was added artificially to the homily. Briefly, three objections have been posed to the integrity of Hebrews and to the authenticity or appropriateness of chap. 13.

(1) The chapter begins abruptly, without apparent link with what precedes. The abruptness is accentuated by a sharp change in tone and theme (cf. Spicq, *ConNT* 11 [1947] 226).

(2) The form of chap. 13 is without parallel in earlier chapters. The exhortation suddenly gives way to a series of catechetical precepts. The opening paragraph, 13:1–6, has been described as a loose collection of general admonitions unrelated to the actual situation of the community or to the specific concerns of the writer (so, e.g., Thompson, *Beginnings of Christian Philosophy,* 143). This series of imperatives exhibits the character of the general parenesis of the early Church as it is known from the letters of the NT (e.g., 1 Thess 5:12–22; Rom 12:9–21; 13:8–10; 1 Pet 3:8–12). A formless collection of the ethical precepts and theological reflections scarcely seems congruous with the careful development of argument in chaps. 1–12. It is noticeably different from the climactic exhortaton of 10:19–12:29. (See further Filson, 'Yesterday', 13–18; Thurén, *Lobopfer,* 49–55, and especially 52, n. 203, for a setting forth of the literary problem.)

(3) The content of chap. 13 clearly distinguishes this section from the remainder of the document. This claim is crystalized in two theses advanced by Nitschke:

In the framework of the New Testament Hebrews 1–12 is an individual solo. Chapter 13 sings as everybody sings. Not only Paul! and not only once in the New Testament!

The ethic contained in chapters 1–12 lacks the concrete. The ethic of chapter 13 goes into the concrete, but lacks the specifically Christian element! (*MPTh* 46 [1957] 179).

(For a summary of Nitschke's argument, and a vigorous response, see J. Thurén, *Das Lobopfer der Hebräer,* 235, n. 814.)

In short, it is asserted that considerations of coherence, form, and content call into question the integrity of Hebrews and the authenticity or appropriateness of chap. 13.

In spite of repeated suggestions that chap. 13, or some parts of it, are an alien intrusion, the integrity of Hebrews can be affirmed with confidence (see *Introduction,* "Integrity"). The affirmation of integrity, of course, is also an assertion of authenticity. It is unnecessary to call into question the authenticity of chap. 13 in the light of the very evident links between this material and the preceding chapters, both in content and thrust. Attention has been called to the character of the vocabulary, to lines of argumentation, to the sustained appeal to texts from the Pentateuch and the Psalms, to the recurrence of key concepts, and to considerations of structure, all of which tend to exhibit the basic homogeneity of chap. 13 with the rest of the document (cf. C. R. Williams, *JBL* 30 [1911] 129–36; Tasker, *ExpTim* 47 [1935–36] 136–38; Spicq, *ConNT* 11 [1947] 226–36; Filson, 'Yesterday', 22–26, 28–29; McCown, "Ο ΛΟΓΟΣ ΤΗΣ ΠΑΡΑΚΛΗΣΕΩΣ," 120–38, 145–49, 177–79; Michel, 478–80; Thurén, *Lobopfer,* 57–70; Vanhoye, *NTS* 23 [1976–77] 121–29). These observations constitute a strong argument for the authenticity of chap. 13.

A further consideration based on style can be added to the arguments for authenticity that have been advanced by others. The length of 13:1–25 is sufficient to provide a clear indication of the distinctive literary style of the writer. In the *Notes,* attention is called to chiastic structure within a sentence or clause (*Notes* c and k on vv 1–6; k and y on vv 7–19), paronomasia or play on words (*Notes* c on v 2; oo and qq on v 18; c on v 20; b on v 22), unusual word order designed to arouse attention (*Notes* f and q on vv 7–19; c on v 20), elegant style (*Note* hh on v 17), linguistic rhythm (*Note* f on v 3), assonance (*Notes* n and o on vv 1–6; h, v, y, and ff on vv 7–19), alliterative arrangements of lines (*Notes* s on v 5; tt on v 19), the conscious use of syntax to display emphasis (*Notes* f, i, l, and s on vv 1–6; h, q, r, bb, and rr on vv 7–19; c on v 20), and the use of classical idioms (*Notes* d and s on vv 1–6; bb and kk on vv 7–19). These elements in combination constitute a distinctive literary signature that serves to identify the writer, as would a set of fingerprints. This is precisely the literary signature recognized in the earlier sections of the homily. These expressions of conscious literary artistry furnish an argument for the authenticity of the entire chapter, since they are drawn from each of its constitutive parts. Heb 13 as a whole was drafted by the writer responsible for Heb 1–12 and was clearly composed to accompany the earlier chapters.

The characterization of chap. 13 as a supplement or a postscript (e.g., Moffatt, 224; Héring, 14, 121, 126; Spicq, 2:415; Strathmann, 152; H. Montefiore, 237–38; for a fuller listing, see Thurén, *Lobopfer*, 51–53) tends to reflect the conviction that it is without inner connection or significance for the homily as a whole. This opinion can be challenged only by showing that this section transmits an essential message that can scarcely be separated from the concerns and themes of chaps. 1–12. Methodologically, an argument for the integration of a document is advanced most effectively by proceeding on the assumption of coherence and allowing that assumption to be tested as rigorously as possible. The argument will be vindicated when the text yields better sense in its parts and as a whole than when a contested unit is regarded as intrusive, poorly connected, or corrupt. It will be shown that chap. 13 is by no means an addendum. Within the structure of the homily it has its own task to fulfill (cf. Riggenbach, xv, 428; Michel, 479; Thurén, *Lobopfer*, 53–55).

The chapter falls into two uneven parts: 13:1–21 furnishes the conclusion to the homily; 13:22–25 has the character of a personal note attached to the homily at the time it was sent because the writer could reach the community only by courier. Questions bearing on form, structure, and setting are appropriate to 13:1–21 because this section is integral to the homily itself.

The connection of 13:1–21 to the preceding section, 12:14–29, is established through 12:28. There the community is summoned to be thankful, and through thanksgiving to serve God in an acceptable manner. At that climactic point in the homily, authentic worship is defined as grateful response to objective covenant blessings already experienced and to the certainty of the future reception of an unshakable kingdom. It is conditioned by a frank awareness of the awesome character of the holiness of God disclosed in the fiery epiphany of Sinai (12:28–29).

The concept of worship, however, is almost certainly to be expanded to include a lifestyle that is pleasing to God at every level. It is to be augmented by active participation in the shared values and witness of the confessing community. The members of the house church are to regard every aspect of their lives as an expression of devoted service to God. What this entails demands the specification that is provided in 13:1–21. The climactic statement in 12:28–29, accordingly, is assigned a double function: it provides closure to 12:14–29, and it serves to focus the attention of the auditors, preparing them for the elaboration of the acceptable service of God in the concluding section of the homily. (It is the merit of Thurén to have shown the extent to which the theme of worship, expressed in 12:28, pervades the entire development of 13:1–21 [*Lobopfer*, 74–90, 105–82, 187–245].)

The importance of 12:28 in preparing for the development in 13:1–21 was recognized over a century ago (1886) by C. F. Keil (378). It has been affirmed more recently by scholars representing a broad spectrum critically and theologically (e.g., Spicq, *ConNT* 11 [1947] 231; Kuss, *TGl* 42 [1952] 193; Strathmann, *TDNT* 4:64; Michel, 479, n. 1; Filson, *'Yesterday'*, 28; Swetnam, *Bib* 55 [1974] 340–41, 347; McCown, "Ο ΛΟΓΟΣ ΤΗΣ ΠΑΡΑΚΛΗΣΕΩΣ," 139; Thurén, *Lobopfer*, 58, 234–35; cf. the heading for chap. 13 in TEV: "Service Well Pleasing to God"; for modifications of this position and alternative proposals see Vanhoye, *La structure*, 210–15; id., *Bib* 55 [1974] 363, 374, 378–79; and id., *NTS* 23 [1976–77] 136–37, who finds in 13:1–18 or 13:1–21 the elaboration of the call to pursue holiness in 12:14; and Bligh, *HeyJ* 5 [1964] 174, who found the announcement of 13:1–6 in 12:16*a*, and of 13:7–18 in 12:16*b*).

Thurén's hypothesis that chap. 13 enjoyed an independent existence and subsequently served as the initial kernel for the composition of the entire work, to which it was then integrated (*Lobopfer*, 53–55, 108, 246–47), cannot be sustained. In a critical response Vanhoye correctly observed that chap. 13 is not a self-sufficient literary unit. The function of introducing the unit cannot be filled by 13:1. Formally it is too brief, and its content is too limited to be the introduction of a major parenetic section; the motif of brotherly love simply does not correspond to the totality of the text. Separated from its immediate context, chap. 13 presents itself as a truncated text deprived of its beginning. It is possible to consider 13:1 only as the beginning of a subdivision of a more extended writing (review of Thurén, *Lobopfer*, in *Bib* 56 [1975] 139–40, and id., *NTS* 23 [1976–77] 130–32, 135–36).

Vanhoye's critical insight is helpful. It suggests that the beginning of the concluding unit of the homily may actually be found in 12:28, with its call for the acceptable service of God (λατρεύωμεν εὐαρέστως τῷ θεῷ, "let us serve God acceptably"). The note of well-pleasing service to God is repeated, with variation, in the petition of 13:21, that the God of peace "may accomplish in us what is pleasing to him" (ποιῶν . . . τὸ εὐάρεστον ἐνώπιον αὐτοῦ). This petition reinforces the double admonition in 13:15–16 to offer the spiritual sacrifices of praise, kindness to others, and generosity, with which God is pleased (τοιαύταις γὰρ θυσίαις εὐαρεστεῖται ὁ θεός, "for with such sacrifices God is pleased"). An *inclusio* is established between 12:28 and 13:21 on the basis of the adverb εὐαρέστως, "acceptably," in 12:28, which occurs only here in the NT, and its cognate εὐάρεστον, "pleasing," in 13:21. This literary device serves to identify 13:1–21 as a self-contained unit of thought within the homily.

The sermon is brought to a close on the note of parenetic instructions. Parenesis is traditional in character (see *Introduction* to 12:14–13:25). An awareness that the auditors are already familiar with the instruction they are receiving is reflected in the continual use of the present imperative (cf. 13:1, 2, 3, 7, 9, 17, 18). Since what is being instilled is not new or unfamiliar instruction, no extended treatment of a particular concern was necessary. It was sufficient to remind the community of what they already knew or were doing, or conversely, to call them to desist from a practice or tendency that was destructive. As a contemporary of the writer commented, "Advice (*admonitio*) is not teaching; it merely engages the attention and arouses us; it concentrates the memory, and keeps it from losing its grip" (Seneca, *Epistles* 94.25). Parenetic instruction reflects a critical and purposeful selection, adaptation, and application of the tradition. A common element in parenetic instruction is the appeal to example. It calls for imitation of qualities of life and conduct exhibited in those who have proved to be models worthy of emulation (cf. 13:7, 12, 17–19). The form that parenetic instruction takes is admonition, advising the audience to act in an appropriate manner or to abstain from a particular course of action.

Heb 13:1–19 is recognizably a parenetic section. The admonitions are traditional in character (cf. Filson, '*Yesterday*', 22–25; Thurén, *Lobopfer*, 57–70). No single topic receives extended treatment. Brief formulations, cast in the form of admonitions, cover the range of Christian responsibilities to one another, to strangers, to the imprisoned or mistreated, to marriage, to the leaders of the community, and to the Lord. Formulations like "Do not neglect" (13:2, 16) or "Remember" (13:3, 7) are calculated to jog the memory into recalling traditional instruction that was thoroughly familiar by this time. The appeal to the example of past leaders and the call to imitate their faith (13:7) is parenetic in character and intention, as is the reference to the exemplary conduct of those who are currently in a position of leadership (13:17–18). These notes are complemented by the appeal to the example of Jesus "who suffered death outside the city gate," followed by the exhortation to emulate him, "bearing the shame he bore" (13:12–13). From the perspective both of form and content, 13:1–19 can be recognized as parenetic in character.

McCown has attempted to define the form of this section with greater precision. He proposes that a distinction be made between 13:1–6, 7–9, 17–19, on the one hand, and 13:10–16 on the other, since these units exhibit two quite different hortatory techniques. McCown classifies 13:1–6, 7–9, 17–19 under the heading of "catechetical precepts" ("*Ο ΛΟΓΟΣ ΤΗΣ ΠΑΡΑΚΛΗΣΕΩΣ*," 145–49). As the name implies, a series of pastoral directives appears to have been drawn from the early Christian catechetical tradition to which the writer referred in 5:12 and 6:1–2. This orally determined didactic material undoubtedly consisted in part of traditional wisdom and advice validated by extensive use. It provided a ready reservoir for pastoral direction (cf. Thyen, *Stil*, 85).

The literary form of "catechetical precept" may be recognized in a series of detached precepts, seemingly without coherence, consisting of concise admonitions of a traditional nature. They tend to be set forth as direct imperatives:

13:1	μένετω	"It must continue"
13:2	μὴ ἐπιλανθάνεσθε	"Do not neglect"
13:3	μιμνήσκεσθε	"Continue to remember"
13:7	μνημονεύετε	"Continue to remember"
	μιμεῖσθε	"imitate"
13:9	μὴ παραφέρεσθε	"Do not be carried away"
13:16	μὴ ἐπιλανθάνεσθε	"Do not neglect"
13:17	πείθεσθε	"Continue to obey"
	ὑπείκετε	"submit"
13:18	προσεύχεσθε	"Continue to pray"

Alternatively, catechetical precepts may be formulated with an introductory adjective of imperatival force or with an imperatival participle:

13:4	τίμιος	"It must be respected"
	ἀμίαντος	"It must be undefiled"
13:5	ἀφιλάργυρος	"It must be free from the love of money
	ἀρκούμενοι	"be content"

There is characteristically an absence of sustained argumentation (as in 13:1–9) and no evidence of catchword association. (McCown, "Ο ΛΟΓΟΣ ΤΗΣ ΠΑΡΑΚΛΗΣΕΩΣ," 145–49, 160, 177–79, 197–200; and for useful background material, W. Schrage, *Die konkrete Einzelgebote in der paulinischen Paränese* [Gütersloh: Mohn, 1961]).

Embedded within this structure, 13:10–16 is a cohesive unit that exhibits a quite different hortatory technique from 13:1–9, 17–19. McCown categorizes 13:10–16 as "explanatory paraenesis" or "hortatory exposition" ("Ο ΛΟΓΟΣ ΤΗΣ ΠΑΡΑΚΛΗΣΕΩΣ," 127–28, 140–43, 148–49, 154–56). These formal descriptions can be applied to an integrated unit in which there is sustained argumentation. The basis of the argument is exposition, although the intention is clearly parenetic. In 13:10–16 the flow of the argumentation is charted by a series of particles. The argument, introduced with the affirmation, "We have an altar," is grounded in an appeal to Lev 16:27, which is expounded in 13:10–12. The writer's parenetic intention, however, is made clear in 13:13–16 when he introduces two hortatory imperatives:

| 13:13 | ἐξερχώμεθα | "let us go out" |
| 13:15 | ἀναφέρωμεν | "let us continually offer." |

In this instance the exposition provides the basis for applying the liturgical directives of Lev 16 to the community by way of descriptive analogy.

The writer used descriptive analogy in earlier sections of the homily (3:1–6; 12:18–29). Basic to this form of exposition is an appeal to an authoritative description in Scripture, the detail of which is applied to Christ or to the community on the basis of redemptive analogy. The primary interest is in the descriptive language of the biblical text, from which the interpreter derives authority for the parenetic appeal (cf. R. Bultmann, "Ursprung und Sinn der Typologie als hermeneutischer Methode," *TLZ* 75 [1950] 212; McCown, "Ο ΛΟΓΟΣ ΤΗΣ ΠΑΡΑΚΛΗΣΕΩΣ," 106–7, 154–56).

In 13:10–16 the appeal to Lev 16:27 serves to clarify the significance that Jesus suffered death "outside the gate" (13:11–12). The OT text furnishes the basis for the exhortation to follow him "outside the camp," bearing the shame he bore (13:13). The biblical text also reflects retrospectively on "the altar" (13:10), which is applied indirectly to Christ's sacrificial death for sin (13:11–12); it is applied directly in the double admonition to offer to God the sacrifice of praise, acts of kindness, and generosity (13:15–16). The biblical and theological character of the argument serves to identify the form of 13:10–16 as hortatory exposition, in distinction from the traditional character of the catechetical precepts. The use of the hortatory subjunctive in 13:1–21 is confined appropriately to 13:10–16.

An analysis of the literary forms within 13:1–19 may be complemented by an appreciation of the structure of the text. The unity and symmetry of 13:1–6 serve to identify this unit as an integrated paragraph. Thurén found in the symmetrical arrangement of 13:1–6 a tripartite structure reflecting a pattern of admonition—warning—Scriptural word (*Lobopfer,* 208, 220–21; for this scheme, but for other reasons, see Dussaut, *Synopse structurelle,* 132, 185, n. 25):

(1) 13:1–3   two double admonitions concerning love;
(2) 13:4–5*a* two double warnings against impurity and idolatry;
(3) 13:5*b*–6 two citations of Scripture, which provide the foundation for 13:5*a* and at the same time serve to round off the whole paragraph.

Although this arrangement is harmonious and throws into bold relief certain aspects of the text, it is artificial. The division made in the middle of 13:5 ignores the coherence between the injunction of v 5*a* and the two OT citations in vv 5*b*–6 that is established with the conjunctions γάρ ("*for* God himself has said") and ὥστε ("*So* we can say"). Moreover, the failure to observe a division between 13:4 and 13:5 obscures the fact that the injunctions in v 4*a* are followed by their own motivation in v 4*b* (correctly observed by Vanhoye, *NTS* 23 [1976–77] 123).

The arrangement proposed by Michel is more faithful to the text. He distinguishes four pairs of single admonitions, "to each of which there is attached a short significant motivation" (479):

(1) 13:1–2   Maintain fraternal love and hospitality!
(2) 13:3   Remember the prisoners and the mistreated!
(3) 13:4   Respect marriage and the marriage bed!
(4) 13:5–[6] Keep yourself from greed and learn to be content, for God will take care of you!

The grouping of single admonitions by pairs may reflect a mnemonic technique analogous to catchword association; terms that were similar in sound or meaning have been brought together (so McCown, "*Ο ΛΟΓΟΣ ΤΗΣ ΠΑΡΑΚΛΗΣΕΩΣ,*" 124):

(1)	13:1–2	φιλαδελφία—φιλοξένιας	brotherly love–hospitality to strangers
(2)	13:3	τῶν δεσμίων—τῶν κακουχουμένων	the prisoners—the mistreated
(3)	13:4	γάμος—κοίτη	marriage—marriage bed
(4)	13:5	ἀφιλάργυρος—ἀρκούμενα τοῖς παροῦσιν	free from the love of money—content with what [you] have

This is an attractive proposal, although 13:3 is not accompanied by a supporting motivation. In fact, it continues to develop the theme of love for brothers and sisters that was introduced in 13:1; it may be readily attached to 13:1–2 to form an integrated unit. The injunction to "continue to remember" in 13:3*a* simply echoes in a positive formulation the caution "do not neglect" in 13:2*a*. It is thus more appropriate to group 13:1–3 together.

A less regulated arrangement that recognizes both the unity and symmetry of 13:1–6 has been proposed by Vanhoye. He finds in the text a tripartite pattern involving two admonitions and a motivation (*NTS* 23 [1976–77] 123–24):

(1)   13:1–2a   two exhortations to love (brothers and strangers)
       2b   —motive (γάρ), with Scriptural allusion
       3   two exhortations to love (prisoners and the mistreated)
(2)   13:4a   two exhortations to marital purity
       4b   —motive (γάρ), with Scriptural allusion
(3)   13:5a   two exhortations to contentment
       5b   —motive (γάρ), with Scriptural citation
       6   —consequence (ὥστε), with Scriptural citation

Vanhoye recognizes that only the central admonitions exhibit in a strict sense the pattern that he identified. The other units each contain an extra component. In 13:1–3 two additional exhortations are attached thematically to the unit, unsupported by a motivational phrase. In 13:5–6 a consequence deduced from the motivation is added, which provides an appropriate conclusion to the paragraph as a whole. According to this arrangement, two fuller units of text frame a briefer one. The result is an arrangement that is symmetrical without being monotonous. The composition of 13:1–6 is both harmonious and purposeful. (For a literary analysis of the compositional detail, see Vanhoye, *NTS* 23 [1976–77] 124–27; cf. Thurén, *Lobopfer,* 68, 220–221; contrast Moffatt, 224, who describes 13:1–7 as "a handful of moral counsels"; similar formulations occur in Kuss, 192; Thompson, *Beginnings of Christian Philosophy,* 143; among others.)

A second integrated paragraph may be recognized in 13:7–19. Within the structure of this paragraph it is necessary to consider 13:7–9 and 13:17–19 together, since they constitute the frame for the explanatory parenesis in 13:10–16. These two small units are shown to belong together initially through the *inclusio* achieved through the reference to "your leaders" and their "conduct":

13:7   Μνημονεύετε τῶν ἡγουμένων ὑμων. . . . ὧν ἀναθεωροῦντες τὴν ἔκβασιν
         τῆς ἀναστροφῆς
         "Continue to remember *your leaders* . . . considering the accomplish-
         ment of *their conduct*"
13:17–18 πείθεσθε τοῖς ἡγουμένοις ὑμῶν . . . Προσεύχεσθε περὶ ἡμῶν πειθόμεθα
         γὰρ ὅτι καλὴν συνείδησιν ἔχομεν ἐν πᾶσιν καλῶς θέλοντες
         ἀναστρέφεσθαι.
         "Continue to obey *your leaders.* . . . Continue to pray for us, for we are
         convinced that we have a clear conscience, since we strive *to conduct*
         [ourselves] commendably in every way."

The injunctions in 13:7 and 13:17–18 complement one another. Moreover, the imperatival statements introduced seem to be paired in an alliterative arrangement:

13:7   μνημονεύετε—μιμεῖσθε   "remember"—"imitate"
13:17–18   πείθεσθε—προσεύχεσθε   "obey"—"pray"

It is natural to associate 13:7–9 conceptually, because the word of God proclaimed by the now-deceased leaders is crystallized in the confessional formulation of 13:8 and is distorted by the various strange teachings to which reference is made in 13:9. These verses function as a unit to introduce the hortatory exposition in 13:10–16. Similarly, since the absent writer groups himself among the leaders to whom obedience is to be rendered and for whom prayer is requested in 13:17–18, it is appropriate to associate 13:19 with these verses as an integral part of the frame (so McCown, *"Ο ΛΟΓΟΣ ΤΗΣ ΠΑΡΑΚΛΗΣΕΩΣ,"* 124–25; Thurén, *Lobopfer,* 71–72, 183–84, 205–6, 208; Dussaut, *Synopse structurelle,* 133–34; cf. Schierse, *Verheissung,* 184–87; Vanhoye, *La structure,* 211–16; Kuss, *MTZ* 7 [1956] 267–68, n. 268; Michel, 485, n. 1, for the argument that the frame is constituted by 13:7 and 13:17–18; the failure to recognize that 13:19 is an extension of 13:17–18 encourages Vanhoye to delete it as a marginal addition [*La structure,* 220–21]; for an alternative proposal to identify an *inclusio* between 13:1–3 and 13:16 on the basis of the repeated injunction μὴ ἐπιλανθάνεσθε; "do not neglect," in vv 2 and 16, see Spicq, *ConNT* 11 [1947] 234–35).

The elaborate building of the frame serves to highlight 13:10–16, which is distinguished as a unit from 13:7–9 and 17–19 by its form and construction. Formally, it consists of exposition, 13:10–12, which grounds the exhortation in 13:13–16. Each constituent part consists of three members arranged chiastically:

A	(13:10)	"We have an altar from which those who serve the tabernacle do not have the right to eat";
B	(13:11)	"For (γάρ) . . . their bodies are burned outside (ἔξω) the camp";
C	(13:12)	"And so (διό) Jesus also suffered death outside (ἔξω) the city gate";
C'	(13:13)	"So then (τοίνυν) let us go out to him outside (ἔξω) the camp, bearing the shame he bore";
B'	(13:14)	"for (γάρ) here we do not have a permanent city, but we are expecting intently the city which is to come";
A'	(13:15–16)	Through Jesus, therefore (οὖν), let us continually offer to God a sacrifice consisting in praise."

The chiastic construction shows that 13:10–12 (A/B/C) provides the ground for 13:13–16 (C'/B'/A').

The assertion in 13:10*a*, "we have an altar" (A) is the determining thesis elucidated and established in 13:11–12 (B/C). The exhortation in 13:15–16 (A') is the decisive demand for which the writer prepares in 13:13–14 (C'/B'). 13:10 (A) and 13:15–16 (A') are clearly related to each other: the proposition that we have an altar fully justifies the exhortation to offer to God the sacrifice that will please him (following Thurén, *Lobopfer,* 74–75; cf. Vanhoye, *La structure,* 211–15, who recognizes a chiasm but locates the middle of the unit between 13:11 and 13:12; Dussaut, *Synopse structurelle,* 132–33, who makes 13:11/13:12/13:13–14 "the three central units" between 13:9–10 and 13:15–16).

The way from 13:10 (A) to 13:15–16 (A') is marked out by transitional conjunctions and particles (B/C/C'/B'/A'), while the incentive for complying with the parenetic instruction is developed by the use of prepositions (B/C/C'). The structural symmetry of 13:10–16 indicates that the climax to the artistically built unit is to be located in the double admonition of 13:15–16. The construction of the unit substantiates that the writer's primary intention is parenesis, which is grounded through the exposition. Progress will be made in the interpretation of these "exceedingly enigmatic" verses (so Kuss, 215, commenting on 13:7–17; cf. Oepke, *Das neue Gottesvolk,* 21) only if close attention is given to the construction of the unit.

In brief, 13:10 (A) develops the antithesis, "we have . . . they have not." The second term of the antithesis is substantiated from the perspective of Day of

Atonement 13:11 (B). 13:11 (B) is then interpreted Christologically in 13:12 (C), which serves as the substantiation for 13:10 (A). The exhortation in 13:13 (C') is motivated through 13:12 (C), while the double admonition in 13:15–16 (A') is motivated through 13:10 (A). 13:11 (B) and 13:14 (B') have the character of interjected explanations; the exhortation in 13:13 (C') is motivated through the explanation in 13:14 (B'). The correspondences must be observed and respected.

The chiastic construction of 13:10–16 does not exhaust the literary artistry of this unit. The final member of the chiasm, the double admonition in 13:15–16 (A'), has also been given a chiastic arrangement by the writer:

A   δι' αὐτοῦ οὖν ἀναφέρωμεν θυσίαν αἰνέσεως διὰ παντὸς τῷ θεῷ
      "Through him, therefore, let us continually offer a sacrifice of praise to God"
B   τοῦτ' ἔστιν καρπὸν χειλέων ὁμολογούντων τῷ ὀνόματι αὐτοῦ
      "this is to say, the fruit of lips that praise his name"
B'   τῆς δὲ εὐποιΐας καὶ κοινωνίας μὴ ἐπιλανθάνεσθε
      "Do not neglect acts of kindness and generosity"
A'   τοιαύταις γὰρ θυσίαις εὐαρεστεῖται ὁ θεός
      "for God is pleased because of such sacrifices"

The first and fourth clauses of the Greek text refer to "sacrifice" and conclude with a reference to "God." The offering of the sacrifice to God is in view in the initial clause, while the final clause refers to the reception of the sacrifice by God. The two clauses are complementary. The interior clauses define the sacrifices that are to be offered to God through Jesus as praise, acts of kindness, and generosity (so Thurén, *Lobopfer,* 105). The care with which 13:10–16 has been composed and framed indicates the importance of this unit within the literary structure of 13:1–21. It is crucial to the writer's pastoral strategy.

The two symmetrically arranged paragraphs, 13:1–6 and 13:7–19, create an effective vehicle for the final instruction in the homily. The prayer-wish that follows in 13:20–21 provides formal closure to the section and to the homily as a whole. The adoption of the participial style and of paraphrastic constructions achieves a noticeable change of rhythm and the solemnity appropriate to the conclusion of the sermon. The prayer is arranged into an invocation, followed by two strophes of four lines each, both of which end with the name of Jesus, and a concluding doxology (see below, *Translation* and *Note* a on v 20, following Michel, 535). The two strophes call attention to parallel movements: the work of God already realized in the Lord Jesus when he was led out from the dead (13:20) and the work of God that must be realized within Christians if they are to do God's will (13:21). These two movements are framed by the invocation of "the God of peace" at the beginning and by the doxology, which is directed to God, at the end (cf. Deichgräber, *Gotteshymnus,* 33–34; for an alternative arrangement of the prayer-wish see Spicq, 2:434, who divides the clauses so as to obtain a fivefold division and who attaches the doxology to its nearest antecedent, "Jesus Christ"; Spicq appeals to the traditional form of the collects of the Church, as traced by J. W. Legg, "Notes on Collects," *JTS* 13 [1912] 558–63). With the "Amen," a period is put to the homily.

It is unnecessary to regard this prayer as a preformulated collect not organic to the thought of Hebrews, as argued by Michel (535, 537). Michel traces the core of the formulation back to an older Palestinian Jewish-Christian tradition of prayer, with formal parallels in *t. Ber.* 3:7; *b. Ber.* 29b (Baraitha, R. Eliezer, c. A.D. 90) (cf. Jewett, *ATR* 51 [1969] 28-30; for a possible model for a history of tradition analysis of the prayer, see Thurén, *Lobopfer,* 222, who compares Heb 13:20–21 with the prayer-wishes in *1 Clem.* 64 and 1 Pet 5:10). The prayer-wish is firmly connected to the preceding paragraphs by the conjunction δέ, "and," is integrated by vocabulary and conception with its setting within the homily (Jewett, *ATR* 51 [1969] 22–23).

The setting of 13:1–21 merits particular attention. The unit brings an elaborately developed homily to its conclusion, justifying the care with which the writer has composed the two integrated paragraphs and the concluding prayer-wish. The symmetry of 13:1–6 and 13:7–19 demonstrates that the writer attached ultimate importance to what he had to say to the community in this section. The status of 13:7–19 as the primary exhortation is clear: the extent of this paragraph, the elaborate framework, and the central position of 13:10–16 all underscore its significance. The importance of 13:1–21 to the pastoral strategy of the writer can be exhibited only after closer examination of the detail of the text. Nevertheless, it is already apparent in the literary artistry of the section and in the specific detail given to the call to worship God in 12:28.

The short unit, 13:22–25, differs from the homily in literary genre and function. It reflects the conventions of a brief personal note or announcement, commending the sermon to the audience (13:22), passing on information they would wish to receive (13:23), and conveying greetings from the writer and his associates (13:24). A familiar blessing (13:25) furnishes an appropriate conclusion to the document as a whole. As an attached note or postscript, 13:22–25 stands outside the basic structure of the work (so Michel, 541; Übelacker, *Appell,* 197–201; for an opposing point of view, see Thurén, *Lobopfer,* 66, who insists that the tradition of the concluding parenesis shows that 13:22–25 is an integral part of the parenetic structure; Thurén argues that 13:15–25 is totally created out of the tradition of the NT [parenetic] letter closing [57–66]).

It has often been suggested that 13:22–25 is a brief letter of recommendation, or a cover letter, appended to the homily by someone other than the writer (e.g., E. Burggaller, *ZNW* 9 [1908] 110–31; Perdelwitz, *ZNW* 11 [1910] 59–78; Schierse, *Verheissung,* 206–7; Vanhoye, *La structure,* 219–22; J. D. Legg, *EvQ* 40 [1968] 220–23). It is not necessary to resort to such a conjecture. The integrity of the homily and the note may be maintained (see pp. 496–97). Dussaut, for example, is confident that the writer of the homily and of the note are one and the same person (*Synopse structurelle,* 134–35). He finds in the correspondence between δέ παρακαλῶ, "And I urge" (13:19), and παρακαλῶ δέ, "And I urge" (13:22), a linking device by which 13:22–25 is joined to the homily, which clearly reflects the literary style of the homilist.

The development of 13:1–21 was motivated by the call in 12:28 to respond to the objective blessings secured in the new covenant with thanksgiving, as the essential condition for the acceptable worship of God. Covenant privilege and obligation imply a level of Christian maturity at which every aspect of life expresses grateful service to God.

The role of 12:28 in determining the development of 13:1–21 is most apparent in 13:10–16. The confessional statement, "We have an altar" (13:10), is supported by reference to Jesus' sacrificial death for sin by which the new covenant people were consecrated to the service of God (13:12). Consecration to God implies committed discipleship (13:13–14). Moreover, the possession of an altar, together with the effective removal of every impediment to authentic worship (13:12), creates the possibility of offering to God the sacrifices that please him (13:15–16). The cultic formulation of the exhortation to worship in 12:28 finds its complement in the elaboration of consecration to God through expressive cultic language in 13:15–16. The verbal link between the foundational pastoral directive in 12:28, "through [thanksgiving] let us serve God *acceptably*" (εὐαρέστως), and the complementary exhortation in 13:15–16 is provided in the confident assertion "for God is *pleased* [εὐαρεστεῖται] with such sacrifice" (13:16). Consecration to God is acknowledged through the offering of "the sacrifice of praise." Life within the confessing community is thankful response to God.

The central unit of explanatory parenesis, 13:10–16, is firmly embedded in its context. Carefully framed by the pastoral directives in 13:7–9 and 17–19, it sheds light on the coherent development of the section as a whole. The identification of acts of kindness and generosity as the sacrifices with which God is pleased (13:16) throws into bold relief the significance of the catechetical precepts calling for expressions of fraternal love in 13:1–3. The service of God becomes visible in service to brothers and sisters. Conversely, sexual impurity and disrespect for the sanctity of marriage or a disposition toward greed and selfishness (13:4–5) would deny the consecration to God affirmed in the sacrifice of praise. The response of faith in the face of adversity in 13:6 provides a specific illustration of God-honoring praise. The initial paragraph, 13:1–6, finds its coherence through the category of the sacrifice of praise.

The community is called to remember their past leaders who proclaimed to them the word of God, to consider the accomplishment of their lives, and to emulate their faith (13:7). The word they proclaimed is crystallized in the confession, Jesus Christ remains the same (13:8). That word is now threatened by teaching foreign to the message the community received (13:9). It is evoked once more in the brief exposition of 13:10–12. In fact, the explanatory parenesis in 13:10–16 is the writer's own response to distortions of the original preaching that appear to have proven attractive to the community. This reading of the text exhibits the coherence in the development from 13:1–16.

On the other side, 13:10–16 is firmly welded to 13:17–19 by reference to the current leadership, including the writer. They exercise a vigilant watch over the community lest it should be subverted and so become disqualified from offering the sacrifice of praise. The concluding prayer-wish in 13:20–21 celebrates the establishment of an irrevocable covenant as the pledge that God himself will complete his work in his people, accomplishing in them *what is pleasing* (τὸ εὐάρεστον) to him. The distinctive formulation of the petition evokes once more the determinative exhortation in 12:28 to "serve God *acceptably*" (εὐαρέστως). The function of 13:1–21 is to give specification to that exhortation. The writer envisions the acknowledgement of consecration to God not only in the formal gatherings of the congregation but in the public and private sectors of life as well. The section as a whole provides a richly orchestrated exhortation to active participation in the shared life and values of the confessing community.

The sequence of (1) concluding parenesis in the form of precepts, pastoral injunctions, and teaching (13:1–19), followed by (2) a formal ascription of praise to God or a prayer-wish (13:20–21), to which there is appended (3) personal information and greetings (13:22–24), ending with a brief blessing (13:25) is not without parallel. It conforms to an early Christian tradition of parenetic closing that can be traced in several of the letters of the NT. (See Filson, '*Yesterday*', 22–25, who called attention to this pattern in 1 Thess 5:12–28; 2 Thess 3:6–18; Gal 6:1–18; Phil 4:10–23; 2 Tim 4:9–22; 1 Pet 5:1–14; Filson's work is advanced and refined by Thurén, *Lobopfer,* 59–70, who finds the closest parallel to the development in Heb 13:1–19 in the sequence of Eph 5:2–6:20.) If it is appropriate to refer to "the model of apostolic paraenesis," as Thurén has done, (*Lobopfer,* 70), it is clear that the writer found in the tradition only certain conventions to which he remained sensitive. His development of the tradition is distinctively his own.

Pastoral Precepts (13:1–6)

Bibliography

See *Bibliography* for 13:1–25 above.

Translation

¹*Brotherly love must continue.*[a] ²*Do not neglect*[b] *hospitality to strangers, for by this means some persons have entertained*[c] *angels without knowing it.*[d] ³*Continue to remember*[e] *the prisoners as if you were fellow prisoners, and those who are mistreated as if you yourselves were*[f] *suffering bodily.*[g] ⁴*Marriage*[h] *must be respected*[i] *by everyone,*[j] *and the marriage bed must be undefiled,*[k] *for God*[l] *will judge those who are sexually immoral*[m] *and adulterers.*[n] ⁵*Your life must be free from the love of money;*[o] *be content*[p] *with what you have,*[q] *because [God] himself has said,*[r] *"I will never fail you; I will never forsake you."*[s] ⁶*So we can*[t] *say with confidence,*

"The Lord is my helper;
I will not be afraid.[u]
What can man do to me?"

Notes

[a] The expression μενέτω is the sole instance of the 3rd person sg imperative in Hebrews. For the strong translation of the imperative see J. Thomas, "The Use of Voice, Moods and Tenses," 48.

[b] The nuance in ἐπιλάνθανεσθαι extends to "neglect," "overlook," "disregard" (BAGD 295). For the suggestion that the present imperative with the negative means, "do not go on being unmindful," see P. E. Hughes, 563, n. 1. This verb occurs with the gen in Heb 6:10; 13:2, 16.

[c] It is impossible in the translation to reflect the striking play on words (paronomasia) between φιλοξενίας, "hospitality to strangers," and ξενίσαντες, "entertained," and between ἐπιλανθάνεσθε, "neglect," and ἔλαθον, "without knowing." The chiastic structure of the exhortation is literary:

2a	τῆς φιλοξενίας	μὴ ἐπιλάθεσθε
	"hospitality to strangers"	"do not neglect"
2b	ἔλαθον	ξενίσαντες
	"without knowing"	"entertained [strangers]."

The ptcp ξενίσαντες supplements the main verb (BDF §413[3]).

ᵈ The construction ἔλαθόν τινες ξενίσαντες, "some have entertained without knowing it," in which the verb ἔλαθον is adverbial to the supplementary act ptcp, is a classical idiom found only here in the NT. The closest parallel in the LXX is found in Tob 12:13 (B A) (so Thurén, *Lobopfer*, 209, n. 717; cf. F. F. Bruce, 387, n. 5). Riddle, *JBL* 57 [1938] 141, offers the suggestive translation: "Do not forget to be hospitable to strangers, for by being so, some, without knowing it, have had angels as their guests."

ᵉ The translation seeks to express the iterative force of the present imperative. In this instance, the present imperative is complemented by the pf ptcp συνδεδεμένοι, "as if you were there with them," i.e., the emphasis is clearly on continued remembrance, as the pf tense of the complementary ptcp indicates.

ᶠ The ptcp ὄντες coupled with αὐτοί is emphatic.

It is impossible in translation to convey a sense of the linguistic rhythm in the formulation of the parallel clauses in v 3*a* and *b:*

3*a*　μιμνῄσκεσθε　　　　　　　τῶν δεσμίων ὡς συνδεδεμένοι
　　　　"Continue to remember　　　*the prisoners as if you were fellow prisoners*
3*b*　　　　　　　　　　　　　　τῶν κακουμένων ὡς καὶ αὐτοὶ ὄντες ἐν σώματι
　　　　　　　　　　　　　　　　the mistreated as if you yourselves were suffering bodily.

ᵍ The idiom ὡς καὶ αὐτοὶ ὄντες ἐν σώματι is difficult. The σύν in 3*a* is implied in 3*b*, i.e., σὺν αὐτοῖς, "together with them." The idiom signifies "as being also yourselves in the body and so liable to similar treatment" (cf. Zerwick and Grosvenor, *Grammatical Analysis*, 687). Andriessen, *En lisant*, 56, suggests that the conj ὡς in 3*b* expresses implicitly a certain causal link: "because you yourselves are in the body." Thurén, *Lobopfer*, 210, renders the idiom "as those who likewise live in the body." Cf. BAGD 799.

ʰ The term γάμος here clearly means "marriage," as in Wis 14:24, 26; Jos., *Ant.* 6.210; Jos., *Life* 4; and often in the papyri. Elsewhere in the NT it signifies a wedding celebration or a wedding banquet (BAGD 151).

ⁱ By virtue of its position at the beginning of the sentence, τίμιος, "respected," is emphatic. The simple adj is used imperatively here, and in 13:5 as well. This is a usage closely related to the imperatival ptcp, which is common in the Koine (see Moule, *Idiom-Book,* 179-80; Hanna, *Grammatical Aid,* 162). Alternatively, the copula ἐστίν can be supplied and the statement read as an ind, as in the AV: "Marriage *is* honourable in all, and the bed undefiled; but." Construing the sentence in this way, however, is inconsistent with the γάρ clause that follows in 4*b* ("for God will judge") and with the immediate context, which consists of a sequence of exhortations (P. E. Hughes, 566).

ʲ The translation assumes that the expression ἐν πᾶσιν is masc ("among all persons," or "in the case of everyone"), with Zerwick and Grosvenor, *Grammatical Analysis*, 687. Alternatively, it can be read as neuter, as it clearly is in Heb 13:18: "in every way," or "in all circumstances" (preferred in v 4 by Andriessen, *En lisant*, 56; H. Montefiore, 240; Buchanan, 228, 231; Jewett, 229). The expression has been suppressed in some MSS (38 460 623 1836 1911*) and by a number of patristic writers (Cyr J Did Eus Epiph Thret Theophilus of Alexandria), presumably in the conviction that celibacy was to be preferred to marriage.

ᵏ The simple adj ἀμίαντος "undefiled," is used as an imperative, i.e., "must be undefiled." The adj is in an emphatic position within its clause. The chiastic arrangement of the clause is literary:

τίμιος　　　　　　　　　　　　　　　ὁ γάμος
　　"respected"　　　　　　　　　　　　"marriage"
ἡ κοίτη　　　　　　　　　　　　　　ἀμίαντος
　　"the marriage bed"　　　　　　　　"undefiled"

ˡ The final position in the sentence given to ὁ θεός, "God," is emphatic: there will be a judgment, and the judge will be God. For this arrangement elsewhere in Hebrews see 4:10; 11:5*a*, 10, 19*a*; 12:7*a*; 13:16.

ᵐ The expression πόρνους clearly describes sexually immoral persons. For the proposal that the reference is to married persons involved in incest or sodomy, see Moffatt, 227. Cf. R. Kempthorne, "Incest and the Body of Christ: A Study of I Corinthians VI, 12–20," *NTS* 14 (1967–68), 568–74, who contends that the cognate term πορνεία in 1 Cor 5–6 consistently refers to incest.

ⁿ It is impossible in translation to convey the sonorous effect achieved by the word endings: τίμιος, "respected," γάμος, "marriage," ἀμίαντος, "undefiled," πόρνους, "sexually immoral persons," μοιχούς, "adulterers," ὁ θεός, "God."

ᵒ The adj ἀφιλάργυρος, "not loving money," "not greedy," is used imperatively, as is the case with the two adjs in 4*a*. By virtue of its position at the beginning of the sentence, the syntax is emphatic. The sonorous effect of ἀφιλάργυρος ὁ τρόπος should also be appreciated.

ᴾ The expression ἀρκούμενοι, "be content," appears to stand on its own as an imperatival ptcp (so Moule, *Idiom-Book*, 179–80; A. P. Salom, "The Imperatival Use of the Participle in the New Testament," *AusBR* 11 (1963) 41–49; Turner, *Grammatical Insights*, 166–67; McCown, "Ο ΛΟΓΟΣ ΤΗΣ ΠΑΡΑΚΛΗΣΕΩΣ," 199). Alternatively, the ptcp may depend upon the preceding imperatival adj for its hortatory force; cf. rsv: "Keep your life free from the love of money *and* be content with what you have" (italics added). The imperatival use of the ptcp is common in lists of ethical admonitions, but not at all common in Hebrews. Note the suggestive translation of Countryman, *Dirt*, 229: "Let your manner of life not be addicted to money; be satisfied with what you have."

۹ For the proposal to translate τοῖς παροῦσιν "the present funds" or "resources," see Vanhoye, *NTS* 23 [1976–77] 126.

ʳ In the introductory formula, αὐτὸς γὰρ εἴρηκεν, "for he himself has said," the αὐτός is emphatic because it is somewhat redundant.

ˢ The use of the double negative οὐ μή (or the triple negative οὐδ' οὐ μή) with the aor subjunctive expresses emphatic future negation. The construction is known in classical Greek and in the papyri (see Moule, *Idiom-Book*, 22, 156–57; Zerwick, *Biblical Greek* §444; BDF §365[3]). The alliterative arrangement of the lines cannot be duplicated in translation, but should be appreciated:

ἀφιλάργυρος ὁ τρόπος,	"Your life must be free from the love of money;
ἀρκούμενοι τοῖς παροῦσιν.	be content with what you have,
αὐτὸς γὰρ εἴρηκεν,	because he himself has said,
οὐ μή σε ἀνῶ οὐδ'	'I will never fail you;
οὐ μή σε ἐγκαταλίπω.	I will never forsake you.'"

ᵗ The ptcp has a causative nuance, calling for the supplying of δύνασθαι, "to be able," in translation. Moule, *Idiom-Book*, 144, finds in 6a evidence of a tendency to *ellipsis* in the use of ὥστε: ὥστε [δύνασθαι] θαρροῦντας ἡμᾶς λέγειν, "so we can say with confidence." The use of ὥστε with the inf to express natural (intended) result does not occur elsewhere in Hebrews.

ᵘ Almost certainly the καί, "and," found in brackets in the critical editions of the Gk. text was originally in the LXX but was omitted in Hebrews (with א* C* P 33 1175 1739 lat syᵖ); its inclusion is supported by P⁴⁶ א² A C² D Ψ 0121b vgᵐ syʰ Cl). On the textual issue, cf. K. J. Thomas, *NTS* 11 [1964–65] 319; McCullough, *NTS* 26 [1979–80] 367, n. 27; Zuntz, *Text of the Epistles*, 172. The effect of the omission is to make the citation more terse. Moulton, *Grammar*, 1:150, correctly identified the durative sense in the fut pass verb φοβηθήσομαι, "be afraid." Cf. Moule, *Idiom-Book*, 10.

Form/Structure/Setting

See 13:1–25 above.

Comment

1 The admonition to maintain brotherly love introduces a coordinated series of pastoral directives purposefully arranged in pairs with a supporting motivation (see above, *Form/Structure/Setting*, on the unity and symmetry of 13:1–6). The expression of love may be regarded as an essential aspect of the pursuit of holiness (12:14) (so Spicq, *ConNT* 11 [1947] 232; cf. Michel, 478, who introduces 13:1–6 under the heading "The Holiness of Our Lives"). It is entirely appropriate that the sober recognition of the holiness of God in 12:28–29 should be followed by the admonition, "Brotherly love must continue."

An appeal for fraternal love (v 1), hospitality (v 2), identification with those imprisoned and mistreated (v 3), indifference to earthly possessions (v 5), and confidence in the presence of hostility (v 6) evokes the exemplary stance that the community had assumed under harsh circumstances in the past (10:32–34). Concurrently, it reiterates and gives specification to the exhortation to love and

good works in 10:24. In the larger context of the homily, v 1 recapitulates expressed concerns and introduces the theme of the following verses. (Cf. Nitschke,
MPTh 46 [1957] 180, who treats 13:1 as a superscription to what follows.)

In v 1 the term φιλαδελφία, "brotherly love," clearly refers to the quality of love
that binds the community together as brothers and sisters within the family of
faith (3:1, 12; 10:19; 13:22, 23; cf. 2:11, 12, 17). In ordinary usage as well as in the
LXX, the Greek term was restricted to the love of those who were actual brothers
and sisters (e.g., Philo, *On Joseph* 218; *The Embassy to Gaius* 87; Jos., *Ant.* 4.26; 4 Macc
13:21, 23, 26; 14:1; 15:10; Plutarch, *Concerning Brotherly Love* [*Moralia* 5.478A];
Lucian, *Dialogues of the Gods* 26.2, 286). In v 1, however, as elsewhere in the NT (1
Thess 4:9; Rom 12:10; 2 Pet 1:7*ab;* cf. *1 Clem.* 47:5; 48:1), the term carries a distinctly Christian nuance that can be traced to Jesus' instruction of his disciples:
"You are all brothers (ἀδελφοί)" (Matt 23:8). This directive together with the
command to love one another (e.g., John 13:34–35; 15:12, 17; cf. 1 Thess 4:9),
served to expand the semantic and social reference in φιλαδελφία to those who
shared a common confession (Schlatter, 260: "In Christianity the confession of
Christ outweighs all other considerations" in the determination of brothers and
sisters; cf. Sedlaczek, *ThQ* 76 [1894] 272–95). The expression of love to brothers
and sisters represented a recognizably Christian response to the holiness code
with its commandment of love for one's neighbor (Lev 19:18). It defines "neighbor" as a member of the confessing community.

It is important to appreciate that this was something new. In the second half of
the second century the satirist Lucian of Samosata explained to a correspondent,
Cronius, that the relationship among Christians is unusual; they are to regard
one another as "brothers." He illustrates his point by calling attention to the
Christian attitude toward material possessions and grounds in the teaching of
Jesus their willingness to share what they own with one another:

> Moreover, their original lawgiver persuaded them that they should be like brothers to
> one another. . . . Therefore, they despise all things equally, and view them as common
> property, accepting such teachings by tradition and without any precise belief (*Peregrinus*
> 13).

Lucian's remarks indicate that an educated person in the second century was
quite unprepared for the Christian notion of φιλαδελφία expressed in the admonition, "Keep on loving each other as brothers." The expansion of the term to
include men and women beyond the immediate family was considered ludicrous.
Ironically, Lucian's choice of the Christian attitude toward personal property to
illustrate Jesus' teaching is insightful. It is precisely a willingness to share possessions unselfishly that is characteristic of the relationship among members of the
same family. New perspectives concerning familial relationships will inevitably have
implications for attitudes toward personal wealth (cf. 13:5) (see Lane, *PRS* 9 [1982]
270).

As in 1 Thess 4:9, the key word φιλαδελφία serves to introduce a cluster of instructions concerning the relationship of the members of the community to one
another as well as to outsiders. Here, as in the case of the Thessalonians, a detailed admonition was not required. The community had demonstrated love to
other Christians in the past and continued to do so at the present time (see

Comment on 6:10). "Brotherly love" is already characteristic of these men and women. It only needs to "remain" (μενέτω) as the hallmark of a distinctly Christian communal lifestyle (Thurén, *Lobopfer,* 209).

2 The admonition to fraternal love is exemplified in vv 2–3. These directives concern hospitality to strangers and ministry to those who have been imprisoned or mistreated. They constitute a plea for unselfishness and for the expression of love as service.

Each of the catechetical precepts introduced in 13:1–6 is rooted in tradition received from those who had heard the Lord himself (2:1–4) and who had delivered the message of the gospel to the community (13:7). That the exhortation to fraternal love in v 1 depends upon Jesus' teaching is clear. A comparison of vv 2–3 with the teaching of Jesus reveals their traditional character as well. It is sufficient to recall Jesus' parable concerning the eschatological judgment in Matt 25:31–46 to locate the parenesis in vv 2–3 in the received tradition:

Heb 13:2	*Matt 25:35*
"Do not neglect hospitality to strangers"	"I was hungry and you gave me food, I was thirsty and you gave me drink, I was a stranger and you welcomed me."

Heb 13:3	*Matt 25:36*
"Remember those in prison" "Remember . . . those who are mistreated"	"I was in prison, and you came to me, I was naked and you clothed me, I was sick and you visited me."

The formulation of the catechetical precepts in Hebrews is, of course, distinctive. Nevertheless, there is a relatively close correlation between the demonstrations of loving service recited by the eschatological Judge and the pastoral directives in Heb 13:2–3. Early in the second century, Ignatius drew upon that same strain of tradition when he observed how "contrary to the mind of God" are those who come with "strange teaching concerning the grace of Jesus Christ" (cf. Heb 13:9). Such persons "have no concern for love, none for the widow, none for the orphan, none for the mistreated, none for the prisoner, nor for the one who has been released from prison, none for the hungry or thirsty" (*Smyrn.* 6:2–3). The pastoral appeal for the community to sustain its concern for the stranger, the prisoner, and the mistreated is grounded in traditional instruction.

The dynamic character of love makes new modes of sharing normative: hospitality to strangers (φιλοξενία) is the corollary of brotherly love (φιλαδελφία). The extension of hospitality provided a practical measure for identifying with brothers and sisters, including many who were as yet unknown (6:10). It served to expand the network of interdependence that unites the family of God. Concurrently, it provided a powerful expression of the quality of life experienced within the Christian communities.

The root ξενίζειν signifies "to receive as a guest" (e.g., Acts 10:23; 28:7). The cognate noun φιλοξενία, "hospitality" (Rom 12:13; Heb 13:2; cf. φιλόξενος, "hospitable," in 1 Tim 3:2; Titus 1:8; 1 Pet 4:9), connotes a delight in the guest/host relationship, through which there can be a mutual exchange of unanticipated gifts that brings refreshment to one another. The term is an intensification of the noun ξενία, which already means "hospitality" (e.g., Acts 28:23: "to come to table as an invited guest"). φιλοξενία stresses the love of hospitality that Koenig describes as "partnership with strangers" (*Hospitality*, 1–10; Koenig argues convincingly that "hospitality" as "partnership with strangers" provides a hermeneutical key for interpreting significant aspects of Jesus' ministry, the missionary practice of Paul, and the structure of the early communities as reflected in Luke-Acts; he adds significantly, "Fundamental to the building of partnerships with strangers is a community that experiences itself as the guests of God" [132]).

For Christians, a delight in the guest/host relationship reflects the expectation that God will play a significant role in the ordinary exchange between guests and hosts. This lends to hospitality a sacramental quality. The fact that hospitality is first and foremost an attitude, not an action, clarifies why v 2 belongs organically with v 1 and v 3. (Cf. Vanhoye, *NTS* 23 [1976–77] 123–24, who notes that the correlation between v 1 and v 2*a* is underscored by the presence of synonymous parallelism: the two qualities commended are semantically related, and the order of the components of each phrase [i.e., substantive-verb] is identical.)

The negative formulation, τῆς φιλοξενίας μὴ ἐπιλανθάνεσθε, "Do not neglect hospitality to strangers," reflects pastoral concern for the guest/host relationship and focuses attention on the role of host that members of the house church must be prepared to assume. The earliest Christian assemblies met in homes, which provided a natural setting for the extension of hospitality to traveling brothers and sisters (Filson, *JBL* 58 [1939] 109–12; for a useful overview of hospitality within the context of the Christian household, see J. H. Elliott, *Home for the Homeless*, 145–50, 165–200; G. Bornkamm, *Early Christian Experience* [New York: Harper & Row, 1969] 123–93). Itinerant teachers, missionaries, emissaries, and refugees from persecution relied upon a network of Christian homes for shelter and provisions (cf. Thurén, *Lobopfer*, 209, who stresses that hospitality belongs to the confession of the early Church in times of persecution). Commonly, in Luke-Acts God's messengers receive food and lodging from those to whom they minister (e.g., Acts 21:4, 7, 16–17). In Luke's frequent reference to "house" and house churches, two facts emerge: (1) the house church was the creative hub for the confessing community; (2) the church can be depicted as a feasting community, celebrating the abundance of God in Christ (cf. H. J. Cadbury, "Lexical Notes on Luke-Acts," *JBL* 45 [1926] 305–22; M. Green, *Evangelism in the Early Church* [London: Hodder & Stoughton, 1970] 81, 207–23, 326).

The specific reference to the entertainment of strangers in v 2 is a reminder that early Christianity shared in the mobility of Roman society and that this was a major factor in the expansion of the Church. (On the comparative ease of travel, cf. Casson, *Travel*, 115–225; Malherbe, *Social Aspects*, 62–68, 94–96; and on the importance of this factor in the spread of Christianity, cf. Riddle, *JBL* 57 [1938] 141–54.) In their travels Christians depended upon private hospitality and appear to have assumed that they would be welcomed wherever they went (e.g., 3 John 5–8; *Did.* 11:1–3; 12:1–2*a*; cf. Lucian, *Peregrinus* 16). (Mathews ["Hospitality and the New Testament Church," 166–74, 230–31] shows that the social conventions of hospitality were reflected in a vocabulary that was virtually technical, which spoke of "receiving" and "sending on one's way." These terms called upon the host to invite the traveler into the family and provide whatever was necessary, even to the extent of making provision for the next leg of the journey [cf. *Did.*

12:1*a*, 2*a*: "Let anyone who comes in the name of the Lord be received. . . . If he comes as a traveler, help him as much as you can"]. For clear reference to hospitality in travel plans, cf. Rom 15:28–29; 16:1–2; 1 Cor 16:10–11; Phil 2:24, 29; Philem 22; see further, Rusche, *Gastfreundshaft*, 37–40.) Shared life had become an integral part of the early Christian message (e.g., 1 Pet 4:8–9, where the catechetical precept "love one another" is exemplified in the directive: "extend hospitality to one another"; Rom 12:13: "Share with God's people who are in need. Practice hospitality"; cf. Heb 13:16).

The supporting motivation in v 2*a* is without parallel in the early literature. The allusion to those who entertained angels as their guests without knowing it reflects the writer's sensitivity to the numinous qualities of hospitality that often enrich its purely social aspects (cf. Koenig, *Hospitality*, 2, 9). It throws into bold relief the element of surprise that is sometimes stressed in the biblical accounts, when mysterious strangers become guests, revealing to their hosts the promise they are carrying with them. The stranger received is disclosed to be a bearer of gifts, God's special envoy who has been sent to bless his children (e.g., Gen 18:1–21; 19:1–3; cf. Tob 12:15–20, 22). The allusion in v 2*a* is almost certainly to the Genesis account of Abraham's encounter with the three mysterious visitors to his tent at Mamre, when he and his wife Sarah received the promise of the birth of Isaac (Gen 18:1–21; cf. *1 Clem.* 10:7). (Thurén, *Lobopfer*, 209, prefers to think of Lot [Gen 19:1–3; *1 Clem.* 11:1], who, as host, sought to protect his guests from violation but was extended their protection in one of those reversals of roles between host and guests that are celebrated in the OT. There is little warrant in the text, however, for the deduction he draws: "So even now, many protectors [of Christians fleeing from persecution] will be saved by their guests.") The emphasis in Hebrews was calculated to stir within the community a disposition to welcome stangers in the expectation that they will be the bearers of God's abundance (Koenig, *Hospitality*, 125).

3 The instruction to sustain a compassionate concern for prisoners and the mistreated further exemplifies the admonition to maintain brotherly love in v 1 (see above, *Comment* on v 1; cf. Thurén, *Lobopfer*, 209–10, who treats v 3 as the development of v 1). The formulation of the pastoral charge evokes the stance of the community at a time when they had been subjected to public abuse, arrest, and the loss of property (10:32–34). On that occasion they had displayed empathy and solidarity with those who were imprisoned or who had suffered abusive treatment (see *Comment* on 10:33–34).

The suggestive allusion to that earlier demonstration of fraternal love is strengthened by the qualifying phrases appended to each part of the admonition: "Remember those in prison *as if you were fellow prisoners*, and those who are mistreated *as if you yourselves were suffering bodily*." Michel asserts that "this usage is properly understandable only within the teaching concerning the 'body of Christ,' which is lacking in Hebrews" (481). It is unlikely, however, that the qualifying phrases are intended to evoke the image of a body. The appeal for $\phi\iota\lambda\alpha\delta\epsilon\lambda\phi\iota\alpha$, "fraternal love," and $\phi\iota\lambda o\xi\epsilon\nu\iota\alpha$, "hospitality to strangers," in the immediate context (13:1–2) points rather to the supportive relationships characteristic of a family (so also Thurén, *Lobopfer*, 210; for the treatment of v 3 as an aspect of hospitality, see Riddle, *JBL* 57 [1938] 144–45). This interpretation is harmonious with the description of the Church as a household in Hebrews (3:6; 10:19–21).

Christians were bound together not only by a common confession but by a common way of life and, as Celsus shrewdly perceived, by their common danger (Origen, *Against Celsus* 1.1). Timothy had only recently been released from prison (13:23), and there were undoubtedly other Christians in custody who were known to the members of the house church (contrast Filson, '*Yesterday*', 78, who finds in v 3*a* a reference to non–Christian prisoners). Although Roman criminal law did not recognize the imprisonment of free persons as a form of punishment, there were both public prisons for brief incarcerations and private domestic prisons in larger households for the imprisonment of slaves. Moreover, during inquiry in a criminal trial the accused could be detained (*custodia reorum*) so as to be at the disposal of the authorities, and condemned persons could be imprisoned to as- sure the execution of their sentence (A. Berger, "Prison," *OCD* 879). Prisoners may have been dependent upon the support of family and friends for their food dur- ing the period of their detainment (cf. Lucian, *Friendship* 31, who speaks of the Cynic Demetrius of Sunium "who, when caring for a friend in prison, worked as a porter, and in this way demonstrated his friendship").

The readiness of Christians to lend material support to brothers in prison is attested not only by the NT and later Christian writers (e.g., Justin, *Apology*, 67.6) but by Lucian, a far from sympathetic witness. Lucian's statements about the manner in which Christians responded when Peregrinus Proteus was arrested and imprisoned in Palestine (*Peregrinus* 12–13) furnish a valuable commentary of the formulation of v 3*a*. His vivid account is a source of insight on the extent to which Christians in the second century rallied their resources to support a brother imprisoned as a confessor. Initially, the Christians did everything within their power to have Proteus released. When that proved impossible, they identified themselves with him in the prison. The detail that certain leaders, "after bribing the guards," slept inside Peregrinus' cell with him suggests that the Church in the second cen- tury sought to honor the admonition to remember those in prison *as if they were fellow prisoners* (ὡς συνδεδεμένοι). They were prepared to share the actual living conditions of an imprisoned brother in order to demonstrate their solidarity with him.

Lucian also refers to the bringing in of meals and to the reading of the Scrip- tures and their exposition. Christians were eager to extend to the prison the communal experiences of the house church gathered around the dinner table. This suggests that the early Church regarded a ministry to Christian brothers in prison as a corollary of the responsibility to practice hospitality. Subsequently, Christians, who were delegated to travel to Palestine "at common expense for the purpose of supporting, defending, and encouraging" Peregrinus, arrived from cities in Asia. This detail is consistent with the measures of support Paul had en- joyed from churches in Macedonia and Asia when he was imprisoned (e.g., Phil 2:25–30; 4:10–18; Titus 3:13; 2 Tim 1:16–18). The response of the churches to Peregrinus' arrest reflects a broad sensitivity to the parenetic concepts expressed in Heb 13:1-3. The details supplied by Lucian serve to interpret the pastoral in- tention of v 3*a*, with its pointed call for identification with those in prison (see further, G. Bagnani, "Peregrinus Proteus and the Christians," *Hist* 4 [1955] 107– 12; Lane, *PRS* 9 [1982] 171–73).

In recalling the community's past exposure to blatant hostility, the writer re- ferred to those who were subjected to public abuse (10:33) and to others who were imprisoned (10:34). This distinction provides the background to the formulation of the parallel clauses in 13:3, where "those in prison" are distinguished from "those who are mistreated." In point of fact, prisoners were rarely exempt from mistreatment, so that the two groups of sufferers specified in v 3*ab* are virtually identical.

The reference in v 3*b*, of course, is to that larger company of men and women who experienced abuse in any form because of their Christian faith. With the choice of the expression τῶν κακουχουμένων, "those who are mistreated," the writer calls to mind the recital of the attested witnesses under the old covenant who "experienced jeering and lashing . . . who went about in sheepskins and goatskins, destitute, oppressed, mistreated" (κακουχούμενοι) (11:36–37). He also evokes the prior reference to Moses, who had preferred mistreatment with the people of God (συγκακουχεῖσθαι) to the enjoyment of sin for a season (11:25). In precisely the same way, the members of the confessing community must take thought for the mistreated, demonstrating a readiness to share their abuse, if that should become necessary. It is presupposed that the Church is a caring fellowship and that Christians are prepared for partnership with those who are mistreated (10:33). The Church must maintain its solidarity with those who have become outcasts, the objects of contempt and ill-treatment, because of their faith (10:32–34; 11:36–38; cf. Filson, *Yesterday'*, 78–79, 81).

The substantiating qualification ὡς καὶ αὐτοὶ ὄντες ἐν σώματι, "as if you yourselves were suffering bodily," introduces the ground for genuine empathy. Whoever experiences life in the body can appreciate the bodily pain of a fellow human being and suffer with him. Schierse astutely compares 2:14 with 13:3*b*: the Son of God assumed a body of flesh and blood in order to be able to experience authentic solidarity with the human family (*Verheissung*, 105). It is unnecessary on this basis, however, to interpret v 3*b* in a gnostic vein, as Schierse does. The real basis of the comparison is the possibility of entering into another's situation with loving empathy (2:17–18; 4:15). (So correctly Thurén, *Lobopfer*, 210–11, n. 721, who draws attention to the relationship between 13:3 and 13:15–16.) When Christians remember one another in suffering with compassionate action, then they can offer to God with integrity the sacrifices of praise, generosity, and kindness with which he is pleased. The fact that those addressed have a body with a capacity for suffering means that they are capable of feeling the pain of those who are mistreated. They can extend help to them as an expression of fraternal love. They should do so in imitation of the Son of God (2:14, 17–18) and of their own earlier courageous example (10:33).

The sequence of 13:1–3 suggests an implied call to full participation in the life of the confessing community. Those who respond in love, providing shelter to persecuted brothers and sisters, visiting them in prison, and caring for them when they are ill-treated, will through these acts acknowledge themselves to be Christian. Their actions will complement and validate their public confessions of Christian faith. In the absence of demonstrations of love to other confessors of Christ, public confession is an empty gesture. Confession in the form of action is indispensable for exhibiting the quality of life within the confessing community. In the context of 12:28–29, the expressions of brotherly love to which the members of the house church are summoned are the responses of gratitude that constitute authentic worship (cf. Michel, 479, n. 1).

4 The allusion to the body and to shared vulnerability in v 3*b* is carried forward in the directive concerning respect for marriage and sexual responsibility in v 4*a*. In Hebrews, unlike Philo, there is no disparagement of the physical body (2:14; 10:5, 10; cf. Williamson, *Philo*, 275–76). Respect for the life of the body is the corollary of an understanding of human sexuality as the gift of God. It is to be honored as an expression of our distinctiveness as persons. Sexual responsibility affirms the lordship of God the Creator over the sphere of bodily life. Consequently, regard for marriage and for the physical intimacy integral to marriage is an essential aspect of the pursuit of holiness to which the community has been called by God (12:14).

The form in which the directive has been cast consists of two injunctions to marital purity (v 4*a*), supported by their own motivation (v 4*b*). The fact of marriage must be respected ἐν πᾶσιν ("by everyone"). Although in principle the writer would undoubtedly desire that society as a whole valued fidelity in marriage, his immediate concern is for those in the redeemed community (so also Filson, 'Yesterday', 79). Marital infidelity is inconsistent with the summons to fraternal love in 13:1. Regard for marriage is an essential expression of the quality of love that binds the community together as brothers and sisters who share a common confession. As a community they must respect marriage as the gift of God and support those who share the marriage relationship with empathy and affection.

Respect for marriage has broad implications concerning sexual relationships, both for those who are married and for those who are not. The formulation ἡ κοίτη ἀμίαντος, "the marriage bed must be undefiled," is a euphemism for preserving the sexual integrity of the marriage relationship. The adjective ἀμίαντος is more commonly associated with things than with persons (e.g., Wis 4:2: "the contest for prizes that are undefiled"; cf. BAGD 46). The term belongs to the cultic idiom (see Thurén, *Lobopfer*, 213–15; Spicq, *ConNT* 11 [1947] 232–33, argues that it is necessary to preserve the cultic nuance here: sexual impurity entails desecration of the sacred). Here it is used of ἡ κοίτη, "the marriage bed," with reference to sexual purity (as in Wis 3:13; 8:19–20; *T. Jos.* 4:6; Plutarch, *Numa* 9.5). The writer appears to inject casually the language of defilement into a non-cultic setting. The explanation for this may be that the injunctions in v 4*a* specify an aspect of the pursuit of holiness, acknowledging the awesome, holy character of God (12:14, 28–29).

Illicit sexual intercourse defiles the marriage bed; it profanes what God has made holy. (On the defiling of marriage by adultery, cf. Gen. 49:4; *T. Reub.* 1:6; Jos., *Ant.* 2.55; for a powerful statement from a contemporary, cf. Horace, *Odes* 3.6: "Full of sin, our age has defiled first the marriage bed, then our children and our homes; springing from such a source, the stream of disaster has overflowed both people and nation. The young girl is eager to learn Ionian dances, and soon acquires the art of flirting; even in childhood she devises impure affairs. Soon she is looking for young lovers, even at her husband's table, and does not even choose out those on whom she will quickly bestow illicit pleasures when the lights are low. When invited, she openly, and not without her husband's knowledge, gets up and goes, whether it is some peddler who calls her or the owner of some Spanish ship, a lavish buyer of shame!") Those who are sexually immoral and adulterers "defile" the marriage bed as they bring with them their defilement. (On the contagious character of defilement, see 12:15.) In calling the members of the house church to sexual purity, the writer demands that they reflect a level of moral sensitivity which, though unusual, was not unknown in Roman Hellenism. For example, among the rules of a private religious association in Philadelphia, dating from the first century B.C., are the provisions that "a man [is not to take] another woman in addition to his own wife . . . nor is he to corrupt a child or a virgin. . . . A free woman is to be pure and is not to know bed or sexual intercourse with any other man except her own [husband]" (W. Dittenberger, ed., *Sylloge Inscriptionum Graecarum*³, 985).

Those who defile marriage through sexual offense can anticipate the certainty of judgment, "for God will judge those who are sexually immoral and adulterers" (v 4*b*). The thought is thoroughly biblical and Jewish (Lev 20:10; Deut 22:20–23; Job 24:15–24; Prov 5:15–23; Sir 15:17–20; 23:18–20, 22–23*a*; Wis 3:16–19; 4:4–16). The descriptive term πόρνοι, "sexually immoral persons," has reference to those who engage in sexual relationships outside of marriage (cf. Countryman, *Dirt*, 229, who suggests that πόρνοι here signifies men who use prostitutes; alternatively, he suggests it may refer to anyone who holds family property in contempt). The word μοιχοί, "adulterers," denotes those who are unfaithful to the vows of commitment expressed in marriage (cf. Sir 23:18*a*: "A man who breaks his marriage vows," followed by a graphic depiction of the husband [23:18–21] and the wife [23:22–27] who commit adultery). (For an analysis of adultery as an offense against sexual property, analogous to theft, with an appeal to Exod 20:14–15, 17, see Countryman, *Dirt*, 157–59, 175–81; see, however, Lev 20:10, where adultery is treated as a violation of purity in the Holiness Code.) Together the two expressions cover all who engage in illicit sexual activity (F. F. Bruce, 392; P. E. Hughes, 566; for the sequence πόρνοι followed by μοιχοί in a traditional Jewish treatment of sexual offenses, see Sir 23:16–27). The warning against impurity is traditionally associated with the concern for holiness, which is the essential condition for the true worship of God (Thurén, *Lobopfer*, 212–17).

Sexual immorality is actually a rejection of the presence and goodness of God who created the human family in its maleness and femaleness. It is an expression of a selfishness blind to the emotional fragility that characterizes every person. The writer warns that those who place personal gratification above responsibility to God and to the community will encounter God himself as Judge (as in 12:23, 29). Implicit in the future tense of κρινεῖ, "[God] will judge," is an allusion to the final judgment that determines human destiny (cf. 6:2; 9:27; 10:25, 27, 29–31, 38–39; 12:23, 27, 29; 13:17). The awesome prospect of the final judgment throws into high relief the ultimate importance of respect for marriage and for sexual integrity. They represent aspects of the pursuit of holiness that are foundational to the worship of God.

5–6 The juxtaposition of v 4 and v 5*a* reflects a common parenetic pattern in antiquity. Warnings against sexual impurity and greed are joined together (e.g., *T. Jud.* 18:2: "Keep yourselves, therefore, my children from sexual impurity and the love of money" [ἀπὸ τῆς πορνείας καὶ τῆς φιλαργυρίας]; *T. Levi* 14:6; Philo, *On the Posterity and Exile of Cain* 34: "all the worst quarrels, both public and private, are due to greed for either a well-formed woman or possessions"; cf. Epictetus, *Enchiridion* 3.7.21). The pattern reflects an awareness that selfishness lies behind both sexual immorality and greed (e.g., Lucian, *Nigrinus* 16: "[The love of pleasure] brings in adultery and the love of money" [μοιχεία καὶ φιλαργυρία]).

The fact that the seventh and eighth commandments occur side by side in the Decalogue (Exod 20:14–15; Deut 5:18–19) encouraged Jewish writers to treat sexual offenses and greed in this order (so Spicq, 2:418). The writer is thoroughly Jewish in his arrangement of the catechetical precepts that have bearing on the pursuit of holiness (12:14) (cf. Sahlin, *ST* 24 [1970] 97, who points to the coherence of Heb 13:4–5*a* with the cardinal sins of the Damascus Document, e.g., CD 4:17–19 [on "the three nets of Belial" with which he captures those who are morally careless]: "The first net is sexual offense, the second greed for profit, and the third is the defilement of sacred things"; CD 6:14–16, 20–7:7 speaks of the sacrifices of brotherly love, hospitality, and nurture of the needy, which must not be defiled through sexual offense and greed; cf. *T. Levi* 14:5–8; *T. Reub.* 4:6, "Sins of promiscuity . . . lead to idolatry," with *T. Jud.* 19:1, "Love of money leads to idolatry"; see further Kosmala, *ASTI* 4 [1965] 98–102, 104–6).

The pastoral concern with impurity and greed in Hebrews reflects the peril of defilement through sexual offense and idolatry, which entails the desecration of that which is holy. (See Thurén, *Lobopfer,* 67, 212–17, who points out that elsewhere in the NT corresponding warnings are placed together under the aspect of "cultic" holiness or under the rubric of avoiding the defilement of the sacrifice of love, as in Eph 5:3, 5; cf. Col 3:5–6.) The joining of injunctions to sexual purity and contentment in 13:4–5*a* constitutes a reminder to preserve the holiness that the members of the house church enjoy through the high priestly action of Christ on their behalf (13:12).

The two imperatival clauses of v 5*a* reinforce one another: a life unhampered by the love of money will reflect a contentment that is theologically grounded. Jesus had spoken sharply concerning the danger of making money the center of one's affection (Matt 6:24; Luke 16:13, in the context of 16:14, where the Pharisees, who scoff at Jesus' teaching, are described as φιλάργυροι, "lovers of money"). He had linked that tendency to a gnawing anxiety that sprang from a basic distrust in God's care and provision for his children (Matt 6:25–34). The love of money and trust in God are mutually exclusive.

The word ἀφιλάργυρος, "free from the love of money," does not occur elsewhere in the NT. The pastoral warning in v 5*a* that life must be free from the love of money (ἀφιλάργυρος ὁ τρόπος) addresses anxiety in the face of a threatening situation. When trouble had erupted on an earlier occasion, the Christians addressed had experienced the loss of property (10:34). That deprivation could occur again. The frightening prospect of renewed suffering (see *Comment* on 12:1–13) may have encouraged the members of the house church to seek to secure their future through the accumulation of material resources. It is at least probable that some Christians wished to amass wealth in order to protect themselves from persecution through money (cf. Riggenbach, 430; Michel, 484; Thurén, *Lobopfer,* 217). The unselfish love to which the community is summoned in 13:1–3 would be thwarted by the love of money (cf. Filson, '*Yesterday*', 79: "The love of money can be an ugly expression of deep-rooted selfishness. . . . It can keep Christians from helping their fellow-men who are in need. It can make them think of protecting their possessions rather than maintaining their solidarity with those who are outcast, despised, and ill-treated"). With pastoral sensitivity, the writer calls his audience to display a contentment with what they possessed that was rooted in God's pledge of his constant presence. A restless concern for money is perceived as a betrayal of trust in God (Thurén, *Lobopfer,* 58).

The directive ἀρκούμενοι τοῖς παροῦσιν, "be satisfied with what you have," reproduces a common Greek phrase for contentment (Democritus, *Fragment* 191; Teles [the Cynic teacher] 11.5; 38.10; 41.12; Cassius Dio 38.8; 56.33, cited by BAGD 107). The conviction that the condition for contentment is the presence of God with his people is thoroughly Jewish. It is reflected in the piety of pre-Christian Pharisaism in a collection of hymns dating to the first century B.C.: "With approval and blessing support me; when you strengthen me, what has been given [by you] is enough for me [ἀρκέσει μοι τὸ δοθέν]" (*Ps. Sol.* 16:12). In Hebrews the injunction to contentment is a call to quietness in the situation, in confident reliance on the presence and provision of a faithful God. Members of the house church are to find their security solely in him.

The call to contentment is grounded in the solemn promise of God's unfailing presence and care, which is asserted emphatically with a quotation from Scripture. It is unnecessary for Christians to place their trust in wealth because they can trust in God, who shares their vulnerability (cf. 1 Tim 6:17). Consequently, greed for wealth is an expression of idolatry (Thurén, *Lobopfer,* 217).

The redundant αὐτός in the introductory formula αὐτὸς γὰρ εἴρηκεν is emphatic ("for he *himself* has said"). The impersonal use of "he says" (8:5) or "he has said" (1:13; 4:4; 13:5b), where the reference is clearly to God and introduces a quotation from Scripture, reflects synagogue praxis (e.g., *m. ʾAbot* 6:2, 7, 9, 10, 11; cf. 1 Cor 6:16; 15:27; 2 Cor 6:2; Gal 3:16; Eph 4:8). The perfect tense of the verb indicates that the affirmations made continue to be in force.

The words cited offer a compelling argument for a life devoid of a desire for material security. Although close parallels to the quotations occur in Gen 28:15; Deut 1:6, 8; Josh 1:5; and 1 Chr 28:20 LXX, the actual form of the citation is unsupported in the MSS of the Old Greek version that have been preserved (for a helpful chart displaying the Greek text in parallel columns, see P. E. Hughes, 568, n. 14). The precise form of the quotation was known, however, to Philo, who also ascribed the words to God (*On the Confusion of Tongues* 166). There is no reason to suspect that the writer of Hebrews was dependent upon Philo for the form of the citation (as argued by Moffatt, 229; Spicq, 1:336). The two writers apply the quotation quite differently. Philo cites the words as a promise that God will never abandon the human soul to its passions (see Williamson, *Philo,* 570–73). The agreement between Philo and Hebrews points rather to a form of the quotation familiar from the preaching or liturgy of the hellenistic synagogues in Alexandria (cf. Delitzsch, 669; Riggenbach, 431; Michel, 483–84 and n. 1; Schröger, *Verfasser,* 194–96).

In seeking the source of the quotation in v 5b, Westcott (434) had already referred to Gen 28:15, which includes the phrase οὐ μή σε ἐγκαταλίπω, "I will never forsake you." P. Katz demonstrated that this was indeed the source of Philo's quotation (*Philo's Bible* [Cambridge: UP, 1950] 72, n. 12). He argued that in Heb 13:5b the text is derived from Gen 28:15 enlarged from the similar passages in Deut 31:6, 8 as found in the recension of the Old Greek version used by both Philo and Hebrews (*ZNW* 49 [1958] 220–21; id., *Bib* 33 [1952] 523–25). Alternatively, it has been proposed that the words are dependent upon Josh 1:5, supplemented by Deut 31:8 (cf. Westcott, 434; H. Montefiore, 240–41; Williamson,

Philo, 570; Thurén, *Lobopfer,* 218). The writer could have understood the oracle as the word of God to a new Joshua who will lead the people into rest (4:8). It is important in any case that the singular of address ("I will never fail *you*; I will never forsake *you*") has in view an individual who represents the whole people. If the writer read the oracle in this manner he may have understood it as the word of God addressed to the Son (so Thurén, *Lobopfer,* 218). Christians share in this word and its response, in so far as they are partners with Christ (cf. 3:14).

The pledge of God's presence prompts the response of faith: "So we can say with confidence, 'The Lord is my helper'" (v 6). The answer to the word of God assumes the form of biblical confession. Michel has observed that "vv 5b and 6 correspond to one another as promise and response of the community"; the pair of quotations reflects the liturgical dialogue between God and the confessing community (483–84). As elsewhere in the homily, the writer has connected a quotation from the Torah with a word from the Psalms (1:6–13; 4:4–5; 7:1–4, 17, 21; cf. Schröger, *Verfasser,* 197).

The experience of the covenant faithfulness of God invites the confident assertion of trust in the Lord in the presence of peril. The quotation is taken from the last of the Hallel psalms, which was well known to the audience as the Passover psalm par excellence (cf. Werner, *Sacred Bridge,* 159). The citation of Ps 117[MT 118]:6 LXX consists of three lines that suggest the setting for confession is the experience of persecution: the first line brings into focus God and the confessor; the third line the oppressor and the confessor; and the intervening second line the confessor alone, who responds with confidence to a threatening situation. The quotation has the sobering effect of establishing a social context for the instruction in v 5a. The writer's concern is not limited to the provision of daily needs. It extends to the confrontation with hostility in society at large.

In the psalm the declaration "The Lord is my helper" is given prominence through repetition (Ps 117[MT 118]:6, 7). The psalm opens with a fourfold summons to thank the Lord for his goodness, which is grounded in the experience of answered prayer (Ps 117[MT 118]:1–5; cf. vv 21 and 28 as well: "I thank you because you have heard me"). The response to this summons assumes the form of confession in v 6. It provides an example of "the fruit of lips that praise [God's] name" (Heb 13:15). The confession reflects the experience of the Lord as helper during the ordeal of testing (cf. Sir 51:1–3a LXX, where the confession assumes the form of a hymn of thanksgiving in praise of God as protector and helper). Although the word βοηθός, "helper," occurs only here in the NT, it was firmly rooted in the liturgy of the early Church as descriptive of Jesus or God in the role of protector (e.g., *1 Clem.* 36:1; 59:3).

Assurance that the Lord is the divine enabler permits the Christian to affirm, "I will not be afraid." The confessor expresses his own fearlessness to the honor of God. This central clause corresponds to the confidence affirmed in the introductory words, "So we can say with confidence" (v 6a). The expressions θαρρεῖν, "to be confident," and μὴ φοβεῖσθαι, "not to be afraid," are interchangeable in the NT, as elsewhere in contemporary Jewish literature (Grundmann, *TDNT* 3:26–27). The logical shift from the monetary concerns expressed in v 5 to confident dependence upon the Lord when threatened in a hostile society is striking. The Christian is to be free both from the love of money and from the fear of death (cf. 2:14–15).

The final clause, "What can man do to me?" is simultaneously an exultant confession and a bold expression of trust in God as helper. As the confessor now considers not only his oppressor but also his relationship to the Lord, he anticipates the vindication affirmed by the psalmist: "I shall look in triumph upon my enemies" (Ps 117[MT 118]:7 LXX; cf. Torrence, *EvQ* 28 [1956] 102–3, who calls attention to the past, the present, and the future in vv 5–7 of the psalm: v 5 refers to the past, when the Lord answered the prayer of distress; v 6 has reference to the present, for "the Lord is at my side"; v 7 looks to the future, when the Lord will vindicate his servant in the presence of those who have hated him). The praise of God and a declaration of trust are mutually complementary here, and elsewhere in the Psalter (e.g., Ps 55:11 LXX [MT 56:12]: "In God I trust. I will not be afraid. What can men do to me?"). Confidence, joy, and thanksgiving merge as the confessor looks away from himself, with the result that his boast expresses confession to God (cf. Bultmann, *TDNT* 3:647).

Each of the three lines of the quotation thus has a special function:

"The Lord is my helper"	Confession
"I will not be afraid"	Expression of confidence
"What can man do to me?"	Boast

The primary matter is the confession of the Lord; the expressions of confidence and boasting are the consequences of confession (following the analysis of Thurén, *Lobopfer*, 218–20).

The function of the quotation in the context of Heb 13:1–6 is to summon the anxious members of the house church to assume their place within the ranks of the confessing community. Like the psalmist, they know the human emotions of fear and insecurity (cf. 2:15). They are to recall past experiences of deliverance as the ground of their confidence as they face an uncertain future, when it was natural to reckon again with loss and deprivation (10:34). The writer encourages them to affirm their trust in God's pledge of his constant presence. This is the ground of the certainty that whatever they experience he will not abandon them. He will share their vulnerability and supply their needs. This assurance provides an appropriate conclusion to the paragraph as a whole.

Explanation

See 13:22–25 below.

Communal Directives (13:7–19)

Bibliography

See *Bibliography* for 13:1–25 above.

Translation

[7]Continue to remember[a] your leaders, as those who spoke[b] the Word of God to you, considering[c] the accomplishment[d] of their conduct, and imitate their faith. [8]Jesus Christ is[e] the same yesterday and today, and forever.[f] [9]Do not be led away whenever[g] various strange teachings[h] arise. For it is good for the heart to be strengthened through grace, not by foods,[i] with which their adherents[j] are not benefited. [10]We have[k] an altar from which those who serve[l] the tabernacle do not have the right to eat.[m] [11]For while the blood of those animals is brought into the Most Holy Place[n] by the high priest[o] for sin,[p] their[q] bodies are burned outside the camp. [12]And so Jesus[r] also suffered death[s] outside the city gate[t] in order to consecrate the people through his own blood. [13]So then,[u] let us go out to him outside[v] the camp, bearing the disgrace[w] he bore. [14]For here we do not have a permanent city, but we are expecting intently[x] the city which is to come.[y] [15]Through Jesus,[z] therefore,[aa] let us continually offer to God a sacrifice consisting in praise,[bb] that is to say, the fruit of lips that praise[cc] his name. [16]Do not neglect acts of kindness[dd] and generosity,[ee] for God is pleased because of such sacrifices.[ff] [17]Continue to obey[gg] your leaders, and submit to their authority,[hh] for they[ii] keep watch for your eternal life[jj] as those who intend to give an account.[kk] Let them do this[ll] with joy, and not groaning, for this would be unprofitable[mm] for you. [18]Continue to pray[nn] for us, for we are convinced[oo] that we have a clear conscience, since we strive[pp] to act commendably[qq] in every way.[rr] [19]I urge you especially[ss] to pray[tt] so that I might be restored to you sooner.[uu]

Notes

[a] The present tense of the imperatives and ptcp is noteworthy. μνημονεύετε is emphatic. The translation, "Continue to remember," seeks to bring out the iterative force of the present tense. The stress is on continued remembrance, especially as this impinges on the present with the summons to μιμεῖσθε τὴν πίστιν, "imitate their faith."

[b] The shift from the present tense of the imperative to the aor tense of the verb ἐλάλησαν, "they spoke," is striking.

[c] The present ptcp ἀναθεωροῦντες stresses continued action, i.e., "look at again and again" (cf. BAGD 54, who translate the clause, "considering the outcome of their lives"). Alternatively, the participial clause can assume a hortatory function by association with and extension of the finite verbal imperative with which the admonition is introduced. In that case, it affirms attendant or coordinate circumstances. This is the understanding of the RSV and NIV: μνημονεύετε . . . ἀναθεωροῦντες . . . μιμεῖσθε, "remember . . . consider . . . and imitate." On any reading of the text, the juxtaposition of ἀναθεωροῦντες with μιμεῖσθε is purposeful.

[d] The term ἔκβασις is ambiguous. It can mean "the end of one's life" (cf. Wis 2:17), but it can also be understood as "[the successful] outcome," "result of one's way of life" (cf. Wis 11:14). Modern translations have tended to favor the latter alternative (RSV, NEB, JB, NASB, NIV: "outcome"; but TEV: "died"). For the translation adopted here cf. Michel, 489–90; P. E. Hughes, 569 and n. 18.

[e] The copula ἐστίν must be supplied, as in the NIV: "Jesus Christ *is* the same." By virtue of its position at the beginning of the sentence, the proper name "Jesus Christ" is emphatic.

[f] Conventions of English style obscure the unusual word order, which seems designed to arouse attention: "Jesus Christ, yesterday and today the same—and forever!"

[g] The translation seeks to recognize the iterative force of the present tense in the prohibition μὴ παραφέρεσθε, "Do not be led away *whenever,*" emphasized by Moulton, *Grammar,* 1:125; cf. Hanna, *Grammatical Aid,* 162. P. E. Hughes, 571, n. 22, finds in the expression the nuance, "Do not go on being led astray," i.e., they are to put a stop to what is already taking place.

[h] Stylistic considerations suggest that the expression ποικίλαις καὶ ξέναις is an instance of hendiadys: "various strange teachings" (cf. NIV: "all kinds of strange teachings"). It is impossible to reflect in translation the sonorous quality of the dative endings, which is rhetorically effective: διδαχαῖς ποικίλαις καὶ ξέναις. The entire phrase stands in an emphatic position in the clause.

ⁱ Although the term βρῶμα, "food," is never used in the LXX for sacrificial meals, the exclusively Jewish cast of the argument that follows suggests the paraphrase "not by *ceremonial* foods."

ʲ The clause ἐν οἷς . . . οἱ περιπατοῦντες, "those who walk in them," i.e., who follow that way of life, is Jewish in its formulation. For the suggestive translation "those who frame their conduct by them," see Countryman, *Dirt*, 130.

ᵏ In the syntax of the sentence, the initial term ἔχομεν, "we have," is emphatic. It introduces an implied chiasm in the construction of the sentence:

[ἡμεῖς]   [ἔχομεν]
"[we]"   "we have"
οὐχ ἔχουσιν   οἱ λατρεύοντες
"they do not have"   "those who serve"

ˡ The nuance of "serving" or of "ministering" in οἱ λατρεύοντες would seem to be beyond question (cf. 8:5; 9:6; and BAGD 366–67, 467). Nevertheless, Sowers, *Hermeneutics*, 73, translates the expression "those venerating," and defends this nuance for λατρεύειν (110).

ᵐ The inf φαγεῖν, "to eat," is used epexegetically to explain the phrase οὐκ ἔχουσιν ἐξουσίαν, "they do not have the right." It is thrown forward in the clause for emphasis.

ⁿ The writer uses the neuter pl with the article to designate "the Most Holy Place" in the tabernacle or its heavenly prototype (e.g., 9:12, 25; but see 9:24 where the anarthrous ἅγια denotes the inner compartment of the sanctuary). Cf. Salom, *AUSS* 5 (1967) 59–70. In 13:11, the writer is actually quoting freely from Lev 16:27.

ᵒ The prep διά used in connection with a person has the transferred sense of agency rather than mediation (Moule, *Idiom-Book*, 204, who cites Esth 8:10 LXX; 1 Cor 1:9; Heb 13:11; Zerwick, *Biblical Greek* §113, suggests there is a causal nuance in διά at this place).

ᵖ The prep περί occurs with the sense of ὑπέρ, "for sin" (BDF §229[1]). Cf. Atkinson, *Prepositions*, 9, who emphasizes the sense of purpose in περί here and paraphrases "to *deal with the matter of sin*." The translation in the NIV ("The high priest carries the blood of animals . . . *as a sin-offering*") has been conformed to Lev 16:27, but there the LXX text reads περὶ τῆς ἁμαρτίας, "for the sin offering," not περὶ ἁμαρτίας, as in Heb 13:11.

ᑫ The construction ὧν . . . τούτων is an example of the emphatic use of the demonstrative pronoun, which serves to throw the weight of the construction on the final clause.

ʳ The name Ἰησοῦς is emphatic in the syntax of the statement.

ˢ Whenever the writer speaks of the death of Jesus he uses the verb πάσχειν, "to suffer," and its derivatives. Consequently, in Hebrews the verb πάσχειν receives the meaning "to die" (cf. Michaelis, *TDNT* 5:917, 934–35; Michel, 508; F. F. Bruce, 412, n. 77). See above on 2:9, 10, 18; 5:8; 9:26.

ᵗ Although P⁴⁶ P 104 boᵃˢ read παρεμβολῆς, "camp," the better attested and more difficult πύλης, "gate," should be read: Jesus suffered death "outside the city gate."

ᵘ Under the influence of the LXX, Hebrews shows a tendency to use coordinating particles as the first word. The inferential hellenistic particle τοίνυν rarely occurs in first place in literary Gk. (cf. Turner, *Grammar*, 4:111). Much like οὖν in 13:15, τοίνυν signifies consequential deduction. Cf. Luke 20:25; 1 Cor. 9:26.

ᵛ Zerwick, *Biblical Greek* §84, suggested that where ἔξω is used instead of the simple ἐκ there is, perhaps, the connotation of a certain idea of remaining outside, as in this instance: ἐξερχώμεθα πρὸς αὐτὸν ἔξω τῆς παρεμβολῆς, "let us go out to him outside the camp" (i.e., "*to a place* outside the enclosure" [italics mine]). The choice of ἔξω in this instance, however, may be simply for the sake of sound: ἐξερχώμεθα . . . ἔξω, "let us go out . . . outside."

ʷ The expression τὸν ὀνειδισμόν is emphatic in its phrase. The term conveys the nuances of reproach, abuse, and shame (cf. NEB: "bearing *the stigma* that he bore"; and see above on 11:26). For an extensive treatment of the clause τὸν ὀνειδισμὸν αὐτοῦ φέροντες in terms of the bearing of "shame," see Thurén, *Lobopfer*, 91–99, and the discussion of this motif in *Comment* below.

ˣ For this nuance in the verb ἐπιζητεῖν, see above on 11:14. The present tense of ἐπιζητοῦμεν indicates a continual, habitual attitude of life (cf. Filson, *'Yesterday'*, 70). For the suggestion that the compound ἐπιζητεῖν was chosen because it can mean "to long for" and also "to go to see," see Thurén, *Lobopfer*, 100, n. 358.

ʸ It is impossible in translation to convey the literary and rhetorical quality of the statement. It is chiastic in structure.:

οὐ ἔχομεν   μένουσαν πόλιν
"we do not have"   "a permanent city"
τὴν μέλλουσαν [πόλιν]   ἐπιζητοῦμεν
"[the city] which is to come"   "we are expecting intently."

Moreover, the arrangement of the sentence is sonorous: ἔχομεν . . . μένουσαν πόλιν . . . .μέλλουσαν ἐπιζητοῦμεν.

ᶻ The prep διά with the gen here appears to have the transferred sense of mediation ("by means of"). Although Moule, *Idiom-Book*, 57, acknowledges that it is difficult to tie down the sense of δι᾽ αὐτοῦ ἀναφέρωμεν θυσίαν, he does not list Heb 13:15 among those passages which use διά in reference to a person in the transferred sense of agency rather than mediation (204). The expression δι᾽ αὐτοῦ, "through him," is emphatic by virtue of its position at the beginning of the sentence. The translation "Jesus" for "him" is adopted for the sake of clarity.

ᵃᵃ Although the UBSGNT³ includes the conj οὖν, it has been assigned a "D" rating by the editors, indicating a very high degree of doubt concerning the reading selected for the text. It is absent from several early and important witnesses to the text (p⁴⁶ ℵ* D* P ψ latᵃ syᵖ). Nevertheless, it is appropriate at this point, and its inclusion is consistent with the writer's careful use of particles and conj. It appears to have been accidentally omitted in transcription (see Metzger, *Textual Commentary*, 676).

ᵇᵇ The expression θυσίαν αἰνέσεως provides an instance of the epexegetical, or explanatory, gen: "sacrifice *consisting in praise*." The use of the gen in the sense of an appositive conforms to classical usage (BDF §167). Cf. NIV: "a sacrifice *of praise*."

ᶜᶜ The nuance in ὁμολογεῖν must be determined by its usage in a clause explanatory of the prior expression θυσίαν αἰνέσεως, "a sacrifice consisting in praise," and by the fact that it is followed by the dative of object: ὁμολογούντων τῷ ὀνόματι αὐτοῦ, "praising his name" (so BAGD 568). Deichgräber insists that the only acceptable translations for the term here are "to praise," "to extol," and "to glorify," because the dative of object is appropriate only to this nuance (*Gotteshymnus*, 117–18; cf. Zerwick and Grosvenor, *Grammatical Analysis*, 689). The writer draws upon a tradition of a song of praise which the community offers to God (Thurén, *Lobopfer*, 107, n. 377, with bibliography; for the background in the Psalter, see especially F. Mand, "Die Eigenständigkeit der Danklieder des Psalters als Bekenntnislieder," *ZAW* 70 [1958] 185–99; Bornkamm, "Lobpreis," 46–63). The alternative translation, "the fruit of lips which *confess* his name" (see NIV), is defended by Michel, *TDNT* 5:209–10. His attempt to interpret the usage of ὁμολογεῖν in v 15 with the aid of Acts 23:8, where he finds the nuance "to make solemn statements of faith," "to confess something in faith," founders on the syntax (so Thurén, *Lobopfer*, 113, n. 406). His concluding statement actually approximates the nuance adopted for the translation: "God's name is mentioned, proclaimed, acknowledged and extolled in prayer and the offering of praise" (210).

ᵈᵈ The term εὐποιΐα, which appears only here in the Greek Bible, is now attested with the nuance of "kindness" in a papyrus (3rd/4th century) (*NewDocs* 1:59 [#18.3, 13] and from a long inscription of Marcus Aurelius for the Athenians, with the nuance "the doing of good deeds," "beneficence" (*NewDocs* 4:83 [#20.90]). It occurs only once in Philo (*On the Change of Names* 24), where it connotes "a good deed." Cf. BAGD 324: "the doing of good."

ᵉᵉ For this nuance in κοινωνία, see BAGD 439. The financial implications of the term in this context have been broadly recognized: J. Y. Campbell, "*KOINΩNIA*," 21–22 ("contribution," as in Rom 15:26; 2 Cor 9:13, only here *the action of contributing*); McDermott, *BZ* 19 [1975] 229 ("collection," a Pauline innovation that became well accepted into the vocabulary of the early Church); cf. Seesemann, *KOINΩNIA*, 24–31. For the financial connotations of the term, see Rom 15:26–27; 2 Cor 8:4; 9:13; cf. Rom 12:13; Gal 6:6; Phil 4:15; 1 Tim 6:18..

ᶠᶠ The dative case in τοιαύταις θυσίαις is causal ("because of such sacrifices"). Cf. BDF §196; Turner, *Grammar*, 3:242, who describes "this dative" as extraordinary. It is not possible in translation to reflect the sonorous quality of the gen and dative endings, which is rhetorically effective: εὐποιΐας καὶ κοινωνίας . . . τοιαύταις γὰρ θυσίαις.

ᵍᵍ The translation stresses the iterative force of the present imperative πείθεσθε.

ʰʰ Although the words "to their authority" do not appear in the text, they are fully justified by the sense of ὑπείκειν, "to submit to someone's authority" (BAGD 838). The construction of the clause is highly literary: πείθεσθε τοῖς ἡγουμένοις ὑμῶν καὶ ὑπείκετε. The two verbs on the outside form a "linguistic sandwich"; to add an obj after ὑπείκετε, as we must do in translation, would spoil the elegance of the clause. The verb ὑπείκειν occurs only here in the NT (cf. 4 Macc 6:35).

ⁱⁱ The force of the pronoun αὐτοί is emphatic (cf. Moffatt, 239: the leaders are men who are *really* concerned for their highest interests).

ʲʲ It is necessary to understand the expression ψυχή in the light of the prior use of the term in 10:39, so that here it has the nuance of "eternal life" (with Michel, 528–29; Laub, *SNTU* 6–7 [1981–82] 178).

kk The phrase ὡς λόγον ἀποδώσοντες appears to preserve a classical idiom that has been missed in current translations. It has been broadly recognized that the particle ὡς with the fut ptcp ἀποδώσοντες expresses objective motive (cf. BDF §425[3]: "as men who," "with the thought that"). This insight has been added to the conviction that the fut tense of the ptcp expresses necessity or obligation (e.g., Turner, *Grammar,* 3:158: "with the thought that they must"; repeated by Hanna, *Grammatical Aid,* 162; Zerwick and Grosvenor, *Grammatical Analysis,* 689: "[who] must render"). The contemporary translations almost uniformly reflect this reading of the text (Moffatt, Berkeley, Beck, RSV, NEB, JB, NCV, LB, TEV, NIV; NASB is neutral ["as those who will give an account"]; only the Basic translation offers a genuine alternative: "for they keep watch . . . ready to give an account"). The dominant renderings obscure the basic subjective-voluntative force of the idiom. The particle ὡς makes clear that the action involved is accepted with intent and purpose. It is preferable, with Wikgren ("Some Greek Idioms," 148), to recognize in the phrase the classical use of ὡς with the fut ptcp to express strong or avowed purpose (cf. BDF §351; Zerwick, *Biblical Greek,* §282). A sufficient number of instances survive in later Gk. to render plausible the presence of the idiom in Hebrews to express strong purpose and intention. The phrase denotes the current leaders "as those who intend to give an account."

ll The translation treats the idiom ἵνα . . . ποιῶσιν as an instance of the imperatival ἵνα (see A. P. Salom, *AusBR* 6 [1958] 123–41, and especially 138 where this verse is discussed; Morrice, *BT* 23 [1972] 326–30, with reference to this occurrence on 329). The idiom has been broadly recognized (AmT, Moffatt, Phillips, RSV, NEB). The NIV treats the ἵνα clause as expressive of purpose, and repeats from the beginning of the complex sentence the exhortation to obedience: "Obey your leaders. . . . Obey them so that their work may be a joy."

mm The term ἀλυσιτελές occurs only here in biblical literature. The translation takes into account the language of commerce in 17b, λόγον ἀποδώσοντες, "give an account," i.e., let their accounting be a pleasant task, and not a painful one, for this would bring you "no profit." Contemporary usage, however, indicates that the term can be used positively in the sense of "harmful" (BAGD 41). In that case, the clause may be translated, "for this would be detrimental to you."

nn The durative force is exhibited in the present imperative προσεύχεσθε. Something already existing is to continue: "Keep praying" (BDF §336[3]).

oo The term πειθόμεθα seems to be a rare instance of the perfective present verb, "we are convinced" (so BDF §322; Stelzenberger, *Syneidēsis,* 65). The form has been corrected to the pf tense πεποίθαμεν in א^c C^c D^bc I K. For the construction πείθομαι ὅτι, "I am convinced that," instead of the inf, parallel to the idiom at Rom 8:38; 2 Tim 1:5, 12; and Heb 13:18, see now *NewDocs* 4:56 (#15), where the construction occurs in a letter from the late first or early second century. It is striking that in the juxtaposition of vv 17–18, πείθεσθε . . . πειθόμεθα, "Obey . . . we are convinced," the same verb is used in the same context with different meanings. This deliberate play on words is missed by Bischoff, *ZNW* 9 (1908) 171–72, who insists that the meaning of the expression in v 18 is determined by the present imperative in v17: "Obey your leaders. . . . Pray for us, because we are obedient."

pp For θέλοντες as a causal ptcp, see Zerwick and Grosvenor, *Grammatical Analysis,* 689; they translate the participle "seeing that we want." For the translation, cf. Stelzenberger, *Syneidēsis,* 65: "since we strive in everything to walk appropriately."

qq It is impossible in translation to convey the play on words between καλήν, "clear [conscience]," and καλῶς, "commendably."

rr The phrase ἐν πᾶσιν, "in every way," is in the emphatic position within the clause.

ss The adv περισσοτέρως, "especially," is probably elative in force without any comparison intended, as in 2:1; 6:17.

tt The translation "to pray" in place of "to do this" (τοῦτο ποιῆσαι) picks up the verb from v 18. The alliteration in the clause is oratorical (περισσοτέρως δὲ παρακαλῶ τοῦτο ποιῆσαι) and is consistent with the writer's style elsewhere in the homily, especially where it concerns the letter π ("p"): e.g., 1:1 (six times); 2:2; 7:25; 11:28 (five); 12:11; 13:18 (four); and 13:19 (three). In conjunction with v 18, the use of alliteration is even more obvious: προσεύχεσθε περὶ . . . πειθόμεθα . . . πᾶσιν . . . περισσοτέρως . . . παρακαλῶ . . . ποιῆσαι.

uu The comparative adv τάχιον appears to have a true comparative sense in this verse: "more quickly," "sooner" (BDF §244[1]). This is denied by P. E. Hughes, 588, n. 43, who prefers the positive force, "soon," as in v 23.

Form/Structure/Setting

See 13:1–25 above.

Comment

7 A second integrated paragraph in chap. 13 is introduced in v 7. Within the structure of 13:7–19, vv 7–9 and vv 17–19 constitute the literary frame for the central unit of explanatory parenesis in vv 10–16 (see *Form/Structure/Setting* for 13:1–25). The references to former leaders, who had preached the word of God to the community (v 7), and to current leaders, whose authority is to be respected (v 17), are complementary. Together they serve to throw into high relief the central section, where the tradition that brought the community to faith is actualized for the strengthening of its resolve to hold firmly to the word received through preaching (so Michel, 485, n. 1).

The members of the house church are admonished to continue to remember their former leaders, who are characterized as preachers of the word of God (v 7*a*). The term applied collectively to the leadership of the church, ἡγούμενοι ("leaders," vv 7, 17, 24), is not technical but broadly descriptive of the role that certain men played in the life of the community from its formative period. The term appears to have originated linguistically in official and administrative language. In a series of papyri, for example, high state officials are designated this way (for evidence see Laub, *SNTU* 6–7 [1981–82] 183–84). The term is not reserved for a specified official position or administrative task but designates a person entrusted with responsibility for leadership, who on the ground of the official position receives authority (Laub, *SNTU* 6–7 [1981–82] 189–90). In the LXX the form is used typically of political and military leaders (e.g., Deut 1:13; Ezek 43:7; Sir 17:17; 30:27; 41:17; 1 Macc 9:30; 2 Macc 14:16).

Within the NT Judas Barsabbas and Silas are designated as ἄνδρες ἡγούμενοι ἐν τοῖς ἀδελφοῖς, "leading men among the brothers" (Acts 15:22). In this instance ἡγούμενοι is not used substantively as a designation of office but rather in its original participial sense of men in any leading position. Suggestive for the use of ἡγούμενοι in the sense of community leadership is the tradition of Jesus' teaching preserved in Luke 22:26. There ὁ ἡγούμενος, "the leader," is interchangeable with ὁ διακονῶν, "the one who serves," in a context addressing leadership or precedence within the community of faith. Subsequent to Hebrews, the Christian use of the collective term ἡγούμενοι, "leaders," or the compound προηγούμενοι, "chief leaders," to designate holders of community office appears to be confined to documents associated with the church in Rome (*1 Clem.* 1:3; 21:6; 37:2; Hermas, *Vis.* 2. 2.6; 3.9.7; on these texts see Laub, *SNTU* 6–7 [1981–82] 186–88).

According to v 7*a*, the function of the ἡγούμενοι consisted in preaching the word of God. From this fact they may be characterized as charismatically endowed leaders, whose authority derived exclusively from the word they proclaimed and whose precedence was enhanced by preaching alone (cf. Michel, 488, 529; Laub, S*NTU* 6–7 [1981–82] 169, 171–73, 189). No other grounding and safeguarding of the position of the leaders is provided than the authority that results from the word proclaimed.

The phrase λαλεῖν τὸν λόγον τοῦ θεοῦ, "to speak the word of God," with which the act of preaching is summoned up, is in the NT a common expression for missionary as well as for community preaching (e.g., Acts 4:29, 31; 8:25; 13:46; Phil 1:14; 1 Pet 4:11; cf. 1 Thess 2:2, 4; *Did.* 4:1; see Riggenbach, 433; Michel 489,

n. 3). The formulation indicates that the leaders were a link in the chain of tradition that accounted for the reliable transmission of the message of salvation to the audience. According to 2:3, the word of salvation began to be spoken by the Lord. Those who heard him subsequently became the preachers who certified to the community the saving word he spoke, God himself endorsing the integrity of their message with signs and wonders (2:3–4). That word was identical with the decisive eschatological speaking of God delivered through the Son (1:1–2*a*). In the word of God the saving action of God himself is actualized.

Within this perspective, tradition retains the character of the living word of God, which confronted the community with the eschatological act of salvation. The expressions "to speak [λαλεῖν] the word of salvation" and "to speak [λαλεῖν] the word of God" are conceptually interchangeable (so E. Grässer, "Das Heil als Wort: Exegetische Erwägungen zu Hebr 2,1–4," in *Neuen Testament und Geschichte*, ed. H. Baltensweiler and B. Reicke [Tübingen: Mohr, 1972] 261–74, especially 268, 273–74). The parallel between 2:3 and 13:7 brings to light a remarkable theology of the word that informs the function and authority of the former leaders (Laub, *SNTU* 6–7 [1981–82] 173–77, 189–90).

The former leaders are now deceased. As those who "spoke [ἐλάλησαν] the word of God," their preaching belongs to the community's past (for the argument that the aorist tense of the verb has reference to the initial proclamation to the audience, see Tasker, *ExpTim* 47 [1935–36] 138). It is probable that the community was gathered in response to the word they proclaimed. It was on the ground of their preaching that the missionaries were elevated to leadership roles (see B. Weiss, 89; Laub, *SNTU* 6–7 [1981–82] 171–77). They were thus the original leaders or founding fathers of the community (so Filson, '*Yesterday*', 31, 74; P. E. Hughes, 569–70; among others).

The members of the house church are to continue to remember their former leaders because of the example of their forward-looking faith (giving to πίστις the same nuance as in 11:1–2). These now deceased preachers of the word of God retain authority for the community because one can refer to their faith, which was validated by the solid accomplishment of their lives (v 7*b*).

In the clause ὧν ἀναθεωροῦντες τὴν ἔκβασιν τῆς ἀναστροφῆς, "considering the accomplishment of their conduct," τὴν ἔκβασιν connotes the triumphant result of their daily behavior (P. E. Hughes, 569, n. 18; cf. F. F. Bruce, 395, n. 43). The accent falls specifically on the firmness of faith, which characterized the exemplary conduct of the leaders throughout their lives (cf. Riggenbach, 433–34; Michel, 489–90). The quality of their faith aligns them with the exemplars of faith under the old covenant, whose faithfulness is celebrated in 11:4–38. Of Abel it was said expressly that his faith (πίστις) continues to speak, even though he is dead (11:4). The steadfast faithfulness of the deceased leaders poses the standard which those who responded to their preaching must emulate.

The call to imitate the exemplary faith of the leaders (μιμεῖσθε τὴν πίστιν) introduces a discipleship motif. In Hebrews discipleship consists in imitating the pattern of response established by past exemplars of faithfulness rather than in "following" Jesus (see *Comment* on 6:12, where the call to "imitate" is first introduced; on the distinctive understanding of discipleship in Hebrews see Laub, *Bekenntnis*, 143–65). The call to perseverance articulated in 12:1–3 is renewed when the writer appeals for the imitation of the faith of the leaders. In the context of v 7*a*, emulation of their faith will be reflected in the firm adherence to the word they preached (so Grässer, *Glaube,* 121–25; Thurén, *Lobopfer,* 124–25).

A common element in parenetic instruction is the appeal to example. An audience is called to emulate the qualities of life and conduct exhibited in those who have proven to be models worthy of emulation. The directive to remember those who preached the word of God to the community and the summons to imitate their faith are parenetic in character and intention.

8 The writer turns abruptly from the example of the past leaders to the person of Jesus Christ. Key to the proper interpretation of v 8 is recognition that the acclamation is not an isolated remark (as argued, for example, by Kuss, 144–45, 218) but functions as the bridge between v 7 and v 9. (The close link between vv 7–9 is recognized by Westcott, 435; Moffatt, 231–32; F. F. Bruce, 395, 397; Michel, 490, 493; among others.) The connection extends backward (v 7) and forward (v 9); in both instances the acclamation in v 8 provides the ground of the intended continuity of faith. It is necessary to associate vv 7–9 conceptually as an exhortation to correct teaching. The word of God that was proclaimed by the deceased leaders (v 7) is crystallized in the confessional formulation of v 8 and is distorted by the "various strange teachings" to which the writer alludes in v 9 (cf. Thurén, *Lobopfer,* 68, 70; Laub, *SNTU* 6–7 [1981–82] 173 and n. 15).

Accordingly, v 8 is not to be interpreted as an acclamation of Jesus' timeless ontological immutability, corresponding to the assertion that the Son remains ὁ αὐτός, "the same," in 1:10–12 (as asserted by H. Montefiore, 242; P. R. Jones, *RevExp* 82 [1985] 400; cf. Grässer, *Glaube,* 23; Buchanan, 233). The reference is rather to the immutability of the gospel message proclaimed by the deceased leaders in the recent past (see Michel, 490 and n. 2; P. E. Hughes, 570–71). Although the preachers change, the preaching must remain the same. The unchangeableness of the revelation is a consequence of the transcendent dignity of Jesus Christ, the originator of the preaching (2:3) (so Thurén, *Lobopfer,* 183).

It has commonly been proposed that in juxtaposing v 7 and v 8 the writer is addressing a crisis of leadership. The intended contrast is between the deceased leaders (v 7), whose absence is felt by the community, and Jesus Christ, who remains perpetually available (e.g., F. F. Bruce, 395; Thompson, *Beginnings of Christian Philosophy,* 143; P. R. Jones, *RevExp* 82 [1985] 401; among others). That proposal fails to give sufficient weight to the plea to "imitate their faith" in v 7. The more probable connection between the two verses is that v 8 encapsulates the proclamation of the former leaders and illumines the nature of their faith. It was specifically faith in Jesus Christ as the decisive figure in the history of salvation and in the enduring efficacy of his redemptive accomplishment. Since he is ὁ αὐτός, "the same," today as he was then, the community may with confidence emulate the faith of the leaders (so Hurst, "Background," 212–13).

If this is a correct reading of the text, the correlation between vv 7 and 8 challenges the assertion that in Hebrews "faith" is "never Christologically focused" (MacRae, *Semeia* 12 [1978] 192; MacRae adds, "Jesus is not the object of faith, but the supreme model of it," 194). The faith of the leaders was not without content but rather was based on the word of God, which finds its culmination in Jesus Christ (see now Hamm, *CBQ* 52 [1990] 270–91, especially 270, 275–76, 286–91).

A contrast is intended by the writer, but it is not between v 7 and v 8. It occurs rather between v 8 and v 9. In contrast to the fluid and changing configurations of "strange teachings" (v 9), the truth concerning Jesus Christ never changes (v 8).

The recognition that the directive in v 7 is christologically grounded in v 8 has implications for the authority of the former leaders. The authorization for the community to continue to remember their past leaders as preachers of the word of God and exemplars of faith is given in the confessional acclamation of v 8. To the extent that Jesus Christ was presented authoritatively in the preaching and the forward-looking faith of the leaders, they themselves have authority in the assembly of the house church, even after their deaths. The relationship between vv 7 and 8 indicates that the standard and legitimation of the former leaders' authority were of a christological nature (cf. Riggenbach, 434–35; Spicq, 2:421–22; Michel, 490–91; Laub, *SNTU* 6–7 [1981–82] 173).

The terse aphoristic style of v 8 is appropriate to a confession of faith (so Kuss, 144–45, 218; H. Montefiore, 242; Michel, 491, suggests that v 8 is to be understood in the light of Exod 3:14). The formulation reflects a creedal, liturgical structure:

Ἰησοῦς Χριστός	"Jesus Christ
ἐχθὲς	yesterday
καὶ	and
σήμερον	today
ὁ αὐτός	the same
καὶ	and
εἰς τοὺς αἰῶνας	forever."

The unusual word order is calculated to arouse and focus the attention. The confession could be an originally independent acclamation. However, the formulation contains within it motifs that are important for the entire homily (cf. F. F. Bruce, 397–98). The community is called to believe and confess what has been preached. This is the relationship between v 7 and v 8 (Lemcio, *JSNT* 33 [1988] 16, n. 15).

The writer has typically used syntax to emphasize the name of "Jesus" (see above on 2:9; 3:1; 4:14; 6:20; 7:22; 10:19; 12:2, 24). In contrast to the placement of the name of Jesus at the emphatic final position throughout the homily, here Ἰησοῦς Χριστός, "Jesus Christ," is emphatic by virtue of its position at the beginning of the sentence. The compound proper name "Jesus Christ" occurs three times in Hebrews (10:10; 13:8, 21).

On the basis of ordinary language ἐχθές, "yesterday," could recall the past of Jesus' historical ministry, and particularly his passion, when he became qualified to make the unrepeatable, fully effective sacrifice as High Priest (as argued by Filson, 'Yesterday', 30–35). Alternatively, it can have reference to the more recent time of the former leaders, whose faith the audience has just been called to emulate (v 7). The intimate relationship between vv 7 and 8 favors the second alternative. Jesus Christ is declared to remain the object of faith for the assembly now ("today") as he was formerly ("yesterday") for those leaders. The exalted Lord who proved fully adequate for them remains so now (so Westcott, 435; P. E. Hughes, 570–71; Michel, 490, n. 4; Thurén, *Lobopfer*, 183–84). The fact that the message concerning Jesus Christ continues ὁ αὐτός, "the same," even εἰς τοὺς αἰῶνας, "forever," furnishes an appropriate argument for heeding the following admonition in v 9. If the former leaders, who "yesterday" declared the word of the Lord (2:3), did not know this diverse teaching (13:9), then the community may not attempt to find salvation through it "today" (Thurén, *Lobopfer*, 183–84).

"Today" thus has reference to the present time when the community is being tempted to exchange the true and saving instruction of "yesterday" for novel "strange teachings" (v 9). "Yesterday" the original leaders preached Jesus Christ, even as the writer does now; the present time can tolerate no other approach to the grace of God (2:9). "Forever" recalls the quality of the redemption secured by Jesus Christ (5:9; 9:12, 14–15; 13:20) and of the priesthood of Christ (7:24–25): it is "eternal." Those who seek to find security in the novel strange teaching have forgotten that the salvation accomplished through Christ's high priestly ministry is "forever." The intent of the acclamation in v 8 is to drive the men and women of the house church back to the foundational preaching received from their original leaders.

9   Vv 9–14 constitute one of the most controversial passages in Hebrews. The major thrust of the text easily becomes lost in the obscurities of proposals and counter-proposals. Two major problems make this text "a source of exegetical difficulty" (following Thompson, *Beginnings of Christian Philosophy*, 141). On the one hand, the writer concentrates in this section several expressions that appear to be distinctive and for this reason are difficult to interpret in the context of the homily as a whole. There is no common agreement on the nuance of the "various strange teachings," the "foods," the Christian "altar," or of going "outside the camp." In fact, as Schierse has observed, "there is scarcely a concept . . . in verses 9–14 which can be reduced to a clear, generally recognized view" (*Verheissung*, 184).

On the other hand, there is the further problem of ascertaining how the several statements in vv 9–14 form a coherent argument. The abundant use of connectives (γάρ, "for," vv 9, 11, 14; διό, "therefore," v 12; τοίνυν, "so then," v 13) indicates a concern for coherence. Yet the connection between these verses continues to be debated. It will be possible to advance the discussion only if the details of the text and the role of the argument within the larger context of Hebrews can be clarified.

The fact that this section conforms to the writer's customary parenetic form supplies an important key to the general interpretation of vv 9–14. It is introduced with the imperative, "Do not be led away" (v 9), which is supported by two statements in the indicative ("we have an altar," v 10; "Jesus . . . suffered death outside the city gate," v 12). These statements are followed by an exhortation in the hortatory subjunctive ("let us go out to him," v 13), which is grounded in an additional statement in the indicative ("For here we do not have a permanent city," v 14). The writer regularly employs a parenetic form in which the indicative is interwoven with the imperative and the hortatory subjunctive (e.g., 4:14–16; 10:19–23; 12:1–3). Comparison of this section with other passages with which it shares a common form will serve to clarify its intention (so Thompson, *Beginnings of Christian Philosophy*, 142).

The tenor of the passage is clear. The word that the former leaders proclaimed is now threatened by teaching that is inconsistent with the message the community received. The "various strange teachings" competing for their attention are incompatible with the original, always valid, instruction delivered by the founding fathers of the community (vv 7–8). Foreign teaching and the grace of God mediated through the new covenant are mutually exclusive.

Structurally, the directives of v 7 and v 9 form a parenetic pair: the components of the warning in v 9 correspond to those of the exhortation in v 7.

Exhortation (v 7)		*Warning* (v 9)	
A	Remember, imitate	A'	Do not allow yourselves to be led away
B	your former leaders	B'	strange [itinerant preachers]
C	the [one] word of God	C'	diverse [human] teachings
D	Considered the accomplishment of their conduct	D'	their adherents are not benefited
E	their faith	E'	foods

Within the unit vv 7–9, "grace" and "word," "foods" and "teachings" belong together as pairs. "To be strengthened" and "to be carried away" constitute an antithesis (cf. Bleek, 2/2:1003, who draws support for the antithesis from Plutarch, *Timoleon* 6).

It was alleged that the competing teachings concerning foods will strengthen the heart and keep it from defection. In reality, they divert the heart from the grace mediated through the word of God, which the former leaders preached and which always remains valid. Their proponents are correct in maintaining that the heart must be strengthened, but they have become destructive of faith when they insinuate their instructions about foods in the place of the word of grace. It is not to be thought that they disparaged the grace of God. It is that they have another conception of grace and of the relationship of grace to prescribed foods than does the writer of Hebrews (so Thurén, *Lobopfer*, 186–87 and n. 646).

Although it is probable that a specific expression of "strange teachings" has determined decisively the formulation and objective of vv 7–9 as a unit, there has been no unanimity in the interpretation of v 9. The intimations in the descriptive phrase ποικίλαις καί ξέναις, "various strange [teachings]," in the notion of strengthening the heart through prescribed foods or ceremonial meals, and in the allusion to the disappointing experience of the adherents of these teachings have prompted a variety of explanations. (For a review of the most important alternative attempts at interpretation see Windisch, 117–18; Filson, *'Yesterday'*, 50–53; Thurén, *Lobopfer*, 185–86, n. 644.) Methodologically, the explanation must proceed from v 9.

This much is clear:

(1) The reference is not to novel teaching. It cannot be said of completely new teachings that they did not bring their adherents the expected benefit. The instruction is for them already familiar. Its results have been observed by the writer for an extended period (cf. H. Montefiore, 248).

(2) More particularly, the teachings called into question the conviction that the heart can be strengthened through grace alone. It did so by commending the strengthening of the heart through prescribed foods or meals. There is an obvious connection (γάρ, "for") between the phrase "various strange teachings" in v 9a and the reference to "[prescribed] foods" in v 9b. (For a contrary point of view, see Thompson, *Beginnings of Christian Philosophy*, 144.)

(3) Syncretistic-gnostic celebrations of meals, at which special foods mediated the divine life for the initiates, is conceivable but certainly not obvious (cf. Windisch, 117; Behm, *TDNT* 1:643; F. F. Bruce, 397–98; Michel, 495–96) and finds no support in the homily as a whole (see Filson, 'Yesterday', 51, who observes that if this were the issue, the writer "could have been expected to react against it with a horror of which 13:9 reveals no trace"). Nor is it a question of syncretistic-ascetic food prohibitions (e.g., Col 2:16; 1 Tim 4:3; as argued by Windisch, 118; W. Manson, 150), since there is no reference to the avoidance of prescribed foods.

(4) The form of argumentation in the immediate context (vv 10–16) tends to show that the allusion is to the consumption of foods in some way connected with Jewish sacrificial meals. The reference must be to foods whose consumption was considered essential to the strengthening of the heart (cf. already Bleek, 2/2:1005, who thinks of the Passover and of other sacrificial meals generally [e.g., Exod 12:8–9; Lev 19:5–6; 22:29–30]).

(5) The interpretation of v 10 depends upon the clarification of v 9.

With these considerations in the foreground, the detail of the text must be considered patiently.

The present imperative μὴ παραφέρεσθε, "Do not be led away whenever," links vv 9–14 to the preceding pastoral directives. It expresses a concern found elsewhere in the early Church (e.g., Col 2:6–8; Eph 4:14–16; 5:6; cf. Michel, 493 and n. 3, 497; Thurén, *Lobopfer*, 68). The verb παραφέρεσθαι, "to be carried away," belongs to the linguistic arsenal developed by church leaders to combat false teaching (Jude 12), as does the variant reading περιφέρεσθαι in some representatives of the Byzantine text (K L et al.; cf. Eph 4:14). It suggests the image of the person who is insufficiently grounded and is liable to be "carried away" by the currents of false teaching (cf. Thompson, *Beginnings of Christian Philosophy*, 143–44, who compares the directive in v 9a with the writer's use of related terms in 2:1; 3:12; 4:1; and 10:35 that reflect his fears for the weary community; Thompson argues that these passages "suggest that the author's major concern is with the endurance of the community and not with a specific heresy" [143]).

The members of the house church are warned not to allow themselves to be led away from the foundational instruction they had received by the various configurations of competing teachings. Whenever "various strange teachings" from itinerant teachers and prophets arise they must not be permitted to challenge the firm conviction of a dependence upon Jesus Christ and his high priestly ministry, as diversified and enticing as they may be (Fascher, *TLZ* 96 [1971] 165).

The plural form διδαχαῖς, "teachings," which occurs only here in the NT, suggests the polyvalent and polymorphous nature of human traditions, in contrast to the singular character of the word of God. The formulation διδαχαῖς ποικίλαις καὶ ξέναις, "various strange teachings," is clearly pejorative. Although ποικίλαις is used positively in 2:4, it is clearly pejorative in Matt 4:24 par.; 2 Tim 3:6; Titus 3:3; James 1:12; 1 Pet 1:6). In v 9a it signifies teachings that are at variance with the truth and incompatible with the faith of the former leaders. Those who remember them and the word they proclaimed (v 7) will not be subverted through alien instructions. The word of God must not be exchanged for mere human traditions.

There is a deliberate contrast in thought between v 9a and v 9b, as the connecting γάρ, "for," indicates. The preventive to being "led away" is to recognize that καλὸν . . . χάριτι βεβαιοῦσθαι τὴν καρδίαν, "it is good for the heart to be strengthened by means of grace." Since the heart is the vital center of an individual's life and personality and the source of both character and conduct (Jacob, *TDNT* 9:626–27; cf. Heb 3:8, 10, 12, 15; 4:7, 12; 10:22), it must be strengthened by God's grace. The verb βεβαιοῦσθαι, "to be strengthened," "to be supported," is antithetical to παραφέρεσθαι, "to be led away," "to be carried away." The writer shows a preference for forms of βεβαι- (3:6, 14; 6:19) and other words for steadfastness and stability (cf. Braun, *TLZ* 96 [1971] 321–30). The use of βεβαιοῦσθαι serves to link vv 9–14 with other parenetic passages in Hebrews (Thompson, *Beginnings of Christianity*, 144).

There is no other documentary evidence, however, for βεβαιοῦν τὴν καρδίαν χάριτι, "to strengthen the heart through grace," or βρώμασιν, "through foods," as opposing expressions. The notion of strengthening the heart through grace can be found elsewhere in the NT (e.g., 2 Thess 2:16–17) and in texts from Qumran (e.g., 1QH 1:31–32; 2:6–10; 4:3–4; 1QS 11:12), but where is there an opposing teaching concerning the strengthening of the heart through foods?

Thurén (*Lobopfer*, 188–96) has brought together a collection of material from the OT, Qumran, and the rabbinic literature demonstrating that eating, joy, and the praise of God at cultic meals, especially the fellowship meal, were associated with the thought of being supported by the grace of God. This was especially true of Second Temple Judaism. The cultic background to many of the biblical statements concerning God's grace (e.g., Ps 90:14; cf. Pss 17:7, 15; 63:4, 6; 65:5) can be found in the thank offering, with the acclamation, "Praise God, because he is God, and his grace endures forever." The goodness and grace and God saved those who were in peril and supported those who were wavering. They and their guests experienced the goodness and grace of God again as participants in a sacrificial meal.

The liturgy at sacrificial meals in the Second Temple period is known only through allusions (*m. Pesah.* 10:6; cf. *Jub.* 32:7; 49:6; and especially 22:3–9 [a description of a festive feast Isaac made for Ishmael]). What can be discerned is a pattern consisting of the blessing of God, thanksgiving in response to the experience of the grace of God, and petition (see Thurén, *Lobopfer,* 189–90). The participants in the meal obtain joy through eating and drinking so as to praise God with power. The generally acknowledged diction was that "there is no joy without eating and drinking" (*b. Moʿed Qat.* 9a). In Jerusalem this joy was experienced in the sacrificial meal times (*b. Pesah.* 109a [Baraita]: "R. Jehuda b. Bathyra [*ca.* 100] said: 'So long as the sanctuary stood, festal joy was found only in food, as it is said, "Sacrifice fellowship offerings there, eating them and rejoicing in the presence of the Lord your God" [Deut 27:7]. Now when the sanctuary does not exist, it resides only in wine, as it is said, "Wine rejoices the human heart" [Ps 104:15]'"; cf. *b. Ber.* 35b). This was the basis for the conviction that God can be praised properly only when his people are strengthened through the feast of joy (cf. Neh 8:9–12; Esth 9:19). It is, accordingly, a religious duty at such a feast to satisfy oneself with eating (*m. Pesah.* 10:5–6; cf. *Jub.* 49–50).

The teaching that the heart can be strengthened by foods was rooted in Scripture. The key statement is found in Ps 104:14–15: "You bring forth food from the earth . . . and bread to strengthen the human heart." This acclamation was evoked in the blessing pronounced before every Jewish meal. The meal began with the breaking of bread and the reciting of the benediction, "Blessed are you, O Lord, King of the world, who bring forth bread from the earth" (*m. Ber.* 6:1). This blessing extended to all the remaining eating (*m. Ber.* 6:3); "bread" signifies in this context "foods." Every Jewish meal was sanctified through the recalling of Ps 104:14–15 (see Thurén, *Lobopfer,* 191–93).

It is unnecessary, therefore, to distinguish sharply between ordinary Jewish meals and special cultic meal times. Every Jewish meal possessed a cultic character. There is merely a distinction of degree among ordinary meals, Sabbath meals, and the Passover meal. The purity of the foods and especially the recalling of the grace of God sanctify all fellowship meal times. (For a rich collection of sources demonstrating that all Jewish meals preserve the notion of a fellowship, or thank offering, meal, see B. Reicke, *Diakonie, Festfreude und Zelos in Verbindung mit der altchristlichen Agapenfeier* [Uppsala: Lundquistska, 1951] 167–200.) Moreover, the table prayer after the meal, the *birkat hammāzôn,* shows how the concepts of grace and of eating were brought together in Jewish thinking. (For a reconstruction of this prayer at the time of Jesus' earthly ministry see Finkelstein, *JQR* n.s. 19 [1928–29] 243–59.)

The plural form βρώματα, "foods," is never used in the LXX in reference to Jewish sacrificial meals, but only to distinguish pure from impure foods (Lev 11:34). Nevertheless, it is known from Josephus that special sacrificial meal times were observed by Diaspora Jews as σύνδειπνα, "fellowship meals," in imitation of the fellowship meals of the Temple. The key statements occur in A*nt.* 14, in a series of decrees and directives addressed by Julius Caesar in 46 B.C. that were designed to protect Jewish interests and praxis (*Ant.* 14.189). For example, in response to an appeal by Jews of Delos who were being prevented locally from celebrating cultic meals, Caesar responded, "Now it displeases me . . . that they should be forbidden to contribute money to common meals [σύνδειπνα] and sacred rites. . . . Gaius Caesar . . . by edict forbade religious societies to assemble in the city [Rome], but these people alone he did not forbid to do so, or to collect contributions of money, or to hold common meals [σύνδειπνα]. Similarly do I forbid other religious societies but permit these people alone to assemble and feast in accordance with their native customs and ordinances" (A*nt.* 14.213–15; see also 257, 260–61). The purity regulations were naturally observed in such cultic fellowship meals, but the accent was placed on the consumption of prescribed foods.

What Thurén (*Lobopfer,* 194–96) has shown is that the biblical expression "to strengthen the heart [with bread]" was commonly used with the meaning "to observe meal time." It was appropriate to connect every meal with Ps 104:15, since Ps 104:14 ("bread to strengthen the heart") was recited as a blessing at the beginning of every meal. Special meal times in the OT and in Judaism were regarded as occasions for festive joy, which in turn prompted the giving of thanks or the recital of God's grace. In this way such meals recalled the thank offering of the Temple. For Jews who lived outside of Jerusalem or of the land of Israel, the association of eating with the giving of thanks became even more important. Those who had not personally experienced the redemptive character of the grace of God found in the provision of food for the meal an always fresh demonstration of the grace of God.

This, then, is the background to the "strange teachings" that the heart must be strengthened with food, resulting in power to praise God for the food as well as for the grace experienced in redemption. The consumption of foods, it was urged, can bring us into the presence of God and actualize his lordship because it provides an occasion for the giving of thanks (so Thurén, *Lobopfer,* 199–200).

The evidence shows an extensively prepared biblical and Jewish conception that the people of God should eat and drink in order to praise him. In the eating of prescribed foods were experienced the goodness and grace of God that rejoices the heart and strengthens it for the praise of God. Every meal time provided the faithful Jew with strength and an occasion to acknowledge the grace of God. At the same time it was a sober reminder that ultimately one can thank God fully for redemption only through the thank offering and the fellowship meal in the presence of the altar in Jerusalem.

The writer of Hebrews rejects this line of argumentation. He declares that the grace of God was not mediated through the celebration of cultic meals. It was useless to imitate the sacrificial meals in Jerusalem, as the Jews of the Diaspora sought to do. The church will not find its security in such earthly assurances. On the contrary, the grace of God is bestowed through the word of promise concerning the redemptive efficiency of the death of Jesus (2:9) and through prayer (4:16). At their altar (13:10) Christians participate in a sacrifice far superior to the Jerusalem sacrifices. They have not yet attained the festive Sabbath joy reserved for the new people of God (4:9). They have assembled themselves outside the camp (13:13). Nevertheless, through Jesus their high priest, his sin offering and his thank offering, they enjoy now access to the real heavenly sanctuary (4:15–16; 10:19–22).

Those who merely praise God for food and for the graciousness exhibited through it, but not for the grace within the heart mediated by the eschatological promise of the gospel, either have not received in their hearts the revelation mediated through Jesus or have forfeited grace through personal carelessness (12:15). Such persons are not qualified to offer the sacrifice of praise through Jesus, the high priest (13:15). Christian tradition affirms that the heart is benefited by grace and not by any material measures, which really are of no spiritual advantage to their adherents.

This basic line of interpretation, first promulgated by Bleek in 1840 (2/2:1005; cf. Riggenbach, 439–42), offers a plausible and attractive explanation for the distinctive formulation of v 9 (so Thurén, *Lobopfer,* 186–87; cf. Westcott, 436; Michel, 495, n. 1; P. F. Hughes, 572–74; Buchanan, 233; among others). The terms βρώμασιν, "[prescribed] foods," and ἐν οἷς . . . οἱ περιπατοῦντες, "those who walk in them," are appropriate to halakhic food regulations and to the connection between v 9 and v 10, with its reference to the possession of an altar and eating. The allusion is to the eating of prescribed foods within a Jewish cultic setting. Those who framed their conduct by such ceremonial meals, then, are Jewish. Such observances have not brought them the eschatological salvation, the writer insists (Michel, 498). The verb used in v 9c, ὠφελεῖν, "to give an advantage," "to benefit," recalls the cognate forms used in 4:2 and 7:8. In each case what is in view is a deficiency in redemptive effect (Moe, *ST* 4 [1950] 103; Theissen, *Untersuchungen,* 76 argues that ὠφελεῖν, used in the absolute sense in Hebrews, consistently refers to the eschatological salvation).

This reading of the text is congruent with the manner in which Hebrews was read in the early second century. The influence of Heb 13:9–10 on the expression of Ignatius in his *Letter to the Magnesians* is evident:

Gather together—all of you—to the one Temple of God, as it were, to one altar, to one Jesus Christ. . . . Do not be led away through strange teachings [ἑτεροδοξίαι] and outmoded fables, which are not useful. If we still go on observing Judaism, we acknowledge that we never received grace; the godly prophets lived Christ Jesus' way. That is why they were persecuted, for they were inspired by his grace (*Magn.* 7:2–8:2).

(Related expressions occur in Ign., *Pol.* 3:1; *Smyrn.* 6:2; *Phld.* 3:3. See J. Rohde, "Häresie und Schisma im ersten Clemensbrief und in den Ignatius-Briefen," *NovT* 10 [1968] 227; Thurén, *Lobopfer,* 85–87, 229.) The proponents of cultic meals inculcate "strange teachings," which are of no advantage to their adherents because such meals are unable to mediate grace.

The admonition in v 9 repeats what had already been asserted in 9:9–10: the gifts and sacrifices offered under the old Levitical arrangement "cannot perfect the conscience of the worshiper," since they are no more than temporary "regulations for the body," which "deal only with food and drink and various washings" (P. E. Hughes, 574). Emphasized is the inadequacy of now obsolete cultic arrangements to mediate the grace that finds its culmination in the sacrifices which genuinely please God (13:15–16; cf. H. Koester, *HTR* 55 [1962] 305–8; Thompson, *Beginnings of Christian Philosophy,* 144–45).

The warning concerning prescribed foods and ceremonial meals is only a detail. It must not be made the lens through which the remainder of the homily is viewed (see Kuss, 22). The unpolemical nature of the homily as a whole suggests that the writer's intention is primarily parenetic rather than polemical (so rightly, Schierse, *Verheissung,* 206, n. 22; Thompson, *Beginnings of Christian Philosophy,* 142–45). The aim is to stress to a tired and oppressed community the significance of the original word of preaching (v 7) and the confession of praise it evoked (vv 15–16; cf. Kuss, 221: "The appearance of spiritual lethargy makes the church susceptible to 'various strange teachings.' The problem was the inner loss of confidence").

The purpose of those who brought the strange teachings concerning the value of ceremonial meals was to stimulate the heart to confession. Their instruction is to be rejected, because eating does not lead to that goal. (Cf. Philo, *On the Special Laws* 2.193–94, 198–99, who argues that the Day of Atonement shows that the occasion of praise is God and his promise, not food, its enjoyment and nourishment. Close parallels to Heb 13:9 occur in Rom 14:17; 1 Cor 8:8. See further Riggenbach, 437.) It is important that the community be grounded in the preaching concerning the one who is "the same" (13:7–8). Since they possess in their deceased leaders, and supremely in Jesus Christ, exemplars of dependability and steadfastness, the teaching that they received should also remain unchanged (Windisch, 106).

The way to offer to God the praise offering with which he is well pleased is to participate in the life and worship of the new covenant community, sharing Jesus' shame (13:12–16). Only through Christ's mediation and through confidence in his promise can the offering of praise be devoted to God (Thurén, *Lobopfer,* 202). According to v 9, the grace of God exhibited in Jesus is the true nourishment of the heart. The heart that is strengthened through grace is the heart grounded in God's redemptive action in Jesus Christ, who "by the grace of God tasted death for everyone" (2:9). The objective benefit of redemptive grace secured through Christ's death is the only ground of assurance for a weary community.

10 The catechetical precepts in vv 7–9 serve to introduce a cohesive unit characterized by sustained argumentation, vv 10–16. This unit is distinguished from the small units with which it is framed (vv 7–9, 17–19) by its form and construction. McCown has identified the literary form of this new section as "explanatory paraenesis" or "hortatory exposition" (see *Form/Structure/Setting* for 13:1–25 above). Although the basis of the argument is the exposition of Scripture, its intention is clearly parenetic. The flow of the argument may be charted by a series of connectives. The initial declaration, "we have an altar," is grounded through an appeal to Lev 16:27, which is expounded in vv 10–12. The exposition provides the basis for exhortation in vv 13–16. The parenetic intention of the argument becomes clear when the hortatory subjunctive is introduced in v 13 and in v 15. Here the writer applies the liturgical directives of Lev 16 to the community on the basis of redemptive analogy. It will be imperative throughout this section to refer to the details of the formal analysis of vv 10–16 offered in *Form/ Structure/Setting* for 13:1–25. The distinctive form and chiastic structure of the section provide essential keys to its interpretation.

Briefly, the emphatic assertion in v 10a, "We have an altar," is the determining thesis, which is elaborated and established in vv 11–12. The declaration is sharpened by the antithesis, "We have . . . they have not." The second term of the antithesis is substantiated through a reference to the Day of Atonement in v 11. The provision for the disposal of the carcasses of the sacrificed animals outside the camp on that solemn day (v 11b) is then applied in v 12 to Jesus who experienced death outside the city gate. This allusion to the event of the cross serves as the substantiation for the thesis, "we have an altar," in v 10a.

The writer's intention in vv 10–16 is to support and develop the point made in v 9bc. The continuation of the thought in v 10 should clearly indicate the alternative urged by the writer to the useless prescribed "foods" mentioned in v 9. It does so by specifying the source of the grace by which the heart is strengthened (cf. Bleek, 2/2.1005; Thurén, *Lobopfer,* 83). Nevertheless, v 10 is one of the most difficult statements in Hebrews to fit into its context. The major question is how this verse relates to what immediately precedes and follows it. Its ambiguities must be recognized as a first step toward their resolution.

It had been argued by the proponents of the "strange teachings" concerning the value of cultic meals that participation in fellowship meals evoked eating at the altar in Jerusalem (see *Comment* on v 9b). The writer's response, ἔχομεν θυσιαστήριον, "we have an altar," is creedal in character. (For the confessional use of ἔχειν, "to have," see 8:1, "we have such a high priest"; cf. 4:14; 10:19–21; see further Moule, *JTS* n.s. 1 [1950] 37: "the whole burden of Hebrews . . . can be epitomized in two resounding ἔχομενs: we *have* a high priest, we *have* an altar: sanctuary and sacrifices are ours"). This confessional response appears to be the elaboration of the term χάρις, "grace," in v 9 (with Thompson, *Beginnings of Christian Philosophy,* 146, 150–51; for the untenable argument that ἔχομεν signifies "we *Jews* have [an altar]," see Spencer, *ExpTim* 50 [1938–39] 284).

The writer has not previously used θυσιαστήριον, "sacrificial altar," "the place of sacrifice" (see now Klauck, *ZNW* 71 [1980] 247–77) in reference to the death of Christ. Nevertheless, the term can be interpreted on the analogy of the sustained use of cultic language in reference to the high priestly work of Christ in Hebrews (cf. 8:1–5; 9:11–14, 24–26; 10:11–12). That the continuation of the text contains a reference to Golgotha in the immediate context (v 12) indicates that the term θυσιαστήριον, "altar," is anchored in history; it is employed metaphorically for the event of the sacrificial death of Christ outside the city gate (cf. 12:2) (so Haensler, *BZ* 11 [1913] 403–9; Spicq, 2:425; Andriessen, *NRT* 94 [1972] 275; W. Manson, 151; H. Montefiore, 244–45; P. Brunner, *KD* 20 [1974] 230–32; Snell, *RTR* 23 [1964] 16–18; among others; for the argument that participation in the offering is bound up in the term itself, see Westcott, 437–38; Michel, 498; for the counter-argument that the close relationship between the creedal formulations in 8:1 and 13:10 suggests that the altar is the heavenly sanctuary and not Golgotha, see Williamson, *NTS* 21 [1975] 308–9; Filson, *'Yesterday'*, 48–49, 53; Theissen, *Untersuchungen*, 76–79; Thompson, *Beginnings of Christian Philosophy*, 146). The term θυσιαστήριον, "altar," appears as metonymy for "sacrifice."

Jesus' death on the cross is the source of the saving and sustaining grace by which the heart is strengthened (cf. F. F. Bruce, 402: "Christ is both the sacrifice and the sustenance of his people"). The consecration of the new covenant people to the service of God is effected not by cultic meals but by the sacrifice of Jesus (9:14; 10:10, 14; 13:12). Jesus' sacrificial death on the cross not only fulfilled the intention of the Levitical arrangement but superseded it by accomplishing the sanctification that the old order called for but could not effect. The writer introduces the image of the altar not merely as a foil for the altar of sacrifice in Jerusalem but to lay the ground for the exhortation in vv 15–16, with its thought of bringing a sacrifice to God (so Thurén, *Lobopfer*, 74–75).

It has frequently been claimed that the confessional statements ἔχομεν θυσιαστήριον, "we have an altar," is an allusion to the Eucharist or to the eucharistic table (Schröger, *MTZ* 19 [1968] 170, lists twenty scholars holding this opinion; for a helpful review of the current discussion see Michel, 498–503, and especially Williamson, *NTS* 21 [1975] 301–9; more recent proponents of the eucharistic interpretation of v 10 include Swetnam, *Bib* 70 [1989] 90, and especially Thurén, *Lobopfer*, 83–91, 204, who concludes that the Lord's Supper is the theme of Hebrews in its entirety, arguing that the writer's intention was to defend the Lord's Supper as the genuine sacrificial meal time against the strange meal celebrations to which reference is made in v 9). Appeal is made to the allusion to eating from the altar in v 10b and to the fact that the altar is described as "the Lord's table" in Scripture (Ezek 41:22; Mal 1:7, 12, cited by Michel, 503). On this understanding, θυσιαστήριον, "altar," is to be understood literally and not figuratively.

This contention cannot be substantiated. There is no evidence for a sacramental interpretation of the Eucharist, in which the Lord's table is described as an altar, until more than a century after the writing of Hebrews. (The one possible exception is the use of θυσιαστήριον in a eucharistic context in Ign., *Phld.* 4, but see Klauck, "θυσιαστήριον in Hebr 13,10 und bei Ignatius," 154–55, who concludes that in this passage the term signifies the event of the cross. For a careful examination of the remaining passages in Ignatius containing θυσιαστήριον [*Eph.* 5:2; *Magn.* 7:2; *Trall.* 7:2; *Rom.* 2:2] see Klauck, 152–58.) If the point of v 9 is that grace is not mediated by sacrificial meals, "the altar" in v 10 cannot be the eucharistic table (with Loader, *Sohn*, 49–54, 178–81; cf. Snell, *RTR* 23 [1964] 16–23;

Williamson, *NTS* 21 [1975] 308–12; P. E. Hughes, 573 and n. 25; 577–78 and nn. 30, 31; H. Koester, *HTR* 55 [1962] 306–7; 312 and nn. 46–48; among others). Those who interpret the "altar" as the Eucharist or the eucharistic table ignore the connection between the confessional formulation, "We have an altar," and other creedal formulations in Hebrews. As Thompson has observed, ἔχομεν θυσιαστήριον, "we have an altar," is the equivalent of ἔχομεν ἀρχιερέα, "we have a high priest" (*Beginnings of Christian Philosophy*, 146).

The phrase stating that those who serve the tabernacle have no right to eat of this altar (v 10*b*) refers to the biblical statute that prohibits the Levitical priests from the eating of the atonement sacrifice (Lev 6:30 LXX: "No sin offering shall be eaten from which any of the blood is brought into the tent of meeting to make atonement in the holy place; it shall be burned with fire"; cf. Lev. 16:27 LXX). By metonymy, the altar that Christians possess is for them an impure place where there can be no sacrificial meal. The antithesis between "we have" and "they do not have" is so striking that any attempt to identify "those who serve the tent" with Christians is precluded (for this attempt see Holtzmann, *ZNW* 10 [1909] 255; Windisch, 118–19; Moffatt, 234–35; Schierse, *Verheissung*, 184–92; H. Koester, *HTR* 55 [1962] 304). The shift from the first person plural in v 10*a* to the third person plural in v 10*b* would seem to speak for itself.

In the descriptive phrase οἱ τῇ σκηνῇ λατρεύοντες, "those who serve the tabernacle," there is expressed an implied contrast with the Christian audience to whom the writer addressed the appeal λατρεύωμεν εὐαρέστως τῷ θεῷ, "let us serve God acceptably," in 12:28. The formulation echoes the prior use of λατρεύειν, "to serve," "to minister," and its cognates for the ministry conducted by the Levitical priests (8:4–5; 9:6) and for the worship of those whom they represented (9:9; 10:1–2). The expression is thus parallel to ἐν οἷς . . . οἱ περιπατοῦντες, "their adherents," "those who frame their conduct by them," in v 9. Since σκηνή, "tent," is unqualified, it must refer to the earthly tabernacle (cf. 8:2; 9:11), not to the heavenly sanctuary (so Michel, 499; P. E. Hughes, 528, n. 32). The writer's customary use of the present tense to describe the cultic activities of the OT furnishes the background for understanding the reference in v 10*b*. These cultic activities only serve as a figurative expression for the present age (9:9) and serve to underscore the inadequacy of the now obsolete cultic arrangements of the old covenant.

The reference to eating in v 10*b* seems to have been suggested by the thought of the strengthening of the heart through "foods" in v 9. The verb φαγεῖν, "to eat," picks up that thought and carries it forward. It is almost certainly to be interpreted metaphorically, as the participle γευσαμένους, "having tasted," is in 6:5 (cf. Kuss, 219). "Eating from the altar" is a figurative expression for participating in the sacrifice. The act of eating from the altar in Jerusalem gave those who participated in the meal a share in what had transpired on the altar (cf. 1 Cor 9:13; 10:18). The declaration that the adherents of the old cultus have no right to eat from the altar asserts that they have no share in the sacrifice of Christ on Golgotha and are excluded from its benefits (so already Bleek, 2/2:1005). Participation in the efficacy of Jesus' sacrifice is limited to those who recognize in the cross-event the source of the grace by which the heart is strengthened.

11 The explanatory γάρ indicates that the following christological argument in vv 11–12 is intended to support the affirmation about the altar in v 10. The prohibition of eating from the altar is tied to the prescription of the law for the annual Day of Atonement, as set forth in Lev 16. In Lev 16:27 it is specified that both animals, whose blood has been brought into the sanctuary for the atonement ritual (Lev 16:11–19), may not be used as sacrificial food (cf. Lev 6:30); their remains must be taken outside the holy precinct of the camp for disposal in a region of cultic impurity by servants of the tabernacle (cf. Lev 16:28). The carcasses of the young bull and the goat were to be burned to prevent their remains from being eaten (cf. Exod 29:14; Ezek 43:21). The writer finds a correspondence between this provision of the Levitical cultus and the fact that Jesus suffered death "outside the city gate" (v 12).

This is the only instance in Scripture where a form of ζῷον, "living being," "animal," designates sacrificial victims. This unique choice of term may have been prompted by the writer's desire to apply the atonement ritual to Jesus in v 12 (so Dussaut, *Synopse structurelle*, 186, n. 27). In paraphrasing Lev 16:27 the writer has also introduced the expression διὰ τοῦ ἀρχιερέως, "by the agency of the high priest." He regards the action of the high priest on the great Day of Atonement as his primary distinctive function (9:7, 25), so that in Hebrews the expression "high priest" customarily signals that the field of reference is the annual atonement ritual (cf. 5:3; 7:27; 8:1–3; 9:7, 11, 12, 24–26). The explicit reference to the action of bringing the blood of the victims into the sanctuary is significant for underscoring the high value that the writer attributes to blood as the medium of access to God (see above on 9:7, 12–14, 18–22, 25). He cannot speak of sacrifice without introducing the thought of the application of blood as "the medium of power" (so Johnsson, "Defilement," 364–65).

The allusion to the regulation governing the disposal of the remains of the atonement sacrifices in v 11b serves to link the argument in vv 9–14 with other passages throughout the homily in which the action of the high priest on this day is regarded as the prototype of the work of Christ (cf. 5:3; 7:27; 8:1–3; 9:7–8, 11, 12, 24–26; 10:1–4). The final phrase concerning the incineration of the carcasses ἔξω τῆς παρεμβολῆς, "outside the camp," provides the point of transition for the speaking of Jesus, who suffered death ἔξω τῆς πύλης, "outside the city gate."

The import of tying together vv 10–11 is clear. Those who serve the tabernacle have no right to eat from the altar, which typically foreshadows the sacrifice of Christ. Those who continue to frame their conduct by the cultic arrangement of the old covenant are excluded from the benefits that Christians enjoy, which result from the fulfillment of the atonement ritual in Jesus' death on Golgotha (so F. F. Bruce, 389; cf. Michel, 499).

12 The direct comparison between the ministration of the old cultus and the new in vv 11–12 exhibits literary symmetry. Corresponding to the sacrificial service of the Levitical high priest on the Day of Atonement, who annually carried the blood of animals into the sanctuary as a sin-offering (v 11a), is the action of Jesus, who through his own blood consecrated the people to the service of God (v 12a). It is significant that the sacrifice of Jesus is expressly set in parallel with the atonement sacrifices on the Day of Atonement. The parallelism presupposes the writer's developed presentation of Jesus as high priest who bore his own blood into the heavenly sanctuary as an offering for sin (8:1–3; 9:12–14, 24–26; cf. Luck, *NovT* 6 [1963] 211). Similarly, the experience of Jesus, who suffered death ἔξω τῆς πύλης, "outside the gate," in v 12b corresponds to the conveyance of the remains of the sacrificial victims ἔξω τῆς παρεμβολῆς, "outside the camp," in v 11 b. The basis of the comparison is expulsion from the sacred precincts. The structural parallelism, so that v 12a corresponds literally to v 11a and v 12b corresponds to v 11b, serves to ground the argument in vv 10–12 christologically.

The initial phrase διὸ καὶ Ἰησοῦς, "and so Jesus also," directs attention to the comparison that is being drawn. The writer is not attempting to show the precise correspondence of the old and the new but is making a homiletical type of comparison. Within the syntax of the sentence, the personal name "Jesus" is emphatic. Its use is appropriate to the human experience of humiliation and crucifixion outside the Jerusalem walls.

The writer alludes to the cross in terms of the sacrificial offerings on the Day of Atonement, on his assumption that Lev 16 gives a reliable preview of its antitype. The parallelism is particularly instructive: Jesus' death on Golgotha corresponds to the removal of the bodies outside the camp. The work of redemption, however, expressed as the sanctifying of the people by Jesus' blood, corresponds to the bringing of the blood of the sacrifices into the Most Holy Place. Jesus in his death on the cross opened up for others access to God, which they themselves and the old Levitical arrangement could not provide. He suffered death as their representative ἵνα ἁγιάσῃ διὰ τοῦ ἰδίου αἵματος τὸν λαόν, "in order to consecrate the people through his own blood." The distinctive formulation evokes the thought of the blood of the covenant rather than of propitiatory blood (cf. 9:18–20; 10:10, 14, 29; so Andriessen, *NRT* 94 [1972] 276).

The notion behind the action of "sanctifying" or "consecrating" the people is that of qualifying them for an approach to God in worship (see above on 10:10, 14, 29; cf. 9:13–14). The writer uses the verb ἁγιάζειν, "to consecrate," "to sanctify," and the cognate noun ἁγιασμός, "consecration," "sanctification," with the nuance of equipping the people for acceptable worship. This usage is consistent with the meaning of these terms in ritual contexts of the OT (e.g., Exod 19:10; 1 Sam 16:5 LXX; cf. Snell, *RTR* 23 [1964] 18–19). The text ascribes to Jesus a unique and unrepeatable action without which the people could not have enjoyed unhindered access to God and the attainment of the "perfection" that will finally culminate in the experience of glory (2:10–11; cf. Silva, *WTJ* 39 [1976] 60–71).

The phrase ἔξω τῆς πύλης ἔπαθεν, which completes the main clause of the sentence ("And so Jesus also . . . suffered death outside the city gate"), contains an implicit reference to the historical event of Jesus' death on Golgotha (John 19:20; cf. Mark 15:20; Matt 27:32; John 19:17; cf. J. Jeremias, *Golgotha* [Göttingen: Vandenhoeck & Ruprecht, 1926] 1–33; Grässer, *ZNW* 56 [1965] 82–87; for the distinctive nuance in the verb πάσχειν, "to suffer," in Hebrews, see above, *Note* s). The factual basis of the gospel comes to expression in the terms πύλης, "city gate," and ἔπαθεν, "suffered death." It was Israelite, Jewish, and Roman practice to perform executions beyond the inhabited area of a town or city (for biblical and Jewish praxis, see Lev 24:14, 23; Num 15:35–36; Deut 17:15; 1 Kgs 21:13; Jos., *Ant.* 4.264, Jos., *J.W.* 4.360; Luke 4:29; Acts 7:58; *b. Sanh.* 42b–43a; *Sipra Lev.* 24:14; *Sipre Deut.* §149 on Deut 17:5, and §242 on Deut 22:24; for the Roman praxis of crucifixion *extra portam* ["outside the city gate"] see Artemidorus, *Dreams* 2.53; Plautus, *Soldier,* 359–60).

The writer's interest is not, however, merely historical. That is clear from the explicit comparison with Lev 16 in vv 11–12. He is concerned to show that Jesus fulfilled the Levitical requirement that the carcass of the bull and the goat sacrificed

on the Day of Atonement be conveyed "outside the camp" and there be inciner-
ated. This ordinance was fulfilled when Jesus, as the sin offering of the new
covenant, died "outside the city gate," i.e., outside the holy city and the sacred
precincts (cf. Lührmann, *ZNW* 69 [1978] 178–86). The "altar" possessed by
Christians (v 10a) is "outside the gate" (cf. H. Koester, *HTR* 55 [1962] 305–6).

The detail of the text indicates that the writer interpreted the crucifixion of
Jesus "outside the gate" of Jerusalem in two ways. First, it fulfilled the intention
of the Day of Atonement. According to the rabbinic regulations in contemporary Judaism, Jerusalem, bounded by its walls, was the counterpart to the sacred
precincts of the wilderness camp. Corresponding to this understanding, the
phrase "outside the camp" (v 11) designates the area outside the walls of
Jerusalem (*Sipre Num.* 1 on Num 5:3; *t. B. Qam.* 1:12; *b. Zebah.* 116b; *Num. Rab.* 7
on Num 5:3). As a point of fact, the remains of the two sacrificial animals were
burned outside the gates of Jerusalem on the Day of Atonement (*b. Yoma* 65 ab).
From the writer's theological perspective, the execution of Jesus outside the city
gate represents the definitive sin offering of the Day of Atonement (cf. Jeremias,
TDNT 6:921–22; Bietenhard, *Die himmlische Welt,* 200). The suffering of death was
the necessary condition for accomplishing the high priestly atonement. Jesus
is the effective high priest who was qualified to make the only adequate offering
for sin (10:12).

Second, the execution "outside the gate" involved the shame of exclusion from
the sacred precincts (cf. 12:2, "despising the shame" [of crucifixion]). From a
Jewish point of view, Jesus was classified with the blasphemer (Lev 24:10–16, 23)
and the Sabbath breaker (Num 15:35) who were to be stoned "outside the camp."
It was precisely for blasphemy that Jesus was officially condemned by the
Sanhedrin, when the court pronounced formally that he had "blasphemed
the Name" (Mark 14:63–64; Matt 27:64–65; cf. Lev 24:11, 16). The writer's juxtaposition of the phrase ἔξω τῆς πύλης, "outside the gate," with ἔπαθεν, "he suffered
death," brings out an element of shame that is not in the verb itself. The fact that
Jesus died as one rejected by his people gave added poignancy to his death. Jesus
was repudiated by the people, and his death appeared to seal his rejection as
final. It was as an outcast that he offered his sacrifice to God (cf. Snell, *RTR* 23
[1964] 19; Thurén, *Lobopfer,* 76, 78).

Only by reference to the theology developed in Heb 8–10 can the allusions to
sacrifice in vv 11–12 be fully understood. When viewed against this background,
the brief data in v 12 fit will with what the writer had said earlier concerning Jesus
as both high priest and sacrifice. The writer to the Hebrews appears to have been
the first theologian to have interpreted the event of the cross from the perspective of Leviticus 16 (so Thurén, *Lobopfer,* 99).

13 The parenetic intention of the argument developed in vv 10–12 is made
explicit when the writer draws the inference to which his argument leads: τοίνυν
ἐξερχώμεθα πρὸς αὐτὸν ἔξω τῆς παρεμβολῆς, "So then, let us go out to him outside
the camp." He frequently uses the hortatory subjunctive when drawing the practical consequences of his theological argument (e.g., 4:11, 16; 10:22, 23, 24; 12:1,
22). It is appropriate in this place to find ἐξερχώμεθα, "let us go out," following
the inferential particle τοίνυν, "so then." The repetition of the phrase ἔξω τῆς
παρεμβολῆς, "outside the camp," has the effect of tying v 13 narrowly to v 11
("outside the camp") and to v 12 ("outside the gate"). It shows that the homiletical

comparison in vv 11–12 was drawn in the service of this moving exhortation. The allusion to Lev 16:27 in v 11 serves to clarify the significance of the fact that Jesus suffered death by crucifixion "outside the gate" (v 12) and furnishes the basis for the admonition to follow him "outside the camp, bearing the shame he bore."

The exhortation to leave the camp and to identify fully with Jesus introduces a distinctive understanding of discipleship. Jesus' action in going "outside the camp" (v 12) set a precedent for others to follow. The task of the community is to emulate Jesus, leaving behind the security, congeniality, and respectability of the sacred enclosure, risking the reproach that fell upon him. Christian identity is a matter of "going out" now to him. It entails the costly commitment to follow him resolutely, despite suffering.

In the context of the allusion to Golgotha in v 12, this summons to discipleship implies following Jesus on the way to the cross (P. Brunner, *KD* 20 [1974] 234–35). The writer appears to be thoroughly familiar with the primitive tradition that associates the "going out" of Jesus with the bearing of his cross (John 19:17; Mark 15:20–21). Since the cross is explicitly connected with "shame" (αἰσχύνης) in Heb 12:2, the exhortation in v 13 appears to be a parenetic adaptation of the familiar call to discipleship in terms of cross bearing (Mark 8:34; Matt 10:38; 16:24; Luke 14:27).

As enunciated by Jesus, the call to discipleship is a call to martyrdom; the phrases "deny himself" (but not Jesus!) and "take up his cross" are parallel. In the Synoptic tradition, the summons to discipleship is linked both with the concept of shame (Mark 8:34–38 par.) and with the severance of social ties (Matt 10:37–38; Luke 14:26–27). The evangelists appear to have understood the requirement of self-denial as synonymous with the bearing of shame (Mark 8:34; Matt 16:24; Luke 9:23–26), just as they have linked cross bearing with confession (Mark 8:38 par.). The distinctive understanding of discipleship that comes to expression in v 13 appears to be informed by this pre-Synoptic strand of the Jesus tradition (so Thurén, *Lobopfer,* 91–93, 98, who argues that the writer shows an awareness of the Jesus tradition, particularly as it has been preserved by the evangelist Luke; similar emphases are connected with the conception of the future city in Herm., *Sim.* 9.14:5–6, which demonstrates that the motifs in Heb 13:13–15 remained current in the Christian community of Rome into the second century; for a discussion of this and related texts in Hermas, see L. Pernveden, *The Concept of the Church in the Shepherd of Hermas* [Lund: Wiksells, 1966] 98–105; Thurén, *Lobopfer,* 97–97).

An aspect of the disgrace Jesus experienced in his death "outside the city gate" (v 12*b*) was expulsion from the sacred precincts (see *Comment* on 12*b*; cf. Luke 6:22, where Jesus connects the notion of "shame" with expulsion from the Jewish community). The shame of expulsion from the camp presupposes the presence of God within the holy enclosure. In fact, the ground for the expulsion of those who had become impure (e.g., Lev 13:46; Num 5:2–4; Deut 23:11) was that God was within the camp (mentioned explicitly in Num 5:3; Deut 23:14) and he is unwilling to look upon any ἀσχημοσύνη, "shamefulness," "defilement" (Deut 23:14 LXX).

Scripture, however, records that after the incident of the golden calf, God chose to demonstrate his presence ἔξω τῆς παρεμβολῆς, "outside the camp":

Now Moses took the tent and pitched it outside the camp [ἔξω τῆς παρεμβολῆς]. . . .
And everyone who sought the Lord would go out to the tent, which was outside the
camp [ἔξω τῆς παρεμβολῆς]. Whenever Moses went into the tent outside the camp
[ἔξω τῆς παρεμβολῆς]. . . . (Exod 33:7–8 LXX).

The erection of the golden calf signified the rejection of God. Consequently, God
departed from the formerly sacred enclosure and displayed his presence only at
the tent pitched "outside the camp" (Exod 33:7–10). An attractive proposal is
that the play on the phrase "outside the camp" in v 11–13 was designed to call to
mind the occasion when God manifested his presence outside the wilderness
encampment. The humiliation of Jesus and his death as an outcast show that
God has again been rejected by his people. His presence can be enjoyed only
"outside the camp," where Jesus was treated with contempt. Anyone who seeks to
draw near to God must go "outside the camp" and approach him through Jesus
(so Michel, 510–12, 514–15; F. F. Bruce, 403; Andriessen, *En lisant,* 58; Thurén,
Lobopfer, 100–4). This is the character of genuine discipleship and the condition
for the acceptable worship of God.

The qualifying phrase in v 13*b*, τὸν ὀνειδισμὸν αὐτοῦ φέροντες, "bearing his
shame," is motivated through the allusion to Jesus' humiliation in v 12*b*. What is
demanded is "shared" reproach (ὀνειδισμὸν αὐτοῦ, "*his* shame"), bearing the same
stigma that Jesus bore. The writer has perceived that there is a form of intimate
sharing that unites Jesus and his followers in the common experience of repudiation and disgrace. Readiness to bear Jesus' shame is an integral part of
discipleship. Earlier he had commended the community for being "sharers"
(κοινωνοί) with those subject to ὀνειδισμοί, "insults," and θλίψεις, "afflictions"
(10:33). They had learned experientially that the price of communal intimacy
was shared suffering. They are now urged to emulate their own bold example,
knowing that identification with the crucified Jesus will invite the same contempt
with which he was treated (so Hurst, "Background," 229–31). Moses took upon
himself τὸν ὀνειδισμὸν τοῦ Χριστοῦ, "the reproach of the Messiah," when he
identified himself with the oppressed people of God (11:26). Christians bear
the shame of Jesus when they are prepared to share with him and with one another the derision, disgrace, and abuse he bore (so Michel, 512). In this light,
the pastoral directive in v 3 anticipates and prepares for the exhortation in v 13
(so Thurén, *Lobopfer,* 210–11).

Among the interpretations of v 13 there are three that deserve consideration.

(1) According to H. Koester (*HTR* 55 [1962] 300–2, 313; similarly, Trudinger,
EvQ 54 [1982] 235–37; P. R. Jones, *RevExp* 82 [1985] 402), the writer is advocat-
ing bearing "the disgrace of worldliness." The key to the interpretation of v 13 is
Lev 16:28, which states that the person who conveyed the remains of the sacrificial animals to the place of burning on the Day of Atonement must wash himself
and his clothes before returning to the camp. The implication is that those
"outside the camp" are unclean. Koester contends that vv 12–13 were formulated
in deliberate contrast to Lev 16:28. The sacrifice of Jesus, which makes people
clean, was performed outside the holy camp. This act of cleansing, accomplished
through the brutal secularity of Golgotha, abolished all cultic performances.
The startling character of Jesus' sacrifice "outside the camp" indicates that the
place of Christians is "not in holy places with the security which is offered in

cultic performances but in the uncleanness of the world" (301). To go "outside the camp" is to identify with the secular world where people are exposed to harsh experiences rather than secluded and protected from them. The implied contrast, insists Koester, is between "the sacred" and "the profane," between "the cultic" and "the secular."

This proposal fails to recognize the pervasiveness of the cultic argument in Hebrews (so correctly, Johnsson, "Defilement," 364–65, n. 244: "Koester's interpretation requires correction in view of the defilement-purgation complex—which renders his explanation of 'outside the camp' as 'the uncleanness of the world' clearly untenable"). The identification of "outside the camp" with "the realm of the profane" is an imposition on the text. The writer's concern is not to advocate a separation from the sphere of the cultic so as to embrace the secularity of the world, but rather the acceptance of the reproach of Christian commitment in a hostile environment (with Johnsson, "Defilement," 364–65; cf. Thurén, *Lobopfer*, 103–4).

(2) Thompson (*CBQ* 40 [1978] 53–63; and *Beginnings of Christian Philosophy*, 147–50) argues that "outside the camp" does not signify "outside Judaism" nor "outside Jerusalem." It implies a call to leave earthly assurances and to pursue the heavenly world where Jesus completed his redemptive action at the heavenly altar. "Outside the camp" connotes outside the earthly sphere, since the writer regarded Christ's offering as made in the heavenly sanctuary. Jesus has opened the way into the heavenly world (10:19–23), and it is the task of the church to follow him, adopting the lifestyle of the pilgrim people of God. Pilgrim existence entails the renunciation of all earthly securities. To "go out" from earthly securities is simultaneously "to enter" the heavenly world. The form that this withdrawal takes is the refusal to rely on any material assurances of stability. The community can endure without any earthly securities because it possesses the promise of the transcendent city that belongs to the heavenly world (13:14).

This is a more nuanced interpretation than the proposal of H. Koester. It has the merit of recognizing the note of pilgrimage that is invoked by the theme of the heavenly city in v 14. Nevertheless, Thompson's vertical dualism of the earthly sphere as opposed to the heavenly sphere is too rigorous; it needs to be qualified more than it is by the horizontal eschatological perspective of present and future that is intrinsic to vv 13–14 (cf. Barrett, "Eschatology," 376, 381; Johnsson, *JBL* 97 [1978] 247–48 and nn. 44–45; Michel, 504–6).

(3) The common understanding finds in v 13 an exhortation to sever the emotional and social ties with the Jewish community that continue to characterize the members of the house church (so Westcott, 441–42; Filson, '*Yesterday*', 61–66; F. F. Bruce, 403; P. E. Hughes, 580–82, among others; cf. Michel, 511). The implied contrast is between a religious attitude centered in the sanctuary in Jerusalem and the sacrificial provisions of the old covenant and a faith that expresses itself in Christian discipleship. Christians are no longer subject to the old order of life and worship. They have become participants in a new order that effects what the old order could only promise. Those who imitate the faith of their former leaders (v 7) cannot continue to pattern their lives in terms of the assurances offered by the old framework. They must leave behind all that belongs to the world of prefiguration and seek the accomplishment of the promise in Jesus.

There is much in the immediate context to commend this interpretation. The argument would be highly relevant to Jewish Christians who could feel the pull of their Jewish heritage at a time when they were growing weary with the necessity of sustaining their commitment to Jesus in a hostile society. Their initial response to the preaching of the gospel had entailed a symbolic going "outside the camp" to identify with Jesus and his shame. Now their resolve was weakening. They are being tempted to turn back in the hope of securing an easier and more respectable existence "inside the camp" (so P. E. Hughes, 580; F. F. Bruce, *ANRW* 25.4 [1987] 3504-5). The writer calls his audience to recognize that those who have been consecrated to the service of God through Jesus' blood have only two possibilities. They can gain *everything* together with Jesus or they can lose *everything* without him. It is for that reason that the writer urges the community to "go out to him" (Grässer, *Glaube*, 18).

14 The supporting motivation for the exhortation to discipleship entailing shame and the severance of social ties is supplied in v 14, which is attached to the main clause by an explanatory γάρ, "for." The hortatory subjunctive ἐξερχώμεθα, "let us go out," is grounded in the indicative with the confessional οὐ γὰρ ἔχομεν, "for we do not have." The sober reminder that "here we do not have a permanent city, but we are expecting intently the city which is to come" introduces the significant theme of pilgrimage to the city of God once more (see above on 11:8-10, 13-16; 12:18-24). The correspondence with the prior development of this theme may be found particularly in the reference to the future city (11:10, 14, 16), which those on pilgrimage are intently expecting. (For this nuance of ἐπιζητεῖν in 11:14 and here, see *Comment* on 11:14.) The "going out" to Jesus, "outside the camp," reaffirms the commitment to be the pilgrim people who leave behind the security of the familiar in order to respond to the call of God. (See *Comment* on 11:8, where "going out" [ἐξέρχεσθαι] is descriptive of Abraham's response to the call of God upon his life.) Sharing Jesus' alienation from one city is symbolic of expecting another, qualitatively different city (cf. Minear, *Apocalyptic*, 150, who treats the conception of the city as part of a broader complex: "City, worship, Christ, suffering—these represent an essential quadrilateral so tightly bound together that no element can be rightly grasped without grasping all four").

Within the structure of the sentence in vv 13-14, the image of the transitory city supplies a second metaphor for sacred space. Discipleship may be described in terms of the pilgrimage of faith not merely from the sacred precincts of the wilderness camp (v 13) but from the city that lacks permanence (v 14a). The explicit identification of the future city as the "heavenly Jerusalem" in 12:22 would seem to imply a veiled reference to the city of Jerusalem in v 14a (so, e.g., de Young, *Jerusalem*, 107-8; Moe, *ST* 4 [1950] 107; P. R. Jones, *RevExp* 82 [1985] 402). That identification is consistent with the implicit reference to Jerusalem in the immediate context, where the writer alluded to Jesus' death by crucifixion outside the walls of the city (v 12b). The repudiation of Jesus unmasked Jerusalem as an ephemeral, transient city and made certain the coming of the future city (so Thurén, *Lobopfer*, 77). The identification is also appropriate to the "strange teachings" that cultic meals in the Diaspora evoke eating at the altar in Jerusalem in the presence of God (see *Comment* on v 9b). The members of the assembly are called to recognize that true sacred space will not be found in Jerusalem, with its impermanent sanctuary and altar, but in the presence of Jesus and in the anticipation of the qualitatively different city to which they have come proleptically (12:22–24).

Thompson astutely observes that a commitment to pilgrimage can be maintained only be "those who have a city (11:9, 10, 16)" (*Beginnings of Christian Philosophy*, 149). The city that the pilgrim people of God desire is not "here" (ὧδε) in this earthly sphere. It belongs to the heavenly world (12:22) and participates in the transcendent character of that realm. As a metaphor for transcendent reality, the πόλις, "city," can be described by the participle μένουσα, "permanent." The verb μένειν, "to remain," "to endure," is descriptive here, as in 12:27, of the permanence and stability of the heavenly world (so Grässer, *Glaube*, 174, who comments that in Hebrews μένειν connotes both durability and stability). The heavenly city is thus essentially equivalent to other terms for transcendent reality in Hebrews, including "the heavenly world to come" (2:5), the heavenly "rest" of God (3:11; 4:1, 8–11), "the age to come" (6:5), and "the kingdom which cannot be shaken" (12:28) (so Grässer, *Glaube*, 174; de Young, *Jerusalem*, 144–45; Vanhoye, *Bib* 45 [1964] 251, n. 2; for a discussion of the parallels between Heb 13:14 and 4 Ezra 7:26; 13:36, see Hofius, *Katapausis*, 92).

The writer underscores the future aspect of the city; it is τὴν μέλλουσαν, "the [city] which is to come." The antithesis in the contrasting spatial metaphor, not the city of Jerusalem but the heavenly Jerusalem, is sharpened by the eschatological antithesis, not present but future. This temporal aspect cannot be bracketed out of v 14 (so correctly, Filson, *'Yesterday'*, 69–70; H. Koester, *HTR* 55 [1962] 303; Thurén, *Lobopfer*, 97, n. 351). The possession of the heavenly city remains an eschatological prospect for Christians. The city exists as present reality in the heavenly world, but the accent in the qualifying participle μέλλουσαν, "coming," is on its future availability. The city can be described as a present realization with a promissory perspective (cf. Bietenhard, *Die himmlische Welt*, 201).

The certainty that the transcendent city of God has been promised to those who respond to his call is the sufficient ground for discipleship. The only security extended to the pilgrim is the assurance that God has prepared a city for his people (11:10, 16). To this extent, v 14 is exactly parallel to 11:13–16. What is new in v 14 is the allusion to the future city within the larger complex vv 9–14. In this context the promised city is an aspect of "the grace" by which "the heart is strengthened" (v 9) and equipped for pilgrimage.

Pilgrimage is impelled by an earnest sense of expectancy, which allows no relaxation of the commitment to the vision of the city of God. The present tense of ἐπιζητοῦμεν, "we are expecting intently," expresses a habitual disposition as the driving force of the disciple's life (see *Comment* on 11:14; cf. Filson, *'Yesterday'*, 70; Hofius, *Katapausis*, 147–49; Thurén, *Lobopfer*, 100, n. 358). The verb is descriptive of an unwavering orientation toward a goal. The goal of going out to Jesus (v 13) is the enjoyment of eschatological salvation in the perfect order of the future age (v 14). Jesus' disciples are those who follow him not only on the way to the cross here and now but ultimately to the final goal of pilgrimage, the future heavenly city. There they will enjoy uninterrupted intimate fellowship with God and will meet Jesus, the mediator of the new covenant (12:24).

De Young has observed that the writer has produced in vv 12–14 two powerful arguments for severing emotional and social ties with a Judaism focused upon the Jerusalem sanctuary. (1) Jerusalem has lost all redemptive significance for

Christians, because Jesus made the definitive sacrifice for sin outside the walls of the city. Salvation can be found only where he is, outside the camp (vv 12–13). (2) Jerusalem has lost all eschatological significance for Christians, because it shares the impermanence that characterizes all human cities. Permanence, stability, and eschatological fulfillment will be found only in the goal of pilgrimage, the future heavenly city of God (v 14) (*Jerusalem*, 108–9).

15 The climax to the artistically built unit of hortatory exposition in vv 10–16 is the double admonition in vv 15–16. The chiastic structure of the unit shows that the determining thesis in v 10 is foundational to the decisive demand in vv 15–16. The confessional statement "we have an altar" fully justifies the admonition to offer to God the sacrifices that please him. At the same time, the exclusiveness of the Christian altar that is asserted in v 10 is clarified in v 15. The symmetry of the structure suggests that the entire unit was composed with the double admonition in mind (see *Form/Structure/Setting* for 13:1–25). The main point of the unit is parenesis, which is developed through exposition and pastoral implication to a weary community (so Thurén, *Lobopfer*, 74–75, who argues that vv 10–14 have no independent significance, but simply prepare for and ground the exhortation in vv 15–16). These verses constitute the theological and practical synthesis of Hebrews (so correctly, Spicq, 2:429).

The interpretation of the double admonition must take into account not only the artistic structure of vv 10–16 as a unit but the chiastic arrangement of the four clauses in vv 15–16 as well (see above *Form/Structure/Setting* for 13:1–25). Corresponding to the concept of the offering of a sacrifice in v 15*a* is the notion of the reception of the sacrifice in v 16*b*. These two clauses are complementary and serve to bracket the interior clauses (vv 15*b*/16*a*), which identify the sacrifices to be offered to God as praise, acts of kindness, and generosity (Thurén, *Lobopfer*, 105).

In the course of the argument, the exhortation to Christian discipleship in vv 13–14 is augmented by the conception of the Christian life as worship in vv 15–16. Consecration to God through Jesus' sacrificial death (v 12) provides the Church with the ground for cultivating the concept of life as devotion to God. True worship consists in the praise of God (v 15) and a shared life of love (v 16). Addressing hellenistic-Jewish Christians who seem to have been vulnerable to reports of the lavish cultic expressions of worship in Jerusalem and who were feeling impoverished by the relative simplicity of the worship within the new covenant community, and especially by the loss of the sacred fellowship meals, the writer responds from a theology of praise. He invests their whole existence, renewed by grace, with the value of authentic devotion to God. He does so by calling the community to the new cultic response to God as opposed to the old, while emphasizing its appropriateness, its spiritual character, and its effectiveness. The striking feature of vv 15–16 is the rich use of OT sacrificial terminology.

The emphatic position of the introductory formula $\delta\iota$ ' $\alpha\dot{\upsilon}\tauο\hat{\upsilon}$, "through him" (i.e., Jesus), gives it prominence. The phrase corresponds to the formula $\delta\iota\dot{\alpha}$ $\tauο\hat{\upsilon}$ $\dot{\alpha}\rho\chi\iota\epsilon\rho\dot{\epsilon}\omega\varsigma$, "through the high priest," in v 11, which suggests that it is to be understood polemically: "through him" and not through some other high priest. (For other proposals, see Thurén, *Lobopfer*, 163.) It is only through the true high priest that the acceptable sacrifice can be offered to God. Conversely, it is only those for whom atonement has been achieved who may bring an acceptable praise offering. Consecration to God through Jesus' shed blood (v 12) is both the ground of praise and the condition for its acceptance by God (Thurén, *Lobopfer*, 77, n. 277; 88). Early Christian documents from Rome and Asia Minor confirm that the formula δι' αὐτοῦ, "through him," was specified in terms of Jesus' high priestly mediation and was used in prayer and praise discourse (e.g., *1 Clem.* 61:3; 64; *Mart. Pol.* 14:3; cf. Hippolytus, *Apostolic Tradition* 4; see further Deichgräber, *Gotteshymnus*, 30–40, 118, 185, n. 5).

The writer's interpretation of the death of Jesus as the perfect sacrifice superseding the sacrifices of the Levitical cultus and sanctuary, was programmatic for his spiritualization of the concept of sacrifice. (See especially, H. Wenschkewitz, "Spiritualisierung," 149–50; Ferguson, *ANRW* 23.2 [1980] 1151–89; Lea, *SWJT* 30 [1988] 15–21; cf. Nikiprowetzky, *Sem* 17 [1967] 98–114). Since Jesus offered the definitive atoning sacrifice, the sacrificial offering of Christians consists initially in the verbal response of praise and gratitude to God (cf. 12:28).

The exhortation in v 15, which abounds in OT sacrificial language, provides a sacrificial interpretation of Christian life consistent with this conviction. The introductory clause in v 15*a* is the legitimate corollary to the argument developed in vv 10–13 (cf. Thurén, *Lobopfer*, 163, who prefers to trace the argument backward, so that v 15 is the logical consequence of vv 13–12–11–10). Through Jesus' sacrifice on Golgotha and his priestly mediation in the heavenly sanctuary, the community enjoys unlimited opportunity to offer to God their praise. Christians must "go out" to Jesus (v 13), not in order to be consecrated to the service of God again but rather because through Jesus' offering for sin they may bring the praise offering. The imagery draws upon the OT provision for the material offering of a sacrifice expressing praise to God (Lev 7:12, 13, 15 LXX). It is descriptive of the Christian celebration of worship as the response of praise to the experience of salvation (cf. Williamson, *Philo*, 176–77).

The formulation θυσία αἰνέσεως (where the genitive is explanatory of the initial term, i.e., "a sacrifice consisting in praise") alludes to Ps 49 [MT 50]:14 LXX. There the expression θυσία αἰνέσεως is used figuratively for the offering of cultic praise to God, which is contrasted with animal sacrifice: θῦσον τῷ θεῷ θυσίαν αἰνέσεως, "offer to God a sacrifice consisting of praise." Only here in the LXX is the phrase θυσία αἰνέσεως connected with τῷ θεῷ, "to God," as in the writer's formulation of the exhortation in v 15. For the verb θύειν, "to slaughter," "to offer," which the translator of the Greek Psalter appears to have chosen for its sonorous quality in Ps 49:14 LXX, the writer substituted a synonym, ἀναφέρειν, "to offer." He altered the form to the hortatory subjunctive ἀναφέρωμεν, "let us offer," in order to stress his solidarity with his audience. He had used this verb in 7:27 (and somewhat differently in 9:28) to denote Jesus' offering of himself as the atonement sacrifice. It may be conjectured that the choice of ἀναφέρειν in v 15 is intended to underscore the homogeneity of the atoning sacrifice and the sacrifice of praise under the new covenant (so Thurén, *Lobopfer*, 106, and n. 135; in 1 Pet 2:5 ἀναφέρειν is used of offering "spiritual sacrifices"; see also Prov 8:6; Sir 8:19; 2 Macc 10:7 LXX).

The qualifying liturgical phrase διὰ παντός, "continually," "unceasingly," has a rich background in the LXX, where the expression occurs especially in cultic legislation (cf. Ps 49[MT 50]:8 LXX, where it is used in reference to animal sacrifices). It can carry the nuance of "regularly," in the sense of each morning and each evening (it occurs fourteen times in Num 28:10–29 LXX in reference to the daily sacrifices; cf. 1 Chr 16:4–6 LXX, where the formula occurs only in v 6, but coordinates the whole arrangement as repeated cultic functions). The source of the expression for the writer is undoubtedly the Pentateuch, which is expounded with the help of the books of Chronicles and the Psalms, just as in the case of the praise offering (so Thurén, *Lobopfer,* 172–75). In v 15 διὰ παντός connotes simply and succinctly that the whole continuous liturgy of the old covenant is fulfilled in the continual praise offering of Christians (cf. Michel, 522–26; Deichgräber, *Gotteshymnus,* 212; Thurén, *Lobopfer,* 175, n. 605).

A continuing offering of praise must have an enduring occasion. Under the old covenant the occasion was the goodness and grace of God demonstrated in his faithfulness to the covenant. The writer undoubtedly reflected upon that fact. In v 9 he speaks of the heart strengthened by grace; in v 12 he refers to the consecration of the people to the service of God; and in v 14 he grounds Christian hope in the promised city of God. The continual offering of praise to God through Jesus is motivated through the experience of his grace and goodness, and is supported by the unchangeableness of his promise.

The phrase τοῦτ᾽ ἔστιν, "that is to say," introduces an explanatory clause. It indicates that v 15*b* has been placed in apposition to v 15*a* and confirms that the expression θυσία αἰνέσεως, "a sacrifice of praise," is to be interpreted figuratively as verbal praise. The presence of τοῦτ᾽ ἔστιν here is consistent with the writer's previous use of a τουτ᾽ ἔστιν clause to clarify OT cultic language for the community: "through the curtain, *that is to say* [τοῦτ᾽ ἔστιν], through his flesh" (see *Comment* on 10:20). At this point in the homily the OT praise sacrifice is further defined with the aid of language borrowed from Hos 14:3 LXX and a variation of a common expression from the Greek Psalter, so that it may retain its significance for the new covenant community.

The expression καρπὸν χειλέων, "[the] fruit of lips," which occurs only here in the NT, contains an allusion to Hos 14:3 LXX:

καὶ ἀνταποδώσομεν καρπὸν χειλέων ἡμῶν
"and we shall give back [to you] the fruit of our lips."

In the context of Hosea the clause appears to refer to a vow of a thank offering (cf. Gordis, *VT* 5 [1955] 88–90) or to the offering of songs of thanksgiving celebrating God's character in corporate acts of praise (so Thurén, *Lobopfer,* 154). In the Psalter, references to the fulfillment of a vow and to the praise of God occur in synonymous parallelism (e.g., Pss 22:25–26; 50:14; 61:8; 65:1; 116:12–14). The "fruit of lips" is a Semitic figure for "speech" (cf. Prov 10:31; 12:14; 13:2; 18:20), but came to be associated with thank offerings and thank offering songs (e.g., Isa 57:18; see further, Thurén, *Lobopfer,* 154–55). The sacrifices that God desires is the praise of his name (cf. Ps 49[MT 50]:23 LXX).

There is no earlier parallel for the writer's precise idiom ὁμολογεῖν τῷ ὀνόματι, "to acknowledge"/ "to praise the Name," although the LXX provides the model in the compound expression ἐξομολογεῖσθαι τῷ ὀνόματι (e.g., Ps 53:8 [MT 54:6] LXX: ἐξομολογήσομαι τῷ ὀνόματί σου, κύριε, "I will praise your name, O Lord," because of deliverance experienced; this was recognized already by Theophylactus, *PG* 125.396; for an intensive linguistic study of the Hebrew and Greek terminology in the Bible and related intertestamental and early Christian texts, see Thurén, *Lobopfer,* 107–52, who suggests that the preference for the simple form of the verb in Heb 13:15 may reflect the writer's Alexandrian education, appealing to an observable tendency in 3 Esd and Philo [108–13, 152]).

Two factors determine the nuance in ὁμολογεῖν in v 15*b*. (1) its usage in a clause explanatory of θυσίαν αἰνέσεως, "sacrifice consisting of praise," and (2) the syntax of the clause, where it is followed by the dative of object ("his name"). The syntax is appropriate only to the nuance of "praise" (see above, *Note* cc on v 15 and the full discussion of Deichgräber, *Gotteshymnus,* 117–18). The writer has drawn upon a biblical and Jewish tradition of the song of praise that is offered to God in response to his grace (cf. 2 Macc 10:7; *T. Levi* 3:6–8; *Ps. Sol.* 15:2–6; Philo, *On Noah's Work as a Planter* 126; *On the Special Laws* 1.272, 275; for the background in the Psalms, see especially F. Mand, "Die Eigenständigkeit der Danklieder des Psalters als Bekenntnislieder," *ZAW* 70 [1958] 185–99; Bornkamm, "Lobpreis," 46–63; cf. Old, *Int* 39 [1985] 20–33, who argues that there was in Judaism a strain of spirituality, which began to value the hymn of praise that accompanied the sacrifice more than the sacrifice itself; he holds that the proclamation of God's glory and grace is the expression of worship in view in Heb 13:15).

The closest parallel to the formulation in v 15*b* occurs in a pre-Christian Jewish hymn preserved in the collection known as the *Psalms of Solomon*:

> For who, O God, is strong except the one who praises you in truth;
> And what person is powerful except the one who acknowledges your name?
> A new psalm with song from a happy heart,
> The fruit of lips from the well-tuned instrument of the tongue,
> The first fruits of the lips from a devout and righteous heart (*Ps. Sol.* 15:2–3).

The connection of the phrases "fruit of lips" and "to acknowledge the name" is attested only in v 15*b* and in *Ps. Sol.* 15:2–3, where the "new Psalm" is the fruit and sacrifice of those who celebrate God in songs of praise (see Thurén, *Lobopfer,* 142–44). The most instructive parallels to v 15 in early Christian literature are found in *1 Clement,* where the "offerings" that Jesus mediates as high priest are expressions of doxology (cf. *1 Clem.* 36:1; 61:3; 64; 65:2). The formulation in v 15 belongs to a Christian tradition of praise in response to the goodness of God. As in the older biblical material, praise is the response of the covenant people to the revelation of the grace of God and is at the same time the decisive condition for the sustaining of covenant faithfulness (see further, Thurén, *Lobopfer,* 152–53).

A number of scholars have found in v 15 an undisguised reference to the Christian Eucharist. They assert that the "sacrifice of praise" is nothing else but the praising answer of the Church to the sacrifice of Jesus, which is celebrated in the Lord's Supper (e.g., Bornkamm, *TBl* 21 [1942] 61–64; Moe, *ST* 4 [1950] 107–8; Snell, *RTR* 23 [1964] 20–21; P. Brunner, *KD* 20 [1974] 233–34, 236–37; among others). There is, however, no detail in the text that makes this eucharistic interpretation compelling. It is better in the context of the homily as a whole to recall 2:12, where the vow of praise in Ps 22:22 is assigned to Jesus. In psalms of lament like Ps 22 there is an observable structure of lamentation followed by the vow of praise, in spite of the fact that nothing has changed. In 2:12 Christ, the singing Champion and Priest, glorifies the Father in the presence of the congregation. In 13:15 the writer summons the members of the house church to join their voices to his. A model for "the fruit of lips that praise his name" is provided in the near context in 13:6, where the Church is invited to break into song confidently (so correctly, Vanhoye, *La structure*, 215).

16 The second component of the well-pleasing sacrificial service of the new covenant people consists of deeds of love. A comparison with v 15 throws into high relief the conciseness of v 16 and the variation from the communal "we" in v 15 to the direct admonitory address in the second person plural, "you." These stylistic features may indicate that there was less urgency for this admonition. The writer knew that exemplary service of fellow Christians was the hallmark of the community in the past (10:33) and continued to characterize them (see *Comment* on 6:10). His concern was that they should persist in demonstrating love for God and for one another through practical helpfulness within the assembly (cf. 10:24; 13:1–3).

The directives to filial love in 13:1–3 are summed up and interpreted in v 16*a* (so correctly Spicq, 2:430; Kuss, 221; Thurén, *Lobopfer*, 211). It may not be accidental that v 2*a* and v 16*a* are constructed in the same way (μὴ ἐπιλανθάνεσθε, "Do not neglect"), since what is involved in both directives is responsible partnership in the gospel. The admonition in v 16 is a more specific expression of the pastoral directive in v 2 (cf. Koenig, *Hospitality*, 9–10). The term εὐποιΐα occurs only here in the Greek Bible. Hellenistic parallels show that it denotes "acts of kindness" that give tangible expression to concern for others (see above, *Note* dd; cf. Mark 14:7, where the related phrase εὖ ποιῆσαι, "to do good," occurs in the context of benevolence to the poor; for the sentiment, cf. Sir 12:1–6). This relatively rare term is clarified by the parallel concept κοινωνία, which in this context carries the nuance of "generosity." Both terms are oriented toward shared life in the community of faith.

The financial connotations of the term κοινωνία have been widely recognized (see above, *Note* ee; cf. Rom 15:26–27; 2 Cor 8:4; 9:13). Partnership with other believers carried economic overtones. The concept of partnership is usually understood in the NT as an expanding category. Shared communal life provided a social context where partnership can find practical expression for mutual encouragement. In v 16 κοινωνία denotes "generosity" in the action of contributing to the support of other believers, as a sign of shared partnership (J. Y. Campbell, "*KOINΩNIA*," 21–22; cf. Thurén, *Lobopfer*, 177 and n. 615, who restricts the nuance of "generosity" in κοινωνία to 2 Cor 9:13 and Heb 13:16). Without the practical demonstration of love to other believers, the praise of God lacks integrity (cf. Thurén, *Lobopfer*, 211).

The double admonition to praise God (v 15) and to engage in acts of kindness and generosity (v 16) reflects the pattern of the OT fellowship offering (see *Comment* on 10:23–25). Those who had experienced the grace of God were to gather with others for the public recital of the wonder and majesty of God's activity on behalf of his covenant people. In the context of vv 10–12, it is the provision of full atonement and consecration to the service of God through Jesus that motivates the praise of God. The corollary to praise and gratitude is mutual encouragement and helpfulness as an incentive and aid to Christian maturity. The combination of praise and deeds of love under the aspect of sacrifice has its source in the praise offering of the old covenant (so Moffatt, 237–38; cf. Thurén,

Lobopfer, 176–78, who traces the bipartite interpretation of the praise offering here to the primitive Christian community in Jerusalem!).

The motivation for the double admonition in vv 15–16*a* is provided in v 16*b*: τοιαύταις γὰρ θυσίαις εὐρεστεῖται ὁ θεός, "for God is pleased because of such sacrifices," recognizing the unusual causal idea in the dative case here (see above, *Note* ff). Although the distinctive formulation εὐαρεστεῖται ὁ θεός, "God is pleased," occurs nowhere else in the NT, the word group of the clause in v 16*b* as a whole belongs to the basic parenetic terminology of early Christianity (e.g., Rom 12:1–2, where Paul interprets the parenesis as the elaboration of a "well-pleasing sacrifice"; cf. Rom 14:8; 2 Cor 5:9; Eph 5:10–11; Phil 4:18; Col 3:20). It is particularly appropriate to the use of cognate terminology in 12:28 and 13:21. The thought of pleasing sacrifices does not appear to have been common outside the NT. Here it pertains to one's total conduct before God and covers both personal piety and corporate responsibility.

Only those who are consecrated to God and who have been made pleasing to him can offer to him a well-pleasing sacrifice. This is the relationship of v 16*b* to its immediate context, and especially to v 12*b*. On the other hand, the sacrifices of praise, acts of kindness, and generosity together constitute the worship that God desires from the new covenant community in response to the experience of saving grace. Christians must glorify God not merely with their mouths but with their works as well (cf. *2 Clem.* 3:2–4: "what is the true knowledge concerning him [i.e., the Father of truth], except that we should not deny him through whom we knew him. And he himself also says, 'Whoever acknowledges me before others I will acknowledge before my Father. . . .' But how do we acknowledge him? By doing what he says, and not disregarding his commandments, and honoring him not only with our lips but 'with all our hearts and all our minds'").

The use of the verbal form εὐρεστεῖται, "to please," evokes the exhortation of 12:28–29, which provides the announcement of the subject for this section (see *Form/Structure/Setting* on 13:1–25). Through these sacrifices the will of God is satisfied and God is properly worshiped; whoever does not worship God acceptably shows that he has no true understanding of the grace of God and risks rejection by God (cf. Thurén, *Lobopfer,* 178). For the writer, the time of the atonement sacrifice is decisively past. The response of praise and the works of love are the only appropriate sacrifices remaining to the redeemed community (so Thurén, *Lobopfer,* 178–82, who reviews possible Jewish parallels to the double admonition in vv 15–16 and concludes that, in its concentration on the bipartite sacrifice of praise, Heb 13:15–16 is a unique unit of early Christian tradition in the NT). The elaboration of consecration to God through the expressive cultic language of vv 15–16 complements the cultic formulation of the exhortation to worship in 12:28.

17 The pastoral concern with the quality of the relationship between the community and their current leaders is congruous with the development of thought in vv 7–17. Former leaders had carried out the preaching of the word of God, which was foundational for the community (v 7). That word, crystallized in the confessional formulation of v 8, was distorted by the "various strange teachings" (v 9), which threatened to move the community from its foundation. The current leadership now exercises a ministry of vigilance for the community, so that they do not forget the word of God or exchange it for mere human tradition. The pastoral injunctions in v 7 and v 17 are complementary to one another.

Although there is a clear interest in v 17 in strengthening a respect for the authority of the leaders, this is a consequence of the theology of the word that undergirds v 7. No other grounding and safeguarding of the position of the community leaders is provided than the authority that derives from the word of preaching (see *Comment* on v 7; cf. Laub, *SNTU* 6–7[1981–82] 189–90).

The intervening unit of expository parenesis in vv 10–16, which is framed by vv 7–9 and vv 17–19 (see *Form/Structure/Setting* for 13:1–25), appears to have been drafted in response to the challenge to the word of God represented by the foreign teaching. It addresses the community in terms of its confession (v 10), its consecration to God (vv 11–12), its call to discipleship (vv 13–14), and its celebrative lifestyle (vv 15–16), inculcating aspects of the word of God that were in danger of being obscured. The members of the house church will be able to offer the sacrificial service desired by God only if they obey their leaders and submit to their authority (so Thurén, *Lobopfer*, 205–6, 208). The strikingly strong exhortation in v 17 is thus an appropriate continuation of an integrated unit of pastoral concern (cf. Riggenbach, 447; Spicq, 2:431).

The members of the house church are admonished to obedience and submission to the authority of the leading men of the community (for the nuance in ἡγούμενοι, "leaders," see *Comment* on v 7a). The distinctive vocabulary selected by the writer is instructive. Normally in the NT the verb ὑποτάσσεσθαι, "to subject oneself," "to obey," is used to call Christians to the acknowledgment of constituted ordinances and authorities (e.g., Rom 13:1–7; 1 Cor 14:33–36; Col 3:18–4:1; Eph 5:22–6:9; 1 Pet 2:13–17, 18–3:7). The writer, however, defines the obligatory conduct of his audience with the verb πείθεσθαι, "to be persuaded," "to obey." This verb certainly demands obedience. But the specific quality of the obedience for which πείθεσθαι asks is not primarily derived from a respect for constituted structures of authority. It is rather the obedience that is won through persuasive conversation and that follows from it (so Laub *SNTU* 6–7 [1981–82] 179–80, who points out that πείθεσθαι in the sense of obey is used in connection with persons of authority comparatively rarely: 4 Macc 6:4; 8:17, 26; 10:13; 12:4–5; 15:10; cf. Jas 3:3).

The writer carries his injunction a step further with the second verb ὑπείκειν, "to submit to someone's authority." Although the verb occurs only here in the NT, it is used frequently in secular Greek in the sense of submission to a person of authority (cf. 4 Macc 6:35; Philo, *On the Special Laws* 2.232; *Moses* 1.156; *On the Sacrifices of Abel and Cain* 105). A cognate term ἐκτικῶς, which denotes a "habitual readiness" to comply, is used in describing military subordination in *1 Clem.* 37:2 (cited by Thurén, *Lobopfer*, 205). The community is summoned to respect the authority with which the leadership has been invested by God.

There is in v 17a an intimation of a strained relationship between the members of the house church and their leaders in the concrete situation of shared communal life. The near context refers to the "various strange teachings" (v 9), which distort the word of God proclaimed in the past and which threaten the stability of the assembly in the present. If there is a direct connection between that disturbance and the admonition in v 17a, this can only mean that tension existed between the members of the assembly and their leaders. The source of that tension was the group's attraction to the "various strange teachings" (so Laub, *SNTU* 6–7 [1981–82] 180–82, 185, who finds additional evidence for the existence of tension in the final clause of v 17, which appears to have been dictated by a specific difficulty). The unequivocal demand for obedience is relative to the importance of the issue at stake and the peril of apostasy to which members of the community were exposed (see *Comment* on 2:1–4; 3:7–12; 5:11–6:12; 10:23–29; 12:12–13, 14–17, 25–29; cf. Riggenbach, 438). The writer's consistent concern is to motivate the members of the house church to persevere in their response of faith to the foundational word they had received.

The motivation for submitting to the authority of the community leaders is provided in v 17*b*. It is grounded in the quality of the leaders' response to the charge to watch for the welfare of the congregation. The emphatic *αὐτοί*, "they themselves," which is placed at the beginning of the clause, gives prominence to the authority and responsibility of the leaders. It seems to imply that their voices, as opposed to other voices to which the community has been listening, need to be heard and respected. It is roughly equivalent to "no one other than they" (so Laub, *SNTU* 6–7 [1981–82] 181, n. 44).

The members of the house church owe obedience and submission, since the leaders *ἀγρυπνοῦσιν ὑπὲρ τῶν ψυχῶν ὑμῶν ὡς λόγον ἀποδώσοντες*, "they keep watch for your eternal life as those who intend to give an account." The clause offers a commendation of the leaders as men with divinely given pastoral authority and responsibility. God has entrusted to their care the other members of the community. The distinctiveness and importance of their task are underlined by the verb *ἀγρυπνεῖν*, "to watch," "to be vigilant." Spicq (2:431) has emphasized the appropriateness of this verb to the shepherd metaphor (cf. Acts 20:28–31, where the synonym *γρηγορεῖν* is used), but the translation "watch for" conveys the intention better than "watch over." Neither in secular Greek nor in the LXX does the verb express an official activity. In the NT the term always connotes eschatological vigilance (cf. Mark 13:33; Luke 21:36; Eph 6:8 in the context of 6:13–17). The leaders function as watchmen for the community, knowing that in the eschatological judgment they intend to give an accounting to God.

The implication is that they have been charismatically endowed with the gift of discernment and were prepared to exercise this gift in the service of the church. The legitimation for their authority is grounded in their responsibility before God in the final judgment (so Laub, *SNTU* 6–7 [1981–82] 177–80, who rightly objects that there is no reference in v 17 to a hierarchical structure of the community and of jurisdiction, as urged by Spicq, 2:431; Zimmermann, *Bekenntnis*, 12–13; Buchanan, 238 [the accounting must be given not merely to God but "to their superior officers"!]; see further Laub's conclusion, 189–90: the authority of the leaders is not officially bestowed but derives directly from the authority inherent in the word of preaching). Leadership of the house churches was a form of service worthy of honor. These Christians should be shown the deference that their leadership plainly deserved.

The fact that the term *ψυχή* can be understood here from the perspective of 10:39, in the sense of "eternal life," indicates that the leaders had imposed upon them by God nothing less than the care for the eschatological salvation of the individual participants in the community (so Michel, 528–29; Schweizer, *TDNT* 9:650–51; *ψυχή* has this significance also in Luke 17:33; 21:19; Jas 1:21; 1 Pet 1:9; 2:25). They intend to justify before God that their service was directed toward the community's attainment of eschatological salvation (so Laub, *SNTU* 6–7 [1981–82] 178).

The phrase ὡς λόγον ἀποδώσοντες appears to preserve a classical idiom. The particle ὡς with the future participle expresses subjective motive ("as men who," "with the thought that"). The action is accepted with intent and purpose. The phrase does not express necessity or obligation (i.e., "as men who *must* render an account") but conforms to the classical usage of ὡς with the future participle to express strong or avowed purpose. It designates the leaders "as those who intend to give an account" of their service to God (see above, *Note* kk). They should be trusted and their authority should be respected because they recognize their place within a structure of accountability to God. This phrase assigns to the task with which they have been entrusted by God an eschatological significance.

The clause in v 17c is introduced with an imperatival ἵνα ("Let them do this"; see above, *Note* ll). The concern that the leaders be allowed to render their account joyfully rather than unhappily (καὶ μὴ στενάζοντες, "and not with groaning") is a further intimation of the tension that exists between the members of the house church and the leadership of the community. The thought is echoed for the Church in Rome in Hermas, *Vis.* 3.9.10: "Have peace among yourselves, that I also may stand joyfully before the Father and give an account of you all to the Lord." The writer is eager for those leaders to have the joy of a willing and loyal response from the men and the women they serve (Filson, '*Yesterday*', 75).

The final clause in v 17d provides as the motivation for compliance ἀλυσιτελὲς γὰρ ὑμῖν τοῦτο, "for this would be unprofitable for you." The term ἀλυσιτελές, which is found only here in biblical literature, appears to be derived from the language of commerce, carrying forward the metaphor of accounting in v 17b (see above, *Note* mm). The clause is a sober reminder that the welfare of the community is tied to the quality of their response to their current leaders. The tensions that exist between the community and their leaders must be resolved.

18–19 A sustained concern to resolve the tension between the community and those in a leadership role accounts for the request for prayer and the appearance of self-commendation in v 18. The formulation of v 18b is clearly apologetic. It defends the integrity of the motives and conduct of the leaders whose counsel and guidance the community appears to have resented. What is striking is the writer's identification with the leaders through the use of the first-person plural forms in v 18, before speaking more directly in the first-person singular in v 19. He is to be included among the ἡγούμενοι, "leaders," to whom obedience and respect for authority are to be tendered (Laub, *SNTU* 6–7 [1948 1–82] 181, 185, 188; Thurén, *Lobopfer*, 208; this has not always been recognized; e.g., Filson, '*Yesterday*', 71: "in each of the three mentions of the leaders [the author] speaks of them as a group to which he does not belong"). The writer directs the members of the house church προσεύχεσθε περὶ ἡμῶν (where the present imperative expresses durative force: "Keep praying for us"). He knew that resentment would be dissolved and tensions relaxed, if the community would continue to intercede earnestly for those entrusted with the pastoral oversight of each of their number.

The request for prayer is grounded in the firm conviction of the leadership: πειθόμεθα γὰρ ὅτι καλὴν συνείδησιν ἔχομεν, "for we are convinced that we have a clear conscience." The rare use of the perfective present πειθόμεθα, "we are convinced," corresponds formally to the note of "boasting" in the letters of Paul (e.g., Rom 5:2, 3,11; 2 Cor 7:14; 10:8, 13, 15–17; 11:16, 18, 30; cf. Bultmann, *TDNT* 3:649, n. 37, who points out that καυχᾶσθαι, "to boast," and πεποιθέναι, "to be convinced," are synonymous; Wrede, *Rätsel,* 51, found the formal pattern for Heb 13:18–19 in 2 Cor 1:11–12). All self-confidence is radically excluded from such boasting. What is prominent is the element of trust: it is a boasting of trust in God. This trust is a presupposition of shared community life (so correctly, Thurén, *Lobopfer,* 206). In the case of the leaders, it proceeds from their sense of ultimate accountability to God (v 17).

In Hebrews the term "conscience" (συνείδησις) has deeply religious overtones. The conscience is directed toward God and embraces the whole person in his relationship to God (see *Comment* on 9:9, 14; 10:2, 22). Apart from this single reference to καλὴ συνείδησις, "a clear conscience," the term has negative connotations; it is the "uneasy conscience" that is in view, with its internal witness that defilement extends to the heart and mind. It is not engaged in moral decision making but in remembering. The defiled conscience is an obstacle to the worship of God and calls for decisive purgation (9:14; 10:22). In the light of this background, the assurance of a "clear conscience" is all the more remarkable. In the dynamic context of community relationships, the assertion of a clear conscience is a particular form of protection against slander and an affirmation of credibility. It signifies "we have a clear conscience" in the specific matter of our conduct toward you. The clause expresses a joyful sense of being in the will of God (cf. *1 Clem.* 45:7: "the Most High is the defender and protector of those who serve his excellent name with a pure conscience").

The integrity of the leadership is substantiated with the causal participle θέλοντες, "since we strive." The clear conscience of the writer and his fellow leaders is based on a decision of the will to conduct themselves appropriately as men called to holiness of life (cf. 12:14) and to a task imposed by God (13:17). The infinitival phrase ἐν πᾶσιν καλῶς . . . ἀναστρέφεσθαι, "to act commendably in every way," is calculated to call to mind the cognate noun ἡ ἀναστροφή, "the manner of life," "the conduct," "the behavior," which was used in reference to the former leaders in v 7. Their conduct was validated by its accomplishment and provides a model for the community to emulate. "To conduct oneself commendably" (καλῶς . . . ἀναστρέφεσθαι) is a typical Semitic expression for a faultless moral conduct (so Stelzenberger, *Syneidēsis,* 65). The community can pray confidently for their leaders since their actions correspond to the irreproachable conduct of the former leaders, whose integrity was beyond question. The aim of the pastoral directives is that those in leadership may continue to discharge their responsibilities in a manner that gives pleasure to God and stability to the church.

The series of pastoral injunctions gains a very personal note when in v 19 the writer asks for the prayers of the community. This brief request for prayer specifies a personal concern to be reunited with the community. The verb of entreaty παρακαλῶ, "I urge [you]," and the nature of the request indicate the depth of affection that the writer felt for the members of the small house church he had apparently visited on a previous occasion. He asks for special prayer in regard to his intense desire to exchange absence for presence. His request is a tacit reminder that he would have preferred to have delivered his homily in person than in written form and that he regarded what he has written as merely a substitute for a personal visit. He is confident that through their prayers he will be restored to them sooner.

It is difficult, if not impossible, to determine the precise relationship that the writer enjoyed with the members of the house church (cf. Filson, 'Yesterday', 71–72; P. E. Hughes, 588). Certainly the purpose clause ἵνα τάχιον ἀποκατασταθῶ ὑμῖν, "so that I might be restored to you sooner," implies that he has been with them previously and knows these Christians personally. This is interesting because it indicates that Hebrews was not originally anonymous, inasmuch as the writer and his audience were known to each other. It is evident that he is eager to return to them as soon as it is possible to do so (see *Comment,* on v 23). He is persuaded that his sphere of leadership extends to the men and women for whom he has expressed such ardent pastoral concern. This deeply personal note conveys a sense of urgency as the writer invites the community to partnership in mission.

Explanation

See 13:22–25 below.

Closing Doxology (13:20–21)

Bibliography

See *Bibliography* for 13:1–25 above.

Translation

20   And[a] may the God of peace,
      who led out from the dead
      the great Shepherd of the sheep,
      by virtue of the blood[b] of the eternal covenant,
      our Lord Jesus,[c]
21   make you complete[d] with everything good[e]
      to do his will,
      accomplishing[f] in us[g] what is pleasing to him[h]
      through Jesus Christ.
      To him[i] be glory forever.[j] Amen.

Notes

[a] The arrangement of the prayer-wish leading to an invocation, followed by two strophes of four lines each and a doxology, is adapted from Michel, 535. For a full treatment of the importance of the particle δέ in the form, see Jewett, *ATR* 51 (1969) 22–23. The particle deserves to be translated because

it bears a connective sense in such units. It implies that the prayer-wish is intrinsically related to the written discourse that precedes it.

b Although it has been proposed that the prep in the phrase ἐν αἵματι seems to have the notion of accompaniment or attendant circumstances (Moule, *Idiom-Book*, 78, who tentatively translates the phrase "with the blood"), the construction of the strophe as well as the text to which an allusion is made, Zech 9:11 LXX, make clear that the expression is to be understood causally, i.e., "by virtue of the blood," or "through the blood." On this important point of grammar as it affects the translation of v 20, see especially Jeremias, *ZNW* 42 (1949) 198; Zerwick, *Biblical Greek*, §119, supplemented by Zerwick and Grosvenor, *Grammatical Analysis*, 689; Thurén, *Lobopfer*, 226.

c The deferred reference to Jesus (τὸν κύριον ἡμῶν Ἰησοῦν) in the strophe is emphatic and is consistent with the writer's habit elsewhere in the homily (see above on 2:9; 3:1; 4:14; 6:20; 7:22; 10:19; 12:2; 12:24).

d The aor optative καταρτίσαι, which is the only optative in the literary Gk. of Hebrews, expresses the notion of wishing: "may God . . . make you complete" (BDF §384; Zerwick, *Biblical Greek*, §355; Hanna, *Grammatical Aid*, 163). Its occurrence here is consistent with the fact that of the thirty-eight proper optatives in the NT, sixteen are found in prayer-wishes or blessings (see Jewett, *ATR* 51 [1969] 23–24, who suggests that the concentration of these optatives in prayer units may have been influenced by LXX usage, since the optative is used there primarily for wishes and blessings). The verb καταρτίζειν possesses a very wide range of meaning. Its nuances include "adjust," "put in order," "restore," "mend," "recommission," "furnish," "equip," "make good," "prepare" (cf. Spicq, 1:23–24 for eleven different usages of the verb). It occurs in 10:5 and 11:3, but in a different sense: 10:5 "to prepare"; 11:3 "to fashion," "to create." The notion of supplying that which is defective or deficient suggests the translation "make complete" (cf. Delling, *TDNT* 1:475).

e The liturgical tone of this prayer probably explains why there are no less than four textual variants in v 21. In the first instance the reading παντὶ ἀγαθῷ is assigned an "A" rating in the UBSGNT³, indicating that the text, supported by p⁴⁶ ℵ D* ψ latt bo, is virtually certain. The addition of ἔργῳ after παντί in the TR, in company with C Dᶜ K M P almost all minuscules and syᵖ·ʰ sa aeth (i.e., "every good work"), is "an obvious homiletic gloss" (Metzger, *Textual Commentary*, 676).

f Although the reading αὐτῷ ποιῶν is strongly attested (ℵ* A C 33* 81 1739ᵐᵍ sa; cf. p⁴⁶ αὐτὸ ποιῶν), the pronoun is unintelligible. It appears to have arisen as a dittogr of the preceding αὐτοῦ (so Zuntz, *Text*, 62; Metzger, *Textual Commentary*, 676). The shorter reading ποιῶν, "accomplishing," is supported by ℵᶜ Dᵍʳ K P ψ 0121b 33ᶜ 88 614 1739* Byz Lect lat vg syᵖ·ʰ saᵐˢ boᵐˢ arm. The translation does not reflect the repetition in the formulation ποιῆσαι . . . ποιῶν, "to do . . . accomplishing."

g The pronoun ἡμῖν, "us," which is strongly supported by p⁴⁶ ℵ A Dᵍʳ K M 33 81 614 1739 syᵖ sa bo arm, was altered in some MSS to read ὑμῖν, "in you," probably to agree with the preceding ὑμᾶς, "make you complete" (Metzger, *Textual Commentary*, 676–77).

h The prep phrase ἐνώπιον αὐτοῦ, which is closer to Hebrew idiom than the simple dative, carries the nuance "in the opinion of him" "in the judgment of him" (BAGD 270[3]). Cf. 4:13, where the same expression has the nuance of "in the sight of him," "in the presence of him" (i.e., "in his presence").

i The translation resolves the ambiguity in the antecedent of the relative pronoun ᾧ, "to him," by placing a period after the second strophe, so that the doxology refers most naturally to "the God of peace" of the invocation, rather than to the closest antecedent, "Jesus Christ." Considerations of structure are decisive in shaping the translation.

j The translation reflects the shorter form of the text (εἰς τοὺς αἰῶνας, supported by p⁴⁶ C³ Dᵍʳ ψ 104 436 1241 1877 2127 2492 2495 Lect syʰ saᵐˢˢ arm Thret). Both the shorter and the fuller formulations are well attested. The addition of τῶν αἰώνων is supported by ℵ A (C*) K P 33 81 614 1739 latt saᵐˢˢ bo aeth Chr Euthalius Thret John of Damascus. Both phrases are to be found in other NT texts. Zuntz, *Text*, 120–21, argued that the shorter form is correct. The knowledge of the fuller formulation, inculcated from liturgical usage, suggested expansion of the shorter form, and this has left its traces in the surviving witnesses of some ancient branches of the tradition. According to Zuntz, "there is no instance of an originally longer form being shortened in witnesses as numerous and ancient as here. But the expansion of an originally shorter form, so far as it did occur at all, was characteristic of the older tradition" (121). The editors of the UBSGNT³ found it difficult to decide whether copyists added the phrase τῶν αἰώνων here to conform with other NT usage or others omitted the phrase "either through carelessness or in imitation of εἰς τοὺς αἰῶνας ["forever"] in Heb 13:8" (Metzger, *Textual Commentary*, 677). The editors decided to retain the addition, but to enclose it with square brackets as an indication that it might well be a gloss.

Form/Structure/Setting

See 13:1–25 above.

Comment

20–21   The request for prayer in vv 18–19 is followed appropriately by engagement in prayer. The fervent prayer-wish in vv 20–21 serves to summarize the concerns of the previous section and provides formal closure to the homily as a whole. The prayer consists of an invocation of God, followed by two strophes of four lines each, both of which end with the name of Jesus, and a concluding doxology, which is directed to God (so Michel, 535; Deichgräber, *Gotteshymnus*, 33–34; Jewett, *ATR* 51 [1969] 20–25). The two strophes of the prayer constitute a colon, i.e., a metrical unit expressing one complete thought (cf. R. Schütz, "Die Bedeutung der Kolometrie für das Neue Testament," *ZNW* 21 [1922] 161–84, especially 172). They provide a kerygmatic recital of divine activity as the ground of the writer's confidence in God's ability and willingness to mature his work within Christians, enabling them to do his will in an acceptable manner.

The prayer-wish is firmly attached to its setting by the connective δέ, "and," which implies that it is intrinsically related to the preceding unit of discourse (Jewett, *ATR* 51 [1969] 22–23, 27–28, who traces the development of the distinctive form of the homiletical benedictions in the NT to hellenistic circles). It is integrated with its immediate setting by vocabulary and conception. The fact that the prayer-wish takes up again central themes from the homily indicates that the formulation was not simply taken over from some pre-formed liturgical expression (as argued by Michel, 535, 537; cf. Jewett, *ATR* 51 [1969] 28–30) but is organically related to the development of the sermon.

The invocation ὁ θεὸς τῆς εἰρήνης, "the God of peace," belongs to a broad group of genitival expressions for God (cf. Deichgräber, *Gotteshymnus* 88–96). It identifies God as the source and giver of peace. The designation "the God of peace" may be of Christian coinage, since it occurs nowhere in the OT. (See, however, *T. Dan* 5:2; "Be at peace, holding fast to the God of peace." The invocation introduces a variation on a blessing used to conclude a worship service, which appears in its simplest form in Rom 15:33: "The God of peace be with you all. Amen" (see Cuming, *NTS* 22 [1975–76] 111–12). The term εἰρήνη, "peace," in the formula often conveys the nuance of eschatological salvation (cf. Foerster, *TDNT* 2:415; see *Comment* on 12:14). On occasion, however, the notion of "rest" or "order" is in the foreground (e.g., Rom 16:20 in the context of 16:17–20; 1 Cor 14:33; 2 Cor 13:11; Phil 4:9; 1 Thess 5:23; cf. 2 Thess 3:16). The occurrence of the epithet in this context is related to the immediate concern with relaxing the tension between the community and its leadership (see above, *Comment* on vv 17–18). This was signalled in the congregation by the wish with which the service of worship was concluded: "The God of peace be with you all." The "peace" of God will be appropriated through the obedience and submission of the community to their leaders (13:17) (so also Spicq, 2:435; F. F. Bruce, 410; Thurén, *Lobopfer*, 222).

The divine predicate is expanded through a participial clause (as in 2 Thess 2:16; 1 Pet 5:10; *1 Clem.* 64:1; on praise in the participial style, see Delling, *ST* 17 [1963] 16–17, 34–35). In v 20 the participial clause points to the objective reality of God's saving deed. The formulation indicates that the writer has been reflecting on Isa 63:11–14 LXX:

Heb 13:20   ὁ ἀναγαγὼν ἐκ νεκρῶν τὸν ποιμένα τῶν προβάτων τὸν μέγαν
             "who led out from the dead the great shepherd of the sheep"
Isa 63:11–14 ὁ ἀναβιβάσας ἐκ τῆς γῆς τὸν ποιμένα τῶν προβάτων … ὁ ἀγαγὼν
             [v. l. ἀναγαγὼν] … Μωϋσῆν …. ἤγαγεν αὐτοὺς …. οὕτως ἤγαγες τὸν
             λαόν σου ποιῆσαι σεαυτῷ ὄνομα δόξης.
             "who brought up out of the land the shepherd of the sheep …. He
             who led forth … Moses …. He led them …. Thus you led your
             people to make for yourself a glorious name."

The reference in Isa 63:11–14 LXX is to God's appointment of Moses as the leader of Israel in the context of the deliverance from Egypt. Moses, the shepherd of Midian (Exod 3:1), is the model for "the great shepherd," Jesus. According to Isa 63:11–14 he was "led forth" not as an isolated individual but as the shepherd of the flock. The entire people are specified as the object of God's leading. This is true of Jesus as well, who was led forth from the realm of the dead. Through him God has begun to lead his flock in order to make a glorious name for himself. That action will be complete when the flock of God is brought to an experience of celebrative rest (cf. Isa 63:14 LXX; Heb 2:10; 4:9). Appointment to the office of "shepherd" is the goal of the leading forth of Jesus from among the dead (cf. Thurén, *Lobopfer*, 225–27).

This is the only direct reference in the homily to the resurrection of Jesus. What is implicit elsewhere (e.g., 7:16, 24) is here made explicit. The resurrection of Jesus demonstrates God's decisive intervention by which he acknowledged and ratified the cross of Christ as the means of the redemption of the human family (see further Cranfield, *SJT* 20 [1967] 438 and n. 2; Michel, 536–37; Thurén, *Lobopfer*, 223–26).

The writer's choice of the verb ἀνάγειν, "to lead," "bring up," to express the powerful intervention of God is consistent with the use of the cognate verb ἄγειν, "to lead," in Isa 63:12–14 LXX. (Cf. also Exod 33:12, 15 LXX, where the compound verb ἀνάγειν is used in God's instruction for Moses to "lead out" the people; Symm. has in Isa 63:11 ὁ ἀναγαγὼν αὐτοὺς ἐκ τῆς θαλάσσης, "who led them out from the sea"). The phrase ἐκ νεκρῶν, "out from the dead," in v 20 appears to be an interpretive rendering of the prepositional phrase in the LXX ἐκ τῆς γῆς, "out of the land." Alternatively, Isa 63:11–14 LXX may have recalled to the writer a pattern of statement found frequently in the Psalms, where the "leading out" from the realm of the dead is actually expressed with the verb ἀνάγειν (e.g., Ps 29[MT 30]:4; 70[MT 71]:20; 85[MT 86]:13; cf. 2 Sam 2:6; Tob 13:2 [B A]; Wis 16:3 LXX; see Thurén, *Lobopfer*, 223–25).

The "leading out" is the fundamental redemptive action of God under both the old and new covenant. Upon it are based the exclusive claims of God to his people's allegiance, on the one hand, and, on the other, the ground for trust in God's power and readiness to stand by his covenant people. The intervention of God in leading his people from Egypt in the Torah (e.g., Exod 6:7; 20:1–2; Lev 19:36; 25:38; 26:13; Num 5:31; Deut 5:6) and in the Prophets (e.g., Isa 64:11–14) and from the realm of the dead in the Psalter (e.g., Ps 30:3; 71:20; 86:13) prefigured his decisive action in raising Jesus from the dead. Jeremiah had prophesied that the old formula that spoke of "leading out" would be replaced by a new one (Jer 16:14–15; 23:7–8), which would belong integrally to the new covenant (Jer 38[MT 31]:31–34 LXX). The comment on Jer 38[MT 31]:31–34 and the full citation of the text in Heb 8:6–13 is recalled in v 20 with the reference to "the eternal covenant." The formulation in v 20 is thus grounded in the conviction that God has established a new covenant with his people through the "leading out" of Jesus from the realm of the dead. The leading forth of Jesus is, for the new and eternal covenant, the fundamental action of God that has replaced the foundational acts of salvation under the old covenant. It provides the ground of the obligation to obey God in a manner "pleasing to him" (v 21). It is also the basis of the writer's confidence that God will hear and respond favorably to his prayer for the community (so Cranfield, *SJT* 20 [1967] 437; Thurén, *Lobopfer,* 225, 227).

The description of Jesus as a shepherd is rooted in early Christian tradition (e.g., John 10:1–18; 1 Pet 2:25; 5:4; cf. Mark 6:34; 14:27; Matt 9:36; 18:12–14; 25:32; 26:31; Luke 15:3–7; cf. Bracewell, "Shepherd Imagery," 90–227). What is significant is the writer's introduction of the words τὸν μέγαν, "the great," which qualify the biblical expression "the shepherd of the sheep" (Isa 63:11). These words serve to stress the incomparable superiority of Jesus, the mediator of the new covenant, to Moses, the mediator of the old covenant. The addition is consistent with the writer's christological use of the adjective "great" earlier in the homily (e.g., 4:14 ἀρχιερέα μέγαν, "a great high priest"; 10:21 ἱερέα μέγαν, "a great priest") and reiterates the definite and sustained comparison between Jesus and Moses throughout the sermon (see *Comment* on 1:1–4; 2:1–4; 3:1–6; 8:1–6; 10:26–31; 12:18–24, 25–29; see especially P. R. Jones, *RevExp* 76 [1979] 102–3). Although Moses is "the shepherd of the sheep" whom God "led out" from the land of Egypt, Jesus is "the great shepherd of the sheep" whom God "led out" from the realm of the dead. He alone is the mediator of an everlasting covenant.

The unusual formulation ἐκ νεκρῶν ἀνάγειν, "to lead out from the dead," is found in Rom 10:7 as well, where Paul finds in Deut 30:12–14 an intimation of the resurrection of Jesus. The verb ἀνάγειν, "to lead," "bring up," is not a typical expression for Paul or for the writer of Hebrews. This fact suggests that both writers were drawing on a common early Christian tradition that used the vocabulary of "leading out from the realm of the dead" to describe Jesus' resurrection. That tradition may have contributed as well the designation κύριος Ἰησοῦς, "Lord Jesus," which occurs only here in Hebrews. In developing the tradition, the writer of Hebrews was clearly independent of Paul in his dependence upon the formulation of Isa 63:11–14 LXX. It is striking that in none of Paul's letters is there a doxology or homiletical benediction in which phrases are woven from the LXX, as in Heb 13:20–21.

The formulation of v 20 has been influenced by Zech 9:11 LXX as well:

Heb 13:20   ἐν αἵματι διαθήκης αἰωνίου
             "by virtue of the blood of an eternal covenant";
Zech 9:11 LXX καὶ σὺ ἐν αἵματι διαθήκης ἐξαπέστειλας δεσμίους σου ἐκ λάκκου
             οὐκ ἔχοντος ὕδωρ
             "And you, because of the blood of the covenant, sent forth your
             captives out of the waterless pit."

The allusion to Zech 9:11 LXX, as well as the construction of the strophe in Heb 13:20, shows that the phrase concerning the eternal covenant is to be understood causally ("because of the blood," "by virtue of the blood") and is to be referred to the participle ἀναγαγών, "who led out . . . because of the blood of the eternal covenant" (see above, *Note* b). Jesus was led out from among the dead by virtue of his unique and unrepeatable pouring out of his own blood (cf. 9:18–28; 10:11–18). The writer correctly interpreted the phrase "the waterless pit" in Zech 9:11 LXX as the realm of the dead (cf., e.g., Pss 27[MT 28]:1; 29[MT 30]:3; 87[MT 88]:4, 6; 142[MT 143]:7 LXX). The term λάκκος, "pit," is connected with the verb ἀνάγειν in Jer 45[MT 38]:10, 13 LXX and is used figuratively in Ps 39[MT 40]:2 (Thurén, *Lobopfer*, 226, n. 786).

The writer understands that Jesus died on the cross as a covenant sacrifice and that he entered into the heavenly sanctuary and there sprinkled his own blood, prior to the resurrection. The resurrection of Jesus occurred by virtue of the sprinkling of the blood in the heavenly sanctuary and the establishment of the new covenant. The phrase ἐν αἵματι διαθήκης αἰωνίου accordingly does not mean "with the blood of the eternal covenant" but rather "by virtue of the blood of the eternal covenant." The decisive consideration is that in cultic thinking the obtaining of the blood and the sprinkling of the blood belong indissoluably together. The offering of the body of Jesus (προσφορὰ τοῦ σώματος, 10:10) and the offering (προσφορά, 9:25) of the blood of Jesus in the heavenly sanctuary are associated but successive actions. As Jeremias has observed, "Good Friday is the great Day of Atonement of the human family with God" (*ZNW* 42 [1949] 198). The blood of the covenant effects the sanctification of the new covenant people (10:29).

The phrase "blood of the covenant" alludes to Jesus' death as a covenant sacrifice (cf. Exod 24:8; Heb 9:20). The qualifying adjective αἰώνιος, "eternal," celebrates the fact that the atoning work of Jesus has eternal validity (Jeremias, *ZNW* 42 [1949] 199). Although the covenant is called "eternal" only here in Hebrews, the general theme of eternal validity has been a matter of persistent importance throughout the homily (1:8; 5:6, 9; 6:20; 9:12, 14, 15; 10:12, 14; the adjective αἰώνιος and its cognate noun have eschatological significance especially in 5:9; 9:12, 15). It is the work and sacrifice of Jesus that are the basis for the eternal covenant. The expression "eternal covenant" is, of course, biblical (Isa 55:3; Jer 39[MT 32]:40; Ezek 37:26; cf. Jer 38[MT 31]:35–37 LXX). It refers to a future event that will bring with it an enduring closeness to God (Michel, 538). The new covenant is the promised "eternal covenant." It replaces the old covenant, which is ready to vanish (see *Comment* on 8:13). The gift of the new covenant is not provisional or temporary, "but God's final, costly forgiveness, which in no way glosses over or condones our sin, but is altogether worthy of God, who in all his ways is holy, righteous and true" (Cranfield, *SJT* 20 [1967] 439).

In v 20 the writer wants to stress two motifs without completely harmonizing them: (1) through his blood the exalted Jesus once for all accomplished the atonement of the people of God and established an eternal covenant; and (2) after his resurrection Christ became the leader of the new covenant community, having satisfied the preconditions for an acceptable worship of God. Christians belong to the fold of "the great Shepherd" because they have been bonded to him by the eternal covenant. The fact that the Church has become the flock of

God, taking the place of old Israel, and that Jesus is "the great Shepherd," surpassing Moses, gives the writer the certainty that God will receive his prayer favorably. The deferral of the reference to "our Lord Jesus" to the end of the strophe is emphatic and is consistent with the writer's practice elsewhere in the homily (see above on 2:9; 3:1; 4:14; 6:20; 7:22; 10:19; 12:2, 24).

The substance of the petition is that God may supply what is defective or deficient within the members of the assembly so that they may live the Christian life in a manner which will please him (v 21). The singular use of the optative καταρτίσαι, "may [God] . . . make complete," is appropriate to the language of prayer (see above, *Note* d). The word group καταρτίζειν and its cognates is associated with petitionary prayer elsewhere in the NT (2 Cor 13:9; 1 Thess 3:10; 1 Pet 5:10) and is narrowly connected with parenetic instruction (2 Cor 13:11; cf. 1 Cor 1:10; Gal 6:1; Eph 4:12). This connection is important for the interpretation of the petition in v 21 (so correctly Michel, 539, n. 1).

The writer prays specifically that God may make the community complete ἐν παντὶ ἀγαθῷ, "with everything good." Some scribes understood "the good" in terms of "good deeds," which accounts for the homiletical gloss in the TR: "in every good work" (see above, *Note* e; cf. Spicq, 2:436: "render you apt to all good things"). The "good" was thus understood as the main aim of ethical action, in keeping with the following lines of the strophe, i.e., as the accomplishment of God's will and the achievement of what is well-pleasing to him. MS Alexandrinus (A) went so far as to fill in the formula from 2 Thess 2:17: "May God make you complete in every good word and work." Here the "good" is interpreted as a reference to the word of God, which strengthens and equips the congregation (cf. Michel, 535–36). The "good" must be ascertained and discerned by the community, but it must also be given and presented by God himself (so Michel, 539).

There is, however, another interpretation that seems to be more appropriate. The "good" is the inner endowment required so that the will of God can be done. Since "God" is the subject of the clause, the "good" is the "good gift" of God (cf. Matt 7:11; Luke 1:53; Gal 6:6; Jas 1:17). In other prayer-wishes the charismatic gifts of God, and sometimes their consequences, are given prominence (e.g., Rom 15:5, 13; 2 Cor 1:3–4; 2 Thess 2:17). This appears to be the case here as well. "Everything good" has reference to the gifts of God as the prerequisite for godly action. This proposal is supported by the structure of the strophe and by the context. It is God who strengthens the heart with grace (13:9), who fills and supports the heart with charismatic gifts (2:4; 6:5; 13:9), so that it neither wavers nor suffers a deficiency but possesses the capacity to do the will of God. The expression "everything good" in v 21a is thus equivalent to the phrase "with all grace" in 1 Pet 5:10. The line of thought is clear: may God himself fill and support the community with every good grace, enabling them to do his will (so Thurén, *Lobopfer*, 227–29). With this petition the Christian life is placed under the sign of obedience as characteristic of the new people of God (cf. 10:5–10, where the vocabulary and conception suggest a parallel to v 21ab).

The petition that God will equip the community to do his will is clarified by the parallel clause in v 21c: God himself will accomplish in the members of the house church that which is well pleasing to him. If the initial lines of the strophe left open the possibility that Christians, once equipped by God, could do his will independently, the subsequent clause establishes that human effort can never be independent of God, who molds the life of his servants into conformity to his will. The two clauses are mutually complementary (Thurén, *Lobopfer,* 221–22). The divine enabling claims men and women for the response of obedience to the revealed will of God.

The key expression τὸ εὐάρεστον, "what is pleasing," picks up the notions of "pleasing service" to God from the programmatic passage 12:28 and of the "pleasing sacrifices" from 13:15–16, which serve to tie the section together as a coherent unit of thought. The exhortation λατρεύωμεν εὐαρέστως τῷ θεῷ, "let us serve God acceptably," in 12:28 is carried forward by the subsequent motivation τοιαύταις γὰρ θυσίαις εὐαρεστεῖται ὁ θεός, "for God is pleased by such sacrifices," in 13:16. It finds its culmination in the assurance that God himself will bless the community through Jesus Christ, creating ἐν ἡμῖν τὸ εὐάρεστον ἐνώπιον αὐτοῦ, "in us that which is pleasing to him." What is pleasing to God will be accomplished "through Jesus Christ" as the mediator of the grace and power of God within the new covenant community.

The emphasis on the mediatorial role of Jesus clearly echoes 13:12–15, where Jesus is portrayed as high priest and mediator of the spiritual sacrifices of the community. The effective, creative blessing of God will be mediated to the community through the agency of Jesus Christ, enabling them to bring to God through Jesus the sacrifices that please him.

The cry of praise with which the prayer concludes was patterned after the traditional doxology in the synagogue, to which the congregation responded with their "Amen" (Michel, 537). It refers most naturally to "the God of peace" (cf. 1 Pet 5:10–11 for the same pattern of prayer). In resolving the ambiguity in the relative pronoun ᾧ, "to him," so that it refers to the invocation rather than to its closest antecedent "Jesus Christ," considerations of structure are decisive (cf. Michel, 535; Deichgräber, *Gotteshymnus,* 33–34; Thurén, *Lobopfer,* 230–33). In a recent examination of a central kerygmatic core that integrates the rich diversity and manifold plurality of the NT, Lemcio has called attention to the theocentric character of the unifying kerygma: God invariably appears as the initiator of the saving event and as the recipient of Christian response (*JSNT* 33 [1988] 13: "A marked theocentricity persists amongst the very writers who have moved Christian thinking in a more Christological direction"; for the treatment of Heb 13:20–21, see ibid., 10, 14). The accuracy of Lemcio's observation is evident here. It is the God of peace who led Jesus out from the realm of the dead to whom Christians respond with the doxological shout, "to whom be glory forever" (adopting the shorter form of the text; see above, *Note* j).

The presence of the homiletical benediction in vv 20–21 indicates the writer's awareness that his homily was to be read aloud as the members of the house church gathered for worship (so Filson, *'Yesterday',* 22, 82; Jewett, *ATR* 5 [1969] 19–22, 30, 34; cf. Schierse, *Verheissung,* 207, who describes Hebrews as "the first liturgical sermon"). The prayer-wish brings the sermon to its conclusion on the note of pastoral prayer for the men and women of the community. A homily ending with such a benediction reminds the congregation that God is giving himself and his blessing in the word as it is presented and applied to the situation of the audience. The final word of the homily is the only adequate one: "Amen."

Explanation

See 13:22–25 below.

Personal Note (13:22–25)

Bibliography

See *Bibliography* for 13:1–25 above.

Translation

[22] *Brothers, I urge you to listen willingly*[a] *to the word of exhortation,*[b] *for in fact*[c] *I have written to you*[d] *briefly.*[e] [23] *Know that our brother Timothy has been released.*[f] *If he comes very soon,*[g] *I will visit*[h] *you with him.*
[24] *Greet all your leaders and all the saints. Those from Italy*[i] *greet you.* [25] *Grace be with you all.*[j]

Notes

[a] The translation of ἀνέχεσθε is crucial, because it tends to color the way in which the descriptive phrase λόγος παρακλήσεως is understood (as reprimand or encouragement, correctly observed by Andriessen, *NRT* 96 [1974] 1063–64). Common translations like "to bear with," "to tolerate" tend to point to a nuance of severity. Andriessen asserts that ἀνέχεσθε signifies rather "submit to," "content yourself with," and translates, "I urge you to content yourself with this word of encouragement" (1063). For the distinctive nuance reflected in the translation, see Acts 18:14; 2 Tim 4:3 (so BAGD 66). There is an iterative force in the present imperative ἀνέχεσθε, as throughout this chap.
[b] The translation fails to reflect the play on words παρακαλῶ . . . παρακλήσεως, "I urge . . . exhortation."
[c] On the particle combination καὶ γάρ, "and in fact," "and further," see the useful comments of J. D. Denniston, *The Greek Particles*, 2nd ed. (Oxford: Clarendon, 1954) 108–9.
[d] The expression ἐπιστέλλειν τινί, "to write to someone," occurs often in Gk. authors, but nowhere else in the NT. The verb can signify "to inform or instruct by letter," or simply "to write" (as in the papyri and the LXX, according to BAGD 300, with the translation "I have written to you [briefly]"). It is difficult to justify the definiteness in the translation of the NEB ("It is after all a short letter") or the NIV ("I have written you only a short letter"). Among alternative proposals that affect translation, two may be noted. Arguing that the reference is to the personal note in 13:22–25, Vanhoye asserts that ἐπιστέλλειν signifies "to send a message," and translates v 22 accordingly: "I ask you, brothers, bear with the discourse of exhortation; and in effect with the brief words *I have sent you*" (*La structure*, 221–22). Trudinger proposes that ἐπιστέλλειν should be given the meaning "enjoin," "instruct," a nuance it often carries in classical Gk. (*JTS* n.s. 23 [1972] 130, with an appeal to LSJ 600; MM 245–46) and that its reference should be restricted to the commands and instructions of chap. 13. For a rejoinder to Trudinger, see P. E. Hughes, 592, n. 47.
[e] The prep phrase διὰ βραχέων denotes attendant circumstances, with the meaning "briefly" (Moule, *Idiom-Book*, 57). It provides an instance of διά with the gen of manner. Zerwick and Grosvenor, *Grammatical Analysis*, 689, propose the translation, "in few words."

ᶠ The precise nuance in the supplementary pass ptcp ἀπολελυμένον is disputed. One proposal is that it connotes "take leave" or "depart," as in Acts 13:13, 15:30, 33; 28:25, i.e., "know that Timothy, our brother, has departed (and is absent) [from me]" (cf. Wrede, *Rätsel,* 57–60; E. D. Jones, *ExpTim* 46 [1934–35] 566; BAGD 96, who add "unless the reference is to a release from imprisonment"; Jewett, 242, who translates "Timothy has been dispatched"). The most frequent sense of ἀπολύειν in the NT is that of "releasing from custody persons who were under arrest or in prison" (P. E. Hughes, 593, n. 51). Cf. Zerwick and Grosvenor, *Grammatical Analysis,* 689, who propose the translation "set free."

ᵍ The comparative adv τάχιον is used for the positive, with the meaning "quickly," "soon," "without delay" (BAGD 807; BDF §244[1]: "if he comes very soon"). For the argument that there *is* an element of comparison in the context and that the phrase ἐὰν τάχιον ἔρχηται may mean "if he comes before I leave," see A. T. Robertson, *Grammar,* 664.

ʰ For this nuance in ὄψομαι see Moffatt, 246, who calls attention to 3 John 14, "I hope to visit (ἰδεῖν) you soon."

ⁱ The precise nuance in the articular prep phrase οἱ ἀπὸ τῆς Ἰταλίας is difficult to determine because during the Koine period ἀπό was in the process of absorbing ἐκ (Moule, *Idiom-Book,* 71) and in Modern Gk. has completely supplanted it. A broad distinction has been attempted, according to which ἐκ means "from within," while ἀπό indicates merely "the general starting point": a man will go ἐκ (ἐξ) a *house,* but ἀπό a *country* (cf. A. T. Robertson, *Grammar,* 577). Although this distinction cannot be validated in the NT generally, Moule concedes that "it may be that *more often than not* the distinction holds, and Heb 13:24 is a specimen of conformity" (*Idiom-Book,* 72). On the other hand, Turner asserts that the articular prep phrase simply means "the Italians" (*Grammar,* 3:15; so also BAGD 87; cf. BDF §437). Zerwick and Grosvenor, *Grammatical Analysis,* 690, offer two alternative translations: "All here send you greetings from Italy," or, "The Italians here send you greetings." The NEB leaves the issue undecided: "Greetings to you from our Italian friends."

ʲ The impact of the later liturgical use of the concluding benediction can be traced in the MS tradition (UBSGNT³ 778). It is apparent most broadly in the addition of ἀμήν, "Amen," in ℵ² A C D H K P Ψ 0121b 81 1739 Byz Lect lat syᵖ·ʰ bo aeth. The intrusion was resisted, however, by several important witnesses, including P⁴⁶ ℵ* Iᵛⁱᵈ 33 vgᵐˢ sa arm. Although the editors of the UBSGNT³ give the text without ἀμήν only a "C" rating, indicating a considerable degree of doubt whether the text or the apparatus contains the superior reading, the addition should be omitted.

Form/Structure/Setting

See 13:1–25 above.

Comment

22 Sustained pastoral concern as well as the sense of separation from his audience encouraged the writer to add a few brief personal remarks. The personal note appended to the homily reflects the conventions of a postscript (see now Übelacker, *Appell,* 197–223). As an attached note or announcement, these lines stand outside the structure of the basic discourse. Their importance lies in the commendation of the homily to the members of the house church, the communication of information the recipients would be eager to receive, and the conveyance of personal and collegial greetings. The concluding blessing provides closure to the document as a whole. The postscript is attached to the homily by a linking device that reveals the literary signature of the writer: corresponding to δὲ παρακαλῶ, "and I urge," in v 19 is the exhortation παρακαλῶ δέ, "and I urge," in v 22 (Dussaut, *Synopse structurelle,* 134–35).

The pastoral appeal παρακαλῶ δὲ ὑμᾶς ἀδελφοί, "and I urge you, brothers," conveys a tone of gentleness and warmth (for the use of the fraternal expression "brothers," see 3:1, 12; 10:19). Concurrently, it expresses an authority appropriate to a church leader addressing a community in crisis. The use of a verb of entreaty to introduce a clear admonition recalls 6:11, where the verb ἐπιθυμοῦμεν, "we desire," occurs (McCown, "Ο ΛΟΓΟΣ ΤΗΣ ΠΑΡΑΚΛΗΣΕΩΣ," 201). Here the appeal is for the members of the house church to "listen willingly" to the homily the writer has delivered (for the significance of ἀνέχεσθε and its nuance, see above, Note a). The sonorous play on words between παρακαλῶ, "I urge," and παρακλήσεως, "of exhortation," is rhetorically effective.

The writer characterizes his discourse as ὁ λόγος τῆς παρακλήσεως, "the word of exhortation." This descriptive phrase recalls the invitation extended to Paul and Barnabas by synagogue officials at Antioch of Pisidia after the reading from the Law and the Prophets: "Brothers, if you have a word of exhortation [λόγος παρακλήσεως] for the people, deliver it now" (Acts 13:15). The expression appears to have been an idiomatic designation for the homily or edifying discourse that followed the public reading from the designated portions of Scripture in the hellenistic synogogues. Similar language occurs in a Palestinian setting in 2 Macc 15:8–11: Judah the Maccabee "exhorted [παρακάλει] his men . . . encouraging them from the Law and the Prophets. . . . He armed them . . . with the encouragement of appropriate words [ἐν τοῖς ἀγαθοῖς λόγοις παράκλησιν]" (cf. 1 Macc 10:24, where λόγους παρακλήσεως signifies "persuasive words"; 2 Macc 7:24: διὰ λόγων ἐποιεῖτο τὴν παράκλησιν, "through which he gave encouragement"). When the writer appeals to the members of the assembly to listen willingly to "the word of exhortation" he has prepared, he uses the customary idiom for a sermon.

The liturgical pattern of the synagogue, in which the public reading of Scripture was followed by preaching, was adopted by the early Church. Evidence for this is provided by the instruction in 1 Tim 4:13: "devote yourself to the public reading [of Scripture], to the exhortation [τῇ παρακλήσει], to teaching." The definite expression "the exhortation" is a synonymous designation for the sermon. It referred specifically to the exposition and application of the Scripture that had been read aloud to the assembled congregation. In a fourth-century description of the liturgy for the consecration of a bishop the homily is designated λόγους παρακλήσεως, "words of exhortation" (Apost. Const. 8.5). This appears to be a fixed expression for the sermon in early Christian circles (so Wills, HTR 77 [1984] 280 and n. 10).

The exhortation consisted of strong encouragement and stern warning. This is precisely the character of Hebrews. The writer prepared his sermon with the intention that it should be read aloud to the assembled members of the house church at a public gathering for worship. The descriptive phrase "word of exhortation" is appropriate to a homily in written form (see Filson, 'Yesterday', 21, 27–30; Lane, SWJT 28 [1985] 13–15). Significant reflection on the oral sermon form, which lies behind the "word of exhortation" in Hebrews, has recently been published (Wills, HTR 77 [1984] 277–99; C. C. Black II, HTR 81 [1988] 1–8; Übelacker, Appell, 214–29; see Introduction, "Defining the Genre" and "Rhetorical Analysis").

The pastoral appeal to listen willingly to the homily is supported by the circumstantial clause καὶ γὰρ διὰ βραχέων ἐπέστειλα ὑμῖν, "for in fact I have written to you only briefly." The clause could suggest an anticipation that the length of the homily might be found wearisome by the audience. The reference to brevity, however, is simply a polite literary convention, with parallels in Jewish (e.g., 2 Macc 2:31–32; 6:17) and early Christian documents (e.g., 1 Pet 5:12: "I have written briefly" [δι᾽ ὀλίγων ἔγραψα]; Ign., *Rom.* 8:2; "I beg you by these few lines" [δι᾽ ὀλίγων γραμμάτων]; *Pol.* 7:3: "I exhort you by these few lines" [δι᾽ ὀλίγων ... γραμμάτων]). *Barnabas,* for example, is twice as long as Hebrews. In the introductory lines the writer says, "I hastened to send you a brief [κατὰ μικρόν] letter" (*Barn.* 1:5; cited by Andriessen, *NRT* 96 [1974] 1064). The structure of the sentence in v 22 clearly implies that the statement "I have written to you briefly" qualifies the phrase "word of exhortation." It thus has reference to the homily and not to the postscript (as argued by Vanhoye, *La structure,* 221–22).

23 The impression is conveyed that the communication concerning Timothy's release will be welcome news to the audience. The designation of Timothy as τὸν ἀδελφὸν ἡμῶν, "our brother," suggests that he was well known to the members of the house church. He is presumably the disciple and traveling companion of the apostle Paul. The notice regarding his release is tantalizingly brief. If the perfect passive participle ἀπολελυμένον means "has been released from prison," it has reference to an otherwise unknown imprisonment (for proposals see F. F. Bruce, *ANRW* 25.4 [1987] 3501, n. 43). The assumption that Timothy has been in custody is supported by the common meaning of ἀπολύειν in the NT, especially when it is used absolutely, as here (see above, *Note* f), and by the writer's concern for those Christians who remain in custody in the near context (13:3). The familiarity with which the writer speaks of Timothy suggests that he himself may have belonged to the Pauline circle.

The writer's own travel plans remain tentative. He is eager to visit the congregation in the near future (13:19), and he would like to have Timothy for a traveling companion. Timothy's arrival, however, has been delayed. The condition that "if he comes very soon" (τάχιον) the writer will visit the community with Timothy sufficiently indicates the urgency with which he regarded his own departure. He will not wait long. If necessary, he will travel alone to implement the exhortations he was forced by circumstances to commit to writing. The inclusion of the brief travelogue is a forceful reminder that the writer regarded what he had written only as a substitute for his own presence. His personal preference was to speak directly with the men and the women for whom he was profoundly concerned.

24–25 The greeting was a distinct literary form intended to establish or affirm a bond of friendship. It was essentially a literary gesture, the equivalent of a wave of the hand or of greeting and embracing in personal encounter. It expressed sincere affection in separation and served to strengthen personal relationships (cf. Windisch, *TDNT* 1:169–97; Mullins, *JBL* 87 [1968] 418). The ἀσπάζεσθαι formula ("greet") came into prominent use during the Roman period, especially from the time of Augustus. In private letters and notes it occurs predominantly as a closing formula, although in Greek private letters it can occur in the opening or body of the letter as well (Baldwin, "The ΑΣΠΑΖΟΜΑΙ Formula," 30–66). The NT exhibits the formula only as a closing convention.

As a literary form, the greeting appears in three types, corresponding to the three persons of the verb. (1) In the first-person type of greeting, the writer extends his own greeting (only Rom 16:22 in the NT). (2) In the second-person type of greeting, the writer indicates that the addressee is to greet others for him. This is the case in v 24*a*. The writer is the greeter, but he enlists the members of the house church as his agents in conveying his greeting to others who are not expected to be present when the homily and its attached note are read aloud.

This type of greeting appears to presuppose a closer relationship between the writer and his immediate audience than he enjoys with those to whom he sends his greetings. However, since the greeting is an expression of warm cordiality, it may indicate a succession of friendly relationships, without specifying the relative degree of closeness between the writer and those to whom he extends greetings. The second-person type of greeting is of value for its indication of relationships that exist beyond the scope of the document. (3) In the third-person type of greeting, the writer relays to the addressee the greetings of a third party. This is the case in v 24*b* (see Mullins, *JBL* 87 [1968] 418–21).

By using a second-person type of greeting in v 24*a*, the writer is able to continue to direct his undivided attention to the group of Christians he has been addressing. He wants them to act as his agent in expressing his greeting to "all your leaders and all the saints." By speaking directly to the members of the house church, he identifies himself with them, even as he enlists them for a gesture that will bring them in close contact with their leaders. If it is correct to detect in the formulation of vv 17–18 evidence of tension between the members of the assembly and their leaders, the greeting formula shows pastoral sensitivity in bringing the two groups together in a context of shared cordiality. The use of the inclusive πάντας, "all [your leaders]," acknowledges the plurality of leaders whose authority is to be acknowledged in the local situation. It implies that none of the leaders is to be excluded from the respect and affection expressed in the extension of greetings.

The members of the community are also to extend the writer's greeting to πάντας τοὺς ἁγίους, "all the saints." The repetition of the word "all" reflects the situation of the house church. As the impact of the gospel was felt in a given locality, a number of house churches would be formed, particularly in larger cities. In his letter to the Romans, for example, Paul seems to know of the existence of perhaps five house churches (Rom 16:5, 10*b*, 11*b*, 14, 15). Generally, house churches must have remained relatively small. Although a lack of information precludes a clear understanding of the interrelationship of the house churches in any given area, it would appear that they were not isolated from each other but regarded themselves as together constituting the church in that center (cf. Filson, *JBL* 58 [1939] 105–12; Malherbe, *Social Aspects*, 70, 100–102).

The multiplicity of house churches suggests why diversity, disunity, and a tendency toward independence were persistent problems in the early Church. Unity and organization became matters of urgent concern. The members of the several house churches in a particular center needed to keep in touch with one another. It was of vital importance that the greetings of the writer be conveyed to "all the saints" (Filson, 'Yesterday', 76). The purpose of the directive in v 24*a* appears to have been to reinforce a sense of unity with the larger group of Christians in that locale, at a time when the members of the house church would have preferred to isolate themselves from other groups in the city. Isolation could only encourage the members of the community to go their own way, rather than drawing on the strength that emerges from the collegiality of Christian groups throughout the city. It was to counter that disposition that the writer directs attention to the larger fellowship of believers. Christians were not to regard themselves as isolated individuals, or as autonomous societies, but as members of the family within the household of God (cf. 3:1–6; 10:19–21).

The third-person greeting in v 24*b*, in which the writer acts as the agent through whom a third party extends their greetings to the community, is intriguing. The ambiguity in the formulation ἀπὸ τῆς Ἰταλίας, "those from Italy," is well known: the Italian Christians could currently be within or outside Italy (see above, *Note* i). The subscriptions found in some MSS of Hebrews stating that the document was written from Rome (ἐγράφη ἀπὸ Ῥώμης: Codex Alexandrinus [A], fifth century) or from Italy (ἐγράφη ἀπὸ τῆς Ἰταλίας: Codex Euthalianus [H], sixth century) show that v 24*b* was interpreted in certain circles as a greeting from within Italy (so also Spicq, 1:261–65). The fact remains, however, that in the only parallel from the NT ἀπὸ τῆς Ἰταλίας clearly means "from Italy" in the sense of outside Italy (Acts 18:2). The text refers to Aquila and his wife Priscilla who were currently in Corinth; they had sailed "from Italy" when Claudius issued a decree expelling Jews from Rome (cf. Suetonius, *Claudius* 25.4). In this instance "Italy" denotes "Rome." This may be the most natural way of reading v 24*b* as well. In the closing lines the writer conveys to the members of the house church the greetings of Italian Christians who are currently away from their homeland. If that is a correct reading of the text, the writer is currently outside of Italy; he prepared his homily for a group of believers in or near Rome (so Harnack, *ZNW* 1 [1900] 16–41; Gutbrod, *TDNT* 3:190–91; Filson, *'Yesterday'*, 10–11, among others; cf. Moffatt, 246–47; F. F. Bruce, 415–16). The significance of the greeting lies in the allusion to a larger group of persons who care, as does the writer, about what is happening on the home base.

The final brief blessing, like the invocation of "the God of peace" in v 20, has its source in the liturgy of the early Church. The benediction "grace be with you all" functioned to bring closure to a service of worship (see Cuming, *NTS* 22 [1975–76] 13–15). Christians discovered that the pronouncement of blessing activates the spiritual power of God to bestow blessing. The shortest possible form of this service ending is used in Col 4:18: "Grace be with you." The form adopted by the writer of Hebrews is found in Titus 3:15 as well (cf. 2 Tim 4:22). The writer understands by χάρις, "grace," the gracious action of God himself. Although the wording of the final blessing is traditional, it is appropriate to Hebrews as a whole, with its celebration of the redeeming and sustaining grace of God (2:9; 4:16; 10:19; 12:15; 13:9). With this closing benediction, the personal relationships and crisis of the community are brought under the aspect of the sufficiency of the inexhaustible grace of God.

Explanation

In 13:1–21 the writer adds the closing section to the discourse he would have preferred to have delivered in person. As the final instruction to the community the paragraphs brought together in this section have been assigned a position of paramount importance. They consist of selected catechetical precepts (13:1–6, 7–9, 17–19) and of an artistically constructed unit of hortatory exposition (13:10–16). The section concludes on the note of prayer (13:20–21), which brings formal closure to the homily. These units constitute an integrated whole that has direct bearing upon the response expected from the members of the community.

This final section of the sermon conveys an essential message concerning the worship of God in the context of shared communal life. The writer struck the thematic note of worship in 12:28, announcing the subject of 13:1–21. There worship was identified as gratitude to God in response to the objective blessings of the new covenant secured by Jesus. That the theme of worship pervades the development of the final section indicates that the writer prepared 13:1–21 as the elaboration of 12:28. The entire section is a skillfully constructed admonition to worship God acceptably.

Authentic worship is an expansive concept that makes sacred all of life. It presupposes the willing adoption of a lifestyle pleasing to God. Worship, accordingly, cannot be restricted to formal or informal expressions of praise and prayer, but infuses every aspect of public and private life with the character of consecrated service to God. The writer focuses the attention of the assembled Christians upon shared life within the confessing community because he perceives worship comprehensively. Identification with the community of the new covenant is itself a declaration of devotion to God that must be validated at the level of fraternal relationships and in the routine of daily life. What this entails demanded the specification provided in 13:1–21.

The writer interpreted the worship of God as the central directive of the apostolic parenesis. This seems clear from two considerations. First, he has placed a double admonition to acceptable worship at the center of his development of the section (13:15–16) and treats it under the aspect of sacrifice (13:10–16). This permitted him to draw upon the resources of the rich sacrificial imagery of the OT. The OT sacrificial cultus, on which the argument in 13:10–16 rests, was an arrangement for worship. The association of the praise of God with deeds of love under the aspect of sacrifice finds its source in the praise or fellowship offering of the old covenant. Only when the detail of the double admonition in 13:15–16 is seen in the light of this type of sacrifice is the section adequately understood.

The writer thinks typologically and proceeds exegetically. The Day of Atonement and the sin offering provide the OT type and parallel for the discussion. As in 10:19–25, the writer leads his audience from the thought of the sacrifice of the sin offering and the Day of Atonement (13:11–12) to the offering of the sacrifice of praise (13:15). The explicit reference to the burning of the bodies of the animals outside the camp (13:11) establishes the background as the sin offering (Lev 4:12, 21; Lev 16:27). As a consequence of the consecration to God which Jesus has effected through his death, Christians are able to offer the sacrifice of praise to God continually (13:15). The writer's expression is deeply rooted in the language of the Psalter and confirms the presence of the language, imagery, and conception of the praise offering.

Second, throughout the final section the writer has carefully selected, arranged, and developed themes congenial to the concern with worship, so that they anticipate, expound, and complement the sacrificial double admonition in 13:15–16.

This second consideration may be illustrated with reference to 13:1–6. The pastoral directives in 13:1–3 specify that drawing near to God entails drawing near to other members of the church (13:1) and to strangers who share the common Christian confession (13:2–3). The service of God (12:28) finds tangible expression in service to brothers and sisters (13:1–3). The corollary to praise and gratitude is mutual encouragement and helpfulness as an incentive and aid to Christian maturity. These specific directives are subsequently summarized in

13:16, when the members of the house church are summoned to engage in acts of kindness and generosity as expressions of sacrificial devotion to God.

In 13:4–5*a* the assembled believers are warned against immorality and greed or idolatry as dispositions that would defile the offering of the sacrifice of praise to God. The pursuit of holiness is the essential condition for the worship of God. The initial paragraph is rounded off in 13:5*b*–6 when the community is reminded that the occasion for worship is the Scriptural promise of the presence of God who shares their vulnerability. This assurance is the ground of the confident and courageous response of faith, which finds expression in the praise of God. The tenor of the directive to praise is then repeated with variation in 13:15, when the community is exhorted continuously to offer to God through Jesus the sacrifice of praise.

The seminal concept of the Christian life as worship is distilled in the double admonition of 13:15–16. These verses may be identified as the theological and practical synthesis of Hebrews. Authentic worship consists in the praise of God and in a shared life of love. It provides the context for the response desired by God to the commandments to love God completely and to love one's neighbor fully. Although the writer makes no explicit allusion to the great love commandments of the old covenant, the commandment to love one's brothers and sisters in the confessing community (13:1–3, 16) represents a recognizably Christian response to the Holiness Code with its directive to love one's neighbor as oneself (Lev 19:18). The love of neighbor is a corollary of the love of God (Deut 6:4–5), which finds a recognizably Christian response in the admonition to offer to God the sacrifice of praise through the priestly mediation of Jesus (13:15).

What is new and distinctive in Hebrews is the explicit exposition of the double commandment to love as sacrifice. True piety is expressed through the offering of praise and gratitude to God from the heart; love for brothers and sisters is expressed through deeds of love and generosity. Heb 13 is the oldest preserved parenetic exposition of this theme. It is the earliest Christian text that purposefully shapes all of life within the confessing community as the double sacrifice of love that brings pleasure to God.

Drawing upon the pattern of the OT fellowship offering, the writer implies that the whole continuous liturgy of the old covenant is fulfilled in the continual praise offering of the Christian community. The time of the atonement offering is decisively past; it was accomplished definitively in Jesus' sacrificial offering of himself upon the cross of Golgotha, "outside the city gate" (13:10–12). Every impediment to worship has been permanently and decisively removed. The community has been consecrated to the service of God (13:12) and is fully qualified to approach God in worship. The response of praise to God and the commended works of love are now the only appropriate sacrifices remaining to the redeemed community. The law written upon the heart under the new covenant (Jer 31:31–34; cf. Heb 13:20–21) produces the praise of God, which is the impulse for the new covenant liturgy.

The remaining units of the section are congenial to this central concern with the acceptable worship of God. The writer appeals to the function of the past and present leaders of the community, who were charged with primary responsibility for the worshiping community (13:7–9, 17–19). Their authority is grounded solely in the word of God they proclaimed. The preaching of the former leaders resulted in the formation of the new covenant community. Although they were now deceased, their exemplary faith, coupled with the vigilance of the current leaders, should deter the assembly from shifting their allegiance to alien teaching (13:7–9). The foreign tradition encouraged an exchange of their commitment to the message of salvation they had received (13:7; cf. 2:3–4) for an approach to worship expressed through cultic meals and focused upon the altar in Jerusalem (13:9). The result could only be a catastrophic distortion of worship. Only the eschatological word of God, not human tradition or cultic practices, creates in a people the quality of being well pleasing to him. The strengthening of the heart for acceptable worship is accomplished through the grace of God revealed in history through Jesus' death on Golgotha. This is the content of the Christian confession, "We have an altar!" (13:9–12).

There is a strong intimation of a strained relationship between the members of the house church and their leaders in the formulation of the directive to obedience and submission to the authority of those currently in leadership (13:17). The source of the tension may be located in the attraction of the house church to Jewish tradition concerning the value of cultic fellowship meals. It was imperative to resolve the tension between the community and its leaders if they were to engage in the acceptable worship of God.

Discipleship is a related aspect of devotion to God. In Hebrews discipleship consists in imitating past exemplars of faithfulness rather than in "following" Jesus. Although the writer did not use the term "to follow in discipleship" familiar from the synoptic tradition of Jesus' words, a discipleship motif is introduced with the call to emulate the exemplary faith of those former leaders who preached the word of God to the community (13:7). Discipleship is exhibited in firm adherence to the word they proclaimed and alignment with the conduct they modelled.

A parenetic adaptation of the familiar call to discipleship in terms of cross bearing can be recognized in the formulation of 13:13, when the community is exhorted to leave "the camp," going out to Jesus and bearing the shame he bore. Jesus' own action in going "outside the camp" set a precedent for others to follow. The task of the community is to emulate Jesus, leaving behind the security, congeniality, and respectability of the sacred enclosure. Discipleship in this context means to become directed by the course of Jesus' life. It entails exposure to shame and the severance of social ties. It is affirmed in the acceptance of the reproach of Christian commitment in a climate of hostility. The allusion to Golgotha in the immediate context (13:12) implies following Jesus on the way to the cross. The path of discipleship is marked out in the patient endurance of suffering.

Concurrently, the "going out" to Jesus "outside the camp" reaffirms a commitment to be the pilgrim people of God who leave behind the security of the familiar in order to respond to the call of God upon their lives. Jesus' disciples are those who follow him not only on the way to the cross here and now, but ultimately to the final goal of pilgrimage, the future heavenly city (13:14). Conversely, the certainty that the transcendent city of God has been promised to those who respond to his call is the sufficient ground of discipleship. With these distinctive nuances the synoptic concept of discipleship has been transposed for the situation of the second-generation community. The course and goal of Jesus' life provide the pattern for breaking loose from the grip of fear and lethargy in which the second generation tends to live.

In developing these emphases the writer sought to invest the whole existence of the community with the value of authentic devotion to God. He does so by calling the members of the house church to the new cultic response to God made possible through Jesus, as opposed to reliance upon the assurances offered under the old framework. In developing this thought he emphasizes its appropriateness, its spiritual character, and its effectiveness in bringing pleasure to God. Security is not to be found in cultic performance, ceremonial meals, or sacred enclosures. Its source is a confident reliance on the presence and provision of a faithful God, to whom the community enjoys unlimited access by virtue of their consecration to the service of God through Jesus' atoning death (13:12). The action of God in raising Jesus from the dead is the ground of the assurance that he will accomplish in them through the risen and exalted Jesus what is pleasing to him (13:20–21).

The significance of 13:1–21 to the pastoral strategy of the writer must be appreciated. His intention throughout the homily has been to stir the members of the house church from their lethargy and to ground them once again in the message of salvation they had received from those who preached to them the word of God. The description of worship under the aspect of sacrifice in the final section of the homily permitted the writer once more to call attention to the significance of the death of Jesus, the perfect sacrifice for sin. The writer's passionate message to the weary believers is that Jesus shared their vulnerability. He died the humiliating death of an outcast. Yet through his death Christians have been consecrated to the service of God (13:12). His death possessed the character of covenant sacrifice, through which the new and eternal covenant was inaugurated and the objective blessings of the new covenant were secured. Vindicated by God through resurrection, he remains the great Shepherd of the flock, the true pastor of the congregation (13:20–21).

Jesus Christ is not absent but present in authentic worship. As the mediator of the praise of God (13:15), he creates the possibility of serving God in a manner wholly pleasing to him. Deviation from the message of salvation proclaimed by the original leaders of the assembly (13:7–9) is incompatible with participation in the shared life of the confessing community and with the response of praise and gratitude to which the congregation has been summoned (12:28; 13:15). Similarly, the persistence of tension between the members of the house church and their current leaders is equally unacceptable. Strained relationships must be repaired if the confession and worship of the community are to have integrity.

There is one further component to the writer's pastoral strategy. He indicates his eagerness to be restored to the community (13:19, 23). He himself will come to implement the word of exhortation he was forced by circumstances to reduce to writing and to entrust to a courier (13:22). His absence now affords the house church time to respond appropriately to this passionate appeal to affirm once more their Christian character as the confessing community.

Index of Authors Cited

Index of Biblical and Other Ancient Sources

A. The Old Testament

B. The New Testament

C. Old Testament Apocrypha and Pseudepigrapha

D. Dead Sea Scrolls

E. Philo

F. Josephus

G. Targums

H. Rabbinic Writings

I. Apostolic Fathers

J. Other Early Christian and Gnostic Writings

K. Other Ancient and Classical Texts

L. Papyri and Inscriptions

Index of Principal Topics